Lecture Notes in Computer Science 1626

Edited by G. Goos, J. Hartmanis and J. van Leeuwen

T0223116

Springer
Berlin
Heidelberg
New York
Barcelona
Hong Kong
London
Milan
Paris
Singapore
Tokyo

Matthias Jarke Andreas Oberweis (Eds.)

Advanced Information Systems Engineering

11th International Conference, CAiSE'99
Heidelberg, Germany, June 14-18, 1999
Proceedings

Springer

Series Editors

Gerhard Goos, Karlsruhe University, Germany
Juris Hartmanis, Cornell University, NY, USA
Jan van Leeuwen, Utrecht University, The Netherlands

Volume Editors

Matthias Jarke
RWTH Aachen, Lehrstuhl für Informatik V
Ahornstr. 55, D-52056 Aachen, Germany
E-mail: jarke@informatik.rwth-aachen.de

Andreas Oberweis
Universität Frankfurt, Lehrstuhl für Wirtschaftsinformatik II
Merton Str. 17, D-60325 Frankfurt, Germany
E-mail: oberweis@wiwi.uni-frankfurt.de

Cataloging-in-Publication data applied for

Die Deutsche Bibliothek - CIP-Einheitsaufnahme

Advanced information systems engineering : 11th international conference ;
proceedings / CAiSE '99, Heidelberg, Germany, June 14 - 18, 1999. Matthias
Jarke ; Andreas Oberweis (ed.). - Berlin ; Heidelberg ; New York ; Barcelona ;
Hong Kong ; London ; Milan ; Paris ; Singapore ; Tokyo : Springer, 1999
  (Lecture notes in computer science ; Vol. 1626)
  ISBN 3-540-66157-3

CR Subject Classification (1998): H.2, H.4-5, J.1, K.4.3, K.6

ISSN 0302-9743
ISBN 3-540-66157-3 Springer-Verlag Berlin Heidelberg New York

Typesetting: Camera-ready by author
SPIN: 10703286   06/3142 – 5 4 3 2 1 0   Printed on acid-free paper

Preface

CAiSE*99 is the 11th in the series of International Conferences on Advanced Information Systems Engineering. The aim of the CAiSE series is to give researchers and professionals from universities, research, industry, and public administration the opportunity to meet annually to discuss evolving research issues and applications in the field of information systems engineering; also to assist young researchers and doctoral students in establishing relationships with senior scientists in their areas of interest.

Starting from a Scandinavian origin in the late 1980's, CAiSE has evolved into a truly international conference with a worldwide author and attendance list. The CAiSE*99 program listed contributions from 19 countries, from four continents! These contributions, 27 full papers, 12 short research papers, six workshops, and four tutorials, were carefully selected from a total of 168 submissions by the international program committee.

A special theme of CAiSE*99 was 'Component-based information systems engineering'. Component-based approaches mark the maturity of any engineering discipline. However, transfering this idea to the complex and diverse world of information systems has proven more difficult than expected. Despite numerous proposals from object-oriented programming, design patterns and frameworks, customizable reference models and standard software, requirements engineering and business re-engineering, web-based systems, data reduction strategies, knowledge management, and modularized education, the question of how to make component-oriented approaches actually work in information systems remains wide open.

CAiSE*99 addressed these issues through invited talks and panels by business and research leaders. The invited talks, held by two of the most influential researcher-entrepreneurs, represent two key trends in information systems engineering, towards object model standardization and towards business domain model standardization. Ivar Jacobson (Rational Software Inc.) reviewed the Unified Process of Component-Based Development, filling a sorely felt gap in the Unified Modelling Language (UML) standardization effort. August-Wilhelm Scheer (Universität des Saarlandes and IDS Prof. Scheer GmbH) investigated the way-of-working leading from business process models to application systems. These talks were complemented by a high-level interdisciplinary panel on Component-Based Information Systems Architectures.

More details on the conference theme were provided by two full-day tutorials on component-based development and on the impact of the Unified Modeling Language. Additional mini-tutorials during the conference itself addressed the emerging questions of advanced workflow systems and infrastructure for electronic commerce.

CAiSE*99 was held in Heidelberg, Germany, not only a beautiful site with the oldest university in Germany, but also close to numerous leading Information

Systems Engineering companies in the Rhein-Main-Neckar area, just an hour away from Frankurt airport. The touristic attraction of the area dates back 500 000 years – the oldest human bones ever found in Europe belong to 'Homo Heidelbergensis'! More recent Heidelberg features include the historic student town with the biggest wooden wine barrel in the world as well as the historic student dungeon for those who had too much of the contents.

Besides summaries of the invited talks, this proceedings volume includes the research papers accepted as long or short papers for the conference. Topics addressed include:

– components, workflows, method engineering, and process modeling
– data warehousing, distributed and heterogeneous information systems
– temporal information systems and information systems dynamics.

Associated pre-conference workshops covered Data Warehousing, Method Evaluation, Agent-Oriented Information Systems, Business Process Architectures, and Requirements Engineering. Papers from these workshops could not be included in these proceedings but are available through the workshop organizers (for more information, consult the web site *http://www-i5.informatik.rwth-aachen.de/conf/caise99/*).

We would like to thank all the institutions and individuals who have made this conference possible, especially our General Chair Wolffried Stucky, the workshop and tutorial co-chairs Gottfried Vossen and Klaus Pohl as well as the CAiSE advisory committee led by Janis Bubenko and Arne Solvberg. Several sponsors and supporters from industry made substantial contributions to the success of the conference. Thanks are also due to all the submitters of papers, tutorials, workshops, and last but not least to our co-workers Kirsten Lenz, Stefan Sklorz, and Irene Wicke without whom the organization would hardly have been possible. Stefan Sklorz also served as Technical Editor of this proceedings volume.

March 1999   **Matthias Jarke and Andreas Oberweis**
Aachen and Frankfurt

CAiSE*99 Conference Organization

Advisory Committee
Janis Bubenko
Royal Institute of Technology, Sweden
Arne Sølvberg
The Norwegian University of Science and Technology, Norway

General Chair	Program Chair	Organizing Chair
Wolffried Stucky	**Matthias Jarke**	**Andreas Oberweis**
University of Karlsruhe,	*RWTH Aachen,*	*University of Frankfurt,*
Germany	*Germany*	*Germany*

Program Committee

Hans-Jürgen Appelrath	Germany	Andreas Opdahl	Norway
Sjaak Brinkkemper	The Netherlands	Maria E. Orlowska	Australia
Meral Binbasioglu	U.S.A.	Michael Papazoglou	The Netherlands
Janis Bubenko	Sweden	Barbara Pernici	Italy
Silvana Castano	Italy	Klaus Pohl	Germany
Panos Constantopoulos	Greece	Naveen Prakash	India
Vytautas Cyras	Lithuania	Bala Ramesh	U.S.A.
Klaus R. Dittrich	Switzerland	Andreas Reuter	Germany
Eric Dubois	Belgium	Colette Rolland	France
Marcel Francksson	France	Thomas Rose	Germany
Wolfgang Hesse	Germany	Matti Rossi	Finland
Stefan Jablonski	Germany	Gunter Saake	Germany
Matthias Jarke (chair)	Germany	Motoshi Saeki	Japan
Christian S. Jensen	Denmark	Amit Sheth	U.S.A.
Manfred Jeusfeld	The Netherlands	August-Wilhelm Scheer	Germany
Leonid Kalinichenko	Russia	Michel Scholl	France
Hannu Kangassalo	Finland	Arie Segev	U.S.A.
Gerti Kappel	Austria	Amilcar Sernadas	Portugal
Kamal Karlapalem	China	Keng Siau	U.S.A.
Gerhard Knolmayer	Switzerland	Elmar J. Sinz	Germany
Frederick H. Lochovsky	China	Arne Sølvberg	Norway
Pericles Loucopoulos	United Kingdom	Stefano Spaccapietra	Switzerland
Kalle Lyytinen	Finland	Wolffried Stucky	Germany
Neil A.M. Maiden	United Kingdom	Rudi Studer	Germany
Robert Meersman	Belgium	Babis Theodoulidis	United Kingdom
Carlo Meghini	Italy	Yannis Vassiliou	Greece
Günter Müller	Germany	Yair Wand	Canada
John Mylopoulos	Canada	Roel Wieringa	The Netherlands
Erich J. Neuhold	Germany	Eric Yu	Canada
Antoni Olivé	Spain		

Additional Referees

Mounji Abdelaziz	Belgium	Dirk Jonscher	Switzerland
Guiseppe Amato	Italy	Yannis Kakoudakis	United Kingdom
Michael Amberg	Germany	Vera Kamp	Germany
Ismailcem Budak Arpinar	U.S.A.	Panos Kardasis	United Kingdom
Sören Balko	Germany	E. Kavakli	United Kingdom
Patrick Baudisch	Germany	Minna Koskinen	Finland
Linda Bird	Australia	Markus Kradolfer	Switzerland
Michael Boehnlein	Germany	Michael Lawley	Australia
Dietrich Boles	Germany	Karel Lemmen	The Netherlands
Markus Breitling	Germany	Mauri Leppänen	Finland
Patrik Budenz	Germany	Weifa Liang	Australia
Ralph Busse	Germany	Jianguo Lu	Canada
Jorge Cardoso	U.S.A.	ZongWei Luo	U.S.A.
Fabio Casati	Italy	Olivera Marjanovic	Australia
Donatella Castelli	Italy	Silvia Mazzini	Italy
Judith Cornelisse-Vermaat	NL	Jens Neeb	Germany
Stefan Decker	Germany	Marian Orlowski	Australia
Martin Doerr	Greece	Boris Padovan	Germany
Ruxandra Domenig	Switzerland	Rainer Perkuhn	Germany
St. Duewel	Germany	Anne Persson	Sweden
Christian Ege	Germany	Ilias Petrounias	United Kingdom
Rolf Engmann	The Netherlands	Nikos Prekas	United Kingdom
Fabian Erbach	Germany	Jaime Ramos	Portugal
Torsten Eymann	Germany	Stefan Rausch-Schott	Austria
Dieter Fensel	Germany	Martin Reichenbach	Germany
Erwin Folmer	The Netherlands	Jörg Ritter	Germany
Chiara Francalanci	Italy	Roland Rolles	Germany
Lars Frank	Denmark	Gregory Rose	U.S.A.
Peter Frankhauser	Germany	Wasim Sadiq	Australia
Matthias Friedrich	Germany	Carina Sandmann	Germany
Hans Fritschi	Switzerland	Mohammad Saraee	United Kingdom
Michael Gebhardt	Germany	Ralf Schamburger	Germany
Christian Ghezzi	United Kingdom	Michael Schlundt	Germany
G. Giannopoulos	United Kingdom	Ingo Schmitt	Germany
Soenke Gold	Germany	Hans-Peter Schnurr	Germany
Paula Gouveia	Portugal	Detlef Schoder	Germany
Tom Gross	Austria	Dirk Schulze	Germany
Peter Haumer	Germany	Kerstin Schwarz	Germany
Olaf Herden	Germany	Roland Schätzle	Germany
Eyk Hildebrandt	Germany	Mikael Skov	Denmark
Martin Hitz	Austria	Steffen Staab	Germany
Stefan Horn	Germany	Umberto Straccia	Italy
Giovanni Iachello	Germany	Juha-Pekka Tolvanen	Finland
Uwe Jendricke	Germany	Dimitrios Tombros	Switzerland

Can Tuerker	Germany	Klaus Weidenhaupt	Germany
Achim Ulbrich-vom Ende	Germany	Patrik Werle	Sweden
Anca Vaduva	Switzerland	Benedikt Wismans	Germany
Alex Vakaloudis	United Kingdom	Shengli Wu	U.S.A.
Kris De Volder	Belgium	J.Leon Zhao	U.S.A.
Rob L.W. v.d. Weg	The Netherlands	Frank-O. Zimmermann	Germany

Organizing Committee

Marcus Raddatz	RWTH Aachen	Kirsten Keferstein	Univ. of Frankfurt
Stefan Sklorz	RWTH Aachen	Kirsten Lenz	Univ. of Frankfurt
Irene Wicke	RWTH Aachen	Jürgen Powik	Univ. of Frankfurt

Supporting and Sponsoring Organizations

Association for Information Systems
European Media Lab (Heidelberg)
Gesellschaft für Informatik e.V.
IBM Deutschland GmbH
Promatis GmbH

CAiSE*99 Tutorials

Tutorial Chair
Klaus Pohl
RWTH Aachen, Germany

UML at Work - From Analysis to Implementation		**Building Component-Based Business Applications**	
Gregor Engels	Germany	Claus Rautenstrauch	Germany
Annika Wagner	Germany	Klaus Turowski	Germany
Martin Hitz	Austria		
Gerti Kappel	Austria		
Werner Retschitzegger	Austria		

Challenges in Workflow Management		**Technological Infrastructure for Electronic Commerce**	
Amit Sheth	U.S.A.	Avigdor Gal	U.S.A.
Christoph Bussler	U.S.A.	John Mylopoulos	Canada

CAiSE*99 Pre-conference Workshops

Workshop Chair
Gottfried Vossen
University of Münster, Germany

6th CAiSE Doctoral Consortium		**Agent-Oriented Information Systems (AOIS'99)**	
Frank Moisiadis	Australia		
Gabrio Rivera	Switzerland	Gerd Wagner	Germany
Antonia Erni	Switzerland	Eric Yu	Canada

Design and Management of Data Warehouses (DMDW'99)		**Software Architectures for Business Process Management (SABPM'99)**	
Stella Gatzi	Switzerland		
Manfred Jeusfeld	The Netherlands	Wil van der Aalst	The Netherlands
Martin Staudt	Switzerland	Jörg Desel	Germany
Yannis Vassiliou	Greece	Roland Kaschek	Austria

4th CAiSE/IFIP8.1 Int. WS on Evaluation of Modeling Methods in Systems Analysis and Design (EMMSAD'99)		**5th International Workshop on Requirements Engineering: Foundation for Software Quality (REFSQ'99)**	
Keng Siau	U.S.A.	Klaus Pohl	Germany
Yair Wand	Canada	Andreas Opdahl	Norway

Table of Contents

XII   Table of Contents

Heterogeneous Databases

IS Dynamics

SHORT PAPERS

The Unified Process for Component-Based Development

Ivar Jacobsen

Rational Software Corporation
ivar@Rational.Com

Abstract. A better development process-in fact, a process unifying the best practices now available-is the key to the software future. The proven Unified Process originally developed by Ivar Jacobson, now incorporating the work of Grady Booch, Jim Rumbaugh, Philippe Kruchten, Walker Royce, and other people inside Rational, answers this long-felt need. Component and object based, the Unified Process enables reuse. Use-case driven, it closes the gap between what the user needs and what the developer does, it drives the development process. Architecture centric, it guides the development process. Iterative and incremental, it manages risk. Represented in the design blueprints of the newly standardized Unified Modeling Language (UML), it communicates your results to a wide audience.

M. Jarke, A. Oberweis (Eds.): CAiSE'99, LNCS 1626, pp. 1-1, 1999.

From Business Process Model to Application System - Developing an Information System with the House of Business Engineering (HOBE)

August-Wilhelm Scheer, Michael Hoffmann

Institut für Wirtschaftsinformatik (IWi) an der Universität des Saarlandes
Im Stadtwald, Geb. 14.1, 66123 Saarbrücken
{scheer, hoffmann}@iwi.uni-sb.de

Abstract. Organizational concepts, like virtual enterprises or profit centers in companies, are ordering new functionality on information systems. Enterprises have to customize their business processes in very short periods because of stronger competition and globalization. Concepts like electronic commerce and supply chain management need a permanent optimization of the business processes along the supply chain. The generating of individual software and model based customizing of ERP-packages offer potentials for more flexibility supporting business processes with information systems. This paper shows a concept for describing and implementing business processes and a software development project using this concept.

1 Flexible Information Systems for Mobile Enterprises

Organizational concepts, like virtual enterprises or profit centers in companies, are ordering new functionality on information systems. The networks between many organizational units in a company and between companies need more flexibility in implementing and customizing information systems.

In the past, information systems had been customized on the basis of organizational structures and business processes once and then not been altered again over a period of many years. Nowadays, enterprises have to customize the business processes in very short periods because of stronger competition and globalization. Concepts like electronic commerce and supply chain management demand a permanent optimization of the business processes along the supply chain.

Companies selling enterprise resource planning packages have realized the necessity to deliver tools reducing the time and the costs spent in implementing and customizing their software products.

Many enterprises expect more flexibility from generating their individual software products on the basis of semantic models and software components working together in a framework. A change of the semantic models automatically takes effect on the configuration of the information system.

With ARIS – House of Business Engineering, chapter 2 introduces a concept for describing business processes from semantic models to implementation. Chapter 3

M. Jarke, A. Oberweis (Eds.): CAiSE'99, LNCS 1626, pp. 2-9, 1999.
© Springer-Verlag Berlin Heidelberg 1999

shows the development of software applications using the HOBE-concept. In chapter 4 future trends are presented.

2 ARIS - House of Business Engineering (HOBE)

ARIS - House of Business Engineering is an integrated concept describing and executing business processes. Furthermore, it is a framework for developing real application software. The next chapters explain the meaning of the different levels shown in Fig. 1.

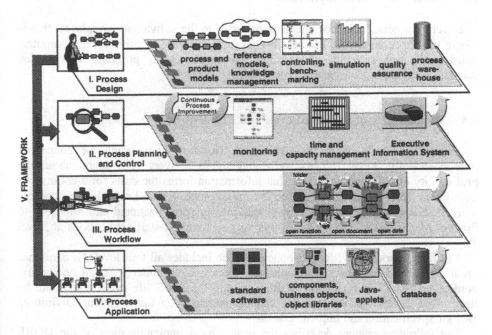

Fig. 1 ARIS - House of Business Engineering

2.1 Level I: Process Design

Level I describes business processes according to the routing. Therefore, the ARIS concept provides a method to cover every aspect of the business process. Methods for optimizing and guaranteeing the quality of processes are available, too.

2.2 Level II: Process Management

Level II plans and monitors every current business process from the "business process owner's" point of view. Various methods of scheduling and capacity control and cost analysis are available. By monitoring the process, the process manager is aware of the status of each process instance.

2.3   Level III: Process Workflow

Level III transports the objects to be processed, such as customer orders with the corresponding documents or insurance claims in insurance companies, from one workplace to the next. The documents are then stored in "folders". Workflow systems carry out the material handling in electronically stored documents.

2.4   Level IV: Process Application

Level IV processes the documents transported to the individual workplaces; that is where the functions of the business process are executed. At this level, computer-aided application systems – from simple word processing programs to complex standard software modules and internet applets – are used.

2.5   Combination of the Four Levels and Framework

Those four levels of ARIS – House of Business Engineering are connected interdependently. Level II (Process Management) delivers information about the profitability of currents processes. That information forms the basis for a continuous adjustment and improvement of the business processes at Level I. The process workflow reports data regarding times, amounts and organizational allocation etc. to Process Management. The workflow systems at Level III start applications at Level IV.

The framework is the fifth component, which includes all four levels. It combines architecture and application knowledge, from which concrete applications are configured. At all levels of the HOBE concept, the ARIS life cycle model can be used. That means that the software can be described by Requirements Definition, Design Specification and Implementation.

The following chapter describes the prototypical implementation of the HOBE Concept.

3   Prototypical Implementation of ARIS – House of Business Engineering

In order to implement the HOBE Concept, the institute for information systems (Institut für Wirtschaftsinformatik – IWi) of the University of Saarland, and the IDS Scheer AG, have launched a project to prototypically implement a sales scenario. This project was supported by CSE Systems Cooperation and NEXUS GmbH. Fig. 2 shows the components used with the implementation.

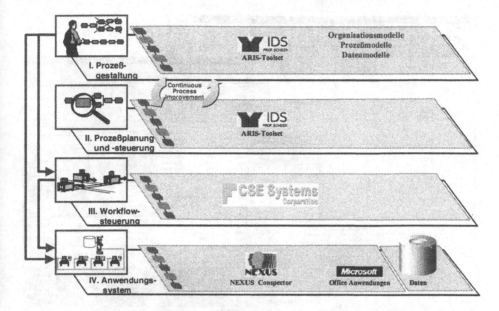

Fig. 2 Components used with the implementation

At Level I, the ARIS Toolset has been used to model the processes, the data structure and the hierarchical organization of the enterprise considered. An organigram has been modeled for the hierarchical organization, as well as an UML class diagram for the data structure and an extended Event Driven Process Chain (eEPC) for the process organization.

3.1 Data Modeling

On the basis of the UML class diagram, a database repository has been generated by using a report and an interface between the ARIS Toolset and the NEXUS Builder. The following rules were observed:

- Each class is represented as an object in the database.
- Each association with the cardinality m:n is represented as an object in the database.
- Associations with the cardinality 1:n are not represented as objects. The attributes of these associations are administered in the subordinate classes.
- Classes are depicted centrally in forms, associated classes are depicted in the detail section.

Filling the generated database with content, one gets the company-wide integrated database/data set for the company considered.

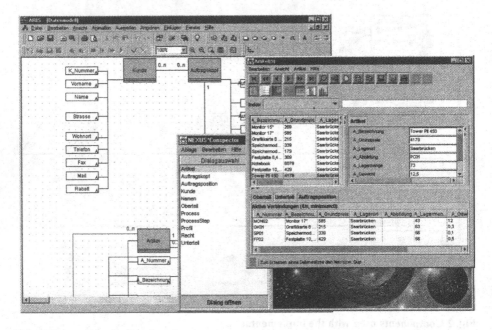

Fig. 3 Generating the Database

Fig. 3 shows part of the data model and the result after the transition to the NEXUS runtime environment. In the center of the generated mask, the class "Artikel" can be seen. In the detail section, the associations "Unterteil" and "Oberteil" can be faded in, which depict the bill of material view respectively. If someone selects the association "Auftragsposition", it will be depicted which order position an item has been assigned to.

3.2   Organizational Structure

Figure 4 shows the organigram of the exemplary company. As shown on the right-hand side of the figure, in CSE-Workflow, the modeled organizational units are depicted as tree-control. The following transition rules have been used:

- An organizational unit in the organigram becomes an organizational unit in CSE-Workflow.
- An internal person is depicted as a user in CSE-Workflow.
- A person type in the organigram determines a role in CSE-Workflow.
- A position describes a synonym.

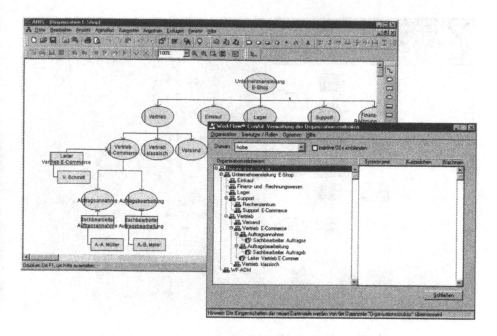

Fig. 4 Generating the Organizational Structure

3.3   Organization of Workflow

Fig. 5 shows the modeling of the workflow organization according to the modeling conventions of the CSE-Workflow filter, and the transition of the eEPC to CSE-Workflow. In the process designer of the CSE-workflow system, events are not depicted. The red-colored ovals stand for activities and correspond to the functions within the eEPC. The first activity is particularly stressed and may not be automated in the workflow.

It is unusual that application systems supporting the execution of a function are not modeled to the respective function, but to the event triggering the function. One reason for this is that events in workflow systems are not modeled and that application systems are opened via internal workflow triggers at the transitions. In Fig. 5 they are shown as exclamation marks on the lines between the activities. The organizational units are assigned to the functions responsible for their execution.

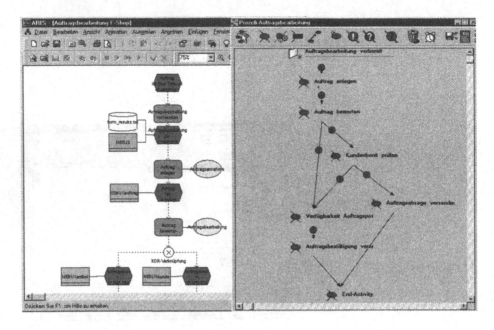

Fig. 5 Generating the Organization of Workflow

Next chapter describes the scenario supported with the developed information system.

3.4   Scenario

We consider an enterprise that sells computers and computer parts on the Internet. A customer can enter his master data in a form on the homepage of the enterprise and generate an order by entering quantities of the desired items. The generated electronic order automatically initiates the instantiation of a workflow. The employee responsible for order acceptance finds the form completed by the customer in the inbox and copies the data down to the NEXUS database generated from the ARIS toolset. When double-clicking on that business event, the database is automatically opened with the respective input mask appearing. Having finished his task, the employee sends the work folder containing the order to the next position according to the workflow model. The information systems required for the processing of the task are, too, opened by double-clicking on the business event. The business event will be forwarded to the next position until it has been worked off. Figure 6 shows the process model modeled with ARIS toolset, the Internet form which – when completed - triggers a workflow, the inbox of the employee responsible for order acceptance and the input mask of the generated enterprise-wide database.

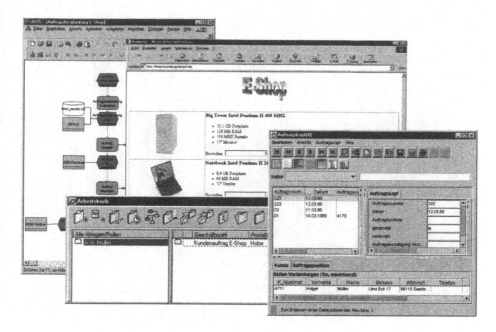

Fig. 6 Order processing with the system developed

4   Outlook

The development of the project shows that future models will not only document software, but also generate and modify it. Thus the importance of a consistent and complete modeling of enterprises on the level of requirements definition is growing. As a change of models automatically generates a change in the underlying software. Enterprise are able to support new business processes with application software or adjust existing business processes nearly without any delay. Thus ,e.g., the instantiation of ad-hoc workflow becomes feasible. New aspects are expected with reverse engineering and reverse customizing. The features of the tool used for modeling are very important. Besides usability, the functionality of the database that records the objects of the models, and the interfaces offered to application software programming environments are decisive for the exhaustion of maximum potentials.

CPAM, A Protocol for Software Composition

Laurence Melloul, Dorothea Beringer, Neal Sample, Gio Wiederhold

Computer Science Department, Stanford University
Gates Computer Science building 4A, Stanford, CA 94305, USA
{melloul, beringer, nsample, gio}@db.stanford.edu
http://www-db.stanford.edu/CHAIMS

Abstract. Software composition is critical for building large-scale applications. In this paper, we consider the composition of components that are methods offered by heterogeneous, autonomous and distributed computational software modules made available by external sources. The objective is to compose these methods and build new applications while preserving the autonomy of the software modules. This would decrease the time and cost needed for producing and maintaining the added functionality. In the following, we describe a high-level protocol that enables software composition. CPAM, CHAIMS Protocol for Autonomous Megamodules, may be used on top of various distribution systems. It offers additional features for supporting module heterogeneity and preserving module autonomy, and also implements several optimization concepts such as cost estimation of methods and partial extraction of results.

1 Introduction

CPAM, the CHAIMS Protocol for Autonomous Megamodules, is a high-level protocol for realizing software composition. CPAM has been defined in the context of the CHAIMS (Compiling High-level Access Interfaces for Multi-site Software) [1] research project at Stanford University in order to build extensive applications by composing large, heterogeneous, autonomous, and distributed software modules.

Software modules are large if they are computation intensive (computation time may range from seconds in the case of information requests, to days in the case of simulations) or/and data intensive (the amount of data can not be neglected during transmissions). They are heterogeneous if they are written in different languages (e.g., C++, Java), use different distribution protocols (e.g., CORBA [2], RMI [3], DCE [4], DCOM [5]), or run on diverse platforms (e.g., Windows NT, Sun Solaris, HP-UX). Modules are autonomous if they are developed and maintained independently of one another, and independently of the *composer* who composes them. Finally, software modules are distributed when they are not located on the same server and may be used by more than one client. We will call modules with these characteristics *megamodules,* and the methods they offer *services.*

In this paper, we focus on the composition of megamodules for two reasons:

- service providers being independent and geographically distant, software modules are autonomous and most likely heterogeneous and distributed,
- because of cost-effectiveness, composition is critical when services are large.

M. Jarke, A. Oberweis (Eds.): CAiSE'99, LNCS 1626, pp. 11-25, 1999.

Megamodule composition consists of remotely invoking the services of the composed megamodules in order to produce new services. Composition differs from integration in the sense that it preserves megamodule autonomy. Naturally, the assumption is that megamodule providers are eager to offer their services. This is a reasonable assumption if we consider the business interest that would derive from the use of services, such as a payment of fees or the cut of customer service costs.

Composition of megamodules is becoming crucial for the software Industry. As business competition and software complexity increase, companies have to shorten their software cycle (development, testing, and maintenance) while offering ever more functionality. Because of high software development or integration costs, they are being forced to build large-scale applications by reusing external services and *composing* them. Global information systems such as the Web and global business environments such as electronic commerce foreshadow a software development environment where developers would access and reuse services offered on the Web, combine them, and produce new services which, in turn, would be accessed through the Web.

Existing distribution protocols such as CORBA, RMI, DCE, or DCOM allow users to compose software with different legacy codes but using CORBA, RMI, DCE, or DCOM as just the distribution protocol underneath. The Horus protocol [6] composes heterogeneous protocols in order to add functionality at the protocol level only. The ERPs, Enterprise Resource Planning systems, such as SAP R/3, BAAN IV, and PeopleSoft, integrate heterogeneous and initially independent systems but do not preserve software autonomy. None of these systems simultaneously supports heterogeneity and preserves software autonomy during the process of composition in a distributed environment.

CPAM has been defined for accomplishing megamodule composition. In the following, we describe how CPAM supports megamodule heterogeneity (section 2), how it preserves megamodule autonomy (section 3), and how it enables optimized composition of large-scale services (section 4). We finally explain how to use CPAM, and provide an illustration of a client doing composition in compliance with the CPAM protocol (section 5).

2 CPAM Supports Megamodule Heterogeneity

Composition of heterogeneous and distributed software modules has several constraints: it has to support heterogeneous data transmission between megamodules as well as the diverse distribution protocols used by megamodules.

2.1 Data Heterogeneity

In order for megamodules to exchange information, data need to be in a common format (a separate research project is exploring ways to map different ontologies [7]). Also, data has to be machine and architecture independent (16 bit architecture versus 32 bit architecture for instance), and transferred between megamodules regardless of the distribution protocol at either end (source or destination). For these reasons, the current version of CPAM requires data to be ASN.1 structures encoded using BER rules [8]. With ASN.1/BER-encoding rules:

1. Simple data types as well as complex data types can be represented as ASN.1 structures,
2. Data can be encoded in a binary format that is interpreted on any machine where ASN.1 libraries are installed,
3. Data can be transported through any distribution system.

It has not been possible to use other definition languages such as CORBA Interface Definition Language or Java classes to define data types because these definitions respectively require that the same CORBA ORB or the RMI distribution protocol be supported at both ends of the transmission.

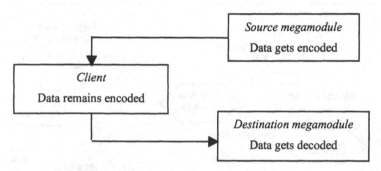

Fig. 1. Data transfer, Opaque data

2.2 Opaque Data

Because ASN.1 data blocks are encoded in binary format, we refer to them as BLOBs (Binary Large OBjects). BLOBs being opaque, they are not readable by CPAM. A client doing composition only (the client gets and transmits the data, with no computation in between) does not need to interpret the data it receives from a megamodule, or sends to another megamodule. Therefore, as shown in Fig. 1, before being transported, data is encoded in the source megamodule; it is then sent to the client where it remains a BLOB, and gets decoded only when it reaches the destination megamodule.

A client that would have the knowledge of the megamodule definition language could convert the blobs into their corresponding data types, and read them. It would then become its responsibility to encode the data before sending it to another megamodule.

2.3 Distribution Protocol Heterogeneity

Both data transportation and client-server bindings are dependent on the distribution system used. CPAM is a high-level protocol that is implemented on top of existing distribution protocols. Since its specifications may be implemented on top of more than one distribution protocol within the composed application, CPAM has to support data transmissions and client-server connections across different distribution systems.

We mentioned that encoded ASN.1 data could be transferred between the client and the megamodules independently of the distribution protocols used at both ends. Regarding client-server connections, CPAM assumes that the client is able to simultaneously support the various distribution systems of the servers it wishes to talk to. The CHAIMS architecture, along with the CHAIMS compiler [9], enables the generation of such a client. This process is described in next section. Currently, in the context of CHAIMS, a client can simultaneously support the following protocols: CORBA, RMI, *local* C++ and local Java (*local* qualifying a server which is not remote).

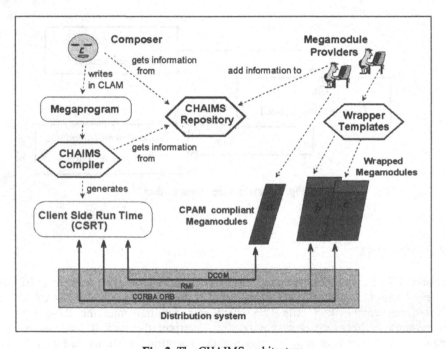

Fig. 2. The CHAIMS architecture

2.4 The CHAIMS Architecture

Figure 2 describes the CHAIMS architecture. In CHAIMS, the client program is the *megaprogram* and the compiled client program is the *CSRT* (Client Side Run Time). Also, server information repositories are currently merged into one unique CHAIMS repository.

The distribution protocol used during a specific communication between the client and a remote server is the one of the server itself, and must be supported by the client. In the context of CHAIMS, the composer writes a simple megaprogram in CLAM

(CHAIMS Language for Autonomous Megamodules) [10], a composition only language. This program contains the sequence of invocations to the megamodules the composer wishes to compose (an example of megaprogram is given in section 5.3). The CHAIMS compiler parses the megaprogram and generates the whole client code necessary to simultaneously bind to the various servers (CSRT). Server specifications such as the required distribution protocol are contained in the CHAIMS repository and are accessible to the CHAIMS compiler.

Both the client and the servers have to follow CPAM specifications. As it is noted in Fig. 2, megamodules that are not CPAM compliant need to be *wrapped*. The process of wrapping is described in section 5.2.

3 CPAM Preserves Megamodule Autonomy

Besides being heterogeneous and distributed, megamodules are autonomous. They are developed and maintained independently from the composer who therefore has no control over them. How can the composer be aware of all services offered by megamodules, and of the latest versions of these services without compromising megamodule autonomy? Also, how do the connections between the client and the server take place? Which of the client or the server controls the connection? After specifying these two points, we will briefly described several consistency rules that will ensure offered services are not updated by the server without the client being aware of it.

3.1 Information Repository

Composition can not be achieved without knowing what services are offered and how to use them. The composer could refer to an application user's guide to know what the purposes of the services available are. He/she could also refer to the application programmer's guide to get the implementation details about the services. Nonetheless, the composer would only get static information such as service description and method input/output parameter names and types. Megamodules being autonomous and distributed, make it compulsory to also retain dynamic information about the services, such as the name of the machines where the services to be composed are located.

CPAM requires that the necessary megamodule information, both static and dynamic, be gathered into one information repository. Each megamodule provider is responsible for making such a repository available to external users, and for keeping the information up-to-date. It is also the megamodule provider's responsibility to actually offer the services and the quality it advertises.

Information Repository Content. The information repository has to include the following information:

1. Logical name of the service (i.e., megamodule), along with the machine location and the distribution protocol used, in order for the client to bind to the server,

2. Names of the services offered (top-level methods), along with the names and nature (input or output) of their parameters, in order for the client to make invocations or preset parameters before invocation.

Scope of Parameter Names. The scope of parameter names is not restricted to the method where the parameters are used, but rather to the whole megamodule. For megamodules offering more than one method, this implies that if two distinct methods have the same parameter name in their list of parameters, any value preset for this parameter will apply to any use of this parameter in the megamodule. CPAM enlarges the scope of parameter names in order to offer the possibility of presetting all parameters of a megamodule using one call only in the client, hence minimizing data flow (see section 4.2).

3.2 Establishing and Terminating a Connection with a Megamodule

Another issue when composing autonomous megamodules is the ownership of the connection between a client and a server. Autonomous servers do not know when a client wishes to initiate or terminate a connection. In CPAM, clients are responsible for making a connection to a megamodule and terminating it. Nonetheless, servers must be able to handle simultaneous requests from various clients, and must be started before such requests arrive. Certain distribution protocols like CORBA include an internal timer that stops a server execution process if no invocations occur after a set time period, and instantly starts it when a new invocation arrives.

CPAM defines two primitives in order for a client to establish or terminate a connection to a megamodule. These are *SETUP* and *TERMINATEALL*. SETUP tells the megamodule that a client wants to connect to it; TERMINATEALL notifies the megamodule that the client will no longer use its services (the megamodule kills any ongoing invocations initiated by this client). If for any reason a client does not terminate a connection to a megamodule, we can assume the megamodule itself will do it after a time-out, and a new SETUP will be required from the client before any future invocation.

3.3 Consistency

Megamodules being autonomous, they can update services without clients or composers being aware of the modifications brought to the services. The best way a client becomes aware of updates in the server is still under investigation (one option could be to have such changes mentioned in the repository). Nevertheless, it should not be the responsibility of the megamodule provider to directly notify clients and composers of service changes since we do want to preserve megamodule autonomy.

Once the composer knows what modifications were brought to the services, he/she can accordingly upgrade the client program. In CHAIMS, the composer upgrades the megaprogram, which the CHAIMS compiler recompiles in order to generate the updated client program.

It is the responsibility of the service provider not to update the server while there are still clients connected to it. The server must first ask clients to disconnect or wait for their disconnection before upgrading megamodules.

The information repository and the connection and consistency rules ensure that server autonomy is preserved and that clients are able to use offered services.

4 CPAM Enables Efficient Composition of Large-Scale Services

CPAM makes it possible to compose services offered by heterogeneous, distributed and autonomous megamodules. Services being large, an even more interesting objective for a client would be to efficiently compose these services. CPAM enables efficient composition in the following two ways:

- Invocation sequence optimization
- Data flow minimization between megamodules [11].

4.1 Invocation Sequence Optimization

Because the invocation cost of a large service is a priori high and services are distributed, a random composition of services could be very expensive. The invocation sequence has to be optimized. CPAM has defined its own invocation structure in order to allow parallelism and easy invocation monitoring. Such capabilities, added to the possibility of estimating a method cost prior to its invocation, enable optimization of the invocation sequence in the client.

Invocation Structure in CPAM. A traditional procedure call consists of invoking a method and getting its results back in a synchronous way: the calling client waits during the procedure call, and the overall structure of the client program remains simple. In contrast, an asynchronous call avoids client waits but makes the client program more complex, as has to be multithreaded. CPAM splits the traditional call statement into four synchronous remote procedure calls that make the overall call behave asynchronously while keeping the client program sequential and simple. These procedure calls have also enabled the implementation of interesting optimization concepts in CPAM, such as partial extraction and progress monitoring.

The four procedure calls are INVOKE, EXAMINE, EXTRACT, and TERMINATE:

1. *INVOKE* starts the execution of a method applied to a set of input parameters. Not every input parameter of the method has to be specified as the megamodule takes client-specific values or general hard-coded default values for missing parameters (see hierarchical setting of parameters, section 4.2). An INVOKE call returns an invocation identifier, which is used in all subsequent operations on this invocation (EXAMINE, EXTRACT, and TERMINATE).
2. The client checks if the results of an INVOKE call are ready using the *EXAMINE* primitive. EXAMINE returns two pieces of information: an *invocation status* and an *invocation progress*. The invocation status can be any of DONE, NOT_DONE, PARTIAL, or ERROR. If it is either PARTIAL or DONE, then respectively part or all of the results of the invocation are ready and can be extracted by the client. Invocation progress' semantics is megamodule specific. For instance, progress information could be quantitative and describe the degree of completion of an

INVOKE call, or qualitative (e.g., specify the degree of resolution a first round of image processing would give).

3. The results of an INVOKE call are retrieved using the *EXTRACT* primitive. Only the parameters specified as input are extracted, and only when the client wishes to extract results, can it do so. CPAM does not prevent a client from repeatedly extracting an identical or a different subset of results.

4. *TERMINATE* is used to tell a megamodule that the client is no longer interested in a specific invocation. TERMINATE is necessary because the server has no other way to know whether an invocation will be referred to by the client in the future. In case the client is no longer interested in an invocation's results, TERMINATE makes it possible for the server to abort an ongoing execution. In case the invocation has generated persistent changes in the server, it is the responsibility of the megamodule to preserve consistency.

Parallelism and Invocation Monitoring. The benefits of having the call statement split into the four primitives mentioned above are parallelism, simplicity, and easy invocation monitoring:

- *Parallelism*: thanks to the separation between INVOKE and EXTRACT in the procedure call, the methods of different megamodules can be executed in parallel, even if they are synchronous, the only restrictions being data flow dependencies. The client program initiates as many invocations as desired and begins collecting results when it needs them. Figure 3 illustrates the parallelism that can be induced on synchronous calls using CPAM. Similar parallelism could also be obtained with asynchronous methods.

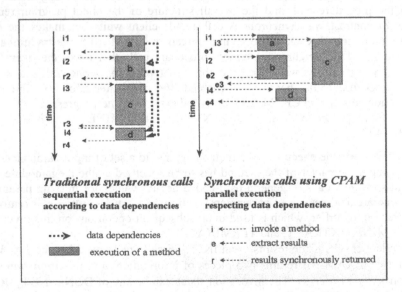

Fig. 3. Split of the procedure call in CPAM and parallelism on synchronous calls

- *Simplicity*: the client program using CPAM consists of sequential invocations of CPAM primitives, and is simple. It does not have to manage any callbacks of asynchronous calls from the servers (the client is the one which initiates all the calls to the servers, including the ones for getting invocation results).

- *Easy invocation monitoring:*

  - *Progress monitoring:* a client can check a method execution progress (EXAMINE), and abort a method execution (TERMINATE). Consider the case where a client has the choice between megamodules offering the same service and arbitrarily chooses one of them for invocation. EXAMINE allows the client to confirm or revoke its choice, perhaps even ending an invocation if another one seems more promising.

  - *Partial extraction:* a client can extract a subset of the results of a method. CPAM also allows progressive extraction: the client can incrementally extract results. This is feasible if the megamodule makes a result available as soon as its computation is completed (and before the computation of the next result is), or becomes significantly "more accurate." Incremental extraction could also be used for terminating an invocation as soon as its results are satisfying, or conversely for verifying the adequacy of large method invocations and maybe terminating them as soon as results are not satisfying.

  - *Ongoing processes:* separating method invocation from result extraction and method termination enables clients to monitor ongoing processes (processes that continuously compute or complete results, such as weather services).

With very few primitives to learn, the composer can write simple client programs, still benefiting from parallelism and easy invocation monitoring. CPAM offers one more functionality in order to optimize the invocation sequence in the client program: invocation cost estimation.

Cost Estimation. Estimating the cost of a method prior to its invocation augments the probability of making the right invocation at the right time. This is enabled in CPAM through the ESTIMATE primitive. Due to the autonomy of megamodules, the client has no knowledge of or influence over the availability of resources. The ESTIMATE primitive, which is provided by the server itself, is the only way a client can get the most accurate method performance and cost information.

A client asks a megamodule for a method cost estimation and then decides whether or not to make the invocation based upon the estimate received. ESTIMATE is very valuable in the case of identical or similar large services offered by more than one megamodule. Indeed, for expensive methods offered by several megamodules, it could be very fruitful to first get an estimate of the invocation cost before choosing one of the methods. Of course, there is no guarantee on the estimate received (we can assume that a service invocation which is not in concordance with the estimate previously provided to a client will not be reused by the client).

Cost estimates are treated in CPAM as *fees* (amount of money to pay to use a service, in electronic commerce for instance), *time* (time of a method execution) and/or *data volume* (amount of data resulting from a method invocation). Since the last two factors are highly run-time dependent, their estimation should be at run-time, as close as possible to the time the method could be invoked. Other application-specific parameters like *server location*, *quality of service*, and *accuracy of estimate* could be added to the output estimate list in the server (and in the information repository), without changing CPAM specifications.

Parallelism, invocation estimates and invocation examinations are very helpful functions of CPAM which, when combined, give enough information and flexibility to get an optimized sequence of invocations at run-time. Megamodule code should return pertinent information with the ESTIMATE and EXAMINE primitives in order for a client to completely benefit from CPAM through consistent estimation and control.

Another factor for optimized composition concerns data flow between megamodules.

4.2 Data Flow Minimization between Megamodules

Partial extraction enables clients to reduce the amount of data returned by an invocation. CPAM also makes it possible to avoid parameter redundancy when calling INVOKE thanks to parameter presetting and hierarchical setting of parameters.

Presetting Parameters. CPAM's *SETPARAM* primitive sets method parameters and global variables before a method is invoked. For a client which invokes a method with the same parameter value several times consecutively, or invokes several methods which have a common subset of parameter names with the same values, it becomes cost-effective to not transmit the same parameter values repeatedly. Let us recall that megamodules are very likely to be data intensive. Also, in the case of methods which have a very large number of parameters, only a few of which are modified at each call (very common in statistical simulations), the SETPARAM primitive becomes very advantageous. Finally, presetting parameters is useful for setting a specific context before estimating the cost of a method.

GETPARAM, the primitive dual, returns client specific settings or default values of the parameters and global variable names specified in its input parameter list.

Hierarchical Setting of Parameters. CPAM establishes a *hierarchical setting of parameters* within megamodules (see Fig. 4). A parameter's default value (most likely hard-coded) defines the first level of parameter settings within the megamodule. The second level is the client specific setting (set by SETPARAM). The third level corresponds to the invocation specific setting (parameter value provided through one specific invocation, by INVOKE). Invocation specific settings override client specific settings for the time of the invocation, and client specific settings override general default values for the time of the connection. When a method is invoked, the megamodule takes the invocation specific settings for all parameters for which the invocation supplies values; for all other parameters, the megamodule takes the client specific settings if they exist, and the megamodule general default values otherwise. For this reason, CPAM requires that megamodules provide default values for all parameters or global variables they contain.

Example: parameters of method "reservation"					
	start-date	end-date	from	to	seats
general default values	1JAN1998	1JAN1998	LAS	BWI	1
client-specific settings for client A	4OCT1998	6OCT1998	SJO	ZRH	
client-specific settings for client B				FRA	2
invocation-specific settings for client A					
actual values used during invocation	4OCT1998	6OCT1998	SJO	ZRH	1
invocation-specific settings for client A		7OCT1998	SFO		
actual values used during invocation	4OCT1998	7OCT1998	SFO	ZRH	1
invocation-specific settings for client B	1DEC1998	9DEC1998			
actual values used during invocation	1DEC1998	9DEC1998	LAS	FRA	2

Fig. 4. Hierarchical setting of parameters

In conclusion, a client does not need to specify all input data or global variables used in a method in order to invoke that method, nor does it need to repeatedly transmit the same data for all method invocations which use the same parameters' values. Also, a client need not retrieve all available results. This reduces the amount of data transferred between megamodules.

Megamodules being large and distributed, invocation sequence optimization and data flow minimization are necessary for efficient composition.

5 How to Use CPAM

We have so far discussed the various CPAM primitives necessary to do composition. Still, we have not yet described the primitives' syntax nor the constraints a composer would have to follow in order to write a correct client program. Another point would concern the service provider: what does he/she need to do in order to convert a module which is not CPAM compliant to a CPAM compliant megamodule that supports CPAM specifications?

CPAM primitives' syntax is fully described and can be found under the CHAIMS Web site at http://www-db.stanford.edu/CHAIMS. In this section, we describe the primitive ordering constraints, the CHAIMS wrapper templates, and provide a client program example which complies with CPAM, and is written in CLAM.

5.1 Primitives Ordering Constraints

CPAM primitives cannot be called in any arbitrary order, but they only have to follow two constraints:

- All primitives apart from SETUP must be preceded by a connection to the megamodule through a call to SETUP (which has not yet been terminated by TERMINATEALL),
- The invocation referred to by EXAMINE, EXTRACT, or TERMINATE must be preceded by an INVOKE call (which has not yet been terminated by TERMINATE).

Figure 5 summarizes CPAM primitives and the ordering relations.

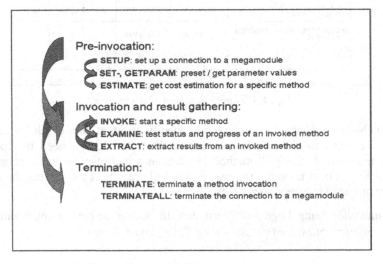

Pre-invocation:
  SETUP: set up a connection to a megamodule
  SET-, GETPARAM: preset / get parameter values
  ESTIMATE: get cost estimation for a specific method

Invocation and result gathering:
  INVOKE: start a specific method
  EXAMINE: test status and progress of an invoked method
  EXTRACT: extract results from an invoked method

Termination:
  TERMINATE: terminate a method invocation
  TERMINATEALL: terminate the connection to a megamodule

Fig. 5. Primitives in CPAM and invocation ordering

5.2 The CHAIMS Wrapper

In case a server does not comply with CPAM specifications, it has to be *wrapped* in order to use the CPAM protocol. The CHAIMS wrapper templates allow a megamodule to become CPAM compliant with a minimum of additional work.

The CHAIMS wrapper templates are currently implemented as a C++ or Java object which serves as a middleman between the network and non-CPAM compliant servers. They implement CPAM specifications in the following way:

1. *Mapping of methods [12] [13] and parameters:* the wrapper maps methods specified in the information repository to one or more methods of the legacy module. It also maps parameters to ASN.1 data structures, preserving default values assigned in the legacy modules (or adding them if they were not assigned).
2. *Threading of invocations:* to ensure parallelism and respect asynchrony in the legacy code, the CHAIMS wrapper spawns a new thread for each invocation.

3. *Generation of internal data structures to handle client invocations and connections, and support hierarchical setting of parameters:* each call to SETUP generates the necessary data structures to store client and invocation related information in the wrapper. Such information includes client-specific preset values, and the status, progress and results for each invocation. The generated data structures are deleted when a call to TERMINATEALL occurs.

4. *Implementation of the ESTIMATE primitive for cost estimation:* for each method whose cost estimation is not provided by the server, the ESTIMATE primitive by default returns an average of the costs of the previous calls of that method. It could also include dynamic information about the server and the network, such as machine server load, network traffic, etc.

5. *Implementation of the EXAMINE primitive for invocation monitoring:* by default, only the status field is returned. For the progress information to be set in the wrapper, the server has to give significant information.

6. *Implementation of all other CPAM primitives:* SETUP, GET/SETPARAM, INVOKE, EXTRACT, TERMINATE, and TERMINATEALL.

The current CHAIMS wrapper templates automatically generate the code to ensure points 2 to 6. Only requirement 1 needs manual coding (except for BER-encoding/decoding, which is automatically done by ASN.1 libraries).

5.3 Example of a Client Using CPAM

A successful utilization of CPAM for realizing composition is the Transportation example implemented within the CHAIMS system. The example consists in finding the best way for transporting goods between two cities. The composer uses services from five heterogeneous and autonomous megamodules. The client program is written in CLAM, and the CSRT generated through the CHAIMS compiler is in compliance with CPAM. A second example is under implementation. It computes the best design model for an aircraft system, and includes optimization functionality as cost estimation, incremental result extraction and invocation progress examination.

Below is given a simplified version of the Transportation megaprogram (Fig. 6). Heterogeneity and distribution characteristics of the composed megamodules are specified as follows: locality (Remote or Local), language, and protocol.

6 Conclusion

CPAM is a high-level protocol for composing megamodules. It supports heterogeneity especially by transferring data as encoded ASN.1 structures, and preserves megamodule autonomy by collecting service information from an information repository, and by subsequently using the generic invocation primitive of CPAM in order to INVOKE services.

Most importantly, CPAM enables efficient composition of large-scale services by optimizing the invocation sequence (parallelism, invocation monitoring, cost estimation), and minimizing data flow between megamodules (presetting of parameters, hierarchical setting of parameters, partial extraction). As CPAM is currently focused on composition, it does not provide support for recovery or security. These services could be obtained by orthogonal systems or by integrating CPAM into a larger protocol.

```
Transportationdemo
BEGINCHAIMS
io   = SETUP ("io")          // Remote, Java, CORBA ORBACUS
math = SETUP ("MathMM")      // Local, Java
am   = SETUP ("AirMM")       // Remote, C++, CORBA ORBIX
gm   = SETUP ("GroundMM")    // Remote, C++, CORBA ORBIX
ri   = SETUP ("RouteInfoMM") // Remote, C++, CORBA ORBIX

// Get type and default value of the city pair parameter
(cp_var = CityPair) = ri.GETPARAM()

// Ask the user to confirm/modify the source and destination cities
ioask = io.INVOKE ("ask", label = "which cities", data = cp_var)
WHILE ( ioask.EXAMINE() != DONE )  {}
(cities_var = Cities) = ioask.EXTRACT()

// Compute costs of the route by air, and by ground, in parallel
acost = am.INVOKE ("GetAirTravelCost", CityPair = cities_var)
gcost = gm.INVOKE ("GetGdTravelCost", CityPair = cities_var)

// Make other invocations (e.g., Check weather)
....

// Extract the two cost results
WHILE ( acost.EXAMINE() != DONE )  {}
(ac_var = Cost) = acost.EXTRACT()
WHILE ( gcost.EXAMINE() != DONE )  {}
(gc_var = Cost) = gcost.EXTRACT()

// Compare the two costs
lt = math.INVOKE ("LessThan", value1 = ac_var, value2 = gc_var)
WHILE ( lt.EXAMINE() != DONE )  {}
(lt_bool = Result) = lt_ih.EXTRACT()

// Display the smallest cost
IF ( lt_bool == TRUE ) THEN
{ iowrite = io.INVOKE ("write", data = ac_var) }
ELSE
{ iowrite = io.INVOKE ("write", data = gc_var)  }

am.TERMINATE()
ri.TERMINATE()
gm.TERMINATE()
io.TERMINATE()
math.TERMINATE()
ENDCHAIMS
```

Fig. 6. CLAM megaprogram to calculate the best route between two cities

In the future, we plan to enable even more optimization through automated scheduling of composed services that use the CPAM protocol within the CHAIMS system. Automation, while not disabling optimizations that are based on domain expertise, will discharge the composer from parallelism or lower level scheduling tasks. In a large-scale and distributed environment, resources are likely to be relocated, and their available capacity depends on aggregate usage. Invocation scheduling and data flow optimization need to take into account such constraints. The CPAM protocol can give sufficient information to the compiler or the client program for enabling automated scheduling of composed software at compile-time, and more significantly, at run-time.

References

1. G. Wiederhold, P. Wegner and S. Ceri: "Towards Megaprogramming: A Paradigm for Component-Based Programming"; Communications of the ACM, 1992(11): p89-99
2. J. Siegel: "CORBA fundamentals and programming"; Wiley New York, 1996
3. C. Szyperski: "Component Software: Beyond Object-Oriented Programming"; Addison-Wesley and ACM-Press New York, 1997
4. W. Rosenberry, D. Kenney and G. Fisher: "Understanding DCE"; OReilly, 1994
5. D. Platt: "The Essence of COM and ActiveX"; Prentice-Hall, 1997
6. R. Van Renesse and K. Birman: "Protocol Composition in Horus"; TR95-1505, 1995
7. J. Jannink, S. Pichai, D. Verheijen and G. Wiederhold: "Encapsulation and Composition of Ontologies"; submitted
8. "Information Processing -- Open Systems Interconnection -- Specification of Abstract Syntax Notation One" and "Specification of Basic Encoding Rules for Abstract Syntax Notation One", International Organization for Standardization and International Electrotechnical Committee, International Standards 8824 and 8825, 1987
9. L. Perrochon, G. Wiederhold and R. Burback: "A compiler for Composition: CHAIMS"; Fifth International Symposium on Assessment of Software Tools and Technologies (SAST '97), Pittsburgh, June 3-5, 1997
10. N. Sample, D. Beringer, L. Melloul and G. Wiederhold: "CLAM: Composition Language for Autonomous Megamodules"; Third Int'l Conference on Coordination Models and Languages, COORD'99, Amsterdam, April 26-28, 1999
11. D. Beringer, C. Tornabene, P. Jain and G. Wiederhold: "A Language and System for Composing Autonomous, Heterogeneous and Distributed Megamodules"; DEXA International Workshop on Large-Scale Software Composition, August 28, 1998, Vienna Austria
12. Birell, A.D. and B.J. Nelso: "Implementing Remote Procedure Calls"; ACM Transactions on Computer Systems, 1984. 2(1): p. 39-59
13. ISO, "ISO Remote Procedure Call Specification", ISO/IEC CD 11578 N6561, 1991

A Process-Oriented Approach to Software Component Definition

Florian Matthes, Holm Wegner, and Patrick Hupe

Software Systems Institute (STS)
Technical University Hamburg-Harburg, Germany
{f.matthes,ho.wegner,pa.hupe}@tu-harburg.de

Abstract. Commercial software component models are frequently based on *object-oriented* concepts and terminology with appropriate binding, persistence and distribution support. In this paper, we argue that a *process-oriented* view on cooperating software components based on the concepts and terminology of a language/action perspective on cooperative work provides a more suitable foundation for the analysis, design and implementation of software components in business applications.

We first explain the relationship between data-, object- and process-oriented component modeling and then illustrate our process-oriented approach to component definition using three case studies from projects with German software companies.

We also report on our experience gained in developing a class framework and a set of tools to assist in the systematic process-oriented development of business application components. This part of the paper also clarifies that a process-oriented perspective fits well with today's object-oriented language and system models.

1 Introduction and Rationale

Organizations utilize information systems as tools to support cooperative activities of employees within the enterprise. Classical examples are back-end information systems set up to support administrative processes in banks, insurances, or processes in enterprise resource planning.

Driven by various factors (availability of technology, group collaboration issues and organizational needs), there is a strong demand for more flexible and decentralized information system architectures which are able to support

- cooperation of humans over time (persistence, concurrency and recovery),
- cooperation of humans in space (distribution, mobility, on/offline users), and
- cooperation of humans in multiple modalities (batch processing, transaction processing, asynchronous email communication, workflow-style task assignment, ad-hoc information sharing).

Another crucial observation is the fact that cooperation support can no longer be restricted to employees (intra-organizational workflows) but also has to encompass inter-organizational workflows involving customers, suppliers, tax authorities, banks, etc.

M. Jarke, A. Oberweis (Eds.): CAiSE'99, LNCS 1626, pp. 26–40, 1999.
© Springer-Verlag Berlin Heidelberg 1999

The objective of our research is to identify abstractions and architectural patterns which help to design, construct and maintain software components in such a "cooperative information system" environment [2, 3]

In Sect. 2, we argue that the successful step in information system engineering from data-oriented to object-oriented information system modeling should be followed by a second step from object-oriented to process-oriented system engineering. Only a process-oriented perspective allows software architects and organizations to identify and to reason about actors, goals, cooperations, commitments and customer-performer relationships which are crucial in a world of constant change to keep the organizational objectives and the objectives of the supporting information systems aligned.

In Sect. 3, we illustrate our process-oriented approach to component definition using three case studies from projects with German software companies. Details of the underlying process and system model are given in Sect. 4 and 5.

2   Approaches to Component Definition in Information Systems

In this section, we briefly review the evolution of information system architectures to highlight the benefits of a process-oriented approach to component definition. Figure 1 summarizes the main result of this section:

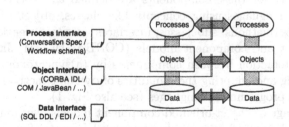

Fig. 1. Three Approaches to Component Definition in Business Information Systems

Interaction between system components in an information system can be understood at three levels, namely at the level of *data* access, *object* interaction and at the level of *process* coupling.

At each level, interfaces between system components should be declared in an abstract, system-independent syntax which also provides a basis for the systematic implementation of vendor-independent middleware. Abstract concepts of the interface language are mapped to concrete implementation concepts of the participating system components. A higher-level interface language includes concepts of the lower-level interface language but often imposes additional restrictions on the use of these concepts. For example, CORBA IDL provides data attributes and attribute types similar to record attributes and SQL domains, but also provides mechanisms for data encapsulation at the object level.

2.1   Data-Oriented Component Definition

Database research and development focused on the entities and relationships of an information system and led to the development of conceptual, logical and physical data models, generic systems and tools as well as software development processes to support the analysis, design and efficient implementation of (distributed) data components.

Today, virtually all organizations have conceptual models of the information available in their back-end information systems and systematic mechanisms to develop and change applications to satisfy new information needs.

For information stored in relational databases, SQL as the "intergalactic dataspeak" [13] provides both, a language for the exchange of vendor-independent data description (schemata, tables, views, . . .) as well as a language for (remote) data access (via APIs like ODBC, JDBC, . . . ; see also Fig. 1).

2.2   Object-Oriented Component Definition

In modern client-server architectures and in cooperating information systems, the information assets of an enterprise are modeled (and implemented) as collections of distributed and persistent objects interacting via messages and events.

The interfaces for these components are defined as enriched signatures in object-oriented languages using concepts like classes, objects, (remote) references, attributes, methods, subclasses, interfaces, events, exceptions etc.

These object and component models (CORBA, DCOM, JavaBeans, etc.) describe the interaction between components by (a)synchronous method invocation extending and adapting the semantics of dynamic method dispatching in object-oriented programming languages (see also Fig. 1).

The advantage of object-oriented component models over pure data models on the one hand side and over purely procedural (remote) function libraries on the other hand is their ability to describe semantic entities which are meaningful already at the analysis and at the design level. The often quoted classes `Customer` and `Shipment` are examples for such high-level entities.

As exemplified by ODMG using CORBA IDL, an object-component model can also be used to describe "data-only" components, simply by omitting elaborate method and message specifications and only providing (set-oriented) get, set, insert and delete methods.

2.3   Process-Oriented Component Definition

An object-oriented component definition is "richer" than a data-oriented component definition since the methods provide a more suitable protocol for the interaction between a client and a server component than a sequence of raw SQL statements working on a shipment table.

However, we still see the following deficiencies of object-oriented component definitions which call for an even richer process-oriented component definition:

- The interface of a software component rarely consists of a single object interface but of a large number of highly interrelated object interfaces.
- Frequently it is necessary for a server to manage multiple execution contexts, for example, one for each concurrent client session. Clients then often have to pass a *session* handle as an extra argument to each of these methods.
- In particular in business applications, it is desirable to enforce restrictions on the admissible execution order of certain method calls ("A shipment can only be send after a payment has been received").
- The lifetime of such execution contexts tends to be longer than the lifetime of the server process. Therefore, it becomes necessary to make such execution contexts first-class persistent and possibly mobile objects.
- If a large system is broken down into autonomous *concurrent* subsystems (a collection of *agents*), synchronization issues can arise

As a solution to these problems we propose not to use object-oriented component interface definitions but process-oriented interface definitions between parts of a business information system following the language/action perspective on cooperative work [15, 4, 12, 1]. For details on our model, see [8, 10, 6, 14].

In a first step, we identify *actors* in a business information system. An actor can either be a human or an active process (thread, task, job, ...) in an information system. For example, a customer, an SAP R/3 application server and a Lotus Notes Domino Server can all be viewed as actors.

In a second step, we identify *conversation specifications* to describe long-term, goal-directed interactions between actors. For example, if a customer can browse through an Internet product catalogue on a Lotus Notes Server to place an order online, we identify a conversation specification called **online shopping**. We also assign *roles* to actors within a conversation. The actor that initiates the conversation (the online shopper) is called the *customer* of the conversation. The actor that accepts conversation requests is called the *performer* of the conversation.

An actor can participate in multiple (possibly concurrent) conversations in different roles. For example, Lotus Notes could use the services of SAP R/3 to check the availability of products. Thus, Lotus Notes would be the customer of SAP R/3 for this particular conversation specification.

Next, we identify *dialog specifications* which are process steps within each of the conversations (catalog/item view, shopping cart dialog etc. for online shopping and a dialog for the availability check). A dialog consists of a hierarchically structured *content specification* plus a set of *request specifications* valid in this particular process step. For example, the shopping cart dialog could aggregate a set of shopping cart items (part identification, part name, number of items, price per item) plus a total, the name of the customer, VAT, etc. In this dialog, only a restricted set of requests can be issued by the customer (leave shop, select payment mode, remove item from cart, etc.).

For each request specification in a dialog there is a specification of the set of admissible follow-up dialogs. If this set contains more than one dialog, the performer can continue the conversation at run-time with any of these dialogs. For example, the addItemToShoppingCart request in the item view dialog could either lead to the shopping cart view or to an out of stock error dialog.

It should be emphasized that a dialog specification fully abstracts from the details and modalities of dialog processing at run-time. For example, the dialog could be carried out synchronously via a GUI interface or via HTTP or asynchronously via email or a workflow-style task manager.

Contrary to object interactions via message passing, this "form-based" or "document-based" style of interaction at the level of dialogs also fits well the (semi-)formal interaction between humans. For example, we are all used to a form-based interaction with public authorities.

We consider the ability to abstract from the modalities of an interaction (local/remote, synchronous/asynchronous, short-term/persistent, involving systems/humans) as a major contribution of our process model since it makes it possible to uniformly describe a wide range of interactions.

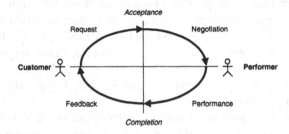

Fig. 2. Phases of typical customer-oriented conversations

Figure 2 illustrates the basic structure of a typical customer-oriented conversation. In the first step, the *request*-phase, a customer asks for a specific service of a performer ("I want to order a hotel-room"). In the second *negotiation*-phase, customer and performer negotiate their common goal (e.g. conditions, quality of service) and possibly reach an agreement. To do this, several dialog iterations may be necessary. In the third *performance*-phase, the performer fulfills the requested activity and reports completion back to the customer ("we accepted your order"). The optional fourth *feedback*-phase gives the customer a chance to declare his/her satisfaction and may also contain the payment for the service.

It should be noted that we deliberately restrict our model to *binary* customer/performer relationships and that we do not follow established workflow models (from CSCW) that focus on process chains involving multiple performers from different parts of the enterprise. For example, in our model a workflow with three specialized performers could be broken down into a coordinator that takes a customer request and that initiates three separate (possibly concurrent) conversations with the three performers involved.

This example also illustrates that conversation specifications are an excellent starting point for component definitions since they help to identify data and control dependencies. Moreover, it becomes much simpler to assign (data, behavior and also process) responsibilities to actors than it is the case for pure data- or object-oriented models.

To summarize, conversation specifications include data specifications (similar to complex object models) and behavior specifications (similar to methods in object models) and they provide additional mechanisms for process modeling:

- Actors and their roles in the network of conversations of an enterprise are modeled explicitly and at a high level of abstraction.
- The context of a request is modeled explicitly. For example, it is possible to access the history or the client of a conversation.
- It is possible to restrict requests to certain steps (dialogs) within a process.
- It is possible to specify (aspects of) the dynamic behavior of the process through the set of follow-up dialogs defined for a requests.

Finally, it should be noted that conversation, dialog, request and content specifications can be used as *static* interfaces between components. Only at runtime, conversations, dialogs, requests and contents are created *dynamically* as instances of these classes. This corresponds to the distinction between schema and database at the data level and the distinction between interface and object at the object level.

3   Three Case Studies

In this section, we illustrate our process-oriented approach to component definition using three case studies from projects with German software companies. The goal of these projects was to investigate whether the abstract process component model described in [8, 10] and successfully implemented in persistent programming languages [6, 14] is also a suitable basis for the implementation of process components using commercially relevant technology.

The conceptual basis for these projects is summarized in Table 1 that shows the (rough) correspondence between the abstract process component model concepts on the one hand side and the implementation concepts of the respective languages or systems used to systematically realize these concepts. We also added a column describing the relationship between Java HTTP-Servlets and our model.

Several cells in the table are marked as "not applicable" (n.a.), since some of the systems lack the required modeling support. However, these concepts can be emulated by a systematic use of other language constructs.

Figure 3 summarizes the agents and conversation specifications of the three case studies. In this diagram, an agent is indicated by a circle with an arrow. A conversation specification between two agents is indicated by a line with two arrows connecting the agent icons. If there are multiple agents that are based on the same conversation specifications, the icons of these agents are stacked.

Model Concept	Implementation Concept				
	SAP R/3 Dynpro Technology	SAP R/3 BAPI Technology	Lotus Notes Technology	Java Server Technology	Microsoft ASP Technology
Agent	R/3 Application Server	R/3 Application Server	Domino / Lotus Server	HTTP-Server + Servlets	HTTP-Server + ASP Extension
Performer Role	Collection of related Dynpros	Collection of related BAPIs	Collection of Agents	Collection of Servlets	Collection of ASPs
Customer Role	n.a.	n.a.	n.a.	n.a.	n.a.
Conversation	R/3 Dynpro	Client Session / SAP Transaction	Session	Servlet-Session	ASP-Session
Dialog	Dynpro Screen	n.a.	Document	HTML-Form	HTML-Form
Request	Modification of GUI Variable	BAPI Method Invocation (RFC)	User Event	HTTP-Request	HTTP-Request
Content	Dynpro Screen Field	BAPI Method Arguments	Content of a document	HTML-Document	HTML-Document
Rule	PBO / PAI-Module	Implementation of BAPI (RFC)	Agent (Event Handler)	Servlet	Embedded Script Code
Conversation Specification	EPC Description of Dynpro	n.a.	n.a.	n.a.	n.a.
Request Spec	EPC Event	n.a.	n.a.	HTML-Form	HTML-Form
Content Spec	(I/O values of EPC transition)	n.a.	n.a.	DTD	DTD

Table 1. Mapping of Process Component Model Concepts to Implementation Concepts

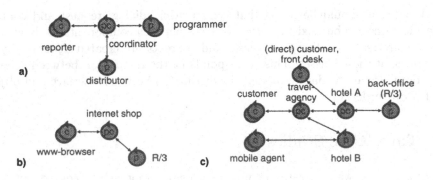

Fig. 3. Agents and Conversations of Three Case Studies

Each agent is annotated with the letter(s) P or C depending on his role(s) in the participating conversations (performer or customer role).

Figure 3 is described in more detail in the following subsections. At this point, we should note that some of the agent *patterns* depicted in this figure (coordinator, mediator, broker) tend to appear in multiple application domains.

3.1   Process-Oriented Modeling of an Internet Shop

In this example, an internet shop was created to support internet customers with HTTP clients and inhouse customers using Lotus Notes clients. The internet shop was implemented using a Lotus Notes Domino server. This implementation is based on a rather generic implementation of the agent model outlined in Sect. 2. This generic subsystem is responsible for managing multiple conversations and to decouple visual details of the user interface from the rule-based agent implementation.

Using this generic infrastructure, the system implementor first defines the conversation specification including dialogs, requests and specifications for the admissible follow-up dialogs in each dialog step. The developer can utilize the standard Notes tools to design the dialogs and their content layout.

In a next step, the application developer implements rules (event handlers) for each request specification that appears in a dialog. This event handler at run time has to return a dialog object to be displayed to the user in the next process step. Each rule has access (via database variables) to the contents and requests of previous dialogs in the current conversation.

The shop also uses a SAP R/3 system for invoices, accounting and product availability checks. All client conversations share a common conversation with the SAP R/3 system which effectively serializes client dialog steps.

3.2   A Workflow Manager for Software Bug Tracking

The next example illustrates how conversation specifications can be used to structure the interaction between multiple human agents within an enterprise.

At StarDivision Inc., a cooperative information system was created for tracking and removing bugs in software (see Fig. 3 a). There are three kinds of human actors and one software actor:

- A reporter is a human agent (a member of the support staff) that is a customer in a conversation *ReportBug*, which starts with a dialog where a description of the bug is entered. This conversation ends when the reporter is informed that the bug has been fixed. There can be multiple reporters.
- The distinguished coordinator agent (a centralized software system implemented with the Microsoft Transaction Manager and Active Server Pages) is the performer for the *ReportBug* conversation but also a customer in two other conversations (*AssignBug* and *RemoveBug*).
- A distributor is a human agent responsible for the correctness of a particular software component. The *AssignBug* conversation is used by the coordinator agent to request the distributor to propose a programmer who may be able to remove the bug. There can be an arbitrary number of distributors.
- A programmer is a human agent that may be able to locate a bug and report successful removal of the bug back to the coordinator.

The task of the coordinator agent is to implement each *ReportBug* conversation by a sequence of *AssignBug* and *RemoveBug* conversations. If a programmer is not able to remove a bug, the bug report is returned to the distributor who has to propose another programmer to solve the bug.

Each human agent has access to a list of the active conversations he is involved in. The list items are grouped by role and conversation specification and also indicate the currently active dialog step of each conversation. A human agent can switch freely between conversations and issue requests (as customer) or create follow-up dialogs from a list of possible follow-up dialogs (as performer).

Similar to the system described in the previous section, this system has been implemented based on a generic subsystem for conversation management and

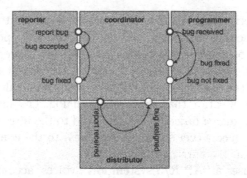

Fig. 4. Agents and Conversation in the Bug Tracker

dialog visualization. Since the main objective of the bug tracking software is to keep track of the state and of the history of problem-solving conversations in the enterprise, only very little code had to be written to implement the performer and customer rules of the coordinator.

Despite the fact that our process model described in Sect. 2.3 is based on purely sequential conversations, the implementation of agents (more precisely the implementation of the customer and performer rules) may introduce concurrency by initiating multiple conversations.

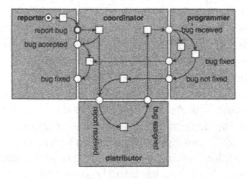

Fig. 5. Petri Net for combined Conversations of Bug Tracker

Figure 4 and 5 illustrate how agents (as process-oriented software components) can be composed systematically via conversation specifications using a Petri-Net formalism:

- In a first step, one draws a state for each dialog in a conversation. The states are drawn at the borderline between two grey boxes. Each grey box corresponds to one of the participating agents. In Fig. 4 there are three conversations with two resp. three dialogs.

– In a second step, one connects a state with its follow-up states via transitions based on the conversation specification.
– In a third step, additional transitions and states (internal to an agent, but possibly connecting multiple of its roles) are added to formally define the desired interaction and synchronization between the agent's conversations. Since agents should be self-contained, autonomous software components, the only way to establish connections between roles of different agents are states corresponding to dialogs of conversations.

The resulting Petri-net (cf. Fig. 5) could be analyzed formally for deadlocks, safety and liveness. Alternatively, simulations could be carried out to detect mismatches between the design and the system requirements.

3.3   A Broker for Hotel Reservations

The last example in this section illustrates the use of process-oriented component specifications in a distributed environment that also supports conversations between *mobile and persistent agents* [7, 9].

The work described here is the result of a cooperation project with SAP AG which is interested in technologies and architectures suitable for the construction of scalable cooperative software architectures [11].

Diagram (c) in Fig. 3 summarizes the agents and conversations in this particular scenario. The main agent developed in this project is a broker agent (e.g., Hotel A) implementing a virtual hotel front desk. This front desk is a performer for a *RoomReservation* conversation that can be carried out via three different communication media, namely a HTML front-end for customers, message passing for remote agents at travel agencies and message passing for mobile agents that visit the front desk through the Internet. The front desk has to be able to use a (legacy) system like SAP R/3 as a back-office system to do controlling, material management etc. which is not an integral part of room reservations.

The mobile agents and the travel agency agent may in turn act as *brokers* on behalf of customers contacting the agency via internet, e.g. to identify the cheapest offer available.

The agent Hotel B in Fig. 3 (c) and 6 illustrates an important aspect of our process model: There can be multiple, possibly different agent implementations for the same conversation specification (*RoomReservation* in our case).

Each of these agents utilizes a common generic object-oriented class framework which provides means of defining (abstract) conversation-specifications, agents, roles, rules etc. [14]. This framework also supports conversations between persistent and mobile agents and is implemented in the programming language Tycoon, a persistent programming language developed by our group.

Moreover, we developed on top of this framework a so-called "generic customer" application, which transparently and automatically visualizes conversations and dialogs (using HTTP) so that a human user can interact directly with any agent in the distributed system.

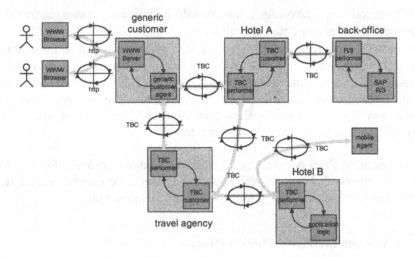

Fig. 6. Scenario for a Hotel Reservation System

4   Building a Generic Conversation Management Framework

In this section we briefly highlight the major steps necessary to build a generic conversation management framework. Details can be found in [14, 8, 6].

The first step is to define (persistent and mobile) representations for conversation specifications that match the object model of Fig. 7. The recursive definition of the class ContentSpec supports complex dialog contents based on atomic types (bool, int, real, string, date, time, currency) and structured types like records, variants, lists, and multiple-choices. All of these constructs may be combined orthogonally. Finally, specifications may appear as the contents of conversations which is useful for "higher-level" (meta-)conversations.

In an object-oriented implementation language, this model maps directly into a class hierarchy. Using the visitor pattern, the construction of generators to dynamically instantiate conversations, dialogs and contents, to visualize conversations, dialogs and contents and to transmit these objects is straightforward.

The implementation of concurrent conversations and the synchronization between multiple concurrent conversations of a single agent is more intricate, in particular, if agents have to be persistent (i.e. outlive individual operating system processes) or if agents are allowed to migrate between address spaces while they are participating in conversations.

A detail from the *RoomReservation* conversation specification of the hotel reservation system is depicted as a state diagram in Fig. 8. The Search dialog has two attributes denoting the date of arrival and the number of days the customer wants to stay at the hotel. The content of the dialog ProductList is a single-choice-list which contains the different products that match the customer's query. In the ProductList dialog, three requests can be issued by the customer:

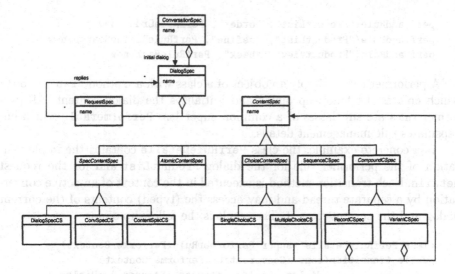

Fig. 7. An Object-Oriented Model for Conversation Specifications

Return to the Search dialog to refine the search, move to the ProductView
dialog to view details of a single product, or order the product selected from the
product list.

Fig. 8. A Detail from the *RoomReservation* Conversation Specification

The actual definition of an agent implementing this conversation as a performer looks as follows:

```
(* create a hotel front-desk agent *)
let agent :Agent = Agent.new("Hotel Front Desk"),
(* use existing RoomReservation specification *)
let convSpec :ConversationSpec = CvSpecFactory.create("Reservation"),
(* create a performer role for this conversation specification *)
let perf :PerformerRole(PerformerContext) =
    PerformerRole.new(agent, convSpec),
(* add rules to the performer for all 3 dialogs *)
perf.addRule("Search", "search", PerfRuleSearch.new ),
perf.addRule("ProductList", "details", PerfRuleDetails.new ),
```

```
perf.addRule("ProductList", "order", PerfRuleOrder.new ),
perf.addRule("ProductList", "refine", PerfRuleRefineSearch.new ),
perf.addRule("ProductView", "back", PerfRuleBack.new ),
```

A performer rule is simply an object of a class with a method `transition()` which creates the follow-up dialog and initializes the dialog content. All performer rules are subclasses of a common superclass `PerformerRule` which encapsulates rule management details.

As a concrete example, the class `PerfRuleDetails` contains the implementation of the performer rule for the dialog `ProductList` and for the request `details`. Each transition method is executed in the context of an active conversation by a separate thread and may access the (typed) contents of the current dialog and the current request. The result is the follow-up dialog.

```
class PerfRuleDetails  super PerformerRule(PerformerContext)
public transition(conv :Conversation(PerformerContext),
                  dialog :Dialog, request :Request ) :Dialog {
   (* create and initialize the follow-dialog *)
   let next :Dialog = conv.newDialog( "ProductView" ),
   (* fetch current product key from current dialog "ProductList" *)
   let product :Product =
       lookupProd(dialog.content["products"].singlechoice.current),
   (* set attributes of next dialog "ProductView" *)
   next.content["description"].str := product.name,
   next.content["salesPrice"].currency := product.price *
       conv.history[''Search''].content.[''numOfStays''].int,
   next.content["picture"].image := product.picture,
   next    (* return the next dialog *)
}
```

5   State-Enriched Type Checking

The rule implementation shown at the end of the previous section exhibits a significant potential for improvements exploiting the static knowledge already present in conversation specifications:

- Type-safe access to the contents of the current dialog should be supported. Thereby, spelling errors and also errors caused by schema changes can be detected at compile-time.
- The validity of the follow-dialog should be checked already at compile-time.
- Warnings should be issued if an implementor writes code to attach rules to requests which are not valid in a given dialog.
- Type-safe access to the dialog contents of earlier steps of a conversation should be supported. This requires a non-trivial control flow analysis of conversation specifications to detect which dialogs are guaranteed to, cannot or may appear in the history. We have formalized this decision procedure using temporal logic formulae [5].

We have implemented these improvements by means of a so-called *state-enriched type checker* which is able to verify the consistency of rule implementations based on the additional knowledge of the dynamics of the system described by an object of class conversation specification. The state-enriched type checker makes use of a (typed) representation of the history and the current dialog.

As a consequence, the body of the rule described in the previous section can be written in a more concise and type-safe way as follows:

```
nextDialog( "ProductView" ),            (* create the next dialog *)
(* fetch current product from the current dialog "ProductList" *)
let product = lookupProd( dialog.products.current ),
(* set attributes of next dialog "ProductView" *)
next.description = product.description,
next.salesPrice = product.price * history.numOfStays,
next.picture = product.picture,
```

The state-enriched type checker ensures that the dialog to be created in the `nextDialog` statement is valid. Similar checks are performed on requests generated in customer rules. The checker also ensures that variables referenced by the identifiers `dialog` or `next` are declared in the corresponding dialogs. In comparison to the former dynamically-typed code, no type information has to be specified; the dialogs' variables are completely statically typed.

One of the biggest advantages of state-enriched type checking becomes apparent when changing conversation specifications, e.g. when extending or refining an existing conversation specification by adding new paths, new dialogs or moving attributes from one dialog to another. Without typechecking, all rule code implementing the specification would have to be verified to check the compliance with the altered specification. In our example, the checker can verify that access to the variable `numOfStays` which is set in a previous dialog, is correct.

6   Concluding Remarks

In this paper we described our *business conversations* model which is based on a process-oriented perspective on software components. We illustrated the use of this model using three practical examples and explained in quite some detail how such software components can be implemented in different technologies using generic conversation management frameworks.

The technology and formalization of state-enriched type checking may have other interesting application areas (e.g., verifying the consistency of a set of interacting Java Servlet implementations or generating strongly-typed access code to CGI-arguments).

A necessary condition for process-oriented component specifications to become practically relevant is the availability of a widely accepted syntax/language to write down and to exchange such specifications in distributed heterogeneous environments. One could either "abuse" CORBA IDL as a starting point for conversation specification or one could utilize SGML/XML documents that conform to an agreed-upon `ConversationSpecification` DTD.

References

[1] J. Austin. How to do things with words. Technical report, Oxford University Press, Oxford, 1962.

[2] Giorgio De Michelis, Eric Dubois, Matthias Jarke, Florian Matthes, John Mylopoulos, Mike Papazoglou, Klaus Pohl, Joachim Schmidt, Carson Woo, and Eric Yu. Cooperative information systems: A manifesto. In Mike P. Papazoglou and Gunther Schlageter, editors, *Cooperative Information System: Trends and Directions*. Academic Press, 1997.

[3] Giorgio De Michelis, Eric Dubois, Matthias Jarke, Florian Matthes, John Mylopoulos, Joachim W. Schmidt, Carson Woo, and Eric Yu. A three-faceted view of information systems. *Communications of the ACM*, 41(12):64–70, December 1998.

[4] F. Flores, M. Graves, B. Hartfield, and T. Winograd. Computer systems and the design of organizational interaction. *ACM Transactions on Office Information Systems*, 6(2):153–172, 1988.

[5] Patrick Hupe. Ein Typsystem zur Analyse dialogorientierter Workflows in kooperativen Informationssystemen. Studienarbeit, Fachbereich Informatik, Universität Hamburg, Germany, November 1998.

[6] Nico Johannisson. Eine Umgebung für mobile Agenten: Agentenbasierte verteilte Datenbanken am Beispiel der Kopplung autonomer "Internet Web Site Profiler". Diplomarbeit, Fachbereich Informatik, Universität Hamburg, Germany, April 1997.

[7] B. Mathiske, F. Matthes, and J.W. Schmidt. On migrating threads. *Journal of Intelligent Information Systems*, 8(2):167–191, 1997.

[8] F. Matthes. Business conversations: A high-level system model for agent coordination. In *Database Programming Languages: Proceeding of the 6th International workshop; proceedings / DBPL-6, Estes Park, Colorado, USA, August 18 - 20, 1997.* Springer-Verlag, 1998.

[9] F. Matthes and J.W. Schmidt. Persistent threads. In *Proceedings of the Twentieth International Conference on Very Large Data Bases, VLDB*, pages 403–414, Santiago, Chile, September 1994. (An extended version of this text appeared as [MaSc94b]).

[10] Florian Matthes. Mobile processes in cooperative information systems. In *Proceedings STJA'97 (Smalltalk und Java in Industrie und Ausbildung)*, Erfurt, Germany, September 1997. Springer-Verlag.

[11] Volker Ripp. Verbesserung der Lokalität und Wiederverwendbarkeit von Geschäftsprozeßspezifikationen: Probleme und Lösungsansätze am Beispiel kundenorientierter Hotelgeschäftsprozesse. Diplomarbeit, Fachbereich Informatik, Universität Hamburg, Germany, March 1998.

[12] J. Searle. Speech acts. Technical report, Cambridge University Press, Cambridge, 1969.

[13] M. Stonebraker, L.A. Rowe, B. Lindsay, J. Gray, M. Carey, M. Brodie, and P. Bernstein. Third-generation data base system manifesto. *ACM SIGMOD Record*, 19, September 1990.

[14] Holm Wegner. Objektorientierter Entwurf und Realisierung eines Agentensystems für kooperative Internet-Informationssysteme. Diplomarbeit, Fachbereich Informatik, Universität Hamburg, Germany, May 1998.

[15] T.A. Winograd. A language/action perspective on the design of cooperative work. Technical Report No. STAN-CS-87-1158, Stanford University, May 1987.

Configuring Business Objects from Legacy Systems

Willem-Jan van den Heuvel, Mike Papazoglou, and Manfred A. Jeusfeld

INFOLAB, Tilburg University, PO Box 90153,
Tilburg 5000 LE, The Netherlands
wjheuvel@kub.nl, mikep@kub.nl, jeusfeld@kub.nl

Abstract. In this paper we present a methodology, called binding Business Applications to LEgacy systems (*BALES*), that allows to blend modern business objects and processes with objectified legacy data and functionality in order to construct flexible, configurable applications, that are able to respond to business changes in a pro-active way.

1 Introduction

As a result of the growing turbulence in which modern organizations operate, the design of information systems is faced with new challenges. The adaption and deployment of information systems needs to be completed in the shortest possible time, amidst changes, as the organizations and their constituting business processes tend to become more complex every day [1]. Accordingly, most organizations are striving to respond to rapid changes by creating modular business processes that can be quickly implemented and re-engineered as the situation may demand [2].

To meet the requirements of modern organizations, and get better reuse from software, distributed business object computing is the preferred solution [3]. Business objects can be the key building block in the re-engineered (process-oriented) enterprise as they can realize domain business processes and default business logic that can be used to start building applications in these domains. Furthermore, domain specific models can be designed as business frameworks so that they can be easily extended and modified, e.g., SAP and IBM's San Francisco business objects [4]. These can be deployed for integrated enterprise-wide applications that can be easily built upon distributed broker architectures such as CORBA. However, most contemporary enterprise information systems are characterized by a rigid (technical) infrastructure and their heritage of data to perform their primary processes. These systems are not able to keep abreast of the rapid organizational and technological changes that occur in a business environment. Such information systems 'that significantly resist modification and evolution to meet new and constantly changing business requirements' can be defined as *legacy systems* [5].

Over the years several strategies to deal with the legacy problem have been proposed: access integration in place, the cold turkey (replace at once) and the gradual migration approach [6], [5]. Access/integration in place requires an environment in which the legacy systems and new business components can coexist and cooperate. For that purpose it uses technologies such as object wrappers [7]. Wrappers are used to objectify legacy systems and expose interfaces over legacy transactions as well as provide meta-data descriptions of legacy data [8]. Such wrapping solutions generally present the following four drawbacks:

M. Jarke, A. Oberweis (Eds.): CAiSE'99, LNCS 1626, pp. 41–56, 1999.
© Springer-Verlag Berlin Heidelberg 1999

1. The object wrapping solution views enterprises from the legacy perspective and assumes that new applications may be developed in terms of legacy objects with perhaps marginal adjustments to the legacy data and functionality. This assumption is not realistic given that the legacy systems are geriatric systems that reflect organizational requirements and objectives of a long time ago.
2. Because of the way that legacy applications are built and continue to be upgraded, they do not only contain data divorced from a business context but they are also seldom consistent with modern business objectives.
3. It is unlikely that this approach would survive in an increasingly fluid environment where (unpredictable) organizational changes and business objectives require frequent adjustment and enhancement of the legacy functionality.
4. Finally, and possibly more importantly, any viable long-term approach to mapping between legacy and target systems must be *methodology-oriented* and be performed on an ad hoc basis as the situation may demand.

In this paper we propose a methodology, called binding Business-Applications to LEgacy Systems (*BALES*). The *BALES* methodology allows to blend modern business objects and processes with legacy objects and processes to construct flexible applications. This methodology allows reusing as much of the legacy data and functionality needed for the development of applications that meet modern organization requirements and policies. This implies "adjusting" (or retrofitting) legacy data and functionality at the enterprise modeling level. In particular, the *BALES* methodology allows to construct configurable business applications on the basis of business objects and processes that can be parameterized by their legacy counterparts. The goal of the *BALES* methodology is to enable organizations to react at business induced changes in a manner that does not disrupt enterprise applications or the business processes that underly them.

The remainder of this paper is organized as follows. In the next section, we present the *BALES* methodology for linking business objects and processes to objectified legacy data and functionality. In section 3, we present a realistic example to illustrate the application of the *BALES* methodology. Finally, section 4 describes our conclusions and future research directions.

2   A Methodology for Binding Business Application Objects and Processes to Legacy Systems

Most of the approaches to integrate legacy systems with modern applications are designed around the philosophy that data residing in a variety of legacy database systems and applications represents a collection of entities that describe various parts of an enterprise. Moreover, they assume that by combining these entities in a coherent manner with legacy functionality and objectifying (wrapping) them legacy systems can be readily used in place. In this way it is expected that the complexities surrounding the modern usage of legacy data and applications can be effectively reduced. Unfortunately, these approaches do not take into account the evolutionary nature of business and the continual changes of business processes and policies. Although part of the functionality of a legacy system can be readily used, many of its business processes and policies may have changed with the passage of time.

A critical challenge to building robust business applications is to be able to identify the reusable and modifiable portions (functionality and data) of a legacy system and combine these with modern business objects in a piecemeal and consistent manner. These ideas point towards a methodology that facilitates *pro-active change management* of business objects that can easily be retrofitted to accommodate selective functionality from legacy information systems. In the following we describe such a methodology that takes into account these considerations. This methodology concentrates on parameterizing business objects with legacy data and functionality. However, the same methodology can be successfully employed for coping with changes to existing business objects and processes.

One important characteristic of business object technology, that also contributes to the critical challenge described above, is the explicit separation of interface and implementation of a class. Business objects technology takes this concept a step further by supporting *interface evolution* in a way that allows the interfaces of classes to evolve without necessarily affecting the clients of the modified class. This is enabled by minimizing the coupling between business components. Client and server classes are not explicitly bound to each other, rather messages are trapped at run-time by a semantic data object that enforces the binding at the level of parameter passing semantics [13]. As we will see in the following, the *BALES* methodology thrives on this key feature of business object technology.

2.1   The *BALES* Methodology

The *BALES* methodology, that is under development, has as its main objective to parameterize business objects with legacy objects (LOs). Legacy objects serve as conceptual repositories of extracted (wrapped) legacy data and functionality. These objects, just like business objects, are described by means of their interfaces rather then their implementation. A business object interface can be constructed from a legacy object interface partition comprising a set of selected attribute and method signatures. All remaining interface declarations are masked off from the business object interface specification. In this way, business objects in the *BALES* methodology are configured so that part of their specification is supplied by data and services found in legacy objects. A business object can thus have a part that is directly supplied from some legacy data and services which it combines with data and services defined at its own level. This means that business object interfaces are parameterizable to allow these objects to evolve by accommodating upgrades or adjustments in their structure and behavior.

The *BALES* methodology borrows ideas from the object-oriented application development literature based on *use cases* [9] and *task scripts* [14]. It also combines ideas from event-driven business process (re-)engineering [15], with concepts from the area of enterprise modeling [11], [16]. *BALES* presents some similarities with contemporary approaches in the field of Enterprise Resource Planning (ERP) package development, e.g., the San Francisco-project of IBM [4]. Lastly, *BALES* draws on recent research to workflows and interoperability, e.g. [30].

The core of the *BALES*-methodology comprises the three phases (see fig. 1): *forward engineering, reverse engineering* and *meta-model linking*. To illustrate the *BALES* mapping methodology a simplified example is drawn from the domain of maintenance and overhaul of aircrafts (see fig. 1). This example was inspired from building block definitions that we currently help develop at the Department of Defense in the Netherlands [17]. The upper part of this figure illustrates the results of the forward engineering of the business domain (phase 1) in terms of workflows, business processes and business objects. As can be seen from this figure the enterprise model is enacted by a *Request-Part* workflow which comprises three business processes: *Request, Prognosis* and *Issue*. The *Request-Part* workflow is initiated by a maintenance engineer who requests parts (for maintaining aircrafts) from a warehouse. A warehouse manager can react in two different ways to such a request.

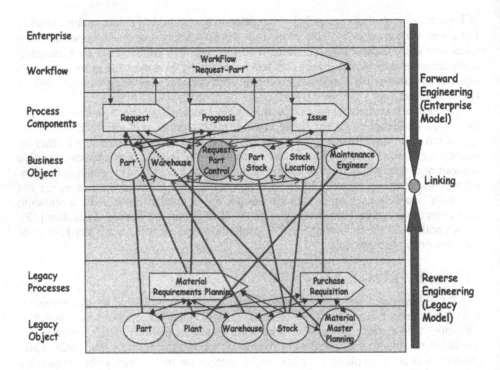

Fig. 1. Developing an enterprise model by means of reusing legacy processes and objects.

Firstly, the manager can directly issue an invoice and charge/dispatch the requested products to the requester. In this case, the workflow will use information from the *Request* process to register the maintenance engineer's request in an order list. This list can be used to check availability and plan dispatch of a specific aircraft part from the warehouse. The *Request* process uses the business (entity) objects *Part* and *Warehouse* for this purpose. Subsequently, the workflow initiates the *Issue* process (see fig. 1). The *Issue* process registers administrative results regarding the dispatching of requested part and updates the part inventory record by means of the *Part-Stock* business object. The business object *Request_Part_Control* is an auxiliary control object used during the execution of the workflow to store and control the state of the running business processes. If the requested part is not in stock then an *Order-Part* workflow is triggered (not shown in this figure). This workflow then orders the requested parts to fulfill the request of the *Request Part* workflow.

Secondly, in case of an 'abnormal' request, for example if the customer informs the warehouse manager about a large future purchase, the manager may decide to run a prognosis. This process scenario first registers the request information provided by the *Request* business process and runs a prognosis on the basis of the availability and consumption history of the requested part. The *Prognosis* process uses information from the *Part* and *Warehouse* business objects for this purpose. After the prognosis has ran successfully the part can be reserved. If the results of the process *Prognosis* are negative, as regards future availability of the requested aircraft part, the workflow *Order-Part* is activated.

The lower part of the picture 1, represents the result of the reverse engineering activity in the form of two processes (wrapped applications and related database(s)) *Material_Requirements_Planning* and *Purchase_Requisition*. These processes make use of five legacy objects to perform their operations. Moreover, figure 1 indicates that the enterprise workflow draws not only on "modern" business objects and processes, but also already existing (legacy) data and functionality to accomplish its objectives. For example, business processes such as *Request* and *Issue* on the enterprise model level are linked to the legacy processes *Material_ Requirements_Planning* and *Purchase_Requisition* as indicated by means of the solid lines. This signifies the fact that the processes on the business level *reuse* the functionality of the processes at the legacy model level. The same applies for business objects at the enterprise model level such as *Part*, *Part-Stock* and *Stock-Location* which are parameterized with legacy objects. In this simplified example we assume that problems such as conflicting naming conventions and semantic mismatches between the enterprise and legacy models have been resolved. A solution to this problem can be found in [18].

Figure 2 represents the individual steps and (intermediate) milestones during the three main phases of the *BALES* methodology. These are described in the following subsections.

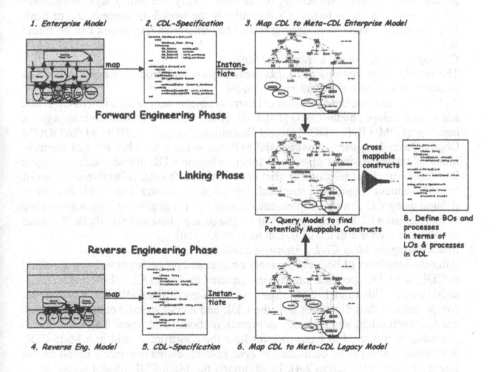

Fig. 2. The *BALES* methodology.

2.2   Forward Engineering the Business

The forward engineering phase transforms a conceptual enterprise model into CDL and maps this CDL definition to a Meta-CDL-Model which serves as a basis for comparison between business and legacy enterprise models. This phase comprises the following activities which correspond to steps 1, 2, and 3 in fig. 2.

1. *Enterprise Modeling:*
   The forward engineering activity starts with the construction of an enterprise model. The enterprise model reveals the activities, structure, information, actors, goals and constraints of the business in terms of business objects, processes and workflows (that can be defined in terms of each-other), and is typified by the enterprise workflow in the upper part of fig. 1.
   As can be seen in this figure, the enterprise model is structured by means of a layered enterprise architecture. This architecture comprises four layers: the (atomic) business objects, business processes, business workflows and business policies/goals. Business objects provide a natural way for describing application-independent concepts such as product, order, fiscal calendar, customer, payment and the like. A business process is used to define a set of interrelated activities that collectively accomplish a specific business objective, possibly, according to a a set of pre-specified policies. The purpose of this layer is to provide *generic business processes* in terms of business object services. The workflow layer assigns activities to actors according to the state of each process in progress and moves the process forward from one activity to the next. Lastly, the policy layer constitutes the business policies in terms of subsequently the workflow, process and/or business objects. An elaborated description of the enterprise framework can be found in [12].

2. *CDL-Specification of the Enterprise Model:*
   The interface descriptions of the business objects and processes need to be constructed on the basis of the enterprise model.
   To formally describe the interfaces of business objects we use a variant of CDL that has been developed by the OMG [19]. CDL is declarative specification language – a superset of OMG IDL, ODGM Object Definition Language (ODL) and the ODGM Object Query Language – that is used to describe composite behavior of communities of related business objects. A specification in CDL defines business object interfaces, structural relationships between business objects, collective behavior of related business objects and temporal dependencies among them [19]. An object defined using CDL can be implemented using any programming language as long as there exists a CDL mapping for that language, e.g., Java and Smalltalk. Practical experiences with use of the CDL can be found in [20].

3. *Instantiating the Meta-CDL Enterprise Model:*
   After the interfaces of both the business objects and processes have been specified in CDL, the CDL specifications are instantiated to a Meta-CDL Enterprise (Business) Model. This model depicts the *instantiations* of the CDL enterprise model components. It thus illustrates how the CDL and model specific constructs are related to each other, and provides information about their types. The CDL meta-modeling step is used as basis to infer how the constructs found in a Meta-CDL Enterprise Model can be connected to (viz. re-use) related constructs found on the Legacy Model (see section 2.4). In summary, the Meta-CDL-Model serves as an 'independent' canonical model to which the forward as well as the reverse engineered CDL models will be linked, superimposed, and compared in order to ascertain which (portions of) legacy processes and objects can be reused at the enterprise model level. In this way, it is possible to parameterize enterprise model business processes and objects with related legacy business processes and objects.

2.3 Reverse Engineering the Legacy System

In the second phase of the *BALES*-methodology, we represent the legacy objects and processes in terms of CDL and link them to a Meta-CDL Legacy Model. The activities during the reverse engineering phase are similar to those performed during the forward engineering phase. The following activities, which correspond to steps 4, 5 and 6 in fig. 2, can be identified:

1. *Reverse Engineered Model:*
   The reverse engineered model represents the wrapped legacy data and functionality. To construct the legacy objects we rely on techniques that combine object wrapping and meta-modeling with semantic schema enrichment [23], [24].
   The legacy object model comprises a distinct legacy object and legacy process layer in the Enterprise Framework (see bottom part of fig. 1).
2. *CDL-Specification of the Legacy Model:*
   The interfaces of the legacy objects and processes are described by CDL in the same way as we explained for business processes and objects.
3. *Instantiating the Meta-CDL Legacy Model:*
   After the CDL-descriptions of the legacy components are available the legacy CDL specifications are instantiated to a Meta-CDL Legacy model much in the same way that we described for the enterprise model.

2.4 Link Phase of the CDL Meta Models

The CDL descriptions of both the forward- and backward-engineered models have to be connected to each other in order to be able to ascertain which parts of the legacy object interfaces can be re-used with new applications. To achieve this, we represent both business and legacy CDL specifications in a repository system. The repository system has a CDL meta model which is capable of representing the CDL constructs and the CDL upgrades that we introduced for representing legacy object interfaces and their components. The advantage of this repository approach is that the content of the repository, viz. Meta-CDL Models, is subject to automated analysis, mainly by means of queries. For this purpose we utilize the ConceptBase system [22] because it has an advanced query language for abstract models (like the CDL meta model) and it uniformly represents objects at any abstraction level (data objects, model components, modeling notations, etc.).

The underlying representation language of ConceptBase is Telos [21]. Telos has a frame syntax to represent classes and objects. An equivalent representation is in form of directed graphs. The content of a ConceptBase repository is subject to queries. The query language is based on deductive rules. In the frame syntax, queries have the form:

```
QueryClass <query-name> isA <class>
   retrieved_attribute
    <attr-name> : <Class>
    ...
   parameter
    <param-name>: <Class>
    ...
   constraint
    <con-name>: <membership-condition>
end
```

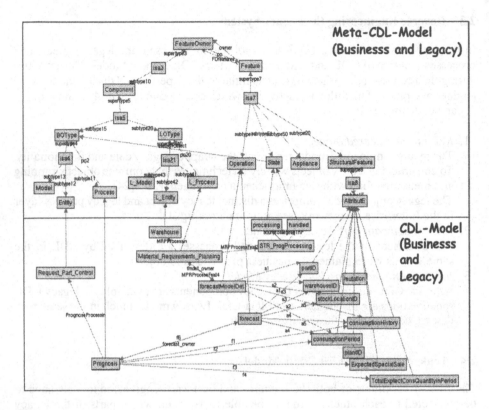

Fig. 3. A snapshot of ConceptBase graph browser containing the Business and Legacy Meta-CDL Models.

The interpretation of a query are all instances of the super class (isA) which fulfill the membership condition. The system will include the retrieved attributes in the answer. If parameters are specified, the user can call a query with values for the parameters. Parameters may appear in the membership condition which itself is a logical formula.

Figure 3 shows an excerpt of the abstract representation of business and legacy objects displayed by the ConceptBase graph browser. The upper half shows the Meta-CDL-Model, i.e. the meta classes to represent CDL constructs. Note the distinction between business object types (*BOType*) and legacy object types (*LOType*). The lower half displays an excerpt of the result of the instantiations of CDL representations to Meta-CDL models for business and legacy objects. Note that *Material_Requirements_Planning* is classified as legacy object type whereas *Prognosis* is instantiated as business object (*BOType*).

After the CDL descriptions of the forward and reverse engineered models have been instantiated to their respective Meta-CDL-Models, the two models can be superimposed and compared (see fig. 3). The following two tasks need to be performed in succession in oder to be able to link legacy objects to business objects.

1. Query the Model to find Potentially Mappable Components
    During this task queries are used to infer potential legacy components that may be connected to business components. For instance, we can identify business object

attributes and/or operations that can be constructed out of legacy object attributes and/or operations. In [25] ConceptBase is successfully deployed for solving a similar problem. Telos queries are used to retrieve exact or partial matches of signatures of requested components that are stored in a repository. As argued in [25], most queries will lead to a *partial solution*, since it is unlikely that two interfaces will match exactly. This type of querying is useful for combining signatures of legacy operations with operations of business objects. However, it raises type safety issues that will be addressed in section 4.

2. Specify Business Objects in CDL in terms of Legacy Objects

The legacy constructs that are returned by the query answers above are subsequently substituted in the CDL business object specifications obtained in step 2 of the forward engineering phase, see fig. 2. For this purpose we have extended the CDL language with a special linking operator '$X \mapsto Y$', where X represents some source construct (for example a Meta-CDL construct for business *Operation*, see fig. 3). Y denotes the target construct (e.g., a Meta-CDL legacy *Operation*) which corresponds to a reused operation from the Meta-CDL legacy model.

The *BALES* methodology results in a CDL specification of business objects and processes in terms of their related legacy counterparts. The mapping statements can be easily adjusted to satisfy new market requirements by, for example, accommodating new packages such as ERP solutions [10], [4].

In the next section, we will illustrate the *BALES* activities and milestones in terms of the aircraft maintenance and overhaul example that we presented earlier.

3 Putting Things Together

3.1 Forward Engineering

In the following, we will explain the forward engineering phase in a step-by-step manner according to what we have outlined in section 2.

1. *Enterprise Modeling:*

During this phase the enterprise model is constructed as already explained in section 2.1.

2. *CDL-Specification of the Enterprise Model:*

The enterprise model represented in fig. 1, serves as a starting point to specify the business object/process in CDL. We shall give an example of a CDL specification involving a business object with interesting dynamic behavior, namely the *Request_Part_Control* in fig. 2. Detailed descriptions of the CDL syntax can be found in [19].

This CDL specification describes the interface of the business control object *Request_Part_Control* (see fig. 1) and shows that this business object encapsulates three business processes: *Request*, *Prognosis* and *Issue*. As can be seen from the CDL specification, the *Request_Part_Control* object is related to the *Part*, *Maintenance_Engineer* and *Warehouse* business objects. This business object can be in three states: '*initial*', '*processing*' or '*handled*'. The business process *Request* can change the state of the business object *Request_Part_Control* from '*initial*' to '*pro-*

cessing' on the basis of the incoming event *request*. Likewise, the *Prognosis* and *Issue* process can change the state of this control object, as described in section 2.1.

```
#include metamodel.cdl
entity Request_Part_Control {
    // cdl description of the control object "request_part_control"
    // this object comprises all three business processes and registers
    // the state of them (initial, processing or handled).
    // static aspects
    attribute workflow_ID, state_description, active_Process;
    relationship for Many Part inverse requested_in;
    relationship by One Maintenance_Engineer inverse requests;
    relationship from Many _Warehouse inverse has;
    // dynamic aspects
    state {initial, processing, handled}

    process Request {
        // process description here
    }; # end str
    }; # end process Request

    process Prognosis {
        attribute consumptionHistory, consumptionPeriod, expectedSpecialSale,
            totalExpectedConsQuantityinPeriod;
        relationship of Many Parts inverse has;
        relationship for Many Warehouse inverse has;
        event register_expected;
        event register_exptected_stock;
        void forecast(in partID, in stockID, in warehouseID, in consumptionPeriod,
                in consumptionHistory);
        void manualReorderPointPlanning (in artID, in stockID, in warehouseID);
    }; # end process Prognosis

    process Issue_Part {
        attribute quantityRequest;
        event issue;
        apply StateTransitionRule IssueProcessing {
            trigger  = {issue}
            source   = processing
            target   = handled
        }; # end str
    }; # end process Issue
}; # end entity Request_Part_Control
```

3. *Instantiating the Meta-CDL Enterprise Model:*
   In this step, the CDL definitions given above are instantiated to a Meta-CDL-Model representing the enterprise. The Meta-CDL-Model is stored in the ConceptBase tool as already explained (see fig. 3), and can be reused each time the Meta-CDL Enterprise/Legacy Model need to be instantiated. The Meta-CDL model represents all CDL modeling constructs such as business objects and business processes and their constituents as already explained.
   The next step is to to link the forward engineered model *Request-Part* to its CDL-Meta-Model in order to be able to map it later on to its reverse-engineered counterpart.
   The Telos specification that follows is a textual representation of the graphical elements of the ConceptBase graph browser depicted in fig. 3.

```
Prognosis in Process with                    forecast in Operation with
    partof                                       owner
        x : Request_Part_Control                     o : Prognosis
    POfeatures                                   usedAttrib
        f1 : consumptionHistory;                     a1 : partID;
        f2 : consumptionPeriod;                      a2 : stockID;
        f3 : ExpectedSpecialSale;                    a3 : warehouseID;
        f4 : totalExptectConsQuantityinPeriod;       a4 : consumptionPeriod;
        f5 : manualReorderPointPlanning;             a5 : consumptionHistory
        f6 : forecast                        end
end
```

The two Telos frames above define features and operations of the process *Prognosis* as part of the BO *Request_Part*, and an operation *forecast* that is executed during this process (forecasting is used to determine the future consumption of a part). These are specified as instances of the Meta-CDL class *Process* and the Meta-CDL class *Operation*, respectively (see fig. 3). In fig. 3, it is shown that the *forecast* operation uses the attributes like *partID, warehouseID,stockID, consumptionPeriod ConsumptionHistory* to perform its objectives. In section 3.3 we will show how the signature of this operation can be parameterized with components of a legacy operation signature.

After the Telos frames that are generated on the basis of the forward engineered CDL-descriptions and connected to the Meta-CDL-Model, we can proceed with the second phase in the *BALES* methodology: the Reverse Engineering Phase.

3.2   Reverse Engineering

1. *Reverse Engineered Model:*
   During this step the reverse engineered model is constructed as already explained in the previous. Reverse engineered legacy processes such as *Material_Recourse_Planning* (MRP) and *Purchase_Requisition* and wrapped objects like *Part, Plant, Warehouse*, etc., are represented in the reverse engineered model as shown in fig. 1. The legacy process *Material_Recourse_Planning* is used to determine the requirements for parts at a maintenance location.

2. *CDL-Specification of the Legacy Model:*
   We can now provide a CDL-specification on the basis of the reverse engineered model. As an example we use the interface of the legacy object *Warehouse*, see bottom part of fig. 2, whose interface is described below in CDL.

   As can be seen from this example the legacy object *Warehouse* encapsulates the legacy process *Material_Requirements_Planning*. This legacy process can be used to plan all the part requirements in the warehouse. For this purpose it uses the legacy operation *forecastDetModel*. The definitions in the LO *Warehouse* will subsequently be used as a basis to construct the interface of the business object *Warehouse*.

```
// Definition of the legacy entity: Warehouse

[keys={orderID}] entity Warehouse {
  relationship ordered_for Many Part inverse ordered_by;
  relationship has Many Plant inverse of;

  attribute int plantID;
  [required] attribute String warehouse_name, warehouse_address, warehouse_place;
  state ordering{initial, planning, planned}

  // Definition of the Material Requirements Planning business process
  process Material_Requirements_Planning {
    // the relations of the process object, with other components
    relationship of References Part;
    relationship for References Plant;
    relationship in References Warehouse;

    // the dynamic behavior
    event register_expected;
    event start_long_term_planning;
    event start_stat_analysis;

    // Methods to implement MRP
    // forecast stock on basis of deterministic planning
    void forecastDetModel (in partID, in stockID, warehouseID,
                            in consumptionPeriod, in consumptionHistory);
    // forecast stock on basis of consumption based planning
    void planProduct (in artID, in stockID, in warehouseID);

    // state transition rule of MRP
    apply StateTransitionRule ProgProcessing {
      trigger = {register_exp_stock}
      source = processing
      target = handled
    }; # end str
  }; // end process Material_Requirements_Planning
}; // end Warehouse entity
```

3. *Linking the CDL specifications to the Meta-CDL Legacy Model:*
   After the CDL definitions are included in the ConceptBase repository, they are instantiated to the appropriate legacy components in the Meta-CDL Legacy-Model. For example, the legacy object *Warehouse* is instantiated from the Meta-CDL Legacy Modeling construct *L_Entity*. Another example is the legacy process *Material_Requirements_Planning* that is represented as instance of the legacy process

construct *L_Process*, see fig. 1. This object would look like as follows in Telos frame syntax:

```
L_Process Material_Requirements_Planning with          Operation forcastModelDet with
    partof                                                 owner
        x : Warehouse                                          o : Material_Requirements_Planning
    FOfeatures                                             usedAttrib
        f1: consumptionPeriod;                                 a1 : partID;
        f2: consumptionHistory;                                a2 : warehouseID;
        f3: STR_ProgProcessing;                                a3 : stockID;
        f4: forecastModelDet                                   a4 : consumptionPeriod;
end                                                            a5 : consumptionHistory
                                                       end
```

The above two Telos frames depict the legacy components *Material_Recourse_Planning* and *forcastDetModel* as instantiations of the Meta-CDL constructs *L_Process* and *Operation*, respectively. The *Material_Recourse_Planning* legacy process features two attributes (*ConsumptionPeriod* and *ConsumptionHistory*), a state-transition rule (called *STR_ProgProcessing*) and a method (*forecastDetModel*).

After both the forward and reverse engineered CDL descriptions have been specified by means of the Meta-CDL-Model in ConceptBase, the actual linking of business objects and processes to legacy objects and processes can take place.

3.3   Parameterizing: Specifying BOs via Cross-Interface Linkages

This phase indicates that business objects like *PartStock* (a business object that describes the statues of a part at the warehouse) and *StockLocation* (the location of the warehouse where the parts are physically stored, e.g., a shelve) are partly implemented by means of the legacy object *Stock*, see fig. 1. Hence, the interfaces of the business objects such as *PartStock* and *StockLocation* can be partially constructed by connecting them to the interfaces of the legacy object *Stock*. In reality there will also be a need to define auxiliary objects that are required to adjust the structure and behavior of the legacy objects to what is expected at the BO level. However, this procedure will not be discussed further in this paper due to reasons of brevity.

To parameterize BOs with legacy objects the following two tasks need to be performed in succession.

Query to find potentially mappable components: The first task in the linking phase consists of identifying potential legacy constructs that can be linked to related business constructs. We will illustrate the process of linking LO interfaces to BO interfaces by means of a ConceptBase query. The query ('OpWithSameAttributes' that is a specialization of the class *Operation*) results in a set of operations that share one or more attributes have an identical signature.

```
QueryClass OpWithSameAttributes isA Operation with
    retrieved_attribute
        owner : LOType
    parameter
        proto_op : Operation
    constraint
        con:
            $ ( forall a/AttributE (this usedAttrib a) ==>
                ( proto_op usedAttrib a))
        and
            ( forall b/AttributE (proto_op usedAttrib b) ==>
                ( this usedAttrib b)) $
end
```

Essentially the query determines those operations in the repository which are owned by a legacy object type and have the same signature (used attributes) as the operation provided as parameter *proto_op* (signifying a prototypical object). The operation supplied as parameter to the query belongs to a business operation described in a Meta-CDL Business Model. This implies that we are looking for a legacy operation to match a business operation. A call *OpWithSameAttributes[forecast/proto_op]* of this query may yield the following result, which indicates a match between the BO operation *forecast* and the legacy operation *forecastDetModel*.

```
forecastDetModel in OpWithSameAttributes[forecast/proto_op] with
   owner
      fmdet_owner : Material_Requirements_Planning
end
```

As can be seen from the above result the legacy operation *forecastDetModel* is a candidate to implement the *forecast* business object operation. The answers obtained by queries are first checked against some simple type-safety criteria (mentioned below) and are also validated by an analyst to resolve semantic mismatches at the operation level. After successful validation, the interfaces of the *forecast* and *forecastDetModel* can be inter-linked.

Parameterize: The results of the queries to find potentially mappable components are used to create the interface specifications of the business objects. For this purpose we use the initial CDL specification for business objects (step-3) as described in fig. 2 where we connect business component specifications with references to equivalent (mappable) legacy component specifications that we identified by means of querying. An example of such a mapping is given below:

```
process Prognosis {
   attribute consumptionHistory, consumptionPeriod, expectedSpecialSale,
      totalExpectedConsQuantityinPeriod;
   event register_expected;
   event register_expected_stock;
   // Mapping of forecasting method to legacy process component MRP
   this.forecast --> Warehouse.Material_Requirements_Planning.
         forecastDetModel(in partID, in stockID, in warehouseID,
               in consumptionPeriod, in consumptionHistory);
   void manualReorderPointPlanning (in int artID, in stockID, in warehouseID);
}; # end process Prognosis
```

This example defines the business object operation *forecast* in terms of the legacy operation *Material_Requirements_Planning* which is embedded in the business object by means of the linking operator ↦.

In many cases it would be possible for methods at the business object level to be passed methods found at the legacy level as arguments or return legacy level functions as results. It is convenient to view such BO methods as *higher order functions* as they can accept legacy functions as parameters or return functions as results. This issue raises type safety problems as we may get runtime errors if we pass and subsequently invoke an inappropriate function from a high order function.

To ensure type safety on method arguments and method results we require the use of *argument contravariance* (expansion) and *result covariance* (restriction). Method results are said to covariant – they vary in the same way as function types. Result types must be more specific for the function type to be more specific. Conversely, argument types are said to contravariant - they vary in the opposite way as the function type. Argument types must be more general for the function type to be more specific [26]. We can informally explain this as follows. Assume we expect a function or method f to have type $t_1 \rightarrow t_2$, where t_1 are its arguments and t_2 its results. Therefore, we consider t_1 arguments as permissible when calling f. Now assume f actually has type $t'_1 \rightarrow t'_2$ with $t_1 \leq t'_1$, where $\leq$ is a special operator denoting a subclass to superclass relationship. Then we can pass all the expected permissible arguments of type t_1 without type violation; f will return results of type t_2' which is permissible if $t_2' \leq t_2$ because the results will then also be of type t_2 and are therefore acceptable as they do not introduce any type violations. The subject of type safety regarding the parameterization of BOs by legacy counterparts is currently under research scrutiny.

4   Conclusions and Future Research

Enterprises need flexible, modular business processes that can easily be configured to meet the demands of business and technology changes. When developing applications based on business objects and processes it is important to address two factors: (a) requirements for change so that business information systems can evolve over time, and (b) the linking of business objects with legacy information systems. The common aim of these two requirements is the ability to combine new and existing (legacy) business components within a running application. In both cases there is a need for the added business components to interoperate seamlessly with components present in the current execution environment. This should happen without the risk of disrupting the application or business process it models, thus, facilitating the graceful, incremental, evolution of complex systems.

In this paper we have described the *BALES* (binding Business Application objects to LEgacy Systems) methodology that we are currently developing. This methodology has as its main objective to inter-link parameterizable business objects to legacy objects. Legacy objects serve as conceptual repositories of extracted (wrapped) legacy data and functionality. These objects are, just like business objects, described by means of their interfaces rather than their implementation. Business objects in the *BALES* methodology are configured so that part of their implementation is supplied by legacy objects. This means that their interfaces are parameterizable (or self-describing) to allow these objects to evolve by accommodating upgrades or adjustments in their structure and behavior.

The results that we have presented are core results in nature. Extensions are needed in several directions to guarantee a practical methodology. For example, problems with regard to granularity need to be solved in a more efficient manner. As can be observed by the 'Request-Part' enterprise workflow, in section 3, the granularity of the legacy system was higher than that of the business model counterpart. Currently, we use simple decomposition techniques to solve this problem. In addition to this, problems in connection with type safety need to be further investigated. In its current form the methodology does not provide yet mechanisms to bind organizational policies to business processes and objects. Research work reported in [16] and [28] seems to be particularly useful for this purpose. Lastly, the evolution of business processes can be compared to software components configuration management [29]. We plan to combine some of the ideas that have been developed in this area with the approach presented herein to in order to accommodate pro-active behavior in our mapping methodology.

References

[1] D.A. Taylor. *Business Engineering with Object Technology*. John Wiley and Sons, Inc., New York, 1995.
[2] M. Hammer and J. Champy. *Re-engineering the Corporation: A Manifesto for Business Revolution*. Harper Collins, New York, 1993.

[3] M.L. Brodie. "The Emperor's Clothes are Object-Oriented and Distributed" in M.P. Papazoglou and G. Schlageter, editors, *Cooperative Information Systems: Trends and Directions*, Academic Press, 1998.

[4] S. Abinavam and et al. *San Francisco Concepts & Facilities*. International Technical Support Organization, IBM, February 1998. SG24-2157-00.

[5] M. L. Brodie and M. Stonebraker. *Migrating Legacy Systems: Gateways, Interfaces and the Incremental Approach*. Morgan Kaufman Publishing Company, 1995.

[6] A. Umar. *Application (Re)Engineering: Building Web-based Applications and Dealing with Legacies*. Prentice Hall, New Jersey, 1997.

[7] R.C. Aronica and D.E. Rimel Jr. "Wrapping your Legacy System", *Datamation*, 42(12):83–88, June 1996.

[8] P. Robertson. "Integrating Legacy Systems with Modern Corporate Applications", *Communications of the ACM*, 50(5):39–46, 1997.

[9] I. Jacobson, M. Griss, and P. Jonsson. *Software Reuse: Architecture, Process and Organization for Business Success*. Addison Wesley, 1997.

[10] T. Curran, G. Keller, and A. Ladd. *SAP R/3 Business Blueprint: Understanding the Business Process Reference Model*. Prentice-Hall, New-Jersey, 1998.

[11] A. W. Scheer. *Business Process Engineering: Reference Models for Industrial Enterprises*. Springer-Verlag, 1994.

[12] M.P. Papazoglou and W.J. van den Heuvel. "From Business Processes to Cooperative Information Systems: An Information Agents Perspective", in M. Klusch, editor, *Intelligent Information Agents*, Springer-Verlag, Feb. 1999.

[13] P. Eeles and O. Sims. *Building Business Objects*. John Wiley & Sons, New York, 1998.

[14] I. Graham. *Migrating to Object Technology*. Addison-Wesley Publishing Company, Workingham, England, 1994.

[15] I. Jacobson and M. Ericsson. *The Object Advantage: Business Process Re-engineering with Object Technology*. ACM Press, Addison-Wesley Publishing Company, Workingham, England, 1995.

[16] E. Yu. *Modeling Strategic Relationships for Process Engineering*. PhD thesis, University of Toronto, 1994.

[17] Department of Defense Netherlands. "Methodiek voor het inrichten van de informatievoorziening op basis van bouwstenen ten behoeve van het ministerie van defensie", Technical Report, Defense Telematics Organization, 1997.

[18] M.P. Papazoglou and S. Milliner. Content-based Organization of the Information Space in Multi-database Networks", in B. Pernici and C. Thanos, editors, *Procs. CAISE'98 Conf., Pisa, Italy*, Springer-Verlag, 1998.

[19] Data Access Technologies. Business object architecture (BOA) proposal. BOM/97-11-09, OMG Business Object Domain Task Force, 1997.

[20] W. Hordijk, S. Molterer, B. Peach, and Ch. Salzmann. "Working with Business Objects: A Case Study", OOPSLA'98 Business Object Workshop, http://jeffsutherland.org/oopsla98/molterer, October 1998.

[21] J. Mylopoulos, A. Borgida, M. Jarke, and M. Koubarakis. "Telos: Representing Knowledge about Information Systems", *ACM Transactions on Information Systems*, 8(4):325–362, 1990.

[22] M.A. Jeusfeld, M. Jarke, H.W. Nissen, and M. Staudt. "ConceptBase: Managing Conceptual Models about Information Systems", in P. Bermus, K. Mertins, and G. Schmidt, editors, *Handbook on Architectures of Information Systems*. Springer-Verlag, 1998.

[23] M.P. Papazoglou and N. Russell. "A Semantic Meta-modeling Approach to Schema Transformation", In *CIKM-95: Int'l. Conf. on Information and Knowledge Management, Baltimore, Maryland*, 1995.

[24] M.P. Papazoglou and W.J. van den Heuvel. "Leveraging Legacy Assets", to appear in M. Papazoglou, S. Spaccapietra, Z. Tari, editors, *Advances in Object-Oriented Modeling*, MIT-Press, 1999.

[25] S. Chen. *Retrieval of Reusable Components in a Deductive, Object-Oriented Environment*. PhD thesis, RWTH Aachen, Information Systems Institute, 1993.

[26] B. Meyer. *Object-Oriented Software Construction*. Prentice-Hall, Englewood Cliffs, 1994.

[27] J. Mylopoulos. "Conceptual modeling and Telos", in P. Loucopoulos and R. Zicari, editors, *Conceptual Modeling, Databases and Case: an Integrated View on Information Systems Development*, J. Wiley, New York, 1992.

[28] P. Kardasis and P. Loucopoulos. "Aligning Legacy Information Systems to Business Processes", in B. Pernici and C. Thanos, editors, *Procs. CAISE'98 Conf., Pisa, Italy*, Springer-Verlag, 1998.

[29] M. Jarke, M.A. Jeusfeld, A. Miethsam, and M. Gocek. "Towards a Logic-based Reconstruction of Software Configuration Management", *7th Knowledge-Based Software Engineering Conference*. IEEE Computer Society Press, Los Alamitos, California, 1992.

[30] Leonid Kalinichenko. "Workflow Reuse and Semantic Interoperation Issues", in: *Workflow Management Systems and Interoperability* (A. Doğaç, L. Kalichenko, M.T. Özsu and A. Sheth eds.), NATO ASI Series, Springer, 1998

Risk Management for IT in the Large

Denis Verhoef[1], Marcel Franckson[2]

[1] ID Research, Groningenweg 6, 2803 PV Gouda, The Netherlands, T.F.Verhoef@idr.nl

[2] Sema Group, 16 rue Barbès, 92126 Montrouge, France, 100716.146@compuserve.com

Abstract: This paper presents a systematic approach to manage the risks within the acquisition of services and systems. The risk management approach is based upon situational factors which are root causes of risks. Strategy options for a service execution approach and a service control approach are offered to mitigate risks in large, complex and uncertain IT undertakings. The resulting service delivery strategy constitutes the preliminaries to plan a sequence of decision points for the acquisition.

The approach allows also to determine actions which attack the root causes of risks which is vital for the success of a risk management approach.

The approach may be used by customer organisations and by supplier organisations.

1. Introduction

1.1. Objective of This Paper

This paper presents a systematic approach to manage the risks within the acquisition of services and systems.

This approach has been elaborated within the ISPL project [10] on the basis of the results of the Euromethod project [1]. These results have been tested in nine real life projects. These projects have evaluated their use of Euromethod as positive.

The major enhancement of the risk management approach of ISPL with respect to the one of Euromethod is a generalisation that allows one to manage risks for ongoing services as well as for projects. This would make the approach suitable for large outsourcing contracts embedding system development projects as well as a variety of services such as maintenance, network management, system operation and configuration management.

In addition, ISPL has an interface with ITIL (Information Technology Infrastructure Library) [11]. ITIL contains a set of manuals providing guidance on how to define and manage services. ITIL has been initially developed by CCTA and is currently distributed by EXIN. It is considered as a *de facto* standard in a lot of countries of North Europe where it has many users.

ISPL is currently a freely available public method.

The design of the risk management approach has been based on an analysis of the existing risk approaches and the contingency approaches, sometimes called situational approaches [2], [3], [4], [6], [9], [15], [18], [19].

M. Jarke, A. Oberweis (Eds.): CAiSE'99, LNCS 1626, pp. 57-72, 1999.

Although the risk management process is not yet standardised, and in particular, a common terminology is not yet used, it is acknowledged that this process contains the following sub-processes (See for example [5], [21], [22]):
- A process that identifies, analyses, evaluates, assesses, estimates the risks
- A process that plans the risk management actions
- A process that tracks, controls, monitors.

In ISPL, the risk management process is made of situation and risk analysis, risk management planning and risk monitoring (See Fig. 1). Risk management planning is decomposed into design of the service delivery strategy and decision point planning.

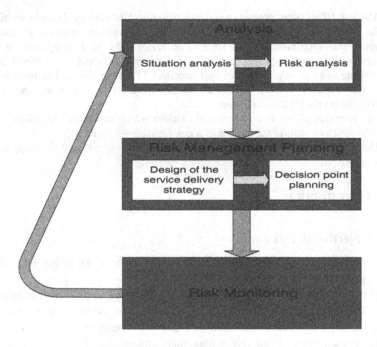

Fig. 1: Risk Management Process

1.2.   What Is an ICT Service Acquisition Process?

The acquisition process is the process of obtaining a system or a service, or any combination thereof, from one or more suppliers.

The acquisition process starts with a customer process, the acquisition initiation process, possibly followed by one or several procurement processes. Each procurement process consists of a series of customer-supplier processes related to one contract: the tendering process, the contract monitoring process and the contract completion process.

Acquisition management includes, but is not limited to: define the acquisition strategy, manage the tendering process, plan the service and system delivery and thus define the decision points and deliverables, monitor contracts, control costs and time-scales, and manage risks.

A service is defined as any process executed by one person or organisation for another one. This paper is restricted to processes in the area of Information and Communication Technology (ICT). Two types of service are distinguished:

- *Projects*: aim at changing processes or systems within an organisation. Examples are system development, system renovation, business process redesign and helpdesk installation.
- *Ongoing services*: aim at executing processes at an agreed service level. Examples are configuration management, network management and the helpdesk function.

1.3.   Structure of This Paper

The remainder of this paper is structured as follows. Section 2 addresses risk analysis and presents how risks are identified through a systematic analysis of the situation. Section 3 addresses the design of a service delivery strategy within a risk management strategy. Section 4 explains how to plan decision points as part of risk management planning. Section 5 analyses the specificity of this approach and suggests some research area that would be useful to improve risk management.

2.   Analysing the Situation and Risks

An important characteristic of the approach is the systematic identification of the risks from an analysis of the situation, using checklists of situational factors. Situational factors are the root causes of risks. Situational factors have already been proposed by the contingency approaches mentioned in Section 1. The framework for classifying the situational factors has been derived from the Leavitts model of organisations [13]. It is also based on the distinction between target domain and project domain considered in the Euromethod Deliverable Model [8].

Some cost estimate methods provide a similar approach to analyse the situation when they consider cost or risk factors in their mathematical model to estimate the costs [17], [12]. The SEI (Software Engineering Institute) proposes an approach which is not very different, although a questionnaire is used instead of situational factors; this questionnaire is based on a taxonomy of risks [20]. Last but not least, it seems that this type of approach is used empirically by experienced project managers as demonstrated in [16].

2.1.   Situation Analysis

The way to analyse the situation is to assign a value to each situational factor that is relevant in the considered situation. Situational factors contribute to the complexity and uncertainty of the service. The situational factors are organised in a two dimensional matrix: the domain and the knowledge characteristics.

The *domain* dimension determines which organisation to investigate. Two domains are considered:

- Target domain: the part of the (customer) organisation, in terms of processes, information and actors, that is affected by the service.
- Service domain: the service organisation that delivers the service.

Target domain	Complexity factor	Uncertainty factor
Business system (including Compute-rised system)	Complexity of requirements	Availability, clarity and stability of requirements
		Quality of existing specifications
		Understanding of business system
		Stability of business system
		Stability of environment
Process	Complexity of business processes	Adequacy of business processes
	Complexity of quality properties of the business processes	Formality of business processes
		Specificity of business processes
Information	Complexity of business information	Formality of business information
	Complexity of quality properties of business information	
Actors	Heterogeneity of business actors	Attitude of business actors
	Complexity of business actors	Ability of business actors
	Size of distribution of business actors	Importance of changes triggered by the project
Technology	Complexity of business technology	Novelty of business technology
		Availability of business technology

Fig. 2: Situational factors related to the target domain

The target domain factors are grouped into four classes:
- Process: properties that characterise the business processes in the target domain.
- Information: properties that characterise the business information in the target domain.
- Actors: properties that characterise the business actors in the target domain; this includes properties of their organisational structure. If the target domain contains computerised systems, it includes properties of the computerised components and the computerised system architecture. In some cases, it is clearer to split these situational factors in factors related to the human system and factors related to the computerised system.
- Technology: properties that characterise the technology (methods, techniques and tools) used in the target domain. If the target domain contains computerised systems, it includes properties that characterise the technology (methods, tech-niques and tools) used in the computerised system. In some cases, it is clearer to split the situational factors in factors related to the human system and factors related to the computerised system.

A factor may concern all aspects of the business systems, e.g. the availability, clarity and stability of requirements concerns processes, information, actors and technology. Such factors are grouped under the heading "business system".

Similarly to the target domain factors, the service domain factors are grouped into four classes:

- Process: properties that characterise the processes that contribute to the delivery of the service.
- Information: properties that characterise the information used to deliver the service.
- Actors: properties that characterise the actors who execute parts of the service; this includes properties of their organisational structure. The service actors may include developers, service managers, experts, users involved in the service execution, sub-contractors, etc.
- Technology: properties that relate to the technology (methods, techniques and tools) used to deliver the service.

This classification into four classes has evolved from the Leavitts model [13]: the "information" class has been added and the former "actor" and "structure" classes have been merged into the current "actor" class. In addition to pragmatic reasons for doing so, the resulting four classes are more in line with the Euromethod Deliverable Model [8].

The other dimension, the *knowledge characteristic*, groups the knowledge about the situation into complexity and uncertainty.

Complexity can be regarded as the difficulty encountered in managing the available knowledge. Uncertainty can be regarded as the lack of available knowledge.

The checklist of target domain situational factors is presented in Fig. 2.

2.2.   Risk Analysis

A risk is the possibility of exposure to the adverse consequences of future events. A risk is characterised by a probability (of the future event) and an impact (the adverse consequence). Both should be quantified.

The risk exposure is defined as the product of the probability and the impact: risk exposure = risk probability * risk impact. Risk exposure is a measure of the criticality of the risk. Critical risks deserve particular attention whilst formulating a service delivery strategy.

Risk analysis consists of risk identification, risk probability assessment, risk impact assessment and critical risk identification.

Risk Identification

Fig. 3 enumerates the most common risks. They are described in terms of their impact. Two classes of risks are considered:

- Risks for the business: those risks have a direct impact on the business performance in terms of quality, costs, non-attainment of stakes, etc.
- Risks for the service: those risks have a direct impact on the service performance in terms of quality, costs, delays, etc. Their impact on the business is only indirect through the increase of probability of some risks for the business.

The word 'system' in the formulation of these risks refers to the result of a project. Be aware that in the case of a service installation project, the word 'system' is actually referring to the service to be installed. A system may then be a business system, an information system, a computerised system, a process, a service, a part of those or a combination of those.

As explained before, situational factors are sources of risks. These relationships between situational factors and risks provide substantial guidance to *identify* the risks inherent to a situation. The table of Fig. 4 presents these relationships for the uncertainty factors in the target domain. Analogous tables have been developed for the other situational factors.

Fig. 5 shows the causality relationships between these risks. Indeed, some risks, if they occur, may cause, as one of their impacts, an increase of probability of other risks. Example: the poor quality of a system will increase the risk of non-acceptance by the business actors.

Risk Probability Assessment

The probability of a risk depends on:
- The number of situational factors having a negative value that contribute to the risk
- The relevance and importance of these situational factors in the specific situation
- The magnitude of the negative value of each of those situational factors.

In some situations, risks may be decreased by situational factors having a positive value.

The probability should be expressed as a real number included between 0 and 1. However, a more qualitative approach can also be used, e.g. a three grades scale such as low, medium, high.

There is no algorithm to compute a risk probability. Expert judgement is required.

Risk Impact Assessment

The impacts of risks are much dependent on, and specific to the context of the service. The risks within the checklist are described by types of impacts, e.g. increased costs, delays in the service or in delivery of deliverables and poor quality of service or deliverables.

This impact is different whether the risk is for the service or the business.

The impact of a risk for the service is measured in terms of an increase of probability of other risks for the service and for the business (Refer to Fig. 4: Risks associated to target domain uncertainty).

The impact of a risk for the business is measured in terms of losses incurred by the business: financial losses, loss of customers of the business, handicap to meet the strategic targets of the business, alteration of the image of the business in the market, threat for the survival of the business, etc.

Critical Risk Identification

Special attention is given to the risks with a high probability and a high impact, i.e. with a high exposure. These risks are called the critical risks. The critical risks should influence the definition of the service delivery strategy and the decision points, and they should be documented in the delivery plan.

Risks for the business

1. Poor quality of service: the delivered service (or system) has not the required quality; it may mean that it is not working, or not adapted to the business needs or that there are shortfalls in some quality properties (functionality, efficiency, reliability, etc.).

2. Delay in system delivery: the system is delivered too late thereby creating problems to the business; this risk is relevant for projects.

3. Service not accepted by business actors: the service (or system) is not accepted by the business actors; the reason may be a poor quality but it may also encompass sociological or human issues.

4. Unpredictable costs for the business: the delivered service or system generates unpredictable costs for the business organisation (target domain); these costs may relate to usage, operation, maintenance, etc. and be due to bad quality or other reasons.

5. Non-attainment of business stakes: the delivered service or system does not contribute to the business stakes at the expected level; reasons may be bad quality, unpredictable costs, delays in the delivery but also more complex combinations of factors.

Risks for the service

1. Unclear service requirements: the requirements to the service (or the system) are not clear or not available.

2. Unstable service requirements: the requirements to the service (or the system) are not stable (they are evolving).

3. Uncertain interfaces (with other processes, systems or services)

4. Lack of business actor participation: the business actors (users, stakeholders, etc.) participate insufficiently in the service execution or in the system development.

5. Shortfalls in sub-contracted tasks: tasks that are sub-contracted are not performed with the required quality.

6. Loss of control of service: the service runs out of control from the management.

7. Delays in deliveries: some deliverables are delivered late; these deliverables may be intermediate deliverables in projects or management deliverables for services in general; the delivery of installed systems is covered under the risk "Delay in system delivery" which is a risk for the business.

8. Poor quality of deliverables: some deliverables are not delivered to the required quality; these deliverables may be intermediate deliverables in projects or management deliverables for services in general; the delivery of installed systems is covered under the risk "Poor quality of service/system" which is a risk for the business.

9. Increased costs of the service: the cost of the service increases.

10. Demotivation of service actors: some actors of the service loose their motivation and commitment for various reasons.

Fig. 3: Checklist of risks

3.   Designing a Service Delivery Strategy

A service delivery strategy consists of individual actions to mitigate risks, strategy options for the service execution approach, and strategy options for the service control approach.

Risks \ Situational factors	Availability, clarity and stability of requirements is low	Quality of existing specifications is low	Understanding of existing business system is low	Stability of business processes is low	Stability of environment is low	Adequacy of business processes is low	Formality of business processes is low	Specificity of business processes is low	Formality of business information is low	Attitude of business actors is negative	Ability of business actors is low	Importance of changes triggered by the project is high	Novelty of business technology is high	Availability of appropriate business technology is high
unclear service requirements	X		X			X	X	X	X	X	X			
unstable service requirements	X			X	X	X				X				
uncertain interfaces	X	X	X	X	X		X		X					
lack of business actor participation						X				X		X		
shortfalls in sub-contracted tasks	X	X											X	X
loss of control of service	X		X	X	X								X	X
delays in the deliveries	X	X	X	X	X	X		X		X	X		X	X
poor quality of deliverables	X	X	X							X	X			
increased costs of the service	X	X	X	X	X	X		X		X	X		X	X
demotivation of service actors	X	X	X			X				X	X		X	X
poor quality of service	X	X	X	X	X	X				X	X	X	X	X
delay in system delivery	X	X	X	X	X	X		X		X	X		X	X
service not accepted by business actors	X		X			X				X	X	X		
unpredictable costs for the business	X	X	X	X	X	X				X	X	X		
non-attainment of business stakes	X		X	X	X					X		X		

Fig. 4: Risks associated to target domain uncertainty

The concepts used for the analysis of situation and risks and for the design of the service delivery strategy are summarised in Fig. 6.

3.1.   Select Actions to Mitigate Risks

The table of Fig. 7 shows examples of actions that are appropriate to mitigate risks. ISPL contains also actions to change individual complexity factors and uncertainty factors.

For a specific situation, a set of actions may be selected to mitigate a set of risks. These actions must be introduced in the plans, in order to allow for monitoring.

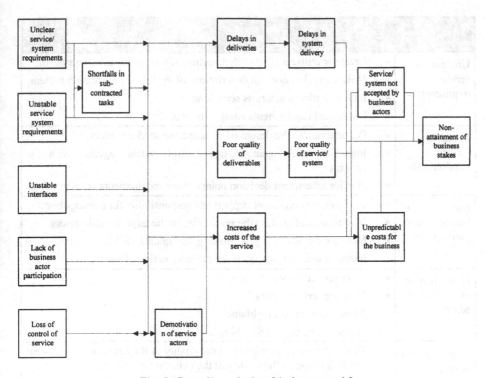

Fig. 5: Causality relationship between risks

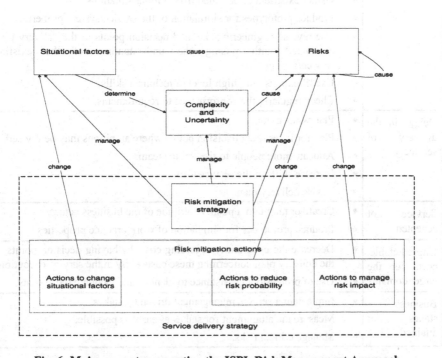

Fig. 6: Main concepts supporting the ISPL Risk Management Approach

Risk	Actions to mitigate risk
Unclear service requirements	• Create or utilise a good understanding, if any, of the existing system. • Make early decisions on descriptions of the future information system. • Include business actors as service actors. • Use formal requirements analysis methods.
Unstable service requirements	• Pay attention to the design of an adaptable service/system. • Implement a stringent change control system together with the customer • Plan for investment decision points where requirements are revised.
Lack of business actor participation	• Get senior management support and responsibility for participation. • Investigate and analyse the motivation of the target domain actors. • Motivate the actors, e.g. by making the benefits visible. • Involve the actors, e.g. increase the information of actors.
Demotivation of service actors.	• Train service actors. • Motivate service actors. • Avoid management by blame. • Produce realistic and feasible plans.
Poor quality of service	• Verify as soon as possible that the quality of the future service/system will be as good as the quality of the existing service/system. • Produce requirements statements, prototypes and specifications. • Gather experiences obtained from similar situations. • Produce prototypes for simulation of the service/system properties. • Use reverse engineering, i.e. add decision points to the delivery plan associated with raising the understanding of the existing service/system. • Use IS-experts with high level of technical skills. • Check regularly the conformance to requirements.
Delays in the delivery of service	• Plan work-arounds. • Plan for investment decision points where ambitions may be revised. • Allocate more people to the service team. • Increase skills in the service team • Revise delivery plan.
Service not accepted	• Create or maintain a positive attitude of the business actors. • Produce prototypes for simulation of work practice properties.
Unpredictable costs for the target domain	• Decrease the uncertainty regarding costs by having decision points in the delivery plan concerning these costs early in the service execution. • Use of professional assistance to identify and evaluate those costs.
Business stakes not attained	• Implement a service management driven by stakes. • Measure the attainment for stakes as early as possible. • Manage critical risks.

Fig. 7: Example of actions to mitigate risks

3.2.   Design Service Execution Approach

The strategy options depend on the type of service, and in particular on whether it is a project or an ongoing service.
This section will consider only projects.
For projects, a service execution approach consists of a description approach, a construction approach, and an installation approach.

Description Approach

A description approach provides the cognitive approach to be followed in producing one or more functional or technical designs, and the social approach required between the service actors and the business actors. The following approaches have been proposed by Mathiassen and Stage in their paper "The principle of limited reduction in software design" [14].
The *cognitive approach* used in producing the system descriptions is the way in which information is processed in order to make the project's design decisions. Two options are distinguished:

- *Analytical approach:* When information is processed analytically, the available information is simplified through abstraction in order to reach a deeper and more invariant understanding. An analytical approach is used to handle the complexity of the information. In an analytical approach the information system is mainly described by use of some degree of formality.
- *Experimental approach*: When using an experimental approach, the service actors learn from experiments generating new knowledge. The purpose is to reduce the uncertainty by generating more information. Experiments can, for example, be based on prototypes, mock-ups, benchmark test of services or other kinds of techniques that make scenarios visible.

The *social approach* is the way in which service actors work together with the business actors during the description task. Two options are distinguished:

- *Expert-driven.* In an expert-driven approach, service actors (the experts) will produce descriptions on the basis of their own expertise, and interviews and observations of business actors. The descriptions can then be delivered to the business actors for remarks or approvals.
- *Participatory.* In a participatory approach, the service actors produce the descriptions in close co-operation with some or all the business actors, e.g. in workshops with presentations, discussions and design decisions. Joint Application Design (JAD) is an example of a technique that can be used in a participatory approach. A participatory approach may allow the acquisition of knowledge, the refinement of requirements and the facilitation of organisational changes.

Construction Approach

A construction approach defines how the system is going to be constructed and tested. The customer and supplier should choose from the following three construction approaches (see also [7]):

- *One shot construction*: The whole system is constructed (and tested) in one version – normally when using 'off the shelf' solutions.

- *Incremental construction*: The system is constructed (and tested) in successive parts. Each part contains a sub-set of the system functionalities. The requirements to the installed system are fully defined before the first construction and will not be changed afterwards.
- *Evolutionary construction*: The system is constructed (and tested) in successive versions. Between two versions, the descriptions of the system can be changed after learning from testing the system. Each version may contain a sub-set or the whole set of functionalities.

Installation Approach

The determination of an installation approach consists of making decisions regarding the parts and the versions of the system that should be installed in the target domain, and the sequence of these installations.

The customer and supplier should choose from the following three options for system coverage:

- *One shot installation*: The whole system is installed (and used) in one version.
- *Incremental installation*: The system is installed (and used) in successive parts. Each part contains a sub-set of the system functionalities. The requirements to the installed system are fully defined before the first installation and will not be changed afterwards.
- *Evolutionary installation*: The system is installed (and used) in successive versions. Between two versions the descriptions of the system can be changed after learning from using the system. Each version may contain a sub-set or the whole set of functionalities.

Orthogonal to these three approaches for system coverage is the geographical coverage within each installation. The customer and supplier should choose from the following two options for geographical coverage:

- *Global installation*. A new version of a system version is installed in all the locations within the target domain in one step.
- *Local installation*. A new version of a system version is installed in several steps covering more and more locations of the target domain.

Social Approach Cognitive Approach	Expert-driven	Participatory
Analytical	When the situation is complex, except when the complexity of the business information or the business processes is high.	When the situation is complex and the complexity of the business information or business processes is high.
Experimental	When the situation is uncertain and participatory approach is not suitable.	When the situation is uncertain and the ability of the business actors is sufficiently high and the adequacy of the schedules is normal.

Fig. 8: General heuristics on the suitability of description approaches

ISPL provides many heuristics to select the most appropriate service execution approach. Fig. 8 and Fig. 9 present the most general heuristics which help to formulate a first 'quick-and-dirty' approach which can be fine-tuned according to more detailed peculiarities of the situation analysis and risk analysis.

Situational Factor			Installation/Construction Approach		
Schedules	*Complexity*	*Uncertainty*	*One Shot*	*Incremental*	*Evolutionary*
Normal	Simple	Certain	X		
		Uncertain			X
	Complex	Certain		X	
		Uncertain			X
Tight	Simple	Certain		X	X
		Uncertain			X
	Complex	Certain		X	
		Uncertain			X
General heuristics: <ul><li>One Shot is suitable when the schedules are normal and the situation is simple and certain.</li><li>Evolutionary is suitable when the situation is uncertain.</li><li>Incremental is suitable when the situation is complex and certain.</li><li>Incremental or evolutionary is suitable when the schedules are tight, i.e. install something as fast as possible.</li></ul>					

Fig. 9: Heuristics on suitability of installation and construction approaches

3.3.   Service Control Approach

Three aspects of service control are considered:
- Frequency: the frequency of customer-supplier decision points within the control process.
- Formality: The degree of formality within organisation, procedures and disciplines used by the control process.
- Customer responsibility. The definition of customer responsibility for processes related to service control. Generally, it is assumed that the supplier is responsible for all processes unless the customer responsibility is explicitly defined in the contract.

High degree of formality in service control can contain for example: periodical approvals of status and plan, well-defined requirements on the content of management reports, well-defined target domain deliverables with deadlines and defined approval procedures, the use of defined metrics for service quality, use of a defined inspection technique to control the quality of code, and well-defined configuration control procedures.

The customer can be defined to be responsible, for example, for: the configuration control of requirements, the quality control of descriptions with respect to requirements and business needs, for the generation of test cases that cover critical situations from the business process perspective, for preparing the organisation for the installation of the new operational information system, and for obtaining any agreements within the organisation, regarding the requirements to the information system.

ISPL provides several heuristics to select the most appropriate service control approach. These heuristics are not presented in this paper.

4.   Planning Decision Points

A decision point within a service is a milestone where the customer, possibly together with the supplier, is making decisions on the service. A decision point is characterised by the decisions that are made, the roles involved in these decisions and the deliverables that are exchanged. These deliverables serve as pre-conditions or as a basis for the decisions to be made.

The input for planning the decision points is the service delivery strategy. The outputs are: the sequence of decision points, and the descriptions of each decision point.

ISPL proposes patterns of sequences of decision points for all the strategy options.

These patterns may be used as a starting point and then tuned to the particular situation.

In particular, the risk mitigation actions that have been selected have generally an influence on the sequence or on the content of decision points.

For each of the decision points, it should be determined which deliverables are required for the decisions to be taken. The customer and supplier should describe their expectation with regard to the deliverables beforehand sufficiently precisely: the deliverables must contain the right information to make the decisions but no more than that; too much information is costly in its production and obscures the picture, thus hampering the decision makers.

5.   Conclusion

The usage of ISPL is expected to be profitable for customer and supplier organisations which manage the acquisition and delivery of services and systems, in particular in large and complex situations. This is due to the following characteristics of ISPL:

1. A rigorous approach is taken to identify risks. The risks are identified through a list of situational factors derived from best practices, and not directly. Situational factors are causes of risks. Consequently, this approach allows to determine actions which attack the root causes of risks which is vital if the course of action to be selected is to be successful.
2. Interactions between risks are taken into account: the effect of one risk may be the cause of another risk.
3. To mitigate risks, actions and strategy options are proposed for each risk. The approach covers then far more than risk analysis.
4. The approach is valid for ongoing services and projects.
5. The approach has been used in practice and experiences have been incorporated. The approach as such has been based upon many underlying best practices.

The improvements of the risk management approach would suggest the following research areas:

- The list of situational factors is not exhaustive; their evaluation is still empirical and their relative importance as a cause of risks is intuitive; empirical research would be needed to increase our knowledge and to bring insight in those issues.
- More heuristics should be elicited and registered with regard to the relationships between situational factors and risks on one hand side and the strategic options and actions to mitigate the risks on the other hand side
- As new technologies will arise and new management practices will evolve, the ISPL approach should evolve continuously to reflect the then current best risk management practice
- Finally, statistical studies should be undertaken to assess the effectiveness of the risk management approaches in general, and the ISPL one in particular, and their influence on acquisition success.

References

1. CEC DGIII and Eurogroup Consortium (July 1996), Euromethod Version 1, also available on the Web (http://www.fast.de/Euromethod)
2. Ahituv N., Hadass M., Neuman S., (June 1984), A Flexible Approach to Information System Development, MIS Quarterly
3. Alter S., Ginzberg M. (Fall 1978), Managing Uncertainty in MIS Implementation, Sloan Management Review, Fall 1978
4. Boehm B., (Jan 1991), Software Risk Management: Principles and Practices, IEEE Software
5. Scarff F., Carty A., Charette R., (1993), Introduction to the Management of Risk, CCTA Library, HSMO Publication Center, London, ISBN 0 11 330648 2
6. Davis G.B., (1982), Strategies for Information Requirements Determination, IBM Systems Journal, Vol 21, No 1
7. Department of Defence USA (Dec 1992), Military Standard Software Development and Documentation (draft), MIL-STD-SDD
8. Franckson M. (1994), The Euromethod Deliverable Model and its contribution to the objectives of Euromethod, in: A.A. Verrijn-Stuart and T.W. Olle (eds.), Elsevier Science B.V. (North Holland), IFIP (Methods and Associated Tools for the Information Systems Life Cycle (A-55))
9. Gibson C.F., Singer C.J., Schnidmann A.A., Davenport T.H., (Jan 1984), Strategies for Making an Information System Fit your Organisation, Management Review
10. ISPL Consortium (March 1999), Risk Management and Delivery Planning
11. CCTA (1997), Information Technology Infrastructure Library, CCTA Library, HSMO Publication Center, London, ISBN 0 11 330691 1 and others
12. Kansala K., (June 1997), Integrating Risk Assessment with Cost Estimation, IEEE Software, Vol 14, N°3
13. Leavitts H., (1964), Applied Organisation Change in Industry: Structural, Technical and Human Approaches, New Perspectives in Organisational Research, John Wiley
14. Mathiassen L., Stage J., (1992), The principle of limited reduction in software design, Information Technology and People, Northwind Publication
15. MacFarlan W., (Jan 1982), Portfolio Approach to Information Systems, Journal of Systems Management

16. Moynihan T., (June 1997), How Experienced Project Managers Assess Risks, IEEE Software, Vol 14, N°3
17. Madachy R., (June 1997), Heuristic Risk Assessment Using Cost Factors, IEEE Software, Vol 14, N°3
18. Ropponen J., (May 1993), Risk Management in Information System Development, Licentiate thesis in Information Systems
19. Saarinen T., (April 1992), Success of Information System Investments – Contingent strategies for development and a multi-dimensional approach for evaluation, Doctoral dissertation (draft)
20. Carr M., Konda S., Monarch I., Ulrich F., Walker C., (1993), Taxonomy-based Risk Identification, SEI Technical Report CMU/SEI-93-TR-6, Software Engineering Institute, Carnegie Mellon, Pittsburgh, Pennsylvania
21. Higuera R., Dorofee A., Walker J., Williams R., (1994), Team Risk Management: A new Model for Customer-supplier Relationship, SEI Technical Report CMU/SEI-94-SR-005, Software Engineering Institute, Carnegie Mellon, Pittsburgh, Pennsylvania
22. Williams R., Walker J., Dorofee A., (June 1997), Putting Risk Management into Practice, IEEE Software, Vol 14, N°3

Linking Business Modelling to Socio-technical System Design

Alistair G. Sutcliffe[1] and Shailey Minocha[2]

[1]Centre for HCI Design, School of Informatics, City University
Northampton Square, London EC1V 0HB, UK
e-mail: a.g.sutcliffe@city.ac.uk
[2]Faculty of Mathematics & Computing
Open University, Milton Keynes MK7 6AA, UK
e-mail: s.minocha@city.ac.uk

Abstract Few methods address analysis of socio-technical system requirements. This paper describes a method for analysing dependencies between computer systems and users/stakeholders in the operational environment. Domain scenarios describing the system and its context are used to create an environment model based on the i* notation. A method is proposed to define business organisational relationships, according to the coupling between agents determined by types of event flows between them, and secondly, by operationalising transaction cost theory to obtain an a priori view of relationships according to the market context for a client and supplier. Coupling metrics are applied to assess the degree of dependencies between the system and the users. High-level requirements are suggested to deal with different types of organisational design. The method is illustrated with a case study of a service engineer support system.

1 Introduction

Few methods have emerged to analyse socio-technical system requirements, even though many problems in requirements engineering are known to have their origins in complex social problems [1], [2]. Ethnographic techniques have been applied to gather data on social issues and requirements do emerge from this process [3]. However, there is little generalisable knowledge, models or analytic methods that can be gleaned from ethnography, so the quality of requirements analysis is dependent on the practitioner's experience.

Some socio-technical models have been proposed for RE, notably the ORDIT project [4] which describes systems in terms of agents, task and roles. Socio-technical systems approaches advocate a human-centric analysis that investigates the impact of computer systems (the technical system) on people and considers ways in which technology can be design more effectively for people. However, few analytic techniques have been reported for such analyses, so the requirements analyst are still dependent on experience for interpreting such models. The Inquiry cycle [5], [6] uses scenarios to investigate barriers to effective use (called obstacles) that may arise in the social domain. However, the Inquiry cycle does not give detailed techniques for analysing socio-technical system dependencies. Analytic guidance has been given in the stakeholder analysis methods (e.g. [1]), which advise modelling requirements according to different user categories or viewpoints. A key problem in socio technical

M. Jarke, A. Oberweis (Eds.): CAiSE'99, LNCS 1626, pp. 73-87, 1999.

systems is how to structure and manage relationships between organisational units. Williamson's theory on transaction cost analysis [7], [8] provides a principled analysis of inter-organisational relationships, yet it does not appear to have been applied to design of business processes and their technological support. A motivation for this paper is to attempt an initial operationalisation Williamson's theory as a method for business organisation design and explore its implications for requirements analysis.

This paper explores the problem of dependency analysis in socio-technical systems by proposing a method for modelling and analysing event flows between users and the intended system in order to derive high level requirements. This extends the work of [9] by addressing workflow problems via a coupling analysis derived from concepts in modular software design [10] and organisational theory [11].

The paper is organised in four sections. The next section introduces the method and this is followed by a more detailed description of two method stages: coupling and transaction cost analysis. A case study of service engineer support system (SESS) runs through these sections to illustrate the method. The paper concludes with a brief discussion.

2 Method Outline and Models

The CREWS-SAVRE (Scenarios for Acquisition and Validation of Requirements) method compares scenarios describing the domain with requirements specifications and models, focusing on events or information flows between the system and its environment. Analysis questions probe the dependencies between people and computers across a tentative system boundary. The system boundaries will change during a requirements investigation as alternative designs emerge; hence there is a single model of the intended system-environment upon which a boundary is imposed. The relationship between scenarios, use cases and the requirements specification is illustrated in Figure 1.

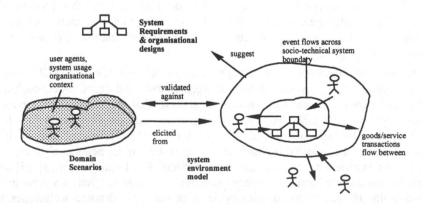

Fig.1. Relationships between Domain Scenarios, Environment Model and the Socio-Technical System Requirements

The method uses "domain" scenarios that contain descriptions of activities in manual systems, interaction with legacy systems, descriptions of agents, roles, and their organisation settings gathered from real-life examples. These are used to elicit facts for the system environment model.

2.1 CREWS-SAVRE Method Outline

The method stages are summarised in Figure 2. The method is iterative, so once the use cases and environment models have been created, all the other stages proceed concurrently.

Stage 1. Use Case and System Modelling
The system environment model is created as an overview model. Then use cases elaborate tasks and interactions between agents to provide more detail. Use case modelling follows standard OO procedures (see [12]), so it is not described further in this paper. Use cases are expressed as interaction diagrams [13] to map out the sequential dependencies of event flows between the agents and the system.

Stage 2. Inbound Event Analysis
Each use case is elaborated by comparing it with one or more domain scenarios and tracing events originating either from human agents or from other objects in the system environment. Each event inbound from the system environment indicates a requirement for a system action, as well as an action in the use case. In this manner the event analysis helps to refine the use cases by identifying events and system responses to deal with the events.

Stage 3. Outbound Event Analysis
Outbound validation is more difficult because the impact on a social system has to be judged. By their nature social systems are complex and unpredictable and the change introduced by a computer system frequently produces unanticipated and undesirable side effects. The outbound event flows are traced to their destination and then questions analyse the acceptability of the system output for the user. First, the domain scenario and use case are cross referenced to ensure output is generated when and where it is needed. Steps in the user's task that imply an information need are identified in the scenario; so if a user needs information at a particular point in the scenario a system output function should exist in the requirements specification.

Stage 4. Coupling Analysis
This assesses the dependencies between the social and technical systems. Coupling analysis is based on software engineering concepts and organisational theory [11], [14] that advises that control based coupling should be avoided. In human organisation control coupling occurs through lines of control, commands, and obligations to carry out activities in response to others. The motivation for avoiding control coupling is twofold. First, it decreases the flexibility of user-system interaction and decreases autonomy. Secondly, too much control imposes the system's goals on the user's working practices, and this may lead to system rejection. The system input and output event flows are classified and counted. The more commands there are, the closer the coupling between the social and technical systems will be. Closely coupled systems are reviewed to either change the design for more automation (computer autonomy) or to increase human control, and design the computer system for an advisory rather than a controlling role.

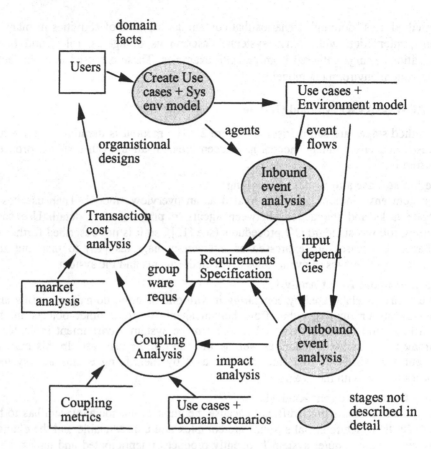

Fig. 2. CREWS-SAVRE method stages and associated models

Stage 5. Transaction Cost Analysis

The market context of the organisations is analysed according to the nature of the goods or services that flow between them. The good/services flows are characterised in terms of volume, values and specificity leading to predictions from Williamson's theory about the type of inter-organisation relationship that should be designed. The technological implications of the inter-organisational design are then investigated.

2.2 System Environment Model

Domain scenarios, captured as narratives or in other media, provide the basis for creating the system environment model. This is an enterprise level model which evolves through different versions as requirements analysis progresses. Rather than invent yet another modelling notation, we have adopted the notion of i* model. This consists of goals, soft goals (non- functional requirements), tasks, agents, and resources (see [9]). The two additions we make are to first, add a socio-technical system boundary, and secondly, relationships to model dependencies between tasks, agents, and objects:

- responsibility: models the association between an agent and an action/task or goal which it has the duty to carry out, e.g. < agent, is-responsible-for, goal | action | task>;
- authority: describes the relationship between two agents in which a dominant agent has authority over the behaviour of a subordinate, or ability of an agent to permit another agent to initiate task or consume some resource; e.g. <agent (x), has-authority-over, agent (y) [task | resource]>;
- accountability: models the relationship by which the achievement of goal or task by an agent is assessed or monitored, e.g. <agent (x), held accountable for, goal,| task, by agent (y)>;
- capability: an agent has the necessary knowledge and abilities for carrying out an action/task, e.g. <agent , has-capability-for, action | task>;

An example of a system environment model is illustrated in Figure 3. This introduces the case study of the SESS (see the use case diagram in Figure 4). Four agents are involved; the controller who receives calls from customers and then allocates the service calls to engineers and schedules their work. The case study focuses on the controller's task and the dependencies between the controller and the engineers in his/her district. The engineer is accountable to the controller for reporting progress on customer calls, and the controller has authority to direct the engineers work.

3 Coupling Analysis

System requirements are discovered by assessing coupling between the required system and its users/stakeholders with the environment model and the use cases. Coupling analysis commences by a qualitative analysis using the scale illustrated in Table I. Events flowing between agents, represented in the context diagram of the top level use case, are counted and each event is assigned a coupling factor. This analysis is performed separately for human to human and human to computer communication as the implications are different for each case. Information coupling is low and makes few impositions on the recipients; however, command coupling places more constraints on actions depending on the type of command. Commands may constrain an agent's freedom to act or take decisions. For instance, the system might set a strategy that dictates how stakeholders must act. Command couples are rated for the strength of the obligation they impose on the recipient agent (optional, mandatory commands, commands with constraints) and the restriction on freedom of action imposed on the recipient. Where high levels of command coupling are apparent these indicate areas of possible conflict and system failure that should be investigated.

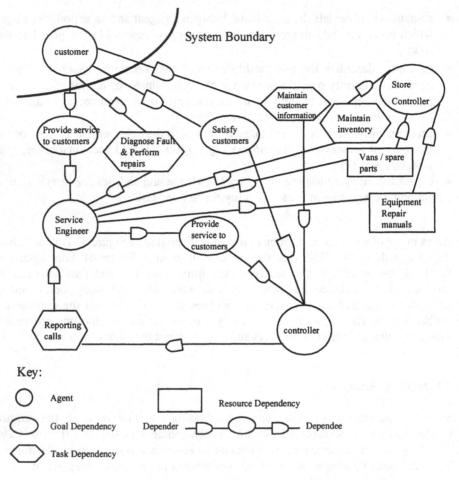

Fig. 3. System Environment model for the SESS, following the i* modelling notation

Table I Coupling Analysis Levels

Weighting	Event Flow- Input (I) or Output (O)	Implications for users / stakeholders
1	O- discretionary information	discretionary use
2	I- discretionary input	discretionary input- may lead to performance problems
3	O- decision-related information	agents needs information to take decisions
4	O- essential information	necessary for task or user action
5	O- indirect command	warning or message that requires attention, and possibly action

6	I- mandatory input	system needs data to continue
7	I- report command	agent must report completion of a task
8	O- command action	agent must carry out an action
9	O- command + constrained actions	agent's way of working is controlled by the system
10	O- command + multiple constraints	command dictates the type/ sequence of another agent's actions
11	O- command + constraints on many agent's actions	one agent's command controls several other agents

Where high levels of command coupling are apparent these should be investigated to reduce commands where possible. Table II summarises some implications of pathological coupling and possible remedies. When coupling scores are high, commands imposed by the system on the user should be reduced; for instance, by reallocating the work so only the user is responsible. Increasing autonomy of agents and decomposing the system into sub systems and also reduce coupling.

Table II Coupling Analysis Implications

Problem	Possible Solutions / Generic Requirements
Agent's ability to respond to commands	check agent's responsibilities, capabilities, workload
Agent's willingness to obey commands	investigate agent's motivation, responsibility and accountability
High coupling scores	Reduce commands, increase local decision making, sub-divide system
Many constrained commands	increase user training, increase local responsibility, control by objectives
Many report commands	monitor by objectives, gather events automatically, increase local responsibility
Many essential inputs	use defaults, reference files, integrate and share databases
Many commands / agents	investigate timing and schedule work, split responsibility
One agent creates many commands	review responsibility and authority, investigate work schedule

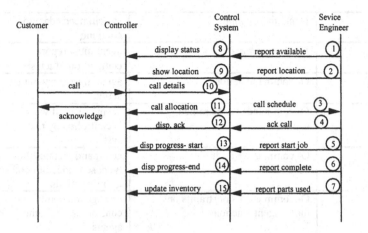

Fig. 4. Use case interaction diagram for the service engineer system (scenario 1). The numbering on the dataflows are used in the subsequent analysis.

A large number of constrained commands indicates that users are not being trusted to carry out their work without direction. Increased training and giving users responsibility should be considered. A large number of reporting commands indicates excessive system monitoring, the necessity of this should be questioned to see whether it benefits the users. Analysis of the convergence of many commands on one agent should trigger a review of responsibilities, workload, and operational schedule.

Case study: Two scenarios are analysed, each represents a different management policy for controlling the system. In the first scenario, control is centralised and all customer calls are sent to a controller who allocates calls to service engineers. The engineers have to report their location and availability to the controller, as well as their progress when undertaking repairs, and other activities such as replenishing spares from the stores. The controller system schedules the work of the engineers who have to obey commands and displays the engineers progress to the controller. The controller's role is to enter details of the customer's call and monitor the performance of the automated call dispatch system. Coupling analysis for this scenario is shown in Table III. Column 1 & 2 give the coupling between the system and the engineer, while columns 3 & 4 give coupling from the controllers viewpoint. The event numbers cross reference to the use case diagram in figure 4.

In this scenario the coupling between the engineer and the controller (see Figure 4) and between the controller and the automated call dispatch system is high. The system commands for call allocation constrain the controller's choice, and in turn the schedule is passed onto the engineer who has no discretion in his or her work. Coupling between the controller and the system could be reduced from 51 to 33 if the system's function is changed to a decision support role (see Figure 5) in which the system displays the engineer's status, locations and customer calls, leaving the controller to decide on the allocation.

Table III Coupling analysis for the SESS (Scenario 1)

Engineer - control system Event	Coupling	Control-system - controller Event	Coupling
1: Availability- I	6	8. Eng availability- O	6
2: Location -I	6	9. Eng location -O	6
3. Call schedule O	8	10.Cust call details-I	6
4. Ack call- I	6	11. Eng-call allocation-O	9
5. Start job- I	6	12. Display acknowledge-O	6
6. Finish job-I	6	13.+14. Report process (start and end)-O	12
7. Report part used- I	6	15. Update inventory-O	6
Total	44	Total	51

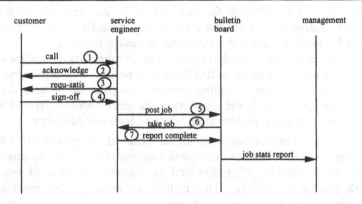

Fig. 5. Use case for the bulletin board (scenario 2) version of the SESS

This reduces the Engineer call allocation coupling to 3 (discretionary decision) and makes the 'Update progress input' unnecessary, hence saving 12 points overall. However, the coupling between the engineer and the controller would remain the same unless some autonomy is granted to the engineers. The high coupling in this scenario indicates a possible brittleness in the system, and more autonomy is desirable. Furthermore, the controller has to handle all the engineers in a branch and this indicates a problem of too many commands converging on one agent.

In the second scenario, a decentralised system is investigated. Small groups of engineers co-operate to handle customer calls in their area. Each engineer is assigned a district and customers call the engineer they have been assigned to directly (see Figure 5). When an engineer receives more calls than he can deal with he posts them onto a bulletin board which is shared with all engineers in the branch. An engineer with no calls who is reasonably close by is expected to take the call, otherwise the customer has to wait. Limited reporting of completed calls is carried out for management statistics. The coupling analysis for this scenario is shown in Table IV.

Table IV   Coupling analysis for the Workgroups Scenario version of SESS

Engineer - customer events	Coupling	Engineer - bulletin board events	Coupling
1.Call-I	6	5.Request -I	2
2.Acknowledge-O	4	6.Take Job-O	3
3.Req Satisfactory- O	4	7.Report complete	2
4. Sign-off-I	4	8.Job Stats	
Total	18	Total	7

In the decentralised scenario, local autonomy, coupling between the customer and the engineer, and between the engineer and the supporting bulletin board is low. Coupling between the service engineer and the controller, who now has a management supervisory role would also be low as this is restricted to discretionary reporting of job statistics. The dramatic differences between the two scenarios demonstrate the work organisations that are possible for this system. To maintain service levels in scenario 2, an incentive system for the engineers to complete jobs as quickly as possible could be implemented and would this increases coupling, but not to the extent of the first centralised control scenario. The coupling analysis shows that a decentralised approach would be more flexible and imposes fewer restrictions on the service engineer's job. However, coupling analysis is no panacea for work design on its own. The advantages of the lower coupling in the second scenario would need to be assessed in light of engineer performance, resource costs and customer satisfaction.

The two scenarios have different requirements for technical system support. The first, centralised control scenario implies functional requirements for an automated call allocation system, a matching algorithm and an accurate database of engineers' location, work activity and training. This in turn necessitates a call reporting and progress tracking system. In contrast the second scenario requires a simpler system composed of an electronic bulletin board to record calls that engineers can not deal with and a limited reporting system to capture details of completed calls for management reports and the incentive scheme. In our ongoing work we are investigating how different patterns of coupling and organisation design can be linked to appropriate requirements templates of co-ordination and workflow systems. These templates are composed of 'generic' requirements which are high level definition of system functionality, or design options that fit a particular type of inter-organisation relationship. These can be used either to involve procurement of appropriate products or to guide further requirements analysis. Generic requirements have been proposed for classes of application domains in other papers (e.g. functionalities for sensing and monitoring applications [15], [16]); however, this paper only deals with generic requirements for workflow and group-co-ordination systems. Some examples of generic requirements for the two scenarios analysed above are:

- Organisation type: High coupling, high automation (scenario 1)

Generic requirements: reliable communications, secure protocols, message logs, message sequence control, system monitors, system status displays, fall-back and recovery procedures, user involvement and responsibility.

- Organisation type: Low coupling, shared information (scenario 2)

Generic requirements: bulletin boards, shared databases, intranets, email logging systems, email broadcast, user motivation for co-operation.

Note that these templates are based on the outcome of the coupling analysis and properties of the organisation design such as information exchange and the degree of automation present in the system. The generic requirements then recommend properties of the technical system e.g. reliable communication), possible system components (e.g. intranets) as well as human factors issues that may need attention (e.g. user motivation). The schema of these templates is still a matter of our current search, as is the range of templates that can be proposed for workflow/groupware applications. Space precludes further treatment of these developing ideas. In the final section of this paper we turn to a variant of coupling analysis motivated by business theory.

4 Coupling Analysis and Organisational Design

While coupling analysis can investigate problems within an organisation, a theoretical framework is required to guide re-design. The theory of transaction costs [7] models the relationships between firms according to how their transactions are organised by cost, frequency and contractual formality. For instance, companies may either compete in a decentralised marketplace, or form synergetic supply chain networks, or bureaucratic hierarchies with more formal control.

Although Williamson's theory has had its critics it has stood the test of time [8], and provides a basis for economic assessment of the relationship between processes and organisation units. This approach is particularly useful when reengineering inter-organisation relationships and outsourcing functions. The transaction cost model asserts that client-supplier relationships depend on the transaction frequency, unit value and specificity of goods, and stability of association between suppliers and customers. Where the product has high value and requires considerable research and development expenditure, more stable process relationships are advisable. When low cost, high volume products are being produced less stability in relationships can be tolerated. Looser process relationships are often desirable as this enables more flexible responses to market changes. More closely coupled relationships imply a hierarchical structure whereas looser coupling suggests a network. The following heuristics are proposed to guide the design of inter-organisation and process relationships according to their control structure.

- If the unit value of goods passed between processes is low then assume low coupling; if high assume high coupling.
- If the volume of goods passed between processes is high assume low coupling and vice versa.
- If the goods are specific to the related processes (i.e. not horizontal, general market products) then assume high coupling, for the opposite assume low coupling.
- If the production time of the goods during the supply chain process is high, assume high coupling.

- If the goods require considerable research and development investment in the supply chain processes, assume high coupling.

One of the problems in operationalising transaction costs is setting the values of high and low value and volume. This depends on domain knowledge and analysis of particular markets. In spite of these limitations, this approach can lead to sector-specific guidance on how to structure process networks for different types of business. We describe a preliminary case study; however, in depth treatment is part of our ongoing research.

Case study: In this section we focus on two scenarios for the customer company relationship in the Service Engineering system. Scenario one is a loosely coupled relationship, in which the customers have either no service contract and maintenance calls are service on demand, or a low priority contract which just assigns a customer to a service engineer with no particular guarantee of service response time. Note that the latter scenario fits with the patchworking scenario used earlier. The second scenario is a closely coupled service contract relationship in which the customer is given a guaranteed level of service. The business analysis question is which relationship might be better suited to the market conditions of the company and then the requirements analysis question is what type of system support is necessary to support the client- service engineer relationship.

The photocopier market has many competitors and the value of machines is relatively high and volumes medium to low, depending on the size of the client company. Applying transaction cost heuristics the following relationship profile is generated:

- Relationship: Photocopier Supplier - customer

- Volume- medium to low, although a major account customer may purchase many machines, most customers only buy 1 or 2.

- Value- moderate to high in terms of the office equipment market.

- Specificity- moderate, there is no substitute for the product, but there are several rival suppliers.

According to transaction cost theory, the low to moderate volume with moderate value and specificity indicates a closely coupled and hierarchically controlled relationship between the client and supplier. This relationship suggests that scenario two is the more appropriate organisational design for the service engineer client relationship as it delivers added value to the customer and hopefully added loyalty to the supplier. The central control model in turn makes the relationship more specific by making the product and service package more specific to the company. The requirements implications are for high transaction support costs as the company will have to develop a call allocation system, customer care monitor and progress tracking for service engineer performance.

5 Discussion

The analytic techniques described in this paper provide the basis for systematically investigating socio-technical system requirements. These build on the i* framework

[9] that analyses requirements by reasoning about relationships between agents, tasks and goals. Models of dependencies between people and systems in the i* framework of enterprise models [9] enables the impact of different technical solutions to be assessed, but it does not provide an analytic method based on any theory of business organisational design. The metric based approach we have adopted complements the i* style analyses. One advantage of the metrics is that they can be applied to high level scenarios of prospective system designs to establish the strengths and weaknesses of different options. Coupling analysis has many applications in organisation design that we are only beginning to explore, such as span of command, and different command structures in organisations [11]. In our future work we will incorporate this analysis into design rationale representations so trade-offs can be assessed in quantitative as well as qualitative terms.

Few theories of organisations give firm design recommendations, apart from transaction cost theory [8] which does have the merit of link properties of the organisation's environment (the market) to recommendation for the organisation's structure. However, such analysis poses several difficulties. Assigning values to the variables of volume, value and specificity is subjective and furthermore depends on the analysts interpretation of the scope of the organisation environment. In spite of these difficulties, we found transactions cost theory to be an instructive tool for thought in organisation design. The coupling analysis complements this analysis as suggests measures for control in organisation hence a business level theory can be integrated with a socio-technical systems analysis. This in turn can provide recommendations for information system requirements. The framework we have proposed is tentative, however, we believe it is a novel attempt to integrate computer systems requirement analysis with business modelling. Some information systems methods have been extended for enterprise modelling and limited business process analysis (e.g. [17]), but no method has incorporated a business theory into the analytic process, nor have other methods integrated requirements analysis with business modelling.

The other contribution of this paper is to suggest how generic requirements could be linked to metric based analyses. Generic requirements (GRs) by their nature are not detailed, hence the utility of such advice needs further evaluation; however, we believe that GRs add value by raising requirements issues, even if they do not always provide solutions. The method spans a wide range of issues which GRs can not deal with in depth, so we see the method as a framework that points the requirements analyst towards other sources for more detailed advice including generic models of requirements for classes of application which we have partially explored for information retrieval [18].

The coupling analysis draws on theories of autonomy and work organisation from management science (e.g.[19]). High level requirements for groupware and workflow systems can be proposed as a result of this analysis, however, we have to improve the connection between generic requirements and organisational design. Furthermore, the recommendations of coupling analysis need to be interpreted in a domain context. While increasing autonomy might help many business organisations the converse may be true for military command and control systems. In producing a method for socio technical organisation analysis we have drawn together several literatures. We have pointed out where business process engineering may profitably benefit from

Williamson's [7] transaction cost model for designing inter-organisational relationships according to a market context and how organisation design can be linked to requirements analysis of technical systems. Design of business relationships will be increasingly vital as more companies outsource functions and concepts of the virtual firm and symbiotic productive networks become a reality (see [20]).

Acknowledgements

This research is funded by the European Commission ESPRIT 21903 'CREWS' (Co-operative Requirements Engineering With Scenarios) long-term research project. The authors wish to thank other members of the CREWS project for their comments and advice.

References

1. Macaulay, L., Requirements Engineering, Springer Verlag, Berlin, (1996).

2. Lubars, M., Potts, C., and Ritcher, C., 'A review of the state of the practice in Requirements Modelling', IEEE Int. Symposium on Requirements Engineering (RE'93), 2-14, (1993).

3. Sommerville, I., and Sawyer, P., 'Requirements Engineering: A Good Practice Guide', John Wiley & Sons, (1997).

4. Harker, S.D.P., Eason, K. D., and Dobson, J. E., 'The Change and Evolution of Requirements as a challenge to the practice of Software Engineering', IEEE Int. Symposium on Requirements Engineering (RE'93), 266-272, (1993).

5. Potts, C., Takahashi, K., and Anton, A. I., 'Inquiry-Based Requirements Analysis', IEEE Software, vol. 11, no. 2, pp. 21-32, (1994).

6. Hsi, I., and Potts, C., 'Towards Integrating Rationalistic and Ecological Design Methods for Interactive Systems', Georgia Institute of Technology, Graphics, Visualisation and Usability Centre *Technical Report*, 1-15, (1995).

7. Williamson, O.E., 'The economics of organisations: The transaction cost approach', American Journal of Sociology, Vol. 87, 548-577, (1981).

8. Williamson, O. E., 'Markets, hierarchies and the modern corporation: an unfolding perspective', Journal of Economic Behaviour and Organisation , Vol. 17, No. 3, 335-352, (1992).

9. Yu, E., 'Modelling Strategic Relationships for Process Reengineering', Technical Report DKBS-TR-94-6, University of Toronto, (1994).

10. DeMarco, T., Structured Analysis and Systems Specification, Englewood Cliffs, New Jersey, Prentice Hall, (1978).

11. Robbins, S. P., 'Organisation theory', Prentice Hall, Englewood Cliffs, NJ, (1990)

12. Jacobson, I., Christerson, M., Jonsson, P., and Overgaard, G., 'Object-Oriented Software Engineering: A Use-Case Driven Approach', Addison-Wesley, (1992).

13. UML, 'Unified Modelling Language: Method', Rational Corporation, (1999). Rational's web site: http://www.rational.com

14. Mintzberg, H.,'The Structuring of Organisations', Prentice-Hall Inc., (1979).

15. Sutcliffe A.G., Maiden N.A.M., Minocha S. and Manuel D., Supporting Scenario based requirements engineering. IEEE Transactions on Software Engineering, Vol. 24, No.12, 1072-1088. (1998)

16. Sutcliffe A.G. and Carroll J.M., Generalising claims and reuse of HCI knowledge. People and Computers XIII Proceedings of the BCS-HCI Conference Sheffield. Editors Johnson H., Nigay L., and Roast C., 159-176, Springer Verlag, (1998)

17.Veryard R. and MacDonald I.G., EMM/ODP: A methodology for federated and distributed systems. In Proceedings of IFIP WG 8.1. Conference, Methods and Associated Tools for the Information System Life cycle, Eds Verrijn-Stuart A. A. and Olle T.W., 241-273, North Holland, (1994).

18.Ryan, M., and Sutcliffe, A. G., 'Analysing Requirements to Inform Design', People and Computers XIII - Proceedings of the BCS-HCI Conference, Sheffield, H. Johnson, L. Nigay and C. Roast (Eds.), Springer Verlag, 139-158, (1998).

19. Clegg, C., Axtell, C., Damodran, L., Farbey, B., Hull, R., Lloyd, R., Nicholls, J., Sell, R., and Tomlinson, C., 'Information Technology: A study of performance and the role of human and organisational factors', Ergonomics, Vol. 40, 851-871, (1997).

20. Holland, C. P., 'Co-operative supply chain management: The impact of interorganisation information systems', Journal of Strategic Information Systems, Vol. 4, No. 2, 117-133, 1995.

Towards Flexible and High-Level Modeling and Enacting of Processes

Gregor Joeris and Otthein Herzog

Intelligent Systems Department, Center for Computing Technologies
University of Bremen, PO Box 330 440, D-28334 Bremen
joeris|herzog@informatik.uni-bremen.de

Abstract. Process modeling and enacting concepts are at the center of work-flow management. Support for heterogeneous processes, flexibility, reuse, and distribution are great challenges for the design of the next generation process modeling languages and their enactment mechanisms. Furthermore, flexible and collaborative processes depend also on unpredictable changes and hence require human intervention. Therefore, high-level process modeling constructs are needed which allow for an easy, adequate, and participatory design of work-flows. We present a process modeling language which covers these require-ments and is based on object-oriented modeling and enacting techniques. In particular, we outline how tasks and task nets are specified at a high level of ab-straction, how flexible and user-adaptable control and data flow specifications are supported, and how reuse of workflow models can be improved. The ap-proach is characterized by the uniform and integrated modeling of workflow schema and instance elements as objects and by the integration of flexible rule-based techniques with the high-level constructs of task graphs. Finally, we pre-sent our object-oriented approach for the distributed enactment of workflow models: A workflow is directly enacted by task agents which may be treated as reactive components, which interact by message passing, and whose execution behavior is derived from the context-free and context-dependent behavior of the tasks defined in the workflow schema.

1 Introduction

Workflow modeling and enacting concepts are at the center of workflow manage-ment. Support for heterogeneous processes (human-centered and system-centered), flexibility, reuse, and distribution are important challenges for the design of the next-generation process modeling languages and their enactment mechanisms (cf. [8, 25]). In particular, flexible and collaborative processes require human intervention. There-fore, a process modeling language on a high level of abstraction is needed which is easy to use and supports the visualization of its elements. In particular, the trade-off between high-level formalisms, such as graph-based modeling approaches, and flexi-ble and executable low-level mechanisms, such as rule-based specifications, has to be resolved.

Based on these design goals and requirements, we have developed a process mod-eling language which supports flexible and user-adaptable control and data flow specifications, as well as dynamic modification of workflows. The approach aims at

M. Jarke, A. Oberweis (Eds.): CAiSE'99, LNCS 1626, pp. 88-102, 1999.
© Springer-Verlag Berlin Heidelberg 1999

combining the flexibility of rule-based techniques with the high-level constructs of task graphs. Our approach is characterized by the uniform and integrated representation of workflow schema and instance elements based on object-oriented technology. Further characteristics are the separate definition of 'what to do' and 'how to do' in the workflow schema, the versioning of the workflow schema, and the separate definition of context-free and context-dependent behavior of tasks within a workflow. All these concepts improve the reusability of workflow models.

In this paper, we concentrate on the workflow modeling and enacting concepts for heterogeneous processes under the given design goals. On a conceptual level, we focus on the specification of complex user-defined control flow dependencies which can be used at a high level of abstraction, which are reusable in different contexts, and which allow for the definition of an adequate and flexible execution behavior in advance. On a technological level, we show how the modeled processes can be enacted by interacting distributed task agents which behave according to the process specification. Instead of interpreting and scheduling processes by a central and monolithic workflow engine, our approach leads to a flexible and distributed architecture.

In section 2, we identify requirements for an advanced and comprehensive approach to workflow management. Section 3 gives an overview on our process modeling approach, and section 4 introduces the basic enactment concepts. Section 5 explains the interplay between modeling and enacting and shows how the execution behavior can be adapted and reused on schema level. Finally, section 6 discusses related work, and section 7 gives a short conclusion.

2 Requirements for Advanced Workflow Management

2.1 Design Goals

In order to apply workflow technology to a broader range of processes and in particular to support dynamic, human-oriented, and distributed processes, we emphasize the following requirements for a comprehensive and integrated process modeling and enacting approach:

Adaptability to heterogeneous processes: Most business processes are rather heterogeneous entities consisting of well-structured and less-structured parts and encompassing transactional and non-transactional. All of them have to be integrated within a single process model. Thus, for adequate process modeling support, different modeling paradigms (net-based and rule-based, proactive and reactive control flow specification, etc.) have to be taken into account and have to be integrated (cf. [20, 25]).

Flexibility: Flexibility of a WFMS comprises two fundamental aspects: (1) The specification of a *flexible execution behavior* to express an accurate and less restrictive behavior in advance: flexible and adaptable control and data flow mechanisms have to be taken into account in order to support ad hoc routing and cooperative work at the workflow level (cf. [8, 15]). (2) The *evolution of workflow models* in order to flexibly modify workflow specifications on the schema and instance level due to process (re)engineering activities and dynamically changing situations of a real process (cf. [4]). Workflow evolution management is an important part of our approach, but it is out of the scope of this paper (see [17] for a detailed overview).

Distribution: Distributed workflow enactment is a key requirement for a scalable and fault-tolerant WFMS (cf. [11]). But distribution and dynamic modifications of workflows cause contradicting architectural requirements. This trade-off has to be resolved for a distributed and flexible WFMS.

Reusability: Increasing business value and complexity of process models require the support of reuse of process specifications (cf. [9, 23]). Thus, a process modeling language should provide abstraction and encapsulation mechanisms.

Ease of use: A very crucial design goal is, that the language is *easy to use*, i.e., it should allow for modeling of processes at a *high level of abstraction,* and it should support the visualization of its elements (cf. [25, 6]) (this is naturally given in a net-based approach; on the other hand, rule-based specifications are hard to understand for people, but provide a great flexibility).

2.2 Advanced Control Flow Modeling

Based on the above presented requirements and design goals we refine the requirements for control flow modeling in order to support heterogeneous and flexible processes. For the representation of heterogeneous processes several *fine-grained inter-task dependencies* have to be supported, which define control flow dependencies between particular states of a task (cf. [1, 21]). Several dependencies of these are well-known from transaction management, e.g., the two-phase commit protocol shows different state-dependencies and also the need for reactive triggering mechanisms in order to commit or abort the corresponding activities. There are many further examples where advanced control flow modeling constructs are useful particularly in order to define an accurate and a priori less prescriptive flow of work, a few of which we are listing in the following (cf. [14, 24]): (1) Our first example is the *SEQ-operator* which forces a set of activities to execute sequentially, but in any order/permutation. In this case, the actor may determine ad hoc the ordering resulting in an a priori more flexible workflow. (2) The so-called *soft synchronization* is useful for dependencies between different branches. Here, an activity may start when the preceding activity is finished or will definitely not be executed. (3) The *deadline* operator says that an activity A can be started only if activity B has not been started. (4) *Simultaneous engineering* is another good example which also shows the need for advanced data flow modeling capabilities (cf. [13, 15]): in this case, dependent activities can overlap and an activity may pass intermediate results to subsequent activities.

In contrast to these requirements, several process modeling languages are based on Petri Net-like or equivalent semantics: an activity is represented as one monolithic block, which consumes all input information once it is started, and produces all outputs, when it has finished. In particular, since control flow dependencies cannot be specified independently for the start and end point of an activity, only end-start dependencies can be defined. Among parallel and conditional splits with corresponding join operators sometimes some special control flow operators are provided. Such approaches support modeling of workflows on a high level of abstraction and the graphical visualization of both workflow schemata and running workflow instances.

However, there is no possibility to model fine-grained inter-task dependencies and to define user-adaptable control flow constructs.

On the other hand, the above listed advanced control flow dependencies can be expressed by more low-level, rule-based formalisms, e.g., by event-condition-action (ECA) rules. Unfortunately, whereas the representation of a workflow model as a set of rules is sufficient for enactment, it is inadequate for workflow design and hardly understandable for people (cf. [2]). Furthermore, the reusability of complex control flow dependency patterns is mostly weak since there is no encapsulation or abstraction mechanism (an exception are the rule patterns of [19]). Therefore, several approaches (e.g., [18, 3, 7, 29, 6]) provide high-level workflow modeling constructs which are transformed into global ECA rules for enactment – in this way the flexibility and expressive power of ECA rules on the modeling level is lost.

To summarize, among the general and well-known requirements of separated control and data flow modeling and provision of multi-paradigmatic control flow mechanisms, a flexible process modeling language should support the specification of fine-grained control flow dependencies, but still provide mechanisms to abstract from these detailed control flow specifications. In particular, an advanced workflow designer should be able to define new control flow dependencies (cf. [14]).

3 Overview of the Processes Meta Model

Our approach to process modeling and enacting is based on object-oriented modeling techniques (not to confuse with an OO process modeling method, where processes would be defined in a product- or object-centered way). All relevant entities are modeled as attributed, encapsulated, and interacting objects. Following the principle of separation of concerns, we divide the overall model into sub-models for tasks and workflows, documents and their versions, and organizational aspects in order to capture the different aspects of processes. We concentrate in the following on the modeling and enacting of tasks and workflows and disregard the integration of document, version, and workspace management capabilities in our approach (see [15, 16] for details). Furthermore, all elements of the organizational sub-model are omitted in this paper. We introduce our object model step by step starting with the definition of task types:

3.1 Task Definition and Task Interface

First of all, a *task definition* (or task type) is separated into the definition of the *task interface* which specifies 'what is to do', and potentially several *workflow definitions* (task body), which specify how the task may be accomplished (how to do) (see figure 1 and 2). Thus, the building block is the class `TaskDefinition` which may contain several `WorkflowDefinitions`. The decision is taken at run-time, which workflow definition of a task definition is used to perform a task (late binding). Every workflow definition has a condition which acts as a guard and restricts the allowed workflows according to the current case. Note, that when talking in the context of our formal meta model, we use workflow definition in the more restricted sense of defin-

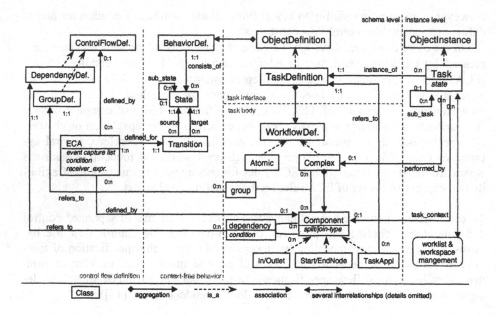

Fig. 1. Functional and behavioral aspects of the process meta model

ing only how a task has to be done (the task body) and use workflow synonymously to workflow definition when misunderstandings are excluded by the context.

The task interface of a task definition is defined by a set of parameter definitions, a behavior definition, and a set of business rules which constrain the valid workflow definitions (parameter definitions and business rules are omitted in figure 1). The behavior definition specifies the external context-free behavior of a task by a state-chart variant (e.g., transactional or non-transactional), whereas the context-dependent behavior is defined by control flow dependencies within a workflow definition (see below). A parameter definition specifies the kind of the parameter (in, out, inout), the type of the parameter, an access type, and a condition, which defines the properties the actual inputs and outputs have to comply with. The access type is based on our integrated workspace management services (see [15] for details).

3.2 Workflow Definition

The basic elements of modeling the control and data flow on a high level of abstraction are well-known from several process modeling languages. Usually, a workflow is modeled in terms of tasks or activities, specific control and data flow dependencies, and branching and synchronization operators. The execution semantics of these workflow-specific terms is mostly defined in workflow-independent terms like Petri Nets, statecharts, or ECA rules. We will follow such an approach, which is based on the high-level constructs of task graphs briefly introduced in this sub-section. In the next sections, we then show how the execution semantics of the control flow dependencies are defined and how user-defined and complex control flow constructs are supported.

A workflow definition may be atomic or complex. An atomic workflow consists only of a process description. A complex workflow is defined in a process-oriented manner by a *task graph* which consists of task components, start and end nodes, and data inlets and outlets, which are linked by control and data flow dependencies:

Components: A *task component* is an applied occurrence of a task definition representing the invocation hierarchy. If a task definition is applicable only in a certain context, it can be locally declared within another task definition, restricting their visibility to this task type. Thus, the declaration and invocation hierarchy of task definitions are separated (as it is well-known from programming languages). For every task component a split and join type can be specified. AND- and OR-splits realize total and conditional branching, respectively. The corresponding join types synchronize the activated branches. In order to provide connectors independently of a task component, *connector components* are predefined which just realize splits and joins. Furthermore, a task graph consists of a start and end node which provide only syntactic sugar.

Control flow dependencies: Task components (and start and end node) are linked by control flow dependencies. Iterations within this task graph are modeled by a special predefined feedback relationship. A condition can be associated to every dependency to support conditional branches (by default, this condition is set to true). We allow to define different control flow dependency types which can be applied and reused within several workflow definitions. The semantics of a control flow dependency type is defined by ECA rules as introduced in the next section. Figure 4 illustrates an example with an end-start dependency and a deadline dependency.

Groups and blocks: Similar to the definition of control flow dependencies we support the definition of groups and block relationship types. A group relationship is used within a workflow definition in order to group arbitrary task components of a task graph; it applies the behavior defined by the group relationship to its components (e.g., to realize mutual exclusion). A block is a group, which contains a subtask-graph with exactly one start and end component (omitted in figure 1). Blocks can be nested. This mechanism is particularly useful for exception handling.

Dataflow relationships: Finally, task components can be linked by dataflow relationships according to the input and output parameters of their task definitions. Furthermore, a data inlet (or outlet) is used in a task graph as a data source (or sink) in order to realize a vertical dataflow between the parameters of the task definition and their use within the workflow.

4 Distributed Enactment by Reactive Components

4.1 Overview on Distributed Workflow Enactment by Reactive Components

This section sketches the basic *execution model* of our approach which is the basis for the detailed consideration of the definition of the execution behavior of a task in the next section. We follow the idea of treating tasks as reactive components (cf. [13, 5, 27, 26]): instead of interpreting a workflow instance by a (centralized) workflow engine, a workflow is directly enacted by distributed task instance agents which interact by event passing.

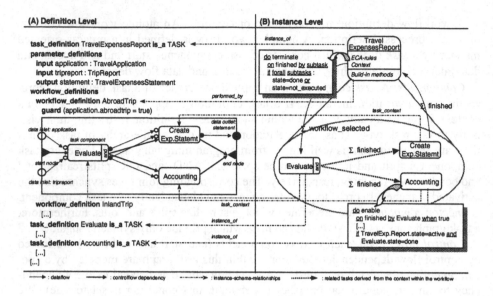

Fig. 2. Example of process definition and enactment

A task has several built-in operations/transitions, which can be categorized into state transition operations, actor assignment operations, operations for handling of (versioned) inputs and outputs, and workflow change operations. For every operation, the task has the knowledge about when to trigger the transition, a condition that must hold for executing the transition, and a list of receivers to which events are passed. Furthermore, the task knows its related tasks (the context of the task, i.e., predecessors, successors, sub-tasks, super-task, supplier of inputs, and consumer of outputs). Thus, workflow enactment is distributed to task agents, which correspond to the components of a workflow definition and behave as defined in the schema. We denote this approach as light-weight agent-oriented, since the knowledge of how to react on events is explicitly represented and decoupled from the built-in operations (corresponding to [10]). On the other hand, task agents lack properties which characterize fully-fledged agents as defined by [28].

Example: A typical workflow enactment with traditional control flows is as follows (see figure 2B): A task is started and in most cases a workflow is selected automatically creating sub-tasks in the case of a complex workflow. An event is passed to the first tasks of this workflow, triggering the evaluation of the 'enable' transition. When a task is enabled, the role resolution is activated if no actor has yet been assigned explicitly. In the case of automatic tasks, the start transition will be directly triggered by the enable event (by the trigger 'on enabled by self'). When a task is terminated, a corresponding event is sent to all successor tasks. This again results in the evaluation of the 'enable' transition. Furthermore, for all tasks which are connected to the end node, the finish event is also sent to the super-task, triggering the termination of the super-task, when all sub-tasks have been terminated.

4.2 Representation of Task Instances

For *instantiation*, neither a copy of a task definition is created (e.g., as it is done in the Petri Net-based approaches) and enriched by execution-relevant information (e.g., assignment of start tokens) nor a compilation into another formalism is used (e.g., as in IBM FlowMark [22], METEOR$_2$ [5]). We rather follow a tightly integrated approach, where a task instance is related to the relevant schema elements and where these interrelationships are explicitly maintained (as illustrated in figure 1 and 2). First of all, a task instance is related to its task definition. Next, when a workflow was chosen for execution at run-time, a 'performed_by' relationship is inserted, the subtasks are created according to the chosen workflow definition, and for every subtask the corresponding component within the workflow definition is identified. Thus, the dynamic task hierarchy is created step-by-step and all execution-relevant information of a workflow schema can be accessed by the instances. Only the execution state of a task instance, the dynamic invocation hierarchy, and the actual dataflow are persistently covered at instance level. The execution behavior, i.e., the ECA rules and the context of a task is cached within the task object, but is not made persistent. The behavior is derived from the context-free behavior of the task definition and the context-dependent behavior of the component that the task plays within a workflow definition. The tight coupling of schema and instances is also reflected by our architecture, which does not distinguish build- and run-time environments. This is the basis to support dynamic workflow changes (see [17] for details).

4.3 Representation and Semantics of the Task Execution Behavior

The *execution behavior* of tasks is defined by a statechart variant by means of states, transitions, and event handling rules. Event-condition-action (ECA) rules determine when an operation/transition is invoked, and when it is applicable. We adopt the concept of ECA rules as follows:

Syntax of ECA rules: First of all, an ECA rule is always associated with an operation/transition, which defines the action part of the rule. Furthermore, there is exactly one ECA rule for every transition. Thus, ECA rules are structured according to the task's transitions, and therefore the transition name is listed at the top of a rule (see BNF of an ECA rule below). Additionally, an ECA rule consists of a list of event captures, a condition, and a receiver expression.

```
ECArule          ::=   "DO" <transition>
                       "ON" <event_capture> { "," <event_capture> }
                       "IF" <transition_condition>
                       "SEND_TO" receiver_expr
event_capture    ::=   <event_name> ["BY" <event_producer_name>]
                                    ["WHEN" <trigger_condition>]
```

Semantics of event handling: Events define when an operation is to be triggered: when a task receives an event that matches an event capture in the event capture list, and when the task is in the source state of the corresponding transition, the event is consumed and the task tries to perform the transition. The invocation of a transition causes the evaluation of the transition condition defined by the ECA rule. This transition acts as a guard, i.e., the transition is performed only when the condition holds (otherwise nothing is done). We allow only the definition of atomic events, which are used only for triggering the evaluation of the transition condition. These state-based semantics avoid the difficulties of defining complex event-based semantics. Moreover, user controllable operations can be invoked externally. In this case, the condition still ensures that the operation is applicable. Thus, invocation and applicability of a transition are strictly separated.

Event capture: The matching of an event with an event capture can be qualified to the causing task, e.g., this allows a task to react differently on the event finished, depending on whether the event was received from a predecessor or from a sub-task (triggering the enable or finish transition, respectively; see figure 2). Furthermore, a trigger condition can be specified within an event capture which must hold for a valid event capture. Otherwise, the next event capture which matches the event is searched.

Event generation and propagation: After an operation is executed, an event is automatically generated for that operation. In contrast to statecharts [12], we use events for inter-object communication and hence do not prescribe a broadcast of events to all tasks in order to avoid communication overhead (note, that a broadcast would not change the execution semantics; therefore and for the sake of readability, we omit the receiver expressions in all examples). The receivers of an event are rather defined by the receiver expression of an ECA rule, taking into account the workflow structure, i.e., passing events horizontally to related tasks as well as vertically among super- and sub-tasks.

5 Behavior Definition and Adaptation

So far, we have introduced how workflows are modeled in terms of a task graph and how tasks are enacted on the basis of event handling mechanisms. But we have not yet presented the interplay of the high-level modeling constructs with the flexible rule-based enacting techniques. In this section, we therefore show how the execution behavior of tasks can be defined and adapted on schema level, how user-definable control flow dependency types and fine-grained state dependencies are represented, and how the execution behavior of a task is configured from this specifications.

5.1 Definition of the Context-Free Behavior of a Task

The context-free behavior of a task is defined by a *statechart variant,* which is encapsulated by the class BehaviorDefinition. The statechart defines the states and the operations/transitions, which can be invoked in that state. We allow for the composition of states into complex states (OR-states), but we disallow concurrent states (AND-states). Furthermore, one context-free ECA rule can be defined for every transition. Further ECA rules can be added by the definition of control flow dependencies types and group relationship types, which we will introduce below.

A task definition can *inherit* from an abstract task definition, i.e., a task definition which has neither parameter definitions nor workflow definitions. Thus, the is_a hierarchy is used to define the behavior classes of tasks (e.g., non-transactional, transactional, etc.; cf. [21, 27] for detailed examples). Within an inherited statechart, new states can be added and atomic states can be refined. Also, transitions can be added and redefined by redefining the source state, refining the target state, and by redefin-

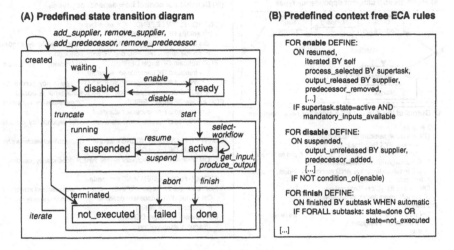

Fig. 3. Predefined context-free execution behavior

ing and adding ECA rules. Every task definition inherits from a *predefined task definition*, which consists of a statechart that defines the basic states, transitions, and context-free ECA rules as illustrated in figure 3. In particular, the activation and termination condition of a task is associated with the enable and finish transition, respectively. The ready state is needed for worklist handling and the truncated state is used to handle the synchronization of dynamically determined parallel branches.

5.2 Definition of Control Flow Types

Different control flow dependency types and group relationship types can be defined by a process engineer. They are defined by a label, an informal description, and a set of ECA rules, which give the semantics of the dependency type. Within the task graph, the control flow dependencies or group relationship can be used by their labels abstracting from the detailed definition and reusing complex control flow schemes. Thus, the ECA rules defined by a control flow type define how to react on events dependent on the context. This leads to a combined approach which integrates the flexibility of rule-based techniques with the high-level constructs of task graphs.

As a first example and omitting the details of defining ECA rules on the schema level, we briefly explain the definition of the standard end-start dependency, which consists of several rules shown in figure 4. We concentrate on the first rule, which defines that the enable transition is triggered 'on finished by predecessor', and that the condition 'source.state=done' must hold. The application of this dependency type in the example of figure 4 results in the following behavior: when 'CloseRegistration' terminates, the corresponding event is sent to the successor tasks (here 'SendProgram'), triggering the evaluation of the enable condition (which requires 'CloseRegistration.state=done', but also that all mandatory inputs are available and that the supertask is active as defined by the context-free behavior), and probably performing the enable transition. Thus, the rules are associated with the target component of a dependency and are merged with other defined rules as introduced below. In a similar

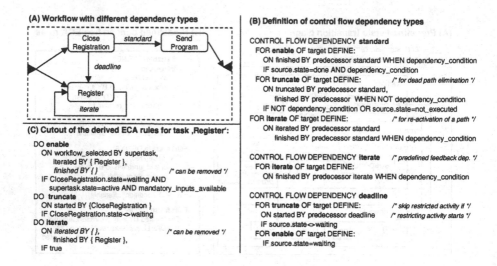

Fig. 4. Examples of the definition and use of control flow dependency types

way, a soft synchronization dependency can be realized with the relaxed enabling condition 'source.state=done OR source.state=not_executed'.

Furthermore, we extend our approach of modeling task graphs by supporting the association of ECA rules directly to a task component. By this mechanism, local adaptations as well as reactions to externally generated events of application systems can be defined within a workflow.

5.3   Definition of ECA Rules on Schema Level

As illustrated in the examples, ECA rules can be partially defined on the schema level by an event capture, a transition condition, or a receiver expression. In the case of dependency types, it is further defined whether the ECA rule is associated with the source or target component of the application of the dependency in a task graph. In addition to the keywords 'source' and 'target', relationships of the workflow structure can be used in the specification of an ECA rule (e.g., to the super- and subtasks, to predecessor and successor task (possibly qualified by a specific dependency type), to task related by the feedback relationship ('iterators'), to consumer and supplier of outputs, to all tasks of a complex workflow or a group). This is essential for reusability since it avoids context-dependent definitions (such as 'on X.done do ...'). Finally, the keyword 'dependency_condition' refers to the control flow dependency condition defined in a task graph, and the keyword 'condition_of' refers to the condition of another transition.

5.4   Configuration of the Execution Behavior of a Task

The (partially) defined ECA rules of the context-free and context-dependent behavior definitions are joined together defining the behavior of a task instance. An ECA rule is relevant for a task T, if

- the ECA rule is defined by the statechart of the task definition of T (context-free ECA rule), or
- T refers to a source (target) component of a control flow dependency of type C in a task graph, and the ECA rule is defined by C for the source (target) component, or
- T refers to a component in a task graph, which is part of a group relationship of type G, and the ECA rule is defined by G (thus, the ECA rules of a group relationship are associated with all members of the group), or
- T refers to a component of a task graph, for which the ECA rule is locally defined.

One ECA rule for every transition is combined from all relevant ECA rules by

- creating the union of the event capture lists of the ECA rules (two event captures are identical, if and only if their event_name, event_producer, and trigger_condition are identical),
- creating the union of the tasks represented by the receiver expressions,
- generating a transition condition as follows (where G is the set of ECA rules which are defined for the transition and which are derived from group relationships, C is correspondingly the set of ECA rules derived from control flow dependencies, $\Theta \in \{\wedge, \vee\}$ depending on the join type of the task):

$$contextfree.condition \wedge \bigwedge_{\forall g \in G} g.condition \wedge \bigodot_{\forall c \in C} c.condition$$

Finally, the relative statements within the ECA rules are resolved according to the structure of the performed workflow. Figure 4 gives an example of this behavior configuration for the 'Register' task (illustrating only the most relevant ECA rules and event captures for this example) and shows an additional dependency type, the deadline dependency.

We finish this section by giving some more examples which show the usage of group relationships: task components that are part of a parallel branch can be related by a SEQ group which declares an enable condition 'forall members: state!=running', and hence guarantees mutual exclusion. Another example is a two-phase commit. First, we have to specify a behavior definition with a new state 'prepared' and redefined transitions for transactional tasks supporting a 2PC protocol. Next, we may group the components of a workflow which are 2PC dependent. For this, we define a 2PC group relationship which ensures by two rules that an abort will cause the abort of all members of the group, and that the final commit is enabled when all members are in the state prepared. Note, that once defined, the workflow modeler can use this complex behavior by grouping task components according to the defined 2PC grouping relationship.

6 Related Work

With respect to the adaptability to heterogeneous processes, flexibility, and modeling of workflows at a high-level of abstraction, APEL and JIL are worth mentioning. JIL [25] provides a rich set of control flow modeling concepts and it combines in particular proactive and reactive mechanisms. APEL [6] is based on object-oriented modeling concepts, provides a graphical process modeling language, and uses state transition diagrams and event-trigger rules for the specification of flexible workflows. However, the specification of user-adaptable control flow dependencies, dynamic modifications of workflows, and distributed enactment of workflows are not addressed by these approaches.

User-defined control flow constructs have been discussed by [14] (MOBILE). The semantics of different control flow constructs are defined by Petri Nets, but without considering the definition of control flow dependencies in the context of a distributed workflow enactment. Furthermore, it is not possible to define fine-grained state-dependencies since the control flow constructs are specified as execution statements/predicates which are independently defined of the execution state of an activity (e.g., deadline(A, and(B,C)) where A, B, and C are elementary/complex workflows).

The idea of treating tasks as reactive components is influenced by our previous work on the DYNAMITE approach [13]. But significant revisions and extensions of the underlying concepts and their integration into a coherent object-oriented framework have been made in our current approach.

With respect to distributed enactment, METEOR$_2$ [5], WASA [27], and EvE [26] follow similar approaches. In contrast to METEOR$_2$, we do not compile the workflow schema into executable code, but we follow an integrated approach for the representation of workflow schemata and instances which supports dynamic modifications of workflow schemata. METEOR$_2$ provides no high-level modeling constructs but supports modeling of fine-grained state dependencies by constructs similar to ECA rules. The WASA model is based on a less complex workflow modeling approach, so that only end-start dependencies have to be synchronized. Both approaches do not support late binding of workflows. Finally, EvE provides a framework for distributed workflow enactment based on distributed event-handling by reactive components, but it is not intended for workflow modeling on a high-level of abstraction. Furthermore, in contrast to our state-based semantics, EvE follows a purely event-based approach.

Finally, ECA rules are used by several WFMS for workflow execution. In those approaches, a workflow specification which is defined in a more high-level workflow modeling language, is transformed into a global set of ECA rules (e.g., WIDE [3], TriGSflow [18], Panta Rhei [7], Waterloo [29], APEL [6]). Thus, different concepts are used for modeling and enacting. The workflow engine is mostly realized using a centralized active database. In our approach, ECA rules can be used on the modeling level in a structured way in order to adapt control flow dependencies and to enhance the flexibility of the WFMS. The rules are encapsulated and hence can be applied at a high level of abstraction for workflow definition. Finally, in contrast to the centralized and transformation-based approaches, we follow a distributed and configuration-based approach, where the ECA rules are derived from the specification for every task instance object and hence define the inter-object communication of the distributed object system.

7 Conclusion

In this paper, we have proposed an object-oriented approach to modeling and enacting of heterogeneous processes that deals with the challenging requirements of flexibility, reuse, distribution, and provision a process modeling language at a high level of abstraction. The encapsulation of a workflow definition by the task interface, the definition of different behavior classes, and the definition of user-adaptable control flow types characterize our modeling formalism and enhance reusability of process models. Furthermore, the combination of rule-based techniques with the high-level constructs of task graphs results in a great flexibility without losing the ability of high-level workflow modeling. The tight integration of schema and instance elements and schema versioning concepts are the basis for supporting dynamic workflow changes. Finally, based on the introduced modeling concepts, distributed enactment is realized in a natural way by distributed and interacting task objects. The presented concepts have been prototypically implemented using CORBA. The architecture of the system will be addressed in subsequent papers.

References

1. Attie, P.C.; Singh, M.P.; Sheth, A.; Rusinkiewicz, M.: "Specifying and Enforcing Intertask Dependencies", in *Proc. of the 19th Int. Conf. on Very Large Databases (VLDB'93)*, Dublin, Ireland, 1993.
2. Belkhatir, N.; Estublier, J.; Melo, W.L: "Adele 2: a Support to Large Software Development Process", in Dowson, M. (ed.): *Proc. of the 1st Int. Conf. on the Software Process*, IEEE Computer Society Press, 1991; pages 159-170.
3. Casati, F.; Ceri, S.; Pernici, B.; Pozzi, G.: "Deriving Active Rules for Workflow Enactment", in Wagner, R.R.; Thoma, C.H. (eds.) *Proc. of 7th Intl. Conf. on Database and Expert System Applications (DEXA'96)*, Zurich, Swiss, Sept. 1996, Springer, LNCS, pp. 94-115.
4. Conradi, R.; Fernström, C.; Fugetta, A.: "A Conceptual Framework for Evolving Software Processes", *ACM SIGSOFT Software Engineering Notes*, Vol. 18, No. 4, 1993; pp. 26-34.
5. Das, S.; Kochut, K.; Miller, J.; Sheth, A.; Worah, D.: "ORBWork: A Reliable Distributed CORBA-based Workflow Enactment System for METEOR_2", Technical Report UGA-CS-TR-97-001, Department of Computer Science, University of Georgia, Feb. 1997.
6. Dami, S.; Estublier, J.; Amiour, M.; "APEL: a Graphical Yet Executable Formalism for Process Modeling", in Di Nitto, E.; Fuggetta, A. (eds.) *Process Technology, Special Issue of the International Journal on Automated Software Engineering*, 5(1), 1998; pp. 61-96.
7. Eder, J.; Groiss, H.: "A Workflow-Management-System based on Active Databases" (in german), Vosser, G.; Becker, J. (eds.) *Geschäftsprozeßmodellierung und Workflow-Management: Modelle, Methoden, Werkzeuge*, Int. Thomson Publishing, 1996.
8. Ellis, C.A.; Nutt, G.J.: "Workflow: The Process Spectrum", in *NSF Workshop on Workflow and Process Automation in Information Systems*, Athens, Georgia, 1996.
9. Estublier, J.; Dami, S.: "About Reuse in Multi-paradigm Process Modelling Approach", in *Proc. of the 10th Intl. Software Process Workshop (ISPW'96)*, Dijon, France, 1996.
10. Genesereth, M.R.; Ketchpel, S.P.: "Software Agents", in *Communications of the ACM*, 37(7), 1994; pp. 48-53.
11. Georgakopoulos, D.; Hornick, M.; Shet, A.: "An Overview of Workflow Management: From Process Modeling to Workflow Automation Infrastructure". *Distributed and Parallel Databases*, 3(2), 1995; pp. 119-153.

12. Harel, D.; Gery, E.: "Executable Object Modeling with Statecharts", in *Proc. of the 18th Int. Conf. on Software Engineering,* Berlin, Germany, 1996; pp. 246-257.
13. Heimann, P.; Joeris, G.; Krapp, C.-A.; Westfechtel, B.: "DYNAMITE: Dynamic Task Nets for Software Process Management", in *Proc. of the 18th Int. Conf. on Software Engineering,* Berlin, Germany, 1996; pp. 331-341.
14. Jablonski, St.; Bussler, Ch.: "Workflow Management - Modeling Concepts, Architecture and Implementation", International Thomson Computer Press, London, 1996.
15. Joeris, G.: "Cooperative and Integrated Workflow and Document Management for Engineering Applications", in *Proc. of the 8th Int. Workshop on Database and Expert System Applications, Workshop on Workflow Management in Scientific and Engineering Applications,* Toulouse, France, 1997; pp. 68-73.
16. Joeris, G.: "Change Management Needs Integrated Process and Configuration Management", in Jazayeri, M; Schauer, H (eds.), *Software Engineering - ESEC/FSE'97,* Proceedings, LNCS 1301, Springer, 1997; pp. 125-141.
17. Joeris, G; Herzog, O.: "Managing Evolving Workflow Specifications", in *Proc. of the 3rd Int. IFCIS Conf. on Cooperative Information Systems (CoopIS'98),* New York, Aug. 1998; pp. 310-319.
18. Kappel, G.; Pröll, B.; Rausch-Schott, S.; Retschitzegger, W.: "TriGSflow – Active Object-Oriented Workflow Management", in *Proc. of the 28th Hawaii Intl. Conf. On System Sciences (HICSS'95),* Jan. 1995; pp. 727-736.
19. Kappel, G.; Rausch-Schott, S.; Retschitzegger, W.; Sakkinen, M.: "From Rules to Rule Patterns", in Constantopoulos, P.; Mylopolous, J.; Vassiliou, Y. (eds.) *Proc. of the 8th Intl. Conf. on Advanced Information System Engineering (CAiSe'96),* Springer, LNCS 1080, 1996; pp. 99-115.
20. M.I. Kellner: "Multiple-Paradigm Approaches for Software Process Modeling", in Thomas, I. (eds.) *Proc. of the 7th Intl. Software Process Workshop - 'Communication and Coordination in the Software Process'.* Yountville, CA, USA, Okt. 1991, IEEE Computer Society Press; pp. 82-85.
21. Krishnakumar, N.; Sheth, A.: "Managing Heterogeneous Multi-system Tasks to Support Enterprise-wide Operations", in *Distributed and Parallel Databases,* 3, 1995; pp. 1-33.
22. Leymann, F.; Altenhuber, W.: "Managing business processes as an information resource", *IBM Systems Journal,* Vol. 33, No. 2, 1994; pp. 326-348.
23. Puustjärvi, J.; Tirri, H.; Veijalainen, J.: "Reusability and Modularity in Transactional Workflows", in *Information Systems,* 22(2/3), 1997; pp. 101-120.
24. Reichert, M; Dadam, P.: "ADEPTflex – Supporting Dynamic Changes of Workflows Without Losing Control", *Journal of Intelligent Information Systems - Special Issue on Workflow Managament,* 10(2), Kluwer Academic Publishers, March 1998; pp. 93-129.
25. Sutton Jr., S.M.; Osterweil, L.J.: "The Design of a Next-Generation Process Language", in Jazayeri, M; Schauer, H (eds.), *Software Engineering - ESEC/FSE'97,* Proceedings, LNCS 1301, Springer, 1997; pp. 142-158.
26. Tombros, D.; Geppert, A; Dittrich, K.R.: "Semantics of Reactive Components in Event-Driven Workflow Execution", in *Proc. of the 9th Intl. Conf. on Advanced Information System Engineering (CAiSe'97),* Springer, LNCS 1250, 1997; pp. 409-420.
27. Weske, M: "State-based Modeling of Flexible Workflow Executions in Distributed Environments", in Ozsu, T.; Dogac, A.; Ulusoy, O. (eds.) *Proc. of the 3rd Biennial World Conference on Integrated Design and Process Technology (IDPT'98), Volume 2 – Issues and Applications of Database Technology,* 1998; pp. 94-101.
28. Wooldridge, M.; Jenings, N.: "Intelligent Agents: Theory and Practice", in *Knowledge Engineering Review,* 10(2), 1995; pp. 115-152.
29. Zukunft, O.; Rump F.: "From Business Process Modeling to Workflow Management: An Integrated Approach", in Scholz-Reiter B.; Stickel E. (eds.) *Business Process Modeling,* Springer-Verlag, Berlin, 1996.

Method Enhancement with Scenario Based Techniques

Jolita Ralyté[1], Colette Rolland[1], Véronique Plihon[2]

[1]CRI, Université de Paris1- Sorbonne, 90, rue de Tolbiac, 75013 Paris
(ralyte, rolland)@univ-paris1.fr
[2]PRISM, Université de Versailles Saint-Quentin 45, av. des Etats-Unis, 78035 Versailles
Veronique.Plihon@prism.uvsq.fr

Abstract. Scenarios have proven useful to elicit, validate and document requirements but cannot be used in isolation. Our concern in this paper is to integrate scenario-based techniques in existing methods. We propose a set of operators to support such an integration. This set is classified in two sub-sets: the one dealing with the integration of the product models of the two initial methods and the one concerned with the integration of their process models. The operators are used to integrate the CREWS-L'Ecritoire approach with the OOSE method. This leads to enhance the use case model construction of the OOSE method with on one hand, the linguistic techniques for scenario authoring and formalisation and on the other hand, the discovery strategies to elicit requirements by scenario analysis of the CREWS-L'Ecritoire approach.

1   Introduction

The aim of analysis methods is to define the specification of a future system. In the new generation of such analysis methods ([1], [2], [3]) scenario-based approaches have been introduced to bridge the gap between the user view and the functional view of the future system and therefore ensure that the future system will meet the requirements of its users. In the CREWS[1] project, four different scenario-based approaches have been developed with the aim of supporting requirements acquisition from real world scenes [4] and from natural language scenario descriptions [5], [6] and requirements validation though scenario walkthrough [7] and scenario animation [8]. The hypothesis of the project is that each of the approaches might be useful in specific project situations which are not well tackled by existing analysis methods and therefore, that it is worth looking for the integration of such approaches in current methods. This shall lead to an enhancement of the existing methods with scenario-based techniques.

In this paper we propose an approach for such a method extension. The CREWS approach that we consider is the one allowing to "acquire requirements from natural language scenario descriptions". In this approach (denoted CREWS-L'Ecritoire), the

---

[1] The work described in this paper is support by the European ESPRIT project CREWS standing for "Co-operative Requirements Engineering With Scenarios".

M. Jarke, A. Oberweis (Eds.): CAiSE'99, LNCS 1626, pp. 103-118, 1999.
© Springer-Verlag Berlin Heidelberg 1999

key concept is the couple (goal, scenario), where the goal is viewed as "something that some stakeholder hopes to achieve in the future", whereas a scenario is defined as "a possible behaviour limited to a set of purposeful interactions taking place among several agents" [6]. The paper illustrates how the CREWS-L'Ecritoire technique is integrated to the part of the OOSE method dealing with the use case model definition.

The approach for method integration is based on the one hand, on a method meta-model which conforms to the traditional view of a method been composed of a product model and a process model and, on the other hand, of a set of operators with associated rules to integrate product model elements and process model elements.

The proposed approach is part of the Method Engineering domain [9], [10]. However whereas assembly approaches focused on the grouping of method fragments belonging to methods which complement one the other [11], [12] we are dealing with the problem of integrating methods which are partially overlapping. In the case at hand, it is obvious that both the CREWS-L'Ecritoire approach and the OOSE approach have the concept of "scenario" but with different meanings. Thus, whereas situational method engineering deals with the assembly of disjoint method fragments, our problem is closer to schema integration in the database area [13].

This paper is organised as follows. We present in the next section our *method meta model* which is instantiated for both the OOSE method and the CREWS-L'Ecritoire approach. Section 3 is dedicated to method integration dealing first with the product models integration and then with the process models integration. In both cases we present and exemplify the *operators* used to perform the integration. Finally, in section 4 some conclusions are drawn.

2   The Method Meta Model

We represent a method as composed of two elements : the *Product Model* and the *Process Model*. The product model represents the class of products obtained as outputs of the use of the method in specific applications. The process model represents the product development process.

2.1   Process Model

We view the process model as composed of two parts : *Map* and *Guidelines*. The map provides a strategic view of the process telling what can be achieved (which process intention) following which strategy. The guidelines define how to apply the strategy to achieve the process intention. These three aspects are described in turn.

Map. A map is a labelled directed graph in which the nodes are the *intentions* and the edges between intentions are the *strategies* (see [14] for more detail). The ordering of intentions and strategies is non-deterministic. The edges in the graph are directed and show which intentions can follow which one. Fig. 1 shows two examples of maps for OOSE and CREWS-L'Ecritoire methods respectively.

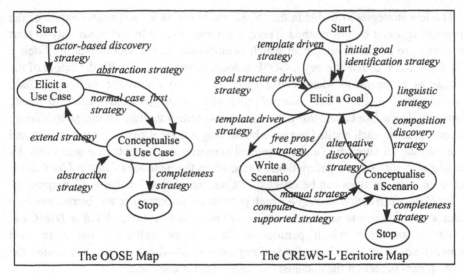

Fig. 1. The OOSE Use Case Model map and the CREWS-L'Ecritoire map

As shown in Fig.1, a map consists of a number of *sections* each of which is a triplet $<i_p, i_p, s_j>$ where i_i is a source intention, i_j is a target intention ant s_{ij} is a strategy defining the way to go from the source to the target intention. There are two distinct intentions called *Start* and *Stop* that represent the intentions to start navigating in the map and to stop doing so. Thus, it can be seen that there are a number of paths in the graph from *Start* to *Stop*. We assume requirements engineering processes to be intention-oriented. At any moment, the requirements engineer has an *intention*, a goal in mind that he/she wants to fulfil. To take this characteristic into account the map identifies the set of intentions *I* that have to be achieved in order to solve the problem at hand. An intention is expressed as a natural language statement comprising a verb and several parameters, where each parameter plays a different role with respect to the verb [15]. For example, the OOSE [1], [16] map (Fig. 1) contains two intentions in addition to *"Start"* and *"Stop"* : *"Elicit a Use Case"* and *"Conceptualise a Use Case"*.

A *strategy* is an approach, a manner to achieve an intention. The strategy, as part of the triplet $<i_p, i_p, s_j>$, characterises the flow from the source intention i_i to the target intention i_j and the way i_j can be achieved. The map identifies the set of strategies *S* which allows to construct different paths in the map.

The specific manner in which an intention can be achieved is captured in a section of the map whereas the various sections having the same intention i_i as a source and i_j as target show the different strategies that can be adopted for achieving i_j when coming from i_i. Similarly, there can be different sections having i_i as source and i_{j1}, i_{j2}, ...i_{jn} as targets. These show the different intentions that can be achieved after the achievement of i_i. The OOSE map is composed of six sections. The triplet *<Elicit a Use Case, Conceptualise a Use Case, Normal case first strategy>* is an example of the section in the OOSE map.

The few strategies available in the OOSE map reflects the sequential nature of the process suggested by this method. There is for example, only one possibility to start the Use Case model development which is embedded in the section <*Start, Elicit a Use Case, Actor based strategy*>. OOSE indeed, proposes to identify the actors of the system as a means to identify use cases. The two sections : <*Elicit a Goal, Conceptualise a Use Case, Normal case first strategy*> and <*Elicit a Goal, Conceptualise a Use Case, Abstraction strategy*> reflect the two OOSE possibilities : to conceptualise each elicited use case by writing a normal case scenario at first and then, writing all alternative and exceptional scenarios or conceptualise a use case by reusing abstract use case descriptions. Then, when the intentions *Elicit a Use Case* is achieved, three sections can be selected : <*Conceptualise a Use Case, Conceptualise a Use Case, Abstraction strategy*> which permits to conceptualise an abstract use case from a set of concrete use cases, <*Conceptualise a Use Case, Elicit a Use Case, Extension strategy*> which permits to identify an extension use case, and <*Conceptualise a Use Case, Stop, Completeness strategy*> which terminates the development process if the obtained use case model is complete.

As shown in the CREWS-L'Ecritoire [6], [14] method map (Fig. 1), there are several flows between two intentions each corresponding to a specific strategy. For example, there are two strategies to *"Write a Scenario"* and two others to *"Conceptualise a Scenario"*. In this sense the map offers *multi-thread flows*. There might also be several strategies from different intentions to reach some intention. For example, there are six strategies *("initial goal identification"*, *"template driven"*, *"linguistic"*, *"goal structure driven"*, *"alternative discovery"* and *"composition discovery")* coming from different intentions to the intention *"Elicit a Goal"*. In this sense the map offers *multi-flow paths* to achieve an intention.

The CREWS-L'Ecritoire method map represents a process to conceptualise a set of scenarios which describe functional system requirements. The complete set of scenarios obtained by this method covers the set of use cases that could be obtained when using the OOSE method. However as illustrated above, the CREWS-L'Ecritoire method map provides more strategies to achieve the process intentions and therefore, offers more flexibility in the scenario conceptualisation process. As depicted in Fig. 1, goal elicitation can be followed by the elicitation of another goal or by scenario writing. Three strategies: *"linguistic"*, *"goal structure driven"* and *"template driven"* are proposed to elicit a new goal. Scenario writing is supported by two strategies, namely the *"template driven strategy"* and the *"free prose strategy"*. The first proposes to write a scenario following a template whereas following the second strategy, the scenario author writes in full prose. Style and content guidelines are proposed in this case to support the scenario writing. Scenario writing can be followed by the scenario conceptualisation. The map proposes two possibilities to conceptualise scenarios : manually (*manual strategy*) or in a computer supported manner (*computer supported strategy*). Finally, scenario conceptualisation can be followed by the elicitation of new goals using two different strategies : *"alternative discovery strategy"* and *"composition discovery strategy"*, or the termination of the development process by verifying the completeness of the obtained model *"completeness strategy"*. The elicitation of new goals using *"alternative discovery strategy"* permits to identify all alternative goals to a given one. The set of corresponding scenarios contains one normal case scenario and all alternative and exceptional scenarios and therefore composes one use case. The elicitation of the new goals using *"composition discovery strategy"* permits to identify the complementary goals to a given one and therefore helps identifying the family of use cases for a given system.

To sum up, a map is a *navigational structure* in the sense that it allows the application engineer to determine a path from *Start* intention to *Stop* intention. The requirements engineer selects dynamically the next intention and /or strategy among the several possible ones offered by the map. The guidelines associated to the map help the engineer in his/her choice. Guidelines are presented in the next section.

Guidelines. Three kinds of guidelines are attached to the map: *"Intention Achievement Guideline"* (IAG), *"Intention Selection Guideline"* (ISG) and *"Strategy Selection Guideline"* (SSG). An *IAG* helps to fulfil the intention selected by the requirements engineer, whereas *ISG* and *SSG* help him/her to progress in the map and to select the right section. For every section $<i_p,i_p,s_{ij}>$ in the map there exists one *IAG*. The *IAG* supports the requirements engineer in the achievement of intention i_j according to the strategy s_{ij}. This *IAG* corresponding to the section *<Elicit a Use Case, Conceptualise a Use Case, Normal case first strategy>* from the OOSE map is shown in Fig. 2. It provides an operational means to fulfil the intention *"Conceptualise a Use Case"*.

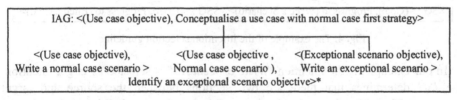

Fig. 2. The example of the intention selection guideline

A number of actions must be performed on the product under development to satisfy this intention. The *IAG* decomposes the initial intention into a set of sub-intentions which themselves may be decomposed till intentions executable through actions on the product are reached. The structure of the guidelines is presented in [14]. It is based on the NATURE contextual approach [17] and its corresponding enactment mechanism [18].

Given two intentions i_p i_j there exists a *SSG* that determines the set of possible strategies s_{ij1} s_{ij2} ..s_{ijn} applicable to i_j and guides the selection of an s_{ijk} thereby leading to the selection of the corresponding *IAG*. For example, given the two intentions *"Elicit a Goal"* and *"Write a Scenario"* from Fig. 1, the *SSG* *<(Goal), Progress to (Write a Scenario)>* is shown in Fig. 3. This *SSG* presents to the requirements engineer two strategies *"template driven"* and *"free prose"*. The engineer picks up the strategy the most appropriate to the situation at hand. Thus, one of two possible sections in the map is selected. Since a unique *IAG* is associated with each section, the *SSG* determines this (Fig. 3).

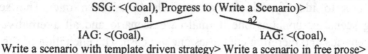

al: Scenario author has to be a scenario writing expert, he/she has to fill a linguistic template.
a2: Scenario author writs scenario in free prose. A set of style and content guidelines are
    provided to support scenario writing.

Fig. 3. The example of the strategy selection guideline

For a given intention i_i, the *ISG* identifies the set of intentions $(i_{j1}, i_{j2}, ..., i_{jn})$ that can be achieved in the next step and helps selecting the corresponding set of either *IAG*s or *SSG*s. The former is valid when there is only one section between i_i and i_j whereas the latter occurs when there are several sections between i_i and i_j. For example, for the intention *"Elicit a Goal"* (Fig. 1) the *ISG* identifies two possible next *intentions "Write a Scenario"* and *"Elicit a Goal"*. The *ISG* then determines whether there is only one section between the source and the selected target intention or whether there are several sections. In the former case, the *IAG* associated with the section is used by the enactment mechanism to achieve the target intention. In the second case, the *SSG* is invoked to determine the strategy to be used in the situation which leads to the determination of an *IAG* and subsequent enactment.

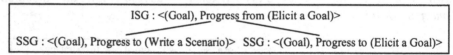

Fig. 4. The example of the intention selection guideline

In our example, if the intention *"Write a Scenario"* is selected as target intention, the *ISG* determines that there are two sections between the source and target intentions. The *SSG* helps to decide which of these strategies shall be used. Thus, the corresponding *IAG* is determined and the intention *"Write a Scenario"* is achieved. If the intention *"Elicit a Goal"* is selected as target intention, the ISG determines that there are tree strategies allowing to fulfil this intention and the corresponding *SSG* is determined (Fig. 4).

2.2   Product Model

The product model is composed of a set of concepts which have properties and can be related through links. We shall use the following notations:
- A *concept* has name c_i and a set of properties $(p_{i1}, p_{i2} ... p_{in})$. Thus it will be denoted $c_i(p_{i1}, p_{i2} ... p_{in})$. For sake of brevity, it is possible to denote a concept only by its name c_i. A set of concepts in the product model is described by C.
- The concepts in the product model are related through the *links*. A *link* has a label l_{ij}, it is an *association*, a *composition* or an *is-a* link. The link is a part of the triplet $<c_i, c_j, l_{ij}>$ where c_i is a source concept, c_j is a target concept and l_{ij} is a link

between these two concepts. A set of the links in the product model is denoted by
L. Therefore, the product model is $PM \subseteq C * C * L$.

The product models of the OOSE method and of the CREWS-L'Ecritoire method
are shown in Fig. 5 and Fig. 6 respectively using ER like notations. *"Actor(Actor
Name, Description)"* is an example of the concepts in the OOSE method. The link
between the *"Actor"* and the *"Use Case Model"* in OOSE product model is denoted
<Use Case Model, Actor, composed_of>.

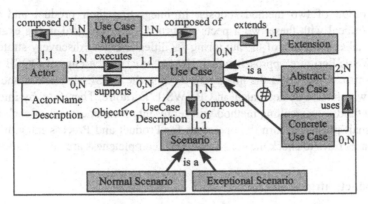

Fig. 5. The OOSE Use Case product model.

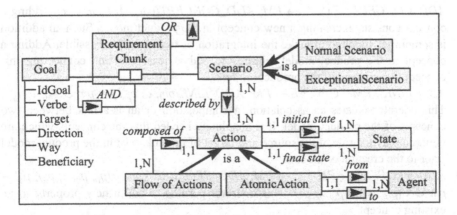

Fig. 6 : The CREWS-L'Ecritoire product model.

The OOSE product model is centred on the concept of a use case. A use case is
composed of a set of scenarios. It can be either concrete of abstract. It can also be
extended by extensions which are themselves considered as use cases. The actor
interacting with the system is related to the use case. Finally, the use case model is a
collection of use cases with their associated actors.

The CREWS-L'Ecritoire product model is centred on the concept of a requirement
chunk, i.e. the coupling of a goal to be achieved and a scenario explaining how the
system will interact with the agents to achieve the goal. The description of a scenario

is based on the notion of action and agent. The definition of a scenario in the CREWS-L'Ecritoire product model is more detailed than the definition provided in the OOSE product model. We will see in the next section how this two product models can be integrated.

3   Method Integration

The integration of two methods consist in integrating their product and process models. We deal with these two aspects in turn. Clearly the goal in the example at hand is to take advantage of the authoring facilities and goal discovery strategies of the CREWS-L'Ecritoire approach which do not exist in the current OOSE method and vice versa, to import in the integrated method the OOSE abstraction and extend strategies which have no equivalent in CREWS-L'Ecritoire. Therefore, by integrating the two methods, the resulting method will represent an enhancement of each isolated one. We shall present in turn the operators for Product and Process integration. For sake of space, rules to check the consistency and completeness are not included.

3.1   Product Integration

Product Integration Operators. Let C be a set of concepts, L a set of links and PM a product model, where $PM \subseteq C * C * L$. The set of operators is as follows:

- $ADD\_CONCEPT : PM * C \rightarrow PM$; $ADD\_CONCEPT(pm, c_i) = pm \cup c_i$. Adding a concept consists in creating a new concept in the product model. Such an addition is sometimes required to make the integration of two concepts possible. Adding a concept in the product model requires to add at least one link connecting this concept to a concept of the product model.

- $ADD\_LINK : PM * C * C * L \rightarrow PM$; $ADD\_LINK(pm, c_p, c_p, l_{ij}) = pm \cup <c_p, c_p, l_{ij}>$. This operator creates an association, a composition or an is-a link between two concepts of the product model. It is absolutely needed that the concepts which are going to play the role of the source and target of the link exist in the product model prior to the creation of the link.

- $ADD\_PROPERTY : PM * C \rightarrow PM$; $ADD\_PROPERTY(pm, c_i(p_{i1}, p_{i2},..., p_{in}), p_{ik}) = pm \cup c_i(p_{i1}, p_{i2},..., p_{ik},..., p_{in})$. This operator permits to add a new property to an existing concept.

- $DELETE\_CONCEPT : PM * C \rightarrow PM$; $DELETE\_CONCEPT(pm, c_i(p_{i1}, p_{i2},..., p_{in}))$ $= pm \setminus c_i(p_{i1}, p_{i2},..., p_{in})$. This operator removes a concept $c_i(p_{i1}, p_{i2},..., p_{in})$ from the schema. Deleting a concept consists in deleting the concept c_i and all its properties $p_{i1}, p_{i2},..., p_{in}$. The concept can be removed from the product model only if all links which were connecting them concept to other concepts have been removed.

- $DELETE\_LINK : PM * C * C * L \rightarrow PM$; $DELETE\_LINK(pm, <c_p, c_p, l_{ij}>) = pm \setminus <c_p, c_p, l_{ij}>$. This operator removes a relationship $<c_p, c_p, l_{ij}>$ from the product model. If one of the related concepts does not have any more links to other concepts, this concept must be removed from the product model or another link must be added to relate this concept to the rest of the schema.

- *DELETE_PROPERTY : PM * C → PM; DELETE_PROPERTY(pm, c_i (p_{i1}, p_{i2},..., p_{ik},..., p_{in}), p_{ik}) = pm ∪ c_i (p_{i1}, p_{i2},..., p_{in}).* This operator removes a property p_{ik} of a concept c_i.

- *OBJECTIFY : PM * C * C* L * C *L * L → PM; OBJECTIFY(pm, <c_i, c_j, l_{ij}>, c_k, l_{ik}, l_{kj}) = pm \ <c_i, c_j, l_{ij}> ∪ <c_i, c_k, l_{ik}> ∪ <c_k, c_j, l_{kj}>.* The *OBJECTIFY* operator transforms a relationship <c_i, c_j, l_{ij}> into an concept c_k and two new links connecting this concept with the two other concepts.

- *RENAME_CONCEPT: PM * C → PM; RENAME_CONCEPT(pm, c_i, c_i') = pm | c_i = c_i'.* This operator changes the name of a concept. This operator is useful in the integration of two overlapping product models.

- *RENAME_LINK: PM * C * C * L * L → PM; RENAME_LINK(pm, <c_i, c_j, l_{ij}>, l_{ij}') = pm ∪ <c_i, c_j, l_{ij} = l_{ij}'>.* This operator changes the name of a link. If two concepts are related by two links having the same name, one of the links must be renamed.

- *RENAME_PROPERTY: PM * C → PM; RENAME_PROPERTY(pm, c_i(p_{i1}, p_{i2},..., p_{ik},..., p_{in}), p_{ik}') = pm ∪ c_i (p_{i1}, p_{i2},..., p_{ik}= p_{ik}',..., p_{in}).* This operator changes the name of a property of a concept c_i from $p_{ik\ i}$ to p_{ik}'. If the integrated concept has two properties with the same name and different semantics, one of these properties must be renamed. If these properties have the same name and the same semantic one of these properties must be removed.

- *SPECIALISE : PM * C * C * C → PM; SPECIALISE(pm, c_i, c_k, c_l) = pm ∪ c_k ∪ c_l ∪ <c_k, c_i, is-a> ∪ <c_l, c_i, is-a>.* This operator specialises the concept c_i into two new concepts c_k and c_l. The two concepts c_k and c_l that play the role of sub-type for c_i are created first and then, the is-a links between c_i and c_k and between c_i and c_l are created. In this definition we make the hypothesis that the concepts c_k and c_l do not exist yet in the product model.

- *GENERALISE : PM * C * C * C → PM; GENERALISE(pm, c_i, c_j, c_k) = pm ∪ c_k ∪ <c_i, c_k, is-a> ∪ <c_j, c_k, is-a>.* This operator permits to generalise two concepts c_i and c_j. into a new concept c_k. A new concept c_k is created first and then, two Is-A links are created. One of them connects c_i with the generalised concept c_k and the second one connects c_j with the generalised concept c_k. Common properties of c_i and c_j are deleted from these concepts and added to the concept c_k.

- *MERGE: PM * C * PM * C *PM * C → PM; MERGE(pm_1,c_1, pm_2,c_2, pm_3,c_3) = pm_3 ∪ c_3.* The *MERGE* operator integrates two concepts c_1 and c_2 from different product models pm_1 and pm_2 respectively into a third one called c_3 in the integrated product model pm_3. The concepts c_1 and c_2 must have the same name prior to their integration. The properties and the links of each merged concept are kept in the new concept.

Example. The application of the product integration operators to the integration of OOSE and CREWS - L'Ecritoire product models is shown in Fig. 7. Some of the concepts of the integrated product model are directly derived from the initial product models, while others are the result of the application of the operators. We comment some examples of concept integration in the following.

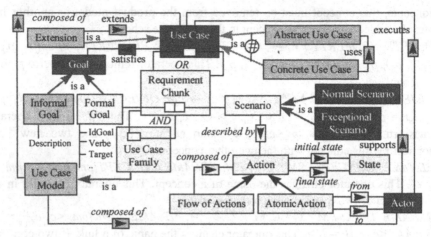

Fig. 7. The integrated product model.

The *"Actor"* concept in the OOSE product model (Fig. 5) and the *"Agent"* concept in the CREWS-L'Ecritoire product model (Fig. 6) have the same semantic but different names. We can rename one of these concepts and then merge them into a new concept in the product model of the integrated method (IM).

- *RENAME_CONCEPT (CREWS-L'Ecritoire, Agent, Actor)*
- *MERGE((CREWS-L'Ecritoire, Actor), (OOSE, Actor), (IM, Actor))*

The concept of *"Use case"* exists only in the OOSE method. However the set of scenarios related through *"OR"* relationships in the CREWS-L'Ecritoire approach is equivalent. The operator *OBJECTIFY* allows us to transform the *"OR"* relationship between two *"RC"* concepts into a new concept called *"Use Case"*.

- *OBJECTIFY(CREWS-L'Ecritoire, <RC, RC, OR>, Use Case)*

Therefore, the *"Use Case"* concept in the integrated method is obtained by merging the *"Use Case"* concept from the OOSE method and the *"Use Case"* concept from CREWS-L'Ecritoire method.

- *MERGE((CREWS-L'Ecritoire, Use Case), (OOSE, Use Case), (IM, Use Case))*

A similar reasoning than the one applied above to the CREWS-L'Ecritoire *"OR"* relationship leads to the reification of the *"AND"* relationship as the concept of *"Use case Family"*. The transformation is as follows :

- *OBJECTIFY(CREWS-L'Ecritoire, <RC, RC, AND>, Use Case Family)*

Finally, the concept of a *"Use Case Model"* is part of the OOSE method but does not exist explicitly in the CREWS-L'Ecritoire product model. However there is a relationship between the use case model and the use case family which leads to add a new Is-A link in the integrated model between the concept *"Use Case Model"* and the concept *"Use Case Family"* .

- *ADD_LINK(IM, < Use case Family, Use Case Model, is-a>)*

The concept of *"Scenario"* belongs to both product models. Merging the two concepts leads to create a new concept whose properties are the union of the properties of both concepts. All the links relating these concepts with the rest of the

product model are kept in the new product model. The same operation is applied on the concepts *"Normal Scenario"* and *"Exceptional Scenario"*.
- *MERGE((CREWS-L'Ecritoire, Scenario), (OOSE, Scenario), (IM, Scenario))*

However, the analysis of the properties and the relationships of the obtained *"Scenario"* concept shows that the role of the *"Description"* property on the one hand and the link *"described-by"* with the concept *"Action"* and the links *"initial-state"*, and *"final-state"* with the concept *"State"* on the other hand, have the same meaning. As a matter of fact, in the CREWS-L'Ecritoire method, a scenario has a set of actions and a final and an initial state. Thus, keeping all these features in the integrated concept of scenario would introduce redundancy. This suggested to us to delete the property *"Description"* from the *"Scenario"* concept.
- *DELETE_PROPERTY (IM, Scenario (Description), Description)*

Finally, the notion of *"Goal"* in the CREWS-L'Ecritoire method represents the objective of the use case in a similar way the property *"Objective"* in the OOSE method does. Therefore, the *"Objective"* must be replaced by the concept *"Informal Goal"* because its structure is different from the *"Goal"* structure in the CREWS-L'Ecritoire method. These two concepts cannot be merged into one single concept. To avoid ambiguities, it was decided to rename the concept *"Goal"* into *"Formal Goal"* and then, to generalise the concepts *"Formal Goal"* and *"Informal Goal"* into the concept *"Goal"*.
- *ADD_CONCEPT (IM, Informal Goal)*
- *ADD_LINK (IM, <Use Case, Informal Goal, Has>)*
- *RENAME_CONCEPT (IM, Goal, Formal Goal)*
- *GENERALISE (IM, Informal Goal, Formal Goal, Goal)*

3.2   Process Integration

Process Integration Operators. The integration of the process models consists in integrating their maps and adapting the corresponding guidelines accordingly. Let I be a set of intentions and S a set of strategies. The map is $Map \subseteq I * I * S$. The set of operators for integrating maps is as follows:
- *RENAME_INTENTION : Map * I * I → Map; RENAME_INTENTION(m, i_p i_j) = m | i_i = i_j*
- *RENAME_SECTION : Map* I * I * S * S → Map; RENAME_ SECTION(m, <i_p i_p s_{ij}>, s_{ij}') = m | <i_p i_p s_{ij} = s_{ij}'>*

These two operators allow to unify the terminology of two overlapping maps by renaming some intentions or strategies of each map. Two intentions from different maps having the same target product must be unified; however, the two intentions must have the same name before their integration. The *RENAME_INTENTION* operator allows to choose the more appropriate intention name. The same kind of operation must be performed on two sections from different maps having the same source and same target intentions. If the corresponding *IAGs* have the same situations (input products) and produce the same target products in the same manner, these sections shall be unified and renamed.

- *ADD_SECTION : Map * I * I * S → Map; ADD_ SECTION(m, i_i, i_j, s_{ij}) = m ∪ <i_i, i_j, s_{ij}>*. This operator allows us to add a new section in the map. More precisely, it permits to introduce a new strategy between two existing intentions. The addition of a new section consists in adding a new *IAG* which defines a new way to achieve the target intention following the new strategy. If there are already several sections having the same input and output intentions, the *SSG* allowing to select one of these sections is modified accordingly. In the contrary, if the added section is the only one between these two intentions, the *ISG* of the source intention must be modified.

- *REMOVE_ SECTION: Map * I * I * S → Map; REMOVE_ SECTION(m, <i_i, i_j, s_{ij}>) = m \ <i_i, i_j, s_{ij}>*. This operator permits to delete one section from the map if its strategy is not relevant in the integrated map or if this section will be replaced by a more appropriate one. The removing of the section from the map consists in removing the corresponding *IAG*. If there are several sections having the same input and output intentions, the corresponding *SSG* must be modified. If the removed strategy was the only strategy available between these two intentions, the corresponding *ISG* must be modified.

- *ADD_INTENTION : Map * I → Map; ADD_INTENTION(m, i) = m ∪ i*. This operator permits to add a new intention in the map. The addition of a new intention in the map implies to add at least one input and one output strategy. Therefore, two sections at least must be added in the map.

- *REMOVE_INTENTION : Map * I → Map; REMOVE_INTENTION(m, i) = m \ i*. This operator allows to remove an intention from the integrated map if this intention is not appropriate or if it is replaced by another one. As the intention might be connected to several other intentions of the map, this operator can be applied only if all sections connecting this intention with other intentions have been removed before. The *ISGs* concerning this intention are modified.

- *MERGE_SECTION : Map * I *I * S * Map * I *I * S * Map * I *I * S → Map; MERGE_SECTION (m_1, <i_{1i}, i_{1j}, s_{1ij}>, m_2, <i_{2i}, i_{2j}, s_{2ij}>, m_3, <i_{3i}, i_{3j}, s_{3ij}>) = m_3 ∪ <i_{3i}, i_{3j}, s_{3ij}>*. This operator allows to merge two sections originating from different maps into one section of the integrated map. The merge of two sections is possible if these sections have the same input and the same output intentions and if the strategies have the same name. The merge of two sections consists in selecting the more complete *IAG* or to merge the two *IAGs* into an integrated *IAG*. In the first case one of two *IAGs* is selected, in the second case a new IAG is defined.

- *MERGE_INTENTION: Map * I * Map * I * Map * I → Map; MERGE_ INTENTION(m_1, i_1, m_2, i_2, m_3, i_3) = m_3 ∪ i_3.* This operator allows to merge two intentions from different maps having the same name. All the sections having this intention as source or target intention are preserved and the corresponding *ISG* is modified. The both *MERGE* operators are especially useful in the integration of two overlapping maps. They allow to integrate two maps without the addition of a new intention or a new section.

- *SPLIT_SECTION : Map * I * I * S * S * S → Map; SPLIT_SECTION(m, <i_i, i_j, s_{ij}>, s_{ij}^1, s_{ij}^2) = m \ <i_i, i_j, s_{ij}> ∪ <i_i, i_j, s_{ij}^1> ∪ <i_i, i_j, s_{ij}^2>*. This operator allows to decompose a section into two parallel sections. It is applicable in the case where the strategy of this section provides two different tactics to satisfy the target intention. The two obtained sections have the same source intention and the same target intention. The *IAG* of this section is decomposed into two *IAGs* and the *SSG* is modified or a new *SSG* is created if it does not existed before.

It shall be noticed that the presented lists of operators for both product and process models integration might be not exhaustive ones.

Example. The application of the operators for integration of the OOSE map and the CREWS-L'Ecritoire map is presented in Fig. 8.

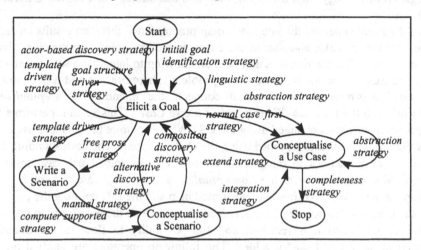

Fig. 8. The integrated map

In the first step of the integration process an effort shall be done to unify the terminology used in the two maps. We need to verify if there are two concepts (intentions or/and strategies) in the different maps having the same name, or similar semantic and thus rename one of the two concepts. We need also to unify the names of concepts having the same semantics but different names. In the case at hand, the intentions *"Elicit Goal"* from the CREWS-L'Ecritoire map and *"Elicit Use Case"* from the OOSE map have different names but are similar in nature. The two intentions refer in fact to the functionality's that the system must provide to its users. The latter emphasises the term *"use case"* whereas the former prefers to put the light of the *"goal"* corresponding to the function. Thus, we rename the intention *"Elicit a Use Case"* of the OOSE map as *"Elicit a Goal"* and then apply the MERGE operator :

- *RENAME_INTENTION(OOSE, Elicit Use case, Elicit Goal)*
- *MERGE_INTENTION((OOSE, Elicit Goal), (CREWS-L'Ecritoire, Elicit Goal), (IM, Elicit Goal))*

The intentions *"Start"* and *"Stop"* should be also merged in the integrated map:

- *MERGE_INTENTION((OOSE, Start), (CREWS-L'Ecitoire, Start), (IM, Start))*
- *MERGE_INTENTION ((OOSE, Stop), (CREWS-L'Ecitoire, Stop), (IM, Stop))*

The intention obtained by applying the operator *MERGE_INTENTION* preserves all sections from the OOSE map and all sections from the CREWS-L'Ecritoire map having the same intention as a source intention. A new *ISG* is constructed for each application of this operator. For example, the merge of *"Elicit a Goal"* intentions implies the construction of a new *ISG* which contains the corresponding *ISG* from the CREWS-L'Ecritoire map and is completed by the progression to the use case conceptualisation, which corresponds to the sections coming from the OOSE map.

The merge of the *"Start"* intentions does not lead to a new *ISG*, because in the two maps, the sections from *"Start"* have the same target intention, namely *"Elicit a Goal"*. In this case a new *SSG* is constructed guiding the selection of one of the two strategies (one strategy from the OOSE map and one strategy of CREWS-L'Ecritoire map).

In the current situation, the integrated map proposes two different results : a set of conceptualised scenarios and a set of use cases. In the integrated map we must obtain only one result. The addition of a new section allowing to integrate a set of scenarios into a use case can be the solution of our problem. Therefore, we add a new section with an *"integration strategy"* which connects the intention *"Conceptualise a Scenario"* with the intention *"Conceptualise a Use Case"*. This section performs the integration of scenarios obtained using the CREWS-L'Ecritoire process into use cases equivalent to the use cases obtained using the OOSE process. The corresponding *IAG* providing the guidelines to integrate a set of scenarios into a use case must be defined. Moreover, the section *<Conceptualise a Scenario, Stop, Completeness strategy>* must be removed from the integrated map and the *ISG* defining the progress from the intention *"Conceptualise a Scenario"* is modified : the possibility to progress to the *"Stop"* intention is removed and the possibility to flow to the intention *"Conceptualise a Use Case"* is added. The following operators are applied on the integrated map :

- *ADD_SECTION (IM, <Conceptualise a Scenario, Conceptualise a Use Case, Integration strategy>)*
- *REMOVE_ SECTION (IM, <Conceptualise a Scenario, Conceptualise a Use Case, Completeness strategy>)*

As the objective of the integration of two maps is to enhance the OOSE process, the section *<Elicit a Goal, Conceptualise a Use Case, Normal case first strategy>* can be removed from the resulting map. This section is replaced by the CREWS-L'Ecritoire *<goal elicitation, scenario conceptualisation>* process which provides richer guidelines than the IAG of the section *<Elicit a Goal, Conceptualise a Use Case, Normal case first strategy>*.

- *REMOVE_ SECTION(IM, <Elicit a Goal, Conceptualise a Use Case, Normal case first strategy>)*

The application of this operator implies to delete the corresponding SSG because there is now only one section coming from the intention *"Elicit Goal"* to the intention *"Conceptualise a Use Case"*.

Discussion on the Map Integration. The representation of the process model by a map and a set of guidelines allows us to provide a strategic view of processes. This view tells what can be achieved (the intention) and which strategy can be employed to achieve it. We separate the strategic aspect from the tactical aspect by representing the former in the method map and embodying the latter in the guidelines. By associating the guidelines with the map, a smooth integration of the strategic and the tactical aspects is achieved.

Traditional stepwise process models have difficulty to handle the dynamically changing situation of a process. The map contributes to solve this problem by constructing the process model dynamically. Therefore, it is easier to represent a process allowing several different ways to develop the product by a map and a set of guidelines than by a set of steps. In the former approach, each step can be performed in several different manners. In the map it is represented by an intention to achieve and a set of strategies. Each strategy describes a different manner to achieve the intention.

Integrating maps is easier than integrating the stepwise process models, especially in the case where the process models overlap. The enhancement of a stepwise process model by another one requires to construct a new process model. On the contrary, the enhancement of a map by an another map does not require to modify all guidelines. Only the guidelines involved in the overlapping parts are modified.

4   Conclusion and Future Work

In this paper we have proposed and illustrated an approach for integrating a scenario-based technique into an existing industrial method. The approach is built upon :
- a set of operators to integrate the product aspects of the two methods on one hand, and to integrate their process aspects in the other hand and,
- a set of rules to check whether if the integrated method is consistent or not.

The motivation for developing such an approach was twofold : first, scenarios have proven useful to requirements engineering but cannot be used in isolation and, secondly, existing methods which cover the entire system life cycle might be enhanced by integrating scenario-based techniques in the requirements engineering step. The paper has shown how to enhance the use case model construction of the OOSE method by integrating the goal discovery and scenario authoring features of the CREWS-L'Ecritoire approach. Vice-versa the rest of the analysis and design process of the OOSE method remains usable.

The approach needs to be validated and improved in other cases. Our goal is to do so in the first place, by integrating the four CREWS scenario-based techniques one with the other and with the OOSE method. We are currently working on the development of a computerised support for facilitating such an integration and to connect this facility with the method base query facilities presented in [19].

Acknowledgements : the authors would like to thank the CREWS project members for their contributions to the development of the ideas presented in the paper.

References

1. I. Jacobson, M. Christerson, P. Jonsson and G. Oevergaard, *Object Oriented Software Engineering: a Use Case Driven Approach*. Addison-Wesley, 1992.

2. Rational Software Corporation, *"Unified Modelling Language version 1.1"*. Available at http://www.rational.com/uml/documentation.html, 1998.
3. J. Rumbaugh, M. Blaha, W. Premerlani, F. Eddy, and W. Lorensen, *Object-Oriented Modeling and Design*. Prentice Hall, 1991.
4. P. Haumer, K. Pohl, K. Weidenhaupt, *Requirements Elicitation and Validation with real world scenes*. IEEE Transactions on Software Engineering, Vol. 24, N°. 12, Special Issue on Scenario Management, December. 1998.
5. C. Rolland, C. Ben Achour, *Guiding the construction of textual use case specifications*. Data & Knowledge Engineering Journal Vol. 25 N° 1, pp. 125-160, (ed. P. Chen, R.P. van de Riet) North Holland, Elsevier Science Publishers. March 1997.
6. C. Rolland, C. Souveyet, C. Ben Achour, *Guiding Goal Modelling Using Scenarios*. IEEE Transactions on Software Engineering, special issue on Scenario Management, 1998.
7. A. G. Sutcliffe, *Scenario-based Requirements Analysis*. Requirements Engineering Journal, Vol (3) N° 1, (ed. P. Loucopoulos, C. Potts), Springer Verlag. 1998.
8. E. Dubois, P. Heymans, *Scenario-Based Techniques for supporting the Elaboration and the Validation of Formal Requirements*, Submitted to RE Journal, 1998.
9. M. Saeki, K. Wen-yin, Specifying Software Specification and Design Methods. Proceedings of Conference on Advanced Information Systems Engineering, CAISE'94, Lecture Notes in Computer Science 811, Springer Verlag, pp. 353-366, Berlin, 1994.
10. C. Rolland, N. Prakash, *A proposal for Context-Specific Method Engineering*, IFIP TC8 Working Conference on Method Engineering, Atlanta, Gerorgie, USA, 1996.
11. S. Brinkkemper, M. Saeki, F. Harmsen, *Assembly Techniques for Method Engineering*. Proceedings of the 10th Conference on Advanced Information Systems Engineering, CAiSE'98. Pisa Italy, 8-12 June, 1998.
12. X. Song, *A Framework for Understanding the Integration of Design Methodologies*. In: ACM SIGSOFT Software Engineering Notes, Vol. 20, N°1, pp. 46-54, 1995.
13. M. Bouzeghoub, I. Comyn, *View Integration by Semantic Unification and Transformation of Data Structures*, Proceedings of the Conference on Requirements Engineering, RE'90, Lausanne, 1990.
14. C. Rolland, N. Prakash, A. Benjamen, *A multi-model view of process modelling*. To appear in the RE journal, 1999.
15. N. Prat, *Goal formalisation and classification for requirements engineering*. Proceedings of the Third International Workshop on Requirements Engineering: Foundations of Software Quality REFSQ'97, Barcelona, pp. 145-156, June 1997.
16. I. Jacobson, *The use case construct in object-oriented software Engineering*. In 'Scenario-based design: envisioning work and technology in system development', John M. Carroll (ed.), John Wiley and Sons, 309-336, 1995.
17. G. Grosz, C. Rolland, S. Schwer, C. Souveyet, V. Plihon, S. Si-Said, C. Ben Achour, C. Gnaho, *Modelling and Engineering the Requirements Engineering Process : an overview of the NATURE approach*. Requirements Engineering Journal 2, pp. 115-131, 1997.
18. S. Si-Said, C. Rolland, G. Grosz, MENTOR :*A Computer Aided Requirements Engineering Environment*. Proceedings of CAiSE'96, Crete, GREECE, May 1996.
19. C. Rolland, V. Plihon, J. Ralyté, *Specifying the reuse context of scenario method chunks*. Proceedings of the 10th Conference on Advanced Information Systems Engineering, CAiSE'98. Pisa Italy, 8-12 June, 1998.

Support for the Process Engineer:
The Spearmint Approach to Software Process Definition and Process Guidance

Ulrike Becker-Kornstaedt[+], Dirk Hamann[+], Ralf Kempkens[+],
Peter Rösch[+], Martin Verlage[+], Richard Webby[*], Jörg Zettel[+]

[+]Fraunhofer Institute for Experimental Software Engineering (IESE),
Sauerwiesen 6, D-67661 Kaiserslautern, Germany
{becker,hamann,kempkens,roesch,verlage,zettel}@iese.fhg.de

[*]Center for Advanced Empirical Software Research (CAESAR), School of Information Systems
The University of New South Wales, Sydney 2052, Australia
r.webby@unsw.edu.au

Abstract The software development process and its related activities are described, implemented, analyzed, and changed by so-called Process Engineers. Process Engineers provide descriptions of software development processes to Process Performers. Because the processes usually are complex, support is needed for both Process Engineers and Process Performers. This paper reports the development and application of the process modeling environment Spearmint[1]. The architecture of Spearmint allows for a flexible definition and addition of views which are used for retrieving filtered and tailored presentations of the process models. One distinct view, namely the Electronic Process Guide used for dissemination of process information and guidance of Process Performers, is discussed in more detail. The Spearmint environment has been validated in industrial process engineering cases.

Keywords: Process Engineering, Process Guidance

1 Introduction

Besides product development, software engineering includes engineering of the software development process. Process improvement and process programming, deal with explicit process representations (i.e., *process models*) in order to analyze process behavior, guide Process Performers, enforce rules, or automate process steps. The process model is the basis for specifying how the process is carried out. It is a vehicle for enabling better understanding and communication of software processes. Various research groups and workshops are addressing process modeling issues under terms

---

1. Spearmint is a registered trademark of Fraunhofer IESE, Kaiserslautern, Germany.

M. Jarke, A.Oberweis (Eds.): CAiSE'99, LNCS 1626, pp. 119–133, 1999.
© Springer-Verlag Berlin Heidelberg 1999

like process-centered software engineering environments and software process management environments.

A *Process Engineer* is responsible for eliciting process knowledge from experts, capturing the processes and process steps in a process model, analyzing both the process models and the real process, disseminating process changes, and for implementing systems to provide automated support to Process Performers. From our experience gained in industrial process modeling case studies, we have found that a typical software process will require modeling up to a hundred entities: process steps, documents, and roles [6]. This cannot be achieved without a well-defined set of guidelines, concepts, and tool support for the Process Engineer.

Software development processes are performed by a large number of people. These processes are very unlikely to be as 'straightforward' as existing process models, for example, the waterfall lifecycle model [6]. Analysis of real software development processes has uncovered, for example, that control flow in software development projects is complicated [16]; the number of process steps high and they are strongly interrelated by means of product flow and control flow [17]. Also, personal interpretation of official process documents may lead to process variants and inconsistent performances by different people [4]. Therefore, support for Process Performers is crucial for the coordination of software development processes.

Most work on support for Process Performers has focused on automated support of the software process ('*enactment*'). Many approaches for the support of Process Performers are influenced by workflow systems. However, experience from industrial projects indicates that automation is only achievable for fine grained, tool-related activities [1,10]. In the context of real-world industrial projects, the understanding of processes, communication and their analysis have much more relevance.

We investigated the capabilities of a number of existing approaches, but found that they all had significant limitations for the purpose of providing practical support for the Process Engineer. This was one major reason why we decided to develop a new approach which we called Spearmint (Software Process Elicitation, Analysis, Review, and Measurement in an INTegrated Modeling Environment) [19]. Spearmint provides an integrated modeling environment using a visual domain-specific process modeling language which is used to describe and define real-world software processes. Among others it supports the generation of a browseable process description (Electronic Process Guide) which is a support tool for Process Performers when performing their tasks.

This paper is structured as follows: Section 2 clarifies tasks and requirements for process engineering. In Section 3 we introduce Spearmint. Section 4 gives an overview of related work. Section 5 discusses the results gained in the application of Spearmint. Section 6 concludes with a summary and an outlook to future work.

2   Support for Process Engineering

The role of a Process Engineer is ideally performed by someone outside of the development team. This may be a member of a software engineering process group

(SEPG) [11], or the Project Manager may be given a set of additional tasks involved by this role, or it may simply refer to a portion of the quality management in an organization. In any case, the Process Engineer deals with more or less formal descriptions of the process, transforms and manipulates them, analyzes them, and packages them for use by other people in his organization. The most relevant tasks the Process Engineer is responsible for are the following (compare also to [15] and [11, page 290]):

- elicitation of process information from both humans and existing process documentation,
- definition of the process as a process model using more or less formal approaches,
- analysis of the process model to check for consistency and dynamic properties,
- design of process models carrying the results of a process change,
- implementation of the process either as a process program or by definition of organizational mechanisms (e.g., measurement forms),
- provision of process models to Process Performers for guidance or enforcement.

To perform these tasks, different approaches to define a process are needed. For example, descriptive process models are used to capture the actual software development process in an organization, whereas prescriptive process models, like standards and guidebooks, require a different approach to the modeling of processes. Using a fine grain process programming language to implement process fragments that are executed or interpreted by a process engine requires other capabilities from a Process Engineer than when re-designing an existing process to reflect changes. Process engineering is often aggravated by the complexity of real-world software processes – and consequently the complexity of their process models.

3 The Spearmint Environment

Spearmint is an integrated environment for modeling, analyzing, and measuring processes (http://www.iese.fhg.de/spearmint). It supports Process Engineers during elicitation, editing, review, and analysis of process models by providing navigation and abstraction support. Internet-browseable views, which constitute the Electronic Process Guide (EPG), for guidance of Process Performers can be generated easily from Spearmint process models. The conceptual schema of Spearmint was influenced by existing approaches (e.g., [2]) as well as experience gained in industrial process modeling case studies.

Experiences from industrial process modeling cases formed the driving forces behind identifying the major requirements for our tools: a comprehensive conceptual schema, a graphical and easily understandable user interface, consistent management of different views of process models, a graphical notation, and the possibility to provide a support for Process Performers during execution.

Section 3.1 introduces a number of requirements for tools aiming at support for process engineers. Section 3.2 describes the main conceptual and user interface aspects of the Spearmint modeling environment. Section 3.3 explains the EPG in more depth. Section 3.4 discusses the integration of the modeling environment and the EPG.

3.1 Views on Process Models

A means to manage the inherent complexity of models of real-world software processes is to divide a process model into *views* [17]. In general, views on a process model can be seen as overlapping subsets of the overall information represented in a process model. Views might be used to concentrate on certain aspects of a process, like control flow, or work breakdown structure (i.e., process hierarchy). Role-specific views, for example, may show only a subset of the process model, namely exactly the information relevant to a particular role. For the Process Engineer, the usage of role-specific views allows to have less complex process models to deal with. For the Process Performer, role-specific views aid in understanding, since they focus only on those parts relevant to the role. Conceptually, we consider a view on a process to be comprised of five characteristics:

- *Objects*: the data to be used for presentation, e.g., activities, artifacts, or roles. A schema is used to represent the objects and their relationships [18].

- *Aspect*: the portion or slice of the process model selected for representation, e.g, product flow, or decomposition. The aspect can be expressed as a subset of the process model schema which is used to represent the objects.

- *Style:* the way in which the data is represented to the user. For the same data set, different representation styles are possible, e.g., product flow between activities and artifacts could for instance be represented using a diagrammatic representation or a table.

- *Synthesizer*: set of functions over the object types that transform the objects for purposes of the required abstraction level. An example for a synthesizer is summarizing effort data from sub-activities into the data of a compound high-level activity.

- *Mechanism*: set of procedures to modify the representation that can be invoked by the user, e.g., simple cut/copy/paste services.

Aspect, style, synthesizer, and mechanism describe a *View Type*. A view type is a general description of what type of objects should be presented to the user, and how they should be presented. View types are instantiated by assigning objects to them.

Process Engineers may use process modeling environments to create and maintain process models. In addition to general requirements (e.g., domain specific schema) which are listed in [9] we consider the following requirements as important in order to cope with process models in industrial environments. These requirements explicitly take into account the use of views.

R1: The process modeling environment must provide and manage different views of a process model. Views filter information (e.g., by not showing all objects) or make it more dense (e.g., show more abstract artifact types than actually accessed by the activity displayed). Hence they reduce complexity.

R2: The process modeling environment must offer predefined view types as well as services to define view types. There is no best set of views available. In our experience it is likely that a new view type is required (e.g., display the relationship between roles and artifacts) when dealing with a new problem.

R3: The process modeling environment must provide concurrent updating mechanisms of objects to keep consistency across views.

R4: The process modeling environment must provide visual cues to track relationships among views, for example, marking process elements in all other views when selected in one view only.

R5: The process modeling environment must provide mechanisms to generate process descriptions, i.e., to export views which are used for guidance of Process Performers.

3.2   Conceptual Schema and Modeling Environment

Spearmint is a new development concentrates on mechanisms to provide different views of a process model to Process Engineers and Process Performers. Spearmint is based on a domain-specific and canonical conceptual schema of process model elements [18]. The most important elements of this schema, the user interface to access process models, and the architecture of Spearmint will be described in this section.

The most important information units needed to describe a real-world software process are mapped onto the following elements of the conceptual schema:

- Artifacts are abstractions of any documents or products that are accessed in a project, as a desired or intermittent result of the project or as an input to an activity in some other form.

- Activities are process steps which may cover software development and maintenance activities as well as project management or quality assurance. Activities consume and/or produce artifacts (product flow).

- Roles are abstractions for a set of responsibilities or skills necessary to perform an activity.

- Tools represent computer programs, or other means that are used to support or automate an activity.

In addition to the concepts mentioned here, the comprehensive conceptual schema contains entities, such as organization, or measurement concepts. (They are discussed in detail in [18]).

The schema is used to define the structure of the *comprehensive process model* which is the union of the objects of all views [17]. The views are used for creating, modifying, and displaying the comprehensive process model or subsets of it. For example, the Process Engineer creates a new, empty part of the comprehensive process model by instantiating an artifact decomposition view type in order to first enter the hierarchy of all artifacts. Whenever he modifies the view displayed (i.e., adding, or renaming an artifact, or specifying an aggregation relationship between artifacts), the comprehensive process model is updated.

The number of concurrently existing views is limited only by available system resources. All views are kept consistent automatically by the system. The view types defined so far in Spearmint are:

124   Ulrike Becker-Kornstaedt et al.

- *product flow view,*
- *properties view,*
- *decomposition view,* and
- *textual view.*

The product flow view is a graph-like interface to the process model, which uses simple icons for entities, connected by lines for relationships. Figure 1 shows an example product flow view. It contains an activity *Implement*, the artifacts used in that activity, a role and a tool assigned to that activity.[1]

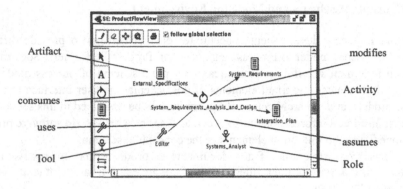

Figure 1. Spearmint: Product flow view

Details of a process model element can be entered using a properties view. This is a dialog, in which general properties like name and description of the element can be edited (see Figure 2). It also supports the flexible definition of *attributes*. Attributes can be dynamically added to and removed from an element. If used in the context of measurement, *values* can be associated with the attributes. In order to better be able to consider the needs for EPGs the Spearmint modeling environment has an extra set of EPG attributes which can be attached to activities, artifacts, or roles. These attributes allow for instance to describe the detailed steps of activities, or to attach links to template documents to artifacts.

Modularity, as a concept for structuring a process model, is supported by the decomposition view (Figure 3). This view allows the user to define and browse the hierarchical decomposition of artifacts, activities, and roles in a representation style familiar to him. The textual view is strongly related to the Electronic Process Guide and will be discussed in Section 3.4.

---

1. This view can be described as follows: Objects = {System_Requirements_Analysis_and_-Design, External_Specifications, System_Requirements, Integration_Plan, Systems_Analyst, Editor}; Aspect = {Activity, Artifact, Role, Tool, Product Flow, Role Assignment, Tool Usage}; Style = {Artifact = 🗐, Role = ⚲, Activity = ⭘ , Tool = 🖋, Product Flow = ⇆ }; Synthesizer = <none>; Mechanisms = {Create Activity, Create Artifact, Create Tool, Create Role, Link, Delete, Cut, Copy, Paste, Print}

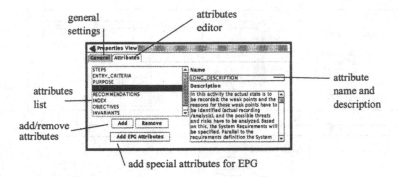

Figure 2. Spearmint: Properties View

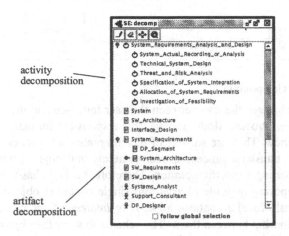

Figure 3. Spearmint: Decomposition View

The implementation of Spearmint uses Java as the technological basis. The integrated software architecture of Spearmint consists mainly of three layers: the Process Model Layer, the Partial Model Layer, and the User Interface Layer. Figure 4 explains the interplay among these in detail.

The bottom layer (Process Model Layer) contains the comprehensive process model, i.e., all process model elements, their attributes, and relationships. This layer is independent from the notation chosen in a specific diagram and forms the canonical basis for all views. The Process Model Layer stores process models using the schema introduced above. In the example used here, the Process Model Layer would comprise the activity *Implement*, the role *Author*, the tool *Editor*, the artifacts used in the product flow and all the relationships among these, and the attribute *Effort* (depicted in Figure 2). We are currently using ObjectDesign/PSE, a simple public-domain file-based object-oriented database, to implement data access services to that layer. This can easily be upgraded to the full functionality of the ObjectStore database system.

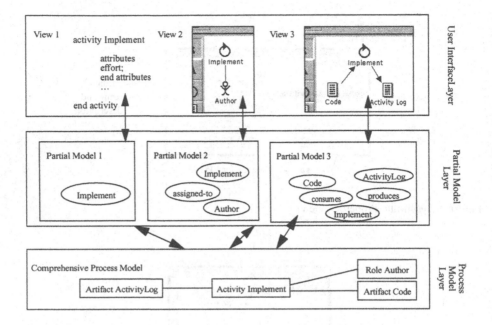

Figure 4. View Management in Spearmint

The Partial Model Layer bridges the gap between the user interface and the comprehensive process model (i.e., Process Model Layer). It is responsible for managing the objects and aspects of a view. They are subsets of the comprehensive process model. The Partial Model Layer translates process model elements into objects, which are more convenient for supporting a specific notation. Therefore this layer has to perform transformations like composing multiple objects into single container objects. In the figure, for example, Partial Model 2 contains an activity *Implement*, the role *Author*, and the *assigned-to* relationship between them. The schema to store the objects is the same as for the comprehensive process model.

The User Interface Layer performs the visualization of process models. The User Interface Layer creates views by assigning view types to Partial Models, manages the views, and provides the user interface. According to the information in the view type the objects of the Partial Model Layer are mapped onto symbols of the presentation which are displayed to the Process Engineer. In addition to the objects and aspects provided by the Partial Model Layer, the User Interface Layer defines the style in which the information is to be presented and provides transformation functions over the data types (synthesizer) as well as modification procedures (mechanism). Each view in the User Interface Layer is related to one Partial Model. In our example, View 2 displays the objects contained in Partial Model 2, but in a user-defined iconic notation, and provides editing services to modify the representation.

Spearmint maintains the consistency between views, Partial Models and the comprehensive process model automatically. This is the basis for a rich set of powerful interactive features at the user-interface level, which are described in more detail in [19]. This architecture allows easy addition of new view types. We found this kind of flexibility very important because in process engineering tasks tailored representations were required (e.g., when Process Performers were accustomed to a particular representation style).

What view types are needed for what process engineering situations is subject to further investigation. Experience with the tool in industrial improvement programs will therefore be incorporated into future increments of the prototype environment.

3.3   Electronic Process Guide

An important process engineering activity is the dissemination of process knowledge. An Electronic Process Guide (EPG) aims to support Process Performers [13]. Typical problems occurring during process performance are related to one of the following:

- staff turnover is high, new team members must become familiar with the process,
- team members must perform activities which they may be unfamiliar with, which may be infrequently performed, or involve many interrupts and context switches,
- communication is impeded due to large development teams or different geographical locations.

In order to overcome these problems and to provide concrete guidance, process-relevant information has to be made accessible to Process Performers in a way that is easy to use for them. In contrast to approaches which use an explicit enactment mechanism and a process engine, the EPG gives *guidance* to the user, that is, it provides the Process Performer with information about the actual state, history, context, and future steps of the process to make informed decisions. The user himself decides what information to access and at what level of detail. This complies with [1] and [10] which advocate that strict enforcement of a prescribed process imposed by many of the enactment mechanisms is not adequate for all tasks in software development.

The technical implementation of the EPG is based on Web-technology. On the one hand this provides a tool and appearance which is already familiar to Process Performers and does not involve a huge investment in new tools. On the other hand this allows to benefit from already existing browser features, like setting bookmarks, or using hyperlinks. In addition to being a web-based process guidebook the EPG provides services like managing personal annotations or links to example and template files. A computer-based guidebook allows fast updating and therefore ensures that Process Performers use a consistent version of the process handbook and the process information needed. Typical usage scenarios for an EPG are:

- A Process Performer familiar with the process needs help in unexpected situations or complex or infrequently performed activities. The EPG may provide additional information, such as manual pages, links to example or template files.

- A novice who joined the team recently needs to become familiar with the most frequent activities and artifacts. The EPG would enable him to navigate and explore the process by following the links and relationships.

- Process performers working at different sites are expected to use a consistent definition of the process. Updated process descriptions can be easily provided even to different geographical sites.

Activities, artifacts, and roles are described on *main pages*. Figure 5 depicts such a main page for the activity *Implement* generated from the example shown in the previous section. The graphical decomposition frame (top left) shows the position of the activity within the decomposition tree. This interactive graphic facilitates navigation. The description (on the right) provides the main information, such as artifacts used. In the description glossary information is integrated as tool-tip information, i.e., when he user rests the mouse pointer on the Φ-icons. Clicking on the on the Φ-icon navigates the user to a whole page providing glossary information. The overview section (bottom left) provides access to the description section via links. In order to provide supplementary information within the same window, the glossary (on the bottom) contains brief descriptions of items referred to in the description section, for instance the artifacts used. Main pages for artifacts and roles have the same structure.

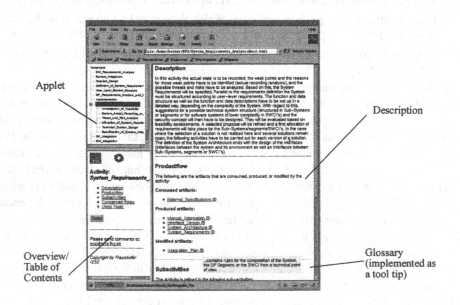

Figure 5. Screenshot of an EPG Activity page

3.4 Technical Integration of Spearmint and Electronic Process Guide

Web-technology used for the EPG allows for updates of the process model in a consistent and cost-effective way, even for multi-site projects and organizations.

We have developed an integrated architecture which addresses the needs of the modeling environment of Spearmint as well as those for the EPG. Figure 6 presents this architecture, showing how the potentially distributed tasks of process definition and process guidance access a common database. On the right side of the figure, a web server provides the EPG as HTML files which are generated from the Spearmint database. Whether the generation is done on a regular basis or dynamically on demand is arbitrary and depends on the application context of the EPG. On the left side, Spearmint provides a special textual view which is a light-weight combination of an EPG generator and a web server. This view provides both an immediate update after process changes as well as navigation features between web browsers showing the EPG and views in the Spearmint environment. Thus the textual view is an excellent aid for the Process Engineer when discussing a process model with one or more Process Performers, or when guiding them through a process. In combination with a telephone, this can even be done over long distances and/or multiple sites.

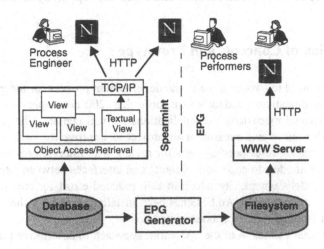

Figure 6. Spearmint and EPG System Architecture

4 Related Approaches

The Process Engineer may be supported by a number of different tools ranging from the very simple to the sophisticated:

- Graphic editors provide simple definition and placement of nodes and edges to create diagrams depicting properties of process models.
- CASE tools and meta-CASE tools (frameworks or generators to create CASE tools) may be used because they provide better drawing capabilities. Sometimes CASE tools have been extended to address process needs, mainly for business process re-engineering, can be also used for software process modeling.
- Simulators, like those based on the idea of System Dynamics [14], may be used to analyze dynamic aspects of processes.
- Specific product development tools, like STATEMATE [12], may be used to support one or a small set of tasks of the Process Engineer, like process analysis by simulating processes.
- Process-sensitive software engineering environments (PSEEs), like Process WEAVER [3], or Workflow Management systems provide some services to create

and manipulate process models. However, often the user interface does not support the Process Engineer adequately and comprehensively, and the focus is not on guidance but on automation.

- Process tools are designed for special tasks of the Process Engineer. For example, the tool Balboa [8] is designed to identify control flow patterns out of event data taken from the actual process performance.

Achievements have also been made in developing a common understanding about what elements should be covered by any of these languages (e.g., the schema by Armitage and Kellner [2]). What has not been tackled extensively in the past is the management of complex process models and especially support by multiple views.

5 Validation of Concepts and Prototype

Spearmint was used to capture a multi-site development process for the evolution of a large telecommunications product where more than 200 developers work on a base product and special extensions like applications for call centers. The process model was used within an overall measurement project to improve the process. The views were used to prepare role-specific views for review with interviewees as well as site-specific process models to cope with variants and interfaces between sites. The views reduced the model's complexity which in turn reduced effort for creating the model compared to former projects. An EPG has been installed recently at the organization's intranet. First feedback is very encouraging.

A major industrial validation of the Spearmint approach to descriptive process modeling was performed recently within the context of a software process improvement effort with an organization developing space software. The company wanted to develop a systematic measurement plan in order to improve its development processes. Based on role-specific interviews a process model was created. It contained some fifty activities, artifacts, and people responsible for the activities, plus the relationships among them. The view concept proved to be very helpful in reducing the complexity of the process model. The resultant descriptive model allowed us to recommend improvements to the current process, which are currently being implemented.

Spearmint and its predecessor MVP-E [5] have been used to formalize prescriptive processes as described in a variety of standards and guidebook, like the IEEE Standard 1074, ISO 12207. Our process modeling environment had been used to review a draft version of a national German standard. Based on the outcome of the consistency checks, major improvements were suggested which have been incorporated into the final version of the standard.

Spearmint was used to analyze the completeness of a real-time systems development process as described in a book in order to determine whether it is possible to create process models out of a technology description [5]. The case was based on [7] which documents the Structured Design Technique (SDL). The purpose was to transform the contents of the book into a formal process to check for consistency and completeness. Using the analysis functions, it was found that major information is lacking (e.g., documents are produced but never used).

The full text of the 1997 version of a national German standard, called 'Das Vorge-hensmodell' (V-Modell), was prepared as an EPG and is available on-line (http://www.iese.fhg.de/VModell). In addition to the public web site, several copies of this instance of the V-Modell EPG are installed at German companies. Positive feedback from the users encourages us to further enhance and improve this technology.

6 Summary and Outlook

The Process Engineer needs support in managing complex process models. In this paper we presented the Spearmint approach which especially focuses on helping in creation of process models and their dissemination. Existing tools seldom address these two responsibilities of the Process Engineer.

The services provided by Spearmint stem from requirements which came up during industrial process modeling cases where tool support was missing. Commercially available tools have been found inadequate at including domain knowledge about soft-ware development processes. Especially they often lack sophisticated services to ana-lyze process models and to check for consistency. Research prototypes in contrast are too specific in the tasks of the Process Engineer they support. Spearmint tries to bridge the gap between commercial process tools and research prototypes. In summary, the unique features of Spearmint are:

- A comprehensive domain-specific schema based on a combination of sophisticated approaches and experience gained in industrial process engineering tasks (e.g. [2, 9]). It also adds its own innovations - for example our schema allows the ability to define parallel abstraction hierarchies for multiple views [17].
- An architecture allowing rapid definition of new view types. Spearmint is not lim-ited to predefined view types, but is easily extendible when the need for a new type of view becomes apparent.
- Concurrent updating of model information. A mechanism for change propagation sends model repository changes to all interested views.
- Visual cues aiding orientation in large process models.
- The possibility to generate EPGs which can be used by Process Performers to nav-igate through complex process information.

This paper has described how Spearmint supports the Process Engineer when creating a process model and disseminating process knowledge using Intranet technology. The future development topics to be addressed in Spearmint include further exploitation of Web-technologies and the improvement of the conceptual schema aimed at supporting process performance in a more explicit way.

Web-technology helps support the communication of process knowledge among the (potentially geographically dispersed) people performing and studying software pro-cesses. Web-based documents are easy to distribute among Process Performers and are accepted because they integrate well at the computer's desktop level. The process model is always up-to-date. Therefore it is more likely to be used than a heap of dust-covered documents on the shelf.

So far, interviews with Process Performers in industrial settings strongly support our preference to concentrate first on a visual, communicative and understandable representation of process models. Our second aim, which is to support process performance, is achieved by providing detailed descriptions of process elements which can be accessed using the EPG. In addition, we will implement services around the EPG like mechanisms for attaching annotations to elements of a process model or search [13] which will be used as a target for the HTML pages generated by Spearmint.

Further research is needed to fully understand the role of the Process Engineer and the potential for process technology such as Spearmint to support this role. Our future research will concentrate on additional view types and other user interface features for dealing with process complexity.

Acknowledgments

We would like to thank Marc Kellner, and Bill Riddle for very fruitful discussions about the EPG. We also thank Andrew Beitz, Lionel Briand, and Louise Scott for their comments, which led to significant improvements to the structure of the paper. We very much appreciate the work by all the students within the development of Spearmint.

References

[1] Jim Arlow, Sergio Bandinelli, Wolfgang Emmerich, and Luigi Lavazza. A fine-grained Process Modelling Experiment at British Airways. *Software Process–Improvement and Practice*, 3(3):105–131, November 1997.

[2] James W. Armitage and Marc I. Kellner. A conceptual schema for process definitions and models. In Dewayne E. Perry, editor, *Proceedings of the Third International Conference on the Software Process*, pages 153–165. IEEE Computer Society Press, October 1994.

[3] Denis Avrilionis, Pierre-Yves Cunin, and Christer Fernström. OPSIS: A view mechanism for software processes which supports their evolution and reuse. In *Proceedings of the Eighteenth International Conference on Software Engineering*, pages 38–47. IEEE Computer Society Press, March 1996.

[4] Sergio Bandinelli, Alfonso Fuggetta, Luigi Lavazza, Maurizio Loi, and Gian Pietro Picco. Modeling and improving an industrial software process. *IEEE Transactions on Software Engineering*, 21(5):440–454, May 1995.

[5] Ulrike Becker, Dirk Hamann, Jürgen Münch, and Martin Verlage. MVP-E: A Process Modeling Environment. *IEEE TCSE Software Process Newsletter*, (10):10–15, Fall 1997.

[6] Ulrike Becker, Dirk Hamann, and Martin Verlage. Descriptive Modeling of Software Processes. In *Proceedings of the Third Conference on Software Process Improvement (SPI '97)*, Barçelona, Spain, December 1997.

[7] R. Bræk and O. Haugen. *Engineering Real-time Systems: An object-oriented Methodology using SDL*. Prentice Hall, New York, London, 1993.

[8] J.E. Cook and A.L. Wolf. Balboa: A framework for event-based process data analysis. In *Proceedings of the Fifth International Conference on the Software Process*, pages 99–110, Chicago, IL, USA, June 1998. ISPA Press.

[9] European Computer Manufacturers Association. Reference model for frameworks of software engineering environments. Technical Report TR–55, ECMA, 114 Rue du Rhone, 1204 Geneva, Switzerland, June 1993.

[10] Volker Gruhn and Juri Urbainczk. Software process modeling and enactment: An experience report related to problem tracking in an industrial project. In *Proceedings of the Twentieth International Conference on Software Engineering*, pages 13–21, Kyoto, Japan, April 1998. IEEE Computer Society Press.

[11] Watts S. Humphrey. *Managing the Software Process*. Addison Wesley, Reading, Massachusetts, 1989.

[12] Marc I. Kellner. Software process modeling support for management planning and control. In Mark Dowson, editor, *Proceedings of the First International Conference on the Software Process*, pages 8–28. IEEE Computer Society Press, August 1991.

[13] Marc I. Kellner, Ulrike Becker-Kornstaedt, William E. Riddle, Jennifer Tomal, and Martin Verlage. Process guides: Effective guidance for process participants. In *Proceedings of the Fifth International Conference on the Software Process*, pages 11–25, Chicago, IL, USA, June 1998. ISPA Press.

[14] Chi Y. Lin, Tarek Abdel-Hamid, and Joseph S. Sherif. Software-engineering process simulation model. *Journal of Systems and Software*, 38(3):263–277, September 1997.

[15] Jaques Lonchamp. A structured conceptual and terminological framework for software process engineering. In *Proceedings of the Second International Conference on the Software Process*, pages 41–53. IEEE Computer Society Press, February 1993.

[16] Dewayne E. Perry, Nancy A. Staudenmayer, and Votta, Jr., Lawrence G. Understanding and improving time usage in software development. In Alfonso Fuggetta and Alexander Wolf, editors, *Software Process*, Trends in Software, chapter 5, pages 111–135. John Wiley & Sons, 1996.

[17] Martin Verlage. An approach for capturing large software development processes by integration of views modeled independently. In *Proceedings of the Tenth Conference on Software Engineering and Knowledge Engineering*, pages 227–235, San Francisco Bay, CA, USA, June 1998. Knowledge Systems Institute, Skokie, Illinois, USA.

[18] Richard Webby and Ulrike Becker. Towards a Logical Schema Integrating Software Process Modeling and Software Measurement. In Rachel Harrison, editor, *Proceedings of the Nineteenth International Conference on Software Engineering Workshop: Process Modelling and Empirical Studies of Software Evaluation*, pages 84–88, Boston, USA, May 1997.

[19] Richard Webby, Peter Rösch, and Martin Verlage. Spearmint - a prototype tool for visualising complex software processes. In *Proceedings of the Third Biennial World Conference on Integrated Design & Process Technology (IDPT'98)*, volume 4, pages 297–304, Berlin, Germany, July 1998.

Managing Componentware Development – Software Reuse and the V-Modell Process*

Dirk Ansorge[1], Klaus Bergner[1], Bernd Deifel[1], Nicolas Hawlitzky[1],
Christoph Maier[2], Barbara Paech[3,**], Andreas Rausch[1],
Marc Sihling[1], Veronika Thurner[1], Sascha Vogel[1]

[1]Technische Universität München, 80290 München, Germany,
{bergner | deifel | rausch | sihling | thurner | vogels}@in.tum.de
as@iwb.mw.tum.de, Hawlitzky@ws.tum.de
[2]FAST e.V., Arabellastr. 17, 81925 München, Germany
cma@fast.de
[3]Fraunhofer Institute for Experimental Software Engineering,
67661 Kaiserslautern, Germany
paech@iese.fhg.de

Abstract. We present the characteristics of component-based software engineering and derive the requirements for a corresponding development process. Based on this, we propose changes and extensions for the V-Modell, the German standard process model for information systems development in the public services. Following this model, we cover not only systems engineering, but also project management, configuration management, and quality assurance aspects.

1 Motivation

Componentware provides the conceptual and technological foundation for building reusable components and assembling them to well-structured systems. However, the problem of creating and leveraging reusable software assets cannot be solved by technology only. It requires a methodological and organizational reuse infrastructure, integrating software engineering and project management issues. This includes, for example, the organization of a company-wide reuse process and the estimation of the costs and benefits involved with reusing or building a certain component. Furthermore, reuse inherently extends the management domain from a single project to multiple projects and from the context of a single company to the context of the global component market.

In this paper, we suggest some solutions for an integrated treatment of components in information system development. We identify the main characteristics that distinguish component software from non-component software, and sketch the resulting requirements for a component-oriented software engineering process. To be able to describe the necessary extensions and changes in a coherent way, we discuss the German standard for information systems development in the public service, called V-Modell [VMod], as a specific example for a "traditional" single-project process

---

* This work was supported by the Bayerische Forschungsstiftung under the FORSOFT research consortium.
** The work was mainly carried out while the author was at the TUM.

M. Jarke, A. Oberweis (Eds.): CAiSE'99, LNCS 1626, pp. 134-148, 1999.
© Springer-Verlag Berlin Heidelberg 1999

model. The V-Modell is highly suitable as a reference model for our purpose as it covers all aspects of traditional software engineering, but was not designed with the componentware paradigm in mind. Although our proposals for extensions and changes are strongly related to the V-Modell, we think that they also apply to many other process models used today. We have, therefore, tried to keep our presentation general enough to be understood by and profitable to people who are not familiar with the V-Modell.

The context of typical software engineering projects ranges from the ad-hoc development of individual information systems within a small company over the distributed development of global information systems to the development of standard software for the global market. Furthermore, different application areas, like distributed systems or production systems in the area of mechanical engineering, impose additional constraints on the development process. In elaborating our proposals, we have tried to leverage the experience and knowledge within the interdisciplinary FORSOFT research cooperative, consisting not only of computer scientists and researchers from mechanical and electrical engineering, but also of economy experts and practitioners from leading companies in each of these four fields.

The paper is structured as follows: Section 2 identifies the main characteristics and requirements associated with componentware, both from the perspective of component users and component producers. Section 3 describes the V-Modell and sketches the overall approach we took in extending and adapting it. The next two main sections contain detailed proposals – Section 4 deals with single projects, while Section 5 treats the multi-project issues brought up by component reuse. A short conclusion rounds off the paper.

2   Componentware – Perspectives and Requirements

In order to discuss the issues involved with componentware process models, it is sufficient to define components as reusable pieces of software with clearly defined interfaces. To be reusable, a component has to be understandable, capturing a generally useful abstraction. Furthermore, its integration into many different, heterogeneous system contexts must be possible in a cost-effective way, implying tool support and interoperability standards, such as [Sam97, Nin96].

To discuss reusability in an appropriate way, two different perspectives must be taken into account: The perspective of the component (re-) user and the perspective of the component producer (cf. Section 2.1, 2.2).

If we try to relate the user and producer perspectives to traditional software engineering and development process concepts, we can find a strong correspondence to the notions of top-down versus bottom-up development. The top-down approach starts with the initial customer requirements and refines them continually until the level of detail is sufficient for an implementation with the help of existing components. Conversely, the bottom-up approach starts with existing, reusable components which are iteratively combined and composed to higher-level components, until a top-level component emerges which fulfils the customer's requirements.

Obviously, a pure bottom-up approach is impractical in most cases because the requirements are not taken into account early enough. However, the top-down approach also has some severe drawbacks: Initially the customer often does not know all relevant requirements, cannot state them adequately, or even states inconsistent requirements. Consequently, many delivered systems do not meet the customer's expectations. In addition, top-down development leads to systems that are very brittle with respect to changing requirements because the system architecture and the involved components are specifically adjusted to the initial set of requirements.

In our eyes, the central requirement for a component-oriented development process is to combine and reconcile the top-down and the bottom-up approaches within a unified process model. In order to capture the requirements for such a process model, the next two subsections will first sketch the perspectives of component users and producers in more detail. The third subsection will discuss possibilities and scenarios for the integration and combination of both viewpoints.

2.1   Using Components for Application Development

Usually, the development process will start with eliciting and analyzing the requirements of the customer. Then, the overall system architecture is designed, and specifications for the involved subsystems and base components are evolved. When a candidate component has been identified, the central question for a component user is whether to make it or to buy it. This decision critically depends on a comprehensive search for existing components. For their assessment, understandable specifications of the involved syntactic and behavioral interfaces are needed.

Sometimes, the available components will not match the customer's requirements or the system architecture exactly. If it is possible to adapt such components with costs lower than the costs for making a substitute, they should be used anyway. The components' properties may also trigger changes to the system architecture or even to the customer's requirements, for example, when the customer decides to standardize his business processes according to a best-practice approach realized by an available standard component.

Using a component bears chances as well as risks. On the one hand, application developers have the chance to focus on their core competencies instead of wasting resources on re-creating readily available components for base services or for the technical infrastructure. By only providing added value on top of existing building blocks, they can considerably reduce their overall costs and their time-to-market. On the other hand, using available components may imply the strategic risk of dependence from certain component producers, and it may mean to give up valuable in-house knowledge in a certain area.

2.2   Producing Marketable Components

The business of a component supplier is the construction and selling of reusable components on the global component market. The customers and system contexts for such commercial off-the-shelf (COTS) components are not known a priori and may differ very much from each other. [CaB95] and [Dei98] present the basic problems arising in the development and requirements engineering of COTS in general.

The large number of potential customers means that the development costs can be distributed over all sold components, and allows the component producer to specialize in a certain area. The cost-effectiveness of component production therefore depends on the reusability of the produced software components. This implies two things:

First, component producers have to know the market and the requirements of their possible customers very well. COTS producers, therefore, have to perform a comprehensive and careful risk analysis and market studies during their requirements elicitation and product definition phase. To receive periodical feedback from their customers and to react directly to their needs, COTS suppliers normally develop their products in short release-cycles. Typically, they also try to acquire and retain customers by offering various license models, for example, for evaluation, non-commercial, and commercial usage.

Second, COTS components should be reusable in as many contexts as possible, and the adaptation costs for customers should be low. This implies that components should be very robust and must be thoroughly tested - implementation and documentation errors will be fatal for many customers and eventually also for the producer. Furthermore, support like design-time customization interfaces, adaptation tools as well as different variants for different hardware and software standards or platforms should be offered.

2.3   Integrating User and Producer Perspectives

Analogous to other markets, there are many possibilities for reconciling and integrating the idealized viewpoints sketched in the previous two subsections. Generally, the distinction between component users and component suppliers is not a strict one.

When components consist of other, lower-level components, both roles blend into each other, as the supplier of such a component also acts as a component user. There may also be companies that are neither true users nor true suppliers because they only act as link between both worlds. An example would be a company that acts as a component broker, identifying the requirements of many customers and elaborating specifications for components that result in orders to dedicated component developers.

Another common example is an in-house component profit center that selects and produces components for a limited number of customers within a certain company. As such in-house producers are only concerned with reuse within the context of a company and its in-house compliance standards, the necessary generality of the components is reduced. In practice, there is often no clear separation between in-house profit centers and COTS suppliers. Before a COTS supplier ships new components, he will usually reuse these components in-house to test them. Conversely, an in-house supplier may decide to sell a component that has been reused in-house successfully as a COTS component on the global market.

We expect that interface organizations like the ones mentioned will play an important role in a fully developed component marketplace, much in analogy to existing distributor hierarchies in established markets.

3   Adapting and Extending the V-Modell

The V-Modell [VMod] is one of the few examples of an integrated treatment of software engineering and project management issues. The overall development process is structured into four different sub-models, namely *Systems Engineering* (SE, "Systemerstellung"), *Project Management* (PM, "Projektmanagement"), *Quality Assurance* (QA, "Qualitätssicherung"), and *Configuration Management* (CM, "Konfigurationsmanagement"). Each sub-model includes a process and detailed guidelines for how to produce the different development products, for example specification documents and source code. Together, all development products make up the so-called *Product Model* ("Erzeugnisstruktur").

In the following two subsections, we will describe the V-Modell's approach in defining the process and its overall structure, and discuss our proposals for general changes and extensions regarding component oriented development.

3.1   Flow-Based vs. Pattern-Based Process Description

The V-Modell's overall approach in defining the process is flow-based. Development products are elaborated within activities and flow into other activities that need them as input. This structure is reflected in the scheme for the activity description:

from		product	to	
activity	**state**		**activity**	**state**
Activity a1	accepted	development result r1	activity a2	processed
...	...	...	...	...

The scheme means that the corresponding development activity receives the development result r1 in state accepted as input from activity a1. After completion of the activity, the state of r1 is set to processed and the result is forwarded to activity a2.

In the V-Modell, this flow-based definition approach is combined with a rather traditional process which is more or less structured into sequential phases. As mentioned above, a sequential process does not fit very well to the bottom-up aspect needed for componentware development. Furthermore, the flow-based formulation of the process model limits the developers' freedom to react flexibly on unforeseen events because the prescribed activity flows must be followed.

The V-Modell tries to alleviate these problems by two measures:

- Feedback loops are introduced into the product flows. This allows to rework and correct products by repeatedly performing certain activities, resulting in an iterative process.
- Informal scenarios provide additional guidance in scheduling the order of activities in the process before the start of a project. With respect to componentware, the scenarios *Use of Ready-Made Components* ("Einsatz von Fertigprodukten") and especially *Object-Oriented Development* ("Objektorientierte Entwicklung") seem to be most adequate.

In our eyes, both measures can only partly solve the above mentioned problems. While the introduction of iterations does not fully remove the rigidity of the prescribed processes of the flow-based model, the scenario approach is very informal and does not match very well with the rest of the process model. Furthermore, the scenario has to be selected before the start of a project and provides no support for modifications during its runtime.

To remedy the deficiencies of the V-Modell, it must be reworked in a more principal way. We propose, therefore, to switch from the current flow-based description to a pattern-based model. Here, the state and consistency of the hierarchical product model together with an assessment of the external market situation form the context for so-called process patterns which recommend possible activities. This way, top-down and bottom-up activities may be selected and performed based on the process manager's assessment of the current development situation. We have motivated and described our pattern-based approach in detail in [BRSV98a,BRSV98b,BRSV98c]. Apart from a high-level description of a suitable product model, we have elaborated a comprehensive catalog of process patterns for component-oriented software engineering.

We think that the V-Modell should be reworked in order to serve as the basis for a complete pattern-based process model with a detailed product model, spanning all activities of the development process. To achieve this, the basic description scheme should be changed. Instead of describing the flow of products between sequential activities, as shown above, the pattern of activities necessary to create products or establish consistency conditions between products should be described without relating to preceding or subsequent activities. The resulting scheme could look like this:

pre		process pattern p1	post	
product	**state**		**product**	**state**
product p1	complete	activity a1	product p2	in progress
...	...	...	...	...

This scheme means that this process pattern is applicable when development product p1 is completed (the conditions related to the external situation are not shown here). After completion of the activities described in the process pattern, the development product p2 is created and set to state in progress.

3.2   Single-Project vs. Multi-project Development

In its current form, the V-Modell aims at the management of single projects, where software is developed more or less "from scratch". Componentware brings up two kinds of new issues:

- There must be support for the reuse of components within a single project. This requires new engineering activities, for example, searching for existent software components. Furthermore, existing activities have to be extended or must change their focus. Testing, for example, now has to deal not only with software that was developed in-house, but also with components from external suppliers.
- The process has to be extended in order to support multi-project issues. This relates, for example, to establishing a company-wide reuse organization, or to maintaining a repository containing components that can be reused by many projects.

The V-Modell uses so-called roles to describe the knowledge and skills necessary for carrying out certain activities appropriately. These roles are then assigned to the available persons on a per-project basis. Some example roles are *System Analyst*, *Controller*, or *Quality Manager*. Similar to our process-changes, we also had to both modify existing roles and introduce new ones in order to reflect the additional and changed skills. The *System Analyst*, for example, is now also responsible for assessing the business-oriented functionality of existing systems and components as a prerequisite for the elicitation of the customer requirements (cf. Section 4.1). An example for a completely new role is the *Reuse Manager* who has to identify the need for new components within a business organization, and propagates the usage of available components within development projects (cf. Section 5.2).

Based on the distinction of single-project and multi-project issues, we propose the following overall approach for extending the V-Modell with respect to component-oriented development:

- The existing V-Modell is slightly extended and modified in order to cope with the additional requirements for componentware. Leaving the structure of the V-Modell intact has the advantage that project managers do not have to adopt a totally new process model, but can build on existing knowledge.
- To deal with multi-project issues, new multi-project counterparts for the existing sub-models are added to the V-Modell. This extension reflects the deep impact componentware has on the organization of a company, but makes it possible for companies to introduce the necessary changes step by step and relatively independent from single projects.

The following figure visualizes the structure of the extended V-Modell:

	Single-Project Issues	Multi-Project Issues
Software Engineering		
Project Management		
Quality Assurance		
Configuration Management		

The next two main sections are organized as follows: Section 4 deals with the four sub-models in the context of a single project, while Section 5 is concerned about the multi-project issues.

4   Single Project Issues

Reuse enforces two basic principles on a software development project. On the one hand, standardization is necessary to support integration of components, and on the other hand flexibility of process and product is important in order to react to the dynamic component market. Standardization in software engineering activities requires, in particular, a well-defined component concept, standardized description techniques, separation between business-oriented and technical issues and a detailed assessment of components to be integrated. Flexibility implies a detailed search for adequate components, a close intertwining of component search, architectural design and requirements capture as well as an emphasis on adaptation and configuration in design and implementation. For project management flexibility in process definition and market activities is required and standards for supplier, contract and variant management. Configuration and quality management need to set standards for a component library, the integration of components and their test.

In the following subsections we discuss the impact of these principles on the activities and roles of the sub-models of the V-Modell.

4.1   Systems Engineering

The sub-model Systems Engineering (SE) subsumes all activities related to hardware and software development as well as the creation of the corresponding documents. It defines nine main activities which are carried out more or less sequentially: Starting with *Requirements Analysis* (SE1), specific software and hardware requirements are analyzed. Then, the system is designed and split up into a hierarchy of logical and physical components (SE2 to SE5). These components are then implemented (SE6) and finally integrated (SE7 to SE8). Finally, the last main activity, *RollOut* (SE9), takes care of how to install the system in its specified environment, and how to configure and execute it properly.

Clear Component Concept: The V-Modell offers a variety of structuring concepts, reaching from *IT Systems* over *Segments*, *Software and Hardware Units*, *Software Substructures*, and *Components* to *Modules*. However, none of these concepts is defined clearly or even formally. This forces each development project to come up with its own incompatible, proprietary interpretations which hinders the reuse of existing components from other projects. To remedy this situation, we recommend to unify the structuring concepts by defining a uniform concept for hierarchical components. A first approach may be found in [BRSV98c].

Standardized Description Techniques: Apart from a clear component concept, reuse requires well-defined, standardized description techniques for the structure and behavior of components. This includes mostly so-called black-box descriptions of the component's external interfaces. During adaptation of pre-fabricated components in some cases also white-box descriptions of the internals of a component are necessary. Proposals for component description languages and graphical description techniques can be found in [UML97,SGW94,HRR98,BRSV98c]. The V-Modell yet only gives some recommendations on what to specify (for example, functionality, data management, exception handling of a component) and which description techniques may be used (for example, E/R diagrams or Message Sequence Charts), but it does not contain guidelines or requirements for component descriptions.

Reuse Activities: Although the V-Modell contains some remarks on reusing existing components in its activity descriptions, a comprehensive treatment of this aspect is missing - system development is mainly seen as starting out from scratch. To provide support for reuse, some activities have to be changed or to be added:

- *Search for Existing Components* should be an explicit activity. Its main purpose is to build an in-project component repository (cf. Section 4.3) based on selecting suitable components from public or in-house repositories (cf. Sections 4.3, 5.2). The V-Modell should provide standard activities for adding, deleting, editing, and searching components and the different versions and variants of these components.
- Based on the criticality of the involved existing components, detailed evaluations have to be carried out in order to assess their suitability and compatibility with the existing design. The *Component Evaluation* activity includes not only validation, verification, process and product tests, but also harmonization of the component and the system quality (cf. Section 4.4). To avoid costly workarounds it should be completed before making the definitive decision to use the respective component. A *Replacement Analysis* may additionally serve to be able to estimate the costs involved with changing architectures and using a substitute component.
- The *Design* and *Implementation* activities change their focus. Instead of designing and coding new software modules, componentware relies mainly on *Composition*, *Instantiation*, and *Adaptation* of existing components and infrastructure systems [Krue92]. In its current version, the V-Modell only covers the special case of a

central database component, which has to be realized and tested, based on the respective database schema.

Controlling: As mentioned in Section 2, existing components may trigger changes to the architecture and even the requirements of the customer. The V-Modell tries to support this via the so-called *Requirements Controlling* activity ("Forderungscontrolling") which is a bottom-up activity in the sense of Sections 2 and 3.1. Based on eventual preliminary architectural considerations, the requirements may possibly changed after the *Requirements Analysis* phase. With componentware requirements should be controlled regularly, especially after the system architecture or key components have been elaborated or changed. Furthermore, if for example new components, standards, or technologies arise on the market also a *Architecture Controlling* activity should be performed

Separation of Business-Oriented and Technical Issues: The V-Modell structures the design into three main activities: During *System Design* (SE2), the overall architecture is designed. *SW/HW Requirements Analysis* (SE3) extends the requirements for the involved hardware and software units. *High-Level SW Design* (SE4) is concerned with designing the internal architecture of software units, and *Low-Level SW Design* (SE5) specifies the interfaces and implementations of the involved software components in detail. With respect to componentware, this scheme has major flaws:

- The combined specification of hardware and software units in the system architecture makes it impossible to separate the business-oriented software design from the technical architecture, consisting of the involved hardware environment and the middleware infrastructure. This is inconsistent with one of the key features of modern component approaches [EJB98], namely, the possibility to employ business-oriented components within different technical system contexts [HMPS98].
- It is not possible to postpone the decision whether a certain component is to be implemented by means of software or by means of hardware.

We therefore propose to abolish the activities SE2 to SE4, replacing them with two activities for *Business-Oriented Design* and for *Technical Design*, which are clearly separated. The hardware/software mapping and the reconciliation and unification of these two architectures into a single, overall architecture may then be done in the subsequent *Low-Level Design* activity, as shown in [BRSV98a,BRSV98b].

4.2 Project Management

The sub-model *Project Management* (PM) consists of three kinds of activities: project initialization activities, planning activities, and execution activities. The *Project Initialization* activity (PM1) comprises basic steps that are performed once before the project starts, like the definition of project goals and the selection of tools. Furthermore, roles have to be assigned to persons and the V-Modell has to be "tailored" with respect to project-specific needs. During the tailoring activity, the project manager decides which activities of the full V-Modell may be discarded. The initialization phase results in an overall *Project Plan*, including a rough expenditure estimate and a time schedule.

Afterwards planning and execution activities start. Typical planning activities are performed periodically for each sub-phase of the project. They include the *Allocation of External Orders* (PM2), the *Management of Suppliers* (PM3), *Detailed Planning*

(PM4) of resources, milestones and expenditures, and *Cost/Value Analysis* (PM5). The resulting data serves as a basis for *Go-/No-Go Decisions* (PM6) for parts of the project. Concurrently, *Risk Management* (PM7), *Controlling* (PM8), and *Reporting* (PM9) activities are performed. Execution activities pertain to *Training and Briefing of Employees* (PM10 and PM13), *Preparation of Resources* (PM11), and *Allocation of Tasks* (PM12).

The final *Project Completion* activity (PM14) results in a final report about progression and project results. *Project Management* roles defined in the V-Modell include the *Project Director*, the *Project Manager*, the *Controller*, the *Legal Adviser*, and the *Project Adviser*.

Flexible Process Redefinition: In principle, the V-Modell already contains all activities necessary for componentware. However, changes on the component market require much more flexible approaches to planning and controlling. Following the pattern-based process model sketched in Section 3.1, the *Project Manager* and the *Project Director* may redefine the project during its runtime by selecting adequate patterns. Similar to the V-Modell's tailoring process, the conditions for the pattern application may be defined before the start of the project.

Dynamic Negotiation of Results: The current V-Modell already provides some facilities for bottom-up information flow and iterative elaboration of results, as described in Section 3.1. The additional flexibility brought by the pattern-based process model leads to a new understanding of the process management role: instead of a pure controlling activity, managing can now be seen as mediating between the customer, the developer, and the external component producers. Mediation relies on activities like *Requirements Controlling* in order to dynamically elicit and define the customer requirements, or *Architecture Controlling* in order to dynamically elaborate a suitable system architecture, taking into account the possible risks, benefits and costs of applying and integrating available components (cf. Section 4.1). The following issues mainly deal with the relation to the external component suppliers.

Market Analysis and Marketing: The initialization phase of sub-model PM has to be supplemented by a market analysis for the corresponding system or component. Component users need information about existing systems mainly in order to elicit the requirements of their customers. For component suppliers, detailed knowledge of the market is a vital precondition, as described in Section 2.2. Therefore, they usually start their development projects with a market study, scanning the market for similar components and analyzing requirements of potential customers. Depending on the results, the supplier estimates the potential income and the strategic value of the planned component. This assessment will in turn be used to further refine the features of the component in order to find an optimum cost/value ratio. In case of novel components and so-called enabling technologies, time-to-market is usually the most important factor – even if not all desirable features are present, the component may open up a new market. In case of more mature markets where components with similar features already exist, the component supplier also has to differentiate the component from those of competitors, either by providing additional features or by offering it for a lower price. Due to the importance of all activities concerned with the market, we propose to add the new role *Marketing Manager* to the V-Modell.

Supplier Management: While marketing is mainly concerned with the possible customers of a system or component, supplier management deals with producers of external components that are to be used within a project. While the V-Modell already includes an activity for *Supplier Management*, it is mainly intended for subcontractor management. Dealing with independent component suppliers involves some additional issues. Besides an evaluation of the price and the features of the offered components, a supplier's reliability and continued support are important to component users, especially in case of critical, non-standard components. During *Risk Management*, corresponding technical and strategic risks must, therefore, be assessed carefully.

Contract Management: After a user has decided to buy a certain component, a contract has to be concluded. Conversely, suppliers must prepare a licensing model for their products. The license model directly influences the profitability of component reuse, for example, by regulating how often license fees have to be paid or whether new releases of components may be bought with certain discounts. Redistribution and copyright issues must also be clarified. It is also important whether the supplier commits himself to a certain roadmap for further development, beyond the usual responsibility for removing errors. Furthermore, the supplier's liability in case of damages caused by a component has to be clarified. Finally, precautions for the bankruptcy of the supplier should be made, for example, by stating in the contract that the source code of the supplied product must be handed over to the user in that case. The management of supplier contracts widens the job of the *Legal Advisor*.

Variant Management: Another important point for both users and suppliers is component variant management. Users should strive to minimize the number of variants, for example, by preferring to reuse existing components against buying modified or compatible ones (cf. Section 4.3). Users also have to check if any of their existing components may be suitable for reuse in a new development project by reviewing the project requirements. For COTS-suppliers, the situation is more complex. On the one hand, having many variants rises the number of potential customers. On the other hand, suppliers can usually only manage a limited range of variants with justifiable effort. To coordinate the development of the variants and especially to avoid duplicated work, we propose the new role *Variant Manager* for component suppliers.

4.3   Configuration Management

The primary goal of the sub-model *Configuration Management* (CM) is to ensure that each part of a product as well as the product itself is identifiable at every time. It includes four main activities: In *Configuration Management Planning* (CM1), guidelines for the configuration, change, build, and archive management have to be established. *Product and Configuration Management* (CM2) deals with the creation, deletion, and change of the product's entities, the product itself, and configurations of the entities. This includes especially the transfer of reusable entities to the central *Configuration Management Services* activity. *Change Management* (CM3) handles error reports, problem reports, and suggestions for improvements. At last, the *Configuration Management Services* (CM4) provide common services like product catalogues, data administration, access control administration, and interface management.

Integration of Component Descriptions: In addition to the traditional hierarchical structure of product models componentware demands for a clear separation of architectural requirements for a certain abstract component from the description of existing components. This allows component users to integrate different, encapsulated components along with their descriptions from external suppliers. Note that the exchange of standardized component descriptions relies on the standardization of the description format as well as of the involved description techniques (cf. Section 4.1).

Component Library Management: Apart from the developed products, *Configuration Management* must also archive components that have been assessed or used in a certain development project. It is also necessary to manage a list of external repositories in order to help developers in searching for reusable components. Note that the management of a component library for a single project doesn't pertain to building a global component repository used by multiple projects (cf. Section 5.3).

Variant Management: For the management of different variants of a single product, one can use concepts and tools for version management that are already available. Branches capture different variants and their history, while configurations may be used to model different internal structures of a component variant. However, due to the complexity introduced by variants, dealing with variants methodically remains an open research question.

4.4   Quality Assurance

The *Quality Assurance* sub-model consists of five main activities: Similar to the project initialization activity in the *Systems Engineering* sub-model, the *QA Initialization* (QA1) results in an overall *QA Plan* which describes the planned tests. *Test Preparation* (QA2) provides a more detailed plan, including the planned measures, test cases, and test procedures. These planning activities are complemented by performing the actual test and quality assurance measures – *Process Tests of Activities* (QA3) corresponds to reviewing and assessing the processed activities, while *Product Test* (QA4) deals with the development documents. *QA Reporting* (QA5) represents the information flow to *Project Management* activities which are informed in case of problems detected during *Quality Assurance*. The structure of activities QA1 to QA5 is similar in that each of them considers constructive as well as analytical measures, in order to both avoid and correct failures.

Component Assessment: Existing QA activities of the V-Modell not always suffice for ensuring the quality of components. As their source code may not be available, the assessment techniques for externally developed components might differ from those employed for assessing software developed in-house. In many situations, one has to resort to black-box tests based on a specification of the component's desired behavior. The *Supplier Management* main activity may also provide some additional information about the quality level of certain component producers. Sometimes, it will even be possible to access the source code, for example, with Open Source Software [Ray98], or when the supplier agrees to provide it. Finally, in contrast to tests of internally developed components, tests of external components should not be delayed until system integration. Rather, they have to be performed during the elaboration of the architecture and the interfaces in order to detect hidden flaws that could require costly workarounds during implementation or might even compromise the whole project (cf. Section 4.1).

5   Reuse Aspects

Reuse inherently expands the development context from a single project to multiple projects. Building a reusable component generally requires more effort which is only worthwhile if it can be sold several times. Therefore it is vital for component users to investigate related current and potential development projects for potential reuse opportunities. Rather than being forced into the organizational framework of a single development project, multi-project activities are generally carried out continuously over longer periods of time by a reuse organization. This organization is responsible for the coordination of all development efforts of the company, and it administers the company's component repository.

In the following, we describe some of the issues involved in the management of such a reuse organization. As sketched in Section 3.2, the principle structure, organization, and processes resemble very much their counterparts in the existing V-Modell. As an example, consider the roles of the new sub-model *Reuse Management* which are more or less isomorphic to the roles of the existing sub-model *Project Management*, only that their context comprehends not only a single project, but also multiple projects and that their tasks usually are more long-term oriented.

The following sections will, therefore, not repeat these foundations again, but only provide some additional recommendations and insights. As with the other activities of the V-Modell, nothing is said about the actual organizational settings – the reuse organization may be a dedicated department or a group of distributed component caretakers working on ordinary projects most of the time.

5.1   Systems Engineering

Reference Architecture and Company Standards: A reuse organization may not only develop reusable components, but also elaborate the company's overall IT architecture and company standards. Clear guidelines help to avoid compatibility problems and ease the work of application developers, as they can start with proven and accepted solutions. Advantages for component suppliers are similar appearance and a common corporate identity on the market.

Identification and Generalization of Reusable Components: Candidate components for (re-)use in multiple projects may be found by examining single in-house projects or by harmonizing product lines based on an overall domain analysis, but also by assessing the properties of components on the component market. Identified component candidates have to go through a reuse analysis which estimates the potential degree of reuse. Normally, in-house components from projects must first be adapted and generalized in order to be usable in a wider context. This may also lead to truly reusable components which may evolve to a stand-alone product for the component market themselves.

5.2   Reuse Management

Assistance for Systems Engineering: Normally, reference architectures and company standards are only proposed and elaborated by *Systems Engineering*. The final decision is usually met by *Reuse Management*. Similar considerations apply for the *Identification and Generalization of Reusable Components*.

Component Propagation: Multi project management has to propagate the usage of components within development projects by actively marketing them within the company. First and foremost, this means to announce already existing components, for example, by organizing systematic publicity campaigns and by informing projects about the company's global component repository.

Rewarding Reuse: Building a reusable component within a project leads to increased costs and efforts. Reuse management therefore has to create a system of incentives for this purpose, for example, by granting additional financial resources to project managers or developers.

Coordinating Development Activities: Sometimes a certain project may intend to use a component which currently is under development in another project. In cases like this, reuse management has to coordinate the development of both projects by harmonizing both project plans accordingly. Especially when time-to-market is a decisive criterion for the success of a software product, component reuse may be profitable even if costs increase compared to in-house development. In such a situation, a component supplier may speed up development within certain limits, if enough resources are available. Reuse management may support the negotiation of costs and development time in order to optimize the total benefits for the company.

Management of Human Resources: Similar to building a portfolio of reusable components, *Reuse Management* may strive to build a portfolio of human resources. This may be achieved by tracking existing abilities of the employees, but also by identifying abilities that are likely to be used in multiple future projects.

5.3   Configuration Management

All issues applying to component *Configuration Management* have already be mentioned in Section 4.3 and apply to *Reuse Configuration Management* analogously, only that the context is the company and not a single project.

5.4   Quality Assurance

Establishing Component Assessment and Quality Standards: In-house assessment standards for components should be developed and established, and assessment rules should be given to the supplier to achieve a common quality level within the company. The standards and rules have to be based on an experience database that has to be built up and refreshed within each new project.

Reusing Test Results: Reuse can reduce the effort for QA activities within similar projects or similar usage contexts. The reason is that certain QA activities must be carried out only once while developing a component. Whenever the component is reused, the focus may then be on integration testing. Even the remaining efforts may be reduced more and more based on the increasing experience with the component.

6   Conclusions

In this paper we have argued that the process models used today, and the V-Modell in particular, is not yet suited to the requirements of a componentware development process. In particular, this concerns the lack of an organizational structure and a process allowing the exchange of information and software either between different, not necessarily concurrent projects within a company or via an open market for components. We have, thus, proposed some modifications and enhancements for the current version of the V-Modell, mainly by introducing new roles and new activities, by evolving a new sub-model concentrating on reuse, and by switching to a pattern-based process definition instead of a flow-based one. In our view, this constitutes the necessary and sufficient foundation for a more detailed elaboration of the V-Modell for component-oriented development.

References

[BRSV98a] K. Bergner, A. Rausch, M. Sihling, A. Vilbig, "A Componentware Development Methodology Based on Process Patterns", Pattern Languages of Programs 1998 (PLOP98), Monticello, Illinois, 1998.

[BRSV98b] K. Bergner, A. Rausch, M. Sihling, A. Vilbig, "A Componentware Methodology based on Process Patterns", Technical Report TUM-I9823, Institut für Informatik, Technische Universität München, 1998.

[BRSV98c] K. Bergner, A. Rausch, M. Sihling, A. Vilbig, "An Integrated View on Componentware - Concepts, Description Techniques, and Process Model", IASTED International Conference Software Engineering '98, Las Vegas, 1998.

[CaB95] E. Carmel, S. Becker, "A Process Model for Packaged Software Development", IEEE Transactions on Engineering Management, Vol. 42, No. 1, 1995.

[Dei98] B. Deifel, "Requirements Engineering for Complex COTS", REFSQ'98, Pisa, 1998.

[EJB98] Sun Microsystems, "Enterprise JavaBeans Specification", Version 1.0, Sun Microsystems, 901 San Antonio Road, Palo Alto, CA94303, 1998.

[HMPS98] W. Hordijk, S. Molterer, B. Paech, Ch. Salzmann, "Working with Business Objects: A Case Study", Business Object Workshop, OOPSLA'98, 1998.

[HRR98] F. Huber, A. Rausch, B. Rumpe, "Modeling Dynamic Component Interfaces", in TOOLS 26, Technology of Object-Oriented Languages and Systems, pp. 58-70, Madhu Singh, Bertrand Meyer, Joseph Gil, Richard Mitchell (eds.), IEEE Computer Society, 1998.

[Krue92] Ch. W. Krueger, "Software Reuse", ACM Computing Surveys, 24,2, 1992.

[Nin96] J.Q. Ning, "A Component-Based Development Model", COMPSAC'96, pp. 389-394, 1996.

[Ray98] E. Raymond, "Open Source: The Future is Here", WWW page http://www.opensource.org, 1998.

[Sam97] J. Sametinger, "Software Engineering with Reusable Components", Springer 1997.

[SGW94] B. Selic, G. Gullekson, P. Ward, "Real-Time Object-Oriented Modeling", John Wiley and Sons Ltd, Chichester, 1994.

[UML97] UML Group, Unified Modeling Language Version 1.1, Rational Software Corporation, Santa Clara, CA95051, USA, 1997.

[VMod] IABG, "Das V-Modell", WWW page http://www.v-modell.iabg.de/, 1998.

Modelling Multidimensional Data in a Dataflow-Based Visual Data Analysis Environment

Frank Wietek

University of Oldenburg, Department of Computer Science
Escherweg 2, D–26121 Oldenburg, Germany
wietek@informatik.uni-oldenburg.de

Abstract. Multidimensional data analysis is currently being discussed in terms like *OLAP*, *data warehousing*, or *decision support*, mainly concentrating on business applications. Numerous *OLAP-tools* providing flexible query facilities for *datacubes* are being designed and distributed. Typical analysis sessions with these kind of systems comprise long and branching sequences of exploratory analysis steps which base upon each other. While concentrating on single functions and processing steps, management of this analysis process as a whole is scarcely supported.
This paper proposes a dataflow-based visual programming environment for multidimensional data analysis (*VIOLA*) as an approach to deal with this problem. Providing a foundation of basic operations, data processing, navigation, and user interaction, an appropriate data model (*MADEIRA*) is developed. Epidemiological studies, i. e. investigations of aggregate data on populations, their state of health, and potential risk factors, will serve as a leading example of a typical application area.

1 Introduction

Especially in the field of business applications, flexible and systematic analysis of fast growing databases has gained more and more general interest in the last few years. Based on *data warehouses*, which collect data from different sources, *OLAP-tools* are oriented towards decision support [1]. Databases analysed by these tools are modelled as a set of multidimensional *dataspaces* or *cubes*. These contain aggregated *fact data* (*measures*, described by *quantifying* or *summary attributes*), e. g. sales or profit, which are classified by a number of *dimensions* (*parameters*, described by *qualifying* or *category attributes*) like product, shop, or time. Instances of parameter values are usually classified in a *category hierarchy*.

Each dimension of a datacube corresponds to a criterion for partitioning base data in different subgroups. A *cell* of a cube describes the group of base data entities defined by the corresponding instances of the cube's category attributes. Since all cell values relate to groups of entities, this kind of data is also called *macrodata*. This contrasts with typically relational *microdata* mostly constituting the base data from which aggregated measures are calculated by *aggregation functions* like count, sum, or average over certain attributes.

M. Jarke, A. Oberweis (Eds.): CAiSE'99, LNCS 1626, pp. 149–163, 1999.
© Springer-Verlag Berlin Heidelberg 1999

Multidimensional data analysis is certainly not restricted to the business domain. In this paper, epidemiological studies (as for example carried out in disease registries) are supposed to serve as an application example. A typical multidimensional dataspace in this domain represents incidence or mortality counts or rates by age, sex, study region, time, and type of disease. Studies typically handle base data of up to some million cases classified in 5–50 dimensions – each of them with two to some thousand different values on usually not much more than ten different aggregation levels. As well as enterprise managers in the "original" OLAP domain introduced above, who navigate through business databases while searching for interesting information, also in the area of epidemiology specialists of different disciplines (social scientists, doctors, health data administrators) are to be provided with intuitive facilities for comfortable, exploratory data analysis.

Most available OLAP-tools (cf. [2]) concentrate on powerful statistical and data management operations and facilities for data visualization, but do hardly support management of this analysis process as a whole by providing the user with an overview of what he has done so far and by offering possibilities to manipulate this exploration history. In this paper, the idea of a dataflow-based visual analysis environment called *VIOLA* (*VIsual On-Line data Analysis environment*) will be proposed to deal with this subject (see Sect. 2).

Corresponding to available tools, existing multidimensional data models (see [3] for a survey) restrict themselves to the database point of view. Additionally, in many cases their design is strongly influenced by the idea of a relational implementation. They provide powerful operations to construct complex database queries, but do not take further steps of data analysis into account.

What we claim is to model the datacube as a data structure for both database queries *and* further processing. Thus, this paper introduces the data model *MADEIRA* (*Modelling Analyses of Data in Epidemiological InteRActive studies*) which

- is independent of a physical (relational) database implementation,
- provides enough information about measures and categories to facilitate intelligent and sensible selection and application of analysis methods to given datasets (especially for, but not restricted to epidemiology), and
- builds a framework for a data analysis environment, which combines different analysis procedures visually and thus keeps track of the whole process of an analysis session – both for complex pre-designed reports and (even more important) for ad-hoc data exploration.

In Sect. 3, some basic ideas, structures and operations of *MADEIRA* will be defined in order to give a solid foundation of the subsequent two sections 4 and 5. These are supposed to show how the idea of dataflow-programming based on a formal logical data model is able to enhance the power and usability of existing OLAP-tools in an "intelligent" way. Different aspects of implementing basic data analysis operations are discussed: execution of visual queries, selection of methods, examples of visual control structures, and interactive data visualization. Section 6 discusses some related approaches to multidimensional data modelling and visual programming in data analysis. Finally, Sect. 7 gives a short summary and points out some ideas for future work.

2   A Dataflow-Based Visual Data Analysis Environment

What is a suitable data analysis environment and what are efficient tools and user interfaces for "good" data analysis? Hand [4] considers a sensible distribution of subtasks between human user and computer-based tools the main goal of performing "intelligent" data analyses. Each one of these two should be able to concentrate on his respective strength: the data analyst on his creativeness, his ability to recognize complex structures and to develop new hypotheses – the computer on management and preparation of data and methods and on processing complex calculations efficiently and systematically.

Visualization of information provides the basic opportunity of integrating the human analyst into the process of data analysis. Especially combined with flexible facilities of modifying parameters and presentation modes as well as selection of data and calculated measures, suitable graphics reveal hidden structures of information. Insights gained in this way lead to new hypotheses and further investigations under new points of view – resulting in an refining analysis cycle.

Many existing tools for data analysis (like SAS, SPSS, or also OLAP-tools) leave the management of this process itself to the user. Thus, he might easily get lost in the course of calculations and produced datasets, not knowing exactly how we got his results and how they relate to the base data. An intelligent system for data analysis should not only provide the user with routines for calculation and visualization, but should also give access to the complete course of a data analysis session to make results interpretable and reproducible and to simplify comparative modifications and repetitions of an analysis sequence.

According to the outstanding role of visualization, dataflow-based visual programming [5] is a suitable paradigm to fulfill these requirements by visualizing the whole process of an analysis. The analysis system *VIOLA* is supposed to implement this concept in the context of OLAP. Different building-blocks, representing data sources and methods of data analysis, management, and visualization, are interconnected in a dataflow-chart corresponding to calculations of intermediate results. Exploratory data analysis is performed by changing datasets or selecting subsets, by interactively modifying parameters of methods, exchanging methods for similar ones, or expanding the flowchart by further analysis steps [6]. Processing multiple datasets "in parallel" in *one* node facilitates flexible reusage and modification of common analysis sequences on multiple datasets and ensures comparability of the respective results. This might additionally be supported by introducing hierarchical subnets of analysis steps.

In our application domain, data exchanged between nodes of an analysis network are multidimensional datacubes. The next section will define some parts of a formal logical data model for datacubes and their processing in order to continue the idea of defining steps of a data analysis process explicitly and making results of an analysis session exactly interpretable.

3   The Multidimensional Data Model *MADEIRA*

The following considerations have been of great importance for the design of the
data model *MADEIRA* as a framework for a visual data analysis environment
and discriminate this model from existing ones:

- In order to guarantee intuitive usability of *VIOLA*, *MADEIRA* is restricted
  to *one* main data structure, namely a multidimensional datacube, and its
  components. Microdata do not play a significant role in *MADEIRA*.
- The most important operation for navigation in datacubes is aggregation.
  In order to support aggregation as good as possible,
    - semantics, especially "disjointness" and "completeness" of categories
      (e. g. all cities of a state do *not* cover the whole state),
    - aggregation levels and hierarchies of categories, and
    - aggregation functions being applicable to a datacube
  need to be modelled explicitly. This is also of great importance for integration of data from different data sources and for consideration of set-valued
  category instances as is sometimes necessary.
- Various metadata, especially object domains described by macrodata as well
  as detailed type descriptions of measures have to be integrated into the model
  to allow exact operator definitions and dataset descriptions for user information. Thus, *MADEIRA* stresses the aspect of *semantic* data definition and
  usage of this knowledge in data processing, whereas most existing multidimensional data models are restricted to the mere *syntax* of datacubes.
- By applying statistical functions to datacubes, complex measures are calculated, which often cannot be further aggregated to higher levels without
  accessing the base data. In order to be still able to facilitate efficient and
  interactive data navigation and also for reasons of flexibility, data of different
  aggregation levels must be combinable in *one* datacube.

In the following, we will at first define categories and dimensions as basic
elements for classifying base data; afterwards dataspaces representing macrodata, which are described by summary and category attributes, are introduced.
Finally, aggregation and restriction of dataspaces are formally modelled.

For a set M, let 2^M denote the set of all subsets of M and $\mathbb{N}^M$ the set of all
multisets on M. Let $a.a_i$ denote a component of a structure $a = (a_1, \ldots, a_n)$.

3.1   Categories and Dimensions

Let $\mathcal{O}$ be a set of OBJECTS to be considered in a data analysis (e. g. persons,
tumours, etc.) and $\mathcal{F}$ be a set of FEATURES, such that each $o \in \mathcal{O}$ is described by
a subset of $\mathcal{F}$ (e. g. persons by sex, age, residence or tumours by some medical
attributes). In the following, a subset $O \subseteq \mathcal{O}$ generally represents a kind of
object-oriented concept (e. g. "all persons"), whereas inst(O) $\subseteq O$ denotes a
particular instance of analysed objects.

Instances of features are described by CATEGORIES (e. g. *Hamburg, 1998*, or
male), which are elements of a set $\mathcal{C}$. $\mathcal{C}$ is partitioned into a set $\mathcal{DO} \subset 2^{\mathcal{C}}$ of

pairwise disjoint DOMAINS (e. g. *region, time, age*, etc.), such that each feature $f \in \mathcal{F}$ is described by categories of one unique domain $D_f \in \mathcal{DO}$ – let $\mathcal{F}_D$ denote the set of all features described by categories of domain D. We will consider categories some kind of logical statements or predicates over features and objects.

$\mathcal{O}_f$ and $\mathcal{O}_{f,c}$ denote the sets of objects in $\mathcal{O}$ which are describable by feature f or for which category $c \in D_f$ holds for f, respectively. We write "$o \vdash_f c$" if $o \in \mathcal{O}_{f,c}$; e. g. if a person x lives in Germany, "$x \vdash_{residence} Germany$" holds.

Two categories c_1, c_2 of one domain D are called EQUIVALENT ("$c_1 \equiv c_2$") if $\forall f \in \mathcal{F}_D : \mathcal{O}_{f,c_1} = \mathcal{O}_{f,c_2}$. Analogously, SUBSUMPTION of categories ("c_1 is finer than (subsumed by) c_2", "$c_1 \preceq c_2$") is defined as $\forall f \in \mathcal{F}_D : \mathcal{O}_{f,c_1} \subseteq \mathcal{O}_{f,c_2}$. c_1 and c_2 are said to be RELATED ("$c_1 \| c_2$") if $c_1 \preceq c_2$ or vice versa. In a similar way, also disjunction ("$c_1 \vee c_2$" satisfying $\mathcal{O}_{f,c_1 \vee c_2} = \mathcal{O}_{f,c_1} \cup \mathcal{O}_{f,c_2}$), conjunction ("$c_1 \wedge c_2$"), and negation ("$\neg c$") of categories are defined intuitively. Finally, we call two categories DISJOINT with respect to a feature f and a set of objects O ("$c_1 \perp_{f,O} c_2$") if $O \cap \mathcal{O}_{f,c_1} \cap \mathcal{O}_{f,c_2} = \emptyset$.

Whereas subsumption is intended to consider general finer-coarser-relationships between categories (e. g. "$Hamburg \preceq Germany$" in the region domain), disjointness needs to be related to single features and object-sets to enable also modelling of set-valued features (with almost no categories being disjoint).

Aggregation levels define groups of categories being typically used together in an analysis for classifying objects described by them. If modelled explicitly, most existing data models (e. g. [7]) consider categories of one level being "of the same granularity". Although covering typical cases (e. g. "all counties of Germany") this approach is to restrictive, e. g. when modelling five-year age-groups with one group "75 and older". Rather often single categories belong to *different* levels of one domain, e. g. cities belong both to a community and a ward level of the region domain. Thus, we only claim a level not to contain *related* categories. (Furthermore, for single-valued features all categories of a level are disjoint.)

Definition 1 (Aggregation levels). *An* (AGGREGATION) LEVEL $le = (D, C)$ *on domain D is given by a finite, non-empty set* $\mathrm{dom}(le) = C \subseteq D$ *satisfying* $\forall c_1 \neq c_2 \in \mathrm{dom}(le) : c_1 \| c_2$. $\mathcal{L}_D$ *is the set of all levels on domain D.*

A relation on levels of one domain can easily be derived from subsumption on categories. This relation focuses on providing sensible aggregation paths from finer to coarser levels. Thus, categories of the higher level must in each case be *completely* disaggregated on the lower one. Furthermore, we distinguish cases in which not a complete level, but just a single category of a level is partitioned (as also proposed in [8]):

Definition 2 (A relation on levels). *A level le is said to be* FINER *than level le' ($le \lhd le'$, cf. Fig. 1) if*

1. $\exists c' \in le' : c' \equiv \bigvee \mathrm{dom}(le)$ *(just one category disaggregated) or*
2. $\forall c' \in \mathrm{dom}(le') : c' \equiv \bigvee \{c \in \mathrm{dom}(le) | c \preceq c'\}$ *(complete level le' disaggregated)*
   – *distinguishing two subcases:*

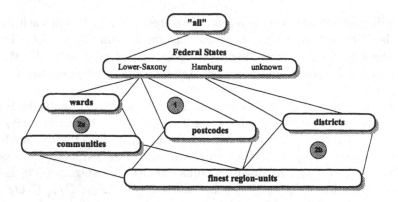

Fig. 1. Example of a category hierarchy on regions

(a) $\bigvee \mathrm{dom}(le) \equiv \bigvee \mathrm{dom}(le')$, *i. e. the levels are "equivalent", or*
(b) this is not the case, i. e. the finer level covers a larger range.

To ensure completeness of disaggregation for a category c', categories subsumed by c' with semantics "c', not otherwise specified" will frequently be introduced in the finer level.

A dimension on domain D primarily defines a category hierarchy of levels covering that part of D which is of interest for the respective application domain.

Definition 3 (Dimensions and category hierarchies). *A* DIMENSION $d = (D, L, le_0)$ *on domain D is defined by*

- *a finite set $L \subseteq \mathcal{L}_D$ of levels and*
- *a* ROOT LEVEL $le_0 \in L$ *satisfying* $\mathrm{dom}(le_0) = \{c_0\}$ *and* $\forall le \in L : \forall c \in \mathrm{dom}(le) : c \preceq c_0$ *(c_0 corresponds to a value "all").*

Relation "$\lhd$" restricted to L is called CATEGORY HIERARCHY *of d.*

Figure 1 outlines a graph-based representation of a category hierarchy on regions showing the respective categories only on state-level. Furthermore, Cases (1), (2a), and (2b) in Definition 2 are marked – with "Hamburg" and "Lower-Saxony" being subdivided in different ways and "finest region units" existing for both of these states.

The sense in defining category hierarchies shall be summarized in the context of using them in a dataflow-based analysis environment: They

1. define typical aggregation paths in multidimensional databases with respect to one category attribute,
2. provide groups of categories aggregating *completely* to another category, and
3. guarantee disjointness of categories (for single-valued features).

Thus, they facilitate correct handling of macrodata – many approaches to summarizability (cf. [9]) and automatic aggregation are made much easier by considering categories statements on features.

3.2   Multidimensional Dataspaces

Macrodata define multidimensional dataspaces, the dimensionality of which is described by category attributes and which contain fact data described by summary attributes in their cells.

Similar to dimensions defining possible values for category attributes, measures define types of summary attributes:

Definition 4 (Measures). *A* MEASURE $m = (T, F)$ *is defined by a set T of possible measure values (e. g. the natural or real numbers, often supplemented by some null-values) and a number of calculation functions defining how m can be derived from different measures. In detail, F is a set of pairs, each consisting of a set of source measures $\{m_1, \ldots, m_n\}$ and a function $f \colon \mathbb{N}^{m_1.T \times \ldots \times m_n.T} \to m.T$.*

An example of a measure is the incidence rate with type "real" and calculation from "case count" and "person years" by division and weighting with $\frac{1}{100,000}$ – in this case, function f is just defined for value-sets with only *one* element pair. Another example would be the age-standardized rate, which aggregates over a *set* of age-specific case and population data in a weighted sum.

Summary attributes are "instances" of measures related to a specific object-set and defining aggregation functions for aggregating summary data to coarser levels or categories.

Definition 5 (Summary attributes). *A* SUMMARY ATTRIBUTE $sa = (m, O, f^{\mathrm{sum}}, f^{\mathrm{aggr}})$ *on measure m is defined by*

- *the set of objects O described by sa,*
- *a (partial)* SUMMARY FUNCTION $f^{\mathrm{sum}} \colon 2^O \to m.T$ *defining the calculation of sa-values for subsets of O,*
- *a family of (partial)* AGGREGATION FUNCTIONS $(f^{\mathrm{aggr}}_{f,O})_{f \in \mathcal{F}, O \subseteq O}$ *with $f^{\mathrm{aggr}}_{f,O} \colon \mathbb{N}^{m.T \times D_f} \to m.T$, i. e. measure values for given categories $c_1, \ldots, c_n$ are aggregated to a value related to the category $c = c_1 \vee \ldots \vee c_n$.*

sa is called SUMMARIZABLE *w. r. t. feature f and object-set O if $f^{\mathrm{aggr}}_{f,O}$ is total, it is called* DISJOINT SUMMARIZABLE *if this function is defined for all sets of pairwise disjoint categories.*

Obviously, f^{sum} and f^{aggr} have to be consistent – we do without a formal definition of this relation here.

Definition 6 (Category attributes). *A* CATEGORY ATTRIBUTE $ca = (O, f, C)$ *is defined by a set of objects O described by a feature f and a set $\mathrm{dom}(ca) = C \subset D_f$ of categories describing f. Let $\mathcal{CA}$ denote the set of all category attributes.*

Note that categories of an attribute are not restricted to one aggregation level as is often the case in existing data models.

Now we are able to define dataspaces describing macrodata:

Definition 7 (Dataspaces). *A* DATASPACE *$ds = (O, CA, sa)$ is defined by the underlying object-set O, a set $CA = \{ca_1, \ldots ca_n\}$ of category attributes describing different features and a summary attribute sa satisfying $sa.O = O = ca.O$ for all $ca \in CA$.*

The instance of a dataspace is given by an object-set $\mathrm{inst}(O) \subseteq O$ and a total function $f^{\mathrm{inst}} \colon \mathrm{dom}(ca_1) \times \ldots \times \mathrm{dom}(ca_n) \to sa.m.T$. This function is derived from the summary function f^{sum} of sa – we leave out the details here.

Let $\mathcal{DS}$ denote the set of all dataspaces.

An example of a dataspace are population data (summary attribute "average yearly population count") by time and region (category attributes) with population count being disjoint summarizable (by addition) over all features except for those relating to the time dimension.

3.3   Aggregation and Restriction of Dataspaces

Aggregation and restriction are the two most important operations on multidimensional dataspaces. Due to preparing definitions in the previous sections, we are able to unite these two neatly in one single operation, namely derivation.

At first, derivation of categories will be introduced, describing how categories are composed of other ones. Based on this composition of categories along one dimension, complete dataspaces can be aggregated from finer ones by grouping values of the respective measure using the associated aggregation function.

Definition 8 (Derivation of categories). *A category c' in domain D is said to be* DERIVABLE *from a set $C \subseteq D$ of categories if $\exists C_{c'} \subseteq C : c' \equiv \bigvee C_{c'}$. If categories of $C_{c'}$ are even pairwise disjoint, then c' is called* DISJOINT DERIVABLE *from C (w. r. t. a feature $f \in \mathcal{F}_D$ and an object-set O).*

Definition 9 (Derivation of dataspaces). DERIVATION *of one dataspace from another is defined by a (partial) function $f^{\mathrm{der}} \colon \mathcal{DS} \times CA \to \mathcal{DS}$. Given a dataspace $ds = (O, CA, sa)$ and a category attribute ca' describing feature f, $f^{\mathrm{der}}(ds, ca') = ds'$ is defined ("ds' is* DERIVABLE *from ds") if*

1. *$ca'.O = O$,*
2. *$\exists ca \in CA \colon ca.f = f$,*
3. *$\mathrm{dom}(ca') \subseteq \mathrm{dom}(ca)$ (only restriction, no aggregation needed) or sa is summarizable over f and O, and*
4. *all categories in ca' are derivable[1] from $\mathrm{dom}(ca)$.*

In this case, $ds' = (O, (CA \setminus \{ca\}) \cup \{ca'\}, sa)$ with its instance satisfying

$$\forall c' \in \mathrm{dom}(ca') \colon f^{\mathrm{inst}'}(\ldots, c', \ldots) = sa.f^{\mathrm{aggr}}(\{(f^{\mathrm{inst}}(\ldots, c, \ldots), c) \mid c \in C_{c'}\})$$

over the same object-set $\mathrm{inst}(O)$ as ds (with $C_{c'}$ – not necessarily unique – as in Definition 8 and f^{inst} denoting the instance of ds).

---

[1] If all categories are disjoint derivable from $\mathrm{dom}(ca)$, disjoint summarizability of sa is sufficient in (3).

Derivation of dataspaces is the basic operation in navigating through multidimensional databases and will be investigated in detail in the next section.

In this section, fundamental concepts of *MADEIRA* have been introduced. We had to skip over many interesting details of the model, as for example

- more than one summary attribute per dataspace,
- more than one object-set (and feature) described by an attribute,
- multiple object-sets, playing certain *roles* for summary attributes,
- null-values, set-valued features, and
- further basic operations on dataspaces (union, join, etc.),

but the ideas described so far will be sufficient to show in the remainder of this paper how this underlying data model can be used to define and improve basic data analysis facilities of *VIOLA*.

4   Interactive Data Processing Based on *MADEIRA*

Interplay of the data model *MADEIRA* and visual dataflow-based analysis in *VIOLA* is essential for describing analysis sessions to the user: The latter provides him with the exact calculation history of (intermediate) results and the former describes the respective meaning of data values by measure definitions, represented object-sets, and their classification by categories modelled independently of a specific dataspace in dimensions and category hierarchies.

But also the definition of the visual programming language provided by *VIOLA* and internal data processing are significantly influenced and supported by the design of *MADEIRA*. In the following, some examples and corresponding ideas will be outlined without formalizing all details but using and motivating the concepts of *MADEIRA*.

4.1   Flexible Data Management

In view of the fact, that navigation in dataspaces, searching for "interesting" subspaces, and comparing subsets of a dataspace amounts to a substantial part of exploratory data analyses, flexible data management support is of crucial importance. Different useful variants of derivation as introduced in Definition 9 should be used to define operators (i. e. types of derivation nodes) of *VIOLA* supporting typical navigation steps in a kind of visual query language.

Figure 2 shows some examples of deriving dataspaces from a one-dimensional spatial dataspace and visualizing the respective results in different ways. The numbers of derivation operators correspond to the types of derivation introduced below. Three spatial aggregation levels are used: *communities* ◁ *wards* ◁ *regional prosperity* (defining groups of wards with similar average income).

A *derivation node* (parameterized with a category attribute ca') applies $f^{der}(\cdot, ca')$ to any dataspace ds to be processed, with ca' being defined by

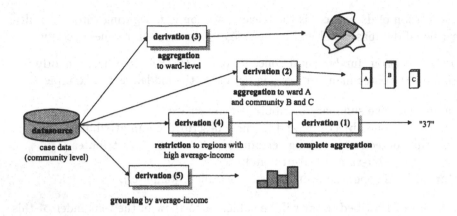

Fig. 2. Instances of derivation in visual queries

- a feature f of an object-set O,
- the corresponding category attribute ca of ds (if existing),
- one of the following five node types (cf. Fig. 2), and
- (in Case 2 to 5) a set of categories $C' \subset D_f$ (e.g. a complete level),

such that $\mathrm{dom}(ca') =$

1. $\bigvee \mathrm{dom}(ca)$ (complete aggregation of one attribute to a total).
2. C' ("pure" derivation).
3. $\{c' \in C' \mid c'$ derivable from $\mathrm{dom}(ca)\}$ (only (disjoint) derivable categories).
4. $\mathrm{dom}(ca) \cap \{c \in D_f \mid c \preceq \bigvee C'\}$ (restriction to categories subsumed by C').
5. $\{\bigvee\{c \in \mathrm{dom}(ca) \mid c \preceq c'\} \mid c' \in C'\}$ (non-complete (as opposed to Case 2) grouping to categories in C').

This list and the corresponding implementation is, of course, open for further instances of derivation.

Thus, we see how explicit modelling of levels and categories (their disjointness and equivalence) on the one hand and summary attributes with differentiated aggregation functions on the other allow intelligent and – above all – automatic aggregation of macrodata.

4.2   Selection of Analysis Methods

Graph nodes in *VIOLA* representing statistical analysis functions are determined by the calculated measure m (cf. Definition 4). Thus, selection of necessary and suitable input data for a node is given by the calculation functions $m.F$.

Correspondingly given a dataspace with a summary attribute for measure m_1, the out-port of the respective graph node may be connected to a node representing measure m if $m.F$ contains a tuple $(M, \cdot)$ satisfying $m_1 \in M$. Additionally, further members of M define further input measures, i.e. dataspaces

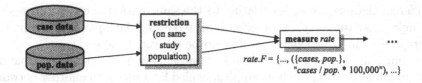

Fig. 3. Calculation of rates from case and population data

needed to calculate m (see the example in Fig. 3). *VIOLA* should help the user to find suitable corresponding graph nodes.

This concept of method selection might be improved by defining a type hierarchy on measures which would allow to group elements of $m.F$. Furthermore, weighting of applicability distinguishing more levels than just "yes" or "no" might be introduced. This extends *VIOLA* to a simple knowledge-based system giving advice which methods are better applicable to a given dataspace than others. For example, some statistical procedures perform "better" on continuous data (measures) than on discrete data or vice versa.

Selection of visualization functions might be supported in a similar way. Additional inclusion of a dataspace's category attributes (their features and dimensions) in rating applicability would be very valuable here, e. g. for specifying that maps are only applicable to spatial data or that certain charts afford one-, two- or three-dimensional data. Finally, *VIOLA* is easily extended with new analysis components by defining a new type of graph node, a new measure and the ways of calculating it from existing measures.

4.3   Caching and Further Query Optimization

Data processing in *VIOLA* is demand-driven. After determining the descriptions (given by summary and category attributes) of requested dataspaces for all nodes of a dataflow-net by propagating descriptions of queries from data sources through all network branches, the calculation of dataspace instances is controlled by output nodes propagating data requests back to the data sources.

Each graph node corresponds to a cache entry in working memory which makes available dataspaces for more efficient processing of further calculations in different parts of a network or even different analysis sessions. Definition 7 provides a semantic description of a cache entry. Before requesting input data due to the network specification and afterwards calculating the result of a node, the cache is searched for dataspaces from which the desired dataspace is derivable (cf. Definition 9). Thus, also cache admission and replacement strategy base on a measure of "generality" of dataspaces, describing how many other (typically requested) dataspaces are derivable from a cache entry.

Definition and types of derivation as introduced in Sect. 4.1 also permit combining subsequent data management procedures in a single derivation step (and dataspace traversal) even w. r. t. different features. Moreover, data source nodes might incorporate subsequent data management steps in a single query unless intermediate results are needed.

Different data source nodes relating to the same database can be processed in a single database query which extends all requested dataspaces to a common "superspace" from which single results can be derived, if necessary.

Summing up, cache management and optimization lead to a transparent transformation of a data analysis graph specified by a user into another network more efficiently processed. This facilitates efficient query processing as multiple queries can be processed in combination, but also poses new questions of how to handle interactive network modifications. Their translation into transformations and extensions of the cache-based derivation graph in an "intelligent" way must combine the paradigm of "dataflow-based visual queries" with known techniques for query optimization.

4.4   Control Structures

MADEIRA also supports control structures allowing for more complex sequences of data analyses. In this paper, we just want to mention loops describing repetitive processing of groups of calculations on different subspaces of a dataspace, e. g. for automatic report generation or incidence monitoring. A "loop counter" can be defined by

- a set of features and respective dimensions,
- an aggregation path consisting of a sequence $le_1 \lhd \ldots \lhd le_n$ of related levels,
- or a level le specifying a set of categories,

the elements of which are used as parameters of a derivation operator in different loop iterations. Besides conditional branching, this defines a simple (especially always terminating), but useful operator supporting typical routine tasks and enhancing the strictly sequential data processing in existing OLAP-tools.

5   Interactive Graphics

Section 4.1 emphasized the importance of data management and navigation in multidimensional dataspaces for performing data analysis flexibly and effectively. This section will propose a different way of implementing these operations aiming at active integration of the user into the exploration process (cf. [10]).

Similar to the idea of visual programming centering around interactive manipulation of the whole process of data analysis, special concepts of interacting with analysis results are needed. Tables and graphics must not only constitute final products, but should also serve as a starting point for further comparative and deepening analyses.

Dynamic queries [11] provide a simple, but powerful example to meet these requirements. They enable the user to restrict dataspaces *interactively* during inspection of results, e. g. using sliders over certain dimensions (or features). This is simply implemented by data management nodes as introduced in Sect. 4.1 (typically of, but not restricted to type (4) or – using appropriate visual grouping operators – (5)) which propagate their results in real-time. This kind of *really*

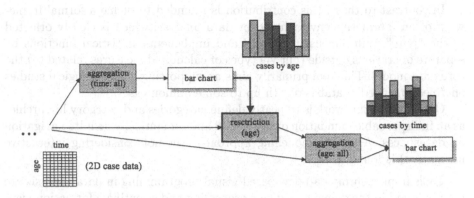

Fig. 4. Linking two charts in a dataflow-programme

interactive navigation facilitates flexible search for interesting subspaces and thus adds a further "dimension" to usually only one- or two-dimensional charts.

Based upon dynamic queries, *linking* of different charts dynamically relates two or more visualization results with each other instead of relating data management and visualization (see e. g. [12]). A typical instance of linking is *linked highlighting*: Subspaces of a dataspace selected in one chart (usually by a subset of one category attribute's elements) are highlighted in another chart that shows a dataspace derived from the former (or a common ancestor). Figure 4 outlines an exemplary implementation in a dataflow-chart: A dataset with case data classified by year of diagnosis and age is visualized in two charts, one after aggregation over each dimension. Selection of age-groups in the first chart highlights the respective shares of cases in all age-groups in the time chart.

Implementations of this concept in existing data analysis systems (e. g. S-Plus or SAS-Insight) are often restricted to linking between charts that show parts of the same dataspace. Besides, they allow no intermediate statistical calculations. Modelling linking in a dataflow-based visual analysis environment as outlined in Fig. 4 provides much more flexibility and can be defined neatly. In terms of Sect. 4.1, the chart serving as the "source" of linking just provides a "normal" data management node with the set C' of categories to define the category attribute for derivation. This node anew can process an *arbitrary* dataspace with a category attribute related to the respective feature. Furthermore, the user is free to carry out further calculations before visualizing the linked dataspace.

6   Related Work

During the last few years, several approaches to modelling multidimensional data have been proposed (cf. [3]). Most of them based on a relational implementation of macrodata in *star schemes*. Powerful operations, also incorporating microdata, especially support queries on very large business databases which make use of various statistical analysis functions.

In contrast to those, this contribution is intended to define a formal framework of an interactive environment for data analysis which is closely oriented to the "pure" multidimensional model and implements statistical functions by separate operations outside (but via types of calculated measures related to) the core data model. This tool primarily aims at supporting epidemiological studies on "medium-sized" databases with up to some million cases.

One focus of this work is to neatly define categories and category hierarchies as an indispensable foundation of structured and semantically definite navigation on dataspaces. A similar modelling approach (yet not considering interactive navigation) is found in [7].

Tools implementing dataflow-based visual programming in data analysis are mainly found in the domains of image processing and scientific information visualization (e. g. IBM Data Explorer [13] or AVS [14]). However, interactive exploration and intelligent processing of multidimensional databases is possible with restrictions only: typical OLAP-operations are not explicitly provided, immediate database support including caching mechanisms is missing, and interactive graphics are not available.

Another similar approach is the project IDEA [15], which also designs an environment for database-supported data exploration, but without taking special requirements of handling multidimensional data into account.

7   Summary and Future Work

In this paper, some basic elements of a visual data analysis environment based on a formal multidimensional data model have been introduced.

Visual language and formal model cooperate and complete one another in making data analyses exactly comprehensible. The dataflow-view provides the user with an appropriate overview of an analysis session and aims at easy operation and intuitive exploration, whereas the data model (especially the formal representation of category hierarchies, measures and aggregation functions) serves an exact definition of data semantics as well as correct and partially automatic application of analysis methods.

However, several tasks are still subject to future work:

- incorporation of even more semantic metadata for better user support,
- complete implementation of *MADEIRA*, possibly based on an existing data warehousing or OLAP tool, which provides efficient management of multidimensional data,
- integration of *MADEIRA* into a dataflow programming language using some kind of formal workflow modelling,
- elaboration and implementation of the ideas introduced in Sect. 4 and 5, and
- evaluation of all concepts within an epidemiological information system for the cancer registry of Lower-Saxony[2] and (later on) in similar domains — especially w. r. t. acceptance among typical user groups, e. g. epidemiologists.

---

[2] Parts of the data model are already successfully implemented and used in routine analysis, processing relational base data stored in an ORACLE database. Further-

The crucial task in system design will be to provide an environment which helps the user to concentrate on the exploratory data analysis process itself, to interact with data and methods *directly*, and *not* primarily to operate a tool.

References

[1] S. Chaudhuri and U. Dayal. An overview of data warehousing and OLAP technology. *SIGMOD Record*, 26(1):65–74, 1997.

[2] E. Woods, E. Kyral, et al. *OVUM evaluates OLAP*. OVUM Ltd, 1996.

[3] M. Blaschka, C. Sapia, G. Höfling, and B. Dinter. Finding your way through multidimensional data models. In *Proc. Int. Workshop on Data Warehouse Design and OLAP Technology (DWDOT), Wien*, 1998.

[4] D. J. Hand. Intelligent data analysis: Issues and opportunities. In *Advances in Intelligent Data Analysis (Proc. IDA'97)*, pages 1–14. Springer Verlag, 1997.

[5] D. D. Hils. Visual languages and computing survey: Data flow visual programming languages. *Journal on Visual Languages and Computing*, 3(1):69–101, 1993.

[6] F. Wietek. Die Epi-Workbench – ein graphischer Editor zur Modellierung deskriptiver epidemiologischer Studien. *KI–Journal. Schwerpunkt KI und Medizin*, 3:27–31, 1997.

[7] L. Cabibbo and R. Torlone. A logical approach to multidimensional databases. In *6th Int. Conf. on Extending Database Technology (EDBT)*, pages 183–197. Springer Verlag, 1998.

[8] W. Lehner, J. Albrecht, and H. Wedekind. Normal forms for multidimensional databases. In *10th Int. Conf. on Scientific and Statistical Database Management (SSDBM)*, pages 63–72. IEEE Press, 1998.

[9] H.-J. Lenz and A. Shoshani. Summarizability in OLAP and statistical data bases. In *9th Int. Conf. on Scientific and Statistical Database Management (SSDBM)*, pages 132–143. IEEE Press, 1997.

[10] R. R. Springmeyer, M. M. Blattner, and N. L. Max. A characterization of the scientific data analysis process. In *Proc. IEEE Visualization 1992*, pages 235–242.

[11] B. Shneiderman. Dynamic queries for visual information seeking. *IEEE Software*, 11(6):70–77, 1994.

[12] W. S. Cleveland and M. E. McGill, editors. *Dynamic Graphics for Statistics*. Wadsworth & Brooks / Cole Advanced Books and Software, Belmont, CA, 1988.

[13] B. Lucas, G. D. Abram, et al. An architecture for a scientific visualization system. In *Proc. IEEE Visualization 1992*, pages 107–114.

[14] C. Upson, J. Faulhaber, et al. The application visualization system: A computational environment for scientific visualization. *IEEE Computer Graphics and Applications*, 9(4):30–42, 1989.

[15] P. G. Selfridge, D. Srivastava, and L. O. Wilson. IDEA: Interactive data exploration and analysis. In *Proc. SIGMOD'96*, pages 24–35, 1996.

more, a prototypical implementation of a visual dataflow-based environment has been applied in evaluating a study of avoidable mortality in Lower-Saxony.

Towards Quality-Oriented Data Warehouse Usage and Evolution

Panos Vassiliadis[1], Mokrane Bouzeghoub[2], Christoph Quix[3]

[1] National Technical University of Athens, Greece, pvassil@dbnet.ece.ntua.gr
[2] University of Versailles and INRIA, France, Mokrane.Bouzeghoub@prism.uvsq.fr
[3] Informatik V, RWTH Aachen, Germany, quix@informatik.rwth-aachen.de

Abstract. As a decision support information system, a data warehouse must provide high level quality of data and quality of service. In the DWQ project we have proposed an architectural framework and a repository of metadata which describes all the data warehouse components in a set of metamodels to which is added a quality metamodel, defining for each data warehouse metaobject the corresponding relevant quality dimensions and quality factors. Apart from this *static* definition of quality, we also provide an *operational* complement, that is a methodology on how to use quality factors and to achieve user quality goals. This methodology is an extension of the Goal-Question-Metric (GQM) approach, which allows to capture (a) the inter-relationships between different quality factors and (b) to organize them in order to fulfil specific quality goals. After summarizing the DWQ quality model, this paper describes the methodology we propose to use this quality model, as well as its impact on the data warehouse evolution.

1 Introduction

Many researchers and practitioners share the understanding that a data warehouse (DW) architecture can be formally understood as layers of materialized views on top of each other. A DW architecture exhibits various layers of data in which data from one layer are derived from data of the lower layer. *Data sources*, also called *operational databases*, form the lowest layer. They may consist of structured data stored in open database systems and legacy systems, or unstructured or semi-structured data stored in files. The central layer of the architecture is the *global* (or *primary*) *DW*. The global DW keeps a historical record of data that result from the transformation, integration, and aggregation of detailed data found in the data sources. Usually, a data store of volatile, low granularity data is used for the integration of data from the various sources: it is called *Operational Data Store (ODS)*. The Operational Data Store, serves also as a buffer for data transformation and cleaning so that the DW is populated with clean and homogeneous data. The next layer of views are the *local*, or *client* warehouses, which contain highly aggregated data, directly derived from the global warehouse. There are various kinds of local warehouses, such as the *data marts* or the *OLAP databases* which may use relational database systems or specific multidimensional data structures.

M. Jarke, A. Oberweis (Eds.): CAiSE'99, LNCS 1626, pp. 164-179, 1999.
© Springer-Verlag Berlin Heidelberg 1999

All the DW components, processes and data are -or at least should be- tracked and administered from a *metadata repository*. The metadata repository serves as an aid both to the administrator and the designer of a DW. Indeed, the DW is a very complex system, the volume of recorded data is vast and the processes employed for its extraction, transformation, cleansing, storage and aggregation are numerous, sensitive to changes and time-varying. The metadata repository serves as a maproad which provides a trace of all design choices and a history of changes performed on its architecture and components. For example, the new version of the *Microsoft Repository* [1] and the *Metadata Interchange Specification* (MDIS) [9] provide different models and application programming interfaces to control and manage metadata for OLAP databases. In figure 1, a generic architecture for a DW is depicted.

As a decision support information system, a DW must provide high level quality of data and quality of service. Coherency, freshness, accuracy, accessibility, availability and performance are among the quality features required by DW users. The metadata repository plays a central role in this concern, as it provides the necessary knowledge to understand, evaluate and analyze current DW architecture in order to predict its behaviour and the resulting quality of service and quality of data.

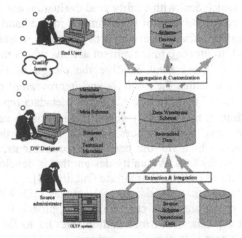

Fig. 1. A generic architecture for a data warehouse

Data quality has been defined as the fraction of performance over expectancy, or as the loss imparted to society from the time a product is shipped [3]. We believe, though, that the best definition is the one found in [13,11,17,14]: data quality is defined as "fitness for use". The nature of this definition directly implies that the concept of data quality is relative. For example, data semantics (the interpretation of information) is different for each distinct user. As [11] mentions "the problem of data quality is fundamentally intertwined in how [...] users actually use the data in the system", since the users are actually the ultimate judges of the quality of the data produced for them: if nobody actually uses the data, then nobody will ever take care to improve its quality.

From the previous it follows that, on one hand, the quality of data is of highly *subjective* nature and should ideally be treated differently for each user. But, on the other hand, the reasons for data deficiencies, non-availability or reachability problems are definitely *objective*, and depend mostly on the information system definition and implementation. Furthermore, the prediction of data quality for each user must be based on objective quality factors which are computed and compared to users' expectations. The question that arises, then, is how to tune the design choices in such a way that all the different, and sometimes opposing, user requirements can be simultaneously satisfied. As the number of users and the complexity of DW systems do not permit to reach total quality for every user, the subsidiary question is how to prioritize these requirements in order to satisfy them with respect to their importance. This problem is typically illustrated by the physical design of the DW where the problem is to find a set of materialized views which optimize user requests response time and the global DW maintenance cost.

In [6] a metadata modeling approach is presented that enables the capturing of all the crucial parts of the architecture of a DW, along with information over different quality dimensions of these components. In this paper, we have refined the quality metamodel with a more detailed linkage between objective quality factors and user-dependent quality goals. Moreover, we have extended the Goal-Question-Metric (GQM) methodology [2] in order (a) to capture the inter-relationships between different quality factors with respect to a specific quality goal, and (b) to define an appropriate lifecycle which deal with quality goal evaluation and improvement.

Our methodology comprises a set of steps aiming, in one hand, to map a high-level subjective quality goal into the measurement of a set of interrelated quality factors, and, in the other hand, to propose improvement actions which may help in achieving the target quality goal. These steps involve the *design* of the quality goal, the *evaluation* of the current status, the *analysis* and *improvement* of this situation, and finally, the *re-evaluation* of the achieved plan. The metadata repository together with this quality goal definition methodology constitute a decision support system which helps DW designers and administrators to take relevant decisions to achieve reasonable quality level which fits the best user requirements. This work is being integrated in a methodology for DW quality design, that is developed in the European DWQ project (Foundations of Data Warehouse Quality) [8].

We want to stress out that we do not follow the ISO 900x paradigm in our approach; rather we try to present a computerized approach to the stakeholder, for both the storage and exploitation of information relevant to the quality of the DW. The objective of this paper is to show how subjective quality goals can be evaluated using more objective quality factors, following an extended GQM approach.

The paper is organized as follows: section 2 describes the DWQ quality metamodel and an example for its instantiation. In section 3, we detail the DWQ methodology for quality management. Section 4 presents some hints on DW evolution. Section 5 summarizes related work and finally section 6 we discusses our results.

2   Metadata Repository and Quality Model

This section summarizes the nature of metadata used in the DWQ framework and gives an overview of the DWQ quality model. The section particularly focuses on the quality dimensions and quality factors associated to the main DW meta objects. As an example, the refreshment process is taken with its corresponding quality factors, because it is an crucial process for the quality of a DW.

2.1   Architecture Components

In the DWQ project we have advocated the need for enriched metadata facilities for the exploitation of the knowledge collected in a DW. In [6], it is shown that the DW metadata should track both architecture components and quality factors.

The proposed categorization of the DW metadata is based on a 3x3 framework, depicted in Figure 2: we identified three *perspectives* (conceptual, logical and physical) and three *levels* (source, DW, client). We made the observation, that the conceptual perspective, which represents the real world of an enterprise, is missing in DW projects, with the risk of incorrectly representing, or interpreting the information found in the DW.

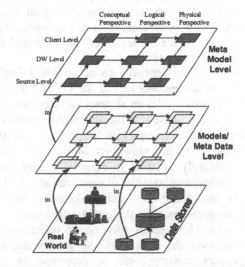

Fig. 2. The Data Warehouse Architecture Meta-Model

The proposed *metamodel* (i.e. the topmost layer in Figure 2) provides a notation for DW generic entities, such as schema, or agent, including the business perspective. Each box shown in figure 2 is decomposed into more detailed DW objects in the metamodel of [6]. This metamodel is instantiated with the *metadata* of the DW (i.e. the second layer in Figure 2), e.g. relational schema definitions or the description of the conceptual DW model. The lowest layer in Figure 2 represents the real world where the actual processes and data reside: in this level the metadata are instantiated with data instances, e.g. the tuples of a relation or the objects of the real world which are represented by the entities of the conceptual model.

2.2   Quality Metamodel

Each object in the three levels and perspectives of the architectural framework can be subject to quality measurement. Since quality management plays an important role in DWs, we have incorporated it in our meta-modeling approach. Thus, the quality model is part of the metadata repository, and quality information is explicitly linked with architectural objects. This way, stakeholders can represent their quality goals explicitly in the metadata repository, while, at the same time, the relationship between the measurable architecture objects and the quality values is retained.

The DWQ quality metamodel [7] is based on the Goal-Question-Metric approach (GQM) of [10] originally developed for software quality management. In GQM, the high-level user requirements are modeled as goals. Quality metrics are values which express some measured property of the object. The relationship between goals and metrics is established through quality questions.

The main difference in our approach resides in the following points: (i) a clear distinction between subjective quality goals requested by stakeholder and objective quality factors attached to DW objects, (ii) quality goal resolution is based on evaluation of the composing quality factors, each corresponding to a given quality question, (iii) quality questions are implemented and executed as quality queries on the semantically rich metadata repository.

Figure 3 shows a simplified conceptual view of the DWQ Quality Model. The class 'DW object type' refers to any meta-object of the DWQ framework depicted in the first layer of figure 2. A *quality goal* is an abstract requirement, defined on DW object types, and documented by a purpose and the stakeholder interested in. This roughly expresses natural language requirements like 'improve the availability of source s1 until the end of the month in the viewpoint of the DW administrator'. *Quality dimensions* (e.g. 'availability') are used to classify quality goals and factors into different categories. Furthermore, quality dimensions are used as a vocabulary to define quality factors and goals; yet each stakeholder might have a different vocabulary and different preferences in the quality dimensions. Moreover, a quality goal is *operationally* defined by a set of *questions* to which *quality factor* values are provided as possible answers. As a result of the goal evaluation process, a set of improvements (e.g. design decisions) can be proposed, in order to achieve the expected quality. A quality factor represents an actual measurement of a quality value, i.e. it relates quality values to measurable objects. A quality factor is a special property or characteristic of the related object wrt. the quality dimension of the quality factor. It also represents the expected range of the quality value, which may be any subset of the quality domain. Dependencies between quality factors are also stored in the repository.

The quality meta-model is not instantiated directly with concrete quality factors and goals, it is instantiated with patterns for quality factors and goals. The use of this intermediate instantiation level enables DW stakeholders to define templates of quality goals and factors. For example, suppose that the analysis phase of a DW project has detected that the availability of the source database is critical to ensure that the daily online transaction processing is not affected by the loading process of the DW. A source administrator might later instantiate this template of a quality goal with the expected availability of his specific source database. Thus, the programmers of the DW loading programs know the time window of the update process.

Based on the meta-model of DW architecture, we have developed a set of quality factor templates which can be used as a initial set for DW quality management. The exhaustive list of these templates can be found in [12]. The following section gives an intuition of some of them which are associated to the DW refreshment process.

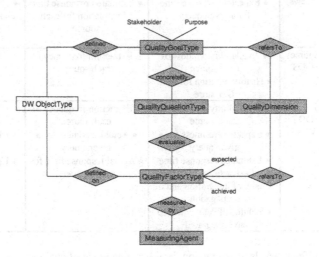

Fig. 3. The DWQ Quality Metamodel (simplified)

2.3   Quality Metamodel Instantiation: The Refreshment Case

As shown in [6], it is not sufficient to describe a DW as layers of materialized views on top of each other. For example, a view definition is not sufficient to capture the semantics of the refreshment process. Indeed, a view definition does not include the information whether this view operates on a history or not, how this history is sampled, which transformations are necessary during the refreshment, whether the changes of a given source should be integrated each hour or each week, and which data timestamp should be taken when integrating changes of different sources. Consequently, based on the same view definitions, a refreshment process may produce different results depending on all these extra parameters which have to be fixed independently, outside the queries which define the views. A detailed description for the refreshment process can be found in [4].

As mentioned before, the refreshment process is one of the main DWs processes for which the quality is an important issue. The associated quality template includes quality dimensions such as coherence, completeness and freshness.

- *Data coherence*: the respect of (explicit or implicit) integrity constraints from the data. For example, the conversion of values to the same measurement unit allows also to do coherent computations.
- *Data completeness*: the percentage of data found in a data store, with respect to the necessary amount of data that should rely there.
- *Data freshness*: the age of data (with respect to the real world values, or the date when the data entry was performed).

Quality Dim.	DW objects	Primary Quality Factors	Derived Quality Factors	Design Choices
Coherence	Sources ODS Views	• Availability window of each source • Expected response time for a given query	• Extraction frequency of each source • Estimated response time of extraction for each source	• Granularity of data • Extraction and cleaning policy • Integration policy
Completeness	Sources ODS	• Availability window of each source • History duration for each DW store	• Extraction frequency of each source	• Extraction policy • Integration policy
Freshness	Sources ODS Views	• Availability window of each source • Expected freshness for a given query • Estimated response time of extraction for each source, of integration and of propagation • Volume of data extracted and integrated	• Extraction frequency of each source • Actual freshness for a given query • Actual response time for a given query	• Extraction policy • Integration policy • Update policy

Table 1. Different levels of abstraction for the management of quality in a data.

Given a quality dimension, several low level quality factors of this dimension may be defined in a DW. For example, one can define quality factors like the *availability window* or the *extraction frequency* of a source, the *estimated values for the response time* of an algorithm or the *volume of the data extracted each time*, etc. However, the quality factors are not necessarily independent of each other, e.g., completeness and coherence may induce a certain accuracy of data. We discriminate between *primary* and *derived* quality factors as well as *design choices*. A primary quality factor is a simple estimation of a stakeholder or a direct measurement. For example, the completeness of a source content may be defined with respect to the real world this source is supposed to represent. Hence, the completeness of this source is a subjective value directly assigned by the DW administrator or the source administrator. On the other hand, derived quality factors are computed as formulae over some other quality factors: for example, the completeness of the operational data store content can be defined as a formula over the completeness of the sources. The design choices are a special kind of quality factors, expressed as parameter values and control strategies which aim to regulate or tune the algorithm followed for the performance of each task in the DW.

We believe that quality dimensions, quality factors and design choices are tightly related. For example, in the case of the refreshment process, the design choice 'extraction policy' is related to the derived quality factor 'extraction frequency' of each source, which is computed from the corresponding primary quality factor 'availability window' of each source. In table 1, we mention several quality factors which are relevant to the refreshment process and link them to the corresponding DW objects and quality dimensions. One can also notice that some quality factors may belong to more than one dimension. Some of them are primary quality factors, arbitrarily assigned by the DW administrator, others are derived. Deriving procedures can be either mathematical functions, logical inferences or any *ad hoc* algorithms. The values of derived quality factors depend on design choices which can evolve with the semantics of the refreshment process. Underlying the design choices are design techniques, that are all rules, events, optimizations and algorithms which implement the strategies on which refreshment activities are based.

3   Exploitation of the Metadata Repository and the Quality Metamodel

This section describes the DWQ methodology to exploit the quality metamodel on the basis of the meta-data repository. We first present the different phases and steps of our methodology.

Our approach extends GQM, based on the idea that a goal is operationally defined over a set of questions. Thus, we provide specific "questions" for the full lifecycle of a goal: this way the DW metadata repository is not simply defined statically, but it can be actually exploited in a systematic manner. Underlying our methodology, we exploit:

Our approach for quality management is based on two folds:

- A metadata repository which provides all the necessary knowledge to understand quality goals, quality factors and their related DW objects. This repository allows to trace design decisions, and to report on the history of quality goals with their successive evaluations and improvements.
- A computational engine composed of all the deriving procedures of quality factors. The techniques underlying this engine can be simple functions and procedures or more sophisticated reasoning mechanisms. In the case of performance evaluation of a given query, a mathematical function is generally sufficient while in the case of coherence validation of a conceptual schema we need a more sophisticated inference mechanism.

Based on this, the DWQ methodology for quality management is composed of three main phases: (i) the design phase which elaborates a quality goal by defining its purpose, the set of questions to solve it and the set of quality factors which answer to these questions; (ii) an evaluation phase which deals with the computation of quality factors; (iii) an analysis and improvement phase which gives an interpretation to the quality goal evaluation and suggests a set of improving actions.

In Figure 4, we graphically present our methodological approach for quality management. This methodology is influenced by the TQM paradigm, which has also been adopted by other approaches such as TDQM [14]. The DWQ methodology suggests four major *steps* (or else *phases of a lifecycle*) when dealing with a quality goal: *design, current status evaluation, analysis and improvement* and *re-evaluation* of a quality goal. In the sequel we provide a detailed presentation of a set of questions corresponding to each step of each process. Before proceeding, we would like to mention that the proposed methodology does not consist of a strict algorithm: one may choose to ignore several steps, according to the specific situation he is tackling.

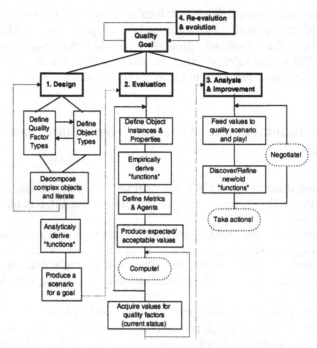

Fig. 4. DW Quality management

3.1   The Design Phase

When dealing with a quality goal, we assume that there is always a first time when the *stakeholder* defines the goal. The *design process* of the goal is the first phase of its interaction with the stakeholder and should result in the selection of the involved object types and their quality factors.

There are two steps which can take place at the same time: *the identification of the object types which are related to the goal* and the respective low level *quality factors*. The identification of the object types, tries to reuse the experience stored in the metadata repository: the metamodel is powerful enough to model the relationships not only at the instance but at the type level as well.

Nevertheless, these steps alone are not sufficient to characterize a quality goal. Since the identified object types are most probably composite (e.g. a schema is composed from several relations) one has to *decompose them at a satisfactory level of detail*. For example, if the examined type is the *refreshment process*, one can try to decompose it into more refined objects such as *data extraction, data cleaning and transformation, data integration and high level aggregation*.

The next step deals with *identification of the inter-relationships between objects and quality factors*. Each object can be viewed as a node of graph. Every node in the graph has input and output arcs, determining the interdependencies of the DW components with respect to their quality factors. Several design choices are by default encapsulated in the figure (e.g. the simple fact that the data of a materialized view stem from source data). The input arc to the graph is the high level quality dimension expressed by the user. The output is the set of specific quality factors which measure this quality dimension.

The goal of this process is, not only to set up a list of the "ingredients" of the problem, but also, to come up with a list of "functions", determining the outcome of the quality of an object, in terms both of its own characteristics and of the quality of other objects affecting it. We call the outcome of the process, the *scenario* of the quality goal.

More specifically, to produce the list of functions, one has to try and analytically define the inter-relationships by inspecting the peculiarities of the problem. For example, one could use either a Pareto diagram [3] to determine the timeliness of a materialized view, or a function taking into respect the availability of the sources, the frequency of updates and queries and the capacity of the propagators.

We do not advocate that these functions can always be derived or discovered in an analytic form: yet (a) as we will show there are truly cases where this can happen, (b) in the absence of an analytical form we can use empirical knowledge and (c) it is important to note that even the existence of an interdependency link can be used as a boolean function to denote dependency.

Example. In the example of Figure 5, we try to quantify a quality dimension: the *believability* of the information delivered to the final user. To achieve this goal, we decide that we have to measure a specific quality factor: the *accuracy* of the data in the views used by the final users. The scenario is composed from all the components participating in the refreshment of a view: the *source database* (which in terms is decomposed to a set of *source relations*), the *transformation agents* converting the data to the desired format and the *DW/ODS views*, each one possibly defined on top of another view. We also provide an analytical function for the accuracy of a view, calculating it from the size and the accuracy of the input data.

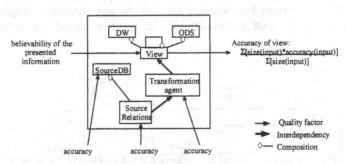

Fig. 5. The scenario of a quality goal

A fascinating feature of a scenario is the tracking of the *inverse relationships* between the quality factors. In other words, by describing the interdependencies of the quality factors, not only do we get a clear view of the way the overall quality of our final "product" is influenced, but also we get a first insight of how to remedy an undesired situation. For example, in Figure 5, we can improve the believability of our information by increasing its accuracy, something which in terms can be achieved through the improvement of the accuracy of the transformation agents or the source relations. In the case of redundant information, one can also increase the volume of the utilized data from a source with higher accuracy. In any case, to generalize this observation, the inverse functions can be either analytical relationships or inverse interdependency path on the scenario.

3.2   The Evaluation Phase

After the design process, the following step is the *evaluation of the current status*. The purpose of the evaluation phase is to construct a detailed *map* based on the constructed scenario, which describes accurately all the interplaying components and factors. This can also be the first step, when a goal has already been defined in the past and a scenario has been developed and is currently reused.

First, we must *determine the specific object instances* of the specific evaluation through a query to the metadata repository. In the example of Figure 5, one can identify two source relations (S_1, S_2), pumping data to two views in the ODS (V_1, V_2), through a respective transformation agent and a final view (V_3), the accuracy of which we have to quantify (Figure 6).

Next, one must take into account several *design choices*, i.e. the properties of the interplaying objects which influence the quality of the outcome. In our example, one can take into account the size of the propagated data, the time windows of the sources, the regularity of the refreshment, etc. For reasons of simplicity of the presentation and since we deal only with the accuracy factor, we retain only the size of the propagated data and the view definitions.

Apart from the component refinement, we can also refine the interrelationships between the quality factors. The refinement can be performed either through the use of analytical formulae or direct instantiations in the scenario, based on the empirical knowledge of a specific situation. Empirical knowledge can be obtained from simple observation or through the use of well-tested techniques such as statistical process control (SPC), concurrent engineering, etc. [3]. In our example, simple sampling could show that in the past, the transformation agent increased the accuracy of the data by 2.

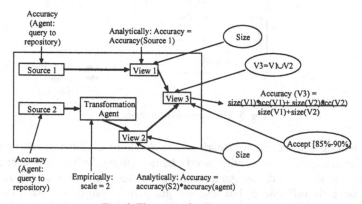

Fig. 6. The map of a quality goal

Then, for each quality factor one should also determine the *metrics* and *measuring agents*. If no measuring agent(s) has ever been defined, one must determine the computation procedure for the actual values of the quality factors. Also, the parameters of the measuring procedures should be set accordingly.

The final step is the addition of *acceptable/expected values for each quality factor*, wherever necessary. This is a crucial step for the evaluation of the current status later on. The accepted range of values will be the basic criterion for the objective judgment of a subjective quality goal. The outcome of this step should provide the stakeholder with a well defined *map* of the problem (see also Figure 6).

With respect to the scenario of Figure 5, the map is enriched with (a) agents for the computation of primary quality factors (e.g. the queries at the metadata repository), (b) formulae for the computation of the derived quality factors, (c) properties of the components such as the view definition or the size of the propagated data and (d) acceptable ranges of values (e.g. accuracy of view 3).

After that, the only thing left is the acquisition/calculation of the specific values of the selected quality factors, though the necessary computation. In Figure 7, a certain instance of our exemplary map is depicted.

The acquisition of these values is performed through the use of the already defined measuring agents. In fact, we anticipate that if the values are regularly (i.e. not on-demand) computed and stored in the metadata repository, then their acquisition can be done through a simple query to the metadata repository.

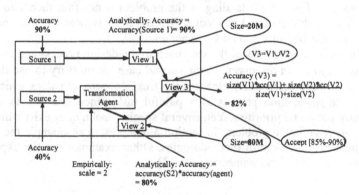

Fig. 7. Instance of a quality map

Here we must clarify again, that several steps can be omitted. In fact, if we consider that the metadata repository is regularly refreshed through an external agent, then some of the intermediate steps of this process can be avoided.

3.3   The Analysis and Improvement Phase

At the end of the second phase, the map of Figure 7 is fully instantiated with actual values. Yet, if the situation is not obviously satisfactory, the stakeholder may choose to react against it. Although this is a process with different characteristics each time, we can still draw some basic guidelines for the steps that can be taken. Consider for example the case in Figure 7, where the computed accuracy for view 3 is not within the accepted range. Obviously there must be some reaction against this undesired situation.

One of the main advantages of our approach is that if we have an understanding of the mechanism that produces the problem, we can attack the problem directly through the use of the inverse quality functions, which have been derived during the design phase or detected during the evaluation phase. Again, by 'inverse functions' we mean both the possible analytical functions and the inverse interrelationships in the map of the problem.

The inverse functions in our example suggest that an increase of 10% for the accuracy of view 3 calls for one of the following actions:

a) Use the analytical formulae directly: increase of 10% to the accuracy of views 1 and 2 (directly through the formula), which in terms implies:

- increase of the accuracy of source 1 by 10%;
- increase of the accuracy of source 2 by 5% or the accuracy of the agent by 10% or a combination of the two.

b) Customize the reaction to the specific characteristics of the situation: Through the use of the specific measurements one could also try to derive a plan taking into account the sizes of the input views. For example, elementary calculations prove that it suffices to increase the accuracy of source 2 to 45%, for the quality of the view 3 to be in the accepted range.

Nevertheless, there is always the possibility that this kind of approach is not directly feasible. If our understanding of the problem is not full, then steps must be taken so that we deepen our knowledge. Moreover, it is possible that the derived solution is not feasible -or is too costly to achieve.

In the first case we must go all the way back to the design process and try to *refine the steps of the function discovery*. In the second case we must try to use the inverse functions in order to *determine which are the feasible limits of values* which we can negotiate. The negotiation process is a painful task, since one has to deal with contradictory goals and priorities. Yet, several specific techniques exist which can be applied to the negotiation problem. In section 5, we present as example the QFD and the Statistical Process Control methodologies. Other examples are the experimental design, the Taguchi quality engineering etc. [3].

4   The Data Warehouse Evolution

A DW is a very complex system whose components evolve frequently independently of each other. Users can create new views or update old ones. Some sources may disappear while others are added. The enterprise model can evolve with the enterprise objectives and strategies. The technical environment changes with products evolution and updates. Design choices at the implementation level can also evolve to achieve users requirements and administration requirements.

In this evolving context, the re-evaluation of a goal and of the strategy to achieve is a strict contingency in a DW environment. There are 3 main reasons for this:

- (a) *evolution reasons*: there are natural changes happening in such a complex environment;
- (b) *failure in the achievement of the desired quality*, and
- (c) *meta-quality:* we can never be sure for the quality of our measuring processes.

In the sequel we will detail the first of these reasons. DWs can evolve in many different ways. The *data stores* can produce changes due to reasons of schema evolution in logical and conceptual perspective, changes to the physical properties of the source (e.g. location, performance etc.), insertions or deletions of a data store, specific reasons due to their nature (e.g. in the sources, the time window for extraction or the data entry process can change). The *software components* can be upgraded, completed, debugged, etc. The *propagation agents* of all types (loaders/refreshers/ wrappers/mediators/source integrators) can obtain new schedules, new algorithms, rules, physical properties, etc. Needless to say that the *user requirements* continuously change, too. New requirements arise, while old ones may become obsolete, new users can be added, priorities and expected/acceptable values change through the time, etc. Moreover, the *business rules* of an organization are never the same, due to real world changes.

As a result of evolution and errors, our goals, components, scenarios and maps are never to be fully trusted. Each time we reuse previous results we must always consider cases like: lack of measurement of several objects, errors in the measurement procedure (e.g. through an agent which is not appropriate), outdated information of the repository with respect to the DW, etc.

A way to control this evolution is to provide a complementary meta-data which tracks the history of changes and provides a set of consistency rules to enforce when a quality factor has to be re-evaluated. To do so, it is necessary to link quality factors to evolution operators which affect them. The idea behind this is to enrich the meta-data repository in order to ease the impact analysis of each evolution operator and its consequences on the quality factor measures.

5   Related Work

There has ben much research on the definition and measurement of data quality dimensions [18,15,17,13]. A very good review is found in [16]. The GQM methodology is best presented in [10,2].

The *TDQM* methodology [14] follows the Total Quality Management approach, adapted for the evaluation of data quality in an information system (by assuming that each piece of produced information can be considered a product). The TDQM methodology also follows the TQM cycle: *Definition, Measurement, Analysis, Improvement*. The Definition part identifies the important quality dimensions and the corresponding requirements. The Measurements step produces the quality metrics. The Analysis step identifies the roots of any quality problems and their interplay, while the Improvement step provides techniques for improving the quality of information.

Negotiation techniques enable the negotiation over the desired quality of a system. *Statistical Process Control* (SPC) is one of the best tools for monitoring and improving product and service quality [3]. SPC comprises of several techniques, such as Pareto diagrams (used to identify the most important factors of a process), process flow diagrams, cause and effect (or Ishikawa) diagrams, check sheets, histograms and control charts.

Quality Function Deployment, (QFD) [5,3] is a team-based management technique, used to map customer requirements to specific technical solutions. This philosophy is based on the idea that the customer expectations should drive the development process of a product. The basic tool used in QFD is the so-called "House of Quality", mapping user expectations to technical solutions, taking into account priorities and conflicts. However, while QFD certainly has a useful role in rough quality planning and cross-criteria decision making, using it alone would throw away the richness of work created by research in measuring, predicting, or optimizing individual DW quality factors.

6   Conclusions

In this paper, we deal with the problem of quality-oriented design, usage and evolution of DWs. As explained also in previous papers we store semantically rich meta information of a DW in our DWQ repository concerning the conceptual, logical and physical perspective of a DW. In addition, the information on the quality of the stored objects is recorded in the repository.

In our view, the quality of the DW is an aggregated view of the metadata and data of the warehouse. For example, the quality of the DW depends on the quality of the sources, the quality of the extraction process and the quality of the DW components itself. One can think of the quality factors as materialized views over the metadata and data of the warehouse; thus the evolution of the DW can be seen as a view maintenance problem on the aggregated quality views. For example, if a source is changed -- either its data or its properties (metadata) -- the quality of the source must be recomputed. All objects and their quality which depends on this source must be adapted to the new situation.

The application of our GQM-like methodology helps us to (a) design and (b) maintain the knowledge about this evolution efficiently. We make extensive use of our metadata repository, so that the information is obtained in a controlled, efficient fashion. We have elaborated on our quality metamodel, in order to track the basic primitives of the interrelationships between DW components and quality factors. We also extend GQM so that we can both take advantage of the interrelationships of components and track the full lifecycle of a stakeholders' requirement.

We exploit the dependencies and computation functions of quality factors. For example, in the case a new source is integrated, we just have to compute the quality of this source and recompute the DW and data mart quality using the information of the process quality, which describes how the data is transformed and what improvement or debasement to the data quality has been made.

In addition to the maintenance process of the quality, the inverse of the computation functions for the quality factors can be used, to find the DW object which has to be improved to reach a certain quality goal. This process can be compared with the view update process in databases systems, where updates to views (here: quality views) are translated to updates in base data (here: quality factors).

As of now, our metamodel and methodology have been validated only partially. As future work, we plan to fully validate and refine them through the development of software tools and application to major case studies.

Acknowledgments. This research is sponsored by the European Esprit Project "DWQ: Foundations of Data Warehouse Quality", No. 22469. We would like to thank all our DWQ partners who contributed to the progress of this work, and especially Prof. Matthias Jake, Manfred Jeusfeld and Maurizio Lenzerini. Many thanks are also due to the anonymous reviewers, for useful comments.

References

1. P.A. Bernstein, Th. Bergstraesser, J. Carlson, S. Pal, P. Sanders, D. Shutt. Microsoft Repository Version 2 and the Open Information Model. *Information Systems* 24(2), 1999.
2. V. R. Basili, G.Caldiera, H. D. Rombach. The Goal Question Metric Approach. *Encyclopedia of Software Engineering - 2 Volume Set*, pp 528-532, John Wiley & Sons, Inc., available at http://www.cs.umd.edu/users/basili/papers.html, 1994
3. D. H. Besterfield, C. Besterfield-Michna, G. Besterfield, M. Besterfield-Sacre, Total Quality Management, Prentice Hall, 1995
4. M. Bouzeghoub, F. Fabret, M. Matulovic, E. Simon. Data Warehouse Refreshment: A Design Perspective from Quality Requirements. Tech. Rep. D 8.5, DWQ Consortium, 1998.
5. E. B. Dean, "Quality Functional Deployment from the Perspective of Competitive Advantage", available at http://mijuno.larc.nasa.gov/dfc/qfd.html, 1997
6. M. Jarke, M.A.Jeusfeld, C. Quix, P. Vassiliadis: Architecture and Quality in Data Warehouses, In *Proc. CAiSE 98*, Pisa, Italy, 1998.
7. M.A. Jeusfeld, C. Quix, M. Jarke: Design and Analysis of Quality Information for Data Warehouses. In *Proc. 17th Intl. Conf. on the Entity Relationship Approach (ER'98)*, Singapore, 1998.
8. M. Jarke, Y. Vassiliou. Foundations of data warehouse quality – a review of the DWQ project. In *Proc. 2nd Intl. Conference Information Quality (IQ-97)*, Cambridge, Mass., 1997.
9. Metadata Coalition: Meta Data Interchange Specification, (MDIS Version 1.1), August 1997, available at http://www.he.net/~metadata/standards/ .
10. M. Oivo, V. Basili: Representing software engineering models: the TAME goal-oriented approach. *IEEE Transactions on Software Engineering*, 18, 10, 1992.
11. K. Orr. Data quality and systems theory. In *Communications of the ACM*, 41, 2, Feb. 1998.
12. C. Quix, M. Jarke, M. Jeusfeld, M. Bouzeghoub, D. Calvanese, E. Franconi, M. Lenzerini, U. Sattler, P. Vassiliadis. Quality Oriented Data Warehouse Evolution. Tech. Rep. D9.1, DWQ Consortium, 1998.
13. G. K. Tayi, D. P. Ballou: Examining Data Quality. In *Com. of the ACM*, 41, 2, Feb. 1998.
14. R. Y. Wang. A product perspective on total data quality management. In *Com. of the ACM*, 41, 2, Feb. 1998.
15. R.Y. Wang, H.B. Kon, S.E. Madnick. Data Quality Requirements Analysis and Modeling. *Proc. 9th Intl. Conf. on Data Engineering*, IEEE Computer Society, Vienna, Austria, 1993.
16. R.Y. Wang, V.C. Storey, C.P. Firth. A Framework for Analysis of Data Quality Research. IEEE Transactions on Knowledge and Data Engineering, Vol. 7, No. 4, August 1995.
17. R.Y. Wang, D. Strong, L.M. Guarascio. Beyond Accuracy: What Data Quality Means to Data Consumers. Technical Report TDQM-94-10, Total Data Quality Management Research Program, MIT Sloan School of Management, Cambridge, Mass., 1994.
18. Y. Wand, R.Y. Wang. Anchoring Data Quality Dimensions in Ontological Foundations. Communications of the ACM, Vol. 39, No. 11, November 1996.

Designing the Global Data Warehouse with SPJ Views*

Dimitri Theodoratos, Spyros Ligoudistianos, and Timos Sellis

Department of Electrical and Computer Engineering
Computer Science Division
National Technical University of Athens
Zographou 157 73, Athens, Greece
{dth,spyros,timos}@dblab.ece.ntua.gr

Abstract. A global Data warehouse (DW) integrates data from multiple distributed heterogeneous databases and other information sources. A global DW can be abstractly seen as a set of materialized views. The selection of views for materialization in a DW is an important decision in the implementation of a DW. Current commercial products do not provide tools for automatic DW design.
In this paper we provide a generic method that, given a set of SPJ-queries to be satisfied by the DW, generates all the 'significant' sets of materialized views that satisfy all the input queries. This process is complex since 'common subexpressions' between the queries need to be detected and exploited. Our method is then applied to solve the problem of selecting such a materialized view set that fits in the space allocated to the DW for materialization and minimizes the combined overall query evaluation and view maintenance cost. We design algorithms which are implemented and we report on their experimental evaluation.

1 Introduction

In the Data Warehousing approach to the integration of data from multiple distributed heterogeneous databases and other information sources, data are extracted in advance from the sources and stored in a repository (Data Warehouse - DW). When a query is issued against the DW, it is evaluated locally, without accessing the original information sources. DWs are used by companies for decision support applications. Therefore, ensuring high query performance is one of the most significant challenges when implementing a DW.

A DW can be abstractly seen as a set of materialized views defined over source relations. When the source relations change, the materialized views need to be updated. Different maintenance policies (deferred or immediate) and maintenance strategies (incremental or rematerialization) can be applied [2]. This choice depends on the needs of the specific application for currency of the data and view maintenance performance.

* Research supported by the European Commission under the ESPRIT Program LTR project "DWQ: Foundations of Data Warehouse Quality"

M. Jarke, A. Oberweis (Eds.): CAiSE'99, LNCS 1626, pp. 180–194, 1999.
© Springer-Verlag Berlin Heidelberg 1999

A typical DW architecture [1] comprises tree layers. The data at each layer is derived from the data of lower layers. At the lowest layer there are the distributed operational data sources. The central layer is the *global* or *principal Data Warehouse*. The upper layer contains the *local DWs* or *Data marts*. The global DW integrates the data from the distributed data sources. Data marts contain highly aggregated data for extensive analytical processing. They are also probably less frequently updated than global DWs. Here we deal with global DWs. In the following, DW refers to the global DW.

In this paper we address the issue of selecting views for materialization in a DW given a set of input queries. This is an important decision in the implementation of a DW. Current commercial products do not provide tools for automatic DW design.

The materialized view selection issue is complex. One of the reasons of its complexity lies on the fact that the input queries may contain subexpressions that are identical, equivalent or more generally subexpressions such that one can be computed from the other. We describe these subexpressions by the generic term *common subexpressions*. Common subexpressions in the input queries need to be detected and exploited in the view selection process. They can significantly reduce the view maintenance cost and the space needed for materialization.

Computing the input queries using exclusively the materialized views requires the existence of a complete rewriting of the queries over the materialized views [7]. Many formulations of the problem of selecting views to materialize in a DW [3, 14], do not explicitly impose this condition.

Contribution. In this paper we present a generic method for designing a global DW. This method detects and exploits common subexpressions between the queries and guarantees the existence of a complete rewriting of the queries over the selected views. We provide a set of transformation rules for Select-Project-Join (SPJ) queries that, starting with the input queries, generate alternative view selections for materialization and a complete rewriting of the queries over the selected views. These transformation rules are sound, minimal and complete; in this sense all the "significant" view selections are non-redundantly generated.

We then address the following problem (called *DW design problem*):
Given a set of queries to be satisfied by the DW, select a set of views to materialize in the DW such that:
1. The materialized views fit in the space available at the DW.
2. All the queries can be answered locally using this set of materialized views.
3. The combination of the query evaluation cost and the view maintenance cost (*operational cost*) is minimal.
Based on the transformation rules, we model the DW design problem as a state space search problem. A solution to the problem can be found (if a solution to the problem exists) by defining equivalent states and exhaustively enumerating all equivalence classes.

Our approach is implemented for a class of SPJ-queries. We design algorithms that significantly prune the search space using cost-based and other heuristics, and we report on their experimental evaluation

This approach was initially adopted in [12] for a *restricted class* of selection-join queries and it is extended here by: (a) considering space constraints in the formulation of the DW design problem, (b) considering a broader class of queries involving projections and "pure" Cartesian products, and (c) implementing the approach and testing the new algorithms experimentally.

Outline. The rest of the paper is organized as follows. The next section contains related work. In Section 3, we formally state the DW design problem after providing some basic definitions. Section 4 introduces the transformation rules. In Section 5 the DW design problem is modeled as a state space search problem. Section 6 presents pruning algorithms and implementation issues. Experimental results are provided in Section 7. Finally, Section 8 contains concluding remarks and possible extension directions.

2   Related Work

The view selection problem has been addressed by many authors in different contexts. [5] provides algorithms for selecting a set of views to materialize that minimizes the query evaluation cost, under a space constraint, in the context of aggregations and multidimensional analysis. This work is extended in [4] where greedy algorithms are provided, in the same context, for selecting both views and indexes. In [3] greedy algorithms are provided for the view selection problem when queries are represented as AND/OR expression dags for multiple queries.

In [9], given a materialized SQL view, an exhaustive approach is presented as well as heuristics for selecting additional views that optimize the total view maintenance cost. [6] considers the same problem for select-join views and indexes. Space considerations are also discussed. Given an SPJ view, [8] derives, using key and referential integrity constraints, a set of auxiliary views other than the base relations that eliminate the need to access the base relations when maintaining both the initial and the auxiliary views (i.e. that makes the views altogether self-maintainable).

[10, 14] aim at optimizing the combined query evaluation and view maintenance cost: [10] provides an A* algorithm in the case where views are seen as sets of pointer arrays under a space constraint. [14] considers the same problem for materialized views but without space constraints. [3] provides a formalization of the problem of selecting a set of views that minimizes the combined cost under a space constraint but it does not provide any algorithm for solving the problem in the general case. [14, 3] consider a DW environment where all the source relations are available locally for computation.

None of the previous approaches requires the queries to be answerable exclusively from the materialized views. This requirement is taken into account in [12, 13] where the view selection problem is addressed with ([13]) and without ([12]) space constraints, but for a class of selection-join queries.

3 Formal Statement of the DW Design Problem

We consider that a non-empty set of queries $\mathbf{Q}$ is given, defined over a set of source relations $\mathbf{R}$. The DW contains a set of materialized views $\mathbf{V}$ over $\mathbf{R}$ such that every query in $\mathbf{Q}$ can be rewritten completely over $\mathbf{V}$ [7]. Thus, all the queries in $\mathbf{Q}$ can be answered locally at the DW, without accessing the source relations in $\mathbf{R}$. Let Q be a query over $\mathbf{R}$. By Q^V, we denote a complete rewriting of Q over $\mathbf{V}$.We write $\mathbf{Q}^V$, for a set containing the queries in $\mathbf{Q}$, rewritten over $\mathbf{V}$. Given $\mathbf{Q}$, a *DW configuration* $\mathbf{C}$ is a pair $< \mathbf{V}, \mathbf{Q}^V >$.

Consider a DW configuration $\mathbf{C} =< \mathbf{V}, \mathbf{Q}^V >$. The *query evaluation cost* of the queries in $\mathbf{Q}^V$, denoted $E(\mathbf{Q}^V)$, is the weighted sum of the evaluation cost of each query rewriting in $\mathbf{Q}^V$. The view maintenance cost of the views in $\mathbf{V}$, denoted $M(\mathbf{V})$, is the weighted sum of the view maintenance cost of each view in $\mathbf{V}$ in the presence of the other views in $\mathbf{V}$. Note that the maintenance cost of a view depends on the presence of other views in the DW [9, 8]. The *operational cost* of $\mathbf{C}$, denoted $T(\mathbf{C})$, is $cE(\mathbf{Q}^V) + M(\mathbf{V})$. The parameter c indicates the relative importance of the query evaluation and view maintenance cost. The *storage space* needed for materializing the views in $\mathbf{V}$, denoted $S(\mathbf{V})$, is the sum of the space needed for materializing each view in $\mathbf{V}$.

The *DW design problem* can now be stated as follows.

Input: A set of queries $\mathbf{Q}$.

The functions: E for the query evaluation cost, M for the view maintenance cost, and S for the materialized views space.

The space available in the DW for materialization t.

A parameter c.

Output: A DW configuration $\mathbf{C} =< \mathbf{V}, \mathbf{Q}^V >$ such that $S(\mathbf{V}) \leq t$, and $T(\mathbf{C})$ is minimal.

4 Transformation Rules

In order to model the DW design problem as a state space search problem we introduce a set of DW configuration transformation rules for a class of SPJ views. These rules operate on a graph representation for multiple views.

4.1 Multiquery Graphs

We consider the class of relational expressions involving projection, selection and join operations that are equivalent to relational expressions of the standard form $\pi_X \sigma_F (R_1 \times \ldots \times R_k)$. The R_is $i \in [1, k]$, denote relations. The formula F is a conjunction of atoms (atomic formulas) of the form $A \ op \ B + c$ or $A \ op \ B$ where op is one of the comparison operators $=, <, \leq, >, \geq$ (but no $\neq$), c is an integer valued constant and A, B are attributes from the R_i's. Atoms involving attributes from only one relation are called *selection atoms*, while those involving attributes from two relations are called *join atoms*. All the R_i's are distinct. X

is a non-empty set of attributes from the R_is. Queries and views considered here belong to this class.

Query rewritings over the views are in addition allowed to contain self-joins (and attribute renaming if the approach to the relational model that uses attribute names is followed).

A view can be represented by a *query graph*. Consider a view $V = \pi_X \sigma_F(R_1 \times \ldots \times R_k) \in \mathbf{V}$. The query graph G^V for V is a node and edge labeled multigraph defined as follows:

1. The set of nodes of G^V is the set of relations $R_1, \ldots, R_k$. Thus, in the following, we identify nodes with source relations. Every node R_i, $i \in [1, k]$, is labeled by an *attribute label for view* V. This is the (possibly empty) set of attributes of R_i in X, prefixed by V. An attribute label $V : *$ on a node R_i denotes that all the attributes of R_i are projected out in the view definition of V.
2. For every selection atom p in F involving one or two attributes of relation R_i, there is a loop on R_i in G^V labeled as $V : p$.
3. For every join atom p in F involving attributes of the relations R_i and R_j there is an edge between R_i and R_j in G^V labeled as $V : p$.

A set of views $\mathbf{V}$ can be represented by a *multiquery graph*. A multiquery graph allows the compact representation of multiple views by merging the query graphs of each view. For a set of views $\mathbf{V}$, the corresponding multiquery graph, $\mathbf{G}^V$, is a node and edge labeled multigraph resulting by merging the identical nodes of the query graphs for the views in $\mathbf{V}$. The label of a node R_i in $\mathbf{G}^V$ is the set containing the attribute labels of R_i in the query graphs for the views in $\mathbf{V}$. The edges of $\mathbf{G}^V$ are the edges in the query graphs for the views in $\mathbf{V}$.

Example 1. Consider the relations $R(K, A, B)$, $S(C, D)$, $T(E, F)$, and $U(G, H)$. Let V_1 and V_2 be two views over these relations defined as follows:
$V_1 = \pi_{KAE}(\sigma_{B<E+2}(\sigma_{K=A}(R) \bowtie_{B=C} \sigma_{C<D}(S) \bowtie_{D \leq E+2} \pi_E(T)))$, and
$V_2 = \pi_{EH}(\sigma_{C \leq D}(S) \bowtie_{D<E} T \bowtie_{E \geq G} \sigma_{H=3}(U))$.
Let $\mathbf{V} = \{V_1, V_2\}$. The multiquery graph $\mathbf{G}^V$ is depicted in Figure 1. This multiquery graph is used as a running example in this paper.

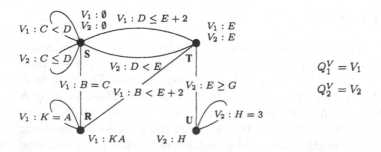

Fig. 1. The multiquery graph for $\mathbf{V}$, and a rewriting of $\mathbf{Q}$ over $\mathbf{V}$

Consider now the query set $\mathbf{Q} = \{Q_1, Q_2\}$, where
$Q_1 = \pi_{KAE}(\sigma_{K=A \wedge B=C \wedge C<D \wedge D \leq E+2 \wedge B<E+2}(R \times S \times T))$, and
$Q_2 = \pi_{EH}(\sigma_{C \leq D \wedge D<E \wedge E \geq G \wedge H=3}(S \times T \times U))$.
The queries in $\mathbf{Q}$ can be rewritten over $\mathbf{V}$ as shown in Figure 1. Thus Figure 1 shows the DW configuration $< \mathbf{G}^V, \mathbf{Q}^V >$, where $\mathbf{Q}^V = \{Q_1^V, Q_2^V\}$. This is the DW configuration $< \mathbf{G}^Q, \mathbf{Q}^Q >$.

4.2   Transformation Rules

We now present five *transformation rules* that can be applied to a DW configuration $< \mathbf{G}^V, \mathbf{Q}^V >$. Each transformation rule consists of two parts. A part that transforms the multiquery graph $\mathbf{G}^V$ and a part that transforms the query set $\mathbf{Q}^V$ by rewriting queries in $\mathbf{Q}^V$ over the new view set. Note that $\mathbf{Q}^V$ is not necessarily the rewriting of $\mathbf{Q}$ over $\mathbf{V}$ that yields the optimal query evaluation cost.

Transformation Rule 1 (Edge Removal). Let V be a view in $\mathbf{G}^V$, and e be an edge between nodes R_i and R_j labeled as $V : p$. Nodes R_i and R_j may coincide in which case e is a loop. Then,

1. $\mathbf{G}^V$ *transformation:*
   (a) If p is not implied by the rest of the atoms of V, replace in $\mathbf{G}^V$ the attribute label $V : Y_i$ $(V : Y_j)$ of R_i (R_j) by $V : Y_i \cup \{A\}$ $(V : Y_j \cup \{A\})$, where A is the attribute of R_i (R_j) occuring in p. In the particular case where R_i and R_j coincide in R_i, replace in $\mathbf{G}^V$ the attribute label $V : Y_i$ of R_i by $V : Y_i \cup Y$, where Y is the set of the attribute or the attributes of R_i occuring in p.
   (b) Replace every occurrence of V in $\mathbf{G}^V$ by a new view name V_1. New view names should not already appear in $\mathbf{G}^V$.
   (c) Remove e from $\mathbf{G}^V$.

2. $\mathbf{Q}^V$ *transformation:*
   Let X be the set of all the attributes appearing in attribute labels for V in $\mathbf{G}^V$. If p is not implied by the rest of the atoms of V, replace any occurrence of V in $\mathbf{Q}^V$, by the expression $\pi_X(\sigma_p(V_1))$. Otherwise, replace any occurrence of V in $\mathbf{Q}^V$, by V_1.

Example 2. Figure 2 illustrates the DW configuration resulting by three applications of rule 1, in sequence, to the edges labeled as $V_1 : B < E+2$, $V_1 : B = C$, and $V_2 : E \geq G$ of the multiquery graph depicted in Figure 1.

Transformation Rule 2 (Attribute Removal). Let V be a view in $\mathbf{G}^V$, X be the set of all the attributes appearing in attribute labels for V, and $A_1, \ldots, A_k, B_1, \ldots, B_k$ be attributes in X. If the atoms $A_1 = B_1, \ldots, A_k = B_k$, where $A_i \neq A_j$, and $A_i \neq B_j$, for every $i, j \in [1, k]$, are implied by the set of the atoms of V, then,

1. $\mathbf{G}^V$ *transformation:*
   (a) Replace every attribute label $V : Y_i$ in $\mathbf{G}^V$ by the attribute label $V : (Y_i - \{A_1, \ldots, A_k\})$.
   (b) Replace every occurrence of V in $\mathbf{G}^V$ by a new view name V_1.

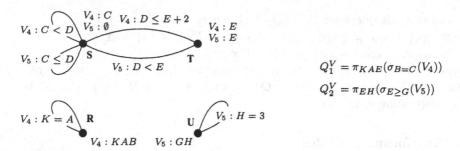

$$Q_1^V = \pi_{KAE}(\sigma_{B=C}(V_4))$$
$$Q_2^V = \pi_{EH}(\sigma_{E \geq G}(V_5))$$

Fig. 2. A DW configuration resulting by three applications of rule 1 (edge removal)

2. $\mathbf{Q}^V$ *transformation:*

Replace any occurrence of V in $\mathbf{Q}^V$, by $V_1 \bowtie_{A_1=B_1} \delta_{B_1 \to A_1}(\pi_{B_1}(V_1)) \bowtie_{A_2=B_2}$ $\dots \bowtie_{A_k=B_k} \delta_{B_k \to A_k}(\pi_{B_k}(V_1))$. The operator δ denotes the attribute renaming operator.

Example 3. The atom $K = A$ of view V_4 is implied by the set of the atoms of V_4 (it is even present in the set), and K and A occur in attribute labels for V_4. Thus rule 2 can be applied to view V_4 of Figure 2. The result of this application is depicted in Figure 3.

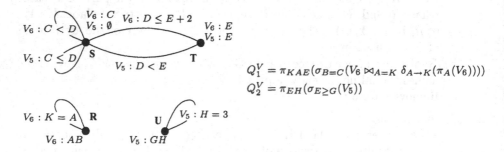

$$Q_1^V = \pi_{KAE}(\sigma_{B=C}(V_6 \bowtie_{A=K} \delta_{A \to K}(\pi_A(V_6))))$$
$$Q_2^V = \pi_{EH}(\sigma_{E \geq G}(V_5))$$

Fig. 3. A DW configuration resulting by an application of rule 2 (attribute removal)

Transformation Rule 3 (View Break). Let V be a view and N_1 and N_2 be two sets of nodes labeled by V, in $\mathbf{G}^V$, such that:

(a) $N_1 \not\subseteq N_2$ and $N_2 \not\subseteq N_1$.
(b) $N_1 \cup N_2$ is the set of all the nodes labeled by V in $\mathbf{G}^V$.
(c) There is no edge labeled by V in $\mathbf{G}^V$, between a node in $N_1 - N_2$ and a node in $N_2 - N_1$.

1. $\mathbf{G}^V$ *transformation:*

(a) Let V_1 and V_2 be new view names. To the label of every node in $N_1 - N_2$ $(N_2 - N_1)$, containing the attribute label $V : Y$, in $\mathbf{G}^V$, add the attribute label $V_1 : Y$ $(V_2 : Y)$. To the label of every node in $N_1 \cap N_2$, in $\mathbf{G}^V$, add the attribute labels $V_1 : *$ and $V_2 : *$.

(b) For every edge between nodes in N_1 (N_2) in $\mathbf{G}^V$, labeled as $V : p$, add an edge between the same nodes labeled as $V_1 : p$ ($V_2 : p$).

(c) Remove from $\mathbf{G}^V$ all the attribute labels for V, and all the edges labeled by V.

2. $\mathbf{Q}^V$ *transformation:*

Let X be the set of all the attributes appearing in attribute labels for V. Replace any occurrence of V in $\mathbf{Q}^V$, by $\pi_X(V_1 \bowtie V_2)$. The operator $\bowtie$ (without subscript) denotes the natural join operator.

Example 4. Consider the DW configuration of Figure 3. Rule 3 can be applied to view V_5 for $N_1 = \{S, T\}$ and $N_2 = \{T, U\}$. The resulting DW configuration is depicted in Figure 4.

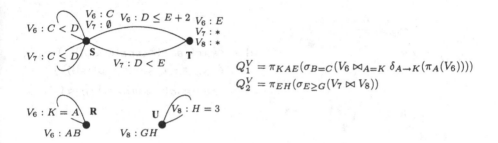

$$Q_1^V = \pi_{KAE}(\sigma_{B=C}(V_6 \bowtie_{A=K} \delta_{A \to K}(\pi_A(V_6))))$$
$$Q_2^V = \pi_{EH}(\sigma_{E \geq G}(V_7 \bowtie V_8))$$

Fig. 4. A DW configuration resulting by an application of rule 3 (view break)

Transformation Rule 4 (View Merging). Let V_1 and V_2 be two views in $\mathbf{G}^V$, and N_1 and N_2 be their sets of nodes respectively such that:

(a) There is no edge labeled by V_1 (V_2) between a node in $N_1 - N_2$ ($N_2 - N_1$) and a node in $N_1 \cap N_2$.

(b) For every atom p of V_1 (V_2) labeling an edge between nodes in N_1 (N_2), p implies or is implied by an atom of V_2 (V_1).

Then, let $\mathbf{F}$ be the set of the atoms p of V_1 such that p is implied by an atom of V_2 and is not implied by a different atom of V_1 and of the atoms p of V_2 such that p is implied by an atom of V_1 and is not implied by a different atom of V_2. Let $\mathbf{F}_1$ ($\mathbf{F}_2$) be the set of all the atoms of V_1 (V_2) in $\mathbf{G}^V$ that are not implied by $\mathbf{F}$, and X be the set of attributes occurring in $\mathbf{F}_1$ or $\mathbf{F}_2$.

1. $\mathbf{G}^V$ *transformation:*

(a) Let V be a new view name. To the label of every node R in $N_1 \cap N_2$ containing the attribute labels $V_1 : Y_1$ and $V_2 : Y_2$, add an attribute label $V : (Y \cup Y_1 \cup Y_2)$, where Y is the set of all the attributes of R in X. To the label of every node in $N_1 - N_2$ ($N_2 - N_1$) containing the attribute label $V_1 : Y_1$ ($V_2 : Y_2$), add the attribute label $V : Y_1$ ($V : Y_2$).

(b) For every atom p in $\mathbf{F}$, labeling an edge between nodes R_i and R_j (R_i and R_j may coincide), add to $\mathbf{G}^V$ an edge between R_i and R_j labeled as $V : p$.

For every atom p of V_1 (V_2) labeling an edge between nodes in $N_1 - N_2$ ($N_2 - N_1$), add to $\mathbf{G}^V$ an edge between the same nodes labeled as $V : p$.

(c) Remove from $\mathbf{G}^V$ all the attribute labels for V_1 or V_2 and all the edges labeled by V_1 or V_2.

2. $\mathbf{Q}^V$ *transformation:*

Replace any occurrence of V_1 (V_2) in $\mathbf{Q}^V$ by $\pi_{X_1}(\sigma_{F_1}(V))$ ($\pi_{X_2}(\sigma_{F_2}(V))$), where X_1 (X_2) is the set of all the attributes in attribute labels for V_1 (V_2), and F_1 (F_2) is the conjunction of the atoms in $\mathbf{F}_1$ ($\mathbf{F}_2$).

Example 5. Consider the DW configuration of Figure 4. Rule 4 can be applied to views V_6 and V_7 for $N_1 = \{R, S, T\}$ and $N_2 = \{S, T\}$. N_1 and N_2 satisfy the premise of the rule. Its application to the DW configuration of Figure 4 results in the DW configuration depicted in Figure 5.

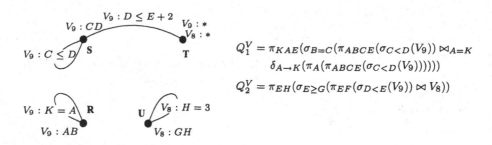

$$Q_1^V = \pi_{KAE}(\sigma_{B=C}(\pi_{ABCE}(\sigma_{C<D}(V_9)) \bowtie_{A=K}$$
$$\delta_{A \rightarrow K}(\pi_A(\pi_{ABCE}(\sigma_{C<D}(V_9))))))$$
$$Q_2^V = \pi_{EH}(\sigma_{E \geq G}(\pi_{EF}(\sigma_{D<E}(V_9)) \bowtie V_8))$$

Fig. 5. A DW configuration resulting by an application of rule 4 (view merging)

Transformation Rule 5 (Attribute Transfer). Let V be a view in $\mathbf{G}^V$, X be the set of all the attributes appearing in attribute labels for V, and $\{A_1, \ldots, A_k\}$ be a proper subset of X. If the atoms $A_1 = c_1, \ldots, A_k = c_k$, where c_i is a constant, $i = 1, \ldots, n$, are implied by the set of atoms of V, then,

1. $\mathbf{G}^V$ *transformation:*
   (a) Let V_1 and V_2 be new view names. To the label of every node containing the attribute label $V : Y$ in $\mathbf{G}^V$ add the attribute labels $V_1 : (Y - \{A_1, \ldots, A_k\})$ and $V_2 : (Y \cap \{A_1, \ldots, A_k\})$.
   (b) For every edge labeled as $V : p$ in $\mathbf{G}^V$ add two edges between the same nodes labeled as $V_1 : p$ and $V_2 : p$.
   (c) Remove from $\mathbf{G}^V$ all the attribute labels for V, and all the edges labeled by V.

2. $\mathbf{Q}^V$ *transformation:*
   Replace any occurrence of V in $\mathbf{Q}^V$, by $V_1 \times V_2$.

Example 6. Consider the DW configuration of Figure 5. The atom $H = 3$ is implied by the set of atoms of V_8 in $\mathbf{G}^V$ (it is even present in this set). The DW configuration in Figure 6 results by the application of rule 5 to V_8, for $k = 1$, and $A_1 = H$.

The set of the previous transformation rules is sound, complete and minimal [11].

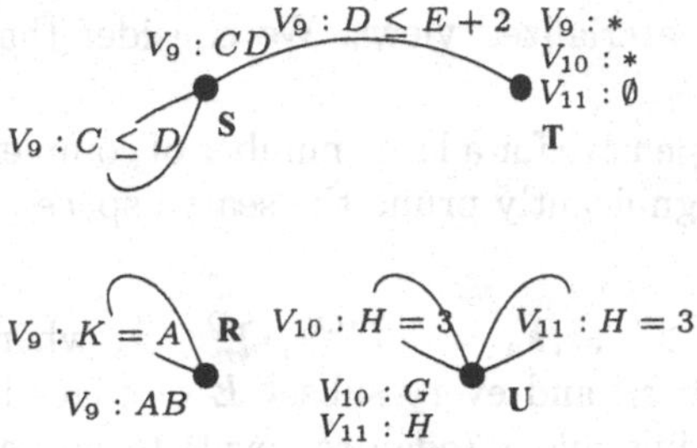

$$V_9 : CD \quad \overset{V_9 : D \leq E + 2}{\qquad} \quad \begin{matrix} V_9 : * \\ V_{10} : * \\ V_{11} : \emptyset \end{matrix}$$

$V_9 : C \leq D \quad \mathbf{S} \qquad\qquad \mathbf{T}$

$$Q_1^V = \pi_{KAE}(\sigma_{B=C}(\pi_{ABCE}(\sigma_{C<D}(V_9)) \bowtie_{A=K}$$
$$\delta_{A \rightarrow K}(\pi_A(\pi_{ABCE}(\sigma_{C<D}(V_9))))))$$

$$Q_2^V = \pi_{EH}(\sigma_{E \geq G}(\pi_{EF}(\sigma_{D<E}(V_9)) \bowtie$$

$V_9 : K = A \quad \mathbf{R} \quad V_{10} : H = 3 \quad V_{11} : H = 3 \qquad (V_{10} \times V_{11})))$

$V_9 : AB \qquad\qquad \begin{matrix} V_{10} : G \\ V_{11} : H \end{matrix} \quad \mathbf{U}$

Fig. 6. A DW configuration resulting by an application of rule 5 (attribute transfer)

5   The DW Design Problem as a State Space Search Problem

We now model the DW design problem as a state space search problem. We define states and transitions between states.

A *state* s is a DW configuration $\mathbf{C} =< \mathbf{G}^V, \mathbf{Q}^V >$. A particular state, the state $< \mathbf{G}^Q, \mathbf{Q}^Q >$ is called initial state and is denoted s_0.

With every state s a cost is associated through the function $cost(s)$. This is the operational cost $T(\mathbf{C})$ of the DW configuration $\mathbf{C}$. Also, a size is associate through the function $size(s)$. This is the space $S(\mathbf{V})$ needed for materializing the views in $\mathbf{V}$.

There is a transition $T(s, s')$ from state $s =< \mathbf{G}^V, \mathbf{Q}^V >$ to state $s' = < \mathbf{G}^{V'}, \mathbf{Q}^{V'} >$ if $< \mathbf{G}^{V'}, \mathbf{Q}^{V'} >$ can be obtained by applying any of the five transformation rules to $< \mathbf{G}^V, \mathbf{Q}^V >$.

Two states s and s' are *equivalent* if there is a renaming of the views in $\mathbf{V}$ that makes $\mathbf{G}^V$ and $\mathbf{G}^{V'}$ identical, and Q_i^V and $Q_i^{V'}$ equivalent, for every $Q_i^V \in \mathbf{Q}^V$.

Viewing the states as nodes and the transitions between them as directed edges, the *search space* is a directed graph determined by the initial state and the states we can reach from it following transitions in all possible ways. Equivalent states are represented in the search space by the same node. Clearly the search space is a rooted at s_0 directed acyclic graph.

The cost and the size of a state is computed *incrementally* when transiting from one state to another. Usually, a transformation rule affects a small number of views in $\mathbf{G}^V$ and of query rewritings in $\mathbf{Q}^V$. Thus, the incremental computation is a substantial improvement in the computation of the cost and a size of new states.

6   Implementation and Algorithms

Our approach is implemented for a class of SPJ-queries. For simplicity, queries and views are as defined in Section 4 but do not contain 'pure' Cartesian products. Query rewritings over the materilalized views are of the same form too. The maintenance cost model takes into account the cost of transmitting data between the DW and the data sources, the cost of computing view changes and the cost of applying the changes to the materialized views. We consider that each view is maintained separately.

An exhaustive algorithm can be very expensive for a large number of complex queries. We outline now algorithms that significantly prune the search space.

Algorithm 1. Pruning algorithm

1. Consider the states $s_1 = <\mathbf{G}^{Q_1}, \mathbf{Q}_1^{Q_1}>, \ldots, s_n = <\mathbf{G}^{Q_n}, \mathbf{Q}_n^{Q_n}>$, where $\mathbf{Q}_1 = \{Q_1\}, \ldots, \mathbf{Q}_n = \{Q_n\}$. For every s_i, and every subset E of edges in $\mathbf{G}^{Q_i}$, we generate new states by applying rule 1 (edge removal) to all the edges in E. From the states thus created, we generate new states by applying exhaustively rule 3 (view break).
   $S_i = \{s_i^1, \ldots, s_i^{k_i}\}$ denotes the set of states created from s_i, $i = 1, \ldots, n$.

2. Consider two states. By combining these states we can create a new state. The combined state is formed by merging their multiquery graphs and unionning their query rewriting sets.
   The second part of the algorithm is explained through the use of a tree depicted in Figure 7. This tree is defined as follows: the nodes of the tree are states and combined states, and the children of the root node are the states $s_1^1, \ldots, s_1^{k_1}$. These nodes are at depth 1. The children of a node s which are at depth d, $d > 1$, are the combined states resulting by combining s with eah of the states $s_d^1, \ldots, s_d^{k_d}$ and all the states resulting by applying transformation rule 4 (view merging) to these combined states (not necessarily once). The leaves of the tree (nodes at depth n) are states (DW configurations) $<\mathbf{G}^Q, \mathbf{Q}^V>$. The algorithm proceeds with the generation of the tree in a depth-first manner. It keeps the state $s_m = <\mathbf{G}^Q, \mathbf{Q}^V>$ that satisfies the space constraint and has the lowest cost, among those generated, along with its cost c_m. s_m and c_m is initially set to $\emptyset$ and ∞ respectively. *The generation of the tree is discontinued below a node if this node does not satisfy the space constraint or if its cost exceeds c_m*. At the end of the process the algorithm returns s_m.

Even though a pruning of the search space is performed, Algorithm 1 always computes a state that satisfies the space constraint and has minimal cost (if it exists). This is due to the fact that, under the assumptions we have made, the cost and the size of a node in the tree depicted in figure 7 are not less than the cost and the size of his descendant nodes.

Algorithm 2. Greedy algorithm

1. The first part is similar to the first part of the pruning algorithm.
2. In this part the algorithm starts by considering the root node of the tree of Figure 7. When a node is considered, all its child-nodes are generated and one with the minimal cost among those that satisfy the space constraint is chosen for consideration. The algorithm stops when no child-node satisfies the space constraint (and returns no answer) or when a leaf node s_m is chosen for consideration (and returns s_m).

Clearly this algorithm is efficient. It may though return no answer even if a solution to the problem exists.

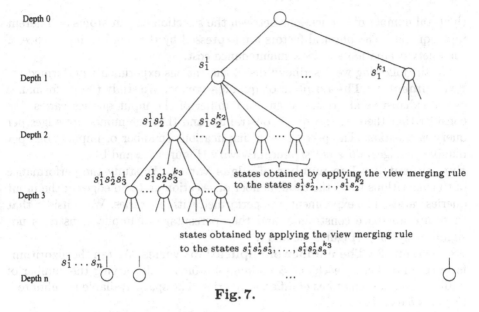

Fig. 7.

Algorithm 3. Heuristic algorithm

1. The first part is similar to the first part of the pruning algorithm.
2. We keep in each S_i, $i \in [1, n]$, only those states s_i that satisfy the space constraint and have minimal cost and those states that when combined with another state $s_j \in S_j$, $i \leq j$, allow the application of the view merging rule to the combined state.
3. This part is similar to the second part of the pruning algorithm.

This algorithm always returns the optimal solution if there are no limitations to the space allocated to the DW. The reason is that the optimal solution is obtained either by combining one optimal state from each S_i, $i \in [1, n]$ or by combining one state from each S_i, $i \in [1, n]$ and applying at least once the view merging rule to an intermediate combined state.

7 Experimental Results

We have performed a sequence of experiments to compare the algorithms presented in the previous section. The comparison is first made with respect to the time required to find the solution. The time required by each algorithm is expressed as CPU time. We also study the greedy algorithm with respect to the quality of the solution returned. This is expressed as the percentage of the cost of the optimal state returned by the pruning algorithm divided by the cost of the final state that the greedy algorithm returns.

The algorithms are compared in terms of the following factors: (a) the complexity of the input query set, and (b) physical factors. The complexity of the query set is expressed by three parameters: the number of input queries, the number of selection and join edges of all the input queries, and the overlapping of the queries in the input query set. The query overlapping is expressed by the total number of implications between the selection or join atoms of different input queries. The physical factors are expressed by the relative importance of the query evaluation and view maintenance cost.

In the following we describe in detail the various experiments performed.

Experiment 1 : The number of queries varies. We study the performance of the exhaustive algorithm when the number of the input queries varies. We consider that there are no space constraints, and that the number of edges per query is constant. The percentage of implications (number of implications per number of edges) does not significantly vary (Figures 8.a and b).

Experiment 2 : The number of edges varies. We study the performance of the algorithms when the total number of selection and join edges of the input queries varies. The experiment was performed with 4 queries. We consider that there are no space constraints, and that percentage of implications does not significantly vary. (Figures 8.c and d).

Experiment 3 : The number of implications varies. We ran the algorithms for a set of 3 queries, each one containing 4 atoms while varying the number of implication between atoms of different queries. The space available is unlimited. (Figures 8.e and f).

Experiment 4 : Parameter c varies. We ran the algorithms for a set of 4 queries, each one containing 4 atoms, while varying the parameter c. The percentage of implications is kept constant. (Figures 8.g and h).

From the previous experiments, we conclude that the heuristic algorithm is the winner when we have no significant restrictions in the space available for materialization. The pruning algorithm is our proposal in cases where significant space restrictions are imposed. The greedy algorithm is a very fast alternative, but it suffers from the fact that in many cases it does not find solutions which are produced by the application of the view merging transformation. Thus, it returns acceptable solutions in the cases where we have limited overlapping between queries, or where the view maintenance cost or the query evaluation cost are important.

8   Conclusion and Possible Extensions

In this paper we have dealt with the issue of selecting a set of views to materialize in a DW. This decision is important when implementing a DW. Current products do not provide tools for automatic DW design.

We provide a generic method that, given a set of SPJ queries to be answered by the DW, generates all the "significant" materialized view selections that answer all the input queries. This is done through the use of a set of transformation rules which detect and exploit common subexpressions between the queries. The rules modify view selections and rewrite completely all the input queries over the modified view selections. Then we address the problem of selecting a set of views that fits in the space available at the DW for materialization, and minimizes the combined view maintenance and query evaluation cost. Using the transformation rules we model the previous problem as a state space search problem and

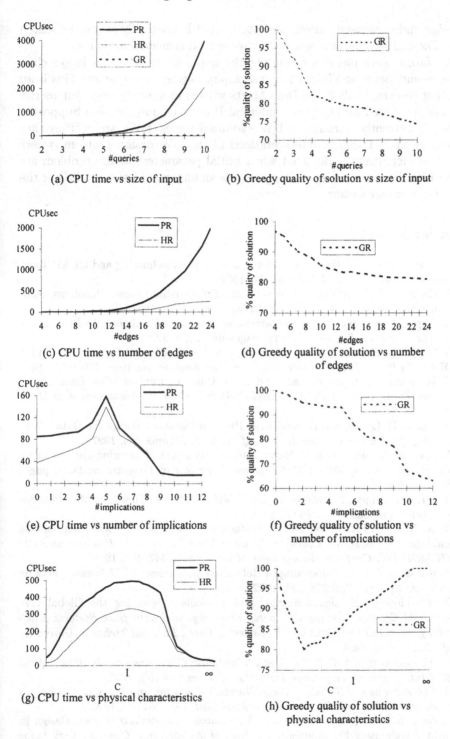

(a) CPU time vs size of input

(b) Greedy quality of solution vs size of input

(c) CPU time vs number of edges

(d) Greedy quality of solution vs number of edges

(e) CPU time vs number of implications

(f) Greedy quality of solution vs number of implications

(g) CPU time vs physical characteristics

(h) Greedy quality of solution vs physical characteristics

Fig. 8. Experimental results

we design and implement various algorithms that heuristically prune the search space. These algorithms are compared through experimental evaluation.

Our future work includes extending the approach to handle a larger class of queries and views, and in particular grouping/aggregation queries. This is an important issue in the design of Data Marts where grouping/aggregation queries are extensively used for On-Line Analytical Processing and Decision Support.

We are currently working on DW evolution issues. DWs are entities that evolve over time. Dynamic interpretations of the DW design problem, where the DW is incrementally designed when initial parameters to the problem are modified (for instance the input query set), is an important issue and it is at the focus of our research efforts.

References

[1] S. Chaudhuri and U. Dayal. An Overview of Data Warehousing and OLAP Technology. *SIGMOD Record*, 26(1):65–74, 1997.

[2] A. Gupta and I. S. Mumick. Maintenance of materialized views: Problems, techniques and applications. *Data Engineering*, 18(2):3–18, 1995.

[3] H. Gupta. Selection of Views to Materialize in a Data Warehouse. In *Proc. of the 6th Intl. Conf. on Database Theory*, pages 98–112, 1997.

[4] H. Gupta, V. Harinarayan, A. Rajaraman, and J. D. Ullman. Index Selection for OLAP. In *Proc. of the 13th Intl. Conf. on Data Engineering*, pages 208–219, 1997.

[5] V. Harinarayan, A. Rajaraman, and J. D. Ullman. Implementing Data Cubes Efficiently. In *Proc. of the ACM SIGMOD Intl. Conf. on Management of Data*, 1996.

[6] W. Labio, D. Quass, and B. Adelberg. Physical Database Design for Data Warehousing. In *Proc. of the 13th Intl. Conf. on Data Engineering*, 1997.

[7] A. Levy, A. O. Mendelson, Y. Sagiv, and D. Srivastava. Answering Queries using Views. In *Proc. of the ACM Symp. on Principles of Database Systems*, pages 95–104, 1995.

[8] D. Quass, A. Gupta, I. S. Mumick, and J. Widom. Making Views Self Maintainable for Data Warehousing. In *PDIS*, 1996.

[9] K. A. Ross, D. Srivastava, and S. Sudarshan. Materialized View Maintenance and Integrity Constraint Checking: Trading Space for Time. In *Proc. of the ACM SIGMOD Intl. Conf. on Management of Data*, pages 447–458, 1996.

[10] N. Roussopoulos. View Indexing in Relational Databases. *ACM Transactions on Database Systems*, 7(2):258–290, 1982.

[11] D. Theodoratos, S. Ligoudistianos, and T. Sellis. Designing the Global DW with SPJ Queries. *Technical Report, Knowledge and data Base Systems Laboratory, Electrical and Computer Engineering Dept., National Technical University of Athens*, Nov. 1998.

[12] D. Theodoratos and T. Sellis. Data Warehouse Configuration. In *Proc. of the 23rd Intl. Conf. on Very Large Data Bases*, pages 126–135, 1997.

[13] D. Theodoratos and T. Sellis. Data Warehouse Schema and Instance Design. In *Proc. of the 17th Intl. Conf. on Conceptual Modeling (ER'98)*, 1998.

[14] J. Yang, K. Karlapalem, and Q. Li. Algorithms for Materialized View Design in Data Warehousing Environment. In *Proc. of the 23rd Intl. Conf. on Very Large Data Bases*, pages 136–145, 1997.

Applying Graph Reduction Techniques for Identifying Structural Conflicts in Process Models *

Wasim Sadiq and Maria E. Orlowska

Distributed Systems Technology Centre
Department of Computer Science & Electrical Engineering
The University of Queensland
Qld 4072, Australia
email: {wasim,maria}@dstc.edu.au

Abstract. The foundation of a process model lies in its control flow specifications. Using a generic process modeling language for workflows, we show how a control flow specification may contain certain structural conflicts that could compromise its correct execution. In general, identification of such conflicts is a computationally complex problem and requires development of effective algorithms specific for target system language. We present a visual verification approach and algorithm that employs a set of graph reduction rules to identify structural conflicts in process models for a generic workflow modeling language. We also provide insights into the correctness and complexity of the reduction process. The main contribution of the paper is a new technique for satisfying well-defined correctness criteria in process models.

1 Introduction

The workflow technology provides a flexible and appropriate environment to develop and maintain next generation of component-oriented enterprise-wide information systems. The production workflows, a subclass of workflows, support well-defined procedures for repetitive processes and provide means for automated coordination of activities that may span over several heterogeneous and mission-critical information systems of the organization. The production workflow applications are built upon business processes that are generally quite complex and involve a large number of activities and associated coordination constraints.

The objective of process modeling is to provide high-level specification of processes that are independent of target workflow management system. It is essential that a process model is properly defined, analyzed, verified, and refined before being deployed in a workflows management system.

A workflow is a set of tasks and associated execution constraints. A workflow management system coordinates the execution of these tasks to achieve some business

* The work reported in this paper has been funded in part by the Cooperative Research Centres Program through the Department of the Prime Minister and Cabinet of the Commonwealth Government of Australia.

M. Jarke, A. Oberweis (Eds.): CAiSE'99, LNCS 1626, pp. 195-209, 1999.

objectives. Generally, tasks in a workflow are inter-related in such a way that initiation of one task is dependent on successful completion of a set of other tasks. Therefore, the order in which tasks are executed is very important. The control flow aspect of a process model captures the flow of execution from one task to another. This information is used by a workflow management system to properly order and schedule workflow tasks. Arguably, the control flow is the primary and the most important aspect of a process model. It builds a foundation to capture other workflow requirements.

The research presented in this paper addresses modeling and verification of production workflows. The Workflow Management Coalition [15] is developing a standard process definition language and an interface specification that could be used to transfer process models between products. The verification issues discussed in this paper are presented using a graphical process modeling language that is based on this standard.

The use of Petri Nets for workflow modeling has been explored in [1] and [7]. However, Petri Nets are not used in any of the major products. A few conceptual modeling languages and methodologies have also been proposed specifically for workflow technology [4] [5] [6] [10] [12] [13].

It is possible to introduce error situations while building large workflow specifications. Such modeling inconsistencies and errors may lead to undesirable execution of some or all possible instances of a workflow. It is essential to rectify such problems at design phase rather than after deploying the workflow application. We have found limited work in literature on workflows verification. In [9] a few verification issues of workflow structures have been examined and complexity of certain verification problems has been shown. In [12] some correctness issues in workflows modeling have been identified. In [1] the application of analysis techniques in Petri Nets domain has been explored for workflow verification.

The work presented in this paper differs from other approaches. It provides an effective approach and algorithm to gradually reduce a workflow graph through a set of reduction rules and allows visual identification of structural conflicts.

2 Process Modeling

To be able to present our reduction technique, we introduce a basic process modeling language that is based on generic modeling concepts as described in [15]. In this language, the process models are modeled using two types of objects: node and control flow.

Node is classified into two subclasses: task and condition. A *task*, graphically represented by a rectangle, represents the work to be done to achieve some objectives. It is also used to build sequential, and-split, and and-join structures. A *condition*, graphically represented by a circle, is used to construct or-split and or-join structures. A *control flow* links two nodes in the graph and is graphically represented by a directed edge.

By connecting nodes with control flows through five modeling structures, as shown in Figure 1, we build directed acyclic graphs (DAG) called workflow graphs where nodes represent vertices and control flows represent directed edges. From now on, we will refer to vertices as nodes and edges as flows.

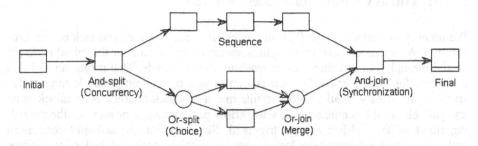

Fig. 1. Process modeling constructs

Sequence is the most basic modeling structure and defines the ordering of task execution. It is constructed by connecting at the most one incoming and one outgoing flow to a task. An *and-split* structure is used to represent concurrent paths within a workflow graph and is modeled by connecting two or more outgoing flows to a task. At certain points in workflows, it is essential to wait for the completion of more than one execution path to proceed further. An *and-join*, represented by more than one incoming flow to a task, is applied to synchronize such concurrent paths. An and-join task waits until all the incoming flows have been triggered.

An *or-split* structure is used to model mutually exclusive alternative paths and is constructed by attaching two or more outgoing flows to a condition object. At run-time, the workflow selects one of the alternative execution paths for a given instance of the business process by activating one of the outgoing flows originating from the or-split condition object. The or-split is exclusive and complete. The exclusive characteristic ensures that only one of the alternative paths is selected. The completeness characteristic guarantees that, if a condition object is activated, one of its outgoing flows will always be triggered. An *or-join* structure is "opposite" to the or-split structure. It is applied to join mutually exclusive alternative paths into one path by attaching two or more incoming flows to a condition object.

Since a workflow model is represented by a directed acyclic graph (DAG), it has at least one node that has no incoming flows (source) and at least one node that has no outgoing flows (sink). We call these *initial* and *final* nodes respectively. To uniquely identify a final node for a workflow graph, we join all split structures. Therefore, a workflow graph contains only one initial and one final node. A workflow instance completes its execution after its final node has completed its execution.

The generic process modeling language [15] also contains additional modeling structures to support nesting, blocks, and iteration. However, these are not discussed in this paper since the modeling approach used for these structures does not impact on the verification algorithm presented here. We recognize the importance of modeling and verifying other aspects like data flow, temporal constraints, execution, roles, and task classifications. However, this paper concentrates only on the verification of structural conflicts.

3   Structural Conflicts in Process Models

We identify two structural conflicts in process models: deadlock and lack of synchronization. As mentioned earlier, all split structures introduced after the initial node are closed through join structures before reaching the final node. That means an and-join is applied for joining and-split paths and an or-join for or-split paths. Joining exclusive or-split paths with an and-join results into a deadlock conflict. A deadlock at an and-join blocks the continuation of a workflow path since one or more of the preceding flows of the and-join are not triggered. Similarly, joining and-split concurrent paths with an or-join introduces lack of synchronization conflict. A lack of synchronization at an or-join node results into unintentional multiple activation of nodes that follow the or-join node.

Figure 2 shows a correct workflow graph and two graphs with deadlock and lack of synchronization structural conflicts. The conflict nodes are highlighted in the incorrect graphs.

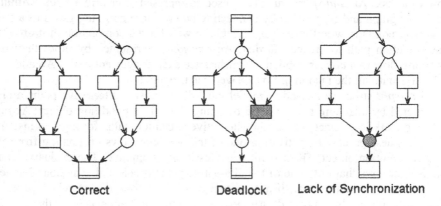

Correct   Deadlock   Lack of Synchronization

Fig. 2. Structural conflicts in workflow graphs

It is important to point out here that structural conflicts are not the only types of errors possible in process models. However, they do represent the primary source of errors in control flow specifications. Other modeling aspects may also affect the correct execution of workflows. For example, data flow modeling captures the data dependencies between activities. A dependent activity may not get the required data from the source activity at run-time because of incorrect modeling. The incorrect data mapping between activities and underlying application components may also cause incorrect execution of workflows. Similarly, control flow specification of a workflow model may not satisfy certain specified temporal constraints.

The existence of other errors in a workflow model does not introduce or remove structural conflicts. Therefore, the identification of structural conflicts in a workflow model can be performed independently from other types of verification analysis. The correctness of a complete workflow specification cannot be guaranteed just by removing structural conflicts from the workflow graph. However, the non-existence of structural conflicts in a workflow model guarantees that control flow specifications conform to a certain correctness criteria.

We partition the verification process for workflow structures into two phases. In first phase, basic syntax checking is performed to ensure that the model conforms to the modeling language syntax and that all necessary properties of its components have been defined. The verification of basic syntax is easy to facilitate and requires local analysis of workflow modeling objects and structures. An example of such verification is checking whether the workflow model is a DAG and is properly connected.

The second phase of verification requires a rigorous analysis of the workflow model. It attempts to identify inconsistencies in the model that could arise due to conflicting use of modeling structures. It is possible that such conflicting structures are placed at distant locations in the workflow graph. In such cases, it is difficult to identify the inconsistencies manually.

We need to define the concept of instance subgraphs before presenting the correctness criteria for workflow graphs. An instance subgraph represents a subset of workflow tasks that may be executed for a particular instance of a workflow. It can be generated by visiting its nodes on the semantic basis of underlying modeling structures. The subgraph representing the visited nodes and flows forms an instance subgraph. Figure 3 shows a workflow graph and its instance subgraphs.

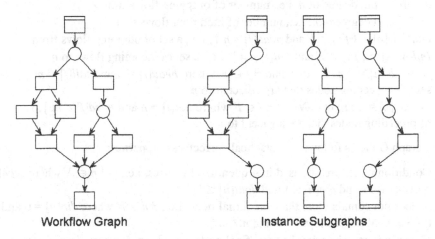

Workflow Graph   Instance Subgraphs

Fig. 3. A Workflow graph and its instance subgraphs

Correctness criteria 1 – deadlock free workflow graphs: A workflow graph is free of deadlock structural conflicts if it does not generate an instance subgraph that contains only a proper subset of the incoming nodes of an and-join node.

Correctness criteria 2 – lack of synchronization free workflow graphs: A workflow graph is free of lack of synchronization structural conflicts if it does not generate an instance subgraph that contains more than one incoming nodes of an or-join node.

The common point in both cases of verification is that in principle, we need to examine all possible instance subgraphs of a workflow. The or-split is the only structure in a workflow graph that introduces more than one possible instance subgraphs. A workflow graph without or-split structures would produce exactly the same instance subgraph as of the workflow graph. A workflow graph with a single or-split structure produces as many possible instance subgraphs as the number of outgoing flows from the or-split structure. However, the number of possible instance subgraphs could grow exponentially as the number of or-split and or-join structures increases in a workflow specification. Therefore, a brute force method to generate all possible instance subgraphs of a workflow graph to ensure correctness is not computationally effective.

We present a formal notation of the workflow graphs that will be used in the verification algorithm as follows.

The workflow graph $G = (N, F)$ is a simple directed acyclic graph (DAG) where

- N is a finite set of nodes
- F is a finite set of control flows representing directed edges between two nodes

For each flow $f \in F$:

- $head[f] = n$ where $n \in N$ represents head node of f
- $tail[f] = n$ where $n \in N$ represents tail node of f

For each node $n \in N$:

- $type[n] \in \{$ TASK, CONDITION $\}$ represents type of n
- $dout[n] =$ out degree of n, i.e., number of outgoing flows from n
- $din[n] =$ in degree of n, i.e., number of incoming flows to n
- $Outflow[n] = \{ f : f \in F$ and $head[f] = n \}$, i.e., a set of outgoing flows from n
- $Inflow[n] = \{ f : f \in F$ and $tail[f] = n \}$, i.e., a set of incoming flows to n
- $Outnode[n] = \{ m : m \in N$ and $\exists f \in F$ where $head[f] = n$ and $tail[f] = m \}$, i.e., a set of succeeding nodes that are adjacent to n
- $Innode[n] = \{ m : m \in N$ and $\exists f \in F$ where $tail[f] = n$ and $head[f] = m \}$, i.e., a set of preceding nodes that are adjacent to n

The graph G meets following syntactical correctness properties:

- Condition nodes are not used in sequential structures, i.e., $\neg \exists n \in N$ where $type[n]$ = CONDITION and $din[n] \le 1$ and $dout[n] \le 1$
- G does not contain more than one initial node, i.e., $\exists n \in N$ where $din[n] = 0$ and
- ($\neg \exists m \in N$ where $din[m] = 0$ and $n \ne m$)
- G does not contain more than one final node: i.e., $\exists n \in N$ where $dout[n] = 0$ and
- ($\neg \exists m \in N$ where $dout[m] = 0$ and $n \ne m$)

3.1 Reduction Rules

In principle, the concept behind the verification approach and algorithm presented in this paper is simple. We remove all such structures from the workflow graph that are definitely correct. This is achieved by iteratively applying a conflict-preserving reduction process. The reduction process eventually reduces a structurally correct workflow graph to an empty graph. However, a workflow graph with structural conflicts is not completely reduced.

The reduction process makes use of three reduction rules – adjacent, closed, and overlapped – as long as they are able to reduce the graph.

Adjacent Reduction Rule

The adjacent reduction rule targets four types of components. We visit all nodes of the graph and check if applying adjacent reduction rule can reduce any of them.

Let us call the node being visited as the current node. We remove the current node from the graph if the number of flows attached to it is less than or equal to one. We also assume that when a node is removed from the graph, all flows attached to it are automatically removed. If the current node is forming a sequential structure, i.e., it has exactly one incoming and one outgoing flow, we change the tail of its incoming flow to the tail of its outgoing flow and remove it from the graph.

If the current node is not removed by first two criteria, it means that it is forming either a split or join structure since it would either have out degree or in degree or both that is more than one. We check if the current node has a single incoming flow and is introducing a split structure by having more than one outgoing flow. If the type of the current node is same as its preceding node, we move outgoing flows of the current node to the preceding node and remove the current node. Finally, if the last criterion is not met, we check if the current node has a single outgoing flow and is introducing a join structure through more than one incoming flow. If the type of the current node is same as its succeeding node, we move incoming flows of the current node to the succeeding node and delete the current node. This step is similar to the previous one except for the fact that it merges join structures whereas the previous step merges split structures. Figure 4 (a) shows examples of applying the adjacent reduction rule.

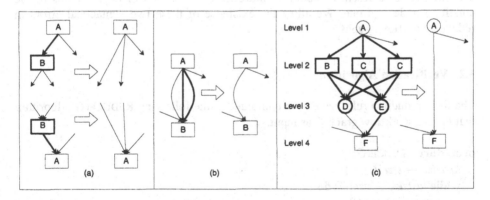

Fig. 4. Examples of reduction rules

Closed Reduction Rule

The application of adjacent reduction rule generally introduces closed components in workflow graphs. A closed component comprises two nodes of the same type that have more than one flow between them. The closed reduction rule deletes all but one flow between such nodes. Figure 4 (b) shows an example of the closed reduction rule. A graph may contain closed components only if some adjacent components are reduced.

Overlapped Reduction Rule

The overlapped reduction rule targets a specific class of components in workflow graphs that has an infrequent occurrence. Therefore, we invoke it only if the adjacent and closed reduction rules are unable to reduce the graph. An overlapped component of a workflow graph meets several properties that ensure non-existence of structural conflicts in it. Such a component has four levels as shown in Figure 4 (c). The source of the component at level 1 is always a condition and sink at level 4 is always a task. It has only task objects at level 2 and only condition objects at level 3. Each of the tasks at level 2 has outgoing flows to each of the conditions at level 3 and has exactly one incoming flow from the source at level 1. Each of the conditions at level 3 has incoming flows only from each of the tasks level 2 and has exactly one outgoing flow to the sink at level 4. The nodes at level 3 and 4 do not have any other control flows attached to them than the ones mentioned above. The overlapped reduction rule identifies components that meet all these properties and reduces them to a single control flow between source and sink of the component.

The workflow graph before reduction is assumed to meet syntactical correctness properties as described in previous section. However, during the reduction process, a reduced graph may not satisfy some of these properties. The adjacent reduction may introduce multiple flows between two nodes, hence transforming the simple graph into a multi-graph. In reduced graphs, multiple flows between two nodes represent existence of more than one reduced path between them. Similarly, the closed and overlapped reduction may introduce sequential condition nodes. Such a sequential condition node represent reduction of more than one or-split or or-join paths of the condition node into one. We allow the existence of these two syntactical errors in reduced workflow graphs.

3.2 Verification Algorithm

The three reduction rules have been combined in the following REDUCE(G) algorithm that takes a workflow graph G as input.

procedure REDUCE(G)
    $lastsize \leftarrow size[G] + 1$
    while $lastsize > size[G]$ **do**
        $lastsize \leftarrow size[G]$
        for each node $n \in N[G]$ **do**   /* Adjacent components */
          if $din[n] + dout[n] \leq 1$ **then**
            delete n
          else if $din[n] = 1$ and $dout[n] = 1$ **then**
            $tail[top[Inflow[n]]] \leftarrow top[Outnode[n]]$
            delete n
            else if $din[n] = 1$ and $dout[n] > 1$ and $type[n] = type[top[Innode[n]]]$ **then**
              for each flow $outflow \in Outflow[n]$ **do**
                $head[outflow] \leftarrow top[Innode[n]]$
              delete n

           else if $dout[n] = 1$ and $din[n] > 1$ and
                $type[n] = type[head[Outnode[n]]]$ **then**
              for each flow $inflow \in Inflow[n]$ **do**
                $tail[inflow] \leftarrow top[Outnode[n]]$
              delete n
if $lastsize < size[G]$ **then**   /* Closed components */
  for each node $n \in N[G]$ **do**
    if $dout[n] > 1$ **then**
      $Nodeset \leftarrow \{\}$
      for each flow $outflow \in Outflow[n]$ **do**
        if $type[n] = type[tail[outflow]]$ **then**
          if $tail[outflow] \notin Nodeset$ **then**
            $Nodeset \leftarrow Nodeset \cup \{ tail[outflow] \}$
        else
          delete $outflow$
if $lastsize = size[G]$ **then**   /* Overlapped components */
  for each node $n \in N[G]$ **do**
    if $type[n] = $ CONDITION and $dout[n] = 1$ and $din[n] > 1$ **then**
      $level4 \leftarrow top[Outnode[n]]$
      $fn \leftarrow head[Innode[n]]$
      if $type[level4] = $ TASK and $din[level4] > 1$ and
          $type[fn] = $ TASK and $dout[fn] > 1$ and $din[fn] = 1$ **then**
        $level1 \leftarrow head[Innode[fn]]$
        if $type[top] = $ CONDITION and $dout[top] > 1$ **then**
          $Level2 \leftarrow Innode[n]$
          $Level3 \leftarrow Outnode[fn]$
          if $\forall$ $node \in Level2$ ($type[node] = $ TASK and
            $Innode[node] = \{ level1 \}$ and
            $Outnode[node] = Level3$) **then**
            if $\forall$ $node \in Level3$ ($type[node] = $ CONDITION and
              $Outnode[node] = \{ level4 \}$ and
              $Innode[node] = Level2$) **then**
              $head[top[Outflow[n]]] \leftarrow level1$
              delete all $node \in Level2$
              delete all $node \in Level3$

A workflow graph is shown in Figure 5 (a). The first application of adjacent rule reduces the workflow graph from (a) to (b). The closed rule removes multiple flows from closed components and transforms the graph to (c). The adjacent and closed rules are applied two more times to get (d). At this point, the adjacent and closed rules cannot reduce the graph any further. Therefore, the overlapped rule is applied to get (e). We get (f) by applying adjacent and closed rules two more times on (e). Finally, a single application of adjacent rule reduces the graph from (f) to an empty graph and hence showing that the workflow graph in (a) does not contain any structural conflicts.

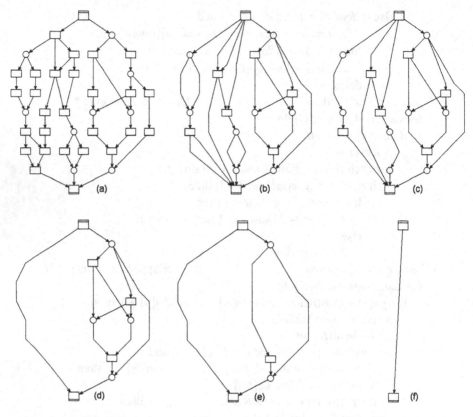

Fig. 5. Reducing a workflow graph containing structural conflicts

Figure 6 (a) shows a workflow graph where we have added an additional control flow to the workflow graph in 5 (a) that introduces a deadlock structural conflict. The reduction procedure is applied on (a) to get (b) that is not reducible any further. The non-reducible graph in (b) shows that a structural conflict exists in (a).

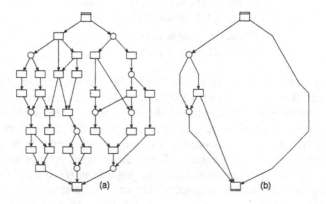

Fig. 6. Reducing a workflow graph with structural conflicts

3.3 Correctness and Complexity

In this section, we look at the correctness and complexity of the REDUCE(G) algorithm. Let the workflow graph G_i is the reduced graph after i iterations of the algorithm on G. We shall prove that:

- the adjacent, closed, and overlapped reduction rules do not generate structural conflicts, i.e., if G_i is correct then G_{i+1} is correct;
- the adjacent, closed, and overlapped reduction rules do not remove structural conflicts, i.e., if G_i is incorrect then G_{i+1} is incorrect; and,
- if G is correct, then reduction algorithm will always reduce G to an empty graph, equivalently, if reduction algorithm can not reduce G to an empty graph then G must contain at least one structural conflict.

First, we will look at individual reduction rules to prove that they meet the first two properties 1 and 2. The adjacent reduction rule targets four types of components as described in section 3.1. The nodes removed by the first two types represent sequential structures that do not introduce any split or join structures in workflow graph. Therefore, they cannot possibly contribute towards a structural conflict. At the same time, they cannot remove any existing structural conflict. The third type of adjacent reduction does not generate new structural conflicts since it only merges the split structure from the current node to the preceding node. The split structures are merged only if the type of the current node and the preceding node is same. If the current node's split structure contributes to a structural conflict that occurs in its succeeding paths, it would not be removed since the split structure is simply moved to the preceding node without any structural differences. At the same time, the current node has only a single preceding node and hence does not take part in a join structure. Therefore, the current node cannot be a part of a structural conflict with a split structure that is in its preceding paths. The fourth type of adjacent reduction is similar to the third one except that it merges join structures rather than split structures. Therefore, it also meets the first two correctness properties on similar basis.

We do not allow multiple flows between two nodes in a workflow graph. However, the adjacent reduction generally introduces components in reduced workflow graph that contain two nodes and more than one flow between them. Such multiple flows imply the existence of more than one path from the head node of the flows to their tail node. If the type of such two nodes is different, then the component represents a case of structural conflict and is not reduced by the algorithm. However, if the type is same, we remove all but one of the multiple flows since they cannot generate structural conflicts or remove existing ones. Multiple flows between two tasks represent concurrent paths and between two conditions represent alternative paths.

The basic property of an overlapped component is that none of the nodes between source and sink of the component are connected to any other nodes of the graph. At the same time, no structural conflict exists between source and sink. Therefore, reducing the whole overlapped component between sink and source of an overlapped component to a single control flow does not generate structural conflicts or remove existing ones.

So far, we have shown that all reduction rules of the algorithm meet first two correctness properties. To prove that algorithm meets the third property, we will show that if the algorithm does not reduce a workflow graph to an empty graph, then it contains at least one structural conflict.

Let G_k be a graph that is not reducible any further after applying k iterations of the reduction algorithm. Non-reducibility of graph G_k implies that it does not contain any sequential structures, i.e., either in degree or out degree or both of each graph node is more than one. It also implies that if a node has an in degree or out degree that is equal to one then the adjacent node attached to the single incoming or outgoing flow is of different type.

It is also possible that graph G_k contains a node that has more than one flow to another node. Non-reducibility of graph implies that such multiple flows could exist only between nodes of different types. Multiple flows from a condition to a task represent deadlock conflict and from a task to a condition represent lack of synchronization conflict. Therefore, if a non-reducible graph contains a node with multiple flows to another node then it always contains a structural conflict.

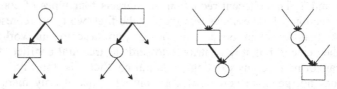

Fig. 7. Structures with single in / out degrees in non-reducible graphs

To proceed, we assume that G_k does not contain a node with more than one flow to another node, i.e., G_k is a simple DAG. We also know that G_k has a single source and a single sink. We know that a simple DAG with a single source and a single sink contains at least one node with a single in degree and another node with a single out degree. This property holds even for complete graphs. Since G_k is non-reducible, then the node on the other side of such a single incoming or outgoing flow is always of a different type, otherwise it would be reducible by adjacent reduction. There are only four possible cases of such structures as shown in Figure 7. It is easy to show that it is not possible to build a non-reducible correct graph with a single source and a single sink that contains any of these four structures. Therefore, a non-reducible graph always contains at least one structural conflict.

Now we look at the time complexity of the algorithm. In each iteration of the algorithm, we visit all nodes to identify and reduce graph objects that meet certain properties of the reduction rules. The checking of whether a graph object meets any of these properties is done in constant time since it takes only those objects into account that are adjacent to the current node. After each iteration, the algorithm continues only if the graph has reduced.

The worst case complexity of the algorithm is $O(n^2)$ where n represents the number of nodes and flows in the workflow graph. The worst case is for a workflow graph that is completely reducible and each iteration of the algorithm is able to reduce at the most one object. However, the average case complexity is much lower than $O(n^2)$, since the first few iterations dramatically reduce the size of a workflow graph and remaining iterations need to work on a much smaller workflow graph than the original graph.

4 Implementation

The algorithm presented in this paper has been implemented in a workflow modeling and verification tool. The tool, called FlowMake, provides workflow analysts and designers a well-defined framework to model and reason about various aspects of workflows. It has been designed to augment production workflow products with enhanced modeling capabilities and to provide a basis for expanding the scope of the verification. Figure 8 shows a screen snapshot of FlowMake where the reduction process is being applied to a process model.

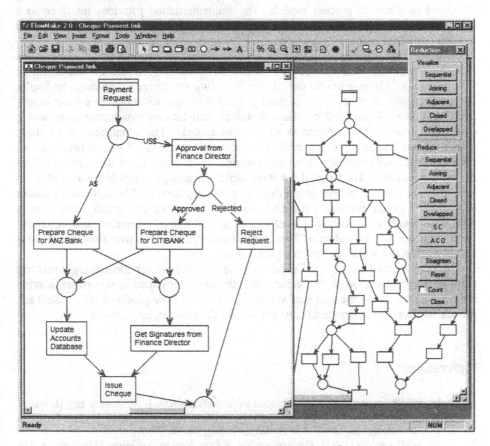

Fig. 8. FlowMake: workflow modeling and verification tool

FlowMake is composed of four major components: the repository, the workflow editor, the verification engine, and the interface. *Repository* maintains workflow models and has been implemented using relational technology. *Workflow Editor* provides a user-friendly graphical environment to maintain large workflow graphs. It is also used to visualize inconsistencies in design. *Verification Engine* implements the algorithms to check the consistency of workflow models. *Interface* component provides linkage to workflow products through import and export of workflow models. Presently, the tool allows importing of process models from IBM workflow product MQ Workflow (previously known as FlowMark), analyzing them for structural conflicts, and exporting them back to the product. More information about FlowMake is available at http://www.dstc.edu.au/DDU/projects/FlowMake/.

5 Conclusions

We report on successful implementation of graph reduction techniques for detecting structural conflicts in process models. The implementation provides interface to a selected workflow product, IBM MQ Workflow, to demonstrate its applicability to a leading workflow management system.

To present the verification approach and algorithm, we introduced a basic process modeling language based on a process definition standard by Workflow Management Coalition. The language makes use of five modeling structures – sequence, and-split, and-join, or-split, and or-join – to build control flow specifications. We have identified two types of structural conflicts, deadlock and lack of synchronization, which could compromise the correctness of process models. The identification of these structural conflicts in workflow models is a complex problem. We have presented an effective graph reduction algorithm that can detect the existence of structural conflicts in workflow graphs. The basic idea behind verification approach is to remove all such structures from the workflow graph that are definitely correct. The algorithm reduces a workflow graph without structural conflicts to an empty graph. However, a workflow graph with structural conflicts is not completely reduced and structural conflicts are easily identifiable. The incremental reduction of workflow model also allows analysis of workflow graph components.

The main contribution of the paper is a new technique for identifying structural conflicts in process models. We believe that the ideas presented in this paper provide a basis for expanding the scope of verification in workflow products. The visual approach for identifying structural conflicts is useful, intuitive, and natural.

References

1. Aalst. WMP van der (1997). Verification of Workflow Nets. In P. Azema and G. Balbo, editors, Application and Theory of Petri Nets 1997, volume 1248 of Lecture Notes in Computer Science, pages 407-426. Springer-Verlag, Berlin, 1997.
2. Aalst. WMP van der (1998). The Application of Petri Nets to Workflow Management. The Journal of Circuits, Systems and Computers, 8(1):21--66, 1998.
3. Butler Report. Workflow: Integrating the Enterprise. The Butler Group, 1996.
4. Reichert M and Dadam P (1997). ADEPTflex - Supporting Dynamic Changes of Workflow without loosing control. Journal of Intelligent Information Systems (JIIS), Special Issue on Workflow and Process Management.
5. Carlsen S (1997). Conceptual Modeling and Composition of Flexible Workflow Models. PhD Thesis. Department of Computer Science and Information Science, Norwegian University of Science and Technology, Norway, 1997.
6. Casati F, Ceri S, Pernici B and Pozzi G (1995). Conceptual Modeling of Workflows. In M.P. Papazoglou, editor, Proceedings of the 14th In-ternational Object-Oriented and En-

tity-Relationship Modeling Conference, vol-ume 1021 of Lecture Notes in Computer Science, pages 341-354. Springer-Verlag.

7. Ellis CA and Nutt GJ (1993). Modelling and Enactment of Workflow Systems. In M. Ajmone Marasan, editor, Application and Theory of Petri Nets, Lecture Notes in Computer Science 691, pages 1-16, Springer-Verleg, Berlin, 1993.

8. Georgakopoulos D, Hornick M and Sheth A (1995) An Overview of Workflow Management: From Process Modeling to Workflow Automation Infrastructure. Journal on Distributed and Parallel Databases, 3(2):119-153.

9. Hofstede, AHM ter, Orlowska ME and Rajapakse J (1998). Verification Problems in Conceptual Workflow Specifications. Data & Knowledge Engineering, 24(3):239-256, January 1998.

10. Kuo D, Lawley M, Liu C and Orlowska ME (1996). A General Model for Nested Transactional Workflow. In Proceedings of the International Workshop on Advanced Transaction Models and Architecture (ATMA'96), Bombay India, pp.18-35, 1996.

11. Rajapakse J (1996). On Conceptual Workflow Specification and Verification. MSc Thesis. Department of Computer Science, The University of Queensland, Australia, 1996.

12. Sadiq W and Orlowska ME (1997). On Correctness Issues in Conceptual Modeling of Workflows. In Proceedings of the 5th European Conference on Information Systems (ECIS '97), Cork, Ireland, June 19-21, 1997.

13. Sadiq W and Orlowska ME (1999). On Capturing Process Requirements of Workflow Based Information Systems. In Proceedings of the 3rd International Conference on Business Information Systems (BIS '99), Poznan, Poland, April 14-16, 1999.

14. Workflow Management Coalition (1996) The Workflow Management Coalition Specifications - Terminology and Glossary. Issue 2.0, Document Number WFMC-TC-1011.

15. Workflow Management Coalition (1998). Interface 1: Process Definition Interchange, Process Model, Document Number WfMC TC-1016-P.

A Multi-variant Approach to Software Process Modelling

Wolfgang Hesse[1] and Jörg Noack[2]

[1] c/o FB Mathematik/Informatik, Philipps-University Marburg/Germany
hesse@informatik.uni-marburg.de
[2] Informatikzentrum der Sparkassenorganisation (SIZ) Bonn/Germany
joerg.noack@siz.de

Abstract: In this article we present a new approach to software process modelling for a large banking organisation. In the past years, the main software development methods and tools of this organisation have migrated from structured to object-oriented technology. Presently, the software process is completely being redefined and adapted to the new goals and requirements. Since there are many kinds of projects differing largely in their goals, requirements and constraints, a two-level approach has been taken: On the base level, the ingredients of processes - activities, results, techniques and tools - are listed and described. These are composed in various ways to form a set of process variants which are defined on the second level. Each variant serves as a sample process for concrete project work. This multi-variant approach meets the requirements of the project managers and developers who demand for a flexible model covering a wide spectrum of projects.

Keynotes: Object-oriented software development, process model, model variants, activities, prototyping, component-based development, phase-oriented development, evolutionary development.

1   Introduction

In the German Savings Banks Organisation (short: GSBO, comprising about 600 savings banks and 13 state banks) information technology (IT) is primarily provided by 10 major   development centres. SIZ, the IT coordination centre, is a service enterprise offering support for these centres. In order to improve organisational and process maturity as well as to enhance   software quality and development performance, SIZ is publishing and maintaining an electronic project handbook called the *application development model* (AD model). This   handbook documents the software processes and best practices collected from several development projects in GSBO and from the literature [11].

During the last years the AD model has continuously been improved to fulfil the requirements of a large banking organisation. A first issue of the handbook covered a waterfall-like process model, structured development techniques like entity-relationship-diagrams or functional decomposition and conventional programming in

M. Jarke, A. Oberweis (Eds.): CAiSE'99, LNCS 1626, pp. 210-224, 1999.
© Springer-Verlag Berlin Heidelberg 1999

COBOL or C. It has primarily been used for large-scale mainframe projects building back-end systems, for example for clearing or accounting.

Meanwhile, the object-oriented approach to software development is becoming more and more popular. Concentration of the banking business has led to many reengineering projects which make it necessary to migrate or redevelop existing monolithic legacy application systems. The growth of the Internet opens up new dimensions of business action like electronic commerce and electronic banking. In order to meet these requirements, SIZ has started a methodology project aiming at a complete new version of its AD model. This version covers object-oriented software development for modern multi-layered software architectures using methodologies, languages and architectures like OMT, UML, JAVA and CORBA.

One kernel piece of the AD model is the object-oriented system life cycle (cf. [4]) described by a process model. In order to support projects of various kinds, goals, size and environments, a customisation approach has been taken: It is based on a toolbox for the construction of processes – the *reference framework* describing activities, results, techniques and roles. On top of this framework, so-called *model variants* act as guided tours through the OO development process. This *multi-variant* approach goes insofar beyond the existing OO methodologies (cf. for example [1], [9], [13] and [6] for a comparison) as it encompasses their model variants and embeds them into a general, customisable process model. This way, a *defined process* (cf. [8]) is achieved which does not force all projects into one single obligatory standard.

Recently, a first release of the AD model has undergone a major revision reflecting the evaluation results from several OO pilot projects in the GSBO. It is still too early to report on experiences of applying the multi-variant approach in a real project environment. However, the experiences of applying the first release of the AD model are discussed in a separate paper (cf. [12]).

2   The Overall Structure of the Development Process

In this section we present the overall *process architecture* (cf. [2]) underlying the AD model. There are several groups of people involved in the software development process which are distinguished by their different tasks and views on a software development project. We use the concept of *roles* to distinguish between these groups and their (complementary) views. To each role belongs an own process – thus the overall software process can be seen as a bunch of *concurrent sub-processes* which are synchronised by means of (milestone-like) revision points (cf. [5], [7]).

The roles and corresponding sub-processes are (cf. fig. 1):

- Development
- Project management
- Quality management
- Configuration management and support
- Use and evaluation

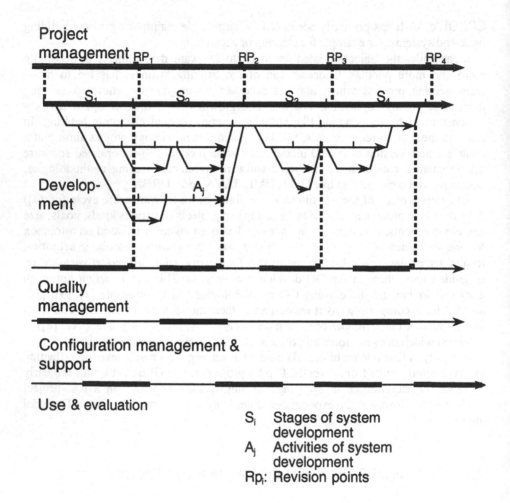

Project management RP₁ ... RP₂ ... RP₃ ... RP₄

S₁   S₂   S₃   S₄

Develop-
ment   Aⱼ

Quality
management

Configuration management &
support

Use & evaluation

Sᵢ   Stages of system
       development
Aⱼ   Activities of system
       development
Rpᵢ: Revision points

Fig. 1. The structure of a typical software process

3   The Process Building Tool Box

Since GSBO is a heterogeneous organisation covering savings banks, state banks, leasing and insurance companies etc. the AD model has to deal with heterogeneous kinds of projects, partners, and applications with special requirements which concern e.g. safety constraints or demands for reuse. For such an organisation a uniform process model is not a realistic option.

On the one hand, tasks should be manageable, components should be exchangeable and projects should be comparable – arguments which suggest to standardise the process as far as possible. Reuse, exchange and sub-contracting of results and components is a major issue for the target institutions – which makes a "real OO process" mandatory for many projects. On the other hand, there are several projects rooted in the tradition of the structured approach which put less emphasis on exchange, reuse or subcontracting. Some projects have relatively fixed and established requirements – others experiment with new solutions or even explore new applications. Projects vary in size, stability of the requirements, complexity of the resulting system and many other factors.

These obviously conflicting requirements have driven our specific approach to process modelling. It is a two-level approach consisting of

(a) a *base level* which comprises all the raw material used for building OO development processes ("the reference model") and

(b) a *composition level* offering several *process variants* based on the ingredients of the base level.

The *reference model* consists of five main components:

- a set of paradigmatic descriptions of *activities*
- a set of descriptions for resulting documents – briefly called *results*,
- a set of *techniques* supporting the elaboration of results,
- a set of *role* descriptions for the various groups of stakeholders in a software development project.
- a set of *guidelines and rules* which are meant to support reading and application of the handbook.

These components are linked by several relationships – as shown in fig. 2. In the following subsections, we briefly summarize the components. Their original presentation consists mainly of (German) text, including graphical figures, tables and examples.

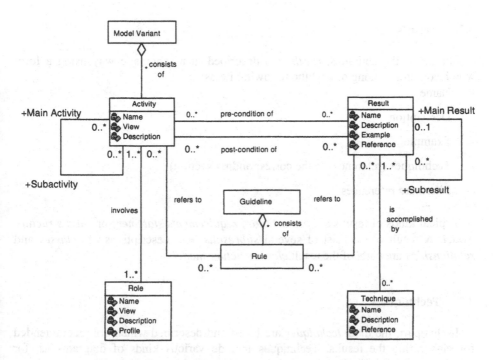

Fig. 2. Metamodel showing the overall structure of the reference model.

3.1   Activities

Activities are the essential building blocks of the process model. In general, their effect is to produce results (which are separately described in the result section). An activity can be decomposed into *subactivities*. These have either to be performed in sequential order or may be carried out in parallel (or in any arbitrary order).

Activities at the first level of the hierarchy are called *main activities*. In its present form, our activity model comprises 24 main activities. Examples of main development activities are *Analyse requirements, Build component, Build architecture, Integrate and test system*. Examples of main management or quality assurance activities are *Start project, Terminate project, Check quality*.

Activities are aggregated forming a tree-like hierarchy. However, sub-activities may be *used* by several main activities - not just by their predecessor activity. All activities are described in a uniform manner following a scheme which contains (among others) the following items:

-   Name

-   View (it belongs to, cf. above)

-   Description

-   Pre- and post conditions

-   Roles (concerned by the activity)

3.2   Results

Similar to the activities, *results* are described in a schematic way using a form which contains (among others) the following items:

-   Name

-   Description

-   Example

-   Techniques (references to the corresponding section)

-   Literature references

Typical kinds of results are *project plan, requirements statement* or *class structure model*. A result can consist of several *subresults*, e.g. descriptions of *classes* and *relationships* are parts of the result *class structure model*.

3.3   Techniques

In this part, the main *techniques* are listed and described which are recommended for elaborating the results. Techniques include various kinds of diagrams as, for example, offered by the Unified Modeling Language (UML) [14], test procedures, management forms etc.

3.4   Roles

In this part, the main *roles* of people involved in a software development project are listed and described. The description includes a profile, i.e. a list of skills and qualifications associated with that role. Typical roles include the *project manager*, the *analyst*, the *designer*, the *programmer*, the *quality specialist*, the *support specialist*, the *user*.

3.5   Guidelines and Rules

Process modelling is just one part of the AD model. Another part consists of *guidelines* which aim to support the activities and to ensure readability, quality, and portability of development results. Examples are guidelines for object-oriented analysis, design, programming, building a software architecture etc. Each guideline consists of several *rules*. In the descriptions of the activities and techniques these rules are addressed in order to support a uniform, comparable and manageable application of the whole framework.

4   The Model Variants: Four Guided Tours through the Development Process

With the ingredients presented in the previous section, processes can be individually composed and cast to the particular project situation they are to be used and to the requirements resulting from that situation. However, experience shows that it is helpful (and sufficient for the major part of situations occurring in practice) to concentrate on a few "typical" processes which cover most of the real-life cases. For these selected processes, a possible line of processing can be predefined and used as a sample for running a concrete project. We call such a sample process a *model variant*.

Given a concrete project with its particular goals, requirements and environment, the most suited model variant can be selected using the criteria given in the subsequent section. The selected variant can then be modified and adapted to the specific needs of the project. In order to cover the majority of current project practices in GSBO, we have selected the following four model variants for detailed presentation in the AD model:

- Incremental development (INC),

- Component-based development (CBD),

- Phase-oriented development (PHA),

- Evolutionary Prototyping (EVP).

All variants are embedded in a general scheme for project management activities depicted in fig. 3:

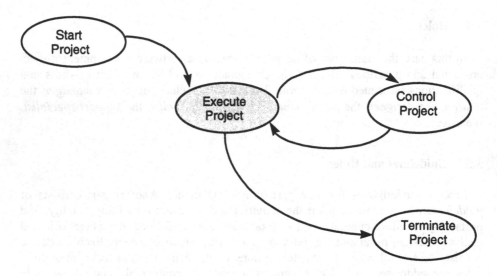

Fig. 3. General management scheme for all model variants

In fig. 3 we have used a very simple ad-hoc diagram technique (so-called *bubble-charts*) to illustrate a process consisting of activities (ovals), subactivities defined at other places (highlighted ovals) and sequence relations (arrows). The same bubble-chart technique will be used as well in the subsequent figures.

In the following sections, the four model variants are depicted by diagrams and briefly explained.

4.1   Incremental Development

This variant is based in the notion of increment. An *increment* is a piece of software which is added to an existing system in order to enhance its functionality or performance. To develop a system incrementally means to start with a relatively small kernel and enhance this kernel step by step by adding increments until the required functionality is reached. An increment may be – but is not required to be - a stand-alone executable unit.

Fig. 4 and 5 show the main steps of incremental development. The development process as a whole is embedded in management activities as shown in fig. 4. Analysis is done as a system-wide analysis (covering all increments) and may (optionally) be supported by developing an explorative prototype (fig. 4).

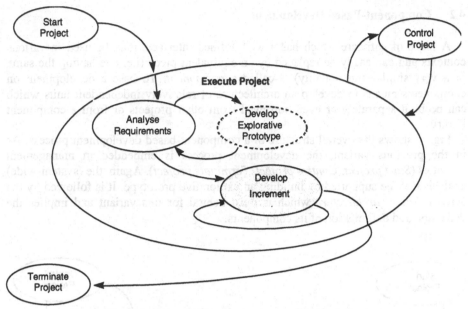

Fig. 4. Incremental development: overall project structure

Analogously, each development of an increment is considered as a kind of "project" with starting, controlling and concluding management activities (fig. 5). The central activity *Build increment* is refined to activities *Model increment, Implement increment* and *Integrate increment into application system* which are main activities of the reference model.

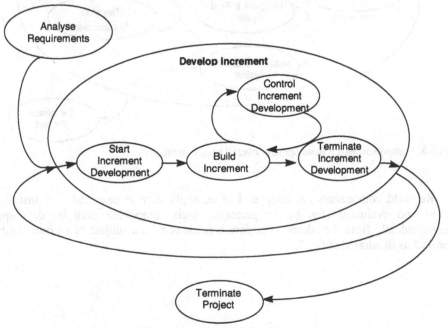

Fig. 5. Development of an increment

4.2   Component-Based Development

A piece of software which has a well-defined interface, may be used in various contexts and can easily be replaced by an equivalent piece (i.e. one having the same or a very similar functionality) is called a *component*. To base a development on components means to develop an architecture of relatively independent units which can be built separately or even borrowed from other projects or from a component library.

Fig. 6 shows the overall structure of a component-based development process. As in the previous variant, the development process is embedded in management activities (*Start project, Control project, Terminate project*). Again, the (system-wide) analysis may be supported by building an explorative prototype. It is followed by the activity *Build architecture* which is most central for this variant and implies the definition and delimitation of its components.

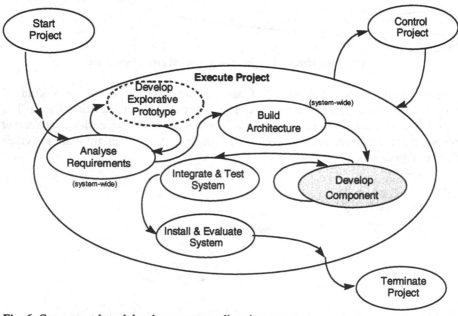

Fig. 6. Component-based development: overall project structure

Released components are integrated to an application system and then installed, used and evaluated (fig. 6). In principle, each component may be developed independently from the others. Therefore it is viewed as a subject of an own (sub-) project as illustrated in fig. 7.

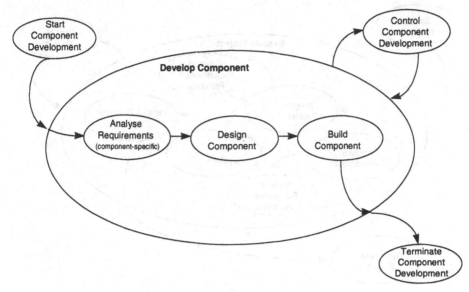

Fig. 7. Development of a component

4.3   Phase-Oriented Development

This is the most traditional of the four model variants. A project is assumed to deal with a rather monolithic system, i.e. one the structure of which is not explicitly reflected by the process structure. Basically, this structure is given by *phases,* i.e. temporal units which follow each other in a sequential manner. On the uppermost level, we distinguish four main phases which correspond to the activity categories introduced in section 3: *Analyse requirements* (with an optional development of explorative prototypes), *Design system* (with an optional development of experimental prototypes), *Build system, Install and evaluate system* (fig. 8).

4.4   Evolutionary Prototyping

Prototyping is a development technique which may be used at many places, in various situations and contexts. Thus we have to distinguish several kinds of prototyping. Following an earlier classification [3] we differentiate between *explorative, experimental and evolutionary prototyping.* Whereas the first two alternatives are rather viewed as supplementary activities supporting the analysis and design steps, resp., *evolutionary prototyping* is considered a technique which constitutes its own kind of process. Therefore, we have it included as a separate model variant.

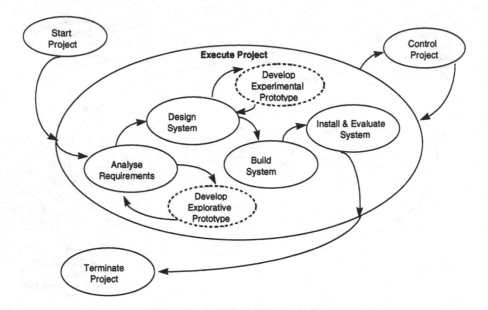

Fig. 8. Phase-oriented development: overall project structure

Evolutionary prototyping applies to projects in an unstable environment, with incomplete, unsafe or not yet defined requirements and constraints. Complex dynamic systems are characterised by the fact that they influence and change their environment which leads to new requirements and eventually results in a chain of feedback loops covering development and use steps [10]. This is reflected by our model variant (fig.'s 9 and 10):

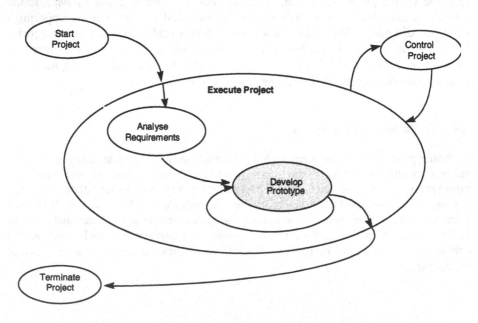

Fig. 9. Evolutionary prototyping: overall project structure

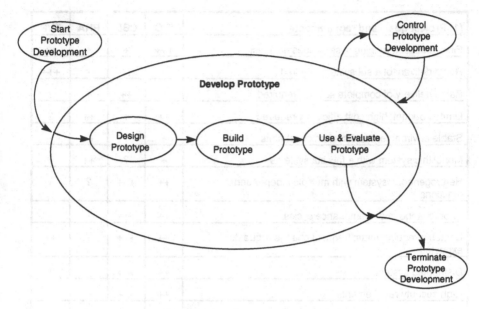

Fig. 10. Development of a prototype

5   Criteria for Variant Selection

In a given concrete situation of an evolving or starting project, it is often not easy to select the most appropriate model variant. In order to support this selection process, we have listed some criteria which normally influence the selection and scored the given model variants with respect to these criteria. Criteria have been classified in two groups:

-    Project goals and requirements

-    Process constraints

Note that the scores given in these tables are mainly based on experience and subjective assessment and are not verified by exact investigations or measurements. Thus they should be handled with care and rather taken as informal hints than as precise, objective rules.

In our present project practice, variants are used with different priority and frequency. Incremental development is often considered the most practicable and most generally applicable variant. Phase-oriented development has still a high preference, mainly for projects building on traditional application systems. Component-based development is considered a rather innovative alternative and still handled with some care and reserve. Evolutionary prototyping is the alternative which so far has least been experienced.

(1) Project goals and requirements	INC	CBD	PHA	EVP
First release, a running system does not exist	+++	+	+	++
Rapid delivery of a subsystem required	++	++	-	+++
Rapid delivery of complete solution required	+	++	+	?
Limited budget, high cost efficiency required	++	+	++	?
Stable environment and system constraints	+	?	++	-
Monolithic system with a few subsystems	+	?	++	?
Heterogeneous system with multiple independent functions	++	+++	?	+
Short change and maintenance cycles	++	+++	-	+
Unstable requirements; frequent change requests expected	++	+++	-	++
Distributed system	++	+++	-	+
High security requirements	++	++	+	?
High quality requirements	++	++	+	+

Fig. 11. Selection criteria: Project goals and requirements

Our selection criteria are rather new and cannot yet been judged reliably. At the moment, we are gathering feedback from the "users" of the AD model (mainly from the project managers and process engineers) in order to check and continuously improve the criteria and the scoring of variants.

(2) Process constraints	INC	CBD	PHA	EVP
Reusable software units or class library to be used	++	+++	?	+
Application is triggered by business processes	++	+	++	?
Business processes are (relatively) independent from each other	++	+++	-	++
Data-centred legacy system is to be integrated	+++	+	+	?
Complex, intertwined data structures	++	+	+	+
Many local, rather few global data	++	+++	?	?
Stable process conditions with a low probability of modifications	+	+	+++	-
Unstable process, requirements have still to be captured	++	++	-	+++
Large, complex system; high distribution of workload	++	+++	+	+
Cooperation project; work is widely shared with partners	+	+++	+	?

Fig. 12. Selection criteria: Process constraints

6   Conclusions

Faced with the requirements and goals of a wide range of different projects and partners in a large banking organisation we have come to the conclusion that there is no chance for a "uniform" software process. In order to cover a broad spectrum of projects we have presented a new approach to software process modelling based on a two-level framework: a base level defining all the raw material (e.g. sets of well-organised activities, techniques, results and roles) and a composition level combining the given material to process variants.

Well-known project variants like incremental, component-based, phase-oriented and evolutionary development can easily be described by using our simple bubble-chart notation. All variants are based on the same framework of activities, result types and techniques and are thus equally supported by the AD model.

Based on our experiences and subjective assessments we have developed an elaborated catalogue of criteria for the selection of the adequate process in a given situation. We believe that both the framework and the catalogue of criteria can easily be adapted to further process variants which might be included in the future. This way, the AD model and handbook constitutes an extensible piece of technology which can always easily be adapted to the current goals, requirements and practices.

The multi-variant approach reduces the average expenses for tailoring the process model to a broad range of projects in GSBO while it guarantees the applicability of several proven process patterns. The positive reaction of our user community, i.e. the project managers and engineers in the development centres in GSBO, is very promising and stimulating for our further work. In a next step we are going to implement our approach in a Web environment using HTML and JAVA for browsing and navigation.

Acknowledgement

We thank our colleagues Klaus Heuer for fruitful discussions and Stephan Düwel for his careful reading of the manuscript.

References

1. G. Booch: Object-Oriented Analysis and Design with Applications. Second Edition, Benjamin/Cummings Publ. Comp. 1994
2. A.M. Christie, A.N. Earl, M.I. Kellner, W.E. Riddle: A Reference Model for Process Technology. In: C. Montangero (Ed.): Software Process Technology, 5th European Workshop, EWSPT 96. Springer LNCS 1149, pp. 3-17 (1996)
3. C. Floyd: A systematic look at prototyping. In: R. Budde, K. Kuhlenkamp, L. Mathiassen, H. Züllighoven (eds.): Approaches to prototyping, Springer 1985
4. B. Henderson-Sellers, J.M. Edwards: Object-oriented software systems life cycle. Comm. of the ACM Vol. 33, No. 9 (1990)
5. W. Hesse: Theory and practice of the software process - a field study and its implications for project management. In: C. Montangero (Ed.): Software Process Technology, 5th European Workshop, EWSPT 96. Springer LNCS 1149, pp. 241-256 (1996)

6. W. Hesse: Life cycle models of object-oriented software development methodologies. In: A. Zendler et al.: Advanced concepts, life cycle models and tools for object-oriented software development. Reihe Softwaretechnik 7, Tectum Verlag Marburg 1997

7. W. Hesse: Improving the software process guided by the EOS model. In: Proc. SPI '97 European Conf. on Software Process Improvement. Barcelona 1997

8. W. Humphrey: Managing the software process. Addison-Wesley 1989

9. I. Jacobson: Object-Oriented Software Engineering - A Use Case Driven Approach. Revised Printing, Addison-Wesley 1993

10. M.M. Lehman: Programs, life cycles, and laws of software evolution. Proceedings of the IEEE. Vol. 68, No. 9, pp. 1060-1076 (1980)

11. J. Noack, B. Schienmann: Designing an Application Development Model for a Large Banking Organization. Proc. 20th Int. Conf. on Software Engineering, IEEE Computer Society Press, Kyoto, pp. 495-498 (1998)

12. J. Noack, B. Schienmann: Introducing Object Technology in a Large Banking Organization. IEEE Software (1999, to appear).

13. J. Rumbaugh, M. Blaha, W. Premerlani, F. Eddy, W. Lorensen: Object-Oriented Modeling and Design. Prentice Hall 1991

14. Unified Modeling Language (UML) Version 1.1 Specification, OMG documents ad/97-08-02 – ad/97-08-09 (1997)

An Ontological Analysis of Integrated Process Modelling

Peter Green[1], Michael Rosemann[2]

[1] University of Queensland, Department of Commerce
Salisbury Road, Ipswich QLD 4035, Australia
p.green@mailbox.uq.edu.au

[2] University of Muenster, Department of Information Systems
Steinfurter Str. 107, D-48149 Muenster, Germany
ismiro@wi.uni-muenster.de

Abstract. Process modelling has gained prominence in the information systems modelling area due to its focus on business processes and its usefulness in different business improvement methodologies. However, process modelling techniques are not without their criticisms. This paper proposes and uses the Bunge-Wand-Weber (BWW) representation model to analyse the four views - process, data, function, and organisation - provided in the Architecture of Integrated Information Systems (ARIS) popularised by Scheer [39, 40, 41]. The BWW representation model attempts to provide a theoretical base on which to evaluate and thus contribute to the improvement of information systems modelling techniques. The analysis conducted in this paper prompts some propositions. Among others, it confirms that the process view alone is not sufficient to model all the real-world constructs required. However, even when considering all four views in combination, problems may arise in representing all potentially required business rules, and specifying the scope and boundaries of the system under consideration, and employing a "top-down" approach to analysis and design.

1 Introduction

Methodological issues surrounding information systems development - the analysis, design, construction and implementation tasks - have long been central to the interest of information systems professionals, practitioners and researchers alike. Hirschheim *et al.* [19, 20], and most recently, Iivari *et al.* [22], and Mylopoulos [29] have reviewed rigorously many methodologies and their underlying philosophies as applied to information systems development. Researchers in information systems development have for years lamented the fact that little theoretical guidance only has been provided to practitioners on several areas involved in IS development [2, 15]. Consequently, methodologies, techniques, and grammars[1] have proliferated over time

---

[1] The terms methodology, technique, and grammar are distinguished in the following way in this paper. A *methodology* provides a comprehensive approach to systems planning, analysis, design, and construction such as Andersen's Method/1. It may include one or more techniques. A *technique* such as data flow diagramming designates a set of concepts and a way of handling them. Within a

M. Jarke, A. Oberweis (Eds.): CAiSE'99, LNCS 1626, pp. 225-240, 1999.

[24, 30]. This situation has contributed to what Banville and Landry [3] describe as the "fragmented adhocracy" of the state of theoretical development in the IS discipline. By contrast, Benbasat and Weber ([6], p. 398) implore the IS community to "not mix up the notions of the *core* of the IS discipline and the *body of knowledge* for the IS discipline." Moreover, Benbasat and Weber [6] go on to advocate that diversity (adhocracy) clearly has its place in IS research but not as an excuse for shirking the fundamental responsibility of a community to build its own theories to account for those *core* phenomena that differentiate the IS discipline from other disciplines.

In an attempt to address this situation, Wand and Weber [47, 48, 49, 50, 51, 52, 53] have developed and refined a set of models that specify what they believe are a set of core phenomena for the IS discipline. These models are based on an ontology defined by Bunge [7] and are referred to as the Bunge-Wand-Weber (BWW) models. These models, in particular their representation model, provide a theoretical basis on which information systems modelling grammars and the scripts prepared using such grammars can be evaluated. As Weber [54] argues, this evaluative aspect of the models persists irrespective of the philosophical assumptions under which the models are applied. His and Wand's central concern is with the goodness of the *representation* of the perception of that portion of the real world that is being modelled. Various researchers have demonstrated the applicability and usefulness of these models for such grammars as data flow diagrams, entity-relationship diagrams, object-oriented schemas, the relational model, NIAM, and grammars in CASE tools [17, 31, 44, 46, 48, 52, 53, 54, 55].

For many years now however, there has been an increased recognition in information systems modelling of the dynamic behaviour of organisations. Process modelling has been embraced as an appropriate approach to describe the behaviour and as a mechanism by which many of the related concerns with the traditional modelling grammars can be overcome [10]. Moreover, process modelling focuses on understanding the underlying business processes which many IS professionals believe is fundamental to the successful implementation of technology-based change in organisations [13]. As Becker *et al.* ([5], p. 821) explain, "process models are ... images of the logical and temporal order of functions performed on a process object. They are the foundation for the operationalisation of process-oriented approaches."

The popularity of concentrating on business processes through process modelling has been fuelled over the last ten years by the prominence of such organisational improvement approaches as Total Quality Management, Time-based Management, Business Process Reengineering (BPR), Value-based Performance Measurement, and Workflow Management. Furthermore, the rapid worldwide take-up over the last five years of enterprise resource planning (ERP) software such as SAP R/3 or BaanERP that rely heavily on reference process models to describe the software functionality and to guide and document implementation has added significantly to the interest and

---

technique, these concepts are represented typically by formal graphical symbols. In this paper, the set of symbols together with its construction rules is called a *grammar*.

perceived usefulness of process modelling. In particular in conjunction with the success of software specific reference models, integrated process modelling that provides various *views* of the process to users has received much attention [9, 14, 28]. However, process modelling is not without its critics who point to such deficiencies as an emphasis on the "hard" factors (who, what, when, and where) to the detriment of the "soft" factors (norms, beliefs, and motives) in the examination and modelling of processes [13].

The aim then of this study is to analyse as an example the integrated process modelling grammar within the ARIS-famework popularised by Scheer [39, 40, 41] using the BWW theory base to determine the ability of this grammar to provide "good representations of the perceptions" of business analysts. Accordingly, this work is motivated by several factors. First, through such an analysis, potential weaknesses of integrated process modelling grammars can be identified. Such an analysis can then potentially contribute to the theoretical development of integrated process modelling. Second, the results of the analysis in this paper may be useful to the implementers and users of comprehensive process-based software systems such as SAP R/3 or BaanERP. SAP has stated that in subsequent versions of its product they intend the implementation/ customisation process to be driven directly by modifications made to the relevant reference process models supplied in the product. In BaanERP it is already possible to derive from the tailored reference model the information necessary for system customisation and authorisation ([45], p. 4). In such a situation, potential weaknesses in integrated process modelling identified in this analysis may provide useful information to the implementers of such software systems. Third, this study provides an opportunity to extend the existing work on the application of the BWW models. To date, the BWW models have in the main been applied to "traditional" information systems analysis and design (ISAD) grammars. This paper extends their application into the dynamic area of process modelling. Fourth, this study will add to the development of the BWW models by extending their application to a different modelling environment. By such a further application, the robustness of the BWW ontological constructs can be examined. Finally, the implications of the analysis can be articulated as hypotheses and empirically tested with a base of integrated process modelling users. The results of such a step will contribute to the development of the BWW models and integrated process modelling.

Consequently, this paper proceeds in the following manner. First, some background on the development of the BWW models and integrated process modelling is given. This section is followed by the analysis of the integrated modelling grammars. Included in this section is a brief discussion of why Scheer's Architecture of Integrated Information Systems was selected for analysis. The analytical methodology is explained using the process view of this integrated modelling grammars as an example. In particular, the ontological implications of examining the views in combination are discussed. Following this work, an initial set of hypotheses is presented. Finally, some conclusions and directions for further research are sketched.

2 Background

2.1 The Bunge-Wand-Weber (BWW) Models

As the number of grammars for information systems modelling has grown over the years, information systems researchers and professionals together have attempted to derive bases on which to compare, evaluate, and determine when to use these grammars [4, 24, 43]. Since the advent of computers, grammars for information systems requirements modelling have progressed from flowcharts, to data flow diagrams, to entity-relationship diagrams, to object-oriented schemas and integrated process modelling systems [29]. Since the early 1980's, however, many IS researchers have lamented the paucity of theoretical foundation for modelling grammar specification.

In an attempt to provide such a theoretical foundation for the design and the evaluation of modelling grammars, Wand and Weber [47, 48, 49, 50, 51, 52, 53] have investigated the branch of philosophy known as ontology (or meta-physics) as a theoretical foundation for understanding the modelling of information systems. Ontology is a well-established theoretical domain within philosophy dealing with models of reality, that is, the nature of the real world ([29], 30-33). Wand and Weber [48, 49, 50, 52, 53] have taken, and extended, an ontology presented by Bunge [7] and applied it to the modelling of information systems. Their fundamental premise is that any modelling grammar must be able to represent all things in the real world that might be of interest to users of information systems; otherwise, the resultant model is incomplete.

The Bunge-Wand-Weber (BWW) [48, 49, 50, 52, 53] models consist of the representation model, the state-tracking model, and the good decomposition model. This work concentrates on the use of the representation model. The representation model defines a set of constructs that, at this time, are thought by Wand and Weber to be necessary and sufficient to describe the structure and behaviour of the real world. To date, however, concerns remain, *inter alia*, with regard to a lack of understandability of the BWW constructs, the problematic application of these constructs to other loosely defined modelling grammars, and the limited empirical testing of the implications of the BWW models [44, 52, 54]. This work attempts to mitigate these concerns in part. Table 1 presents definitions for the constructs of the BWW representation model.

Table 1. Ontological constructs in the BWW Representation model

Ontological Construct	Explanation
THING*	A thing is the elementary unit in the BWW ontological model. The real world is made up of things. Two or more things (composite or simple) can be associated into a composite thing.
PROPERTY*: -IN GENERAL -IN PARTICULAR -HEREDITARY -EMERGENT -INTRINSIC -NON-BINDING MUTUAL -BINDING MUTUAL -ATTRIBUTES	Things possess properties. A property is modelled via a function that maps the thing into some value. For example, the attribute "weight" represents a property that all humans possess. In this regard, weight is an attribute standing for a property in general. If we focus on the weight of a specific individual, however, we would be concerned with a property in particular. A property of a composite thing that belongs to a component thing is called an hereditary property. Otherwise it is called an emergent property. Some properties are inherent properties of individual things. Such properties are called intrinsic. Other properties are properties of pairs or many things. Such properties are called mutual. Non-binding mutual properties are those properties shared by two or more things that do not "make a difference" to the things involved; for example, order relations or equivalence relations. By contrast, binding mutual properties are those properties shared by two or more things that do "make a difference" to the things involved. Attributes are the names that are used to represent properties of things.
CLASS	A class is a set of things that can be defined via their possessing a single property.
KIND	A kind is a set of things that can be defined only via their possessing two or more common properties.
STATE*	The vector of values for all property functions of a thing is the state of the thing.
CONCEIVABLE STATE SPACE	The set of all states that the thing might ever assume is the conceivable state space of the thing.
STATE LAW: -STABILITY CONDITION -CORRECTIVE ACTION	A state law restricts the values of the properties of a thing to a subset that is deemed lawful because of natural laws or human laws. The stability condition specifies the states allowed by the state law. The corrective action specifies how the value of the property function must change to provide a state acceptable under the state law.
LAWFUL STATE SPACE	The lawful state space is the set of states of a thing that comply with the state laws of the thing. The lawful state space is usually a proper subset of the conceivable state space.
CONCEIVABLE EVENT SPACE	The event space of a thing is the set of all possible events that can occur in the thing.
TRANSFORM- ATION*	A transformation is a mapping from one state to another state.
LAWFUL TRANSFORM- ATION -STABILITY CONDITION -CORRECTIVE ACTION	A lawful transformation defines which events in a thing are lawful. The stability condition specifies the states that are allowable under the transformation law. The corrective action specifies how the values of the property function(s) must change to provide a state acceptable under the transformation law.
LAWFUL EVENT SPACE	The lawful event space is the set of all events in a thing that are lawful.
HISTORY	The chronologically-ordered states that a thing traverses in time are the history of the thing.
ACTS ON	A thing acts on another thing if its existence affects the history of the other thing.
COUPLING: BINDING MUTUAL PROPERTY	Two things are said to be coupled (or interact) if one thing acts on the other. Furthermore, those two things are said to share a binding mutual property (or relation); that is, they participate in a relation that "makes a difference" to the things.
SYSTEM	A set of things is a system if, for any bi-partitioning of the set, couplings exist among things in the two subsets.
SYSTEM COMPOSITION	The things in the system are its composition.
SYSTEM ENVIRONMENT	Things that are not in the system but interact with things in the system are called the environment of the system.
SYSTEM STRUCTURE	The set of couplings that exist among things within the system, and among things in the environment of the system and things in the system is called the structure.
SUBSYSTEM	A subsystem is a system whose composition and structure are subsets of the composition and structure of another system.

Table 1. Ontological constructs in the BWW Representation model	
Ontological Construct	**Explanation**
SYSTEM DECOMPOSI-TION	A decomposition of a system is a set of subsystems such that every component in the system is either one of the subsystems in the decomposition or is included in the composition of one of the subsystems in the decomposition.
LEVEL STRUCTURE	A level structure defines a partial order over the subsystems in a decomposition to show which subsystems are components of other subsystems or the system itself.
EXTERNAL EVENT	An external event is an event that arises in a thing, subsystem, or system by virtue of the action of some thing in the environment on the thing, subsystem, or system.
STABLE STATE*	A stable state is a state in which a thing, subsystem, or system will remain unless forced to change by virtue of the action of a thing in the environment (an external event).
UNSTABLE STATE	An unstable state is a state that will be changed into another state by virtue of the action of transformations in the system.
INTERNAL EVENT	An internal event is an event that arises in a thing, subsystem, or system by virtue of lawful transformations in the thing, subsystem, or system.
WELL-DEFINED EVENT	A well-defined event is an event in which the subsequent state can always be predicted given that the prior state is known.
POORLY-DEFINED EVENT	A poorly-defined event is an event in which the subsequent state cannot be predicted given that the prior state is known.

*Source: [49, 53, 54] with minor modifications. * indicates a fundamental and core ontological construct.*

2.2 Integrated Process Modelling

A process can be defined as the sequence of functions that are necessary to transform a business-relevant object (*e.g.,* purchase order, invoice). From an information systems perspective, a model of a process is a description of the control flow. Process modelling is not a new phenomenon. Indeed, the research into process modelling predates that of data modelling if Chen's milestone article [8] about the E-R model represents the birth of data modelling. The basic grammar of most process modelling approaches derives from Petri's doctoral thesis [33]. Since that time, intensive research on this topic has been undertaken. Today, many different, often highly sophisticated, Petri-net approaches exit [32, 34]. All in all, regarding the methodology the Petri-net related research appears to be well developed, however, it lacked a realistic business application.

At the beginning of this decade, the idea of process management gained significant prominence [11, 12, 18, 19, 42]. From a strategic business viewpoint, process management advocated a radical change from a functional focus to a (business) process orientation to cope successfully with new challenges like customer focus and technological development. The publications of Hammer [18, 19] and Davenport [11] in particular triggered intensive research on process management. Accordingly, it would seem now that a process orientation is achieving popularity not only in the business administration discipline but also within the information systems community. For example, workflow management systems [16, 23] represent a new process-oriented middleware.

Process modelling for the various purposes of process management faces three main (new) requirements. First, the process model must include more information than just a representation of the control flow. In addition to the control flow, a comprehensive process model should include at least:

1. Information about the *organisational units* (*e.g.* internal and external persons, departments, (project) groups) that are involved in the process by having to execute certain tasks or be responsible for the performance of those tasks;
2. the *data* that are necessary for a function to process - input data - and the data that result from the execution of a function - output data; and
3. references to existing repositories that describe the *functions* within an enterprise. As Curtis *et al.* (1992, p. 75) explain, "Process modelling is distinguished from other types of modelling in computer science because many of the phenomena modelled must be enacted by a human rather than a machine." Thus a process model should also include manual functions.

Further requirements of business process modelling include the integration of business objectives, business partners such as customers and vendors, temporal aspects (*e.g.* deadlines), involved knowledge, and/or resources such as application systems.

Second, a process model should not only be comprehensive but it must also be *easy to understand*. Only in this case it can be used as a platform for communication with business people who are not familiar with process modelling. Current elaborated Petri-nets cannot fulfil this requirement as they are developed from method experts for method experts. Third, process models should be *based on a meta model* to serve as a well-defined starting point for the development of software like workflow-based applications [26]. Further applications of process models as a result of the requirements engineering that require a runtime component are animation or simulation. All in all, process models, that are not only used for the purpose of developing software must be comprehensive, understandable and formal at the same time.

3 The Analysis

3.1 Why Analyse Scheer's [39, 40, 41] Work?

The increasing prominence of process management together with insufficient existing Petri-net approaches has motivated a significant amount of research in the business process modelling area. One of the most successful grammars for process modelling is *event-driven process chains (EPC)*. This grammar is embedded in the *Architecture of Integrated Information Systems (ARIS)* [1, 25, 39, 40, 41]. Like Petri-nets, event-driven process chains are bipartite graphs with active nodes (functions, designed as soft rectangles) and passive nodes (events, designed as hexagons). In addition to the facilities of Petri-nets, event-driven process chains express explicitly the logic of the control flow, *viz.*, joining and splitting points. Three connectors are used to describe the logical AND, the exclusive OR (A or B), and the inclusive OR (A or B or (A and B)). These connectors represent a principal point of differentiation from most Petri-net based grammars. In summary then, an event-driven process chain depicts who (organisational view) is responsible for which function (functional view), what input data is needed, and what output data is produced by the transformation of which business objects (data view). Figure 1 shows this integrated process modelling approach embedded in the so-called ARIS house and without the output view [39, 40, 41], which includes the output of every function. This view is substituted by representing the process object (here: purchase order), which is related to the data view ([35], 76-84).

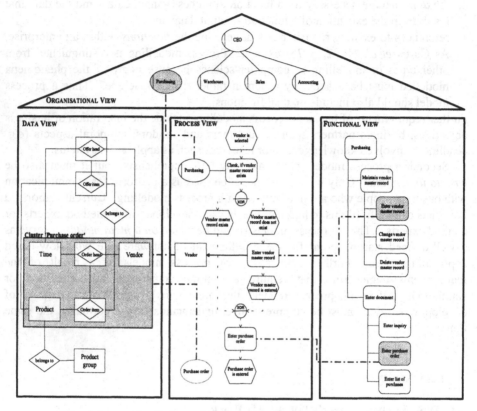

Fig. 1. Integration in the Architecture of Integrated Information Systems

The integration of four views and the relatively easy-to-understand resultant process models are not the only reasons the ARIS-approach was selected to exemplify an ontological analysis of integrated process modelling. Other reasons include:

1. ARIS-Toolset 4.0 provides a "cutting-edge" upper CASE tool that supports the Architecture of Integrated Information Systems. With more than 10,000 licences worldwide, there appears to be a large, mature user base against which the implications of the analysis in this work can be tested. Furthermore, on extending the analysis in future work to cover the implementation aspects of process modelling, again a mature user base will be available for verification of hypotheses.

2. One of the world's most popular ERP software packages, SAP R/3, also uses the grammar that is employed principally within ARIS to describe processes - the event-driven process chain [9, 28]. Within SAP R/3, more than 800 event-driven

process chains explain the functionality of the software - the so-called business blueprint. Consequently, it appears to be a relatively straightforward task to extend the ontological analysis to the software-specific reference models of this ERP-software.

First attempts at integrating event-driven process chains with object-oriented approaches such as UML have been reported [27]. Consequently, this *de facto* object-oriented language represents an area of potential interest for ongoing research stemming from the work reported in this paper.

3.2 Analysis Performed

The aim of this work is to extend the BWW ontological analysis to "state of the art" business process modelling grammars.

Table 2 presents the ontological analysis of the ARIS views (process, data, function, organisation). To explain the application of the analytical methodology, the process view of the Architecture of Integrated Information Systems will be used as an example. A *thing* as an elementary ontological construct is not a part of the original meta model of event-driven process chains.[2] Because a function type within an event-driven process chain can be seen as the transformation of a business relevant object, an EPC function type can be interpreted to represent a *property in general* of that object. Attribute types in EPC represent *attributes* in the BWW representation model. The ontological construct *class*, however, is not represented in the EPC-grammar.

As opposed to grammars that depict the structure of a system (*e.g.*, the Entity-Relationship (E-R) model), process modelling languages focus on the behavioural aspects of what is being modelled. Consequently, the ontological constructs *state*, *transformation*, and *event* are most relevant. *Transformations* are represented by function types in the event-driven process chains while *states* are depicted as event types. Accordingly, the triple, event type – function type – event type, in an EPC represents the ontological construct *event*, and usually *internal events* that are *well-defined*. The homonym between the EPC event type and the ontological *event* requires careful attention during the analysis. Similarly, a *state law* can be represented by the triple, function type – connector – event type, while a *lawful transformation* can be represented by the pattern, event type – connector – function type. An *external event* may be represented by the start event type at the beginning of an EPC while the final *stable state* (of an object) may be represented by the end event type at the bottom of an EPC.

---

[2] The original work of Scheer [41] is referenced here. Further approaches that extend this meta model with business objects (*e.g.*, [27, 35]) are not analysed in this study.

Ontological Construct	Process View	Data View	Function View	Organisational View
		Table 2. BWW Representation Model Analysis of Integrated Process Modelling Views		
THING				User, department (instances)
PROPERTY: IN PARTICULAR IN GENERAL INTRINSIC MUTUAL EMERGENT HEREDITARY ATTRIBUTES	Function Type Attribute type	 Attribute type	Function Type Attribute type	 Attribute type
CLASS		Entity type		Organisation type
KIND		Specialisation/generalisation (IS-A)	Specialisation/generalisation (IS-A)	Organisation type
STATE	Event type (only the state variables that trigger the function)			
CONCEIVABLE STATE SPACE				
STATE LAW	Function type → connector → Event type	Specialisation/generalisation descriptors; [Min., max.] cardinalities	Specialisation/generalisation descriptors	
LAWFUL STATE SPACE				
EVENT	Event type → Function type → Event type			
PROCESS	Process model Function type		Function type Process oriented function decomposition	
CONCEIVABLE EVENT SPACE				
TRANSFORM-ATION	Function type		Function type	
LAWFUL TRANSFORM-ATION	Event type → connector → Function type			
LAWFUL EVENT SPACE				
HISTORY				
ACTS ON				
COUPLING: BINDING MUTUAL PROPERTY		Relationship type (no symbol for relationship in grammar)		
SYSTEM				
SYSTEM COMPOSITION		Cluster		
SYSTEM ENVIRONMENT				
SYSTEM STRUCTURE				
SUBSYSTEM		Cluster		Organisational hierarchy
SYSTEM DECOMPOSI-TION	Function type decomposition indicator Event type decomposition indicator			Organisational hierarchy
LEVEL STRUCTURE	Series of function type or event type decomposition indicators		Series of function type decomposition indicators	

Ontological Construct	Process View	Data View	Function View	Organisational View
Table 2. BWW Representation Model Analysis of Integrated Process Modelling Views				
EXTERNAL EVENT	Start event type (no ingoing arrow)			
STABLE STATE	End event type (no outgoing arrow; event types generally have one ingoing & one outgoing arrow)			
UNSTABLE STATE				
INTERNAL EVENT	Event type → Function type → Event type			
WELL-DEFINED EVENT	Event type → Function type → Event type			
POORLY-DEFINED EVENT				

4 Some Propositions

In the light of an *isolated analysis of the process view*, some propositions can be made:

1. Because there are no direct representations for thing, class, and/or kind, users will lack conceptual clarity regarding the object(s) in the real world to which the EPC relates. The EPC can represent indirectly attributes of the thing (business object) as attributes of the function type but not the thing itself. As Weber [54] explains, the world is made up of things. Things in the world are identified via their properties; not the other way round. Accordingly, some other symbol/grammar/view will be needed in conjunction with the process view to overcome this ontological deficiency.

2. Because the process view does not have representations for *conceivable state space, lawful state space, conceivable event space*, and *lawful event space*, a sufficient focus to identify all important state and transformation laws may not be present during modelling. These laws are the basis of what are known in systems analysis as business rules. Accordingly, problems may be encountered in capturing all the potentially important business rules of the situation. Again, some other symbol/grammar/view may need to be employed in combination with the process view to overcome this shortage.

3. Because the process view does not have representations for *system, system composition, system environment, system structure, subsystem, history, acts on, unstable state*, and *poorly-defined event*, the process view's usefulness for defining the scope and boundaries of the system being analysed is undermined. Moreover, the usefulness of the process view for undertaking "good decompositions" (see [53], for example) during analysis is undermined. Again, the use of some other symbol/grammar/view would appear necessary to overcome this deficiency.

Scheer's [39, 40, 41] integrated process modelling is designed around the four views to reduce complexity during the analysis and design task. Accordingly, the views are intended to be used in combination during a project. Moreover, this combined use of the views is encouraged by Scheer's [41] claims that, when determining which views to use, relationships within views are high while the relationships between the views are relatively simple and loosely linked.

When the *analysis of the four views in combination* in Table 2 is considered, some interesting propositions issue.

4. Even across the four views, no representations exist for *conceivable state space, lawful state space, conceivable event space,* or *lawful event space.* Again, a sufficient focus to identify all important state and transformation laws may not be present during modelling. Accordingly, problems may be encountered in capturing all the potentially important business rules of the situation. Now, some other symbol/grammar/view *in addition to the integrated process modelling system* may need to be employed to overcome this deficiency.

5. Across the four views, no representations exist for *system, system environment, system structure, history, acts on, unstable state,* and *poorly-defined event.* Again, its usefulness for defining the scope and boundaries of the system being analysed is undermined. Moreover, the usefulness of integrated process modelling for undertaking "good decompositions" during analysis would seem undermined. Indeed, because of this situation, integrated process modelling would appear more useful in modelling existing situations to be modified (*i.e.,* where a bottom-up approach is appropriate) as opposed to novel situations (*i.e.,* where a top-down approach might be more appropriate).

Of course, other explanations may exist for the fact that representations for the ontological constructs mentioned in propositions 4 and 5 do not exist in any of the four views. First, the BWW theory may be misspecified or simply wrong. This question however can only be answered after substantially more empirical testing has been performed on the models. Second, for practitioners in the real world, the cost of having and using symbols for these particular ontological constructs in the process modelling views may outweigh the representational benefits that they provide. This question refers to the economical efficiency of modelling activities [36] and is also one that must be answered with empirical evidence.

Green [17] investigated the use of information systems analysis and design (ISAD) grammars in combination within upper CASE tools. In that work, he operationalised a concept known as *minimal ontological overlap (MOO).* This concept was proposed by Weber and Zhang [55] when they concluded from their field work that users would find most useful combinations of grammars in which the grammars overlapped minimally in terms of ontological constructs. Green [17] proposed that, to form a MOO-set of grammars, *inter alia,* one would select a starting grammar and add grammars to it until the set was as ontologically complete as possible (*maximal ontological completeness (MOC)*). Following the rule of parsimony, this set of grammars would be formed using as few grammars as possible. Applying these concepts to the views in Table 2, if the process view is selected as a starting point, then the data view and the organisational view would need to be employed to form the MOO set. The function view however appears to be ontologically redundant when compared to the MOO-set of grammars. This situation suggests the following proposition:

6. Because the function view is ontologically redundant when compared to the combination of process view, data view, and organisational view, its use with the other views will undermine clarity and may cause confusion to users. Accordingly, limited usefulness and use of the function view is expected.

5 Conclusion and Future Directions

This paper has analysed the event-driven process chain popularised by Scheer using the BWW theory base to determine the ability of this grammar to provide a "good representation of the perceptions" of business analysts. Through such an analysis, it has identified some areas where potential contributions can be made to the theoretical development of integrated process modelling. Moreover, this study has extended the existing work on the application of the BWW models. To date, the BWW models have in the main been applied to "traditional" information systems analysis and design (ISAD) grammars. This paper has extended their application into the area of process modelling. Results of the analysis in this work have drawn into question the robustness of certain BWW ontological constructs *e.g.*, *conceivable state space, lawful state space, conceivable event space*, and *lawful event space*. Finally, the implications of the analysis have been articulated as a set of propositions. In further work, it is intended to operationalise these propositions into a set of hypotheses that can be tested in the field against a mature integrated process modelling user base.

The work in this paper exemplifies two concerns that have consistently arisen within the information systems research community over the time that the BWW ontological models have been developed and used. First, the understandability of the constructs within the models has been criticised by various sections of the research community. Wand and Weber [49] originally defined the constructs using a rigourous set-theoretic language. Even though in many subsequent works the researchers attempted to simplify and clarify the explanation of the constructs by defining them using plain English, the criticism of lack of understandability has remained. Second, Wand and Weber [52], Weber and Zhang [55], and Weber [54] concede the difficulty in applying the models to grammars and scripts produced using those modelling grammars. This difficulty stems from the fact that, although the Wand and Weber constructs have clearly defined set-theoretic definitions, the grammars and scripts to which they are applied have at best loose definitions. Consequently, the analysis performed using the BWW models rely to a large extent on the knowledge and experience of the researcher(s) performing the analysis. Such a situation leads to limitations on the results of work in the area.

In an attempt to address these concerns, further work out of this paper will involve the development of a meta model for the BWW representation constructs. The meta language that has been selected for use is an extended form of the Entity-Relationship (E-R) model [41]. Meta models using a similar meta language have proved popular in explaining the constructs of modern modelling techniques, for example, workflow models [37] and object-oriented schemas [38]. Work is well progressed in this direction. As a part of ongoing research work, the entire meta model for the BWW ontological constructs will be compared with existing meta models for different process modelling grammars. With regard to the level of abstraction, the BWW meta model can be viewed as a meta-meta-model. Relationship meta models between the BWW meta model and the grammar-specific meta models will project the results of the ontological analysis. Situations such as construct excess, redundancy, or overload (*e.g.*, [53]) will be transparent in the models.

Acknowledgement

The authors are indebted to Ron Weber, University of Queensland, Brisbane, Australia, Andreas L. Opdahl, University of Bergen, Norway, and participants at the workshops on ontological issues in information systems at the University of Queensland in 1998 for their helpful comments.

References

[1]   van der Aalst, W.M.P.: Formalization and Verification of Event-driven Process Chains. In: Backhouse, R.C., Baeten, J.C.M. (eds.): Computing Science Rep. 98/01. University of Technology, Eindhoven (1998)

[2]   Bansler, J.P., Bodker, K.: A reappraisal of structured analysis: Design in an organizational context. ACM Transactions on Information Systems 11 (1993) 2, 165-193

[3]   Banville, C., Landry, M.: Can the field of MIS be disciplined? Communications of the ACM 32 (1989) 1, 48-60

[4]   Batra, D., Hoffer, J.A., Bostrom, R.P.: Comparing representations with relational and EER models. Communications of the ACM 33 (1990) 2, 126-139

[5]   Becker, J., Rosemann, M., Schütte, R.: Business-to-business process integration: Functions and methods. In: Galliers, R. *et al.* (eds.): Proceedings of the 5th European Conference on Information Systems (ECIS '97), Vol. II, Cork, Ireland (1997), 816-827

[6]   Benbasat, I., Weber, R.: Research commentary: Rethinking "diversity" in information systems research. Information Systems Research 7 (1996) 4, 389-399

[7]   Bunge, M.: Treatise on Basic Philosophy: Volume 3: Ontology I: The Furniture of the World, Reidel, Boston (1977)

[8]   Chen, P.P.-S.: Entity-Relationship Model: Towards a Unified View of Data. ACM Transactions on Database Systems 1 (1976) 1, 9-36

[9]   Curran, Th., Keller, G.: SAP R/3 Business Blueprint. Prentice Hall, New Jersey (1998)

[10]   Curtis, B., Kellner, M.I., Over, J.: Process Modeling. Communications of the ACM 35 (1992) 9, 75-90

[11]   Davenport, T.H.: Process Innovation. Reengineering Work through Information Technology, Boston (1993)

[12]   Davenport, T.H., Stoddard, D.B.: Reengineering: Business Change of Mythic Proportions? MIS Quarterly 18 (1994) 2, 121-127

[13]   Ellison, M., McGrath, G.M.: Recording and analysing business processes: An activity theory based approach. The Australian Computer Journal 30 (1998) 4, 146-152

[14]   van Es, R.: Dynamic Enterprise Innovation, 3rd ed., Ede (1998)

[15]   Floyd, C.: A comparative evaluation of system development methods. In: Information Systems Design Methodologies: Improving the Practice, North-Holland, Amsterdam (1986), 19-37

[16] Georgakopoulos, D., Hornick, M., Sheth, A.: An Overview of Workflow-Management: From Process Modeling to Workflow Automation Infrastructure. Distributed and Parallel Databases 3 (1995) 2, 119-153

[17] Green, P.: Use of Information Systems Analysis and Design (ISAD) Grammars in Combination in Upper CASE Tools – An Ontological Evaluation. In: Siau, K., Wand, Y., Parsons, J. (eds.): Proceedings of the 2nd CAiSE/IFIP8.1 International Workshop on the Evaluation of Modeling Methods in Systems Analysis and Design (EMMSAD'97), Barcelona, Spain (1997), 1-12

[18] Hammer, M.: Reengineering Work: Don't Automate, Obliterate. Harvard Business Review 68 (1990) 7-8, 104-112

[19] Hammer, M., Champy, J.: Reengineering the Corporation. A Manifesto for Business Revolution, New York (1993)

[20] Hirschheim, R., Klein, H.K., Lyytinen, K.: Information Systems Development and Data Modeling: Conceptual and Philosophical Foundations. Cambridge University Press, New York (1995)

[21] Hirschheim, R., Klein, H.K., Lyytinen, K.: Exploring the intellectual structures of information systems development: a social action theoretic analysis. Accounting, Management and Information Technologies 6 (1996) 1/2, 1-64

[22] Iivari, J., Hirschheim, R., Klein, H.K.: A paradigmatic analysis contrasting information systems development approaches and methodologies. Information Systems Research 9 (1998) 2, 164-193.

[23] Jablonski, St., Bussler, Chr.: Workflow Management, Thomson, London et al. (1996)

[24] Karam, G.M. & Casselman, R.S.: A cataloging framework for software development methods. IEEE Computer, Feb. (1993), 34-46

[25] Langner, P., Schneider, C., Wehler, J.: Petri Net Based Certification of Event driven Process Chains. In: Desel, J., Silva, M. (eds.): Application and Theory of Petri Nets 1998. Lecture Notes in Computer Science, Vol. 1420. Springer-Verlag, Berlin (1998)

[26] Leymann, F., Roller, D.: Workflow-based Applications. IBM Systems Journal 36 (1997) 1, 102-133

[27] Loos, P., Allweyer, Th.: Process Orientation and Object-Orientation - An Approach for Integrating UML and Event-Driven Process Chains. Institut für Wirtschaftsinformatik. Paper 144. Saarbrücken (1998)

[28] Meinhardt, St., Popp, K.: Configuring Business Application Systems. In: Bernus, P., Mertins, K., Schmidt, G. (eds.): Handbook on Architectures of Information Systems. Springer-Verlag, Berlin (1998), 651-666

[29] Mylopoulos, J.: Characterizing Information Modeling Techniques, In: Bernus, P., Mertins, K., Schmidt, G. (eds.): Handbook on Architectures of Information Systems. Springer-Verlag, Berlin (1998), 17-57

[30] Olle, T.W., Hagelstein, J., Macdonald, I.G., Rolland, C., Sol, H.G., Van Assche, F.J.M., Verrijn-Stuart, A.A.: Information Systems Methodologies: A Framework for Understanding. Addison-Wesley, Wokingham (1991)

[31] Parsons, J., Wand, Y.: The object paradigm as a representational model. Working Paper. The University of British Columbia. Vancouver (1992), 1-22

[32] Peterson, J.-L.: Petri Net Theory and the Modeling of System, Prentice-Hall, NJ (1981)

[33] Petri, C. A.: Kommunikation mit Automaten, Bonn (1962) (in German)

[34] Reisig, W.: Petri Nets: an introduction. Springer-Verlag, Berlin (1985)

[35] Rosemann, M.: Komplexitätsmanagement in Prozeßmodellen. Gabler-Verlag, Wiesbaden (1996) (in German)

[36] Rosemann, M.: Managing the Complexity of Multiperspective Information Models using the Guidelines of Modelling. In: Fowler, D., Dawson, L. (eds.): Proceedings of the 3rd Australian Conference on Requirements Engineering (ACRE '98). Geelong, Australia (1998), 101-118

[37] Rosemann, M., zur Mühlen, M.: Evaluation of Workflow Management Systems – a Meta Model Approach. Australian Journal of Information Systems 6 (1998) 1, 103-116

[38] Saeki, M.: Object-Oriented Meta Modelling. In: Papazoglou, M.P. (ed.): Proceedings of the 14th International Conference on Object Oriented and Entity Relationship Modelling. Berlin (1995), 250-259

[39] Scheer, A.-W.: ARIS–Business Process Frameworks. 2nd edn. Springer-Verlag, Berlin (1998)

[40] Scheer, A.-W.: ARIS – Business Process Modeling. 2nd edn. Springer-Verlag, Berlin (1998)

[41] Scheer, A.-W.: Business Process Engineering. 3rd edn. Springer-Verlag, Berlin (1998)

[42] Scherr, A. L.: A new approach to business processes. IBM Systems Journal 32 (1993) 1, 80-98

[43] Seligmann, P.S., Wijers, G.M., Sol, H.G.: Analyzing the structure of I.S. methodologies: An alternative approach. In: Maes, R. (ed.): Proceedings of 1st Dutch Conference on Information Systems (1989), 1-28

[44] Sinha, A.P., Vessey, I.: End-user data modeling: An ontological evaluation of relational and object-oriented schema diagrams. Working Paper. Indiana University. Indiana (1995)

[45] Verbeek, M.: On Tools & Models. In: van Es, R. (ed.): Dynamic Enterprise Innovation. 3rd edn. Ede (1998)

[46] Wand, Y., Wang, R.: Anchoring Data Quality Dimensions in Ontological Foundations. Communications of the ACM 39 (1996) 11, 86-95

[47] Wand, Y., Weber, R.: A model of control and audit procedure change in evolving data processing systems. The Accounting Review LXIV(1) (1989), 87-107

[48] Wand, Y., Weber, R.: An ontological evaluation of systems analysis and design methods. In: Falkenberg, E.D., Lindgreen, P. (eds.): Information System Concepts: An In-depth Analysis. North-Holland (1989), 79-107

[49] Wand, Y., Weber, R.: An ontological model of an information system. IEEE Transactions on Software Engineering 16 (1990) 11, 1281-1291

[50] Wand, Y., Weber, R.: Mario Bunge's Ontology as a formal foundation for information systems concepts. In: Weingartner, P., Dorn, G.J.W. (eds.): Studies on Mario Bunge's Treatise. Rodopi, Atlanta (1990), 123-149

[51] Wand, Y., Weber, R.: A unified model of software and data decomposition. In: DeGross, J., Benbasat, I., DeSanctis, G., Beath, C.M. (eds.): Proceedings of the 12th International Conference on Information Systems (ICIS `91) (1991), 101-110

[52] Wand, Y., Weber, R.: On the ontological expressiveness of information systems analysis and design grammars. Journal of Information Systems 3 (1993) 4, 217-237

[53] Wand, Y., Weber, R.: On the deep structure of information systems. Information Systems Journal 5 (1995), 203-223.

[54] Weber, R.: Ontological Foundations of Information Systems, Coopers & Lybrand Accounting Research Methodology. Monograph No. 4. Melbourne (1997)

[55] Weber, R., Zhang, Y.: An analytical evaluation of NIAM's grammar for conceptual schema diagrams. Information Systems Journal 6 (1996) 2, 147-170

Design of Object Caching in a CORBA OTM System

Thomas Sandholm[1], Stefan Tai[2], Dirk Slama[1], and Eamon Walshe[1]

[1] IONA Technologies plc
The IONA Building, Shelbourne Road, Dublin 4, Ireland
{tsndhlm, dslama, ewalshe}@iona.com
[2] Technische Universität Berlin
Sekr. E-N 7, Einsteinufer 17, D-10587 Berlin, Germany
stai@cs.tu-berlin.de

Abstract. CORBA Object Transaction Monitors (OTM) refer to a middleware technology that enable the building of transactional, object-oriented information systems running in distributed and heterogeneous environments. In this paper, we address large-scale OTM-based systems and focus attention on the important quality factors of system performance, system scalability, and system reliability. We develop an object caching strategy that employs OTM concepts such as distributed transactions and asynchronous event multicast, and show how this strategy improves an existing distributed CORBA system wrt. performance and scalability. We further describe our object caching solution as a transferable, reusable architectural abstraction, and demonstrate the application of software architectural concepts for design modeling of CORBA systems that introduce object caching.

1 Introduction

Software systems implemented in distributed and heterogeneous environments are becoming increasingly common as a result of the availability of communication technologies like the Internet and component technologies like distributed object middleware. This observation in particular holds for large-scale information systems, where data is distributed with software components to different nodes in a network. An important requirement here is to keep the distributed data consistent and to guarantee performance of the system.

In this paper, we focus attention on the development of a *CORBA Object Transaction Monitor (OTM)*-based system. CORBA OTM refers to an advanced middleware technology that has been adverted a major trend for next-generation distributed transaction processing [11]. CORBA OTM consists of the standard *object request broker (ORB)* providing mechanisms for remote object invocation [9], and a set of object services for distributed systems and data management, including the *CORBA Object Transaction Service (OTS)* [10].

We develop an object caching strategy that can be introduced to large-scale CORBA OTM-based systems [12]. The major objective is to improve system performance, while assuring system scalability and system reliability. The caching

M. Jarke, A. Oberweis (Eds.): CAiSE'99, LNCS 1626, pp. 241–254, 1999.
© Springer-Verlag Berlin Heidelberg 1999

solution is described using the software architectural modeling concept of a *connector*, and its application is demonstrated with an example scenario that has been implemented using IONA's OrbixOTM product [7]. The work presented has been carried out as part of the project *"CORBA Object Transaction Monitor Experimentation"*, a cooperation between IONA Technologies Dublin and Technische Universität Berlin.

The paper is structured as follows. First, we introduce CORBA OTM and concepts relevant to improve system performance. Second, we present an object caching strategy and its implementation and test results for a sample OTM-based system. Third, we develop the software architectural connector "Object Caching with Transactional Replication" capturing interfaces and interoperation patterns of our caching solution, and show how this connector can be used to describe caching in CORBA OTM-based systems.

2   CORBA OTM

With the Object Management Group's (OMG) *Common Object Request Broker Architecture (CORBA)* [9], a standard middleware technology for the integration and interoperation of diverse software components in distributed and heterogeneous environments has been proposed. *CORBA Object Transaction Monitors* address *enterprise computing* based on CORBA, and provide additional support for security, transactions, availability, or manageability.

CORBA OTMs comprise a variety of (standard and non-standard) *object management services*, of which the CORBA Object Transaction Service (OTS) and the CORBA Events Service [10] are important examples. The OTS provides utilities for distributed transaction processing, i.e. for transaction management, transaction propagation, and for driving the two-phase commit protocol to coordinate different distributed resources, including databases. The Events service enables loosely coupled, asynchronous messaging between multiple event suppliers and multiple event consumers using event channels (being standard CORBA objects), based on a publish/subscribe paradigm.

CORBA OTMs can be compared to Transaction Processing (TP) Monitors of traditional client/server systems, but take the concept of a TP Monitor from procedural to open distributed object computing. A thorough treatment of enterprise computing with CORBA and CORBA OTM can be found in [14].

3   Improving Scalability and Performance

In large-scale distributed systems, special attention has to be paid to possible bottlenecks, due to the fact that a large number of concurrent requests have to be processed. Three main techniques can be used to circumvent this scalability and performance problem: *load balancing, replication,* and *caching.*

Load balancing involves duplicating processing in the system, e.g. by having many servers offering the same service. The main goal is to increase throughput, i.e. the number of successfully served requests, when multiple clients send requests concurrently. In [5], different schemes that can be used for spreading the load between servers transparently to the clients are demonstrated.

If the servers have state (manage local data), then some techniques have to be considered regarding how to replicate the data among the distributed servers [2]. Data can be replicated both to increase availability and to improve performance due to service localization. The main problem with replication is how to keep the replicas mutually consistent. Two main approaches exist here: the replicas can be updated *synchronously*, e.g. within a transaction for absolute consistency, or, the updates can be sent out *asynchronously* to trade off consistency with performance and scalability. Further, either only one replica can be updated (*master/slave* replication), or all replicas can be updated (*peer-to-peer* replication).

Object caching in a distributed environment naturally relates to load balancing and replication, but has as its main goal the improvement of performance, or user response time. Two important issues here are (a) where to locate caches, and (b) which objects to put in the caches. A list of possible cache location levels, e.g. per-process, per-node, and per-node group is presented in [18]. Many different cache location levels can coexist for the same object, as shown in [4]. The decisions taken will influence which clients can share the same objects. Shared objects must be read frequently and be updated infrequently in order for the caching to be successful.

Keeping caches accurate and consistent with the source is of predominant importance when caching objects at distributed servers. The same *update approaches* as with replication can be used: asynchronous, or synchronous. The asynchronous approach can be compared to optimistic locking in the database field, and must handle the case when two conflicting updates are made concurrently. Careful attention has to be paid to what information should be sent with the updates in order to minimize network traffic, while keeping the caches accurate at all times. Network traffic can also be decreased by using the multicast protocol for propagating the updates [8].

Further important issues that have to be considered when implementing an object caching strategy are *object faulting* and *object lifetime* (eviction). Object faulting concerns how to fetch the accurate value from the source and place it in the cache transparently to the client. This mechanism can, for instance, be implemented by detecting operating system page faults, as demonstrated in [8]. The problem with this approach is, however, that pages are cached, but not objects, which results in non-object-oriented trade-offs in the code. Further, such an implementation is also very operating system dependent. The object lifetime policy to choose, i.e. when to evict objects from the cache, is determined (limited) by the cache memory available. Common lifetime policies are: FIFO, TTL (Time To Live), LRU (Least Recently Used), transaction based (object lifetime equals transaction lifetime), and application server based (object lifetime equals application server lifetime) [4], [2].

4   Object Caching Strategy

4.1   Example Scenario

We use a geographically distributed travel agency as a sample CORBA OTM-based system, which is to be improved with an object caching strategy.

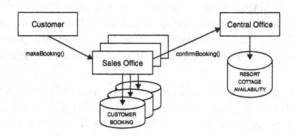

Fig. 1. A Distributed Travel Agency

The system architecture of the travel agency is shown in Fig. 1. `Customers` can book `Cottages` residing in `Resorts`, and browse `Cottage`, `Resort`, and cottage `Availability` information. Multiple `SalesOffices` have been introduced to decrease the load on the `CentralOffice`. Each *booking* for a cottage must first be issued on a `SalesOffice`; the *booking* is then confirmed at the `CentralOffice`. The `CentralOffice` manages persistent `Resort`, `Cottage`, and cottage `Availability` data in a relational database. The `SalesOffice` manages local `Customer` information, and maintains all `Bookings` that are made at the `SalesOffice`.

We assume that the system has one million `Customers`, and that one *booking* can be made each second in the system. For each *booking*, multiple queries on `Resort`, `Cottage`, and cottage `Availability` (`Booking`) information typically are issued. We assume that the average *booking* during peak system load consists of 12 queries, followed by one update (= a booking session).

4.2   Introducing Caching

The first decision concerns to cache `Resort` and `Cottage` objects (as these are frequently read objects, but updated infrequently) and to replicate cottage `Availability` data as `Booking` data at the distributed `SalesOffices`. Two different consistency policies are chosen to keep the cached objects and the replicated data consistent with the data in the `CentralOffice`.

Asynchronous propagation (optimistic approach) is used for keeping the cached objects accurate and consistent with the source. Asynchronous multicast propagation is selected because of performance and scalability reasons. The problem of concurrent updates here is handled when confirming *bookings* at the

CentralOffice. The CentralOffice detects when an inaccurate cache has been used, and returns an exception that the *booking* cannot be made.

Synchronous propagation (pessimistic approach) is used for updating the replicated data (Bookings). When a *booking* is to be made, a distributed transaction is started at the local SalesOffice. Within this transaction, the *booking* is confirmed at the CentralOffice, is made persistent in the Availability table, and is replicated locally in the Booking table. The data in the two databases are hence kept synchronous by the two phase commit protocol. This approach is more time consuming, and does not scale as well as the asynchronous approach. The approach, however, assures that the local data is always consistent with the source at any point in time. This enables book keeping or invoicing tasks, for example, at the local SalesOffices without contacting the CentralOffice. We use master/slave propagation, i.e. all changes must be made at the CentralOffice first. By doing so, we avoid conflicts that can occur due to concurrently propagated updates.

Two different strategies are implemented for updating the caches, once an update event has arrived at the SalesOffice. The source can be contacted to get the currently most accurate value, or local updates can be made using object information sent with the event. Source updates are safer when concurrent updates are made. Additionally, if the original transaction aborts after the notification has been sent away, the caches will still be valid when using the source update approach, as they will read the source data in a transaction scheduled after the original one. Local updates have a significant performance advantage, though.

If an object that is not in the cache is accessed, then it is fetched from the source transparently to the clients. Once the object is fetched, it remains in the cache for the lifetime of the SalesOffice servers. When a particular Cottage is queried, the cache is filled with information for all Cottages in the same Resort. SalesOffices thus only need to cache some Resorts, which compensates the fact that no direct object eviction is implemented. Furthermore, the Availability data are decreased (and thereby also the size of the caches) as more Cottages are booked.

In order to minimize network traffic, a proper *event granularity* must be chosen. In our example, we use only one event channel for propagating *bookings*, but send object information with the events to enable updates of single cache entries (for a single object). The SalesOffices are event consumers, and the CentralOffice is the only event supplier.

The caching strategy is summarized in Table 1.

This object caching strategy has been implemented and tested by simulating the assumptions about system usage. The relation between the number of queries, and the number of updates (12 to one) is crucial to the success of the caching implementation. The more queries that are made, the more does the caching pay off. The tests were carried out by simulating both peak system load, and twice that load, in order to measure scalability of the solution. The peak system load, i.e. one booking session is started every second, was derived from

Table 1. Caching strategy summarized

Problem	Solution
Cached Objects	Resort and Cottage objects
Cache Location	Application server
Replica Consistency	Synchronous propagation
Cache Consistency	Asynchronous multicast propagation
Update Policy Replication	Master/Slave
Update Policy Caches	Update from source/local updates
Object Faulting	Clients access objects via application servers that transparently fetch source state
Cache Eviction	Application server based
Event Granularity	One event channel per class of objects that can be modified, events carry object level information

assumptions made on how the one million customers use the travel agency system. Further, the system was tested before and after the introduction of caching, and local updates were compared to updates from source. Throughput (reliability), i.e. number of successful *bookings*, and the response time for the *bookings* (performance) were measured.

A client test suite was developed for the simulations. Each client in the suite implemented a *booking* session as follows: (1) a query to get all Resorts was made, and one of these Resorts was picked at random; (2) all Cottages for this Resort were collected in a query, and 10 Cottages in the chosen Resort were picked randomly; (3) availability data were retrieved for each of these Cottages; (4) finally a booking was attempted for one week chosen at random from the retrieved availability data. One of these clients was started asynchronously from a shell script each second. Information on the time it took for each client to complete its *booking* session (user response time), and whether the booking attempt in (4) was successful was traced. Further details on test environment are available in [12]. The results are depicted in Fig. 2.

The caching strategy improved reliability, scalability, and performance of the system compared to the system without caching. The caching strategy using local updates scaled better than the solution updating from source. Notable from the tests is that only half of the booking attempts were successful in twice peak system load when caching wasn't used.

The caching strategy could further be improved by redirecting clients accessing the same Resorts to the same SalesOffice. This functionality could be combined with a general load-balancing scheme to dynamically spread the load on the SalesOffice servers by using e.g. OrbixNames [7]. Also, a group of replicated CentralOffice servers could be introduced into the system, so that the CentralOffice no longer can become a bottleneck and single-point of failure.

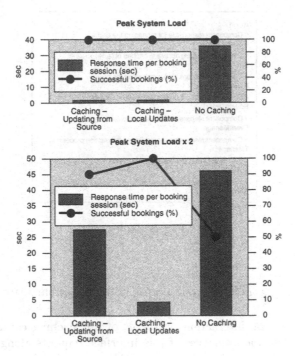

Fig. 2. Object Caching Test Results

5 Software Architectural Design

In the following, we present our object caching solution as a transferable, reusable *connector* abstraction for software architectural system design. The notion of connectors for modeling component collaborations has been mentioned in a variety of work in the area of software architecture [13], [1].

5.1 Connector "Object Caching with Transactional Replication"

Our particular connector concept has been proposed in [16], and has been exemplified for modeling CORBA object services in [15], [3]. Connectors are pattern-like descriptions of complex component collaborations. A connector comprises the definition of *roles, role interfaces*, and *interaction protocols*.

Fig. 3 depicts the roles of our caching connector. Each role describes a collaboration responsibility, which is taken on by components in the software architecture of a particular system.

For each role, a set of role interfaces is defined (Fig. 4). These interfaces must be provided by any particular component playing the role. The role interfaces are declared using OMG IDL [9]. OID in Fig. 4 refers to a secondary identifier of an object, which is not the object reference itself, but an identifier used to

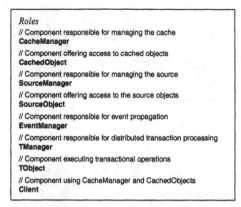

Fig. 3. Roles

map the object to a unique external entity (e.g. a primary key in a relational database).

Fig. 5 depicts the interaction protocols of our caching connector. Interaction protocols describe sequences of role interface requests along with pre- and postconditions. They are described using UML sequence diagrams [19].

The *Cache Initialization and Use* interaction describes the basic cache functionality. A component in role of *Client* sends a request for an object. If there is a valid object in the cache, it is returned directly by the component in role of *CacheManager*. Otherwise, the accurate state of the source object is fetched from the source. The state is used to create a cached object (cache initialization). A reference to the *CachedObject* is returned to the client. The next operation on the object will use the cache if it hasn't been invalidated.

The *Replicated Data Modification* interaction shows how the source data is kept consistent with the locally stored data. When a client wants to modify a value, a transaction is started. Within this transaction, a confirmation with the component in role of *SourceManager* is done, and the local database is updated. Since these operations are performed in an "all-or-nothing" fashion, the replicated data is always kept consistent. The confirmation with the *SourceManager* serves to detect whether other clients have updated the source concurrently, and a conflict thereby has occurred. (In our example scenario, such a conflict occurred when two clients selected the same `Cottage` from the cache, and then tried to book it concurrently for the same calendar week.) A conflict leads to a race condition where the first transaction to execute will succeed, and the second one will roll back.

The interaction *Cache Update* depicts how caches are updated by using event notifications. The events are pushed from the component in role of *Source-Manager* to the component in role of *EventManager* when a *SourceObject* has changed. The *EventManager* then pushes the events to the registered *Cache-*

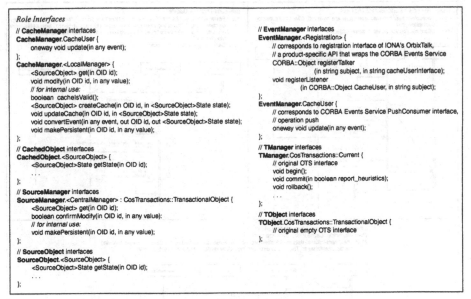

```
Role Interfaces

// CacheManager interfaces
CacheManager.CacheUser {
    oneway void update(in any event);
};
CacheManager.<LocalManager> {
    <SourceObject> get(in OID id);
    void modify(in OID id, in any value);
    // for internal use:
    boolean cacheIsValid();
    <SourceObject> createCache(in OID id, in <SourceObject>State state);
    void updateCache(in OID id, in <SourceObject>State state);
    void convertEvent(in any event, out OID id, out <SourceObject>State state);
    void makePersistent(in OID id, in any value);
};

// CachedObject interfaces
CachedObject.<SourceObject> {
    <SourceObject>State getState(in OID id);
    ...
};

// SourceManager interfaces
SourceManager.<CentralManager> : CosTransactions::TransactionalObject {
    <SourceObject> get(in OID id);
    boolean confirmModify(in OID id, in any value):
    // for internal use:
    void makePersistent(in OID id, in any value);
};

// SourceObject interfaces
SourceObject.<SourceObject> {
    <SourceObject>State getState(in OID id);
    ...
};


// EventManager interfaces
EventManager.<Registration> {
    // corresponds to registration interface of IONA's OrbixTalk,
    // a product-specific API that wraps the CORBA Events Service
    CORBA::Object registerTalker
                        (in string subject, in string cacheUserInterface);
    void registerListener
                        (in CORBA::Object CacheUser, in string subject);
};
EventManager.CacheUser {
    // corresponds to CORBA Events Service PushConsumer interface,
    // operation push
    oneway void update(in any event);
};

// TManager interfaces
TManager.CosTransactions::Current {
    // original OTS interface
    void begin();
    void commit(in boolean report_heuristics);
    void rollback();
    ...
};

// TObject interfaces
TObject.CosTransactions::TransactionalObject {
    // original empty OTS interface
};
```

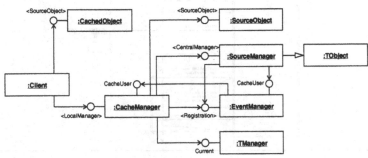

Fig. 4. Role Interfaces

Managers. The *CacheManagers* must filter the event to find out whether the object that has changed is in the cache. If it is in the cache, the value can be updated in two ways. First, it can be updated by getting the state from the source. Second, it can be updated locally by using the value passed by the event. The pros and cons of the two approaches were discussed in section 4.2.

5.2   Modeling the Example Scenario

We describe the software architecture of our example system by using the architectural framework of *components*, *connectors*, *abstract architectures*, and *concrete architectures* [17].

Components are design-time abstractions of computational system parts. Components are described using multiple views: the *core functionality view*, and

250   Thomas Sandholm et al.

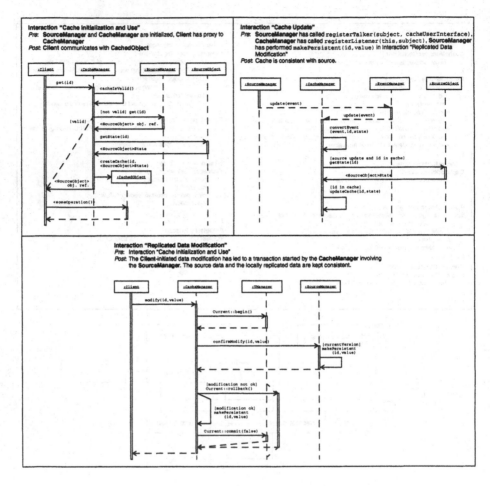

Fig. 5. Interaction Protocols

various component *collaboration views*. The core functionality view models the domain-oriented component features.

For our travel agency system, we can define the three application components `SalesOffice`, `CentalOffice`, and `Customer`, and the two service components `OrbixOTS` and `OrbixTalk` (off-the-shelf components implementing the CORBA OTS and Events Service, respectively) as design-time components. Fig. 6 depicts the exported and imported (required) system-level interfaces of the core functionality view of the `SalesOffice` component.

An *abstract architecture* of connector-based component composition is shown in Fig. 7. The components of our particular system are related by means of the generic connector "Object Caching with Transactional Replication", i.e. the connector roles are distributed to the components. This describes a requirement on the components to implement the respective role interfaces, and characterizes

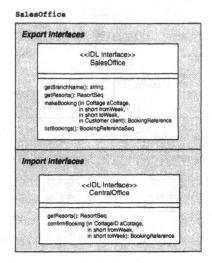

Fig. 6. Component SalesOffice – Core Functionality View

the component to interact with the other components as specified with the connector interaction protocols. Abstract architectures are software architectural descriptions on a very high level of abstraction.

Fig. 8 shows the "object caching with transactional replication" view on the SalesOffice component, i.e. the collaboration view resulting from the abstract architecture of Fig. 7. The caching view exhibits all component features that have been introduced because of the caching rationale (as opposed to the core functionality view). The caching functionality is now exposed with new exported and imported interfaces, such as the provided CacheUser interface, or the required OTS Current interface to start, commit and abort distributed transactions. The SalesOffice component now imports and exports the Resort and Cottage interfaces unchanged.

Fig. 8 also shows the SalesOffice component's *representation* and export and import *representation-map*[1], i.e. the internal realization design and program-level interfaces of the component. This diagram describes implementation details of the component as a distributed, transactional CORBA server, and is expressed using UML class modeling. In the representation part, we can e.g. see that the cache is structured in a hierarchical containment tree. The SalesOffice contains a collection of cached Resorts, and each cached Resort contains a collection of cached Cottages.

The set of all component descriptions of the same (object caching) view is called a *concrete architecture* to an abstract architecture. The software architecture of a particular system is thus described on two different levels of abstraction.

---

[1] We adapted the terminology of representation and representation-map from the ACME ADL [6].

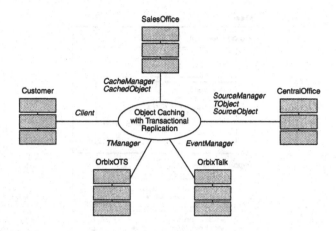

Fig. 7. Abstract Architecture of Travel Agency System

Overall, the architectural framework of design-time components, connectors, abstract and concrete architectures employs a clear separation of modeling concerns, and enables a pattern-oriented, structured approach to architectural software system representation.

6   Conclusion

In this paper, we developed an object caching strategy for CORBA OTM-based systems which addresses system reliability, system scalability, and, in particular, system performance. We demonstrated object caching for a sample distributed, transactional CORBA system, and showed how the caching solution proposed increased system performance notably. We abstracted the caching functionality and interoperation patterns into a software architectural connector, which was used to model the complex component collaborations of our example system, and also serves as a reusable design solution to object caching that can be applied to other CORBA OTM-based systems.

The caching solution can be summarized as follows:

Reliability of the solution was assured by asynchronous updates of the caches, and by synchronous modification of the replicated data. In terms of our connector, this behavior is captured as follows: the *SourceManager* sends an update event through the *EventManager* to the *CacheManagers* (interaction protocol "Cache Update"), and data modified in the database of the *SourceManager* is replicated in the *CacheManager*'s database within a distributed transaction started by the *CacheManager* (interaction protocol "Replicated Data Modification").

Scalability was improved by service localization. All queries can be performed locally because of the caches, which thereby improve load balancing. This is captured in the connector interaction protocol "Cache Initialization and Use". The

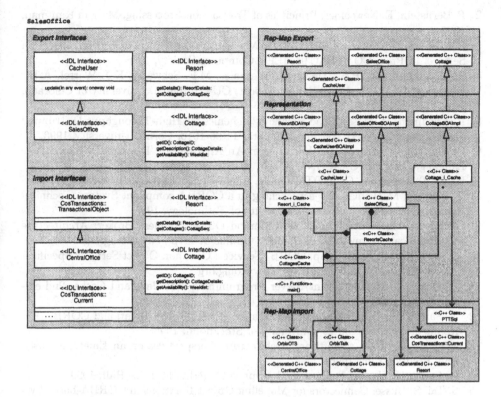

Fig. 8. Component SalesOffice – Object Caching with Transactional Replication View

CachedObject offers the same interface as the *SourceObject*, and the *CacheManager* is responsible for localizing the *SourceObject*, i.e. converts the *SourceObject* into a *CachedObject*. Service localization is also achieved by data replication, as mentioned previously.

Performance of the system was notably improved through the caches, and has been addressed in line with system scalability and system reliability. The design decisions regarding performance are hence documented in all three interaction protocols of our caching connector.

Acknowledgements. We would like to thank Prof. Herbert Weber, TU Berlin, and Fiona Hayes, IONA Technologies Dublin, for their continuous project support. We would also like to thank Prof. Janis Bubenko, University of Stockholm, for co-supervising the thesis underlying this paper.

References

1. L. Bass, P. Clements, R. Kazman. Software Architecture in Practice. Addison-Wesley, 1998.

2. P. Bernstein, E. Newcomer. Principles of Transaction Processing. Morgan Kaufman, 1997.
3. S. Busse, S. Tai. Software Architectural Modeling of the CORBA Object Transaction Service. In Proc. COMPSAC'98, IEEE Computer Society, 1998.
4. A. Chankhunthod, P.B. Danzig, C. Neerdales, M.F. Schwartz, K.J. Worrel. A Hierarchical Object Cache. Technical Report, CU-CS-766-95. University of Colorado, 1994.
5. R. Friedman, D. Mosse. Load Balancing Schemes for High-Throughput Distributed Fault-Tolerant Servers. Technical Report, TR96-1616, Cornell University, 1996.
6. D. Garlan, R. Monroe, D. Wile. Acme: An Architecture Description Interchange Language. In Proc. CASCON97, 1997.
7. IONA Technologies. OrbixOTM Guide. IONA Technologies plc., 1998.
8. R. Kordale, M. Ahmad. Object Caching in a CORBA compliant System. Technical Report, GIT-CC-95-23, Georgia Institute of Technology, 1995.
9. Object Management Group. The Common Object Request Broker: Architecture and Specification, rev.2.2. OMG, 1998. On-line at http://www.omg.org
10. Object Management Group. CORBAServices: Common Object Services Specification. OMG, 1997. On-line at http://www.omg.org
11. R. Orfali, D. Harkey. Client/Server Programming with Java and Corba, 2nd edition. Wiley, 1998.
12. T. Sandholm. Object Caching in a Transactional, Object-Relational CORBA Environment. Masters Thesis, University of Stockholm, 1998.
13. M. Shaw, D. Garlan. Software Architecture: Perspectives on an Emerging Discipline. Prentice-Hall, 1996.
14. D. Slama, J. Garbis, P. Russell. Enterprise CORBA. Prentice-Hall, 1999.
15. S. Tai, S. Busse. Connectors for Modeling Object Relations in CORBA-based Systems. In Proc. TOOLS 24, IEEE Computer Society, 1997.
16. S. Tai. A Connector Model for Object-Oriented Component Integration. In Proc. ICSE'98 Workshop on Component-Based Software Engineering, 1998.
17. S. Tai. Constructing Distributed Component Architectures in Continuous Software Engineering. PhD Thesis, TU Berlin, 1999. to appear.
18. D. Terry. Distributed Name Servers: Naming and Caching in Large Distributed Computing Environments. Technical Report, CSD-85-228. University of California, Berkeley, 1985.
19. UML Partners. The Unified Modeling Language, v1.1. OMG, 1997. On-line at http://www.omg.org

Constructing IDL Views on Relational Databases

Kim Jungfer[1], Ulf Leser[2], and Patricia Rodriguez-Tomé[1]

[1]EMBL Outstation, The European Bioinformatics Institute,
Wellcome Trust Genome Campus,
Cambridge CB10 1SD, United Kingdom
{jungfer, tome}@ebi.ac.uk
[2]Technische Universität Berlin, Einsteinufer 17,
D-10587 Berlin, Germany
leser@cs.tu-berlin.de

Abstract. Data collections are distributed at many different sites and stored in numerous different database management systems. The industry standard CORBA can help to alleviate the technical problems of distribution and diverging data formats. In a CORBA environment, data structures can be represented using the Interface Definition Language IDL. Manually coding a server, which implements the IDL through calls to the underlying database, is tedious. On the other hand, it is in general impossible to automatically generate the CORBA server because the IDL is not only determined by the schema of the database but also by other factors such as performance requirements. We therefore have developed a method for the semi-automatic generation of CORBA wrappers for relational databases. A declarative language is presented, which is used to describe the mapping between relations and IDL constructs. Using a set of such mapping rules, a CORBA server is generated together with the IDL. Additionally, the server is equipped with a query language based on the IDL. We have implemented a prototype of the system.

1 Introduction

Integration of data from multiple, distributed and autonomous data sources is a challenging problem in many domains. Semantic and technical heterogeneity is common and data structures are often complex and evolve over time. The field of Molecular Biology can serve as an example. Historic development and organizational obstacles have prevented the definition and proliferation of standards, leaving end users confronted with an overwhelming diversity in data formats, query languages and access methods. Several proprietary systems like SRS [4] and Entrez [15] have been developed for the integration and distribution of molecular and genomic data. A Biologist nowadays has to find an access method to the desired data source, typically on the WWW. Then he has to understand and use the interface, e.g. by typing in keywords in a form, and finally he has to analyze the results, for instance by parsing

M. Jarke, A. Oberweis (Eds.): CAiSE'99, LNCS 1626, pp. 255-268, 1999.
© Springer-Verlag Berlin Heidelberg 1999

HTML pages. Evolving data structures on the other hand, leave the developers of user interfaces with the tedious task of keeping their Web sites up-to-date.

Clearly, this approach will not be able to cope with the increasing complexity, diversity and amount of data. Several research groups, e.g. [14], have therefore started to apply CORBA to alleviate some of the problems described. CORBA [10], [16], as a middleware platform, has many advantageous features: it offers language, location and platform transparency, which means that clients such as analysis programs and visualization tools can access remote information as if they were local objects. In a CORBA environment, data can be represented using the Interface Definition Language (IDL). This allows clients to work with domain-specific data structures and permits a flexible combination of data sources with different visualization and analysis tools [7].

In this scenario, a CORBA server has to implement a mapping between database structures and their IDL representation. Usually, this mapping is implemented manually: the developer first specifies appropriate IDL definitions, lets the IDL compiler generate the skeletons, and then adds the necessary implementation, mainly code to access the database through a database gateway such as JDBC. However, implementing a new CORBA server for each application and maintaining it in the presence of evolving IDL definitions and database schemas is tiresome. Furthermore, it is completely unclear how ad hoc queries can be supported in such a setting.

Another possibility is the automatic generation of IDL and CORBA server based on the schema of the underlying database. But such an IDL is normally not what we need for our concrete application. One reason is that in order to allow for the interoperation of independently developed clients and servers it is advantageous to agree on a common IDL [1]. Another reason is - as detailed in chapter 3 - that there are many different ways to represent data in IDL. The different representations have different advantages and disadvantages, and can significantly influence the performance of a distributed system. The IDL is therefore highly application specific and cannot be derived from a database schema only.

In this paper, we describe a system that offers a partial solution to these problems for the case of relational databases. Many major and minor data collections in molecular biology, like EMBL [17] or IXDB [9], utilize a relational database management system. Furthermore, relational databases provide a powerful view mechanism, which can be exploited to facilitate the mapping task. This also allows for a higher degree of independence between the CORBA server and the schema of the database.

The central idea of our approach is to automatically generate the server source code based on a set of rules, which describe the mapping from a relational schema to a target IDL. The generated server implements a query language, which is purely based on the IDL definitions. Therefore, the user does not need to know the schema of the relational database. The server can either be used directly, or the code can be exploited as a skeleton for further customizations.

The following example, depicted in Figure 1, will be used throughout the text. The schema represents a very simple model of a genome map. A genome map has a name, the name of the represented chromosome and a set of markers (e.g. genes). Each marker has a name, a position on the map, and the information indicating whether the marker belongs to the framework of the map or not.

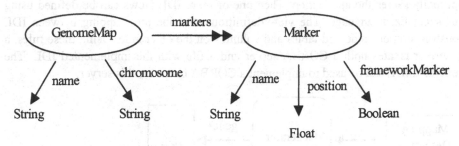

Fig. 1. Example schema for genome maps and markers.

The following IDL is *one* possibility to represent this schema. The genome map is represented by an interface, while markers are represented by structs. This has the advantage, that the application can download all markers belonging to a map with only one remote method invocation.

```
module Example {

  struct Marker {
    string name;
    float position;
    boolean frameworkMarker;
  };

  typedef sequence <Marker> Markers;

  interface GenomeMap {

    readonly attribute string name;
    readonly attribute string chromosome;
    readonly attribute Markers markers;

  };

}; // End of module Example
```

The rest of the paper is organized as follows. The architecture of the system is described in section 2, the mapping language is presented in section 3, query possibilities of the system are examined in the section 4, related work and further issues are discussed in section 5 and 6.

2 Architecture

Figure 2 depicts an overview of the architecture of the system. The process of generating a CORBA wrapper is as follows: The first step is to decide what IDL optimally serves the application. Then one or more IDL views can be defined using our specialized language. The view definitions describe the mapping between IDL constructs on one side and tables and columns on the other side. Using these rules, a generator creates both a CORBA server and a file with the implemented IDL. The generated IDL can be used to implement a CORBA client for this server.

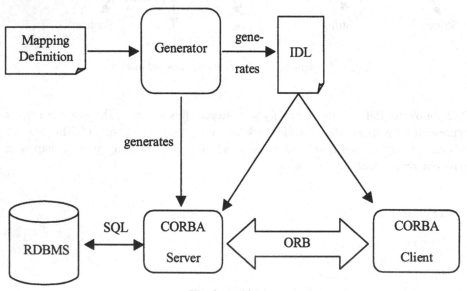

Fig. 2. Architecture

The client can query the server using a query language, which is based on the generated IDL. The queries are translated to SQL queries using the definitions of the mapping language. The results are then translated back in the required IDL representation and returned to the CORBA client.

3 Mapping of a Relational Schema to IDL

We can distinguish between approaches that use CORBA only for the infrastructure of the system, treating data objects and queries basically as strings or bit-streams, and others that also model the data itself in IDL. While the former is for instance followed by [3], we adopt the latter possibility. The main advantage of this solution is the reduced impedance mismatch. The ultimate goal is that clients can be developed based purely on the automatically generated stubs, without having to decode bit-streams or strings into domain objects.

There are a number of different possibilities to represent data in IDL. For example it is possible to model database entries either as structs or as interfaces. Both approaches have advantages and disadvantages. Interfaces can resemble a conceptual data model very naturally, but are often too slow since every method invocation goes over the network. Structs in contrast are copied by value and then accessed locally. Structs are therefore more suitable for bulk data transfers. On the other hand, structs neither support inheritance nor associations. If such concepts are used, they need to be circumscribed. This can for instance occur if an extended entity-relationship model is used as the starting point for the IDL development. The optimal representation of a relational schema in IDL is strictly application dependent. To offer maximum flexibility, our system supports both structs and interfaces.

We will first present the concepts of the mapping language and its grammar, then we give an example, and finally we discuss the generated IDL of the CORBA server.

3.1. The Mapping Language

In this section we describe a high-level language, which can define mappings between relations and columns on one side and different IDL types on the other. The IDL is completely specified by the mapping definitions. To facilitate the task, we restrict the language to the most often used constructs of IDL: modules, the basic types long, float, string, boolean, the constructed type struct, the template type sequence, and interfaces. Interfaces are restricted to read-only attributes. To keep the mapping language simple and without loss of generality we assume that relational views can be used to get closer to the needed IDL. This means that mapping possibilities, which can be expressed by a relational view are not considered here. More specifically:

- Every simple type in the IDL (long, float, string, boolean,) is represented directly by one table attribute. No null-values are permitted.
- All single-valued members (attributes) of a struct (interface) can be found in the same table.
- Multi-valued members (attributes) of a struct (interface) are stored in a different table, which is connected to the base table by foreign keys.

Views

The top-level construct of the mapping language is the view definition. A view has a name and is associated with a table and the mapping for an IDL type, which is either a struct or an interface (xxx_mp in the grammar means: mapping definition for xxx). Different views can use the same IDL types based on different tables.

```
view ::= (view <view_name>
            table <table_name>
            <interface_mp> | <struct_mp>)
```

Interfaces

The mapping definition for interfaces specifies first the IDL name of the interface together with all interface names from which it inherits. All interface names are scoped to specify the appropriate IDL module. The extended interfaces are merely necessary to define the IDL type - they do not affect the mapping. Especially they do not imply any set inclusion properties between different views represented by these interfaces. Then the primary key for the table is given. The key is necessary to allow the CORBA object adapter to keep track of the connection between object references and database entries. For each attribute, the attribute name and the mapping for the attribute type is given. All attributes have to be specified here, including those inherited from other interfaces.

```
interface_mp ::= (interface <scoped_interface_name>
                  extends (<scoped_interface_name>*)
                  keys (<column_name>*)
                  (<attribute_name> <data_type_mp>)+)
```

Structs

For every struct the scoped struct name is specified as well as the mapping for each member. Since structs are passed by-value, there is no need for keys.

```
struct_mp ::= (struct <scoped_struct_name>)
              (<member_name> <data_type_mp>)+)
```

Data Types

The type of an attribute or struct member is either a basic type or an object reference or a struct or a sequence.

```
data_type_mp ::=   <basic_type_mp>
               |   <reference_mp>
               |   <struct_mp>
               |   <sequence_mp>
```

Basic Types

Every type mapping is defined in the context of a table. All basic types are directly represented by one of the table's columns. The only exception is the type boolean, which does not exist in some relational databases. In this case it is necessary to give additionally the value which represents true.

```
basic_type_mp ::=   (boolean <column_name> <true_value>)
                |   (long    <column_name>)
                |   (float   <column_name>)
                |   (string  <column_name>)
```

References

This type represents object references. The corresponding interface has to be defined in a separate view. In this case it is necessary to specify the connection between the current table and the table of the referenced view. This is done by giving the primary / foreign keys of the two involved tables.

```
reference_mp ::= (reference <view_name>
                  keys (<column_name>+)
                       (<column_name>+))
```

Sequences

The data, which belongs to a sequence, is multi-valued and therefore stored in a different table. Again we have to specify the connecting columns of the two tables. In the case where the subtype is an object reference, it is sufficient to give the view name instead of a complete reference mapping as described above. The reason is that the connecting columns are already specified in the sequence mapping. Since sequences are ordered it is additionally necessary to specify an order-by-clause.

```
sequence_mp ::= (sequence <scoped_sequence_name>
                 table <table_name>
                 keys (<column_name>+) (<column_name>+)
                 <sequence_type_mp>
                 order_by <order_by_clause>)

sequence_type_mp ::=   <struct_mp>
                     | <sequence_mp>
                     | <basic_type_mp>
                     | <view_name>
```

3.2 Example

The example is based on the schema and IDL given in the introduction. We define a mapping using the tables of the relational schema depicted in Figure 3. The attribute *map_id* in the table *map_markers* is the foreign key of the table *maps*.

Table: maps   Table: map_markers

id	chromosome

id	position	fw	map_id

Fig. 3. Relational schema.

The mapping definition directly reflects the nested interface-sequence-struct structure of the IDL given in section 1. Note that in the opposite case, where a struct contains a reference to an interface, the interface would be defined in a separate view. Also note that the nesting of IDL modules does not have to be the same as the nesting of the mapping language. For example, it is possible that a struct contains another struct from a completely different module.

```
( view GenomeMaps
  table maps
  ( interface Example::GenomeMap
    extends ()
    keys (id)
    ( name (string id) )
    ( chromosome (string chromosome) )
    ( markers
      ( sequence Example::Markers
        table map_markers
        keys (id) (map_id)
        ( struct Example::Marker
          ( name (string id) )
          ( position (float position) )
          ( frameworkMarker (boolean fw T) ) )
        order_by position
      )
    )
  )
)
```

3.3 The Generated IDL

Given the mapping definitions in section 3.2, a set of IDL definitions can be automatically generated. The first part of this IDL represents the data as specified in the mapping language. In our example it is identical with the IDL given in the introduction. The second part specifies the API for the database itself and defines methods for querying and data retrieval. This works as follows: The *Evaluator* interface has a *get* method defined for each view. The client can specify here a where-clause similar to SQL queries (see next section). The evaluator returns a reference to an iterator. Again, there is a separate iterator specified for each view. The iterator has a *next* method, which returns object references or structs of the type defined in the view. Additionally there are methods *count* and *next_n* to allow the client to optimize the data retrieval. For our example the following IDL is generated:

```
module Views {

    exception NoMoreElements {};
    exception InvalidQuery {};
```

```
interface Iterator {
   boolean more();
   void close();
};

typedef sequence<Example::GenomeMap> GenomeMapSeq;

interface GenomeMaps: Iterator {
   Example::GenomeMap next() raises(NoMoreElements);
   GenomeMapSeq next_n(in long n);
};

interface Evaluator {
   long count(in string viewName, in string where)
        raises (InvalidQuery);
   GenomeMaps get_GenomeMaps(in string where)
              raises (InvalidQuery);
};

}; // End of module Views
```

Note that the *count* method can be used for all views implemented by the server whereas each *get* method is defined for only one view.

4 Queries

Our approach maps a relational schema into IDL, thereby alleviating the infamous impedance mismatch between application code and relational database. Query results are always represented by a predefined type, either structs or object references. This is naturally achieved by class specific *get* methods and iterators as described above. Using this approach, we can avoid the usage of the generic IDL type any. Anys are less efficient for the data transfer and inconvenient to use in client programs. However, using fixed result types inevitably restricts the query power, as arbitrary joins and projections have to be disallowed. In practice this restriction is of little significance and shared by many other applications such as digital libraries.

The *get* methods of the *Evaluator* interface takes as input parameter a string, which is comparable to a SQL where-clause. The predicates of the query are formulated using attribute names and member names of the IDL interfaces and structs. Client code depends therefore only on the IDL and is immune against most schema changes in the database.

4.1 The Query Language

We introduce the language informally using some examples. Conditions on basic types can be specified using the predicates '<', '>', '<=', and '>='. Predicates can be combined using 'and', 'or' and 'not'. If a member or attribute contains a sequence then the quantifiers 'exists' and 'all' can be used. Queries can contain nested subqueries to specify embedded structs or referenced objects.

Examples:

We assume that a view for markers exists for the IDL in the main example. The following where-clauses could be specified in the *get_Markers* method. Note that in this case structs and not object references would be returned. If, as in Q4, several member conditions are specified, then all conditions have to be true.

Q1:   "All markers"
→   " "

Q2:   "The markers with the name 'RH2345' and 'RH5432' "
→   `(name (or 'RH2345' 'RH5432'))`

Q3:   "All markers except the marker with the name 'RH2345' "
→   `(name (not 'RH2345'))`

Q4:   "All non-framework markers with a position greater than 100"
→   `(frameworkMarker false) (position (> 100))`

Q5:   "All markers with a position between 20 and 30"
→   `(position (and (>= 20) (<= 30)))`

For the view *GenomeMaps*, as defined in the last section, the following queries are possible. The *GenomeMap* attribute *markers* contains a sequence of structs. At this place the quantifiers *exists* and *all* can be used. Inside the quantifier a specification for the struct has to be given, which is a list of member conditions as in Q1-Q5.

Q6:   "All maps which contain the marker with the id 'RH3456' "
→   `(markers (exists (name 'RH3456')))`

Q7:   "All maps which contain only framework markers"
→   `(markers (all (frameworkMarker true)))`

4.2 Query Mapping

The translation of our query language to SQL is based on the mapping rules. As these rules always associate each struct or interface with one table, this translation is fairly straightforward. Nested queries are translated to nested SQL statements using the predicate 'in'. We give the translation of queries Q2 and Q6 as examples. Again we assume the relational schema in 3.2.

```
Q2: select distinct id, position, fw from map_markers
    where id='RH2345' or id='RH5432'
```

```
Q6: select distinct id from maps
    where id in (select map_id from markers
                 where id='RH3456'))
```

Note, that in Q2 all information on the markers is retrieved whereas in Q6 only the key. The reason is that in Q2 a struct is returned, which has to contain all data, while in Q6 only an object reference is returned.

5 Related Work

We are not aware of any other project that follows our track of generating CORBA servers and IDL based on a set of declarative mapping rules. However, a number of research areas share problems. For instance, mapping relations to IDL interfaces is related to object-relational mapping (e.g. [12], [18], [20]). The mapping step, consequently called "semantic enrichment" in [6], can in general not be automated because the relational schema simply does not carry the necessary information. Hence, the mapping rules must be specified by a human operator, as done in our approach.

The translation of object-oriented queries into a query against a semantically equivalent relational schema is covered in depth in [5] and [13]. The approach of [5] is similar to ours in that they also assume that each (object-oriented) class is represented by exactly one (relational) table. However, our query language is only a subset of theirs, as we do not treat path expressions. [13] considers extensional relationships in inheritance hierarchies by mapping the translation into DATALOG programs, which are used as a mediator between the query and the database. In contrast, for our mapping we do not require nor guarantee any relationships between extents of interfaces that are in a specialization relationship.

Another related research area is the integration of database systems in a CORBA framework. [8] discusses several design issues in this context, including the consequences of using structs or interfaces for object representation. They clearly point out that it is in general very difficult to achieve full relational query power through CORBA, mainly due to the static type system. The OMG itself has contributed to this area through the "Object Query Service Specification" [11]. However, as detailed in [8] and [19], this specification has severe pitfalls, and, to our knowledge, has not been implemented by any of the commercial ORB vendors. For instance, it does not support any representation of domain objects on the CORBA level.

There are only few commercial tools available, which support the generation of CORBA access layers for relational databases. For example Persistence TM[1] defines an object-oriented schema on top of a relational schema. A programming library is generated which makes the data accessible through a set of C++ classes. Additionally the tool can generate a CORBA server, which maps the OO schema into IDL and uses

---

[1] http://www.persistence.com

the library to access the database. The main problem with this tool is the limited influence the developer has in the choice of the generated IDL. It is purely interface-based with no support for struct-based representations, which are essential to ensure sufficient performance. Hence, in real-life applications, it is necessary to change the generated CORBA server to a great degree by hand. But these changes are not visible for the query processor. A similar approach is taken be the OPM project [2]. We believe that our method is a more direct and flexible way of achieving a CORBA interface to an existing relational database.

6 Discussion

We have presented a method for the semi-automatic generation of CORBA wrappers for relational databases. Compared to the two other major approaches – hand-coding or completely automatic generation – our system offers many advantages. CORBA views can be defined easily, allowing many applications to share data, each with its own IDL. It is straightforward to generate redundant IDL definitions, for instance containing both a struct and an interface for the same data. This leaves it to the client application to choose the most convenient access method.

The server is equipped with a query language, which can express complex conditions. Usage of this query language does not require any knowledge of the schema of the underlying database, but is entirely based on the IDL itself. The client code is therefore completely independent of schema changes, provided that the mapping rules are adjusted. Although, it is clear that our query language can only express a limited set of queries, it proved to be sufficient in our application domain.

Using a set of mapping rules, the system generates JAVA source code for the server. We have chosen this compilation strategy for several reasons. Firstly, it offers a considerably better performance compared to an interpretation of the rules at run-time. Secondly, the code can be used as a template for further customizations. Finally, it allows the usage of skeleton code generated by the IDL compiler, which significantly simplifies the code generation task. The disadvantage is that every change in the mapping rules requires the regeneration of the server. However, the choice between interpretation and compilation is an implementation detail, which does not touch the principal of our approach.

Some problems remain when specifying a query based on IDL definitions. They stem from the fact that IDL was designed to specify an API and not to model data. An example is the usage of inheritance. If an interface A specializes an interface B then a query against B does not necessarily return a superset of the same query against A. Such a behavior can be enforced using the mapping language and appropriate relational views, but it is not visible from the IDL alone. Other problems can occur when the requirements for querying are not identical to the requirements for data retrieval. For instance we might not want to retrieve the information indicating whether a marker belongs to the framework of a map but still be able to use it in a query. These problems would vanish if we use the schema and query language of the underlying relational database and IDL merely represents query results. The disadvantage would be that then the user has to know the relational schema, the IDL and the mapping between the two.

Future investigations will go into extensions of the mapping language. For example we will include a possibility to express simple inheritance on structs through the use of unions. We also aim to improve the query language by adopting a more SQL like syntax.

Acknowledgements

We would like to thank Richard Göbel, Philip Lijnzaad, Jeremy Parsons, and Anastasia Spiridou for their ideas and comments. Ulf Leser was supported by the German Research Society, Graduate School in Distributed Information Systems (DFG grant no. GRK 316).

References

1. Barillot E., Leser U., et al.: A proposal for a standard CORBA interface for genome maps. Bioinfomatics, **15**. Oxford University Press. (1999) 157-169
2. Chen I.M.A., Kosky A.S., et al.: Advanced Query Mechanisms for Biological Databases. Proc. of the 6th Int. Conf. on Intelligent Systems for Molecular Biology (ISMB), Montreal, Canada. AAAI Press, Menlo Park (1998)
3. Dogac A., Dengi C., et al.: A Multidatabase System Implementation on CORBA. 6th Int. Workshop on Research Issues in Data Engineering: Nontraditional Database Systems, New Orleans, Louisiana (1996)
4. Etzold T., Ulyanov A., Argos P.: SRS: Information Retrieval System for Molecular Biology Data Banks. Methods in Enzymology, Vol. 266. Academic Press (1996) 114-128
5. Fahl G., and Risch T.: Query Processing over Object Views of Relational Data. The VLDB Journal **6**(4). Springer-Verlag (1997) 261-281
6. Hohenstein U.: Using Semantic Enrichment to Achieve Interoperability of Relational and ODMG Databases. International Hong Kong Computer Society Database Workshop (1996) 210-232
7. Jungfer K., and Rodriguez-Tomé P.: Mapplet: A corba-based genome map viewer. Bioinformatics, **14**(8). Oxford University Press (1998) 734-738
8. Leser U., Tai S., Busse S.: Design Issues of Database Access in a CORBA Environment. Workshop on Integration of Heterogeneous Software Systems, Magdeburg, Germany (1998)
9. Leser U., Wagner R., et al.: IXDB, an X Chromosome Integrated Database. Nucleic Acids Research., **26**(1). Oxford University Press (1998) 108-111
10. Object Management Group: The Common Object Request Broker: Architecture and Specification. John Wiley & Sons, New York (1995)
11. Object Management Group: CORBAServices: Common Object Service Specification: Query Service Specification. http://www.omg.org (1997)
12. Papazoglou M., Tari Z., and Russell N.: Object-Oriented Technology for Interschema and Language Mappings. Object-Oriented Multidatabase Systems: A Solution for Advanced

Applications, Bukhres O.A., Elmagarmid A.K. (eds.) Prentice Hall, New Jersey (1996) 203-250

13. Qian X., and Raschid L.: Query Interoperation among object-oriented and relational databases. 11th Int. Conference on Data Engineering, Tapei, Taiwan. IEEE Computer Soc. Press (1995)

14. Rodriguez-Tomé P., Helgesen C., Lijnzaad P., and Jungfer K.: A CORBA server for the Radiation Hybrid Database. Proc. of the 5th Int. Conf. on Intelligent Systems in Molecular Biology (ISMB). AAAI Press (1997) 250-253

15. Schuler G.D., Epstein J.A., et al.: Entrez: Molecular Biology Databases and Retrieval System. Methods in Enzymology, Vol. 266. Academic Press (1996) 141-162

16. Siegel J.: CORBA Fundamentals and Programming, John Wiley & Sons (1996)

17. Stoesser G., Moseley M.A., et al.: The EMBL Nucleotide Sequence Database. Nucleic Acids Research, 26(1). Oxford University Press (1998) 8-15

18. Tari Z., Stokes J.: Designing the Reengineering Service for the DOK Federated Database System. Proc. of the IEEE Int. Conf. On Data Engineering (ICDE'97), Birmingham (1997) 465-475

19. Wells D. L., and Thompson C. W.: Evaluation of the Object Query Service Submissions to the Object Management Group. IEEE Quarterly Bulletin on Data Engineering, 17(4). (1994) 36-45

20. Wiederhold G.: Views, Objects and Databases. IEEE Computer, Vol. 19(12). (1986) 37-44

The Design of Cooperative Transaction Model by Using Client-Server Architecture

Am-suk Oh

Department of Multimedia Engineering
Tongmyong University of Information Technology
Pusan 608-711, Korea
asoh@tmic.tit.ac.kr

Abstract. Engineering design applications require the support of long transactions in cooperative environments. The problem of the existing copy/update/merge approaches is that the partial effects of a committed transaction may be not part of the merged version. This paper introduces a new cooperative transaction model, which allows updates to be progressively notified or propagated into other transactions accessing the same object. To support incremental update propagation and notification, we use the term dynamic dependency to define the intertransaction dependency relationships among all the objects checked out from the public database. Consistency in multiple copies of the same object is achieved by a two-phase delta-merge protocol. Our model provides a synchronization of cooperative updates performed in several workspaces without using locking mechanisms.

The final, formatted version of this paper did not reach the Editors in time to be included in this volume.

M. Jarke, A. Oberweis (Eds.): CAiSE'99, LNCS 1626, pp. 269–269, 1999.
© Springer-Verlag Berlin Heidelberg 1999

A Multilevel Secure Workflow Management System

Myong H. Kang,[1] Judith N. Froscher,[1] Amit P. Sheth,[2] Krys J. Kochut,[2]
and John A. Miller[2]

[1]Information Technology Division
Naval Research Laboratory
[2]LSDIS Lab, Department of Computer Science
University of Georgia
http://lsdis.cs.uga.edu

Abstract. The Department of Defense (DoD) needs multilevel secure (MLS) workflow management systems to enable globally distributed users and applications to cooperate across classification levels to achieve mission critical goals. An MLS workflow management system that allows a user to program multilevel mission logic, to securely coordinate widely distributed tasks, and to monitor the progress of the workflow across classification levels is required. In this paper, we present a roadmap for implementing MLS workflows and focus on a workflow builder that is a graphical design tool for specifying such workflows.

1 Introduction

The constant aspect of today's military challenge is change due to the need for operational response to new threats in completely different environments. For example, today's military supports disaster relief, drug interdiction, peace-keeping missions in worldwide regional skirmishes, treaty enforcement, as well as the traditional role of national defense against weapons of mass destruction and aggression against the United States. At no other time in the nation's history has the military relied so heavily on information technology (IT) for all of its operations, including command and control, logistics, surveillance and reconnaissance, personnel management, finances, etc. This dependence means that these systems must be easily configurable and secure.

The operational requirement for DoD is to pull together coalitions quickly and use US military systems as well as coalition partners' systems to achieve a common goal. Each mission has different mission logic and deals with different data sets. For example, the data for disaster relief are different from the data for biological weapons attack. To achieve the needed flexibility, the military should be able to react to different situations quickly and without procuring new IT resources for each crisis. Hence, there is a need to be able to specify the mission logic in terms of existing DoD and coalition resources and applications, and enact that logic with the applications to

M. Jarke, A. Oberweis (Eds.): CAiSE'99, LNCS 1626, pp. 271-285, 1999.
© Springer-Verlag Berlin Heidelberg 1999

achieve the mission. A workflow management system (WFMS) is a key enabler for such a capability.

A WFMS enables the automated coordination, control, and communication of tasks performed by people and/or computers. Although a majority of commercial off-the-shelf (COTS) WFMSs use a client server model, our requirements call for a WFMS that runs in a distributed, heterogeneous computing environment spanning one or more enterprises, as well as supporting integration with independent (legacy) software. We can view such a WFMS as a software layer above the user interface or application layer in the open systems model. For the commercial world, this is the business logic layer; for DoD, it is the mission logic layer.

However, current WFMSs lack capabilities that stem from the following unique operational requirements for DoD:

- The organizations that participate in dynamic coalition may be located in different security classification domains.
- The guidelines for sharing and exchanging information among organizations in different classification domains are stricter than those for organizations in the same classification domain.

To address those problems, the Naval Research Laboratory (NRL), in cooperation with the Large Scale Distributed Systems Lab at the University of Georgia, has embarked upon an R&D project to build a *multilevel secure (MLS) workflow* management system [1]. The goal of the project is to develop tools and security critical components that allow enterprises to harvest emerging COTS technology and still rely on legacy resources with reduced risk. Since our approach to solving the MLS workflow problem requires workflow interoperability, we have introduced extended workflow interoperability capabilities to our MLS WFMS. They are:

- A new workflow interoperability model (i.e., cooperative model),
- A mechanism to communicate to other independent worflows (i.e., synchronization nodes), and
- A new way to model workflow interoperability in a workflow design environment (i.e., foreign task).

This paper presents an approach for developing an MLS WFMS. In section 2, we briefly describe the overview of our 5-step strategy to implement an MLS WFMS. The detailed plan for the first two steps—choosing an MLS architecture and a strategy for dividing an MLS workflow into multiple single-level workflows are presented in section 3. Section 4 discusses the third step that involves executing single level workflows and reconstructing an MLS workflow from multiple single-level workflows. The tools that support building an MLS workflow using our approach are discussed in section 5. We conclude this paper by describing future work in section 6.

2   Technical Approach for an MLS WFMS

An MLS WFMS should support functionality equivalent to a single-level WFMS for users with different clearances but prevent unauthorized access to resources. Tasks that may be single-level individually but operate in different classification domains have to cooperate to achieve a higher-level mission.

Multilevel secure domains can be defined as follows. There is a lattice S of classification domains with ordering relation $<$. A classification domain S_i *dominates* a domain S_j if $S_i \geq S_j$. There is a labeling function L that maps each user, session, task, and data (object) to a classification domain. The classification levels a user can access are determined by his clearance and enforced by the underlying MLS architecture.

To provide MLS services in a distributed and heterogeneous computing environment, the following information flow requirements must be enforced:

- High[1] users must have access to low data and low resources,
- High processes must have access to low data, and
- High data must not leak to low systems or users.

The development of high-assurance software necessary to provide separation between the lowest security level (unclassified) and the highest security level (Top Secret) information has proven to be both technically challenging and very expensive through 20 years of computer security history. Today's fast paced advances in technology and the need to use COTS products make the traditional MLS approach untenable.

To implement an MLS workflow management system using the architectural approach, the following technical approach has been established:

1. Choose an MLS distributed architecture where multiple single-level workflows can be executed.
2. Choose a strategy for dividing an MLS workflow into multiple single-level workflows.
3. Select a single-level workflow management system to execute single-level workflow in each classification domain and devise a way to glue together single-level workflows to provide multilevel functionality.
4. Implement the necessary tools to support MLS workflow.
5. Extend the single-level workflow enactment service to accommodate communication among tasks in different classification domains.

3   MLS WFMS through Multiple Single-Level WFMSs

In this section, we explain in detail the approach, outlined in section 2, for implementing the first two steps of our strategy for supporting MLS workflow.

---

[1] The term high[low] user/process/data stands for high[low]-level cleared/classified user/ process/data.

3.1   MLS Distributed Architecture

Our approach depends on an MLS architecture to separate multiple single-level WFMS to achieve a multilevel secure WFMS. Therefore, multilevel security does not depend on individual WFMS but rather on the underlying MLS distributed architecture.

The MLS distributed architecture:

- Consists of physically or logically separated multiple single-level networks, each containing information at a given level and below.
- Hosts single-level applications and workflows that access information at that level and below, and
- Provides conduits to pass information among tasks in different classification domains.

The MLS distributed architecture is based on a security engineering philosophy: A few trusted devices in conjunction with information release and receive policy servers to enforce the information flow policy among the classification domains, and single-level systems and single-level engineering solutions to provide other functionality, including single-level security services.

In this architecture, switched workstations (e.g., Starlight [2]) enable a user to access resources in multiple classification domains and create information in domains that the user is authorized to access. One-way devices (e.g., a flow controller such as an NRL Pump [7]) together with information release and receive policy servers provide a secure way to pass information from one classification domain to another domain. A detailed description of the multilevel infrastructure and services can be found in *Towards an Infrastructure for MLS Distributed Computing* [8].

The workflow specification at each classification level is derived from the MLS workflow specification that a workflow designer provides through an MLS workflow builder. The next subsection describes how an MLS workflow specification can be decomposed into multiple single-level workflow specifications.

3.2   MLS Dependency and MLS Workflow Decomposition Strategy

An MLS WFMS should support the same kind of intertask dependencies as in a single-level WFMS.[2] However, some dependencies in an MLS workflow may be specified across classification boundaries; these are called MLS dependencies. In other words, state information and some values may have to move across classification boundaries during workflow execution. Hence, it is important to understand what the vulnerability is, whether it is easily exploitable, and how to reduce it.

In our MLS WFMS, all information that has to move across classification domains must go though information release and receive policy servers, and high-assurance

---

[2] To enable the use of different WFMS products at different classification levels, restricted communication along the line of SWAP or OMG/jFlow standards may be adopted.

flow controllers (e.g., Pump or downgrader). We can decompose a transition between two tasks in different classification domains into many transitions. Consider a transition from a task in domain 1 (T_{D1}) to a task in domain 2 (T_{D2}). This transition will be decomposed into transitions from T_{D1} to P_{D1}, P_{D1} to P_{D2}, and P_{D2} to T_{D2} as in Figure 1. Note that there is a flow controller between P_{D1} and P_{D2} where P_{D1} and P_{D2} are proxies that combine the function of flow controller wrappers and policy servers. Flow controller wrappers take care of any protocol translation between an application and a flow controller, and policy servers determine whether the information should be released to or received from another domain. For example, P_{D1} combines a flow controller wrapper and information release policy server, and P_{D2} combines a flow controller wrapper and information receive policy server. Note that domain policies may not allow flow controller wrappers and information policy servers to be combined. In that case, we can decompose transitions further.

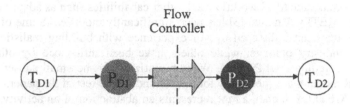

Flow
Controller

Fig. 1. Indirect transition through a flow controller and policy servers

In this way, an MLS workflow will be transformed into multiple single-level workflows. The single-level workflows neither communicate directly nor recognize single-level workflows from other classification domains. The minimum number of single-level workflows that will be generated is equal to the number of classification domains in the MLS workflow. An example of an MLS workflow design and its decomposition are illustrated in section 5.1.

4   A Single-Level WFMS and an MLS Workflow Model

A centerpiece of our strategy for implementing an MLS workflow is to coordinate single-level workflows in the MLS distributed architecture that we described in section 3.1. Therefore, achieving MLS functionality largely depends on interoperability among single-level workflows. In this section, we present an interoperability model that we plan to support as well as an MLS workflow model and primitives that we are implementing to support MLS workflow. In this section, we focus on the third item of our technical approach.

4.1   An MLS Workflow Model

We have chosen the METEOR system [4] as a starting point to build our MLS WFMS. The METEOR Enterprise Application Suite (EAppS) consists of four components: EApp ▶ Builder, EApp ▶ Repository, EApp ▶ Enactment, and EApp ▶ Manager. EApp ▶ Enactment includes two services: ORBWork and WebWork. Both ORBWork and WebWork use a fully distributed open architecture. *WebWork* [9] is a comparatively light-weight implementation that is well-suited for traditional workflow, help-desk, and data exchange applications. *ORBWork* [10] is better suited for more demanding, mission-critical enterprise applications requiring integration with legacy applications and data, high scalability, robustness and dynamic modifications. These features make the METEOR system with ORBWork enactment service a good starting point for extending capabilities to support MLS workflow.

To accommodate MLS workflow and other capabilities such as adaptive workflow, the earlier METEOR model [3] has been significantly modified. Some of the revised features have been influenced by our experience with building realistic workflows with our industry partners, while others have been influenced by other relevant research, including ADEPT [11]. We summarize only the small subset of the new METEOR model that is necessary for understanding the rest of the paper.

In the METEOR model, a *task* represents an abstraction of an activity. A task can be regarded as a unit of work, which is performed by a variety of processing entities, depending on the nature of the task. A task can be performed by (*realized by*) a human, or by performing a computerized activity through executing a computer program, a database transaction, or possibly by a network (workflow or subworkflow) of interconnected tasks. Hence, a task provides one level of abstraction (view) and its realization provides a lower level of abstraction (view). This also directly maps to the nested sub-process concept of jFlow (see section 4.2). Since the realization of a task may contain many tasks at different levels of abstraction, a task is a recursive reference in the METEOR model.

In this paper, we categorize tasks into two types:

- *Foreign task:* A task whose realization (i.e., strategy for implementation) is unknown to the workflow designer. It represents a task that is a part of cooperating independent autonomous workflow. It is required for a designer to declare a foreign task explicitly and provide a hint to the METEOR runtime code generator. A foreign task should have a minimal information set that we will specify in section 4.2 (e.g., invocation, output, where to send the request).
- *Native task:* A task for which the realization is known or the realization will be provided before the runtime-code generation (i.e., all other tasks except the foreign tasks).

A network task represents the core of the workflow activity specification. Since a network task is one of the realizations of a task, it is always associated with a task, called its *parent task*. A single network defines a relationship among workflow tasks, transferred data, exception handling, and other relevant information. It is a collection of either foreign or native tasks and transitions from one task to another.

Figure 2 shows a simplified version of two levels of abstractions (views) where *Task2* is the parent task of the workflow W_i which contains tasks 4, 5, 6, and 7, and transition t_j represents a transition from *Task1* to *Task2*. In Figure 2, *Task1, Taks2,* and *Task3* may belong to different classification domains. Hence, the MLS METEOR model can be thought of as follows: along the xy-surface, there are tasks in different domains and along the z-axis, there are different levels of abstraction.

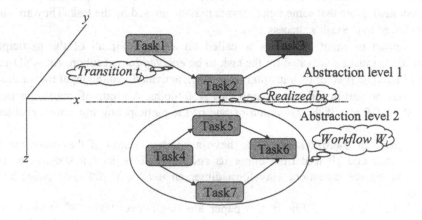

Fig. 2. MLS METEOR model

A task may play the role of a source task or a destination task (e.g., *Task1* is the source task and *Task2* is the destination task of the transition t_j in Figure 2) for a number of transitions. All of the transitions for which a task is the destination task are called the *input transitions* for that task (e.g., transition t_j is an input transition for *Task2*). Likewise, all of the transitions for which a task is the source task are called its *output transitions* (e.g., transition t_j is an output transition of *Task1*). A transition may have an associated Boolean condition, called its *guard*. A transition may be activated only if its guard is true. When there is a transition from task T_i to task T_j where T_i and T_j are in different classification domains, we call this an MLS *transition* from T_i to T_j.

An *external transition* is a special type of a transition in which the two participating tasks (source and destination) are not in the same workflow (i.e., transition to and from a foreign task). An implied external transition may lead to a start task of another workflow. Similarly, an implied transition leads from the final task and is used to notify the external entity that the network has terminated. Note that an MLS transition is turned into an external transition when an MLS design is decomposed into multiple single-level workflows for runtime.

External transitions are also used to specify synchronization points with some external events. Typically, external transitions may be used to specify communication and synchronization between two independent workflows. Here, an external transition leading into a task in the workflow is assumed to have an implied source task (outside of the workflow). Similarly, an external transition leading out of a task in the workflow is considered to have an implied destination task (outside of the workflow). External transition is a cornerstone of our strategy to support MLS workflow.

The classes (i.e., types of objects) that are associated with an input transition to a task are called the task's *input classes*, and those appearing on an output transition are called *output classes* of that task. A task's output class, which is not its input class, is *created* by the task. Specifically, an object instance of the specified class is created by the workflow runtime. A task's input class, which is not its output class, is *dropped (consumed)*. Note that some input classes may be unused by the task. They are simply transferred to the task's successor(s).

A group of input transitions is called an *AND-join* if all of the participating transitions must be activated for the task to be *enabled* for execution. An AND-join is called *enabled* if all of its transitions have been activated. All the input transitions of a task may be partitioned into a number of AND-joins. A group of input transitions is called an *OR-join* if the activation of one of the participating transitions enables the task.

A group of transitions is said to have a *common source* if they have the same source task and all lead from either its success state or its fail state. A group of common source transitions may form either an *AND-split*, *OR-split* (selection), or *Loop*.

All tasks that we define in this paper are single-level tasks. What we mean by single-level task is that it receives input from one classification level and produces output at the same classification level. There are four special tasks: *begin, success, failure,* and *synchronization*. The synchronization tasks represent external transitions to and from other workflows. In general, workflow designers do not manipulate synchronization nodes directly. They are automatically generated by the system based on the specification of foreign tasks, and input and output transitions to and from the foreign tasks.

An MLS *workflow* is a network of interconnected single-level (foreign or native) tasks from more than one classification domain. Note that we call a task single-level from one particular level of abstraction (view). Since a single-level task may be realized by an MLS workflow at a lower level of abstraction, it may have side-effects on different classification domains at lower abstraction levels. Hence, our distinction between single-level and multilevel is purely from the perspective of a specific abstraction level.

An MLS workflow that is the realization of task T_i where $L(T_i) = S_a$ must obey the following constraints:

- The *begin, success,* and *fail* nodes of the MLS workflow must be $L(begin) = L(success) = L(failure) = S_a$ and
- It may have tasks in other classification domains; however, if the $L(T_j) = S_b$ where S_a does not dominate S_b, then T_j must be a foreign task. In other words, only tasks in S_c where $S_a \geq S_c$ may have realizations.

If the workflow designer creates an MLS workflow from the highest classification level with a complete view of the workflow being designed, then the complete MLS workflow with realizations of all its tasks can be specified. However, if the workflow designer creates an MLS workflow that requires input from (output to) higher classification levels, then he may only know the interfaces to the tasks at the higher levels but not the detailed workflow process at that level. Hence, in such cases, foreign tasks can be used to define communication and synchronization with a task at higher classification levels.

4.2 Workflow Interoperability

There are two aspects of workflow interoperability:

1. The interoperability protocol between independent WMFSs.
2. The ability to model the interoperability in a workflow process definition tool (i.e., workflow builder).

A standards body such as OMG (e.g., jFlow [5]) can handle the first aspect. However, the second aspect should be handled by each WFMS.

OMG's jFlow introduces two models of interoperability: nested sub-process and chained processes. In nested sub-process workflow structures, a task in workflow A may invoke workflow B as the performer of a task and then wait for it to complete. Hence, the task in workflow A is a requester, and the task that is realized by the sub-processes can serve as the synchronization point for interaction between the two workflows. In chained workflow structures, one task may invoke another, then carry on with its own business logic. The workflows terminate independently of each other; in this case, the task registered with the sub-process would be another entity that is interested in the results of the sub-process.

These two models provide powerful mechanisms for interoperability. However, we would like to extend them to support a richer interoperability model: *cooperative processes*. Consider two independent autonomous workflows that need to cooperate. Let's assume that there are agreements among organizations that participate in the cooperation. Organization A is in charge of workflow A and Organization B is in charge of workflow B. Tasks in workflow A and workflow B can communicate and synchronize with each other as shown in Figure 3. In this example, two workflows may have independent starting and ending points.

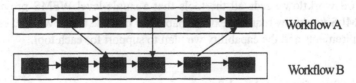

Fig. 3. Cooperative processes

There is another situation that we want to support in the context of cooperative processes. In general, the designer of workflow A does not need to know the structure of workflow B and vice versa. This may be because organization A does not want organization B to know the structure of its workflow process and vice versa. In conjunction with MLS principles, the designer of a workflow may not be allowed to know the detailed workflow structure of a higher level workflow. For example, the designer of the workflow, whose classification level is M, may not be allowed to know the workflow structure that is in domain H where H dominates M.

However, there is a minimal set of information that is required for communication and synchronization among tasks in cooperating autonomous workflows. These include:

1. Where and how to send/receive requests (i.e., the location and invocation method of tasks) and
2. How and where to receive replies (i.e., expected outputs and the return address).

Therefore, the above specification has to appear in the workflow design so that proper runtime code can be generated. Hence, we need a primitive that represents this situation in the design tool. The foreign task, introduced in section 4.1, can accommodate this need.

5   Workflow Tools for MLS Workflow

As we mentioned in section 4.1, a workflow management system consists of, in general, four components. The EApp ▶ Builder, sometimes called a workflow process definition tool, is a distributed programming tool with a graphical user interface. Users should be able to express mission logic in terms of input, output, and external transitions, guards, input and output classes, and conditions for enabling each task, etc. Once a user specifies the mission logic, the runtime code for the EApp ▶ Enactment can be generated. The EApp ▶ Enactment is responsible for task scheduling, enforcing dependencies among tasks, passing data from one task to another, and error recovery based on the generated code. The workflow monitor that is a part of EApp ▶ Manager is a convenient tool to track and monitor the progress of work.

An MLS workflow needs all the tools that a single-level WFMS provides. However, an MLS workflow requires extra capabilities in those tools. We will examine the extra requirements and the capability we plan to support for each tool.

5.1   A Builder for MLS Workflow

An MLS workflow designer should be able to specify MLS mission logic graphically using this tool. In other words, this tool should provide:

– A global picture of the MLS workflow process (mission logic);
– Appropriate views for different users at different levels of abstractions;

- A way to express input and output classes, a guard for each transition, the structure of input and output transitions (e.g., AND-join, Loop) among tasks in the same and different classification domains; and
- Capabilities to define domains and to specify dominance relationships among domains (e.g., Top Secret > Secret > Unclassified).

Each task that will be specified in the tool may be either a foreign or native task. If it is a native task, it has a realization as described in section 4.1. This tool provides the capability to expand a task whose realization is a workflow to see the detailed specification.

To support the design of information flow among classification domains, this tool allows a workflow designer to divide the design region into many classification domains. It allows users to add tasks to a domain. Once a task is added to a domain, it recognizes the classification of the domain and associates that classification level to the task. In our MLS workflow builder, all tasks are single-level tasks at this abstraction level. However, a task in a classification domain may be realized by an MLS workflow at a lower abstraction level. If a user wants to see other levels of abstraction, he can do so by expanding a specific task that was realized by a workflow. The reasons for allowing only single-level tasks in our MLS workflow process definition tool are as follows:

- An MLS task can be decomposed into single-level tasks,
- Each task that was not realized by a workflow must run at a single host and site that are single-level.

Hence, it is more natural to map real-world tasks into single-level tasks in a workflow than to map them into multilevel tasks.

The MLS workflow builder also allows users to add transition arcs between tasks where the tasks may be in the same domain or in two different domains. If there is a transition arc from a task in one classification domain to a task in another classification domain, then there is an information flow between two classification domains. During the runtime code generation stage, the code generator recognizes information flow across classification domains and generates the special code that was described in section 3.2.

A designer of an MLS workflow, working at level S_a, often has a need to specify an interaction with a task T_i at S_a to another task T_j at S_b where S_a does not dominate S_b. Since S_a does not dominate S_b, the designer is not allowed to know the detailed description of T_j. For example, when a secret level workflow designer designs a workflow, the secret workflow may need data from a top secret level task. The secret level designer may not be allowed to know how the top secret task generates the answer, but he knows how to send a request and how to receive an answer when the top secret task sends information. Hence, the top secret task is a foreign task to the secret level designer. Even if S_a dominates S_b in the above example, the MLS workflow designer at S_a may not wish to specify (or does not know the details about) the workflow at S_b, and therefore, may treat T_j at S_b as a foreign task.

Let us give a concrete example that involves cooperative processes and foreign tasks in an MLS workflow design as in Figure 4 where multi-lined arrows represent information flow across classification boundaries, ovals represent tasks, and B (begin), S (success), and F (fail) are special nodes.

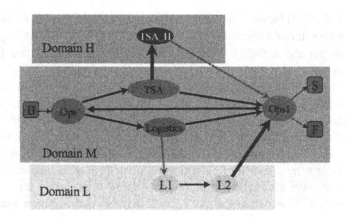

Fig. 4. A workflow that has a cooperative process and a foreign task

Logistics starts a workflow in domain L and *Ops1* receives information form the workflow in domain L. If the designer of the workflow in domain M does not want to specify the details of the workflow in domain L, he can declare *Logistics_L*, which is the combination of tasks *L1* and *L2*, as a foreign task.

Since this particular workflow is designed in domain M, all tasks in domain M may be native tasks. Since the designer of the workflow in domain M may not know the detailed structure of the workflow in domain H, he can declare the *TSA_H* as another foreign task. The transitions, *TSA* to *TSA_H*, *TSA_H* to *Ops1*, *Logistics* to *L1*, and *L2* to *Ops1*, and input and output classes that are associated with each transition define when and what kinds of data will be passed to other workflows at different classification domains. The specification of foreign task expresses interfaces (i.e., invocation methods and outputs) and where to send requests. The runtime code generator uses that information (i.e., specification of foreign tasks and transition spec-ification to and from other tasks) and generates two single-level workflows as in Figure 5 using the principles that were presented in section 3.2. Hence, shaded proxies in Figure 5 represent the combination of policy server, flow controller wrapper and synchronization nodes that represent external transitions. No code will be generated for the workflow in domain H because *TSA_H* is a foreign task.

Note that even though this tool allows workflow designers to specify information and control flow among tasks in different domains, the operational environment of the tool will be system-high (i.e., workflow builder neither accesses sensitive data in multiple domains nor passes it around). Hence, although this tool has to be trusted in the sense that the tool does what it is supposed to do, it can be run in a single-level platform.

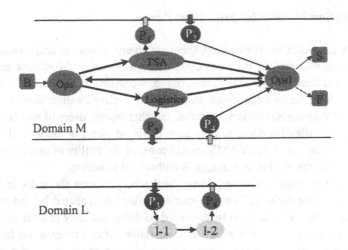

Fig. 5. An outcome of code generation from a workflow design specification

5.2 Enactment Service for MLS Workflow

An MLS workflow enactment service is responsible for executing a workflow in a correct and secure way. As we presented earlier, our approach depends on:

- The services in the underlying MLS distributed architecture to coordinate information and control flow among tasks in different classification domains and
- Secure use of multiple single-level COTS workflow enactment services with or without modifications.

Since there will be no direct communication among workflow enactment services at different classification levels, there is no special MLS requirement for a workflow enactment service itself. On the other hand, the underlying MLS distributed architecture and its security devices must provide the necessary assurance for multi-level security. However, our approach depends on workflow interoperability among multiple single-level workflow enactment services to achieve MLS workflow. This is why we extended the workflow interoperability model, introduced external transitions in the MLS METEOR model, and supported them in the METEOR enactment service.

One question that arises from our approach is "can we use other COTS WFMS enactment services to achieve MLS workflow function?" As long as a WFMS understands the concept of external transitions, we can in principle use any COTS WFMS at each classification level. In that case, the METEOR design tool can be used as an integration tool for designing a workflow comprising several independent workflows.

5.3   Workflow Monitor for MLS Workflow

When an MLS workflow is executed, there are many automatic and human computer tasks that are executed in different classification domains. Workflow managers in different classification domains (assuming a workflow manager per classification level) may have knowledge about tasks in their classification domain and other domains that they are authorized to access. In other words, users of an MLS workflow in different classification domains may have different views of the workflow that they are sharing. Hence, an MLS WFMS should provide the ability to monitor activities in all domains that the workflow manager is authorized to access.

Monitoring may include when, where, and who performs the tasks in the case of human tasks. Since the workflow designer specifies the expected behavior of a work-flow, the workflow monitor can be designed to detect security critical events as well as unexpected behavior. For example, system failure or communication failure can be reported to a workflow manager through a workflow monitor. Also, if a task has not completed within a given time (i.e., deadline), those anomalies can be reported.

A WFMS that runs at each classification level is a single-level WFMS in our strategy for MLS WFMS. A single-level workflow monitor cannot provide all the capabilities that are desired for an MLS workflow monitor. The MLS workflow monitors at different classification levels should have different views of the workflow depending on the dominance relationship among classification domains. Our strategy for an MLS monitor is to send lower level status information (i.e., workflow control data) from the monitor at a lower classification level to a monitor at a higher classi-fication level. The higher level monitor can present a unified execution status of the workflow in its classification domain and other domains that it is authorized to view.

Another natural question in the context of heterogeneous workflow is "what if the COTS WFMS monitor is not equipped to send status information to the outside?" In that case, we can create dummy tasks at higher classification levels to receive status information from lower-level tasks. Higher level workflow managers can monitor lower level activities through those dummy tasks.

6   Conclusion and Future Work

MLS workflow is a new research area that combines workflow and security tech-nology. In this paper, we presented a technical approach to MLS workflow and the necessary techniques for our approach. We introduced a cooperative model and foreign task for workflow interoperability. We also described a new METEOR work-flow model and the focus of our current development effort, a new MLS *EApp ▶ Builder*. The current builder saves design in the form of XML [6]. These XML files are used by *EApp ▶ Enactment* to generate runtime code and by *EApp ▶ Manager* to monitor and manage applications. Our immediate future work includes the modification of *EApp ▶ Enactment* to fully support a new MLS METEOR model and to develop graphical user interfaces for workflow monitors.

References

1. Atluri ,V., Huang, W-K., and Bertino, E.: An Execution Model for Multilevel Secure Workflows. 11th IFIP Working Conference on Database Security (August 1997)
2. Anderson, M., North, C., Griffin, J., Milner, R.., Yesberg, J., Yiu, K.: Starlight: Interactive Link. 12th Annual Computer Security Applications Conference, San Diego, CA (1996)
3. Krishnakumar, N., Sheth, A.: Managing Heterogeneous Multi-system Tasks to Support Enterprise-wide Operations. Distributed and Parallel Database Journal, 3 (2) (April 1995)
4. METEOR project home page. http://lsdis.cs.uga.edu/proj/meteor/meteor.html
5. OMG jFlow submission. ftp:///fpt.omg.org/pub/bom/98-06-07.pdf
6. Extensible Markup Language (XML) 1.0. World-Wide-Web Consortium. http://www.w3.org/TR/1998/REC-xml-19980210.html
7. Kang, M., Moskowitz, I., Lee, D.: A Network Pump. IEEE Transactions on Software Engineering, Vol. 22, No. 5 (1996) 329 - 338
8. Kang, M., Froscher, J., Eppinger, B.: Towards an Infrastructure for MLS Distributed Computing. 14th Annual Computer Security Applications Conference, Scottsdale, AZ (1998)
9. Miller, J., Palaniswani, D., Sheth, A., Kochut, K., Singh, H.: WebWork: METEOR's Web-based Workflow Management System. Journal of Intelligent Information Systems, Vol 10 (2) (March/April 1998)
10. Kochut, K., Sheth, A., Miller, J.: ORBWork: A CORBA-Based Fully Distributed, Scalable and Dynamic Workflow Enactment Service for METEOR, UGA-CS-TR-98-006, Technical Report. Department of Computer Science, University of Georgia (1998)
11. Reichert, M., Dadam, M. and P.: ADEPT$_{flex}$ - Supporting Dynamic Changes of Workflows Without Losing Control. Journal of Intelligent Information Systems, Vol. 10 (2) (March/April 1998)

Time Constraints in Workflow Systems

Johann Eder*, Euthimios Panagos, and Michael Rabinovich

AT&T Labs - Research
180 Park Avenue
Florham Park, NJ 07932
eder@acm.org, {thimios, misha}@research.att.com

Abstract. Time management is a critical component of workflow-based process management. Important aspects of time management include planning of workflow process execution in time, estimating workflow execution duration, avoiding deadline violations, and satisfying all external time constraints such as fixed-date constraints and upper and lower bounds for time intervals between activities. In this paper, we present a framework for computing activity deadlines so that the overall process deadline is met and all external time constraints are satisfied.

1 Introduction

Dealing with time and time constraints is crucial in designing and managing business processes. Consequently, time management should be part of the core management functionality provided by workflow systems to control the lifecycle of processes. At build-time, when workflow schemas are developed and defined, workflow modelers need means to represent time-related aspects of business processes (activity durations, time constraints between activities, *etc.*) and check their feasibility (i.e., timing constraints do not contradict each other). At run-time, when workflow instances are instantiated and executed, process managers need pro-active mechanisms for receiving notifications of possible time constraint violations. Workflow participants need information about urgencies of the tasks assigned to them to manage their personal work lists. If a time constraint is violated, the workflow system should be able to trigger exception handling to regain a consistent state of the workflow instance. Business process re-engineers need information about the actual time consumption of workflow executions to improve business processes. Controllers and quality managers need information about activity start times and execution durations.

At present, support for time management in workflow systems is limited to process simulations (to identify process bottlenecks, analyze activity execution durations, *etc.*), assignment of activity deadlines, and triggering of process-specific exception-handling activities (called *escalations*) when deadlines are missed at run time [10,8,7,18,2,3,17]. Furthermore, few research activities about workflow and time management exist in the literature. A comparison with these efforts is presented in Section 7.

Our contributions in this paper include the formulation of richer modeling primitives for expressing time constraints, and the development of techniques for checking

---

* On leave from the University of Klagenfurt, Austria

M. Jarke, A. Oberweis (Eds.): CAiSE'99, LNCS 1626, pp. 286–300, 1999.
© Springer-Verlag Berlin Heidelberg 1999

satisfiability of time constraints at process build and instantiation time and enforcing these constraints at run time. The proposed primitives include upper and lower bounds for time intervals between workflow activities, and binding activity execution to certain fixed dates (e.g., first day of the month). Our technique for processing time constraints computes internal activity deadlines in a way that externally given deadlines are met and no time constraints are violated.

In particular, at build time, we check whether for a given workflow schema there exists an execution schedule that does not violate any time constraints. The result is a *timed activity graph* that includes deadline ranges for each activity. At process instantiation time, we modify the the timed activity graph to include the deadlines and date characteristics given when the workflow is started. At run time, we dynamically recompute the timed graph for the remaining activities to monitor satisfiability of the remaining time constraints, given the activity completion times and execution paths taken in the already-executed portion of a workflow instance.

The remainder of the paper is organized as follows. Section 2 describes our workflow model and discusses time constraints. Section 3 presents the workflow representation we assume in this paper. Section 4 presents the calculations that take place during build time. Section 5 shows how these calculations are adjusted at process instantiation to take into account actual date constraints. Section 6 covers run time issues. Section 7 offers a comparison with related work and, finally, Section 8 concludes our presentation.

2 Workflow Model and Time Constraints

A workflow is a collection of *activities, agents,* and *dependencies* between activities. Activities correspond to individual steps in a business process. Agents are responsible for the enactment of activities, and they may be software systems (e.g., database application programs) or humans (e.g., customer representatives). Dependencies determine the execution sequence of activities and the data flow between these activities. Consequently, a workflow can be represented by a workflow graph, where nodes correspond to activities and edges correspond to dependencies between activities.

Here, we assume that execution dependencies between activities form an acyclic directed graph. We should note that we do not propose a new workflow model. Rather, we describe a generic workflow representation for presenting our work. In particular, we assume that workflows are *well structured*. A well-structured workflow consists of m sequential activities, $T_1 \ldots T_m$. Each activity T_i is either a primitive activity, which is not decomposed any further, or a composite activity, which consists of n_i parallel conditional or unconditional sub-activities $T_i{}^1, \ldots, T_i{}^{n_i}$. Each sub-activity may be, again, primitive or composite. Typically, well structured workflows are generated by workflow languages that provide the usual control structures and adhere to a structured programming style of workflow definitions (e.g., Panta Rhei [4]).

In addition, we assume that each activity has a duration assigned to it. For simplicity, we assume that activity durations are deterministic. Time is expressed in some basic time units, at build-time relative to the start of the workflow, at run-time in some calendar-time. Some time constraints follow implicitly from control dependencies and activity durations of a workflow schema. They arise from the fact that an activity can only start when its predecessor activities have finished. We call such constraints the *structural time constraints* since they reflect the control structure of the workflow.

In addition, *explicit time constraints* can be specified by workflow designers. These constraints are derived from organizational rules, laws, commitments, and so on. Such explicit constraints are either temporal relations between events or bindings of events to certain sets of calendar dates. In workflow systems, events correspond to start and end of activities. For temporal relationships between events, the following constraints exist:

Lower Bound Constraint: The duration between events A and B must be greater than or equal to δ. We write $lbc(A, B, \delta)$ to express that δ is a lower bound for the time-interval between source event A and destination event B.

Upper Bound Constraint: The distance between events A and B must be smaller than or equal to δ. We write $ubc(A, B, \delta)$ to express that δ is an upper bound for the time-interval between source event A and destination event B.

An example of lower-bound constraint includes a legal workflow with activities of serving a warning and closing a business, with the requirement that a certain time period passes between serving the warning and closing the business. Another example is that the invitation for a meeting has to be mailed to the participants at least one week before the meeting. Upper-bound constraints are even more common. The requirement that a final patent filing is done within a certain time period after the preliminary filing, or time limits for responses to business letters, or guaranteed reaction times after the report of a hardware malfunction provide typical examples of upper-bound constraints.

To express constraints that bind events to sets of particular calendar dates, we first need to provide an abstraction that generalizes a, typically infinite, set of dates such as "every other Monday" or "every fifth workday of a month". Examples of such constraints include: vacant positions are announced at the first Wednesday of each month; loans above USD 1M are approved during scheduled meetings of the board of directors; inventory checks have to be finished on December 31st.

Fixed-Date Type: A fixed-date (type) is a data type F with the following methods: $F.valid(D)$ returns true if the arbitrary date D is valid for F; $F.next(D)$ and $F.prev(D)$ return, respectively, the next and previous valid dates after D; $F.period$ returns the maximum distance between valid dates; and $F.dist(F')$ returns the maximum distance between valid dates of F and F', (with $F.period$ as default value).

Fixed-Date Constraint: Event B can only occur on certain (fixed) dates. We write $fdc(B, T)$, where T is a *fixed-date*, to express the fact that B can only occur on dates which are valid for T.

In the remainder of the paper, we assume that at most one fixed-date constraint can be associated with an activity.

3   Workflow Representation

Our techniques for time constraint management are based on the notion of the *timed activity graph*. This graph is essentially the same as the workflow graph where each

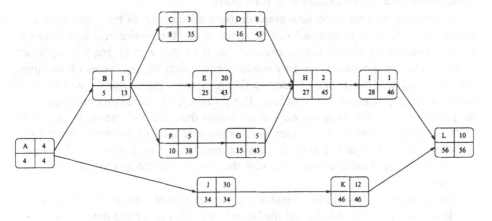

Activity Name	Activity Duration
Earliest Finish Time	Latest Finish Time

Fig. 1. Activity node of a timed workflow graph

Fig. 2. Example timed workflow graph

activity node n is augmented with two values that represent termination time points for activity executions[1].

- $n.E$: the earliest point in time n can finish execution.
- $n.L$: the latest point in time n has to finish in order to meet the deadline of the entire workflow.

Figure 1 shows the representation of an activity node in the timed workflow graph. Without explicit time constraints, E and L values can be computed using the Critical Path Method (CPM) [14], a well known project planning method that is frequently used in project management software. CPM assumes that activity durations are deterministic. We are aware that this assumption does not hold for many workflows, and that for these workflows a technique dealing with a probability distribution of activity durations like the Project Evaluation and Review Technique (PERT) [14] would be more appropriate. However, we chose CPM because it allows us to present the concept more clearly without the math involved with probability distributions.

Figure 2 shows the timed workflow graph we use in the rest of the paper. The interpretation of E- and L-values is as follows. The earliest point in time for activity F

---

[1] Since activity durations are assumed to be deterministic, we do not need to represent activity start points. These time points can be computed by subtracting activity durations from activity termination times.

to terminate is 10 time units after the start of the workflow. If F is finished 38 time units after the start of the workflow, the duration of the entire workflow is not extended. Activity L is the last activity of the workflow, and the earliest and latest completion times are the same, 56. This also means that the entire workflow has a duration of 56 time units. The distance between the E-value and the L-value of an activity is called its buffer time. In our example, activity F has a buffer of 28 time units. This buffer, however, is not exclusively available to one activity, but it might be shared with other activities. In our example, the buffer of F is shared with B, G, H, and I. If B uses some buffer-time, then the buffer of F is reduced.

Computing the timed workflow graph delivers the duration of the entire workflow, and deadlines for all activities such that the termination of the entire workflow is not delayed. Incorporating explicit time constraints into the timed activity graph is explained in detail later. For simplicity, we only consider constraints for end events of activities. Therefore, we will use a shortcut and say that an activity (meaning "the end event of the activity") participates in a constraint. The following additional properties are used for representing workflow activities: $n.d$ represents the activity duration; $n.pos$ represents whether the activity n is a start, end, or internal node of the workflow; $n.pred$ represents the predecessors and $n.succ$ the successor activities of n; $n.deadline$ holds the externally assigned deadline of n; $n.tt$ the actual termination time of an activity instance.

For an upper- or lowerbound-constraint c we represent the source activity with $c.s$, the destination activity with $c.d$ and the bound with $c.\delta$. For a fixed-date constraint f, we write $f.a$ for the activity on which f is posed and $f.T$ for the fixed-date.

Since we assume well structured workflows, in the remainder of the paper we assume that for all upper and lower bound constraints the source node is before the destination node according to the ordering implied by the workflow graph.

4   Build-Time Calculations

At build time, our goal is to check if the set of time constraints is satisfiable, i.e., that it is possible to find a workflow execution that satisfies all timing constraints. We start from the original workflow graph and construct a timed workflow graph such that an execution exists that satisfies all constraints. Initially, all fixed-date constraints are transformed into lower-bound constraints. Then, the E- and L-values of all activity nodes in the timed graph are computed from activity durations and lower-bound constraints, using a straightforward modification of the CPM method. Finally, upper-bound constraints are incorporated into the timed graph. The resulting timed graph has at least two (possibly not distinct) valid executions. These executions are obtained if all activities complete at their E-values or all activities complete at their L-values. There may be other valid combinations of activity completion times within (E, L) ranges. We say that a timed graph *satisfies* a constraint if the executions in which all activities complete at their E- or L-values are valid with respect to this constraint.

4.1   Fixed-Date Constraints

The conversion of fixed-date constraints into lower-bound constraints is done using worst-case estimates. This is because at build time we do not have calendar value(s) for the start of the workflow and, thus, we can only use information about the duration between two valid time points for a fixed-date object. At process-instantiation time we will have more information concerning the actual delays due to fixed-date constraints.

Consider a fixed-date constraint $fdc(a, T)$. Assume that activities start instantaneously after all their predecessors finish. In the worst case, activity a may finish at $T.period + a.d$ after its last predecessor activity finishes. Indeed, let t_1 and t_2 be valid dates in T with the maximum time-interval between them. i.e., $t_2 - t_1 = T.period$, and let b be the last predecessor activity to finish. The time-interval between end-events of b and a is the longest if b finishes just after time $t_1 - a.d$, because then a cannot start immediately (it would then not finish at valid date t_1), and would have to wait until time $t_2 - a.d$ before starting. In this case, the distance between b and a is $\delta = (t_2 - t_1) + a.d$ $= T.period + a.d$, assuming b itself does not have a fixed-date constraint associated with it. If b has a fixed-date constraint $fdc(b, T')$, one can use similar reasoning to obtain $\delta = T.dist(T')$ if $a.d \leq T.dist(T')$ and $\delta = a.d + T.period$ otherwise.

To guarantee the satisfiability of all time constraints at build-time, without knowing the start date of the process, the timed graph must allow the distance of at least δ between a and all it's predecessors, where δ is computed for each predecessor as shown above. Consequently, the fixed-date constraint $fdc(a, T)$ is replaced by a lower-bound constraint $lbc(b, a, \delta)$ for every predecessor b of activity a.

4.2   Lower-Bound Constraints

The construction of the timed workflow graph that includes structural and lower-bound constraints is presented below. We should note that due to the way we carry out the computations, the activities in the resulting graph satisfy all lower-bound constraints.

Forward Calculations

```
for all activities a with a.pos = start
     a.E := a.d
endfor
for all activities a with a.pos ≠ start
    in a topological order
    a.E := max({b.E + b.d | b ∈ a.pred},
                {m.s.E + m.δ | m = lbc(s,a,δ)})
endfor
```

Backward Calculations

```
for all activities a with a.pos = end
     a.L := a.E
endfor
for all activities a with a.pos ≠ end
    in a reverse topological order
    a.L := min({s.L - s.d| s ∈ a.succ},
                {m.d.L - m.δ | m = lbc(a,d,δ)})
endfor
```

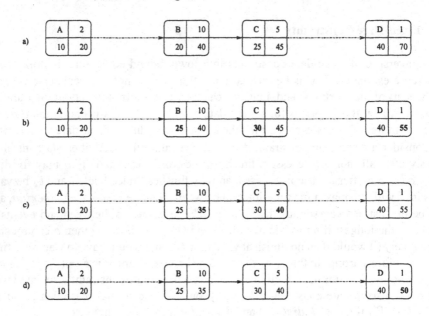

Fig. 3. Incorporating upper-bound constraints

4.3   Upper-Bound Constraints

In the timed workflow graph constructed during the previous step, an upper-bound constraint $ubc(s, d, \delta)$ is violated when either $s.E + \delta < d.E$ or $s.L + \delta < d.L$. In this case, we can use the buffer times of s and d to increase the E-value of s and decrease the L-value of the d in an attempt to satisfy the constraint. However, buffer time availability is a necessary but not sufficient condition for satisfying an upper-bound constraint. For example, in the workflow graph shown in Figure 2, the upper-bound constraint $ubc(B, C, 8)$ cannot be satisfied because the value of $C.E$ is always increased by the same amount as $B.E$.

A necessary condition for constraint $ubc(s, d, \delta)$ to be satisfiable is that the *distance* between s and d is less than δ. The distance is the sum of the durations of the activities on the longest path between s and d, and it can be computed by using the forward or backward calculations presented in the previous section, with s the starting node and d the ending node. We should note that for well structured workflows this distance does not change when the deadline of the entire workflow is relaxed and, therefore, more buffer becomes available for each activity. Consequently, extending the deadline of the whole workflow does not help us in satisfying violated upper-bound constraints.

One can show that if there is a node n between s and d with less buffer than both of them, then the buffer of s and the buffer of d can be reduced without influencing the E-values or L-values of the other node by: $min(buffer(s) - buffer(n), buffer(d) - buffer(n))$. Instead of finding the "safe" value by which the buffer of one end-point of the constraint can be reduced without affecting E and L values of the other end-point, we follow a more constructive approach.

If an upper-bound constraint is violated, we set the E-value of the source node to the value of $d.E - \delta$. If this value is greater than $s.L$, the upper-bound constraint is violated. Otherwise, we recompute the E-values of the timed graph starting at s and if the E-value of d does not change, the constraint is satisfied. In a similar way, we decrease the L-value of the destination node by δ and if this value is not less than $d.E$, we recompute the L-values of all predecessors of d. If the L-value of s does not change, the constraint is satisfied.

While the above can be used for individual upper-bound constraints, it is not enough for handling multiple upper-bound constraints. Figure 3 shows an example that demonstrates this problem. Figure 3a) shows the starting timed graph. Figure 3b) shows the timed graph after the integration of $ubc(B, D, 15)$. When $ubc(A, C, 20)$ is integrated, $ubc(B, D, 15)$ is violated at the L-values, as shown in Figure 3c). Finally, Figure 3d) shows the successful integration of both constraints.

We address this problem by checking whether an already incorporated upper-bound constraint is violated when new upper-bound constraints are incorporated into the timed graph. The following unoptimized algorithm summarizes this procedure. In this algorithm, the re-computation of the timed graph involves the forward and backward computations presented in the previous section.

```
repeat
     error := false
     for each m = ubc(s,d,δ)
           if m.s.E + m.δ < m.d.E            (* violation at E *)
                if m.s.L > m.d.E - m.δ      (* slack   at m.s  *)
                     m.s.E := m.d.E - m.δ
                     recompute timed graph
                     if m.d.E changes
                           error := true
                     endif
                else
                     error := true
                endif
           endif
           if m.s.L + m.δ < m.d.L            (* violation at L *)
                if m.d.E < m.s.L + m.δ       (* slack   at m.d  *)
                     m.d.L := m.s.L + m.δ
                     recompute timed graph
                     if m.s.L changes
                           error := true
                     endif
                else
                     error := true
                endif
           endif
     endfor
until error = true or nothing changed
```

This algorithm for the incorporation of upper-bound constraints has the following properties:

1. *Termination:* The algorithm terminates.
   At each loop there is at least one node x for which x.E is increased or x.L is decreased by at least one unit. Since there is a finite number of nodes, and the E- and L-values are bound, the algorithm must terminate.

2. *Admissibility:* A solution is found if there exists a timed graph satisfying all constraints.

   For an upper-bound constraint $m(s, d, \delta)$, $m.d.E - m.\delta$ is less than or equal to $m.s.E$ and $m.s.L + m.\delta$ is greater than or equal to $m.d.L$ for any timed graph satisfying the constraints. Since we set $m.s.E$ and $m.d.L$ to these values and, moreover, we know that the algorithm terminates, we can conclude that the algorithm will compute a solution, if one exists.

3. *Generality:* The algorithm finds the most general solution, if one exists.

   Let G and G' be timed graphs which differ only in the E- and L-values. We call G more general than G', if for every activity a the following condition holds: $a_G.E \leq a_{G'}.E$ and $a_G.L \geq a_{G'}.L$. Following the discussion of admissibility, it is easy to see that the timed graph generated by the algorithm above is more general than any other timed graph satisfying the constraints.

4. *Complexity:* The worst-case complexity of the algorithm is $O(m * d * n)$, where m is the number of upper-bound constraints, d is the largest buffer, and n is the number of activities.

   We can give an upper bound for number of iterations of this algorithm as follows: in each iteration there is at least one E-value increased or one L-value decreased at least by one unit. If there are m upper-bound constraints, and d is the largest buffer, then the number of iterations is $m * d * 2$ in the worst case. The recalculation is linear with the number of nodes.

5   Calculations at Process Instantiation Time

At process instantiation time, an actual calendar is used in order to transform all time information which was computed relative to the start of the workflow to absolute time points. It is also possible at this procedure to set the *a.deadline* value for an activity a, and increase or decrease the buffers computed at build time. Based on the calculations performed at build time, a deadline for an activity a is valid if it is greater than or equal to $a.E$. Fixed-date constraints are also resolved at process instantiation time, since they rely on absolute time points. (We used worst case estimates for these constraints during build time).

The computations that take place at process instantiation time are presented below, assuming that the variable *start* corresponds to the start-time of the workflow instance.

Forward Calculations

```
for all activities a with a.pos = start
    a.E := start + a.d
endfor
for all activities a with a.pos ≠ start
    in a topological order
    a.E := max({b.E + b.d | b ∈ a.pred},
               {m.s + m.δ | m = lbc(s,a,δ)})
    if there exists dc = fdc(a,T)
        a.E := dc.T.next(a.E)
    endif
endfor
```

Backward Calculations

```
for all activities a with a.pos = end
    if a.deadline < a.E
          raise exception
    else
          a.L := a.deadline
endfor
for all activities a with a.pos ≠ end
    in a reverse topological order
    a.L := min({s.L - s.d| s ∈ a.succ},
                {m.d - m.δ | m = lbc(a,d,δ)})
    if exists a.deadline and a.deadline < a.L
          a.L := a.deadline
    endif
    if there exists dc = fdc(a,T)
          a.L := dc.T.prev(a.L)
    endif
    if a.L < a.E
          raise exception
    endif
endfor
```

Incorporation of Upper-Bound Constraints: **incorporate()**

```
repeat
    error := false
    ok    := true
    for each m = ubc(s,d,δ)
          if m.s.E + m.δ < m.d.E          (* violation at E *)
                m.s.E := m.d.E - m.δ
                ok    := false
                if there exists dc = fdc(m.s,T)
                      m.s.E := dc.T.next(m.s.E)
                endif
                if m.s.E > m.s.L
                      error := true
                endif
          endif
          if m.s.L + m.δ < m.d.L          (* violation at L *)
                m.d.L := m.s.L + m.δ
                ok    := false
                if there exists dc = fdc(m.d,T)
                      m.s.L := dc.T.prev(m.d.L)
                endif
                if m.d.E > m.d.L
                      error := true
                endif
          endif
    endfor
    if ok = false and error = false
          error := recompute();
    endif
until error = true or ok = true
```

Timed Graph Re-computation: **recompute()**

```
for all activities a in topological order
    a.E := max({b.E + b.d | b ∈ a.pred},
                {m.s + m.δ | m = lbc(s,a,δ)}, a.E)
```

```
    if there exists dc = fdc(a,T)
        a.E := dc.T.next(a.E)
    endif
    if a.L < a.E
        return false
    endif
endfor
for all activities a in reverse topological order
    a.L := min({s.L - s.d | s ∈ a.succ},
                {m.d - m.δ | m = lbc(a,d,δ)}, a.L)
    if there exists dc = fdc(a,T)
        a.L := dc.T.prev(a.L)
    endif
    if a.L < a.E
        return false
    endif
endfor
return true
```

There is a possibility of optimizing the re-computation procedure by starting at the first node where an E-value was changed. However, there is additional overhead associated with this. Finally, the algorithm for incorporating upper-bound constraints into the timed graph has the same properties as the corresponding one presented in Section 4.

6   Time Management at Run-Time

6.1   General Computations

During the execution of a given workflow instance, we have to ensure that deadlines are not missed and any time constraints attached to activities are not violated. In order to achieve this, we may have to delay the execution of some of the activities that are either sources of upper-bound constraints or destinations of lower-bound constraints. Figure 4 shows a workflow segment having the upper-bound constraints $ubc(C, I, 18)$ and $ubc(G, H, 7)$. In this example, if F ends at 10 and C ends at 25 and, thus, D will end at 33 and H at 35, G must not start before 28 because the upper-bound constraint will be violated.

Even when we can immediately start the execution of an activity that is the source of some upper-bound constraint, it can be advantageous to delay its enactment so that the remaining activities have more buffer. In the example of Figure 4, if C starts at 7, it will finish at 10 and the buffer for all other activities is reduced. In particular, E, H, and I will have no buffer available since they have to finish at their E-values to satisfy the upper-bound constraints.

Selecting an optimal delay value for an activity is part of on-going work. Furthermore, existing work [11,12,13] can be used for distributing available buffer and slack times to activities and avoid time exceptions – assign-deadline() corresponds to this in the algorithm presented below. Buffer distribution addresses the distribution of extra buffer time that results from the assignment of an overall workflow deadline that is greater than the L-values of all activities with no successors. Slack distribution addresses the distribution of slack time that becomes available when activities finish before their L-values.

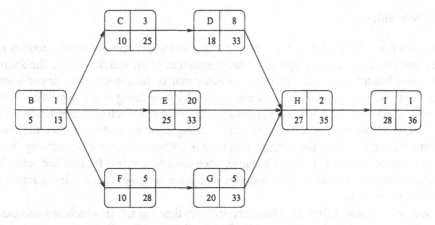

Fig. 4. Workflow segment with $ubc(C, I, 18)$ and $ubc(G, H, 7)$

The algorithm presented below assumes that activities finish within the interval defined by their E- and L-values (this implies that the termination of an activity should be delayed until, at least, its E-value. Allowing activities to finish before their E-values is subject of on-going work). When activity a finishes in the interval $(a.E, a.L)$, we may have to recompute the timed graph and re-incorporate upper-bound constraints before modifying the L-values of the ready activities according to the buffer and slack distribution algorithm. In addition, the re-computation of the timed graph should use the L-values of any active activities for computing E-values in order to avoid upper-bound constraint violations.

```
if a.tt ≤ a.L        (* a.tt = actual termination time *)
     a.L  := a.tt
     a.E  := a.tt
     done := false
     if a is the source of a lower-bound constraint
            recompute()
            incorporate()
            done := true
     endif
     for each b in a.succ that is ready for execution
            if b is source of an upper-bound constraint
                    if done = false
                            recompute()
                            incorporate()
                    endif
                    b.L := assign-deadline(b)
                    recompute()
                    incorporate()
                    done := true
            else
                    b.L  := assign-deadline(b)
                    done := false
            endif
            launch b for execution
     endfor
else
     invoke escalation process, deadline was missed
endif
```

6.2 Schedules

The execution of a workflow instance according to the procedures above requires re-computation of the timed graph after the completion of an activity that is the source of a lower-bound constraint or has a successor that is the source of an upper-bound constraint. We can avoid these re-computations by sacrificing some flexibility in the timed graph. Recall that the timed graph specifies ranges for activity completion times such that there *exists* a combination of activity completion times that satisfies all timing constraints and in which each completion time is within the range of its activity. Run-time re-computation was required because, once completion time for finished activities has been observed, not all completion times within the ranges of the remaining activities continue to be valid.

We define a *schedule* to be a (more restrictive) timed graph in which *any* combination of activity completion times within $[E, L]$ ranges satisfies all timing constraints. In other words, given a schedule, no violations of time constraints occur as long as each activity a finishes at time within the interval $[a.E, a.L]$. Consequently, as long as activities finish within their ranges, no timed graph re-computation is needed. Only when an activity finishes outside its range must the schedule for the remaining activities be recomputed.

It follows directly from the schedule definition that, for every upper-bound constraint $ubc(s, d, \delta)$, $s.E + \delta \geq d.L$ and for every lower-bound constraint $lbc(s, d, \delta)$, $s.L + \delta \leq d.E$; the reverse is also true, i.e., the timed graph that satisfies these properties is a schedule (compare this property with the two inequalities that are incorporated into the timed graph in Section 4). From the way we compute E- and L-values for the activities in a timed workflow graph, the E- and L-values already qualify as schedules. Consequently, when every workflow activity finishes execution at its E-value, there is no need to check for time constraint violations. The same is true when activities finish execution at L-values.

The development of algorithms for computing schedules with various characteristics is subject of ongoing research.

7 Related Work

The area of handling time-related issues and detecting potential problems at build, instantiation, and run time has not received adequate attention in the workflow literature. Existing workflow systems offer some limited abilities to handle time. For example, they support the assignment of execution durations, and deadlines to business processes and their activities, and they monitor whether deadlines are met.

In [9], an ontology of time is developed for identifying time structures in workflow management systems. They propose the usage of an Event Condition Action (ECA) model of an active database management system (DBMS) to represent time aspects within a workflow environment. They also discuss special scheduling aspects and basic time-failures. We used parts of their definitions as basis of our concept.

In [11,12,13], the authors propose to use static data (e.g., escalation costs), statistical data (e.g., average activity execution time and probability of executing a conditional activity), and run-time information (e.g., agent work-list length) to adjust activity deadlines and estimate the remaining execution time for workflow instances. However, this work can be used only at run-time, and it does not address explicit time constraints.

[1] proposes the integration of workflow systems with project management tools to provide the functionality necessary for time management. However, these project management tools do not allow the modeling of explicit time constraints and, therefore, have no means for their resolution.

In [15], the authors present an extension to the net-diagram technique PERT to compute internal activity deadlines in the presence of sequential, alternative, and concurrent executions of activities. Under this technique, business analysts provide estimates of the best, worst, and median execution times for activities, and the β-distribution is used to compute activity execution times as well as shortest and longest process execution times. Having done that, time constraints are checked at build time and escalations are monitored at run-time. Our work extends this work by providing a technique for handling both structural and explicit time constraints at process build and instantiation times, and enforcing these constraints at run-time.

In [6,16], the notion of explicit time constraints is introduced. Nevertheless, this work focused more on the formulation of time constraints in workflow definitions, the enforcement of time constraints through monitoring of time constraints at run-time and the escalation of time failures within workflow transactions [5]. Our work follows the work described in [6,16] and extends it with the incorporation of explicit time constraints into workflow schedules.

8   Conclusions

Dealing with time and time constraints is crucial in designing and managing business processes.

In this paper, we proposed modeling primitives for expressing time constraints between activities and binding activity executions to certain fixed dates (e.g., first day of the month). Time constraints between activities include lower- and upper-bound constraints. In addition, we presented techniques for checking satisfiability of time constraints at process build and process instantiation time, and enforcing these constraints at run-time. These techniques compute internal activity deadlines in a way that externally assigned deadlines are met and all time constraints are satisfied. Thus the risk of missing an external deadline is recognized early and steps to avoid a time failure can be taken, or escalations are triggered earlier, when their costs are lower.

Our immediate work focuses on: (1) using the PERT-net technique for computing internal deadlines to express deviations from the average execution duration of activities; (2) addressing conditionally and repetitive executed activities by providing execution probabilities to estimate average duration and variance for workflow executions; (3) considering optional activities and pruning the workflow graph when such activities should be eliminated to avoid time exceptions; and (4) addressing the different duration values that could be used at build time: best, average, and worst case execution times and turn-around times, which include the time an activity spends in the work-list and the time between start and end of an activity.

References

1. C. Bussler. Workflow Instance Scheduling with Project Management Tools. In *9th Workshop on Database and Expert Systems Applications DEXA '98*, Vienna, Austria, 1998. IEEE Computer Society Press.

2. CSESystems. *Benutzerhandbuch V 4.1 Workflow*. CSE Systems, Computer & Software Engineering GmbH, Klagenfurt, Austria, 1996.

3. CSE Systems Homepage. http://www.csesys.co.at/, February 1998.

4. J. Eder, H. Groiss, and W. Liebhart. The Workflow Management System Panta Rhei. In A. Dogac et al., editor, *Advances in Workflow Management Systems and Interoperability*. Springer, Istanbul, Turkey, August 1997.

5. J. Eder and W. Liebhart. Workflow Transactions. In P. Lawrence, editor, *Workflow Handbook 1997*. John Wiley, 1997.

6. Johann Eder, Heinz Pozewaunig, and Walter Liebhart. Timing issues in workflow management systems. Technical report, Institut f'ur Informatik-Systeme, Universit"at Klagenfurt, 1997.

7. TeamWare Flow. Collaborative workflow system for the way people work. P.O. Box 780, FIN-00101, Helsinki, Finland.

8. InConcert. Technical product overview. XSoft, a division of xerox. 3400 Hillview Avenue, Palo Alto, CA 94304. http://www.xsoft.com.

9. Heinrich Jasper and Olaf Zukunft. Zeitaspekte bei der Modellierung und Ausführung von Workflows. In S. Jablonski, H. Groiss, R. Kaschek, and W. Liebhart, editors, *Geschäftsprozeßmodellierung und Workflowsysteme*, volume 2 of *Proceedings Reihe der Informatik '96*, pages 109 – 119, Escherweg 2, 26121 Oldenburg, 1996.

10. F. Leymann and D. Roller. Business process management with flowmark. In *Proceedings of the 39th IEEE Computer Society International Conference*, pages 230–233, San Francisco, California, February 1994. http://www.software.ibm.com/workgroup.

11. E. Panagos and M. Rabinovich. Escalations in workflow management systems. In *DART Workshop*, Rockville, Maryland, November 1996.

12. E. Panagos and M. Rabinovich. Predictive workflow management. In *Proceedings of the 3rd International Workshop on Next Generation Information Technologies and Systems*, Neve Ilan, ISRAEL, June 1997.

13. E. Panagos and M. Rabinovich. Reducing escalation-related costs in WFMSs. In A. Dogac et al., editor, *NATO Advanced Study Institue on Workflow Management Systems and Interoperability*. Springer, Istanbul, Turkey, August 1997.

14. Susy Philipose. *Operations Research - A Practical Approach*. Tata McGraw-Hill, New Delhi, New York, 1986.

15. H. Pozewaunig, J. Eder, and W. Liebhart. ePERT: Extending PERT for Workflow Management Systems. In *First EastEuropean Symposium on Advances in Database and Information Systems ADBIS 97*, St. Petersburg, Russia, Sept. 1997.

16. Heinz Pozewaunig. Behandlung von Zeit in Workflow-Managementsystemen - Modellierung und Integration. Master's thesis, University of Klagenfurt, 1996.

17. SAP Walldorf, Germany. *SAP Business Workflow©Online-Help*, 1997. Part of the SAP System.

18. Ultimus. Workflow suite. Business workflow automation. 4915 Waters Edge Dr., Suite 135, Raleigh, NC 27606. http://www.ultimus1.com.

TOGA—A Customizable Service for
Data-Centric Collaboration

Jürgen Sellentin[1,2], Aiko Frank[2], Bernhard Mitschang[2]

[1] DaimlerChrysler AG, Research & Technology, Dept. CAE-Research (FT3/EK),
P.O. Box 2360, D-89013 Ulm, Germany
Juergen.Sellentin@DaimlerChrysler.COM

[2] Universität Stuttgart, Fakultät für Informatik, IPVR,
Breitwiesenstr. 20-22, D-70565 Stuttgart, Germany
{Aiko.Frank, mitsch}@informatik.uni-stuttgart.de

Abstract. Collaboration in cooperative information systems, like concurrent design and engineering, exploits common work and information spaces. In this paper we introduce the TOGA service (Transaction-Oriented Group and Coordination Service for Data-Centric Applications), which offers group management facilities and a push model for change propagation w.r.t. shared data, thus allowing for group awareness. Through TOGA's customizability and its layered architecture the service can be adapted to a variety of different collaboration scenarios. Multiple communication protocols (CORBA, UDP/IP, TCP/IP) are supported as well as basic transaction properties. Our approach enables the evolution of a set of separate applications to form a cooperative information system, i.e., it provides a technique towards component-oriented system engineering. In this paper we report on design issues, implementation aspects, and first experiences gained with the TOGA prototype.

1. Introduction

Concurrent and simultaneous engineering (see [2], [3]) is perceived an enabling technology to faster and better design of complex products as e.g. engineered artifacts. From a system point of view this technology refers to a whole spectrum that ranges from multiple and efficient communication protocols [29] to activity coordination (as e.g. provided by workflow systems [17]) and to appropriate support for collaboration techniques (as for example known as computer supported cooperative work [5]).

In contrast to administration and business scenarios these concepts and techniques are not directly applicable to the overly complex area of design, especially engineering design. There, existing system structures, proven processing scenarios, and chosen design methodologies have to be observed and effectively supported. The reason for that is the complexity of the heterogeneous application environment (e.g. CAD systems or FEM systems), its (often) proprietary data structures and data formats that obstruct data exchange, and finally the applied proprietary design process and design methodology itself. As a consequence, effective and practical support for concurrent and simultaneous engineering has to act as a kind of glue to flexibly combine these separate system components to form a cooperative information system, thereby still supporting the existing and well-established design methodology.

M. Jarke, A.Oberweis (Eds.): CAiSE'99, LNCS 1626, pp. 301-316, 1999.

1.1 CAD Application Area

Divide and conquer is the underlying technique that allows to cope with the inherent complexity of engineering design. As depicted in Figure 1, this strategy refers to a decomposition of the artifact under design into separate design items and to the delegation of design tasks to separate design teams, with each design team being responsible for the design of the assigned design item.

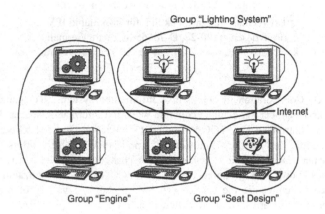

Fig. 1. Design Decomposition: Separate Design Groups and Associated Design Items

To be able to concurrently work within a team on those partitions without interfering or avoiding to interfere with other designers is a demanding task. Therefore it is necessary to organize groups of designers who share a set of design items. Their work should be coordinated automatically to avoid inconsistencies, even if users are spread all over the world (using workstations connected through the Internet).

Unfortunately, current distributed CAD environments often suffer from a lack of coordination among the ongoing design activities. Participants in design have to cooperate mostly by other means than their current design environment; they often have to resort to personal communication methods (like e-mail or telephone) or have to follow certain external design guidelines in order to coordinate their work and to resolve conflicts. Since these rules and design guidelines are specified outside the system, integrity cannot be controlled automatically, leading to manual and error prone design control. This scenario is depicted in Figure 2a.

It is exactly the focus of our work to remedy these grievances. Though there are already a lot of research activities considering similar scenarios, we are not aware of a system that covers all of the properties listed below (see also Section 3). In this paper we report on the design, implementation, and first experiences of our system approach called TOGA. As depicted in Figure 2b, TOGA provides a number of necessary services and system properties. Among the most important ones are:

- TOGA treats participating information systems, as e.g. CAD systems, as separate components within a distributed, collaborative environment, i.e., it supports component-oriented system engineering.

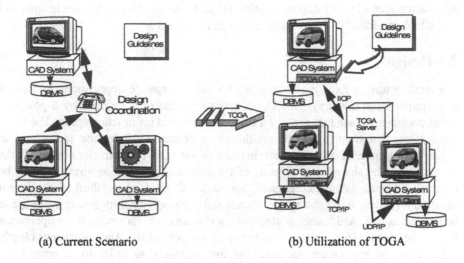

(a) Current Scenario   (b) Utilization of TOGA

Fig. 2. Introduction of TOGA

- TOGA is customizable in such a way that the system behaves according to the given design guidelines. These guidelines cover the operations and undo-operations, the object granules, the conflict situations and associated resolution strategies that altogether make up the desired collaboration model.
- TOGA is group-oriented and data-centric as opposed to user- and process-oriented.
- TOGA delivers a synchronous collaboration approach combined with a distributed, shared work and information space.
- TOGA synchronizes (by means of operation coordination) the state of all data objects that are part of the shared information space.
- TOGA automatically controls this integrity of shared data using a transaction-oriented protocol.
- TOGA consists of an application-specific component for customization and a generic (and thus reusable) middleware/server component.
- TOGA supports multiple communication protocols.

1.2 Overview of the Paper

In this paper we introduce the different layers of TOGA and discuss all aspects that have to be decided upon for customization w.r.t. a certain collaboration model. Due to space restrictions, we focus on the system approach, but not on a (formal) model or methodology on how to map particular design processes and their design guidelines onto our system.

The following section covers the design issues of the layered architecture, describing the interfaces of client layers as well as the underlying CORBA service. Readers that are not familiar with CORBA at all should refer to [13], [19] or [25] first. Section 3 contains a discussion on related work covering similar services as well as workflow and CSCW technology. In Section 4 we present decisions and experiences that are related to our prototype implementation. It consists of a generic, CORBA-based TOGA Service as well as a simple test application. A discussion of more complex application scenarios our implementation might be adopted to, some conclusions and an outlook to additional future work are given in Section 5.

2. Design

Our architecture enables the evolution of a set of separate applications to form a cooperative information system. The cooperation concept is realized by a powerful collaboration approach that exploits a common work and information space. The set of applications that want to collaborate through a common information space have to decide on a number of critical aspects in order to use TOGA effectively. First of all, the contents, i.e. the shared data objects, of the common information space have to be defined. Second, the object granule has to be decided upon, third, the relevant operations (and corresponding undo operations) to change the information space are to be defined as well, and fourth, strategies to decide on conflicts among these operations have to be specified (conflicts are treated by aborts, see below). These decisions clearly depend on the application scenario, but are necessary in order to determine the particular collaboration support TOGA is asked for. For example, considering object rotation in several dimensions, each rotation in a single dimension or only the final state may be synchronized, or, creating a new module, the creation of each (partial) item or only the creation of the (final) module may be synchronized. Choosing the right granule of data objects and operations is the key issue in defining the appropriate level of collaboration.

Once the common work and information space is defined, its consistency is automatically controlled by transaction-oriented processing: Each operation that effects the common information space is encoded into an event and sent to the TOGA server, which utilizes a 2-Phase-Commit protocol (2PC, see [6]) to distribute this event to all group members and to ensure that they all have performed the encoded operation successfully. If an application is not able to perform such an operation, it votes "abort" and TOGA notifies all group members to undo this operation.

In order to support various environments, our service has a layered architecture as displayed in Figure 3. The top level interface is written in C++ (since most CAD applications are written in C++)[1] and offers the integrated functionality needed by the application. It hides the underlying implementation, which may in principal consist of one or several components that utilize other services and communicate via CORBA, or directly via TCP/IP or UDP/IP etc. The prototype implementation described in this paper is based upon a single, integrated CORBA service and several CORBA clients.

The application layer (Section 2.2) contains all information specific to a particular application scenario and has to be developed as part of the customization process. E.g., it is responsible for the encoding of application-specific operations into generic events (and vice versa). Next comes the session layer (Section 2.3), which has a slim, but powerful interface. It will propagate (generic) event data received from the application

---

[1] We are aware of the fact that not all CAD systems provide suitable APIs for their integration into a TOGA environment, yet. Nevertheless, considering our experiences at DaimlerChrysler, we assume that the vendors of such systems will offer those APIs once proof of concept is done and a strong demand for this technology arises among participating enterprises.

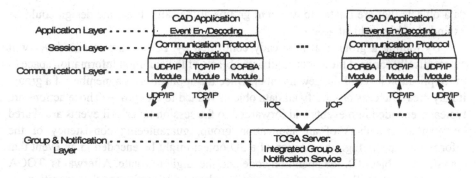

Fig. 3.:Overall Architecture of TOGA

layer to the actual communication layer (and vice versa). This layer is necessary since we want to transparently support direct usage of low level communication protocols like TCP/IP and UDP/IP, but also more powerful middleware like CORBA. The underlying communication layer (Section 2.4) is split into three different modules with specific interfaces. Since this paper is focussed on a CORBA-based server for TOGA, we will not describe interfaces to the TCP/IP and UDP/IP modules in detail. The interface of the group and notification layer (Section 2.5) is defined using the Interface Definition Language (IDL) of CORBA. This enables a component-based architecture and thus the integration of existing software (that is wrapped by specific CORBA skeletons) or the development of new services (like the TOGA server described here).

A simple processing example is presented in the next subsection. It is followed by a more detailed description of each layer, using this example to illustrate the realized functionality. Finally two figures are presented that describe the flow of events through all layers. Please note that these figures are specific to the example as well.

2.1 Overall Processing Example

Let us assume two applications working on the same set of data (e.g. the two applications working on the "lighting system" in Figure 1). According to the design decomposition, they shall become members of the same group. Furthermore, application 1 wants to perform an object rotation that is, according to the customization, an operation to be controlled by TOGA. How does it work?

In our approach, any kind of data and event processing has to be started by opening a new session at the client site. We propose to attach this step to the initialization phase of each application. The desired communication type (CORBA, TCP/IP, or UDP/IP) has to be specified as a parameter. After that, the chosen protocol is not visible any more. It is encapsulated by the session layer. Though each client chooses a single communication protocol, a server might support multiple ones.

In a next step, the application will join a group. Since the application layer is responsible for the relationship between data objects and group definitions (thus it can decide which operation influences which groups' information space), an application may in principal be part of several groups. Defining our architecture, we decided that an application has to be part of exactly one group, though. If it is necessary to access data objects that are related to different groups at the same time, the design could be extended to hierarchical groups.

By joining a group that is already controlled by TOGA, the session layer will automatically forward the status of all data objects of the common information space to the application layer of the new member. Once the application is a member of a group, it may create, access or modify all data objects related to this group. Those actions are typically encoded into events and forwarded to the session layer. All events are shared between all members of an application group, guaranteeing consistency of the information space. E.g., the rotation of a 3D object might be encoded in an event that contains the object ID, the operation code and the angle to rotate. Afterwards, TOGA ensures that either all or none of the group members have performed this operation.

2.2 Application Layer

The application layer realizes the customization. It has to bridge the gap between the application and the generic TOGA components presented in this paper. Thus it has to be aware of the current design decomposition, related data objects, operations and corresponding undo operations. All this information is neither available to the TOGA server nor to the session or communication layer (since these components have a generic interface).

Knowing the design decomposition, the application layer defines groups and related sets of data objects. In addition, it has to define which operations have to be synchronized immediately and which (sequence of) operations can be performed locally before the next synchronization step is necessary.

Once the application has joined a group already known and controlled by the TOGA server, or it has created (and implicitly joined) a new group using the session layer's operations[2], the application layer realizes a (virtual) information space for that particular group. Any changes to the information space are propagated to all group members via TOGA.

Vice versa, the application layer has to decode each event received from the session layer (method messageUp, see next section) and to check if the encoded operation is in conflict with other operations that were already performed locally. In case of no conflict, the application layer initiates the execution of the encoded operation and sends a "vote commit" message to the session layer, otherwise the operation is not performed and the application layer votes to abort. For each (sequence of) operation(s) that is to be synchronized, the application layer has to define undo operations, which have to be performed if any other group member initiates an abort.

Since all these tasks are very application-specific, they can not be moved to or controlled by the TOGA server. Thus, all semantic aspects of the collaboration and its customization are encapsulated within the application layer, whereas the underlying client layers and the TOGA server offer technical, generic collaboration support (that is

---

[2] The session layer can only be used to query for groups that are currently known to and processed by the TOGA server, but the server does not know about the original design decomposition. Since the application layer is aware of the design decomposition, it might initiate the activation of a group (within the TOGA server) that is responsible for another design task.

described in the following subsections). In order to exploit this support, it is very important that each client application contains an application layer with the same (or a compatible) customization model! Please keep in mind that a formal description of this model is out of scope of this paper. However, for our test application (see Section 4.1) we hand-crafted a particular customization.

2.3 Session Layer

The session layer has a slim interface that covers three different issues: The propagation of event data (received from the application layer) to the communication layer, processing and forwarding of group operations, and upcalls (to the application layer) due to event data received from the communication layer. The session layer's interface comprises the C++ class Session and two global methods makeSession and destroySession to start and end a session of work. The class Session defines generic data structures and methods for sending events (sendData), propagating context information (sendAllData), group administration (AddToNewGroup, addToGroup), voting (voteAbort, voteCommit), receiving events by upcalls (messageUp, see below), and additional convenience functions. makeSession initializes a global context (see Section 2.1) whereas destroySession ensures that the application will be removed from its group. In addition, it notifies the communication layer to cancel all connections in a consistent manner. Since our architecture focuses on a generic approach that should also support low-level protocols, there is no need for a more complex object-oriented design. Even more, the introduction of additional classes might lead to additional IDL interfaces at the CORBA level that will reduce performance of communication [24].

Since the session layer realizes only a pure push model for events (see e.g. [14]), there is only a single (asynchronously called) method messageUp for forwarding events and related data. Though this method is declared as part of the session layer's interface, it has to be defined (and thus implemented) by the application layer. Actually, it is only called by the session layer to forward events to the application layer. Considering the application scenario mentioned above, we do not expect that there is a need for a pull model. More precisely, we assume that an application will not wait for an event, but it will perform operations that initiate events (using the push model).

If the application layer generates a new event due to an operation of the application, it will call the method sendData to forward this event to all other group members. Thereby it will pass all necessary data (e.g. the operation ID for object rotation, the object ID and the rotation angle - see Section 2.1) encoded in an instance of dataType.

2.4 Communication Layer

The communication layer consists of three modules that establish a connection to the server component based on the actual protocol (CORBA, TCP/IP, or UDP/IP) selected. All modules have the same interface that is very similar to the session layer's (and is therefore omitted here). During an open session, only one communication module is active at a time (as specified in Section 2.1).

The CORBA module consists of a CORBA client stub for propagating events to the TOGA server (based upon interface c2s of Figure 4), a CORBA server object to receive events from the TOGA server (implementing `interface s2c` of Figure 4) and some methods that map between those objects' interfaces and the interface of the communication layer. E.g. the methods `sendData`, `sendAllData`, `voteCommit` and `voteAbort` are mapped to the single method `sendData` of the TOGA server.

2.5 TOGA Server

The TOGA server (**T**ransaction-**O**riented **G**roup and Coordination Service for Data-Centric **A**pplications) is an integrated CORBA service that manages transaction-oriented event processing as well as related group administration. Its interface is presented in Figure 4. The server itself implements `interface c2s` (client to server), whereas `interface s2c` (server to client) is implemented by the communication layer of each participating application.

Data structures presented in Figure 4 are used in both components. Since the TOGA server is a CORBA-based service (see Figure 3), we can assume reliable communication. The other modules will have more complex protocols.

Interface `c2s` is very slim and reflects the generic architecture: It has only one method for event propagation and three methods for group management. We decided to define only a single, generic method for event operations since the main part of processing will be the same for all kind of events. Thus it is much easier to handle threads of control and related transaction processing within the service.

```
interface c2s {
    short addToNewGroup(in long commNr,
                        in short groupId,
                        in string20 groupName,
                        in short memberId,
                        in string20 memberName);
    short addToGroup( in long commNr,
                      in short groupId,
                      in string20 groupName,
                      in short memberId,
                      in string20 memberName);
    void removeFromGroup( in long commNr,
                          in short memberId);
    short sendData( in long commNr,
                    in long msgNr,
                    in dataMap data);
    // ... additional methods for initialization
};
```

```
interface s2c {
    void addNewGroup  ( in short groupId,
                        in string20 groupName,
                        in short memberId,
                        in string20 memberName);
    void addToGroup   ( in short groupId,
                        in short memberId,
                        in string20 memberName);
    void removeFromGroup ( in short memberId);
    short sendData    ( in long commNr,
                        in long msgNr,
                        in dataMap data);
};
```

```
// Data Structures used by TOGA

typedef string<20> string20;

enum flagMap{ SHORT_TAG, USHORT_TAG,
              INT_TAG, UINT_TAG,
              LONG_TAG, ULONG_TAG,
              CHAR_TAG, FLOAT_TAG,
              DOUBLE_TAG };
union partMap switch (flagMap) {
    case SHORT_TAG  : short dataShort;
    case USHORT_TAG : unsigned short
                      dataUShort;
    case INT_TAG    : short dataInt;
    case UINT_TAG   : unsigned short
                      dataUInt;
    case LONG_TAG   : long dataLong;
    case ULONG_TAG  : unsigned long
                      dataULong;
    case CHAR_TAG   : char dataChar;
    case FLOAT_TAG  : float dataFloat;
    case DOUBLE_TAG : double dataDouble; };
typedef sequence<partMap> dataMap;

struct memberMap( short id;
                  string20 name; );
typedef sequence<memberMap> memberList;
struct groupMap ( short id;
                  string20 name;
                  memberList members; );
typedef sequence<groupMap> groupList;
```

Fig. 4. IDL Interface of the TOGA Service (server and client components)

Interface s2c is similar to c2s since events will be directly propagated from the communication layer to the application layer, except for group events (related to changes of a group composition) that will be processed within the session layer.

The overall architecture of TOGA ensures that participating applications will act as event supplier and event consumer. Thus it realizes a symmetric event model. Furthermore, from a logical point of view, the TOGA server is a central server that is responsible for all known applications based upon the architecture displayed in Figure 3. Nevertheless, the actual implementation may consist of several, distributed servers that use additional protocols to achieve consistency of operations (i.e. defining a global state of group compositions).

2.6 Processing Example

A processing example of a possible initialization phase is presented in Figure 5: Application 1 (see left hand side) initializes its session (thereby choosing the TOGA communication module), retrieves all information describing current groups and members and requests to become a member of one group. Processing this request, the TOGA server retrieves all data related to this group from application 2 (which is already a member of that group), propagates it to application 1, notifies all members of that group (including the new member) that the group composition has changed and replies that the operation has succeeded.

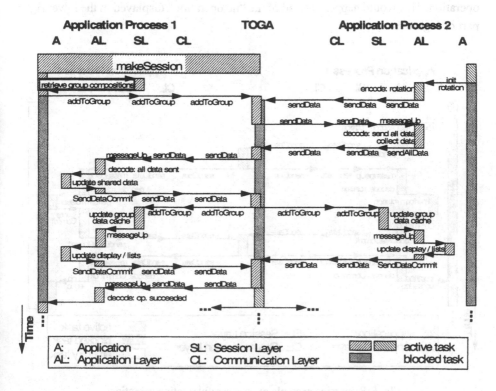

Fig. 5. Processing example of the initialization phase

Figure 5 contains also a request for a rotation operation of application 2 (see right hand side). Since the request of application 1 refers to the same group, the operation request of application 2 is automatically deferred until the first request is processed. If both operations would have been processed in parallel, and the rotation would have been executed by application 2 before it replies to the request for all data, and application 1 would have received the rotation request after having received all data, then the rotation would have been performed twice on the data of application 1, but only once on the data of application 2. Of course, more detailed synchronization protocols (preventing this problem) are possible within our architecture. E.g. the TOGA server might "know" that the rotation has already been performed on the data, and therefore the rotation event must not be propagated to application 1. As one can see, the granularity of shared data has to be well-defined in order to ensure a scalable architecture.

Another example describing the overall processing for a successful rotation operation is presented in Figure 6. Any operation is performed due to a received event, even within the initiating application process. First, this enables the usage of multicast protocols instead of multiple operation invocations. Second, it simplifies the application (otherwise the application code would have to distinguish between user-requests and events).

Considering a third application that could not perform the requested operation, and thus votes abort, application 1 and 2 would have to undo the already performed operation. This would happen instead of the "no operation" displayed in the lower right part of Figure 6.

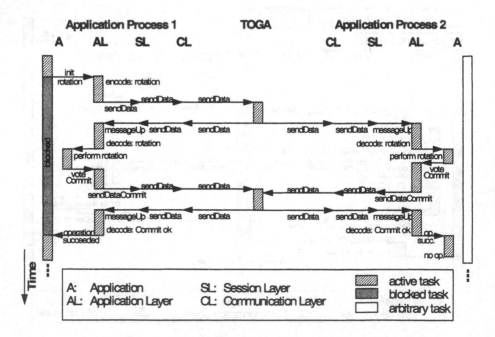

Fig. 6. Processing example of a successful rotation operation

3. Relationship to Existing Technology

TOGA was developed since other approaches don't fulfil the full set of requirements that are associated with a consistent and distributed collaboration in a heterogeneous environment by means of common information spaces, especially for concurrent engineering (see Section 1). TOGA can manage shared data objects consistently among the possibly heterogeneous applications that belong to a group. This leads to a component-based approach showing tight coupling, high group awareness, and consistent work data. Nevertheless, since there exist many different mechanisms for communication and collaboration in distributed environments, we want to show how they relate to our approach.

3.1 Comparison to Existing Communication Services

The simplest approach of communication is defined by the primitives send/receive [29]. It can be used to build higher level communication systems, as e.g. the TOGA service.

Messaging and queuing systems offer functionality to handle messages between two parties in a distributed environment, without being linked by a private, dedicated, logical connection [18]. Thus this approach enables asynchronous communication as used for e.g. bulk message processing or mobile computing. In contrast, our approach ensures communication for synchronous work among a given set of parties and in dedicated Intranets.

Persistent queues (usually) offer reliable asynchronous message exchange and sometimes they can also ensure the order in which messages are received (FIFO, etc., see e.g. JPMQ [26]). This is actually more closely related to our approach which offers guarantees in event and data handling as well as synchronization of events. Message queues could be one way to implement TOGA, with high level functionality like event and group management still to be added.

Since TOGA was implemented using CORBA, we want to show how it relates to existing *CORBA Common Object Services*. The *CORBA Event Service* offers event channels to suppliers and consumers of events. Both can subscribe to such a channel in order to receive or initiate events, either using the push or the pull model. Since the pull model is somehow comparable to polling, and thus inappropriate for our application scenario, we will look only at the push-based event channels. There are generic events which have to be interpreted by the application, and typed events which are defined via IDL. A generic event channel with push consumers and suppliers is similar to our approach. However, in TOGA the group composition is known and accessible to all group members and additional group functionality is available (see Section 2), which is not the case for the *CORBA Event Service*, where suppliers and consumers are connected to the event channel without knowing of each others existence [14], [19]. Furthermore TOGA clients are both suppliers and consumers (per definition), whereas clients connected to an event channel can be suppliers, consumer, or both. Last but not least, it would take considerably more effort to implement a comparable service with event channels, since more service logic has to be implemented. In particular, it is necessary to provide implementations for PushConsumer, ProxyPushConsumer, ConsumerAdmin, EventChannel, PushSupplier, and SupplierAdmin. All in all the *Event Service* shows less transparency of event processing and much more administration overhead. Finally, the *Event Service* doesn't (necessarily) support transaction-like behavior, order of events, and lacks further guarantees (see e.g. [19]).

Transaction-like handling of objects in a CORBA environment could be achieved by deploying the *CORBA Event, Object Transaction* and *Concurrency Control Services*. One major drawback is that the objects to be handled, have to be first class CORBA objects, which causes a lot of overhead (see [19], [24]). In addition, the relationship between applications, events, event channels and transactions is difficult to model. We prefer TOGA as a low level service, which might be used to build an advanced object model adapted to a particular design scenario on top of it.

3.2 Comparison to CSCW Technologies

Since we aim at supporting distributed collaborative work environments, it is obvious that we offer functionality that can be found in CSCW (*Computer Supported Cooperative Work*).

Workflow Management Systems realize process coordination and enactment especially for asynchronous work. Our approach enacts (ad hoc) coordination of synchronous work on shared data objects, but not directly the flow of work activities, since it is not process-oriented.

TOGA more closely resembles a CSCW service for synchronous distributed applications such as e.g. multi-user editors ([11], [22]). CSCW focuses on issues like groups, group awareness, human interaction and common information spaces in order to support cooperation. TOGA does not include support for groups of people like a generic group service would, but groups of applications, where one group is characterized by sharing a common set of data objects. This is due to the data-centric approach of this service and thus it is not user-centric. So we clearly focus on common work and information spaces. In doing 2PC combined with a push model, we also allow for an accurate group awareness, since all actions of a member are directly reflected in all group member applications (see Section 2). This is one of the major points where we differ from approaches like [10] and [27], which support cooperation of asynchronously and possibly disconnected users. To support these users, techniques like versioning, replication, inconsistency detection, and merging are being applied. Since we support synchronous work, such mechanisms become obsolete. We have to cope only with short periods of inconsistency while a commit phase is going on. Afterwards all common data objects are again synchronized, which is the so-called quiescent phase as described in [4]. But in contrast to TOGA, the algorithm presented in [4] relies on transforming conflicting operations to reach the convergence of the shared objects, while TOGA shows a more generic and transaction-oriented behavior. There exist other approaches, which developed formal models to handle concurrency control in synchronous applications (mainly multi user editors), e.g. [16],[21]. Especially [28] seems to be a very comprising work. Numerous criteria have been defined and corresponding algorithms presented in order to support controlled concurrent work. TOGA only offers the basic services to couple different applications by customizing information spaces and the necessary operations. Though it would be a good idea to implement the before-mentioned algorithms into the application layer. For example, one could implement the functionality of the ORESTE-Algorithm (Optimal RESponse TimE, [1]), which is used in synchronous groupware tools (i.e. GroupDesign, [1]).

Another service for distributed collaborative work is realized by the Corona Server [9] and the DistView [20] package. DistView is a toolkit for synchronizing views at the granule of single GUI windows, which is generally coarser than what can be achieved with our architecture. The Corona server was built to support publish/subscribe (P/S) and peer group (PG) communication. The P/S paradigm is related to the CORBA event channel notion (see above). The PG functionality supports group communication and can distinguish between different roles for users (principals and observers), whereas there is no difference for application users in TOGA, since it focuses on symmetrically propagating work activities which are relevant to all applications and doesn't implement direct inter-person communication support (e.g. for email or chat). Furthermore in [9], P/S and PG can be distinguished by means of anonymous versus named communication. TOGA lies in between because the TOGA protocols allow to access and propagate group (composition) information, but on the other hand it broadcasts all events regarding the shared data.

At last we want to point out some differences to GroupKit ([8], [23]), which is a Tcl/Tk-based toolkit offering core technology for implementing synchronous and distributed conferencing systems. In contrast, TOGA is a service for already existing applications. One of the GroupKit core technologies is the support for shared data. Concurrency control is only rudimentarily implemented, since it has to support a wide range of applications (see also [7]). Thus it might be necessary to implement a transactional protocol, like the one of TOGA, for GroupKit. Data sharing and synchronized views are enabled through the choice between three abstractions: multicast RPC, events, and environments. The environment concept is closest to the information space aspect of TOGA. It uses a structured model for name/value pairs. Users can register, to be notified when any changes have been made. However, there is no voting phase as in TOGA to ensure the validity of the modifications.

Because TOGA centers on shared, distributed data it might be interesting to compare it to federated database technology. However, TOGA does not provide a common data storage facility. Instead, it synchronizes (by means of coordination of the operations) the state of only those data objects that are part of the common information space.

4. Prototype Implementation

A prototype implementation has been built to prove the concepts presented in Section 2. It consists of a single TOGA server and several clients that include a simple test application as described in Section 4.1. All components are written in C++ and have been tested on a cluster of SUN Ultra 1 workstations, connected via a 10 MBit Ethernet. The underlying CORBA system is IONA's Orbix, version 2.3MT.

4.1 Test Application

A simple application has been developed to test the functionality and performance of the TOGA server as well as its related client layers. Collaborative work is simulated by

5 coins that can be moved on a fixed desktop. If a single user performs a move operation (using the mouse), our system ensures that this operation will be propagated to all other applications which belong to the same group. If this move operation is in conflict with an operation performed by other group members, it will be undone. Please note that our desktop with the 5 coins symbolizes the common information space and the movements resemble the design operations to simulate a collaborative work scenario on shared data objects. For example, in the real world scenario of Figure 1, the information space for the "engine construction" comprises objects like transmission (as depicted), gear, and motor.

4.2 Client Layers

The application layer as described in Section 2 has been integrated into the application code. The session and communication layer are realized by a class hierarchy that omits unnecessary method implementations. More precisely, the session layer contains only declarations of virtual methods that are implemented by the communication layer. Upcalls from the TOGA server are processed by the communication layer and either directly propagated to the application layer (events due to application operations) or further processed within the session layer (caching of group data).

4.3 TOGA Server

Implementing the prototype, we decided to build a single, central TOGA server only. Though this might reduce scalability, it omits additional protocols for synchronization and distributed event handling. Parallel processing of events can be enabled by choosing the appropriate thread mode of the TOGA server: Using mode 1, the entire server process is single threaded. Mode 2 shows one thread per group and mode 3 refers to one thread per event.

4.4 Experiences

In addition to the graphical application described in Section 4.1, we have developed a script-based client. It has been used to initiate a well defined number of events for measurements. Since a workstation has only a single mouse and keyboard, each graphical application has been run on a separate host (guaranteeing a realistic scenario). The TOGA server and script-based clients have been run on other hosts.

In a first test, we have determined differences between thread modes, thereby using three groups with three applications[3]. In theory, assuming linear scalability, the throughput of each mode should be three times higher than before. In practice, we measured a slightly lower factor (appr. 2.5). Since the server has been run on workstations with a single CPU, threads can only be used for parallel communication, but not for parallel execution of code within the TOGA server. Thus we conclude that the different thread modes achieved very positive and acceptable results.

The next test has been set up to measure scalability related to the number of applications per group (using thread mode 3). It turned out that the throughput

---

[3] One script-based application to initiate events and two passive, graphical applications that receive events.

decreased by 10-15% for a group that had five instead of a single member. Once again, we think that this is a promising result.

Finally, please keep in mind that pure system measurements do not provide a comprehensive assessment of TOGA. In real-world scenarios it is not expected that applications initiate events every millisecond. The main factors comprise thinking time of the user, processing time for operations and undo operations, as well as the amount of conflicting actions that result into conflicting events. The acceptance discussion of TOGA will not be decided w.r.t. the performance at the event level (as e.g. number of events processed per second), but w.r.t. the effectiveness and appropriateness of the semantical support for collaboration.

5. Summary and Outlook

TOGA has been developed in order to meet the demand for coupling existing engineering applications. Thus the TOGA service provides a particular technique towards component-oriented system engineering. It offers customizable group management and collaboration facilities to stand-alone application systems in order to set up a cooperative information system. Our collaboration approach is characterized by the coordination of synchronous work on a common information space. The collaboration model can be adapted to application needs by specifying first, the shared data objects that comprise the common information space, second, the operations that manipulate these data, and third, the conflict as well as conflict-resolution scenarios (i.e. undo algorithms). This conceptual flexibility is further enhanced by its layered and modular architecture that enables implementation flexibility as multiple communication protocols and basic transaction properties can be easily supported. Furthermore, these flexibility issues are the primitives towards extensibility. As discussed in Section 3 it is a platform to implement sophisticated algorithms for concurrent work as needed for certain environments.

We are currently investigating into several directions. One refers to extensions to the collaboration model. We view TOGA as a basic layer that provides the necessary functionality to build higher-level collaboration features as e.g. hierarchical groups referring to hierarchically organized information spaces, or more sophisticated conflict management functionality. Another direction of further work concentrates on implementation issues like multi-protocol communication, multi-threading, and other performance enhancing measures. The third direction of current and future research deals with questions on how to efficiently integrate the TOGA service and its enhancements into different kinds of application systems. Here we want to gain more knowledge on how to customize TOGA and how to integrate it via its application layer to existing application systems. So far, we concentrated on a modular and extensible architecture and therefore only hand-crafted this customization, but in the long run a methodology and clear model seems to be useful or even necessary. Last but not least, we want to employ TOGA within typical application areas of workflow and CSCW systems as for example business process applications or multi-user editors. Therewith, we want to investigate whether a system like TOGA can be used as a basis to a new generation of systems that integrate workflow and CSCW issues.

References

[1] M. Beaudouin-Lafon, A. Karsenty: *Transparency and Awareness in a Real-Time Groupware System*, Proc. of the ACM Symposium on User Interface Software and Technology (UIST'92), Monterey, CA., 1992.

[2] D. E. Carter and B. S. Baker: *Concurrent Engineering: The Product Development Environment for the 1990's*, Addison-Wesley Publishing Company, New York, NY, USA, 1991.

[3] D. Gerwin and G. Susman: *Special Issue on Concurrent Engineering*, IEEE Transactions on Engineering Management, Vol. 43, No. 2, May 1996, pp. 118-123.

[4] C. A. Ellis, S. J. Gibbs: *Concurrency Control in Groupware Systems*, Proc. of the ACM SIGMOD 1989, pp. 399-407, Seattle, Washington, USA, 1989.

[5] C. A. Ellis, S. J. Gibbs, G. L. Rein: *Groupware - Some Issues and Experiences*, CACM, 1991.

[6] J. Gray, A. Reuter: *Transaction Processing: Concepts and Techniques*, Morgan Kaufmann Publ., 1993.

[7] S. Greenberg, D. Marwood: *Real Time Groupware as a Distributed System: Concurrency Control and its Effect on the Interface*, Proc. of the ACM CSCW'94, Oct. 22-26, N. Carolina, USA, ACM Press, 1994.

[8] S. Greeenberg, M. Roseman: *Groupware Toolkits for Synchronous Work*, in *Trends in CSCW*, edited by M. Beaudouin-Lafon, Jon Wiley & Sons Ltd., 1996.

[9] R. W. Hall et al.: *Corona: A Communication Service for Scalable, Reliable Group Collaboration Systems*, Proc. of the ACM Conf. on CSCW '96, Boston, USA, 1996.

[10] J. Klingemann, T. Tesch, J. Wäsch: *Enabling Cooperation among Disconnected Mobile Users*, Second IFCIS Intl. Conference on Cooperative Information Systems (CoopIS '97), Kiawah Island, USA, June 1997.

[11] M. Koch: *Design Issues and Model for a distributed Multi-User Editor*, CSCW, Intl. Journal, 5(1), 1996.

[12] R. Mayr: *Entwurf und Implementierung einer Event-Behandlung in CORBA-Umgebungen*, Diplomarbeit, Technische Universität München, 1996 (in German).

[13] Object Management Group: *The Common Object Request Broker Architecture: Architecture and Specification*, Revision 2.2, http://www.omg.org/corba/corbiiop.htm, Upd. February 1998.

[14] Object Management Group: *The Common Object Request Broker Architecture: Common Object Services Specification*, http://www.omg.org/corba/sectrans.htm, Upd. December 1997.

[15] Object Management Group: *Workflow Management Facility, Request for Proposal (RFP)*, http://www.omg.org/library/schedule/Workflow_RFP.htm, May 1997.

[16] J. Munson, P. Dewan: *Concurrency Control Framework for Collaborative Systems*, Proc. CSCW'96, ACM, Cambridge, MA, USA, 1996.

[17] S. Jablonski, C. Bussler: *Workflow Management, Modeling Concepts, Architecture and Implementation*, Intern. Thomson Computer Press, London, 1996.

[18] R. Orfali, D. Harkey, J. Edwards: *Essential Client/Server Survival Guide*, Van Nostrand Reinhold, 1994.

[19] R. Orfali, D. Harkey, J. Edwards: *Instant CORBA*, Wiley Computer Publ., 1997.

[20] A. Prakash, H. S. Shim: *DistView: Support for Building Efficient Collaborative Apllications using Replicated Objects*, ACM Conference on CSCW, Oct. 1994, pp. 153-164, 1994.

[21] M. Ressel, D. Nitsche-Ruhland, R. Gunzenhäuser: *An Integrating, Transformation-Oriented Approach to Concurrency Control and Undo in Group Editors*, Proc. CSCW'96, ACM, Cambridge, MA, USA, 1996.

[22] N. Ritter: *Group Authoring in CONCORD—A DB-based Approach*, Proc. ACM Symposium on Applied Computing (SAC), San Jose, California, February 1997.

[23] M. Roseman, S. Greenberg: *Building Real Time Groupware with GroupKit, A Groupware Toolkit*, ACM Transactions on Computer Human Interaction, 1996.

[24] J. Sellentin, B. Mitschang: *Data-Intensive Intra- & Internet Applications — Experiences Using Java and CORBA in the World Wide Web*, in: Proceedings of the 14th IEEE International Conference on Data Engineering (ICDE), Orlando, Florida, February 1998.

[25] J. Siegel: *CORBA: Fundamentals and Programming*, Jon Wiley & Sons, 1996.

[26] H. P. Steiert, J. Zimmermann: *JPMQ—An Advanced Persistent Message Queuing Service*, in: Proc. of the 16th British National Conference on Databases (BNCOD16), Cardiff, July 1998.

[27] R. Sturm, J. A. Müller, P. C. Lockemann: *Collision of Constrained Work Spaces: A Uniform Concept for Design Interactions*, 2nd Intl. Conf. on Coop. Information Systems (CoopIS '97), Kiawah Island, USA, 1997.

[28] C. Sun, X. Jia, Y. Zhang, Y. Yang, D. Chen: *Achieving Convergence, Causality Preservation, and Intention Preservation in Real-Time Cooperative Editing Systems*, ACM Transact. on HCI, Vol. 5(1), 1998.

[29] A. S. Tanenbaum: *Computer Networks*, 3rd Ed., Prentice-Hall, Amsterdam, 1988.

A Practical Approach to Access Heterogeneous and Distributed Databases

Fernando de Ferreira Rezende, Ulrich Hermsen, Georgiane de Sá Oliveira,
Renata Costa Guedes Pereira, and Jochen Rütschlin

DaimlerChrysler AG – Research and Technology – Dept. FT3/EK – P.O.Box 2360
89081 Ulm – Germany
jochen.ruetchlin@daimlerchrysler.com

Abstract. A common problem within most large corporations nowadays is the diversity of database systems that are employed by their many departments in the development of a product. Usually, the total corporate data resource is characterized by multi-vendor database servers which, unfortunately, have no ability to relate data from heterogeneous data sources. In this paper, we present a database access interface which allows users to formulate SQL2 queries in a homogeneous way against a federation of heterogeneous databases. The database heterogeneity is not only completely hidden from the user, but what the user really perceives is a global database schema which can be queried as though all data reside in a single local database when, in fact, most of the data are distributed over heterogeneous, autonomous, and remote data sources. Further, the users can navigate through the database complex and compare, join, and relate information via a single graphic interface.

1 Introduction

Large corporations are often penalized by the problem of diversity of software systems. The many departments involved in the development of a product usually use different software tools; of course, each of them employs its own and familiar tools which help them to solve their problems, or their part of the complete product development work, in some way. Particularly in the field of the *engine development*, such tools vary mainly among simulation, CAD, testbenchs, and calculation tools. On the other hand, this diversity problem, or in other words the heterogeneity problem, is reflected in the many different sources of data used by the engineers to collect the necessary data for the product development as well. Usually, but by no means in all the cases, these data are managed by *Database Management Systems* (DBMSs) and stored in *databases* (DBs). Hence, the data are distributed along departmental and functional lines, leading to fragmented data resources. Such data distribution contributes to the emergence of the so-called *islands of information*. Thus, the data are lastly organized and managed by a mix of different DB systems (DBSs) from different software vendors. At both levels of this software diversity – the tools and DBSs levels – there exists the problem of communication between the software. The tools usually do not understand or are able to communicate with each other. And further, the autonomous DBSs have no ability to relate data from the heterogeneous data sources within the organization. The keyword to solve the heterogeneity problem at all levels is *integration* – tool as well as DB integration.

M. Jarke, A. Oberweis (Eds.): CAiSE'99, LNCS 1626, pp. 317-332, 1999.

In the project MEntAs (*Engine Development Assistant*) – an innovation project at DaimlerChrysler Research and Technology – we have to cope with both sides of this heterogeneity problem. On one side, the several software tools employed by the engineers must be integrated; in the sense that the data produced by one tool can be automatically consumed by the next tools used in the engine development process. This data production and consumption among the tools generates a kind of data- and workflow, which is then managed and controlled by a *Workflow Management System*. On the other side, the several DBs must be integrated as well. In this paper, we will particularly give emphasis to this side of the software integration in the project MEntAs. We show how we have solved the DB heterogeneity problem in MEntAs in a very user-friendly way. We leave the discussion of our panacea to the problem of software tool integration in MEntAs to a later opportunity.

The problem that the engineers mainly have with the DB heterogeneity is to collect the information in the many data sources and, additionally, to correlate and to compare the data. The DBs are usually encapsulated by the applications, so that the engineer cannot have direct access to the data stored in them. Hence, they must use the many different interfaces provided by such applications to each DB. Furthermore, such interfaces are limited to a number of pre-defined queries that can be executed against a single DB. Since the process of designing and developing a new engine concept is extremely creative, the engineers often feel themselves limited in their creativity because such interfaces are not satisfactory in providing data from different data sources, in comparing and joining these data.

Our solution to this problem in MEntAs is based upon a *DB Middleware System* [1]. On top of a DB middleware system, we have designed and implemented a DB access interface which allows engineers to formulate queries in a homogeneous way against a federation of heterogeneous DBs. The queries follow the ISO standard SQL2 (*Structured Query Language* [2, 3]) for DB manipulation. By means of a *Graphic User Interface* (GUI), the engineers are friendly guided in the process of creating their own queries which may even traverse the boundaries of a DBS and involve the DB complex integrated in the federation. On processing the queries, the DB heterogeneity is not only completely hidden from the users. But what they really perceive is a global DB schema which can be queried as though all data reside in a single local DB when, in fact, most of the data are distributed over heterogeneous and remote data sources. Further, the engineers can navigate through the DB complex and compare, join, and relate information via a single, homogeneous graphic interface. By such a means, the right data are put available to the engineer much more comfortably and, most importantly, much faster than in usual developing environments.

This paper is organized as follows. In Sect. 2, we sketch the architecture of our DB access interface and explain its components separately. In Sect. 3, we deliberate on the functionality of the interface, showing how it looks like and how the engineer interacts with it. Finally, we conclude the paper in Sect. 4.

2   The Client/Server Architecture of the DB Access Interface

For the DB access interface in MEntAs, we have chosen a client/server architectural approach. This decision was mainly taken due to three reasons: scalability, parallelism, and multi-tier characteristic. Client/server architectures can scale up very well by simply adding to them new hardware power or software components whenever necessary. In addition, client/server computing has a natural parallelism: many clients submit many independent requests to the server that can be processed in parallel, and furthermore, parallelism directly means better performance and so faster results. Finally, client/server architectures have the important feature of being multi-tier; they can be integrated to and take part in other architectures, new components can be added or dropped out, the server can play the role of a client, and the other way around, a client can be a server, etc.

Client/server architectures may be differentiated according to the way the data are transferred and the distribution of tasks is organized. The three most important forms are: *Page Server*, *Object Server*, and *Query Server* (the reader is referred to [4, 5, 6, 7] for more details on these approaches). We consider the client/server architecture of the MEntAs DB access interface as being a simple but very effective example of a query server approach (Fig. 1).

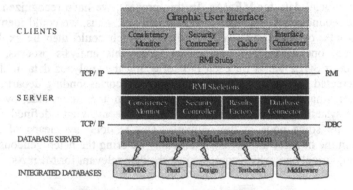

Fig. 1. Architecture of the MEntAs DB access interface.

Essentially, a query server works on the basis of contexts. A context normally comprises a set of complex objects and may be specified for example by means of MQL or SQL/XNF statements [8]. In the case of MEntAs, the contexts can be viewed as the SQL2 statements created by the own engineers via the GUI. The evaluation of such statements takes place in the server, where the objects are derived and stored in a transfer buffer. By means of operations such as projections, selections, and joins, the object views are tailored to the necessities of the users. In MEntAs, the essential functionality and power of the SQL2 language is put available to the engineer to create such operations. Hence, the volume of information to be transferred and fetched into the client cache is significantly reduced and optimized. Additionally, this approach is insensitive to cluster formations. Thus, ill-formed clusters do not affect the whole parallelism and concurrency of the system, because no objects are unnecessarily transferred to the client cache. Therefore, we hold the opinion that this approach mostly fulfils the necessities of MEntAs due to all its distinguishing qualities. This approach is a big research challenge, and up to now, it was followed only by prototype systems. Examples are: AIM-P [9], PRIMA [10], ADMS-EWS [11], XNF [8], Starburt's Coexistence Approach [12], Persistence [13], KRISYS [14], and PENGUIN [15].

Another important implementation decision we have taken during the design of the MEntAs DB access interface was the choice of an adequate programming language.

Due to the broad range of hardware platforms and computer architectures employed by the mechanical engineers in the engine development (the heterogeneity at the level of hardware and software tools), we have committed for using *Java* as the development environment and programming language, not only the client side but also the server side. This has shown later to be the right decision, since the development time was significantly reduced due to all facilities offered by Java, in comparison with for example C or C++, and its platform independence.

2.1   Integrated Databases

The *Integrated Databases* are the many data sources integrated in MEntAs. In the actual stage of the MEntAs development, these are all relational DBs [16].[1] Fig. 2 illustrates how the interconnection of heterogeneous DBs in MEntAs works. In order to construct a global DB schema for the engine development, we have analyzed together with the mechanical engineers the data models of each such DBs in order to identify the crucial data for MEntAs. In this process, we have recognized semantic differences, redundancies, synonyms, and homonyms. Thus, we could identify some common points, or better, overlapping objects, which could then be exploited for cross-DB join operations (DB navigation). After this analysis process, we have defined a set of SQL2 views for each DB reflecting the analyzed data model. Those views are created on top of the original DB by the corresponding department's DB administrator (mainly due to security reasons). On the other side, we tell the middleware system in our DB server that there are some views defined for it in a remote DB on some node in the network. This is done by means of nickname definitions in the middleware. By such a means, we bring the heterogeneous schemas into a global, virtual one, which contains just the data relevant for MEntAs.

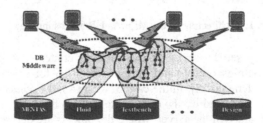

Fig. 2. The MEntAs approach towards integration of heterogeneous schemas in a global one.

2.2   Database Server

There are a lot of DB middleware systems commercially available in the market. The choice of the most appropriate one for MEntAs was based on a very detailed comparative analysis and performance evaluation. The complete results of our evaluation have been thoroughly reported in [17, 1, 18]. In particular, we have committed for using IBM's DataJoiner in MEntAs [19]. However, it is convenient to notice here that the client/server architecture of the MEntAs DB access interface is independent of the middleware system being used. This is so because the

---

[1] We did not detect the use of object-oriented DBSs in any department involved in the engine development process. Nevertheless, the integration of DBSs other than relational, as for example hierarchical or network DBs, can be coped with by the DB middleware system either, but with some limitations.

communication between the MEntAs server and the DB server, where the middleware is located on, is performed via JDBC (*Java Data Base Connectivity*), a Java standard for the access to relational DBs supporting the functionality and power of the SQL2 standard. Therefore, MEntAs can apply any DB middleware system which offers a JDBC API without requiring great programming efforts for the modifications. Currently, practically all DB middleware systems provide a JDBC API.

2.3   Communication

2.3.1   Server/Database Server Communication
In the case of MEntAs, the use of the JDBC API for the communication between the server and the DB server is an adequate alternative since it is tailored to relational data sources [20, 21] (refer to Fig. 1). In addition, practically all well-known DB vendors offer a corresponding JDBC driver for their products. We can employ either a JDBC driver of *Type 2* or *Type 3* [20]. Fig. 3 presents both approaches. In simple words, as type 2 JDBC drivers are classified the ones which convert any JDBC operation to the equivalent operation supported by the client API of the corresponding DBS. Due to this particular feature, in order to apply a type 2 JDBC driver in the MEntAs architecture, we need to install an instance of the DB (middleware) client together with the MEntAs server (Fig. 3a). This type of driver has pros and cons. On the one hand, the platform independence of our MEntAs server is limited, becoming then restricted to the ones supported by the middleware vendor for its DB client. In addition to that, a type 2 JDBC driver is only partially implemented in Java, since many of its functionalities are provided by C libraries which are integrated in Java by means of the JNI (*Java Native Interfaces*) API. Lastly, we have unfortunately found out in the practice that the type 2 JDBC driver offered by our DB middleware vendor cannot execute queries in parallel. It serializes all concurrent queries being performed via all DB connections. In contrast, the type 2 JDBC drivers' implementations have shown to be more mature and stable than the type 3 drivers.

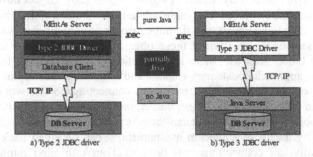

Fig. 3. JDBC driver variations in the implementation of the MEntAs server.

In turn, the type 3 JDBC drivers are implemented in pure Java. They are able to receive JDBC calls made via a DB independent network protocol (e.g., TCP/IP) and pass them on to a special component located at the server side, usually called *Java Server*, which then converts those calls to the corresponding operations understandable by the particular DBS (Fig. 3b). By using this type of driver, we were able to send concurrent queries to the DB server through different DB connections and it has processed all of them in parallel without problems. Unfortunately, the stability of the type 3 JDBC driver provided by our middleware vendor is not at all so high as its counterpart type 2 driver.

In MEntAs, the use of a type 3 JDBC driver is certainly the better approach, due to both its parallel query processing skills as well as its pure Java implementation. In the practice however, we were forced to implement and thus support both variations of the JDBC drivers in our architecture because of the low stability of the type 3 driver currently available. Which of both driver variations is employed in MEntAs can be set up by an input parameter when launching the MEntAs Server.

2.3.2   Client/Server Communication

The *Remote Method Invocation* (RMI) API is an efficient alternative for implementing the communication between distributed Java applications [22]. By means of RMI, distributed objects can be easily and elegantly implemented. Based on the ISO standard TCP/IP protocol, tools and APIs are put available to the software designer which enable a distribution at the object level. In comparison with for example a distribution at the network level via sockets, the distributed objects approach significantly shortens the development and implementation times, and in addition, it drastically reduces maintenance costs.

In comparison with other approaches at the object level, like for example CORBA [23, 24, 25], we believe that the performance of the RMI solution is better. In addition, since in the MEntAs architecture only homogeneous (Java) objects are distributed between clients and server, and hence just such objects must be considered for the integration, the power of the CORBA approach to integrate heterogeneous objects in a distributed environment is irrelevant in our particular case.

2.4   Database Connector

Management of DB Resources

In order to speed up the accesses to the DBs by the different components and at the same time to guarantee a global control over the DB resources, the DB connector manages *connection objects* by means of *object buffers* [26]. Object buffers allow the sharing of instantiated objects. The main advantage of using object buffers is that, since different calls to an object type do not cause a reinstantiation of such objects, no time is dispensed for the creation of those objects. In addition, since the objects are returned to the buffer after use, there is a reduction in the time spent for the garbage collection. This approach boosts performance and minimizes memory use.

Our implementation of the object buffer for connecting objects works as follows. By checking an object out of the object buffer, one receives an exclusive reference to a connection object. This connection can then be used to process an SQL2 statement, and thereafter by means of a checkin mechanism, it can be given back to the object buffer. Generally, all connections can be reused an unlimited number of times. However, in our case we have implemented a kind of timeout mechanism for the connections. After a connection has been used a pre-defined and adjustable number of times, we discard it and open a new again. In [26], a similar mechanism was suggested using timestamps.

Management of Queries

The JDBC drivers' implementation guidelines state that any Java object, which is no longer being used and which consumes DB resources, should free all used DB resources at the time it is caught by the Java's garbage collector. Additionally, it is supposed that the resources used during the execution of a statement should be implicitly freed or reused with the next statement's execution. By this way, the JDBC API handling should be simplified, since the software designer would be alleviated from the tasks of managing DB resources. Notwithstanding, unfortunately there exist implementations of JDBC drivers which fulfil those guidelines only partially. Moreover, the close coupling of the garbage collector with the management of DB resources may be problematic and has shown us some disadvantages in the practice. As a matter of fact, the Java's garbage collector is automatically started whenever a Java process becomes memory bound. At this same time, it releases then the corresponding DB resources. On the other way around, the garbage collector is not started when the DB resources, e.g. connections, must be released due to a high overhead at the DB side. Hence, the triggering time for the garbage collector is merely dictated by memory bound situations of Java processes and not of DB processes. Due to that and to the fact that in MEntAs the overhead difference among the Java and DB processes may vary enormously, we follow the approach of explicitly freeing all DB resources by our own after each operation execution, independently of the JDBC driver being used. Hence, on the one hand, we are not subject to the faults of some driver implementations, and on the other hand, we have a better control about the use of the DB resources.

2.5 Results Factory

The successful processing of a query by the DB connector activates the results factory (Fig. 1). This component is used to create the result sets which are shown to the engineer at the client. On the basis of the DB cursor, the results factory fills its result object with a pre-defined, adjustable quantity of tuples by reading (*next*) the cursor repeatedly. By this way, the results of a query are transported to the client neither all at once nor tuple by tuple. On the contrary, the whole result table is divided into small parts, the *result sets*, which are then sent asynchronously to the client. The time that the engineer spends to visualize a result set is exploited by a prefetcher at the client side to load more result sets into the client cache in background. Thus, the engineer can smoothly navigate through the results, without having to wait an unnecessarily long time for the next result sets from the server.

2.6 Interface Connector

Management of the Global Schema's Meta-Information
The *Interface Connector* (Fig. 1) begins its work when the GUI is started at the client. At login time, it establishes a connection with the server. By means of the server's RMI registry, the client receives a reference to a *server object* which is used as a starting point for all other connections with the server. Via the server object, many other objects are loaded into the client containing meta-information about the integrated data sources in the DB server. The global schema's meta-data comprehend: *Table* - name, attributes, and commentary; *Attribute* - name, commentary, and data type. On the basis of these meta-data, a well-defined interface to the GUI is created, by which means the GUI can show to the end-user the attributes of a table, can present the commentary of an attribute/table as a help function, etc. Furthermore, with the information about the data types of the attributes, the GUI can correlate each attribute with its type-specific comparison operations.
Management of Error Codes and Messages
The error messages employed by the GUI to alert the end-user about any mal-function in the system are caught by the interface connector at initialization time either. The

many different failure situations are characterized by an error code and its corresponding error message. This code and message correspondence is stored in the DB of the middleware and is loaded into a Java *properties object* at initialization time.

Management of Queries

As soon as the engineer has finished the interaction with the GUI to create a query, the GUI produces a string containing the corresponding SQL2 statement. Thereafter, the interface connector asynchronously sends the query to the server for processing. At this time, the thread implementing this object blocks waiting for an answer from the server. On receiving the awaited answer, this object produces an event of the AWT (*Abstract Window Toolkit*) whose identifier carries information about the success or failure of the query processing. In case of success, the GUI receives the first result set, and in case of failure it receives an appropriate error code to inform the engineer about his query's fate. After showing the first result set, the interface connector starts prefetching the next result sets from the server. Such a prefetching runs in an own thread and creates cache objects containing the next result sets.

Storing Select Statements and Result Sets/Tables

The interface connector offers methods to store the generated SQL2 statement in the DB of the middleware. This option to store pre-formulated SQL2 statements has received a good acceptance from the engineers, since they do not need to formulate frequently used queries over and over again. They only need to open the previously saved select statements, and on the basis of an identifier and a commentary given by their own, the complete select statement is sent to the server for processing by means of a single mouse click. Besides the select statement, the result table can be similarly stored in a text file for further visualization and processing by the user.

2.7   Cache

As shortly mentioned, the interface connector manages a cache at the client side for temporarily storing the results of the queries (Fig. 1). The current implementation of the MEntAs client generates for each executed query an instance of the cache class (let us call it *mini-cache*). Such a mini-cache stores then the results of a single query. This mini-cache also embodies a prefetcher, by means of which result sets are fetched from the DB server even beyond the actual cursor position seen by the engineer. Although this implementation of the cache contains sufficient functionality for the first beta version we have delivered of MEntAs, it has proven to be too simple and sometimes even ineffective in some cases. On the one hand, our actual cache storing algorithms have had storage capacity problems whenever handling huge amounts of data produced by some iceberg queries during the test phases. In addition, the independent management of the results of different queries is not the best approach, since each of them performs the same tasks in principle. A last point our cache is still lacking of is the possibility to store and manage mapping information. We intend to overcome these drawbacks in the next version of MEntAs by extending the actual functionality of the cache with an implementation of the *CAOS Cache* approach [27].

2.8   Consistency Monitor

There are mainly two potential sources of problems to be coped with during DB integration – schematic differences in the DBs as well as differences in the data representations. To cope with these problems is the main goal of the local and global consistency monitors (Fig. 1).

Management of Entry Points

In order to support the very important feature of DB navigation, we have identified in the integrated DBs' data models common data which serve the purpose of *entry points*. In simple words, for our purposes DB entry points are entities' attributes which carry the same semantic information. Being so, they can be used for join operations which can cross DBs' boundaries.

Parser

The consistency monitor takes care of differences in the data representations of the integrated DBs. As an example of such differences, the identification of an engine in the MENTAS DB has been modeled according to the standard created by Mercedes-Benz, namely an engine must be identified by a *Type*, an *Specification*, and a *Sample of Construction*. Hence, we have simply created three attributes in the engine table to accommodate such information. Unfortunately, this standard and simple engine identification is, in surprisingly all cases, not at all followed by the data models of the integrated DBs. In a DB, one can find the engine type concatenated with the sample of construction by a dot in a single attribute, in another hyphens are used instead of dots to merge the engine type with the specification, in another there are no dots or hyphens at all and the engine type is merged with the specification in a single attribute whereas the sample of construction is represented in a completely different attribute, and so forth. All these peculiarities must be considered by the consistency monitor in order to make the navigation through the integrated DBs possible. On the one hand, without the intervention of the consistency monitor, the middleware is in most cases simply not able to compare the data due to the so different data representations, and thus the joins result in no matches. On the other hand, by using simple rules to resolve schematic heterogeneity of the type one-to-many attributes, as suggested by [28] where an operator for concatenating attributes is proposed to solve such problems, the middleware cannot join the data either, because many special characters are commonly used as separators in the attributes. And worse, in particular cases such separators seem to be simply ad-hoc chosen by the input data typewriter.

In order to bridge this heterogeneity, the consistency monitor manages complex grammatical rules which bring the DB schemas as well as the different data representations into a platform common to all DBs, on which basis the data can be securely compared, joined, and related to each other. These rules have been defined during the data modeling activities which resulted in the MEntAs global schema construction. However, notice that this common data representation is not followed in the integrated DBs' data models (with exception of the MENTAS DB itself). These are autonomous DBs and should not be changed to fulfil the MEntAs requirements. Thus, the consistency monitor must not only parse the input data to this common representation but also the corresponding data in the integrated DBs. Otherwise, the data as entered by the user and parsed could not be compared to the original data representations. Furthermore, since it would be very inefficient to parse all the huge amount of data in the tables where the entry points are contained in every time a navigation is taking place, we employ mapping tables. These are managed in the DB of the middleware and store the entry points previously parsed. All this functionality builds the basis to drive the navigation between the DBs.

Management of Mapping Tables

The mapping tables are automatically generated when the MEntAs server is firstly started. At this time, the consistency monitor scans all the entry points in the affected tables in the remote, integrated DBs, parses them accordingly, and finally generates the mapping tables containing the entry points in the pre-defined common representation. In addition to that, the mapping tables also contain an attribute for the entry points as represented in the original DBs. These are then used as a kind of pointer to the tuples in the original tables. Hence, whenever a navigation is requested by the engineer, the (parsed) entry point as defined in the where clause is compared to the corresponding data in the mapping tables. Furthermore, by means of the attribute containing the entry point as originally represented, i.e. the pointers, the whole tuples can be found in the original tables. Hence, our mapping tables allow for a very efficient DB navigation because the entry points are all contained in those in the exact same representation as required for the navigation.

Another advanced feature of our consistency monitor is the shadow mechanism used in the generation of the mapping tables. For each entry point requiring schema mapping, the consistency monitor manages two mapping tables – a *current* and a *shadow* version. The current mapping tables give support to all MEntAs clients during the DB navigation. On the other hand, since the mapping tables' generation can be a time consuming operation depending on the original table's size, whenever asked for the consistency monitor starts asynchronous threads which generate the mapping tables in background using their shadow counterparts. When they have finished, it simply changes the current information it manages about the mapping tables, marking the current as shadows and the shadows as current. Of course, synchronization aspects and deadlock problems are appropriately coped with by the consistency monitor by means of refined routines employed in the table generation. By such a means, during the generation of the mapping tables, the engineers are blocked in their DB navigation operations only for a very short period of time, namely the time required to change the mapping table current information – a simple, single DB write operation.

2.9   Security Controller

Essentially, the main tasks of the local security controller are to manage the users' access rights as well as to encrypt and decrypt any data for the network transport (Fig. 1). On the other hand, the security controller plays a kernel role at the server side. It is responsible for managing the user data, access rights to the DBs, and for encrypting the data to the transport to the clients. The security controller is built upon the security mechanisms provided by both the operating system, namely UNIX at the server side [29], and Java [30]. Furthermore, it exploits the DB access controls and the corresponding fine granularity access rights' granting mechanisms supported by the DBMS. These mechanisms provide the basis for the security management in MEntAs.

3   The Functionality of the Graphic User Interface

3.1   The Data Representation

Nowadays, even with innumerous object models being proposed in the literature [31, 32, 33, 34, 35], the *Entity Relationship Model* (ER model [36]) is still spread out and employed in the industry for modeling DBs, and herewith relational DBs [16]. In MEntAs, we have chosen the ER model as the main mechanism for the data representation. Essentially, the data model of each integrated DB is shown to the engineer in the main interface of the GUI (refer to Fig. 4). By means of clicking with the mouse in the presented ER model, the engineer can start formulating his own SQL2 queries. It contains the following components: *Menu list* comprehends the main system commands; *Schema field* shows the ER diagram of the current DB; *Query field* shows the current select statement that is being built by the user (editable); and *Help display*: shows a helping text according to the current mouse position.

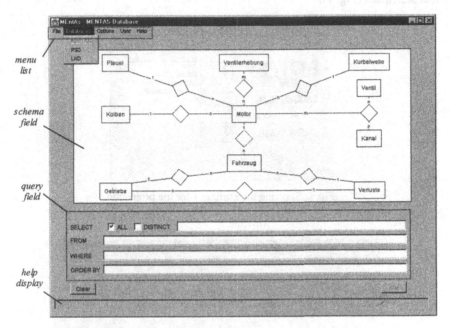

Fig. 4. The main window of MEntAs's DB access interface.

3.2 Formulating the Queries

In order to formulate a query, the user must focus the desired entity with the mouse and right click it. On doing that, a *popup menu* is activated with the following options (Fig. 5): *Select* specifies the projection for the select statement; *Where* defines the condition of the select; *Order by* specifies a sort ordering for showing the results; and *Other Databases* enables the navigation through the other integrated DBs.

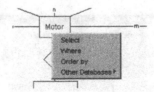

Fig. 5. Popup menu in the entities for formulating the queries.

3.2.1   Select/From

On choosing the select item in the popup menu of the schema field (refer to Fig. 5), the user receives a window containing all the attributes of the entity (Fig. 6). In particular, this same component is reused every time the user is asked to select some items of a list (let us generically refer to it as the *select window*). By means of mouse clicks, the user can select the attributes for the projection.

328   Fernando de Ferreira Rezende et al.

3.2.2   Where

On choosing the where item in the popup menu (Fig. 5), the select window is firstly shown to the user (Fig. 6). After that, the user can exactly define the condition for his select statement (Fig. 7).

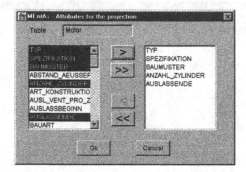

Fig. 6. Showing the attributes for the projection.

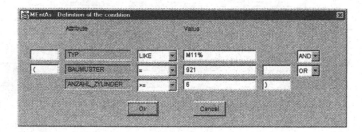

Fig. 7. Showing the attributes for the condition definition.

3.2.3   Order by

The order by item of the popup menu (Fig. 5) allows the user to define a sort ordering for attributes. Similarly as before, the user firstly selects the attributes for the order-by definition (Fig. 6). Thereafter, he can choose the order of sorting (Fig. 8).

Fig. 8. Showing the attributes for the sort ordering.

3.3   The Results Interface

The results are presented to the user by means of the *results interface* (Fig. 9). Its components are: *Menu list* is similar to the main interface; *Query field* shows the user-formulated select statement as executed by the DB server; *Table/Attribute field* presents the table and attribute names of the query's projection; and *Results field* presents the current result set in form of a table.

3.4   Joining Relations

The DB access interface of MEntAs allows users to make joins in a very friendly way, without even having to know the semantic meaning of primary and foreign keys. In principle, any relations that are related via a relationship can be joined. The only things the user needs to do for this are, firstly, to formulate a query on one entity as described in the previous sections, and secondly, to focus another related entity and perform similar steps. By such a means, the join condition, namely primary (foreign) key equals foreign (primary) key, is automatically generated by the GUI and appended to the complete select statement.

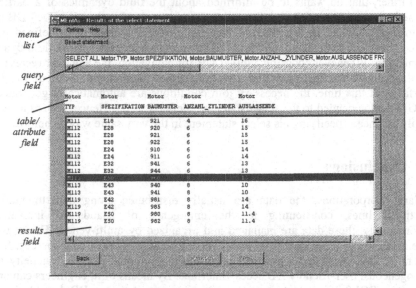

Fig. 9. The results interface.

In a very simple example, consider the ER diagram sketched in Fig. 4, and furthermore, suppose the engineer clicks the entity *engine* (*Motor*) and defines a projection on the engine's type and a condition to find all engines with *Type* equals *M111*. Now, if he clicks the entity *automobile* (*Fahrzeug*), chooses for the projection the automobile's class, and confirms with the OK button, he will lastly receive all automobile classes where the engine *M111* is built in. Internally, the GUI transforms these interactions to the following SQL2 statement:

```
SELECT   engine.type, automobile.class
FROM     engine, automobile
WHERE    engine.type = 'M111' AND
engine.pk_engine = automobile.fk_engine_automobile;
```

where *pk_engine* is the primary key of the entity engine, and *fk_engine_automobile* is a foreign key of automobile referring to the engine's primary key. This procedure of joining two relations can be recursively cascaded to neighbor relations. Extending the above example, if the engineer further clicks on the *gear* (*Getriebe*) and defines a projection containing its *Type*, he will receive not only the automobile classes using the engine *M111* but also the respective gear types of those automobiles.

3.5   The Database Navigation

The DB navigation is based upon the concept of entry points. The DB entry points create a kind of spatial relationships between the entities of the data models of the integrated DBs. By selecting the *Other Databases* item in the popup menu of the main interface (Fig. 5), the user indicates that he wants to make cross-DB join operations via the entry point defined in the clicked entity. This is a very powerful feature by means of which the engineer can catch from another DB any information of a particular entity that is not contained in the current DB.

As a simple example, suppose the engineer currently queries the MENTAS DB, and further, that he wants to be informed about the fluid dynamics of a particular engine he is working on. Such information is not contained in the MENTAS DB itself but in the Fluid DB. In this case, he can exploit the DB entry point defined in the engine entity and navigate to the Fluid DB in order to select the desired fluid dynamic information. Whenever choosing another DB for navigation, the engineer receives the ER diagram of the corresponding DB sketched in the schema field of the main interface. At this time, the necessary join conditions are automatically generated by the GUI and appended to the select statement defined so far. Hence, the engineer can simply go ahead specifying his select statement in the very same way as before.

4   Conclusions

In large corporations, the data are usually distributed along departmental and functional lines, contributing to the emergence of islands of information. Unfortunately, these data are managed and organized by multi-vendor DBSs, which have no ability to relate data from heterogeneous and distributed data sources. In this paper, we have presented a practical approach to overcome DB heterogeneity via a homogeneous, user-friendly DB access interface. By means of it, engineers can create their own SQL2 select statements which may even traverse DB boundaries. On processing the queries against the DB federation, the DB heterogeneity is completely hidden from the engineers which only perceive a global DB schema. This allows the engineer to use his creativity and to find the right information much faster than in usual developing environments.

Our interface is based upon a client/server architectural approach. The *DB middleware system* provides a uniform and transparent view over the *integrated databases*. The *DB connector* manages the communication connections with the middleware system by using JDBC. The *results factory* produces sets of objects containing parts of the whole result tables of the SQL2 statements, giving support to the cache's prefetcher. The *interface connector* intercepts the SQL2 statements produced by the GUI and sends them to the server for processing via RMI. The *cache* serves the purpose of temporarily storing result sets, allowing for a smooth navigation through those. The *consistency monitor* allows for cross-DB operations. It brings the data to a common platform by means of the parser's grammatical rules, and employs mapping table mechanisms which support a secure DB navigation. The *security controller* manages users, authorizations, access rights, and encrypts/decrypts the data for the transport. Finally, our platform independent *GUI* interacts with the engineers in a very friendly way, and guides them in the process of generating their own SQL2 select statements against a federation of heterogeneous DBs transparently.

References

1. Rezende, F.F., Hergula, K.: The Heterogeneity Problem and Middleware Technology: Experiences with and Performance of Database Gateways. In: *Proc. of the 24th VLDB*, USA, 1998. pp. 146-157.
2. Melton, J. (Ed.): *Database Language SQL 2*. ANSI, Washington, D.C., USA, 1990.
3. Date, C.J., Darwen, H.: *A Guide to the SQL Standard*. Addison-Wesley, 4th Ed., USA, 1997.
4. Härder, T., Mitschang, B., Nink, U., Ritter, N.: Workstation/Server Architectures for Database-Based Engineering Applications (in German). *Informatik Forschung & Entwicklung*, 1995.
5. Rezende, F.F., Härder, T.: An Approach to Multi-User KBMS in Workstation/Server Environments. *In: Proc. of the 11th Brazilian Symposium on Data Base Systems*, São Carlos, Brazil, 1996. pp. 58-72.
6. DeWitt, D.J., Maier, D., Futtersack, P., Velez, F.: A Study of Three Alternative Workstation/Server Architectures for Object-Oriented Databases. In: *Proc. of the 16th VLDB*, Australia, 1990. pp. 107-121.
7. Rezende, F.F.: Transaction Services for Knowledge Base Management Systems - Modeling Aspects, Architectural Issues, and Realization Techniques. infix Verlag, Germany, 1997.
8. Mitschang, B., Pirahesh, H., Pistor, P., Lindsay, B., Südkamp, S.: SQL/XNF-Processing Composite Objects as Abstractions over Relational Data. In: *Proc. Int. Conf. on Data Engineering*, Austria, 1993.
9. Küspert, K., Dadam, P., Günauer, J.: Cooperative Object Buffer Management in the Advanced Information Management Prototype. In: *Proc. of the 13th VLDB*, Brighton, U.K., 1987. pp. 483-492.
10. Härder, T., Hübel, C., Meyer-Wegener, K., Mitschang, B.: Processing and Transaction Concepts for Cooperation of Engineering Workstations and a Database Server. *DKE*, Vol. 3, 1988. pp. 87-107.
11. Roussopoulos, N., Delis, A.: Modern Client-Server DBMS Architectures. *ACM SIGMOD Record*, Vol. 20, No. 3, Sept. 1991. pp. 52-61.
12. Ananthanarayanan, R., Gottemukkala, V., Käfer, W., Lehman, T.J., Pirahesh, H.: Using the Coexistence Approach to Achieve Combined Functionality of Object-Oriented and Relational Systems. In: *Proc. of the ACM SIGMOD Int. Conf. on the Management of Data*, USA, May 1993. pp. 109-118.
13. Keller, A., Jensen, R., Agrawal, S.: Persistence Software: Bridging Object-Oriented Programming and Relational Database. In: *Proc. of the ACM SIGMOD Int. Conf. on the Management of Data*, Washington, D.C., USA, May 1993. pp. 523-528.
14. Thomas, J., Mitschang, B., Mattos, N.M., Dessloch, S.: Enhancing Knowledge Processing in Client/Server Environments. In: *Proc. of the 2nd ACM Int. Conf. on Information and Knowledge Management* (CIKM'93), Washington, D.C., USA, Nov. 1993. pp. 324-334.
15. Lee, B., Wiederhold, G.: Outer Joins and Filters for Instantiating Objects from Relational Databases Through Views. *IEEE Transactions on Knowledge and Data Engineering*, Vol. 6, No. 1, 1994.
16. Cood, E.F.: A Relational Model of Data for Large Shared Data Banks. *Communications of the ACM*, Vol. 13, 1970. pp. 377-387.
17. Rezende, F.F., Hergula, K., and Schneider, P.: *A Comparative Analysis and Performance of Database Gateways*. Technical Report Nr. FT3/E-1998-001, DaimlerChrysler, Ulm, Germany, March 1998.

18. Hergula, K., and Rezende, F.F.: *A Detailed Analysis of Database Middleware Technologies* (in German). Technical Report Nr. FT3/E-1998-002, DaimlerChrysler, Ulm, Germany, June 1998.
19. IBM Corporation: DB2 DataJoiner Administration Guide. IBM, 1997.
20. Sun Microsystems Inc. http://java.sun.com/products/jdbc/overview.html, 1998.
21. Hamilton, G., Cattell, R., Fisher, M.: *JDBC Database Access with Java: A Tutorial and Annotated Reference*, Addison-Wesley, USA, 1997.
22. Sun Microsystems Inc. http://java.sun.com/products/jdk/rmi/index.html, 1998.
23. Object Management Group. The Common Object Request Broker Architecture and Specification (CORBA), OMG, Framingham, USA, 1992.
24. Object Management Group. *The Common Object Request Broker Architecture and Specification – Rev. 2.0*, Technical Report, OMG, Framingham, USA, 1995.
25. Orfali, R., Harkey, D., Edwards, J.: *The Essential Distributed Objects Survival Guide*. John Wiley & Sons, USA, 1994.
26. Davis, T.E.: Build your own Object Pool in Java to Boost Application Speed. *JavaWorld*, http://www.javaworld.com/javaworld/jw-06-1998/jw-06-object-pool.html, Jun. 1998.
27. Hermsen, U.: Design and Implementation of an Adaptable Cache in a Heterogeneous Client/Server Environment (in German). M.S. Thesis, Univ. of Kaiserslautern, Germany, 1998.
28. Kim, W., Choi, I., Gala, S., Scheevel, M.: On Resolving Schematic Heterogeneity in Multidatabase Systems. In: Kim, W. (Ed.), *Modern Database Systems – The Object Model, Interoperability, and Beyond*, Addison-Wesley, USA, 1995. (Chapter 26).
29. Garfinkel, S., Spafford, G.: *Practical Unix & Internet Security*. O'Reilly & Associates Inc., USA, 1996.
30. Fritzinger, J.S., Mueller, M.: *Java Security*. White Paper, Sun Microsystems Inc., 1996.
31. Atkinson, M., Bancilhon, F., DeWitt, D., Dittrich, K., Maier, D., Zdonik, S.: The Object-Oriented Database System Manifesto. In: Bancilhon, F., Delobel, C., Kanellakis, P. (Eds.), *Building an Object-Oriented Database System: The Story of O2*, Morgan Kaufmann, USA, 1992. pp. 3-20. (Chapter 1).
32. Cattell, R.G.G. (Ed.): *The Object Database Standard: ODMG-93*. Morgan Kaufmann, USA, 1994.
33. Kim, W.: *Introduction to Object-Oriented Databases*. The MIT Press, Massachusetts, USA, 1990.
34. Loomis, M.E.S., Atwood, T., Cattell, R., Duhl, J., Ferran, G., Wade, D.: The ODMG Object Model. *Joop*, Jun. 1993. pp. 64-69.
35. Stonebraker, M., Rowe, R.A., Lindsay, B.G., Gray, J.N., Carey, M., Brodie, M., Bernstein, P., Beech, D.: Third-Generation Database System Manifesto. *ACM SIGMOD Record*, Vol. 19, No. 4, Dec. 1990.
36. Chen, P.P.: The Entity-Relationship Model: Toward a Unified View of Data. *ACM Transactions on Database Systems*, Vol. 1, March 1976. pp. 9-37.

A Uniform Approach to Inter-model Transformations

Peter McBrien and Alexandra Poulovassilis

Dept. of Computer Science, King's College London,
Strand, London WC2R 2LS
{alex,pjm}@dcs.kcl.ac.uk

Abstract. Whilst it is a common task in systems integration to have to transform between different semantic data models, such **inter-model transformations** are often specified in an ad hoc manner. Further, they are usually based on transforming all data into one common data model, which may not contain suitable data constructs to model directly all aspects of the data models being integrated. Our approach is to define each of these data models in terms of a lower-level hypergraph-based data model. We show how such definitions can be used to automatically derive schema transformation operators for the higher-level data models. We also show how these higher-level transformations can be used to perform inter-model transformations, and to define inter-model links.

1   Introduction

Common to many areas of system integration is the requirement to extract data associated with a particular **universe of discourse (UoD)** represented in one modelling language, and to use that data in another modelling language. Current approaches to mapping between such modelling languages usually choose one of them as the **common data model (CDM)** [16] and convert all the other modelling languages into that CDM.

Using a 'higher-level' CDM such as the ER model or the relational model greatly complicates the mapping process, which requires that one high-level modelling language be specified in terms of another such language. This is because there is rarely a simple correspondence between their modelling constructs. For example, if we use the relational model to represent ER models, a many-many relationship in the ER model must be represented as a relation in the relational model, whilst a one-many relationship can be represented as a foreign key attribute [7]. In the relational model, an attribute that forms part of a foreign key will be represented as a relationship in the ER model, whilst other relation attributes will be represented as ER attributes [1].

Our approach is to define a more 'elemental', low-level modelling language which is based on a hypergraph data structure together with a set of associated constraints — what we call the **hypergraph data model (HDM)**. We define a small set of primitive transformation operations on schemas expressed in the HDM. Higher-level modelling languages are handled by defining their constructs

M. Jarke, A. Oberweis (Eds.): CAiSE'99, LNCS 1626, pp. 333–348, 1999.
© Springer-Verlag Berlin Heidelberg 1999

and transformations in terms of those of the HDM. In common with **description logics** [5,6] we can form a union of different modelling languages to model a certain UoD. However, our approach has the advantage that it clearly separates the modelling of data structure from the modelling of constraints on the data. We note also that our HDM differs from graph-based conceptual modelling languages such as Telos [13] by supporting a very small set of low-level, elemental modelling primitives (nodes, edges and constraints). This makes the HDM better suited for use as a CDM than higher-level modelling languages, for the reasons discused in the previous paragraph.

Our previous work [14,10] has defined a framework for performing semantic **intra-model transformations**, where the original and transformed schema are represented in the same modelling language. In [14] we defined the notions of schemas and schema equivalence for the low-level HDM. We gave a set of primitive transformations on HDM schemas that preserve schema equivalence, and we showed how more complex transformations may be formulated as sequences of these primitive transformations. We illustrated the expressiveness and practical usefulness of the framework by showing how a practical ER modelling language may be defined in terms of the HDM, and primitive transformations on ER schemas defined in terms of composite transformations on the equivalent HDM schemas. In [10] we showed how schema transformations that are automatically reversible can be used as the basis for the automatic migration of data and application logic between schemas expressed in the HDM or in higher-level languages.

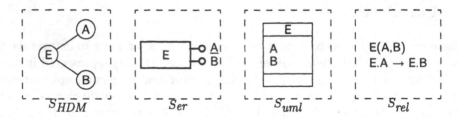

Fig. 1. Multiple models based on the HDM

Here we extend our previous work by providing a generic approach to defining the semantics of modelling languages in terms of the HDM, which in turn allows the automatic derivation of transformation rules. These rules may be applied by a user to map between semantically equivalent schemas expressed in the same or different modelling languages. In combination with the work in [10], this allows us to automatically transform queries between schemas defined in different modelling languages. Also, our use of a unifying underlying data model allows for the definition of inter-model links, which support the development of stronger coupling between different modelling languages than is provided by current approaches.

The concept is illustrated in Figure 1 which shows three high-level schemas each of which is represented by the same underlying HDM schema. The constructs of each of the three higher-level modelling languages (UML, ER and relational) are reduced to nodes associated by edges in the underlying HDM schema. In particular, the three schemas illustrated have a common HDM representation as a graph with three nodes and two edges, as well as some (unillustrated) constraints on the possible instances this graph may have.

The remainder of the paper is as follows. We begin with an overview of our low-level framework and the HDM in Section 2. In Section 3 we describe our general methodology for defining high-level modelling languages, and transformations for them, in terms of the low-level framework. We illustrate the approach by defining four specific modelling languages — an ER model, a relational model, UML static structure diagrams, and WWW documents. In Section 4 we show how to perform **inter-model transformations**, leading to Section 5 where we demonstrate how to use our approach to handle combinations of existing modelling languages, enhanced with **inter-model links**. A summary of the paper and our conclusions are given in Section 6.

2   Overview of the Hypergraph Data Model

In this section we give a brief overview of those aspects of our previous work that are necessary for the purposes of this paper. We refer the reader to [14,10] for full details and formal definitions.

A **schema** in the Hypergraph Data Model (HDM) is a triple $\langle Nodes, Edges, Constraints \rangle$. A **query** q **over a schema** $S = \langle Nodes, Edges, Constraints \rangle$ is an expression whose variables are members of $Nodes \cup Edges$[1]. $Nodes$ and $Edges$ define a labelled, directed, nested hypergraph. It is nested in the sense that edges can link any number of both nodes *and* other edges. $Constraints$ is a set of boolean-valued queries over S. Nodes are uniquely identified by their names. Edges and constraints have an optional name associated with them.

An **instance** I of a schema $S = \langle Nodes, Edges, Constraints \rangle$ is a set of sets satisfying the following:

(i)   each construct $c \in Nodes \cup Edges$ has an extent, denoted by $Ext_{S,I}(c)$, that can be derived from I;
(ii) conversely, each set in I can be derived from the set of extents $\{Ext_{S,I}(c) | c \in Nodes \cup Edges\}$;
(iii) for each $e \in Edge$, $Ext_{S,I}(e)$ contains only values that appear within the extents of the constructs linked by e (domain integrity);
(iv) the value of every constraint $c \in Constraints$ is true, the **value** of a query q being given by $q[c_1/Ext_{S,I}(c_1), \ldots, c_n/Ext_{S,I}(c_n)]$ where $c_1, \ldots, c_n$ are the constructs in $Nodes \cup Edges$.

We call the function $Ext_{S,I}$ an **extension mapping**. A **model** is a triple $\langle S, I, Ext_{S,I} \rangle$. Two schemas are **equivalent** if they have the same set of instances. Given a condition f, a schema S **conditionally subsumes** a schema

---

[1] Since what we provide is a framework, the query language is not fixed but will vary between different implementation architectures. In our examples in this paper, we assume that it is the relational calculus.

S' w.r.t. f if any instance of S' satisfying f is also an instance of S. Two schemas S and S' are **conditionally equivalent** w.r.t f if they each conditionally subsume each other w.r.t. f. We first developed these definitions of schemas, instances, and schema equivalence in the context of an ER common data model, in earlier work [9,11]. A comparison with other approaches to schema equivalence and schema transformation can be found in [11], which also discusses how our framework can be applied to schema integration.

We now list the primitive transformations of the HDM. Each transformation is a function that when applied to a model returns a new model. Each transformation has a proviso associated with it which states when the transformation is **successful**. Unsuccessful transformations return an "undefined" model, denoted by ϕ. Any transformation applied to ϕ returns ϕ.

1. *renameNode* $\langle fromName, toName \rangle$ renames a node. Proviso: *toName* is not already the name of some node.
2. *renameEdge* $\langle \langle fromName, c_1, \ldots, c_m \rangle, toName \rangle$ renames an edge. Proviso: *toName* is not already the name of some edge.
3. *addConstraint* c adds a new constraint c. Proviso: c evaluates to true.
4. *delConstraint* c deletes a constraint. Proviso: c exists.
5. *addNode* $\langle name, q \rangle$ adds a node named *name* whose extent is given by the value of the query q. Proviso: a node of that name does not already exist.
6. *delNode* $\langle name, q \rangle$ deletes a node. Here, q is a query that states how the extent of the deleted node could be recovered from the extents of the remaining schema constructs (thus, not violating property (ii) of an instance). Proviso: the node exists and participates in no edges.
7. *addEdge* $\langle \langle name, c_1, \ldots, c_m \rangle, q \rangle$ adds a new edge between a sequence of existing schema constructs $c_1, \ldots, c_m$. The extent of the edge is given by the value of the query q. Proviso: the edge does not already exist, $c_1, \ldots, c_m$ exist, and q satisfies the appropriate domain constraints.
8. *delEdge* $\langle \langle name, c_1, \ldots, c_m \rangle, q \rangle$ deletes an edge. q states how the extent of the deleted edge could be recovered from the extents of the remaining schema constructs. Proviso: the edge exists and participates in no edges.

For each of these transformations, there is a 3-ary version which takes as an extra argument a condition which must be satisfied in order for the transformation to be successful. A **composite transformation** is a sequence of $n \geq 1$ primitive transformations. A transformation t is **schema-dependent (s-d)** w.r.t. a schema S if t does not return ϕ for any model of S, otherwise t is **instance-dependent (i-d)** w.r.t. S. It is easy to see that if a schema S can be transformed to a schema S' by means of a s-d transformation, and vice versa, then S and S' are equivalent. If a schema S can be transformed to a schema S' by means of an i-d transformation with proviso f, and vice versa, then S and S' are conditionally equivalent w.r.t f.

It is also easy to see that every successful primitive transformation t is reversible by another successful primitive transformation t^{-1}, e.g. *addNode* $\langle n, q \rangle$ can be reversed by *delNode* $\langle n, q \rangle$, etc. This reversibility generalises to successful composite transformations, the reverse of a transformation $t_1; \ldots; t_n$ being $t_n^{-1}; \ldots; t_1^{-1}$.

3 Supporting Richer Semantic Modelling Languages

In this section we show how schemas expressed in higher-level semantic modelling languages, and the set of primitive transformations on such schemas, can be defined in terms of the hypergraph data model and its primitive transformations. We begin with a general discussion of how this is done for an arbitrary modelling language, M. We then illustrate the process for three specific modelling languages — an ER model, a relational model, and UML static structure diagrams. We conclude the section by also defining the conceptual elements of WWW documents, namely URLs, resources and links, and showing how these too can be represented in the HDM.

In general the constructs of any semantic modelling language M may be classified as either extensional constructs, or constraint constructs, or both. **Extentional constructs** represent sets of data values from some domain. Each such construct in M must be built using the extentional constructs of the HDM *i.e.* nodes and edges. There are three kinds of extentional constructs:

- **nodal** constructs may be present in a model independent of any other constructs. The **scheme** of each construct uniquely identifies the construct in M. For example, ER model entities may be present without requiring the presence of any other particular constructs, and their scheme is the entity name. A nodal construct maps into a node in the HDM.
- **linking** constructs can only exist in a model when certain other nodal constructs exist. The extent of a linking construct is a subset of the cartesian product of the extents of these nodal constructs. For example, relationships in ER models are linking constructs. Linking constructs map into edges in the HDM.
- **nodal-linking** constructs are nodal constructs that can only exist when certain other nodal constructs exist, and that are linked to these constructs. Attributes in ER models are an example. Nodal-linking constructs map into a combination of a node and an edge in the HDM.

Constraint constructs represent restrictions on the extents of the extentional constructs of M. For example, ER generalisation hierarchies restrict the extent of each subclass entity to be a subset of the extent of the superclass entity, and ER relationships and attributes have cardinality constraints. Constraints are directly supported by the HDM, but if a constraint construct of M is also an extentional construct, then the appropriate extensional HDM constructs must also be included in its definition.

Table 1 illustrates this classification of schema constructs by defining the main constructs of ER Models and giving their equivalent HDM representation. We discuss this representation in greater detail in Section 3.1 below.

The general method for constructing the set of primitive transformations for some modelling language M is as follows:

(i) For every construct of M we need an *add* transformation to add to the underlying HDM schema the corresponding set of nodes, edges and constraints. This transformation thus consists of zero or one *addNode* transformations, the operand being taken from the Node field of the construct definition (if any), followed by zero or one *addEdge* transformations taken from the Edge field, followed by a sequence of zero or more *addConstraint* transformations taken from the Cons(traint) field.

(ii) For every construct of M we need a *del* transformation which reverses its *add* transformation. This therefore consists of a sequence of *delConstraint* transformations, followed possibly by a *delEdge* transformation, followed possibly by a *delNode* transformation.

(iii) For those constructs of M which have textual names, we also define a *rename* transformation in terms of the corresponding set of *renameNode* and *renameEdge* transformations.

Once a high-level construct has been defined in the HDM, the necessary *add*, *del* and *rename* transformations on it can be **automatically** derived from its HDM definition. For example, Table 2 shows the result of this automatic process for the ER model definition of Table 1.

Table 1. Definition of ER Model constructs

Higher Level Construct		Equivalent HDM Representation
Construct **entity** (E)		
Class	nodal	Node $\langle er{:}e \rangle$
Scheme	$\langle e \rangle$	
Construct **attribute** (A)		Node $\langle er{:}e{:}a \rangle$
Class	nodal-linking,	Edge $\langle \_, er{:}e, er{:}e{:}a \rangle$
	constraint	Links $\langle er{:}e \rangle$
Scheme	$\langle e, a, s_1, s_2 \rangle$	Cons makeCard$(\langle \_, er{:}e, er{:}e{:}a \rangle, s_1, s_2)$
Construct **relationship** (R)		Edge $\langle er{:}r, er{:}e_1, er{:}e_2 \rangle$
Class	linking,	Links $\langle er{:}e_1 \rangle, \langle er{:}e_2 \rangle$
	constraint	Cons makeCard$(\langle er{:}r, er{:}e_1, er{:}e_2 \rangle, s_1, s_2)$
Scheme	$\langle r, e_1, e_2, s_1, s_2 \rangle$	
Construct **generalisation** (G)		Links $\langle er{:}e \rangle, \langle er{:}e_1 \rangle, \ldots, \langle er{:}e_n \rangle$
Class	constraint	$e{:}g[\forall 1 \leq i < j \leq n \,.\, e_i \cap e_j = \emptyset];$ Cons $e{:}g[\forall 1 \leq i \leq n \,.\, e_i \subseteq e];$
Scheme	$\langle pt, e, g, e_1, \ldots, e_n \rangle$	if $pt = $ **total** then $e{:}g[e = \bigcup_{i=1}^{n} e_i]$

3.1   An ER Model

We now look more closely at how our HDM framework can support an ER model with binary relationships and generalisation hierarchies ([14] shows how the framework can support ER models with n-ary relations, attributes on relations, and complex attributes). The representation is summarised in Table 1. We use some short-hand notation for expressing cardinality constraints on edges, in

Table 2. Derived transformations on ER models

Transformation on er	Equivalent Transformation on HDM
$rename_E^{er}\langle e, e'\rangle$	$renameNode \ \langle er{:}e, er{:}e'\rangle$
$add_E^{er}\langle e, q\rangle$	$addNode \ \langle er{:}e, q\rangle$
$del_E^{er}\langle e, q\rangle$	$delNode \ \langle er{:}e, q\rangle$
$rename_A^{er}\langle a, a'\rangle$	$renameNode \ \langle er{:}e{:}a, er{:}e{:}a'\rangle$
$add_A^{er}\langle e, a, s_1, s_2, q_{att}, q_{assoc}\rangle$	$addNode \ \langle er{:}e{:}a, q_{att}\rangle; \ addEdge \ \langle\langle \_, er{:}e, er{:}e{:}a\rangle, q_{assoc}\rangle;$ $addConstraint \ \mathsf{makeCard}(\langle \_, er{:}e, er{:}e{:}a\rangle, s_1, s_2)$
$del_A^{er}\langle e, a, s_1, s_2, q_{att}, q_{assoc}\rangle$	$delConstraint \ \mathsf{makeCard}(\langle \_, er{:}e, er{:}e{:}a\rangle, s_1, s_2);$ $delEdge \ \langle\langle \_, er{:}e, er{:}e{:}a\rangle, q_{assoc}\rangle; \ delNode \ \langle er{:}e{:}a, q_{att}\rangle$
$rename_R^{er}\langle\langle r, e_1, e_2\rangle, r'\rangle$	$renameEdge \ \langle\langle er{:}r, er{:}e_1, er{:}e_2\rangle, er{:}r'\rangle$
$add_R^{er}\langle r, e_1, e_2, s_1, s_2, q\rangle$	$addEdge \ \langle\langle er{:}r, er{:}e_1, er{:}e_2\rangle, q\rangle;$ $addConstraint \ \mathsf{makeCard}(\langle er{:}r, er{:}e_1, er{:}e_2\rangle, s_1, s_2)$
$del_R^{er}\langle r, e_1, e_2, s_1, s_2, q\rangle$	$delConstraint \ \mathsf{makeCard}(\langle er{:}r, er{:}e_1, er{:}e_2\rangle, s_1, s_2);$ $delEdge \ \langle\langle er{:}r, er{:}e_1, er{:}e_2\rangle, q\rangle$
$rename_G^{er}\langle e, g, g'\rangle$	$renameConstraint \ \langle er{:}e{:}g, er{:}e{:}g'\rangle$
$add_G^{er}\langle pt, e, g, e_1, \ldots, e_n\rangle$	if $pt = \mathbf{total}$ then $addConstraint \ e{:}g[e = \bigcup_{i=1}^n e_i];$ $addConstraint \ e{:}g[\forall 1 \le i \le n \,.\, e_i \subseteq e];$ $addConstraint \ e{:}g[\forall 1 \le i < j \le n \,.\, e_i \cap e_j = \emptyset]$
$del_G^{er}\langle pt, e, g, e_1, \ldots, e_n\rangle$	if $pt = \mathbf{total}$ then $delConstraint \ e{:}g[e = \bigcup_{i=1}^n e_i];$ $delConstraint \ e{:}g[\forall 1 \le i < j \le n \,.\, e_i \cap e_j = \emptyset];$ $delConstraint \ e{:}g[\forall 1 \le i \le n \,.\, e_i \subseteq e]$

that $\mathsf{makeCard}(\langle name, c_1, \ldots, c_m\rangle, s_1, \ldots, s_m)$ denotes the following constraint on the edge $\langle name, c_1, \ldots, c_m\rangle$:

$$\bigwedge_{i=1}^m (\forall x \in c_i \,.\, |\{\langle v_1, \ldots, v_m\rangle \mid \langle v_1, \ldots, v_m\rangle \in \langle name, c_1, \ldots, c_m\rangle \wedge v_i = x\}| \in s_i)$$

Here, each s_i is a set of integers representing the possible values for the cardinality of the participating construct c_i e.g. $\{0, 6..10, 20..N\}$, N denoting infinity. This notation was identified by [8] as the most expressive method for specifying cardinality constraints.

Entity classes in ER schemas map to nodes in the underlying HDM schema. Because we will later be mixing schema constructs from schemas that may be expressed in different modelling notations, we disambiguate these constructs at the HDM level by adding a prefix to their name. This prefix is *er*, *rel*, *uml* or *www* for each of the four modelling notations that we will be considering.

Attributes in ER schemas also map to nodes in the HDM, since they have an extent. However, attributes must always be linked to entities, and hence are classified as nodal-linking. The cardinality constraints on attributes lead to them being classified also as constraint constructs. Note that in the HDM schema we prefix the name of the attribute by its entity's name, so that we can regard as distinct two attributes with the same name if they are are attached to different entities. The association between an entity and an attribute is un-named, hence the occurrence of _ in the equivalent HDM edge construct.

Relationships in ER schemas map to edges in the HDM and are as classified linking constructs. As with attributes, the cardinality constraints on relationships lead to them being classified also as constraint constructs. ER model

generalisations are constraints on the instances of entity classes, which we give a textual name to. We use the notation *label*[*cons*] to denote a labelled constraint in the HDM, and provide the additional primitive transformation *renameConstraint*⟨*label*, *label*′⟩. Several constraints may have the same label, indicating that they are associated with the same higher-level schema construct.

Generalisations in ER models are uniquely identified by the combination of the superclass entity name, e, and the generalisation name, g, so we use the pair $e{:}g$ as the label for the constraints associated with a generalisation. Generalisations may be partial or total. To simplify the specification of different variants of the same transformation, we use a **conditional template transformation** of the form 'if q_{cond} then t', where q_{cond} is a query over the schema component of the model that the transformation is being applied to. q_{cond} may contain free variables that are instantiated by the transformation's arguments. If q_{cond} evaluates to true, then those instantiations substitute for the same free variables in t, which forms the result of the template. Otherwise the result of the template is the identity transformation. Templates may be extended with an else clause, of the form 'if q_{cond} then t else t'', where if q_{cond} is false then the result is t'.

Table 3. Definition of relational model constructs

Higher Level Construct	Equivalent HDM Representation
Construct **relation** (R)	
Class nodal	Node ⟨$rel{:}r$⟩
Scheme ⟨r⟩	
	Node ⟨$rel{:}r{:}a$⟩
Construct **attribute** (A)	Edge ⟨_, $rel{:}r$, $rel{:}r{:}a$⟩
Class nodal-linking,	Links ⟨$rel{:}r$⟩
constraint	if (n = null)
Scheme ⟨r, a, n⟩	Cons then makeCard(⟨_, $rel{:}r$, $rel{:}r{:}a$⟩, {0, 1}, {1..N})
	else makeCard(⟨_, $rel{:}r$, $rel{:}r{:}a$⟩, {1}, {1..N})
Construct **primary key** (P)	Links ⟨$rel{:}r{:}a_1$⟩, ..., ⟨$rel{:}r{:}a_n$⟩
Class constraint	$x \in \langle rel{:}r \rangle \leftrightarrow x = \langle x_1, \ldots, x_n \rangle$
Scheme ⟨$r, a_1, \ldots, a_n$⟩	Cons ∧ ⟨x, x_1⟩ ∈ ⟨_, $rel{:}r$, $rel{:}r{:}a_1$⟩ ∧ ...
	∧ ⟨x, x_n⟩ ∈ ⟨_, $rel{:}r$, $rel{:}r{:}a_n$⟩
Construct **foreign key** (F)	Links ⟨$rel{:}r{:}a_1$⟩, ..., ⟨$rel{:}r{:}a_n$⟩
Class constraint	⟨x, x_1⟩ ∈ ⟨_, $rel{:}r$, $rel{:}r{:}a_1$⟩ ∧ ...
Scheme ⟨$r, r_f, a_1, \ldots, a_n$⟩	Cons ⟨x, x_n⟩ ∈ ⟨_, $rel{:}r$, $rel{:}r{:}a_n$⟩ → ⟨$x_1, \ldots, x_n$⟩ ∈ r_f

3.2   The Relational Model

We define in Table 3 how the basic relational data model can be represented in the HDM. We take the relational model to consist of relations, attributes (which may be null), a primary key for each relation, and foreign keys. Our descriptions for this model, and for the following ones, omit the definitions of the primitive transformation operations since these are automatically derivable.

Relations may exist independently of each other and are nodal constructs. Normally, relational languages do not allow the user to query the extent of a relation (but rather the attributes of the relation) so we define the extent of the relation to be that of its primary key. **Attributes** in the relational model are similar to attributes of entity classes in the ER model. However, the cardinality constraint is now a simple choice between the attribute being optional (null $\rightarrow$ $\{0,1\}$) or mandatory (notnull $\rightarrow \{1\}$). A **primary key** is a constraint that checks whether the extent of r is the same as the extents of the key attributes $a_1, \ldots, a_n$. A **foreign key** is a set of attributes $a_1, \ldots, a_n$ appearing in r that are the primary key of another relation r_f.

Table 4. Definition of UML static structure constructs

Higher Level Construct		Equivalent HDM Representation
Construct **class** (C)		
Class	nodal	Node $\langle uml{:}c \rangle$
Scheme	$\langle c \rangle$	
Construct **meta class** (M)		
Class	nodal,	Node $\langle uml{:}m \rangle$
	constraint	Cons $c \in \langle uml{:}m \rangle \rightarrow \langle c \rangle$
Scheme	$\langle m \rangle$	
Construct **attribute** (A)		Node $\langle uml{:}c{:}a \rangle$
Class	nodal-linking,	Edge $\langle \_, uml{:}c, uml{:}c{:}a \rangle$
	constraint	Links $\langle uml{:}c \rangle$
Scheme	$\langle c, a, s \rangle$	Cons $makeCard(\langle \_, uml{:}c, uml{:}c{:}a \rangle, s, \{1..N\})$
Construct **object** (O)		Links $\langle uml{:}c \rangle, \langle uml{:}c, uml{:}a_1 \rangle, \ldots, \langle uml{:}c, uml{:}a_n \rangle$
Class	constraint	Cons $c{:}o[\begin{smallmatrix}\exists i \in uml{:}c \,.\, \langle i,v_1 \rangle \in \langle uml{:}c, uml{:}a_1 \rangle \\ \wedge \ \ldots \wedge \langle i, v_n \rangle \in \langle uml{:}c, uml{:}a_n \rangle \end{smallmatrix}]$
	$\langle c, o, a_1, \ldots, a_n, $	
Scheme	$v_1, \ldots, v_n \rangle$	
Construct **association** $(Assoc)$		Edge $\langle uml{:}r{:}l_1{:}\ldots{:}l_n, uml{:}c_1, \ldots, uml{:}c_n \rangle$
Class	linking,	Links $\langle uml{:}c_1 \rangle, \ldots, \langle uml{:}c_n \rangle$
	constraint	makecard($\langle uml{:}r{:}l_1{:}\ldots{:}l_n,$
	$\langle r, c_1, \ldots, c_n,$	Cons $uml{:}c_1, \ldots, uml{:}c_n \rangle, s_1, \ldots, s_n$)
Scheme	$l_1, \ldots, l_n, s_1, \ldots, s_n \rangle$	
		Links $\langle uml{:}c \rangle, \langle uml{:}c_1 \rangle, \ldots, \langle uml{:}c_n \rangle$
Construct **generalisation** (G)		if disjoint $\in cs$
Class	constraint	then $c{:}g[\forall 1 \leq i < j \leq n \,.\, c_i \cap c_j = \emptyset]$;
Scheme	$\langle cs, c, g, c_1, \ldots, c_n \rangle$	Cons if complete $\in cs$ then $c{:}g[c = \bigcup_{i=1}^{n} c_i]$;
		$c{:}g[\forall 1 \leq i \leq n \,.\, c_i \subseteq c]$

3.3 UML Static Structure Diagrams

We define in Table 4 those elements of UML class diagrams that model static aspects of the UoD. Elements of class diagrams that are identified as dynamic in the UML Notation Guide [4] e.g. operations, are beyond the scope of this paper.

UML **classes** are defined in a similar manner to ER entities. **Metaclasses** are defined like classes, with the additional constraint that the instances of a metaclass must themselves be classes. **Attributes** have a **multiplicity** associated with them. This is a single range of integers which shows how many instances of the attribute each instance of the entity may be associated with. We represent this by a single cardinality constraint, s. The cardinality constraint on the attribute is by definition $\{1..N\}$. Note that we do not restrict the domain of a in any way, so we can support attributes which have either simple types or entity classes as their domain. A more elaborate implementation could add a field to the scheme of each attribute to indicate the domain from which values of the attribute are drawn. An **object** in UML constrains the instances of some class, in the sense that the class must have an instance where the attributes $a_1, \ldots, a_n$ take specified values $v_1, \ldots, v_n$. We model this an HDM constraint, labelled with the name of the object, o, and the class, c, it is an instance of.

UML supports both binary and n-ary **associations**. Since the former is just a special case of the latter [4], we only consider here the general case of n-ary associations, in which an association, r, links classes $c_1, \ldots, c_n$, with role names $l_1, \ldots, l_n$ and cardinalities of each role $s_1, \ldots, s_n$. We identify the association in the HDM by concatenating the association name with the role names. The **composition** construct is special case of an association. It has $\{1\}$ cardinality on the number of instances of the parent class that each instance of the child class is associated with (and further restrictions on the dynamic behaviour of these classes). Finally, UML **generalisations** may be either incomplete or complete, and overlapping or disjoint — giving two template transformations to handle these distinctions.

3.4   WWW Documents

Before describing how WWW Documents are represented in the HDM, we first identify how they can be structured as conceptual elements. URLs [2] for Internet resources fetched using the IP protocol from specific hosts take the general form $\langle$scheme$\rangle$://$\langle$user$\rangle$:$\langle$password$\rangle$@$\langle$host$\rangle$:$\langle$port$\rangle$/$\langle$url-path$\rangle$.

We can therefore characterise a URL as an HDM node, formed of sextuples consisting of these six elements of the URL (with _ used for missing values of optional elements). A WWW document resource can be modelled as another node. Each resource must be identified by a URL, but a URL may exist without its corresponding resource existing. Each resource may link to any number of URLs. Thus we have a single HDM schema for the WWW which is constructed as follows:

   $addNode$ $\langle www\text{:}url, \{\} \rangle$;
   $addNode$ $\langle www\text{:}resource, \{\} \rangle$;
   $addEdge$ $\langle\langle www\text{:}identify, www\text{:}url, www\text{:}resource\rangle, \{0..1\}, \{1\}, \{\}\rangle$;
   $addEdge$ $\langle\langle www\text{:}link, www\text{:}resource, www\text{:}url\rangle, \{0..N\}, \{0..N\}, \{\}\rangle$;

Notice that we have assigned an empty extent to each of the four extensional constructs of the WWW schema. This is because we model each URL, resource, or link in the WWW as a constraint construct — see Table 5 — enforcing the existence of this instance in the extension of the WWW schema.

Table 5. Definition of WWW Constructs

Higher Level Construct		Equivalent HDM Representation
Construct **url** (u)		Links $\langle www{:}url \rangle$
Class	constraint	Cons $\langle s, us, pw, h, pt, up \rangle \in \langle www{:}url \rangle$
Scheme	$\langle s, us, pw, h, pt, up \rangle$	
Construct **resource** (r)		Links $\langle www{:}url \rangle$
Class	constraint	Cons $\langle \langle s, us, pw, h, pt, up \rangle, r \rangle \in$
Scheme	$\langle \langle s, us, pw, h, pt, up \rangle, r \rangle$	$\langle www{:}identify, www{:}url, www{:}resource \rangle$
Construct **link** (l)		Links $\langle www{:}url \rangle$
Class	constraint	Cons $\langle r, \langle s, us, pw, h, pt, up \rangle \rangle \in$
Scheme	$\langle r, \langle s, us, pw, h, pt, up \rangle \rangle$	$\langle www{:}link, www{:}resource, www{:}url \rangle$

4   Inter-model Transformations

Our HDM representation of higher-level modelling languages is such that it
is possible to unambiguously represent the constructs of multiple higher-level
schemas in one HDM schema. This brings several important benefits:

(a) An HDM schema can be used as a unifying repository for several higher-level
schemas.
(b) Add and delete transformations can be carried out for constructs of a modelling language M_1 where the extent of the construct is defined in terms of the
extents of constructs of some other modelling languages, $M_2, M_3, \ldots$. This
allows **inter-model transformations** to be applied, where the constructs
of one modelling language are replaced with those of another.
(c) Such inter-model transformations form the basis for automatic **inter-model
translation** of data and queries. This allows data and queries to be translated between different schemas in interoperating database architectures such
as database federations [16] and mediators [17].
(d) New **inter-model edges** which do not belong to any single higher-level
modelling language can be defined. This allows associations to be built between constructs in different modelling languages, and navigation between
them. This facility is of particular use when no single higher-level modelling
language can adequately capture the UoD, as is invariably the case with any
large complex application domain.

Items (a) and (d) are discussed further in Section 5. Item (c) follows from
our work in [10] which shows how schema transformations can be used to automatically migrate data and queries. We further elaborate on item (b) here. We
use the syntax $M(q)$ to indicate that a query q should be evaluated with respect
to the schema constructs of the higher-level model M, where M can be *rel*, *er*,
uml, *www* and so forth. If q appears in the argument list of a transformation
on a construct of M, then it may be written simply as q, and $M(q)$ is inferred.
For example, $add_C^{uml}\langle man, male \rangle$ is equivalent to $add_C^{uml}\langle man, uml(male) \rangle$, meaning add a UML class man whose extent is the same as that of the UML class
male, while $add_C^{uml}\langle man, er(male) \rangle$ would populate the instances of UML class
man with the instances of ER entity male.

Example 1 A Relational to ER inter-model transformation

The following composite transformation transforms the relational schema S_{rel} in Figure 1 to the ER schema S_{er}. $rel(q)$ indicates that the query q should be evaluated with respect to the relational schema constructs, and $er(q)$ that q should be evaluated with respect to the ER schema constructs. $getCard(c)$ denotes the cardinality constraint associated with a construct c.

1. $add_E^{er}\langle E, rel(\{y \mid \exists x.\langle x, y\rangle \in \langle \_, E, A\rangle\})\rangle$
2. $add_A^{er}\langle E, A, getCard(\langle \_, rel{:}E, rel{:}E{:}A\rangle), rel(\{y \mid \exists x.\langle x, y\rangle \in \langle \_, E, A\rangle\}), rel(\langle \_, E, A\rangle)\rangle$
3. $add_A^{er}\langle E, B, getCard(\langle \_, rel{:}E, rel{:}E{:}B\rangle), rel(\{y \mid \exists x.\langle x, y\rangle \in \langle \_, E, B\rangle\}), rel(\langle \_, E, B\rangle)\rangle$
4. $del_P^{rel}\langle E, A\rangle$
5. $del_A^{rel}\langle E, B, getCard(\langle \_, er{:}E, er{:}E{:}B\rangle), er(\{y \mid \exists x.\langle x, y\rangle \in \langle \_, E, B\rangle\}), er(\langle \_, E, B\rangle)\rangle$
6. $del_A^{rel}\langle E, A, getCard(\langle \_, er{:}E, er{:}E{:}A\rangle), er(\{y \mid \exists x.\langle x, y\rangle \in \langle \_, E, A\rangle\}), er(\langle \_, E, A\rangle)\rangle$
7. $del_R^{rel}\langle E, er(\{y \mid \exists x.\langle x, y\rangle \in \langle \_, E, A\rangle\})\rangle$

Notice that the reverse transformation from S_{er} back to S_{rel} is automatically derivable from this transformation, as discussed at the end of Section 2, and consists of a sequence of transformations $add_R^{rel}, add_A^{rel}, add_A^{rel}, add_P^{rel}, del_A^{er}, del_A^{er}, del_E^{er}$ whose arguments are the same as those of their counterparts in the forward direction.

Whilst it is possible to write inter-model transformations such as this one for each specific transformation as it arises, this can be tedious and repetitive, and in practice we will want to automate the process. We can use template transformations to specify in a generic way how constructs in a modelling language M_1 should be transformed to constructs in a modelling language M_2, thus enabling transformations on specific constructs to be automatically generated. The following guidelines can be followed in preparing these template transformations:

1. Ensure that every possible instance of a construct in M_1 appears in the query part of a transformation that adds a construct to M_2. Occasionally it might be possible to consider these instances individually, such as in the first transformation step of Example 2 below. However, usually it is combinations of instances of constructs in M_1 that map to instances of constructs in M_2, as the remaining transformation steps in Example 2 illustrate.

2. Ensure that every construct c of M_1 appears in a transformation that deletes c, recovering the extent of c from the extents of constructs in M_2 that were created in the addition transformations during Step 1 above.

We illustrate Step 1 in Example 2 by showing how the constructs of any relational model can be mapped to constructs of an ER model.

Example 2 Mapping Relational Models to ER Models

1. Each relation r can be represented as a entity class with the same name in the ER model, using its primary key to identify the instances of the class:
   if $\langle r, \_, \ldots, \_\rangle \in$ primarykey then $add_E^{er}\langle r, rel(\langle r\rangle)\rangle$

2. An attribute set of r which is its primary key and is also a foreign key which is the primary key of r_f, can be represented in the ER Model as a partial generalisation hierarchy with r_f as the superclass of r:

if $\langle r, a_1, \ldots, a_n \rangle \in$ primarykey $\land$ $\langle r, r_f, a_1, \ldots, a_n \rangle \in$ foreignkey
then $add_G^{er}\langle$partial, $r_f, r\rangle$

3. An attribute set of r which is not its primary key but which is a foreign key that is the primary key of r_f, can be presented in the ER Model as a relationship between r and r_f:

if $\langle r, b_1, \ldots, b_n \rangle \in$ primarykey $\land$ $\langle r, r_f, a_1, \ldots, a_n \rangle \in$ foreignkey $\land$
$\{a_1, \ldots, a_n\} \neq \{b_1, \ldots, b_n\}$
then $add_R^{er}\langle a_1 : \ldots : a_n, r, r_f, \{0, 1\}, \{0..N\}, \{\langle\langle y_1, \ldots, y_n\rangle, \langle x_1, \ldots, x_n\rangle\rangle \mid \exists x$.
$\langle x, y_1 \rangle \in rel(\langle r, b_1\rangle) \land \ldots \land \langle x, y_n \rangle \in rel(\langle r, b_n\rangle) \land$
$\langle x, x_1 \rangle \in rel(\langle r, a_1\rangle) \land \ldots \land \langle x, x_n \rangle \in rel(\langle r, a_n\rangle)\}\rangle$

4. Any attribute of r that is not part of a foreign key can be represented as an ER Model attribute:

if $\langle r, a \rangle \in$ attribute $\land \neg\exists a_1, \ldots, a_n$. $(\langle r, \_, a_1, \ldots, a_n\rangle \in$ foreignkey $\land$
$a \in \{a_1, \ldots, a_n\})$
then $add_A^{er}\langle r, a, \{0, 1\}, \{1..N\}, \{x \mid \exists y . \langle y, x \rangle \in rel(\langle r, a\rangle)\}, rel(\langle r, a\rangle)\rangle$

5   Mixed Models

Our framework opens up the possibility of creating special-purpose CDMs which mix constructs from different modelling languages. This will be particularly useful in integration situations where there is not a single already existing CDM that can fully represent the constructs of the various data sources. To allow the user to navigate between the constructs of different modelling languages, we can specify inter-model edges that connect associated constructs. For example, we may want to associate entity classes in an ER model with UML classes in a UML model, using a certain attribute in the UML model to correspond with the primary key attribute of the ER class. Based on this principle, we could define the new construct *common class* shown in Table 6.

This technique is particularly powerful when a data model contains **semi-structured data** which we wish to view and associate with data in a structured data model. For example, we may want to associate a URL held as an attribute in a UML model, with the web page resource in the WWW model that the URL references. In Figure 2 we illustrate how information on people in a UML model can be linked to the person's WWW home page. For this link to be established, we define an inter-model link which associates textual URLs with url constructs in the WWW model. This is achieved by the **web page** inter-model link in Table 6, which associates a resource in the WWW model to the **person** entity class in the UML model by the constraint that we must be able to construct the UML url attribute from the string concatenation (denoted by the 'o' operator) of the url instance in the WWW model that identifies the resource.

We may use such inter-model links to write inter-model queries. For example, if we want to retrieve the WWW pages of all people that work in the **computing** department, we can ask the query:

Table 6. Two Examples of Inter-model Constructs

Higher Level Construct		Equivalent HDM Representation
Construct **common class**		Edge $\langle \_, er{:}e, uml{:}c \rangle$
Class	linking,	Links $\langle er{:}e \rangle, \langle uml{:}c \rangle$
	constraint	Cons $\langle _, er{:}e, uml{:}c \rangle = $
Scheme	$\langle e, c, a \rangle$	$\{ \langle x, x \rangle \mid x \in er{:}e \wedge \exists y. \langle y, x \rangle \in \langle \_, uml{:}c, uml{:}a \rangle \}$
		Edge $\langle \_, www{:}r, uml{:}a \rangle$
Construct **web page**		Links $\langle www{:}r \rangle, \langle uml{:}a \rangle$
Class	linking,	$\langle \_, www{:}r, uml{:}a \rangle = \{ \langle r, a \rangle \mid \exists z, s, us, pw, h, pt, up.$
	constraint	$\langle \langle s, us, pw, h, pt, up \rangle, r \rangle \in$
		Cons $\quad \langle www{:}\mathsf{identity}, www{:}\mathsf{url}, www{:}\mathsf{resource} \rangle \wedge$
Scheme	$\langle r, c, a \rangle$	$a = s\text{'}{:}//\text{'}ouso\text{'}{:}\text{'}opwo\text{'}@\text{'}oho\text{'}{:}\text{'}opto\text{'}/\text{'}oup \wedge$
		$\langle z, a \rangle \in \langle \_, uml{:}c, uml{:}a \rangle \}$

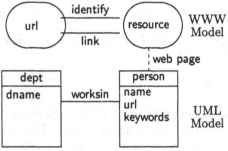

Fig. 2. Linking a semantic data model with the WWW

$\exists d, p, u \,.\, \langle d, \text{'computing'} \rangle \in \langle \mathsf{dept}, \mathsf{dname} \rangle \wedge \langle d, p \rangle \in \langle \mathsf{worksin}, \mathsf{person}, \mathsf{dept} \rangle \wedge$
$\langle p, u \rangle \in \langle \mathsf{person}, \mathsf{url} \rangle \wedge \langle r, u \rangle \in inter(\langle \mathsf{resource}, \mathsf{person}, \mathsf{url} \rangle)$

We may also use the inter-model links to derive constructs in one model based on information held in another model. For example, we could populate the keywords attribute of person in the UML model by using the HTMLGetMeta(r,n) utility which extracts the CONTENT part of a HTML META tag in resource r, where the HTTP-EQUIV or NAME field matches n [12].

$add_A^{uml} \langle \mathsf{person}, \mathsf{keywords}, \{0..N\}, \{1..N\}, \{ \langle p, k \rangle \mid \exists u, r \,.\, \langle p, u \rangle \in \langle \mathsf{person}, \mathsf{url} \rangle \wedge$
$\langle r, u \rangle \in inter(\langle \mathsf{resource}, \mathsf{person}, \mathsf{url} \rangle) \wedge k \in \mathsf{HTMLGetMeta}(r, \text{'Keywords'}) \} \rangle$

6   Conclusions

We have presented a method for specifying semantic data models in terms of the constructs of a low-level hypergraph data model (HDM). We showed how these specifications can be used to automatically derive the transformation operations for the higher-level data models in terms of the operations of the HDM, and how these higher-level transformations can be used to perform inter-model transformations. Finally, we showed how to use the hypergraph data structure to define inter-model links, hence allowing queries which span multiple models.

Our approach clearly distinguishes between the structural and the constraint aspects of a data model. This has the practical advantage that constraint checking need only be performed when it is required to ensure consistency between models, whilst data/query access can use the structural information to translate data and queries between models.

Combined with our previous work on intra-model transformation [9,14,10], we have provided a complete formal framework in which to describe the semantic transformation of data and queries from almost any data source, including those containing semi-structured data. Our framework thus fits well into the various database integration architectures, such as Garlic [15] and TSIMMIS [3]. It complements these existing approaches by handling multiple data models in a more flexible manner than simply converting them all into some high level CDM such as an ER Model. It does this by representing all models in terms of their elemental nodes, edges and constraints, and allows the free mixing of different models by the definition of inter-model links. Indeed, by itself, our framework forms a useful method for the formal comparison of the semantics of various data modelling languages.

Our method has in part been implemented in a simple prototype tool. We plan now to develop a full-strength tool supporting the graphical display and manipulation of model definitions, and the definition of templates for composite transformations. We also plan to extend our approach to model dynamic aspects of conceptual modelling languages and to support temporal data models.

References

1. M. Andersson. Extracting an entity relationship schema from a relational database through reverse engineering. In *Proceedings of ER'94*, LNCS, pages 403–419. Springer-Verlag, 1994.

2. T. Berners-Lee, L. Masinter, and M. McCahill. Uniform resource locators (URL). Technical Report RFC 1738, Internet, December 1994.

3. S.S. Chawathe, H. Garcia-Molina, J. Hammer, K. Ireland, Y. Papakonstantinou, J.D. Ullman, and J. Widom. The TSIMMIS project: Integration of heterogeneous information sources. In *Proceedings of the 10th Meeting of the Information Processing Society of Japan*, pages 7–18, October 1994.

4. UML Consortium. UML notation guide: version 1.1. Technical report, Rational Software, September 1997.

5. G. DeGiacomo and M. Lenzerini. A uniform framework for concept definitions in description logics. *Journal of Artificial Intelligence Research*, 6, 1997.

6. P. Devanbu and M.A. Jones. The use of description logics in KBSE systems. *ACM Transactions on Software Engineering and Methodology*, 6(2):141–172, 1997.

7. R. Elmasri and S. Navathe. *Fundamentals of Database Systems*. The Benjamin/Cummings Publishing Company, Inc., 2nd edition, 1994.

8. S.W. Liddle, D.W. Embley, and S.N. Woodfield. Cardinality constraints in semantic data models. *Data & Knowledge Engineering*, 11(3):235–270, 1993.

9. P.J. McBrien and A. Poulovassilis. A formal framework for ER schema transformation. In *Proceedings of ER'97*, volume 1331 of *LNCS*, pages 408–421, 1997.

10. P.J. McBrien and A. Poulovassilis. Automatic migration and wrapping of database applications — a schema transformation approach. Technical Report TR98-10, King's College London, 1998.
11. P.J. McBrien and A. Poulovassilis. A formalisation of semantic schema integration. *Information Systems*, 23(5):307–334, 1998.
12. C. Musciano and B. Kennedy. *HTML: The Definitive Guide*. O'Reilly & Associates, 1996.
13. J. Mylopoulos, A. Borgida, M. Jarke, and M. Koubarakis. Telos: Representing knowledge about information systems. *ACM Transactions on Information Systems*, 8(4):325–362, October 1990.
14. A. Poulovassilis and P.J. McBrien. A general formal framework for schema transformation. *Data and Knowledge Engineering*, 28(1):47–71, 1998.
15. M.T. Roth and P. Schwarz. Don't scrap it, wrap it! A wrapper architecture for data sources. In *Proceedings of the 23rd VLDB Conference*, pages 266–275, Athens, Greece, 1997.
16. A. Sheth and J. Larson. Federated database systems. *ACM Computing Surveys*, 22(3):183–236, 1990.
17. G. Wiederhold. Forward to special issue on intelligent integration of information. *Journal on Intelligent Information Systems*, 6(2–3):93–97, 1996.

OTHY: Object To HYpermedia

Franck Barbeau[1] and José Martinez[2]

[1]MAIF – Service Bureautique, 200, Av. Salvador Allende
79038 Niort Cedex 9 – France
Franck.Barbeau@irin.univ-nantes.fr
[2]IRIN – Université de Nantes, IRESTE – La Chantrerie – BP 60601
44306 Nantes Cedex 3 – France
Jose.Martinez@irin.univ-nantes.fr

Abstract. In this paper, we present a Web-based universal browser for heterogeneous and non federated databases. Recently appeared hypermedia methods are at the core of this system. However, contrary to these methodologies, our tool directly supports the conception, the navigation, and the presentation phases without requiring any modification of the databases. It is mostly based on the OTHY framework, which is a library of classes to develop different kinds of presentation based on well-established hypertext concepts. The design of our tool and a first implementation resulted in a prototype under the O_2 OODBMS. This implementation was convincing. Consequently, a Java development and two querying and relational database retro-engineering modules are on the path to be added to this prototype.

1   Introduction

MAIF (*Mutuelle Assurance des Instituteurs de France*) is a French insurance company devoted to teachers. It is quite large with over one hundred agencies, approximately 4,500 employees and as many computers. In the short term, all the applications will use the Web technology. MAIF needs allow us to stress three important characteristics required by users of an heterogeneous and non-federated information system. These characteristics are (1) to navigate on the data, (2) to query them with an intuitive, non formal interface, and (3) to present different views on the data for different users and even for a given user.

Hypertext [6] and more recently hypermedia [24], [10] are not isolated research domains. Indeed, outside "classical" applications, like help, documentation, or workgroup, hypertext concepts have been adopted by many application areas. Thereby, their flexibility is greatly enhanced. More precisely, Web user-friendliness is nowadays demanded by users. Conversely, a review of the proposed architectures, including the seminal Dexter model [9], highlights the fact that hypermedia systems need database functionalities. As an example, Hyperwave is an hypermedia system based on an object-oriented database engine. In the field of databases mature methodologies such as RMM, OOHDM, EORM, etc., have emerged [16].

In a way, our proposition merges these two complementary approaches by (1) offering an hypertextual view of databases and (2) offering a customisable set of hy-

M. Jarke, A. Oberweis (Eds.): CAiSE'99, LNCS 1626, pp. 349-363, 1999.
© Springer-Verlag Berlin Heidelberg 1999

permedia tools and concepts. The basic aim of the work is to allow conventional database accesses with an hypermedia interface. This interface must not be intrusive, i. e., it must not impact the used databases.

This paper is organised as follows: First, we detail user needs at MAIF, but they may be generalised to any important organisation. Then, we present related work: methodologies and tools for navigating/querying databases. In section 4, we present the first part of our proposal: the system architecture based both on hypermedia and database concepts, in an Internet/Intranet-based platform. In section 5, we see in details the principal tool of this project: a Java applet. This applet is composed of four modules, the most important of which is OTHY, a framework developed to present information to the user by translating database instances into "pages." Section 6 validates our approach by presenting our V0 prototype. In fact, in order to alleviate the initial programming effort, OTHY was implemented under the O_2 OODMBS [1]. The conclusion points out important issues in the development of the on-going V1 operational prototype: (1) reverse engineering, (2) query possibilities, and (3) schema integration.

2   The Needs

The architecture synoptic of the information system of many organisations may be as follow. A single desktop computer has to access a lot of independent sub-systems (different databases, files, different kinds of database management systems), located on different servers, sometimes physically distant. This is true at MAIF with contract databases (textual data), precious object databases (with pictures and descriptions of sold objects with their auction prices), etc.

A study of the users' needs at MAIF highlighted three main requirements: The most important need is the possibility to navigate easily among this information mass, with the ease offered by the Web technology. This *navigation* must be possible not only in one database, but also between databases with common or related elements. In other words, users demand a single interface to the whole information system.

However, navigation alone is not sufficient; some techniques of database *querying* must be added to the system. But experience demonstrated, through some old systems based on classical querying, that too formal queries are supplanted by manual querying, e. g., users preferred to access directly to the printed version of a textual database! Queries are envisaged solely as a means to retrieve rapidly an entry point close to the wanted information, therefore avoiding a lengthy and tortuous initial navigation.

Finally, the system should offer to the user the possibility to customise his or her *view* of the information, an extension of the well-known concept in relational database management systems.

3   Related Work

Some authors claim that an hypertext is not a database [22]. On the one hand, they are right, because data managed by hypertext are often poorly structured, if not at all. On the other hand, the use of the database approach is still the best means to organise a collection of data as far as we are concerned. A database stores information with relationships between them. Data and relationships are modelled by conceptual schemas presenting common concepts. These concepts may be network, relational, entity-relationship, semantics or object-oriented notions like aggregation, generalisation, etc. [2]. An hypertext model is a complicated model that needs high level tools. [29] recommend the use of an OODBMS as the more rational solution to store hypertext data. An underlying structure to the hypertext exists and it is usually clearly translated by the interface. The real difficulty is the intensive use of texts, i. e., semi-structured data, which are badly managed by DBMS. This lack is emphasised by the current growth of the forms of semi-structured data: images, videos, and audio. However, this pitfall is being solved thanks to meta-modelling, e. g., SGML (*Standard Generalized Mark-up Language*) for texts [30], MULTOS for office documents [20], HyTime for multimedia documents [23].

We shall detail some methodologies and tools that influenced are design and tool.

3.1   RMM (Relationship Management Methodology)

RMM [11], [3] is a conceptual method for the design and construction of hypermedia applications. It is based on the entity-relationship conceptual model. It introduces hypertextual navigation concepts during the logical description step of a database schema.

To simplify, each entity type has a corresponding page model, or sometimes several pages (slices) if the number of information is too large. Each entity instantiates the page model with its attribute values.

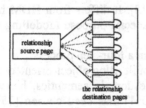

Fig. 1. A guided tour   **Fig. 2.** An indexed tour

Each relationship role has zero, one or more anchors according to its cardinality. A zero-valued cardinality is translated into a text indicating the role absence. A one-valued cardinality is translated into an anchor representing the relationship nature. A multi-valued cardinality can give rise to different presentation of the relationships, namely a guided tour, an indexed tour, or a guided indexed tour. A guided tour (Fig. 1), unidirectional or bi-directional, allows the user to follow sequentially all the related (and linked) instances of the source object, possibly with a direct return to the initial object. An indexed tour (Fig. 2) needs a discriminating element, e. g., at the best a foreign key in relational terms. A multiple but limited cardinality can be translated into a page containing all the accesses to the linked elements. Too large a cardinality would give rise to a separate page. Moreover, a very important cardinality would give birth to a hierarchical index. Finally, it is possible to combine guided tours and indexed tours (Fig. 3)

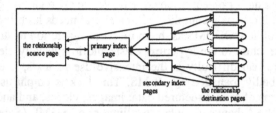

Fig. 3. The most complicated case of navigation between a source and related destinations

The slice concept avoids scrolling in windows. One slice is selected as the entry point of the object (in general, it is the slice containing the key.) (Notice that index pages may be considered as object slices.)

A relationship may itself be viewed as an object. Therefore, it is possible to create pages for relationship instances. These pages are composed of main slices of each object participating in the relationship. (Furthermore, that if we encompass sets of relationships instances in the definition, we merely obtain the classical tabular view in relational databases.)

3.2   OOHDM (Object-Oriented Hypermedia Design Model)

OOHDM [27], [28] is a direct descendant of HDM [8]. It differs from HDM both in its object-oriented nature, and in its integration of special purpose modelling primitives for navigational and interface design.

With OOHDM, a hypermedia application is built in a four-step process.

In the conceptual phase, an application model is built using object-oriented modelling principles. The main concern is to capture the domain semantics, hence, any object-oriented method may be used, in practice OMT has been chosen [25]. The single extension is the possibility to offer several types for one attribute [28].

During the navigational design step, the structure of an hypermedia application is described in terms of navigational context (classes such as *nodes, links, indexed tours, guided tours*.) Different navigational models may be built for the same conceptual schema to express different *views* on the same domain. Nodes are defined as object-oriented views of conceptual classes, links reflect relationships intended to be explored by the final user and are considered as views on relationships.

The abstract interface model is built by defining perceptible objects (*picture, city map* ...) in terms of interface classes. These interface classes are built as aggregations of primitive classes (*text fields, buttons*.) The aim of this step is to define the way in which different navigational objects are going to appear.

The last step maps interface objects to implementation objects. This step may implement interface objects in different platforms like Director, HTML, etc.

RMM and OOHDM are methodologies, i. e., they give guidelines. Our tool takes into consideration the general rules of these methods but introduces a great deal of freedom through extensibility of the OTHY object-oriented framework. The framework that is to be presented in the sequel supports the well-established concepts of hypertext design, but can be customised for very special requirements too.

3.3   HyperWave

HyperWave [19] is an hypermedia system, conceived to be a distributed Web-server, that is based on the principle of recursive collections. A collection is a composite object, and may contain objects or other collections [14], [15]. To further improve navigation tools in a HyperWave site, the notions of clusters and sequences were added. Clusters permit to partition documents of a given collection with respect to some attribute value, e. g., presenting either the French, or the English pages of a large multi-lingual document. Sequences organise documents as doubly linked list, thereby offering guided tours.

Each object of HyperWave has system-specific attributes (title, author, keywords, creation and modification dates ...) These attributes or meta-information are used to perform more accurate queries. Links between documents are stored in a document independent database. They are bi-directional, i. e., they allow to find document sources from document destinations.

HyperWave is based on the principle that users may be contribute to the server life. This involves that the system is multi-users, multi-developers. This allows registered users to own a personal collection where they may store bookmarks, history, etc.

In our opinion, the problem with HyperWave is that the schema model has been fixed. We believe that the system must adapt to the initial organisation of the data rather than the reverse. OTHY relies on this hypothesis.

3.4   PESTO (Portable Explorer of Structured Objects)

PESTO is a user interface that supports browsing and querying of object databases [4] [1]. It allows users to browse classes of objects and to navigate across the relationship that exist among them.

All attributes of a given class are shown in the same window: simple attributes are presented as being contained in the object window, reference attributes are presented as buttons that bring up new windows for displaying the referenced objects.

In addition, users may formulate complex object queries through an integrated query paradigm (*Query in Place*) that presents querying as an extension of browsing.

With PESTO, all the objects are presented according to a default presentation: a window with lists of attribute/value pairs. Contrary to our system, PESTO does not afford views, which is a severe limitation for end-users who do not want to deal with the totality of the information stored in a database.

---

[1] This paper gives a nice (short) survey of the history of querying/browsing tools since the seminal QBE (*Query By Example*) system.

As a consequence, PESTO querying capabilities are much like conventional database ones, i. e., formal though graphical. In addition, PESTO works in a single environment. We plan a more intuitive way to query an heterogeneous set of databases, based on information retrieval techniques.

4   System Architecture

Our proposition is based on the architecture presented in Fig. 5. The possibility for desktop computers in one organisation to access to different conceptual and physical sources of information, requires the use of a "universal client." Therefore, we use a Java applet to obtain this uniqueness. A side effect, and an important advantage of using a Java-enabled browser is that there is no software deployment during the system installation step, nor the forthcoming modification, nor the progressive integration of new information sub-systems. At the very most, only the browser needs some upgrades from time to time. At MAIF, this is undoubtedly a desirable feature.

For reasons that will become clear in the sequel, we adopted object orientation [21]. In contrast, the information sub-systems are heterogeneous and certainly not based on a single conceptual, nor physical model. Therefore, specific integration modules are responsible for reverse engineering of the underlying database meta-schemas. Currently, we are working on two such integration modules. Since relational database management systems (RDBMS) are wide-spread, it is an important issue to access them with our tool. Fortunately, all of them conform to the JDBC/ODBC standard. Therefore, any vendor-specific RDBMS is now accessible as a standard and unique model. But, this module is always required since it must translate meta-schemas from first normal form relations to non-normalised classes. This module will implement an algorithm developed by our research team [26].

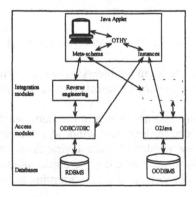

Fig. 4. System architecture

The major alternative to relational technology is object-orientation (equivalently, object-relational.) We hope that the progressive adoption of the ODMG standard [5] will make this module unnecessary in the future. In the first version of the applet, only the O_2 OODBMS and its *O2Java* binding module are to be used, which facilitates our work.

Finally, the "Java applet", i. e., the run-time intensive part of the whole architecture, is still a complex module. It is composed of four sub-modules. First, the meta-schema is in charge of loading the database meta-schemas, and to federate them in order to allow for inter-database navigation.

The accessed instances have to be interpreted by the applet, i. e., they will be split up into their very basic components: basic data types (integer, boolean, char ...), type constructors (list, set, tuple ...), as well as simple methods (observers, which return a view of the object without modifying it.)

Then, the OTHY module, which is at the core of our proposition, is responsible for translating instances into "pages."

Lastly, the user interface presents "pages" as visual components (widgets), and constitutes the visible part of the iceberg.

5   The Applet Architecture

Now, let us detail two sensitive aspects of the applet architecture to develop: (1) the meta-schema and (2) the OTHY framework. Our tool works at the meta-level; it has to manipulate instance components, hence it has to know about their structure and relationships. We rely on an object-oriented meta-schema. Then, the OTHY framework uses this information, as well as the hypermedia concepts that it incorporates, to translate database objects into "pages."

5.1   The Meta-schema

Fig. 5 presents the proposed meta-schema. It is relatively usual but it contains some interesting details: The first important notion is the use of simple inheritance, which is easier to understand and to implement. With simple inheritance, we do not care about attribute and method conflicts. Contrary to the last proposal of the ODMG, neither is the interface concept retained at that time.

Next, we use an external object identifier, i. e., a key in the relational world. The identifier is a set of particular attributes that permits naturally to distinguish an object from other objects on the same class hierarchy. More loosely, this identifier can be only a local key, i. e., a value differentiating instances that are related to a given instance. In the worst case where no key exists, this "identifier" is still useful: it allows our application to present a significant anchor to the user rather than the mere instance class name. However, this default behaviour can be overridden for special application needs.

Then, this meta-schema stresses the relationship and role concepts. More precisely, we are interested in the cardinalities of the roles. Knowing their values makes it possible to choose between different kinds of navigation detailed in section 5.2 (guided tour, indexed tour, direct access; separated pages or anchor incorporation in the source object.)

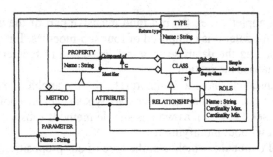

Fig. 5. An object-oriented meta-schema model

The applet meta-schema will contain several separated schemas. A long-term idea is to create relationships between these different schemas. For instance, the system may retrieve identifiers with the same name and may consider that this information comes from the same source, but is replicated in different databases. Such obvious situations arise with the employee number, or his or her first and last names. This is part of the issues to be explored in order to improve navigation and thereby to reduce the recourse to querying.

5.2   The OTHY Framework

OTHY, the core of our proposal, can be seen as a framework [12], [13], [7], [17] for translating objects into hyper-linked components. The aim of OTHY is to create a presentation "page" (with information and anchors to navigate) from a specific instance.

The OTHY framework implements prominent points of the RMM and OOHDM methodologies: (1) guided tours, indexed tours from RMM, and (2) the use of the objet-orientation, and the concept of views from OOHDM (See Sect. 3.) The philosophy of RMM is to construct hypermedia applications on top of a database conceptual model. We saw in section 2 that we are typically in this application case. Nevertheless, this method is too rigid, because it is impossible to express external views of a database application. Nevertheless, this point is taken into account by OOHDM which introduces navigational models on top of the conceptual schema. From a schema, several views may be defined.

In mathematical terms, the main function of OTHY consists in translating an instance into a "page," with respect to a given view:

$$\text{OTHY} : \text{DB} \times \text{View} \times \text{Object} \rightarrow \text{Page} \qquad (1)$$

Fig. 6 presents the needed framework skeleton to perform this transformation! This framework integrates most of the concepts of RMM and OOHDM. But, above all, it realises all the steps from navigation to implementation without requiring any modification of the database, nor development of code in the framework, except for very specific needs.

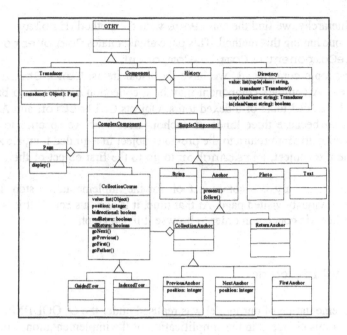

Fig. 6. The OTHY framework

Navigational Views

The class `Transducer` is the essential support of the transformation function. This class is a generic class and allows to transform any object into a page. It is the root of a concrete and/or abstract class hierarchy. This is very useful for extensibility and adaptability; each class may own a specific transducer. To go ahead, the system is able to manage several transducers for each class: specific, generic or parametric transducers.

The relationship between the transducer and the application class is made via the `Directory` class, which manages an associative relationship between class types (or, more precisely, the names of the class instances in the meta-schema) and transducer instances. Each known class name in the meta-schema is linked with a transducer reference. Each (kind of) user may obtain a distinct directory, where he or she may use both different transducers for the same instances, and different presentations or navigation according to his needs. This is the way we implemented view and user profile concepts.

Interfaces

The most important hierarchy, in terms of number of classes only, is for the hypermedia presentation of data. There are usual page concepts, anchors, guided tours, indexed tours and different kinds of media (*text, string, picture ...*) Instances of these classes are the result of applying a transducer to a data instance. This result is presented to the user for browsing. Properties extracted from an object can be attributes or observers without parameters. (In the case of query extension, we should take into account other observers to allow users to provide parameters at run-time.)

In this hierarchy, we find the class `Page` with the method `display()`. This class is the only one having this method. This page amalgamates `Components` which may be `SimpleComponent` or `ComplexComponent`.

Among simple components, we have the usual items: `Text`, `String`, `Photo`, `Anchor`, etc. A complex component may be a collection of objects to browse. The tours may be guided tours or indexed tours. Objects `Collection` and `Anchor` are closely linked because three kinds of anchors over four are specific to collections (`PreviousAnchor` to return to the previous object in a guided tour, `NextAnchor` to go to the next object, `FirstAnchor` to go to the first object of the collection to browse).

The class `History` is a common tool, for the implementation step. It allows to return to a previously visited page. At that time, it is only a stack. But it is possible to extend this historic concept in order to browse it like a graph.

6   The V0 Prototype

A first implementation of our model was realised under the O_2 OODBMS. The major advantage of this choice is in the simplification of the implementation. This was done to validate our approach before the development of the full tool. More precisely, advantages are three-fold: (1) homogeneity, (2) direct use of the O_2 meta-schema, and (3) less need to interpret the instances. Using a single environment eliminates connections and the "impedance mismatch" between a host language and the database. The implementation was achieved with the native O_2 meta-schema, though it does not have all the needed characteristics. More precisely, the notion of natural key is still absent and we choose to use the value of the first attribute as the anchor value in a page. Also, the development was easier because instances are directly accessible as objects. In the final version, we will have to decompose objects as they contain components (attributes and methods.)

A simple application was coded. There are five classes (`Author`, `Publication`, `Book`, `Magazine` and `Publisher`) linked by two relationships (`Wrote` and `Published`) or by inheritance. Note that the O_2 classes do not reference OTHY, as implied by the principle of total independence that we impose to ourselves (See Table 1)

OTHY is already a usable framework but –and this is one advantage of the object-oriented approach– it is possible to extend it. This is really true for the instance presentation definition. Consequently, we added some subclasses for `Publication`. Relationships between these classes and application classes are notified to OTHY through a directory.

At run-time, link between an application instance and the instance of an OTHY transducer is made via the directory associative memory. There are two input points: the instance of the directory used (function of the user connected) and an application object. First, from this object, thanks to a generic O_2 method named `title` that returns the instance class name, we obtain the string "`Author`." Secondly, this name is transferred from the application domain to the OTHY framework. This step uses a `Directory` object . It is an associative memory that is able to retrieve the instance of `Transducer` that has been previously associated by the user (or a default one if such an association has not been specified.) Thirdly, the retrieved transducer is applied to the initial instance. This returns a page, using either a generic, or a specific layout, by instantiating standard components (labels, drawings ...) and using values from the object (attributes or method results.) The sub-object `Asimov-Books` allows the user to perform a guided tour of all the books of this author. Notice that it is allowed to manipulate references from the OTHY domain to the application domain. Anchors and references allow us to launch the same process for one book if the user desired so.

Table 1. Some O_2 classes of our example

```
class Author                        class Publication
private type tuple(                 Private type tuple(
  read FirstName: string,             read Title: string,
  read LastName: string,              dateP: Date,
  dateB: Date,                        read WrittenBy:
  dateD: Date,                            unique set(Author),
  read Photo: Image,                  read EditedBy:
  read Biography: Text)                   unique set(Publisher))
method                              end;
  public BirthDate: string
  public DeathDate: string          class Book
  public Wrote:                       inherit Publication
          unique set(Book)          private type tuple(
end;                                  read Cover: Image,
                                    end;
```

Fig. 7 gives an example of standard presentation with the O_2 browser (`display(Asimov)` or `Asimov->display()`). This is to be compared to a presentation obtained by using our framework, in Fig. 8. The presentation is obtained by a call to `OTHY(BibliograhicDirectory, Asimov)->display()`[2]. The code of this function consists of a single line of code, as follows:

```
function body OTHY(dir: Directory, inst: Object): Page
{ return (dir->map(inst->title)->transduce(inst)); }
```

The function signature conforms to the mathematical one of section 5.2 except for the DB parameter which is implicit. Though the current presentation is not yet really attractive, its use to navigate in a database is really eloquent. First, the O_2 browser forces to open a new window for each sub-object. All opened windows are stacked and must be closed in reverse order. In contrast, OTHY manages automatically the erasure of windows and allows a return to the previous windows (the history), like a Web browser. This decreases considerably the user concentration, and increases the freedom of move around the objects of the database.

---

[2] Another version of this function uses a default directory, set for the user session in a global variable (named a root of persistence in O_2.)

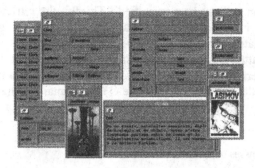

Fig. 7. The standard presentation with the O_2 browser

(a)   (b)

Fig. 8. The OTHY presentation of (a) an author and (b) a book

Note that taking into account methods allows cross navigation between related objects. The O_2 browser relies only on attributes; therefore it is possible to go from a book to its authors but not the reverse way because this role has been implemented by a method.

Another difference is that each attribute is presented in a separate panel with the O_2 browser whereas we are free to mix labels and values in OTHY, e. g., the name followed by constant strings and dates in Fig. 8(a).

Guided tours (Fig. 1) are represented by a next and a previous button (respectively "Livre précédent" and "Livre suivant" in Fig. 8(b) that allow to browse Asimov's books.

Indexed tours (Fig. 2) are not implemented in our example, but they are represented by one (or several) index page(s.) In turn, these pages access to the desired pieces of information. In the case of *Authors*, if one author is very prolix, it is very interesting to group his or her books according to different criteria (date of publication, alphabetic order ...) Also not presented here is the possibility to incorporate parts of the related objects into the currently displayed instance page. In fact, since transducers can be derived for very specific needs, their result can be composed of anything that is reachable from the instance parameter[3].

7   Conclusion and Future Work

We saw that there exist needs for large organisations to browse through their heterogeneous information system. Browsing has to be independent both of localisation and of the kind of storage and retrieval systems (object, relational, or object-relational databases, specific systems, even simple files.) Other demands have been made by the users but are not addressed by this paper.

We decided to develop a framework to display objects contained in several databases in the manner of an hypermedia application. This framework is totally independent from the storage sub-systems and from the data models. Localisation independence and hypermedia conviviality is to be achieved through the use of a Web browser.

A first prototype allowed us to validate our approach. Indeed, it is now possible to create an application without taking care of how this application will be browsed. This is very important to decrease the time devoted to the user interface construction (thanks to a default transducer, it can even be reduced to zero.) The OTHY framework integrates the main concepts of hypermedia design (consistency of the presentation, links and anchors, guided and/or indexed tours, history.) However, it is possible to customise our framework by providing additional transducers up to particularising each object presentation. Furthermore, users may choose themselves convenient presentations to obtain particular "views."

We are on the path to develop the V1 prototype. This tool is a Java applet integrating the access layers described in Section 4. It must manage the additional problems of instance interpretation (splitting them into their basic components), user identification and loading of his or her profile. Moreover, a graphical tool to describe pages has to be developed to allow users to customise themselves their views of the information system.

From the theoretical point of view, at least three issues have to be investigated: reverse engineering, querying, and integration. First, our framework is object-oriented whereas the information sub-systems are heterogeneous. Therefore, reverse engineering is mandatory to be able to use the framework for any kind of data. This is currently being added, based on previous works of our research team [26].

The second issue is to incorporate query capabilities. They will be based on information retrieval concepts and techniques, rather than on (almost) formal queries, which were rejected by the end-users in past experiences. In the long term, it is envisaged to integrate also multimedia retrieval capabilities, since they are being studied in our research team [18].

---

[3] In another application, the visualisation of a class with a single attribute and a recursive relationship leads to the extreme case where the value of the object and the values of all the related objects (used as anchors) were presented in a single window.

The last envisaged issue is schema integration. Effectively, considering the different databases as isolated islands of information is poor practice. The system has to find implicit relationships between the different databases that belong to the information system of the same organisation because they necessarily share common subschemas, objects, or simply attributes. Integration would greatly improve browsing and postpone the moment when user is obliged to query the system.

8   Acknowledgements

We would like to thank Cyril Tiollier, and more particularly Pejman Parandi, engineer students at IRESTE, who implemented part of the V0 OTHY framework in the context of a second year student project. The example of *"Asimov"* is theirs.

9   References

1. Bancilhon, F., Delobel, C., Kannelakis, P.; Building an Object-Oriented Database System: The Story of O_2; Morgan-Kaufmann, 1992
2. Batini, C., Ceri, S., Navathe, S.B.; Conceptual Database Design: An Entity-Relationship Approach; The Benjamin/Cummings Publishing Company, Inc., 1992, 470 p.
3. Bieber, M., Isakowitz, T.; Designing Hypermedia Applications; Communications of the ACM, August 1995, Vol. 38, No. 8, pp. 26-29
4. Carey, M., Haas, L., Maganty, V., Williams, J.; PESTO: An Integrated Query/Browser for Object Databases; Proc. of the 22nd Int'l Conf. On Very Large Data Bases (VLDB'96), Mumbai (Bombay), India, 1996, pp. 203-214
5. Cattel, R. G. G., Barry, D., Bartels, D., Berler, M., Eastman, J., Gamerman, S., Jordan, D., Springer, A., Strickland, H., Wade, D.; The Object Database Standard: ODMG 2.0; Morgan Kaufmann Publishers, Inc., San Francisco, California, 1997, 270 p.
6. Conklin, J.; Hypertext: An Introduction and Survey; IEEE Computer, September 1987, pp. 17-41
7. Fayad, M. E.; Schmidt, D. C.; Object-Oriented Application Frameworks; Communications of the ACM, October 1997, Vol. 40, No. 10, pp. 32-38
8. Garzotto, F., Paolini, P., Schwabe, D.; HDM – A Model-Based Approach to Hypertext Application Design; ACM Transaction on Information Systems, Vol. 11, N° 1, January 1993, pp. 1-26
9. Halasz, F., Schwartz, M.; The Dexter Hypertext Reference Model; Communications of the ACM, February 1994, Vol. 37, No. 2, pp. 30-39
10. Hardman, L., Bulterman, D.C.A., Van Rossum, G.; The Amsterdam Hypermedia Model: Adding Time and Context to the Dexter Model; Communications of the ACM, February 1994, Vol. 37, No. 2, pp. 50-62
11. Isakowitz, T., Stohr, E. ; Balasubramanian, P. ; RMM: A Methodology for Structured Hypermedia Design; Communications of the ACM, August 1995, Vol. 38, No. 8, pp. 34-44
12. Johnson, R.E., Foote, B.; Designing Reusable Classes; JOOP, Vol. 1, n° 2, June/July 1998, pp. 22-35
13. Johnson, R.E.; Frameworks = (Components + Patterns); Communications of the ACM, October 1997, Vol. 40, No. 10, pp. 39-42
14. Kim, W., Banerjee, J., Chou, H.-T., Garza, J. F., Woelk, D.; Composite Object Support in an Object-Oriented Database; Proc. of the ACM Int'l Conf. on Object-Oriented Programming, Systems, Languages, and Applications (OOPSLA'87), 1987, pp. 118-125

15. Kim, W., Bertino, E., Garza, J. F.; Composite Objects Revisited; Proc. of the ACM SIG Int'l Conf. On the Management of Data (SIGMOD'89), Portland, Oregon, 1989, pp. 337-347

16. Losada, B., Lopistéguy, P., Dagorret, P.; Etude de la Conception d'Applications Hypermédias (in french); Actes du XVe Congrès INFORSID, June 1997, Toulouse, France, pp. 133-146

17. Manhes, S.; La réutilisabilité: Patterns et Frameworks (in french); M. Sc. Thesis, IRIN, University of Nantes, 1998

18. Martinez, J., Marchand, S.; Towards Intelligent Retrieval in Image Databases; Proc. of the Int'l Workshop on Multi-Media Data Base Management Systems (MMDBMS'98), Dayton, Ohio, August 1998, pp. 38-45

19. Maurer, H. (ed.); HyperG is now HyperWave: The Next Generation Web Solution; Addison-Wesley Publishing Company, 1996

20. Meghini, C., Rabitti, F., Thanos, C.; Conceptual Modeling of Multimedia Documents; IEEE Computer, October 1991, pp. 23-30

21. Meyer, B.; Object-Oriented Software Construction; Prentice Hall, 1988

22. Nanard, J., Nanard, M.; Hypertext Design Environments and the Hypertext Design Process; Communications of the ACM, Vol. 38, No. 8, August 1995, pp. 49-56

23. Newcomb, S.R., Kipp, N.A., Newcomb, V.T.; "HyTime": The Hypermedia/Time-based Document Structuring Language; Communications of the ACM, November 1991, Vol. 34, No. 11, pp. 67-83

24. Nielsen, J.; HyperText and HyperMedia; Academic Press, Inc., San Diego, California, USA, 268 p.

25. Rumbaugh, J., Blaha, M., Premerlani, W., Eddy, F., Lorensen, W.; Object-Oriented Modeling and Design; Prentice Hall, 1991

26. Saoudi, A.; Une approche terminologique pour l'interopérabilité sémantique des systèmes de bases de données hétérogènes; Ph. D. Thesis, November 1997, IRIN, University of Nantes

27. Schwabe, D., Rossi, G., Barbosa, S.D.J.; Abstraction, Composition and Lay-Out Definition Mechanisms in OOHDM; Proc. of the ACM Workshop on Effective Abstractions in Multimedia, San Francisco, California, November 4, 1995

28. Schwabe, D., Rossi, G., Barbosa, S.D.J.; Systematic Hypermedia Application Design with OOHDM; Proc. of The 7th ACM Conf. on Hypertext, Washington D.C., March 16-20, 1996, pp. 116-128.

29. Smith, K.E., Zdonik, S.B.; InterMedia: A Case Study of the Differences between Relational and Object-Oriented Database Systems; Proc. of the Int'l Conf. on Object-Oriented Programming Systems, Languages, and Applications (OOPSLA'87), Orlando, Florida, October 1987

30. Van Herwijnen, E.; Practical SGML; Kluwer Academic, 1994

Modeling Dynamic Domains with ConGolog⋆

Yves Lespérance[1], Todd G. Kelley[2], John Mylopoulos[2], and Eric S.K. Yu[2]

[1] Dept. of Computer Science, York University,
Toronto, ON Canada, M3J 1P3
lesperan@cs.yorku.ca
[2] Department of Computer Science, University of Toronto
Toronto, ON, Canada M5S 3G4
{tgk,jm,eric}@ai.toronto.edu

Abstract. In this paper, we describe the process specification language *ConGolog* and show how it can be used to model business processes for requirements analysis. In *ConGolog*, the effects of actions in a dynamic domain are specified in a logical framework. This supports modeling even in the absence of complete information. The behavior of agents in the domain is specified in a concurrent process language, whose semantics is defined in the same logical framework. We then describe a simulation tool implemented in terms of logic programming technology. As well, we discuss a verification tool which is being developed based on theorem proving technology.

1   Introduction

Models of dynamic aspects of the world constitute an essential ingredient of information systems engineering. Such models are useful during requirements analysis where the operational environment of a system-to-be needs to be described, along with the role the system will play within that environment. Dynamic models also play a key role during design when the functions of the system and its major components are specified.

Existing dynamic models come in two flavors. State-based models describe the processes of a dynamic world in terms of states and (state) transitions. Finite-state machines, Petri nets [14], statecharts [7], and workflows are examples of modeling frameworks which adopt a state-oriented view of the world. A major advantage of state-based models is that they can be simulated, showing the sequence of state transitions that will take place for a particular sequence of input signals. Alternatively, predicative models [1, 20] describe processes in terms of pre/post-conditions, i.e., in terms of a condition that has to be true before a process is launched (the precondition) and a condition that will be true once the process execution has been completed (the postcondition). Predicative models

---

⋆ This research received financial support from Communications and Information Technology Ontario (and its earlier incarnation ITRC) and the Natural Science and Engineering Research Council of Canada. A longer version of the paper appears at www.cs.yorku.ca/~lesperan.

M. Jarke, A. Oberweis (Eds.): CAiSE'99, LNCS 1626, pp. 365–380, 1999.
© Springer-Verlag Berlin Heidelberg 1999

admit a type of formal analysis where properties of a process can be verified. For example, one can show that a certain invariant is preserved by a process in the sense that if the invariant holds before the process begins, it will also hold at the end of the process.

Predicative models typically do not support simulation and state-based models do not support formal property analysis. This paper describes a modeling framework for dynamic worlds that supports both simulation and verification. The framework is based on the language *ConGolog*, originally developed as a high level language for programming robots and software agents [3].[1] *ConGolog* is based on a logical formalism, the situation calculus, and can model multi-agent processes, nondeterminism, as well as concurrency. Because of its logical foundations, *ConGolog* can accommodate incompletely specified models, either in the sense that the initial state of the system is not completely specified, or in the sense that the processes involved are nondeterministic and may evolve in any number of ways. These features are especially useful when one models business processes and open-ended real world situations.

Section 2 of the paper introduces the framework and how it is used for modeling states, actions, and processes, and presents a simple example involving the handling of orders by a business. Section 3 demonstrates the ability of the framework to support both simulation and verification, while section 4 describes the semantics of *ConGolog* and the formal theory on which it is based. Finally, section 5 summarizes the contributions of this research and suggests directions for further research.

2   Modeling a Domain in *ConGolog*

In the *ConGolog* framework, an application domain is modeled *logically* so as to support reasoning about the specification. A *ConGolog* model of a domain involves two components. The first component is a specification of the *domain dynamics*, i.e. how the states are modeled, what actions may be performed, when they are possible, what their effects are, and what is known about the initial state of the system. This component is specified in a purely declarative way, in a language called the *Golog Domain Language (GDL)*.[2]

The second component of a *ConGolog* domain model is a specification of the *processes* that are unfolding in the domain; this can also be viewed as a specification of the behavior of the agents in the domain. Because we are interested in modeling domains involving complex processes, this component is specified procedurally in the *ConGolog* process description language.

Both GDL and the *ConGolog* process language have formal semantics defined in a language of predicate logic called the *situation calculus*. Various mechanisms

---

[1]   *ConGolog* is an extended version of the Golog (AlGOl in LOGic) language described in [10]. Earlier work on modeling business processes in Golog appeared in [15].

[2]   GDL is related to Gelfond and Lifschitz's action language $\mathcal{A}$ [6]; one significant difference though, is that GDL is a first-order language, while $\mathcal{A}$ is essentially a propositional language.

for reasoning about properties of a domain have been implemented using this situation calculus semantics. We outline the semantics in section 4.

To illustrate the use of the framework to model a domain, we use a running example involving a simple mail-order business. We assume that the business sells only one product. We also assume that there are only two agents in the business, who could be single people or whole departments:

- the *order desk operator*, who processes payment for orders while waiting for the phone to ring, and when it does, receives an order from a customer; and
- the *warehouse operator*, who fills the orders that the order desk operator has received, and ships orders for which the order desk operator has processed payment; whenever a shipment is delivered by a supplier, the warehouse operator receives the shipment.

Orders can be processed in two possible ways as described in the diagram in Figure 1. The example is kept artificially simple so that it can be presented in its entirety.

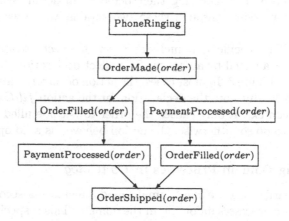

Fig. 1. An diagram showing the two possible paths in the life-cycle of an order.

2.1   Modeling Domain Dynamics in GDL

The first component of a *ConGolog* model is a specification of the dynamics of the domain and of what is known about its initial state. For this, our framework uses GDL. In our models, we imagine the world as starting out in a particular initial *situation* (or state), and evolving into various other possible situations through the performance of *actions* by various agents. Situations are described in terms of *fluents*. *Relational fluents* are relations or properties whose truth value can vary from situation and to situation and *functional fluents* are functions whose value varies from situation to situation. For instance in our example, we use the action term *shipOrder(agt, order)* to represent the action of agent *agt* shipping

order, and the relational fluent *OrderShipped(order)* to represent the property
that *order* has been shipped. This fluent might be false in the initial situation,
but true in a situation that is the result of the action *shipOrder(agt, order)*.

The modeler chooses the fluents and actions in a domain model according to
the desired level of abstraction. A GDL domain specification starts with a set of
declarations for the fluents used in the model. Each *fluent declaration* specifies
the name of the fluent, the number of arguments it takes and whether it is a
functional fluent or not. Optionally, one can also specify what value the fluent
has in the initial situation. The GDL fluent declarations for our example domain
appear in Figure 2. Note that orders are identified by a number determined by
the value of the *orderCounter* fluent when the order is received.

Next, a GDL domain specification includes *action declarations*, one for each
primitive action. These specify the name of the action, the arguments it takes,
and action's preconditions, i.e. the conditions under which it is possible. The
GDL action declarations for our example domain appear in Figure 2. The last
two represent actions performed by customers and suppliers that impact on the
business. We view customers and suppliers as agents that are outside the system
and are not interested in modeling their behavior in detail. We only consider
their effect on the system through these two actions, which we call *exogenous*
actions.

Finally, a GDL specification includes a set of *effect declarations*, one for
each fluent that is affected by an action. The effect declarations for our example
domain appear in Figure 3. In most cases, the action occurrence **always** produces
the specified effect. But note the declaration for the action *fillOrder*; its effects
depend on the context: it only causes the order to become filled **when** there is
sufficient stock to do so; otherwise, the action behaves as a no-op.

2.2 Modeling Domain Processes in *ConGolog*

As mentioned earlier, a *ConGolog* domain model includes a second component
that describes the processes unfolding in the domain. This is specified in a procedural sublanguage where actions can be composed into complex processes, possibly involving concurrency and nondeterminism. This *ConGolog* process specification language provides the constructs listed in Figure 4.

Let us go over some of the less familiar constructs in the language. The
nondeterministic constructs include $(\sigma_1 \mid \sigma_2)$, which nondeterministically choses
between processes σ_1 and σ_2, $\pi x[\sigma]$, which nondeterministically picks a binding
for the variables in the list x and performs the process σ for this binding of x,
and σ^*, which means performing σ zero or more times. Concurrent processes
are modeled as interleavings of the actions involved. The actions themselves are
viewed as atomic and cannot be interrupted. A process may become blocked
when it reaches a primitive action whose preconditions are false or a wait action
ϕ? whose condition ϕ is false. Then, execution of the system may continue provided another process executes next. In $(\sigma_1 \rangle\!\rangle \sigma_2)$, σ_1 has higher priority than
σ_2, and σ_2 may only execute when σ_1 is done or blocked. $\sigma^\|$ is like nondeterministic iteration σ^*, but the instances of σ are executed concurrently rather

Fluent Declarations

fluent *PhoneRinging()*   % the phone is ringing
    initially *False*;
fluent *OrderMade(order)*   % *order* has been made
    initially *False*;
fluent *PaymentProcessed(order)*   % payment for *order* has been
    initially *False*;   % processed
fluent *OrderFilled(order)*   % *order* has been filled
    initially *False*;
fluent *OrderShipped(order)*   % *order* has been shipped
    initially *False*;
fluent *SuppliesAtShippingDock()*   % incoming supplies are at
    initially *False*;   % the shipping dock
functional fluent *orderQuantity(order)*   % the quantity of items requested
    initially 0;   % in *order*
functional fluent *orderCounter()*   % the value of the order counter
    initially 1;
functional fluent *stock()*   % the quantity of items in stock
    initially 10;
functional fluent *incomingOrderQuantity()*   % the quantity of items requested
    initially 0;   % in the incoming order
functional fluent *incomingSuppliesQuantity()*   % the quantity of items delivered
    initially 0;   % in the incoming shipment

Action Declarations

action *receiveOrder(agt)*   % *agt* receives the incoming phone order
    possible when *PhoneRinging()*;
action *processPayment(agt, order)*   % *agt* processes payment for *order*
    possible when *OrderMade(order)*;
action *fillOrder(agt, order)*   % *agt* fills *order*
    possible when *OrderMade(order)*;
action *shipOrder(agt, order)*   % *agt* ships *order*
    possible when *OrderMade(order)* $\land$ *OrderFilled(order)*;
action *receiveSupplies(agt)*   % *agt* receives supplies at the loading dock
    possible when *SuppliesAtShippingDock()*
    $\land$ *stock()* + *incomingSuppliesQuantity()* < 100;
exogenous action *mkOrder(cust, q)*   % customer *cust* makes an order for *q* items
    possible when $\neg$*PhoneRinging()*;
exogenous action *deliverSupplies(supp, q)*
                            % supplier *supp* delivers *q* items of new stock
    possible when $\neg$*SuppliesAtShippingDock()*;

Fig. 2. Example GDL domain specification – part 1.

Effect Declarations

occurrence *receiveOrder(agt)* **results in** *OrderMade(orderCounter())* **always**;
occurrence *receiveOrder(agt)* **results in**
  orderCounter() = orderCounter() + 1 **always**;
occurrence *receiveOrder(agt)* **results in** ¬*PhoneRinging()* **always**;
occurrence *receiveOrder(agt)* **results in**
  orderQuantity(orderCounter()) = incomingOrderQuantity() **always**;
occurrence *processPayment(agt, order)* **results in**
  PaymentProcessed(order) **always**;
occurrence *receiveSupplies(agt)* **results in** ¬*SuppliesAtShippingDock()* **always**;
occurrence *receiveSupplies(agt)* **results in**
  stock() = stock() + incomingSuppliesQuantity() **always**;
occurrence *fillOrder(agt, order)* **results in** *OrderFilled(order)*
  when *orderQuantity(order) < stock()*;
occurrence *fillOrder(agt, order)* **results in**
  stock() = stock() − orderQuantity(order)
  when *orderQuantity(order) < stock()*;
occurrence *shipOrder(agt, order)* **results in** *OrderShipped(order)* **always**;
occurrence *mkOrder(c, q)* **results in** *PhoneRinging()* **always**;
occurrence *mkOrder(c, q)* **results in** *incomingOrderQuantity() = q* **always**;
occurrence *deliverSupplies(su, q)* **results in** *SuppliesAtShippingDock()* **always**;
occurrence *deliverSupplies(su, q)* **results in**
  incomingSuppliesQuantity() = q **always**;

Fig. 3. Example GDL domain specification – part 2.

α	primitive action
ϕ?	wait for a condition
$(\sigma_1; \sigma_2)$	sequence
$(\sigma_1 \mid \sigma_2)$	nondeterministic choice between actions
$\pi\, x\, [\sigma]$	nondeterministic choice of arguments
σ^*	nondeterministic iteration
if ϕ **then** σ_1 **else** σ_2 **endIf**	conditional
while ϕ **do** σ **endWhile**	loop
$(\sigma_1 \parallel \sigma_2)$	concurrent execution
$(\sigma_1 \rangle\!\rangle \sigma_2)$	concurrency with different priorities
$\sigma^{\parallel}$	concurrent iteration
$< x : \phi \to \sigma >$	interrupt
proc $\beta(x)$ σ **endProc**	procedure definition
$\beta(t)$	procedure call
noOp	do nothing

Fig. 4. Constructs in *ConGolog* process specifications.

than in sequence. Finally, an interrupt $< x : \phi \rightarrow \sigma >$ has a list of variables x, a trigger condition ϕ, and a body σ. If the interrupt gets control from higher priority processes and the condition ϕ is true for some binding of the variables, the interrupt triggers and the body is executed with the variables taking these values. Once the body completes execution, the interrupt may trigger again. With interrupts, it is easy to write process specifications that are reactive in that they will suspend whatever task they are doing to handle given conditions as they arise.

Let us look at how this language can be used to specify the processes in our mail-order business domain; the specification appears in Figure 5. The whole

Process Specifications

proc $runOrderDesk(odAgt)$
　　$< phoneRinging \rightarrow receiveOrder(odAgt) >$
　　$\rangle\rangle$
　　$< order : OrderMade(order) \wedge \neg paymentProcessed(order)$
　　　$\rightarrow processPayment(odAgt, order) >$
endProc

proc $runWarehouse(wAgt)$
　　$< SuppliesAtShippingDock \rightarrow receiveSupplies(wAgt) >$
　　$\rangle\rangle$
　　$< order : OrderMade(order) \wedge OrderFilled(order)$
　　　$\wedge PaymentProcessed(order) \wedge \neg OrderShipped(order)$
　　　$\rightarrow shipOrder(wAgt) >$
　　$\rangle\rangle$
　　$< order : OrderMade(order) \wedge \neg OrderFilled(order)$
　　　$\rightarrow fillOrder(wAgt) >$
endProc

proc $main$
　　$runOrderDesk(OrderDeskAgt) \parallel runWarehouse(WarehouseAgt)$
endProc

Fig. 5. Example *ConGolog* process specification.

system is specified by the *main* procedure. It executes two concurrent processes, one for each agent in the domain. The agents in our system are very reactive. Their behavior involves monitoring the progress of orders, and when certain conditions hold, performing some step in the processing of the order. So we specify their behavior using interrupts. The behavior of the order desk operator is specified by the *runOrderDesk* procedure. This agent has two responsibilities: receiving an order when the phone rings and processing payments for orders. Each of these is handled by an interrupt. Since receiving orders when the phone rings is more urgent than processing payments, the interrupt for receiving orders runs at higher priority than the one for processing payments. The interrupt for processing payment nondeterministically picks an order for which payment has not yet been processed, and processes its payment.

The *runWarehouse* procedure specifying the behavior of the warehouse operator involves three interrupts each running at a different priority. At the highest priority, the operator should receive an incoming shipment when the shipping door bell rings. When there is no shipment to receive, the next highest priority is to ship orders that are ready to ship (orders that are filled and for which payment is processed), if there are any, picking at random. At the lowest priority, the operator should fill any order that has been received but not yet filled, picking the order arbitrarily.[3]

3   Analyzing Domain Specifications Using *ConGolog* Tools

3.1   Validation through Simulation

Simulation is a useful method for validating domain models. We have developed a tool for incrementally generating execution traces of *ConGolog* process specifications. This tool can be used to check whether a model executes as expected in various conditions. For example, our simulation tool can be used to confirm that our model of the mail-order business domain can process a single order in two different ways, either filling the order before payment is processed, or vice versa. In Figure 6, we see a trace of the first execution of the specification, where a single order by customer $c1$ for 3 items ($mkOrder(c1, 3)$) is made and where payment is processed on the order before it is filled. The figure shows the simulation tool at the end of the execution. A list of executed actions appears at the top right of the viewer, with later action occurrences at the top. The (partial) state of the system is displayed at the top left of the viewer. A trace of a second execution of the specification where the order is filled before payment can also be obtained.

Our simulation tool is based on a logic programming technology implementation of the *ConGolog* framework. It involves two main components:

- the *GDL compiler*, which takes a domain specification in GDL and produces a Prolog implementation of the corresponding situation calculus domain theory;
- the ConGolog *interpreter*, which takes a *ConGolog* process specification and a domain theory, and generates execution traces that satisfy the process specification given the domain theory; the interpreter uses the domain theory in evaluating tests and checking whether action preconditions are satisfied as it generates the execution traces; the Prolog implementation of the interpreter is described in [4].

---

[3] Note that the action *fillOrder* succeeds in filling the order only if there is sufficient stock and the agent may do it repeatedly until it succeeds. It is easy to refine the program to favor orders for which there is sufficient stock.

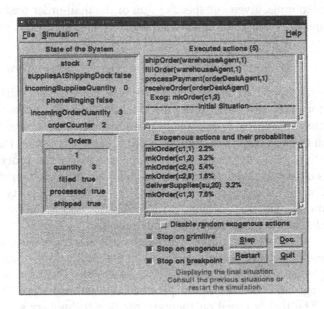

Fig. 6. The *ConGolog* simulation tool at the end of a first execution of the mail-order domain specification.

These two components are at the core of a toolkit. The kit includes a *graphical viewer*, shown in Figure 6 for displaying simulations of *ConGolog* process specifications. This tool, which is implemented in Tcl/Tk, displays the sequence of actions performed by the *ConGolog* process specification and the value of the fluents in the resulting situation (or any situation along the path). The process execution can be stepped through and exogenous events can be generated either manually or at random according to a given probability distribution. The manner in which state information is displayed can be specified easily and customized as required. X The toolkit also includes a module for *progressing* the initial situation, i.e. updating the specification of the initial situation to make it correspond to a later situation [12]; this improves the system's efficiency.

The logic programming technology implementation of the *ConGolog* framework is fairly efficient and can be used for both simulation and for deploying actual applications when one provides implementations for the actions used. However, the current implementation is limited to specifications of the initial situation that can be represented as logic programs, which are essentially closed-world theories. This is a limitation of the logic programming implementation, not the *ConGolog* framework. Note also that we are currently working on extending the implementation to support limited types of incompleteness.

3.2 Verification

One may be interested in verifying that the processes in a domain satisfy certain properties. The *ConGolog* framework supports this through its logic-based semantics. For example, given our specification of the mail-order business domain, we may be interested in showing that no order is ever shipped before payment is processed, i.e.

$$\forall order.\ OrderShipped(order) \supset PaymentProcessed(order).$$

In fact, we can prove that if the above property holds in the initial situation, it will hold for every situation during an execution of our process specification. Intuitively, this is the case because (1) once payment is processed for an order no action can cause it to become unprocessed, (2) the only action that can cause an order to have been shipped is *shipOrder*, and (3) in the process specified, *shipOrder* is only performed when payment has been processed on the order. We give a proof of the property in section 4.4. Note that the property follows even if the domain specification includes no information about the initial situation other than the fact that the property holds initially.

A user-assisted verification tool that can handle arbitrary *ConGolog* theories, i.e. incompletely specified initial situations and specifications of agents' mental states (knowledge and goals), is being developed [19]. The user would provide a proof strategy and the tool would produce the detailed steps of a proof automatically. The tool is based on theorem proving technology and relies on an encoding of the *ConGolog* semantics in a form that the PVS program verification system can reason with.

4   *ConGolog* Semantics

4.1   The Situation Calculus and the Semantics of GDL

As mentioned earlier, the semantics of GDL and of the *ConGolog* process specification language are specified in the *situation calculus* [13], a language of predicate logic for representing dynamic domains. The reasoning performed by our tools is also based on the situation calculus. Let us briefly introduce this language. In the situation calculus, all changes to the world are the result of named *actions*. A possible world history, which is simply a sequence of actions, is represented by a first order term called a *situation*. The constant S_0 is used to denote the initial situation, namely that situation in which no actions have yet occurred. There is a distinguished binary function symbol *do* and the term $do(\alpha, s)$ denotes the situation resulting from action α being performed in situation s. Actions may be parameterized. So for example, $do(receiveOrder(agt), s)$ would denote that situation resulting from agt having received the incoming phone order when the world was in situation s.

In the situation calculus, properties and relations whose truth value varies depending on the situation are called *relational fluents* and are represented by predicate symbols that take a situation term as their last argument. For example, the formula $\neg\exists order\ OrderMade(order, S_0)$ would be used to represent the fact no order has been made in the initial situation, and

$$OrderMade(1, do(receiveOrder(OrderDeskAgent),\\ do(mkOrder(Customer1, 2), S_0)))$$

would be used to represent the fact that order number 1 has been made in the situation obtained after customer *Customer*1 makes an order for 2 items and the order desk agent receives it. Similarly, functional fluents are represented by function symbols that take a situation as their last argument, as in *orderQuantity(order, s)*, i.e., the quantity of items requested in *order* in situation *s*. In GDL specifications, the situation argument of fluents is suppressed to make the notation less verbose.

The semantics of GDL maps GDL declarations into situation calculus axioms that capture the meaning of the declarations. GDL fluent declarations can include information about the value of the fluent in the initial situation in an **initially** clause. If such a clause is present, it is mapped into an *initial situation axiom*. For example, the fluent declaration for *PhoneRinging* in Figure 2 is mapped into the initial situation axiom $\neg PhoneRinging(S_0)$.

A GDL action declaration specifies the preconditions of the action, i.e. the conditions under which it is physically possible to perform it. Such a declaration is mapped by the GDL semantics into an *action precondition axiom*. These axioms use the special predicate *Poss*, with $Poss(\alpha, s)$ representing the fact that action α is physically possible (i.e. executable) in situation s. For example, the action declaration for *receiveSupplies* in Figure 2 is mapped into the following action precondition axiom:

$$Poss(receiveSupplies(agt), s) \equiv SuppliesAtShippingDock(s)$$
$$\wedge\ stock() + incomingSuppliesQuantity() < 100$$

Finally, we also have GDL effect declarations which specify how actions affect the state of the world. These declarations are mapped by the GDL semantics into *effect axioms*. Effect axioms provide the "causal laws" for the domain of application. For example, the effect declarations in Figure 3 that involve the fluent *PhoneRinging* are mapped into the following effect axioms:

$$\neg PhoneRinging(do(receiveOrder(agt), s))$$

$$PhoneRinging(do(mkOrder(customer, quantity), s))$$

The full syntax and semantics of GDL are defined in [9].

4.2   Addressing the Frame Problem

The sort of logic-based framework we have described allows very incomplete information about a dynamic domain to be specified. But this creates difficulties in reasoning about action and change Effect axioms state what must change when an action is performed, but do not specify what aspects of the domain remain unchanged. One way to address this is to add *frame axioms* that specify when fluents remain unchanged by actions. For example, an agent *agt* filling *order* does not cause new supplies to appear at the shipping dock:

$$\neg SuppliesAtShippingDock(s) \supset$$
$$\neg SuppliesAtShippingDock(do(fillOrder(agt, order), s))$$

The frame problem arises because the number of these frame axioms is very large, in general, of the order of $2 \times \mathcal{A} \times \mathcal{F}$, where $\mathcal{A}$ is the number of actions and $\mathcal{F}$ the number of fluents. This complicates the task of axiomatizing a domain and can make automated reasoning extremely inefficient. Most predicative approaches do not address this problem [2].

To deal the frame problem, we use an approach due to Reiter [17]. The basic idea behind this is to collect all effect axioms about a given fluent and make a *completeness assumption*, i.e. assume that they specify all of the ways that the value of the fluent may change. A syntactic transformation can then be applied to obtain a *successor state axiom* for the fluent, for example:

$$PhoneRinging(do(a, s)) \equiv$$
$$\exists customer, quantity\; a = mkOrder(customer, quantity)$$
$$\vee\; PhoneRinging(s) \wedge \neg\exists agt\; a = receiveOrder(agt)$$

This says that the phone is ringing in the situation resulting from action a being performed in situation s if and only if a is some customer making an order or if the phone was already ringing in situation s and a is not some agent receiving the order. Therefore, no other action has any effect on $PhoneRinging$. This approach yields a solution to the frame problem — a parsimonious representation for the effects of actions. Note that it relies on quantification over actions.[4]

Given a GDL domain specification, successor state axioms are generated automatically by the GDL compiler. The result is a theory of the following form:

- Axioms describing the initial situation, S_0.
- Action precondition axioms, one for each primitive action α, characterizing $Poss(\alpha, s)$.
- Successor state axioms, one for each fluent F, stating under what conditions $F(x, do(a, s))$ holds as function of what holds in situation s.
- Unique names axioms for the primitive actions.
- Some foundational, domain independent axioms [11, 18].

4.3 Semantics of the *ConGolog* Process Description Language

In [3], a semantics for the *ConGolog* process description language is developed within the situation calculus. This semantics, a kind of structural operational semantics [16], is based on the notion of *transitions*, i.e. "single steps" of computation. A step here is either a primitive action or testing whether a condition holds in the current situation. Two special predicates are introduced, *Final* and *Trans*, where $Final(\sigma, s)$ is intended to say that process σ may legally terminate in situation s, and where $Trans(\sigma, s, \sigma', s')$ is intended to say that process σ in situation s may legally execute one step, ending in situation s' with process σ' remaining.

---

[4] This discussion assumes that there are no state constraints; a treatment for these that is compatible with the above approach is presented in [11].

Final and *Trans* are characterized by a set of axioms, each depending on the structure of the first argument.[5] Let us only list a few of these axioms to illustrate the approach. For *Final*, we have:

- $Final(\mathbf{nil}, s) \equiv True$,
  i.e., if what remains to execute is the empty process we are done;
- $Final(\alpha, s) \equiv False$,
  i.e., if what remains to execute is a primitive action we are not done;
- $Final([\sigma_1; \sigma_2], s) \equiv Final(\sigma_1, s) \wedge Final(\sigma_2, s)$, i.e. a sequence can be considered done in a situation s if both components are done in s.

The axioms for *Trans* include:

- $Trans(\alpha, s, \delta, s') \equiv Poss(\alpha, s) \wedge \delta = \mathbf{nil} \wedge s' = do(\alpha, s)$,
  i.e., if we are in situation s and the process remaining is a primitive action α, we can do a transition to the situation $do(\alpha, s)$ with the empty process remaining provided that α is possible in s;
- $Trans([\sigma_1; \sigma_2], s, \delta, s') \equiv Final(\sigma_1, s) \wedge Trans(\sigma_2, s, \delta, s')$
  $\qquad \vee \exists \delta'.\delta = (\delta'; \sigma_2) \wedge Trans(\sigma_1, s, \delta', s')$,
  i.e. a sequence $[\sigma_1; \sigma_2]$ can do a transition by performing a transition from its first component σ_1 or by performing a transition from its second component σ_2 provided that the first component is already done.

With *Final* and *Trans* in place, one can complete the semantics by defining a predicate Do, where $Do(\sigma, s, s')$ means that process specification σ, when executed starting in situation s, has s' as a legal terminating situation. The definition of Do is:

$$Do(\sigma, s, s') \stackrel{\text{def}}{=} \exists \delta. Trans^*(\sigma, s, \delta, s') \wedge Final(\delta, s')$$

where $Trans^*$ is the transitive closure of *Trans*. In other words, $Do(\sigma, s, s')$ holds if and only if it is possible to repeatedly single-step the process σ, obtaining a process δ and a situation s' such that δ can legally terminate in s'.

When a domain contains exogenous actions, we are usually interested in executions of the process specification where instances of the exogenous actions occur. From the GDL action declarations, one can define using a predicate Exo, which actions can occur exogenously. For our domain, we would have:

$$Exo(a) \equiv \exists cust, q \; a = mkOrder(cust, q)$$
$$\vee \exists supp, q \; a = deliverSupplies(supp, q)$$

Then, we define a special process for exogenous actions: $\delta_{EXO} \stackrel{\text{def}}{=} (\pi a. Exo(a)?; a)^*$. Executing this program involves performing zero, one, or more nondeterministically chosen exogenous actions. Then we make the user-specified process δ run

---

[5] Note that these quantify over process specifications and so it is necessary to encode *ConGolog* process specifications as first-order terms; see [5] for the details. Here, we simply use process specifications within formulas as if they were already first-order terms.

concurrently with this, i.e. $\delta \parallel \delta_{EXO}$. In this way we allow exogenous actions whose preconditions are satisfied to asynchronously occur (outside the control of δ) during the execution of δ.

A more detailed description of the *ConGolog* process language and its formal semantics appear in [3, 4]. One limitation of the semantics is that it does not handle non-terminating processes.

4.4 Using the Semantics in Verification

Now that we have outlined the semantics of *ConGolog* let us show how it can be used in verification. We show that our mail-order business domain specification satisfies the property that no order is shipped before payment is processed (provided that this is true initially). Formally, we want to prove that:[6]

$$\forall s, s'.[\forall o.\ OrderShipped(o, s_0) \supset PaymentProcessed(o, S_0)]$$
$$\land\ Do(main \parallel \delta_{EXO}, S_0, s) \land s' \leq s \supset$$
$$[\forall o.\ OrderShipped(o, s') \supset PaymentProcessed(o, s')].$$

We prove this by contradiction. Suppose that there exists a situation s' that is during an execution of *main* $\parallel \delta_{EXO}$ such that $OrderShipped(o, s')$ and $\neg PaymentProcessed(o, s')$. We can also suppose that s' is the earliest such situation, since if this is not the case, we can always move to an earlier situation. Now $s' \neq S_0$ since we are given that no order has been shipped without payment being processed initially. So $s' = do(a, s'')$ for some a and s'' and

$$OrderShipped(o, s'') \supset PaymentProcessed(o, s''),$$

since s' is the earliest situation where this doesn't hold. As well, since $\neg PaymentProcessed(o, s')$, it follows that $\neg PaymentProcessed(o, s'')$ by the successor state axiom for *PaymentProcessed*, i.e.

$$PaymentProcessed(o, do(a, s)) \equiv$$
$$\exists agt\ a = processPayment(agt, o) \lor PaymentProcessed(o, s).$$

Therefore $\neg OrderShipped(o, s'')$. By the successor state axiom for *OrderShipped*, i.e.

$$OrderShipped(o, do(a, s)) \equiv$$
$$\exists agt\ a = shipOrder(agt, o) \lor OrderShipped(o, s)$$

the only action that can cause $OrderShipped(o, s')$ to become true is $shipOrder(agt, o)$, thus $s' = do(shipOrder(agt, o), s'')$.

Now using the complete semantics of the *ConGolog* process language, it can be shown that

$$\forall s, s'', agt, o.Do(main, S_0, s) \land do(shipOrder(agt, o), s'') \leq s \supset$$
$$PaymentProcessed(o, s'')$$

---

[6] $s \leq s'$ means that s' can be reached by performing some sequence of actions in s such that each action is possible when it occurs.

i.e. the process never performs $shipOrder(agt, o)$ in a situation when payment has not been processed on order o in the situation. Intuitively, this is because the only place where $shipOrder$ appears in the process specification is in the body of the second interrupt of $runWarehouse$ and $PaymentProcessed(o)$ is one of the conjuncts of the trigger condition of the interrupt. A contradiction follows. Notice that the proof does not require anything to be known about the initial situation other than the fact that the property wasn't already false there.

5 Conclusion

The *ConGolog* framework is an attempt to develop a middle ground between state-oriented and predicate-oriented models of dynamic domains. The paper has illustrated how *ConGolog* combines elements of both approaches to support the modeling of complex dynamic domains and analyze such models through simulation and verification. Our work on applying *ConGolog* to requirements analysis and process modeling is part of a larger project dealing with process reengineering and modeling the rationale for various design alternatives [21].

The closest rival to this work is the SCR (Software Cost Reduction) framework of formal specification [8], which allows both proofs of formal properties and simulation. Unlike *ConGolog*, the SCR framework is based on a vector representation for states and a collection of finite state machines for processes. In this respect, the *ConGolog* framework is more general and more readily applicable to business process and enterprise modeling.

The most pressing task for future research is to complete the development of the *ConGolog* verification tool so that it can support a designer in verifying properties of process specifications along the lines described in sections 3 and 4. Even though *ConGolog* has been used to model and analyze several example domains, we plan to experiment with the scalability of the *ConGolog* tools by trying them out on larger and more realistic examples. We are also investigating ways of combining the *ConGolog* framework with the design rationale modeling formalism described in [21].

References

[1] D. Bjorner and C.B. Jones. *The Vienna Development Method: The Metalanguage*, volume 61 of *LNCS*. Springer-Verlag, 1978.

[2] A. Borgida, J. Mylopoulos, and R. Reiter. ...and nothing else changes: The frame problem in procedural specifications. In *Proc. ICSE-93*, 1993.

[3] Giuseppe De Giacomo, Yves Lespérance, and Hector J. Levesque. Reasoning about concurrent execution, prioritized interrupts, and exogenous actions in the situation calculus. In *Proceedings of the Fifteenth International Joint Conference on Artificial Intelligence*, pages 1221–1226, Nagoya, Japan, August 1997.

[4] Giuseppe De Giacomo, Yves Lespérance, and Hector J. Levesque. ConGolog, a concurrent programming language based on the situation calculus: Language and implementation. Submitted, 1999.

[5] Giuseppe De Giacomo, Yves Lespérance, and Hector J. Levesque. ConGolog, a concurrent programming language based on the situation calculus: Foundations. Submitted, 1999.

[6] M. Gelfond and Lifschitz. Representing action and change by logic programs. *Journal of Logic Programming*, 17(301–327), 1993.

[7] D. Harel. Statecharts: A visual formalism for complex systems. *Science of Computer Programming*, 8, 1997.

[8] C. Heitmeyer, R. Jeffords, and B. Labaw. Automated consistency checking of requirements specifications. *ACM Transactions on Software Engineering and Methodology*, 5(5), July 1996.

[9] Todd Kelley and Yves Lespérance. The Golog Domain Language: an abstract language for specifying domain dynamics. In preparation, 1999.

[10] Hector J. Levesque, Raymond Reiter, Yves Lespérance, Fangzhen Lin, and Richard B. Scherl. GOLOG: A logic programming language for dynamic domains. *Journal of Logic Programming*, 31(59–84), 1997.

[11] Fangzhen Lin and Raymond Reiter. State constraints revisited. *Journal of Logic and Computation*, 4(5):655–678, 1994.

[12] Fangzhen Lin and Raymond Reiter. How to progress a database. *Artificial Intelligence*, 92:131–167, 1997.

[13] John McCarthy and Patrick Hayes. Some philosophical problems from the standpoint of artificial intelligence. In B. Meltzer and D. Michie, editors, *Machine Intelligence*, volume 4, pages 463–502. Edinburgh University Press, Edinburgh, UK, 1979.

[14] J.L. Peterson. *Petri Net Theory and the Modeling of Systems*. Prentice Hall, Englewood Cliffs, NJ, 1981.

[15] Dimitris Plexousakis. Simulation and analysis of business processes uning GOLOG. In *Proceedings of the Conference on Organizational Computing Systems*, Milpitas, CA, August 1995.

[16] G. Plotkin. A structural approach to operational semantics. Technical Report DAIMI-FN-19, Computer Science Dept., Aarhus University, Denmark, 1981.

[17] Raymond Reiter. The frame problem in the situation calculus: A simple solution (sometimes) and a completeness result for goal regression. In Vladimir Lifschitz, editor, *Artificial Intelligence and Mathematical Theory of Computation: Papers in Honor of John McCarthy*, pages 359–380. Academic Press, San Diego, CA, 1991.

[18] Raymond Reiter. Proving properties of states in the situation calculus. *Artificial Intelligence*, 64:337–351, 1993.

[19] Steven Shapiro, Yves Lespérance, and Hector J. Levesque. Specifying communicative multi-agent systems with ConGolog. In *Working Notes of the AAAI Fall 1997 Symposium on Communicative Action in Humans and Machines*, pages 75–82, Cambridge, MA, November 1997.

[20] J. M. Spivey. *The Z Notation: A Reference Manual*. Prentice Hall, 1989.

[21] Eric K.S. Yu, John Mylopoulos, and Yves Lespérance. AI models for business process reengineering. *IEEE Expert*, 11:16–23, August 1996.

Towards an Object Petri Nets Model for Specifying and Validating Distributed Information Systems

Nasreddine Aoumeur* and Gunter Saake

Institut für Technische und Betriebliche Informationssysteme
Otto-von-Guericke-Universität Magdeburg
Postfach 4120, D–39016 Magdeburg
Tel.: ++49-391-67-18659, Fax: ++49-391-67-12020
{aoumeur|Saake}@iti.cs.uni-magdeburg.de

Abstract. We present first results towards a tailored conceptual model for advanced distributed information systems regarded as open reactive and distributed systems with large databases and application programs. The proposed model, referred to as CO-Nets, is based on a complete integration of object oriented concepts with some constructions from semantical data modeling into an appropriate variant of algebraic Petri Nets named ECATNets. The CO-Nets behaviour is interpreted into rewriting logic. Particularly, it is shown how CO-Nets promote incremental construction of complex components, regarded as a hierarchy of classes, through simple and multiple inheritance (with redefinition, associated polymorphism and dynamics binding). Each component behaves with respect to an appropriate intra-component evolution pattern that supports intra- as well as inter-object concurrency. On the other hand, we present how such components may be interconnected, through their interfaces, with respect to an inter-component interaction pattern that enhances concurrency and preserves the encapsulated features of each component. Moreover, by interpreting the CO-Nets behaviour into rewriting logic, rapid-prototypes can be generated using rewrite techniques and current implementation of the MAUDE language particularly. The CO-Nets approach is presented through a simplified Staff management system case study.

1 Introduction and Motivation

Due to an ever-increasing in size and space of present-day organizations, both system designers and users of information systems —that are intended to represent and then computerize accurately (the most part of) such realities— are nowadays confronted by challenging problems. Indeed, while the size-increasing has resulted in more and more complex and multi-layered systems those components are loosely connected and behaving mostly in a true concurrent way,

---

* This work is supported by DAAD grant.

M. Jarke, A. Oberweis (Eds.): CAiSE'99, LNCS 1626, pp. 381–395, 1999.
© Springer-Verlag Berlin Heidelberg 1999

the space dimension is reflected by a high distribution of such systems over different (geographical) sites, where different forms of (synchronous/asynchronous) communication are often required.

With the aim to master such challenging dimensions that go beyond the traditional information systems specification models — including, data-oriented models in general [EM85] [HK87], process-oriented models (CCS [Mil89], Petri nets [Rei85]) or even 'sequential' object oriented (OO) models— recent research advocates particularly the *formal* integration of the *object paradigm* with *concurrency* as basic requirement for advanced conceptual modeling [FJLS96] [ECSD98].

The great efforts undertaken in the last decade, towards providing the (concurrent) OO paradigm with theoretical underpining foundation, have forwarded very promising OO formalisms. More particularly, OO foundations are based on the algebraic setting in the general sense including HSOA [GD93]; DTL (Distributed Temporal Logic) [ECSD98] and rewriting logic [Mes92]. OO formalisms based on (high level) Petri nets have also been proposed recently including: OPNet [Lak95], CLOWN [BdC93], CO-OPNets [Bib97].

However, we claim that much work remains ahead and there is up-to now no ideal approach that fulfills all the expected requirements. Indeed, besides a sound formalization of OO concepts and constructions, an appropriate approach for the distributed information systems should be, among others, appropriate for validation /verification purpose and more or less easy to be understand to non-experts users. Last but not least database aspects like views and queries are also important.

On the basis of these motivations, we present in this paper the first results of our investigation towards a suitable conceptual model, for specifying distributed information systems, that fulfills (as more as possible) the above requirements. The model, referred to as CO-Nets, is based on a complete and a sound integration of OO concepts and constructions into an appropriate variant of algebraic Petri nets [Rei91] named ECATNets [BMB93]. The semantics of the CO-Nets approach is expressed in rewriting logic [Mes92]. In some details, particular to the CO-Nets approach are the following features:

- A clean separation between *data* —specified algebraically[1] and used for describing object attributes (values and identifiers) and message parameters— and *objects* as indivisible and uniquely identified units of structure and behaviour.
- The modeling of simple and multiple inheritance, with possibility of methods overriding, is achieved in a straightforward way using subsorts and an appropriate 'splitting and recombination' axiom (inherent to the CO-Nets semantics) of the object state at a need. In the sequel, a hierarchy of classes will be referred to as a *component*.
- For capturing the notion of a class, rather as a module, we distinguish between local, and hence hidden from the outside features (as a part of the object state as well as some messages) and external, observed and possibly

---
[1] Using ordered sorted algebra(OSA).

modifiable from the outside features. The local behaviour of each module is ensured by an appropriate intra-component evolution pattern that enhance intra- as well as inter-object concurrency, while the interaction between different (external features of) modules follows an inter-component communication pattern that enhance concurrency and preserve the encapsulated features of each module.

- The CO-Nets semantics is interpreted in rewriting logic that is a *true-concurrent* operational semantics allowing particularly rapid-prototyping using concurrent rewriting techniques in general and current implementation of the MAUDE language specifically.

The rest of this paper is organized as follows: In the second section we informally introduce the simplified staff management case study. In the third section, using this case study and without entering into technical details (that can be found in [Aou99]), we show how the CO-Nets approach allows for specifying (independent) templates and classes. The fourth section deals with the semantics aspects of the CO-Nets approach. In the next section, we introduce how more advanced abstraction mechanisms, with mainly inheritance and interaction, are modeled in the CO-Nets. Some concluding remarks are given in the last section.

For the rest of the paper we assume the reader is familiar with some basic ideas of algebraic Petri nets and rewriting techniques. Good references for these topics are [EM85, Rei91] for the algebraic setting and algebraic Petri nets, and [DJ90, Mes92] for rewriting techniques. We use for algebraic descriptions an OBJ notation [GWM+92]. Moreover, due to space limitation, a deep introduction to the ECATNets model can be found in [Aou99]

2   The Staff Management Case Study

This section presents a simplified form of a general case study dealing with a staff management more tailored to the (Algerian) universities staff systems [Aou89]. The staff management we consider concerns the employees-career management and the employee payment system; however, due to space limitation we present only the first system. Depending on their different functionalities, we find three classes of employees: The lecturer (and the researchers), the administrators and the technical and security staff. For sake of simplicity, we abstract away from this difference, and only deal with their common characteristics.

According to the 'states' through which can pass each employee, the staff management system can be informally described as follows:

- Each person, verifying some conditions like the (minimal) age, the required degree (or necessary formation), etc, can apply for a job at the university. The minimal information that should be provided in this case are: the name, the surname, the birth-day, the diploma, the address, his/her familiar situation and so forth. If (s)he is accepted as a new employee (i.e. if there is sufficiently budget items corresponding to the inquired function and the administrative committee estimate this recruitment positively), (s)he becomes an employee (as probationer) at the university. In this case some further information is systematically added like the function, the reference number (for uniquely identifying each employee), the department name to which (s)he is appointed and the recruitment date.

- After some period that go from nine months to two years and only if the employee have had in this (probation) period no caution, (s)he is appointed as a titular; in which case, further informations will be added like the number of rungs (initialized by 1), (administrative) responsabilities if any, etc. Also, we note that each titular employee may progress (with one unit) in the rung after a period that go from one to three years.
- Each employee, on probation or titular, can go on a leave; where, two kinds of leaves are possible: regular leaves, that are granted to all employees, with a fixed, same period and date (generally, at the beginning of July for 45 days). The exceptional leave such as sick leave necessitates in addition to the period and the date, the matter of such leave.
- After some professional misconducts, the employee may be subject to disciplinary measures that go from salary diminution or a warning to a complete dismissal.
- Each employee may leave temporary or completely the university when necessary. Partial leaves are for example scientific leave to another university (for researcher) or improvement leave (for the administrators and lecturers). The complete leaves, are for example resignation, pensioned off, etc.

3   CO-Net: Template and Class Specification

This section deals with the modelling of the basic concepts of the object oriented paradigm, namely objects, templates and classes. We first present the structure or what is commonly called the 'object' signature templates [EGS92], then we describe how 'specification' templates and classes are specified.

3.1   Template Signature Specification

The template signature defines the structure of the object states and the form of operations that have to be accepted by such states. Basically, in the CO-Nets approach, we follow the general object signature proposed for MAUDE [Mes93]. That is to say, object states as regarded as terms —precisely as a tuple— and messages as operations sent or received by objects. However, apart from these general conceptual similarities, and in order to be more close to the aforementioned information system requirements, the OO signature that we propose can be informally described as follows:

- The object states are terms of the form $\langle Id|atr_1 : val_1, ..., atr_k : val_k, at\_bs_1 : val'_1, ..., at\_bs_{k'} : val'_s \rangle$; where Id is an observed object identity taking its values from an appropriate abstract data type OId; $atr_1, .., atr_k$ are the local, hidden from the outside, attribute identifiers having as current values respectively $val_1, .., val_k$. The observed part of an object state is identified by $at\_bs_1, ..., at\_bs_s$ and their associated values are $val'_1, ..val'_s$. Also, we assume that all the attribute identifiers (local or observed) range their values over a suitable sort denoted AId, and their associated values are ranged over the sort $Value$ with $OId < Value$ (i.e. OId as subsort of $Value$) in order to allow object valued attributes.

- In contrast to the indivisible object state proposed in MAUDE that avoid any form of intra-object concurrency, we introduce a powerful axiom, called 'splitting / recombination' axiom permitting to split (resp. recombine) the object state out of necessity. As will be more detailed later, this axiom, that can be described as follows: $\langle Id|attrs_1{}^2, attrs_2\rangle = \langle Id|attrs_1\rangle \oplus \langle Id|attrs_2\rangle$, allows us in particular, first, to exhibit intra-object concurrency[3]. Second, it provides a meaning to our notion of observed attributes by allowing separation between intra- and inter-component evolution (see later). Third, it allows us to simplify drastically the conceptualization of the inheritance.
- In addition of conceiving messages as terms —that consists of message's name, the identifiers of the objects the message is addressed to, and, possibly, parameters— we make a clear distinction between internal, local messages and the external as imported or exported messages. Local messages allow for evolving the object states of a given class, while the external ones allow for communicating different classes using exclusively their observed attributes.

All for all, following these informal description and some ideas from [Mes93], the formal description of the object states as well as the classes structures, using an OBJ [GWM+92] notation, takes the form presented in figure 1:

Remark 1. The local messages to a given class Cl have to include at least the two usual messages: messages for creating a new object state and messages for the deletion of an existing object; we denote them respectively by Ad_{Cl} and Dl_{Cl}.

Example 1. As informally described, each employee (on probation) have to be characterized, at least, by his name (shortly, Nm), surname(Sn), birthday(Bd), address(Ad), diploma(Dp), function(Fc) and recruitment date(Dr). Hence, w.r.t. our state structure, the employee structure takes the form $\langle Id|Nm : N_i, Sn : S_i, Bd : B_i, Ad : Ai, Dp : Dp_i, Fc : F_i, Dr : Dr_i\rangle$; where $N_i, S_i, B_i, A_i, Dp_i, Dr_i$ are the actual values of the attributes and Id is a logical identity representing the employee reference number. Besides this state structure, the main operations (regarded as messages) that we consider are: the departure on leave, $Lv(Id, Dt, Pd, Mt)$, where Id is the identity of the concerned employee, Dt the date, Pd is the period and Mt is the matter. The sanction operation, $Sc(Id, Mt,$

---

[2] $attr_i$ stands for a simplified form of $atr_{i1} : val_{i1}, ..., atr_{ik} : val_{ir}$.

[3] In the sense that two messages sent to the same object and acting on different attributes can be performed (i.e. rewritten) parallely by splitting the two parts using this axiom.

Dg), with Mt as the matter and Dg is the kind of the sanction[4]. Also, we give the possibility for an employee to change his/her address, $Chg(Id, Nad)$, with Nad as a new address. With respect to the operation of leave, first we associate another message for controlling the respective (date of) return to the work; second we introduce a new attribute denoted as Lv that indicates if an employee is on leave or not. Similarly, we add a new attribute Sc that keeps the sanction information.

obj Object-State is
  sort AId .
  subsort OId < Value .
  subsort Attribute < Attributes .
  subsort Id-Attributes < Object .
  subsort Local-attributes External-attributes < Id-Attributes .
  protecting Value OId AId .
  op _:_ : AId Value $\rightarrow$ Attribute .
  op _,_ : Attribute Attributes $\rightarrow$ Attributes [assoc. commu. Id:nil] .
  op $\langle$_|_$\rangle$: OId Attributes $\rightarrow$ Id-Attributes .
  op _$\oplus$_ : Id-Attributes Id-Attributes $\rightarrow$ Id-Attributes
   [assoc. commu. Id:nil] .
  vars Attr: Attribute ; Attrs$_1$, Attrs$_2$: Attributes ; I:OId .
  eq1 $\langle I | attrs_1 \rangle \oplus \langle I | attrs_2 \rangle = \langle I | attrs_1, attrs_2 \rangle$.
  eq2 $\langle I | nil \rangle = I$ **endo.**

obj Class-Structure is
  protecting Object-state, s-atr$_1$,...,s-atr$_n$, s-arg$_{11,1}$,..., s-arg$_{l1,l1}$,
       ...,s-arg$_{i1,1}$,...,s-arg$_{i1,i1}$ ...
  subsort Id.obj < OId .
  subsort Mes$_{l1}$, Mes$_{l2}$,...,Mes$_{ll}$ < Local_Messages .
  subsort Mes$_{e1}$, Mes$_{e2}$,...,Mes$_{ee}$ < Exported_Messages .
  subsort Mes$_{i1}$, Mes$_{i2}$,...,Mes$_{ii}$ < Imported_Messages .
  sort Id.obj, Mes$_{l1}$, . . . ,Mes$_{ip}$
  (* local attributes *)
   op $\langle$_$| atr_1 :$ _,$...$, $atr_k :$ _$\rangle$: Id.obj s-atr$_1$ ...s-atr$_k$
    $\rightarrow$ Local-Attributes.
  (* observed attributes *)
   op $\langle$_$| atrbs_1 :$, $...$, $atrbs_{k'} :$ _$\rangle$: Id.obj s-atbs$_1$ ...s-atbs$_{k'}$
    $\rightarrow$ External-Attributes.
  (* local messages *)
   op ms$_{l1}$: s-arg$_{l1,1}$ ...s-arg$_{l1,l1}$ $\rightarrow$ Mes$_{l1}$ . ...
  (* export messages *)
   op ms$_{e1}$: s-arg$_{e1,1}$ ...s-arg$_{e1,e1}$ $\rightarrow$ Mes$_{e1}$ . ...
  (* import messages *)
   op ms$_{i1}$: s-arg$_{i1,1}$ ...s-arg$_{i1,i1}$ $\rightarrow$ Mes$_{ip}$ . ...
endo.

Fig. 1. The template signature specified in an OBJ notation

---

[4] With the convention that $Dg = 1$ corresponds to a warning and $Dg = 2$ to a complete dismissal.

Respecting the general template schema described above, the employee template
may be described as follows:

```
obj employee is
 extending Class-structure .
  protecting nat    string    date .
  sorts Emp    LV SC    CHG    PYM RET .
 subsort Local-Emp Observed-Emp < Emp .
 subsort Id.emp < OId .
 (* Hidden attributes *)
 op 〈_|Dr : _, Ad : _, Dp : _, Lv : _, Sc : _〉 : Id.emp date
    string string bool nat→Local-Emp.
 (* Observed attributes (by the payment system) *)
 op 〈_|Nm : _, Sn : _, Bd : _, Fc : _〉 :
    Id.emp  string string  date  string → Observed-Emp.
 (* Local messages *)
 op Lv : Id.emp    date    nat    string → LV .
 op Sc : Id.emp    string    nat → SC .
 op Chg : Id.emp    string → SC .
 op Ret : Id.emp    date → RET .
 (* Exported messages *)
 op Py : Id.emp    string    nat    → PYM .
endo.
```

3.2 Template and Class Specification

On the basis of the template signature, we define the notion of *template specification* as a CO-Net and the notion of class as a marked CO-Net. Informally the
associated CO-Net structure, with a given template signature, can be described
as follows:

- The places of the CO-Net are precisely defined by associating with each
  message generator one place that we called 'message' place. Henceforth, each
  message place have to contain message instances, of a specific form, sent to
  the objects (and not yet performed). In addition to these message places,
  we associate with each object sort one 'object' place that has to contain the
  current object states of this class.
- The CO-Net transitions reflect the effect of messages on the object states to
  which they are addressed. Also, we make distinction between local transitions
  that reflect the object states evolution and the external ones modeling the
  interaction between different classes. The requirements to be fulfilled for
  each transition form are given in the subsection below. The input arcs are
  annotated by the input conditions, while the output arcs are labelled by the
  created tokens. Both inscriptions are defined as multisets of terms respecting
  the type of their input and/ot output places—the associated union operation
  is denoted by ⊕.
- Conditions may be associated with transitions. They involve attribute and/or
  message parameters variables.

Example 2. For the staff management system that we consider here we have just the employee class. Following the above class definition, the CO-Net describing this class is composed of an object place denoted by *Emp* containing the employee state and of five message places denoted by *Leav*, *Punish* and *Chg*, *return* and *del* corresponding respectively to the (go on)leave, (being) punished, change of the address, the return from a leave and possibly the fire. The effect of each message is described by a transition that takes into account just the relevant attributes. For example, the message *Chg(Id, Nad)* that allows to change the address of an employee identified by *Id* enters into contact with just the address component of this employee state. This is possible only due to the 'splitting / recombination' axiom. Following this, the CO-Net representing the employee class is depicted in figure 2. The symbol ϕ denotes $\emptyset$ as in the ECATNets model [BMB93], and it means that the invoked tokens should not to be deleted.

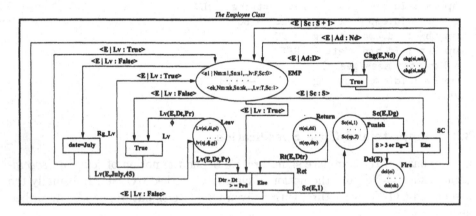

Fig. 2. The Employee Class Modeled as CO-ATNet

4   CO-Nets: Semantical Aspects

After highlighting how CO-Nets templates, as description of classes, are constructed, we focus herein on the behavioural aspects of such classes. That is, how to construct a *coherent* object society as a community of object states and message instances, and how such a society evolves only into a *permissible* society. By coherence it is mainly meant the respect of the system structure, the uniqueness of object identities and the non violation of the encapsulation property.

Objects Creation and Deletion. For ensuring the uniqueness of objects identities in a given class denoted by *Cl*, we propose the following conceptualization:

1. Add to the associated (marked) CO-Net (modeling a class) a new place of sort *Id.obj* and denoted by *Id.Cl* containing *actual objects identifiers* of object states in the place *Cl*.

2. Objects creation is made through the net depicted in the left hand side of figure 3. The notation ~, borrowed from the ECATNets model, captures exactly the intended behaviour (i.e. the identifier Id should not already be in the place $Id.Cl$). After firing this transition, there is an addition of this new identifier to the place $Id.Cl$ and a creation of a new object, $\langle Id|atr_1 : in_1, ..., atr_k : in_k\rangle$, with $in_1, ..., in_k$ as optional initial attributes values.

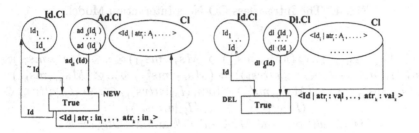

Fig. 3. Objects Creation and Deletion Using OB-ECATNets

Evolution of Object States in Classes. For the evolution of object states in a given class, we propose a general pattern that have to be respected in order to ensure the encapsulation property—in the sense that no object states or messages of other classes participate in this communication — as well as the preservation of the object identity uniqueness. Following such guidelines and in order to exhibit a maximal concurrency, this evolution schema is depicted in Figure 4, and it can be intuitively explained as follows: The contact of the just relevant parts of some object states of a given Cl, —namely $\langle I_1|attrs_1\rangle^5$;..; $\langle I_k|attrs_k\rangle$— with some messages $ms_{i1}, .., ms_{ip}, ms_{j1}, .., ms_{jq}$—declared as *local or imported* in this class— and under some conditions on the invoked attributes and message parameters results in the following effects:

- The messages $ms_{i1}, .., ms_{ip}, ms_{j1}, .., ms_{iq}$ vanish;
- The state change of some (parts of) object states participating in the communication, namely $I_{s1}, .., I_{st}$. Such change is symbolized by $attrs'_{s1}, .., attrs'_{st}$ instead of $attrs_{s1}, .., attrs_{st}$.
- Deletion of the some objects by explicitly sending delete messages for such objects.
- New messages are sent to objects of Cl , namely $ms'_{h1}, .., ms'_{hr}, ms'_{j1}, .., ms'_{jq}$.

Rewriting Rules Gouverning the CO-Nets Behaviour In the same spirit of the ECATNets behaviour, each CO-Net transition is captured by an appropriate rewriting rule interpreted into rewrite logic. Following the communication pattern in figure 6, the general form of rewrite rules associated with this intra-component interaction model, takes the following form:

---

[5] $attrs_i$ is simplified notation of $atr_{i1} : val_{i1}, .., atr_{ik} : val_{ik}$.

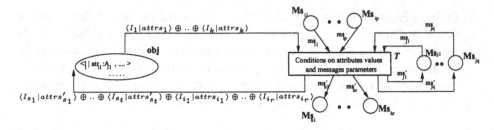

Fig. 4. The Intra-Class CO-Nets Interaction Model.

$$T : (Ms_{i1}, ms_{i1}) \otimes .. \otimes (Ms_{ip}, ms_{ip}) \otimes (Ms_{j1}, ms_{j1}) \otimes .. \otimes (Ms_{jq}, ms_{jq}) \otimes$$
$$(obj, \langle I_1|attrs_1 \rangle \oplus .. \oplus \langle I_k|attrs_k \rangle) \Rightarrow (Ms_{h1}, ms'_{h1}) \otimes ... \otimes (Ms'_{hr}, ms'_{hr}) \otimes$$
$$(Ms_{j1}, ms'_{j1}) \otimes .. \otimes (Ms'_{jq}, ms'_{jq}) \otimes (obj, \langle I_{s1}|attrs'_{s1} \rangle \oplus .. \oplus \langle I_{st}|attrs'_{st} \oplus$$
$$\langle I_{i1}|attrs_{i1} \rangle \oplus .. \oplus \langle I_{ir}|attrs_{ir} \rangle)$$
$$if\ Conditions\ and\ M(Ad_{Cl}) = \emptyset\ and\ M(Dl_{Cl}) = \emptyset$$

Remark 2. The operator $\otimes$ is defined as a multiset union and allows for relating different places identifiers with their actual marking. Moreover, we assume that $\otimes$ is distributive over $\oplus$ i.e. $(p, mt_1 \oplus mt_2) = (p, mt_1) \otimes (p, mt_2)$ with mt_1, mt_2 multiset of terms over $\oplus$ and p a place identifier. The condition $M(Ad_{Cl}) = \emptyset$ and $M(Dl_{Cl}) = \emptyset$, in this rule, means that the creation and the deletion of objects have to performed at first: In other words, before performing this rewrite rules the marking of the Ad_{Cl} as well of the Dl_{Cl} places have to be empty. Finally, noting that the selection of just the *invoked parts* of object states, in this evolution pattern, is possible only due to the splitting /recombination axiom—that have to be performed in front and in accordance with each invoked state evolution.

Example 3. By applying this general form of rule, it is not difficult to generate the rules corresponding to the employee class (depicted in figure 2).

LEAVE [6]$:(Emp, \langle E|Lv : False \rangle) \otimes (Leav, lv(E, Dt, Pr))$
$\Rightarrow (Emp, \langle E|Lv : True \rangle) \otimes (Leav, lv(E, Dt, Pr))$[7]

RETURN $:(Emp, \langle E|Lv : True \rangle) \otimes (Leav, lv(E, Dt, Pr)) \otimes (Return, rt(E, Drt)) \Rightarrow$
$\quad if\ (Dtr - Dt \le Pr)\ then\ (Emp, \langle E|Lv : False \rangle)$
$else \quad (Emp, \langle E|Lv : False \rangle) \otimes (Punish, Pnsh(E, 1)$[8]$)$

PUNISH $:(Emp, \langle E|Sc : S \rangle) \otimes (Punish, pnsh(E, Dg))$
$\quad \Rightarrow if(S + 1 > 3\ or\ Dg = 2)$
$\quad\quad then\ (DEL, del(E))\ else\ (Emp, \langle E|Sc : S + 1 \rangle)$

---

[6] The label corresponds to the transition identifier.
[7] The leave message has not to be deleted in order to use it for controling the corresponding return.
[8] When the employee does not respect the Period of leave (s)he is punished.

CHG $:(Emp, \langle E|Ad : D\rangle) \otimes (Chg, chg(E, Nd)) \Rightarrow (Emp, \langle E|Ad : Nd\rangle)$

RG_LEAV $: (Emp, \langle E|Lv : False\rangle)$
$$\Rightarrow (Emp, \langle E|Lv : True\rangle) \otimes (Leav, lv(E, July, 45)) \; if \; Date = July$$

Remark 3. In this application we have the possibility for exhibiting intra-object concurrency. This is the case for the messages Lv, Sc and Chg that can be performed at the same time, when they are sent to the *same employee*.

5   CO-Nets: More Advanced Constructions

So far, we have presented only how the CO-Nets approach allows for conceiving independent classes. In what follows, we give how more complex systems can be constructed using advanced abstraction mechanisms, especially inheritance and interaction between classes. However, due to the space limitation only the simle inheritance case and the interaction pattern (without an illustrative example) would presented.

5.1   Simple Inheritance

Giving a (super) class Cl modeled as a CO-Net, for constructing a subclass that inherits the structure as well as the behaviour of the superclass Cl and exhibits new behaviour involving additional attributes, we propose the following straightforward conceptualization.

- Define the structure of the new subclass by introducing the new attributes and messages. Structurally, the new attributes identifiers with their value sorts and the message generators are described using the *extending* primitive in the OBJ notation.
- As *object place* for the subclass we use the *same* object place of the superclass; which means that such place should now contains the object states of the superclass as well as the object states of the subclass. This is semantically sound because the sort of this object place is a supersort for objects including more attributes.
- As previously described, the proper behaviour of the subclass is constructed by associating with each new message a corresponding place and constructing its behaviour (i.e. transitions) with respect to the communication model of figure 4 under the condition that at least one of the additional attributes has to be involved in such transitions.

Remark 4. Such conceptualization is only possible because of the splitting / recombination operation. Indeed this axiom permits to consider an object state of a subclass, denoted for instance as $\langle Id|attrs, attrs'\rangle$ with $attrs'$ the additional attributes (i.e. those proper to the subclass), to be also an object state of the superclass (i.e. $\langle Id|attrs\rangle$). Obviously, this allows a systematic inheritance of the structure as well as the behaviour. The dynamic binding with polymorphism is systematically taken in this modeling. Indeed, when a message is sent to a hierarchy of classes we can know only after the firing of the associated transition to which class in the hierarchy the concerned object belong.

Example 4. As informally described, the titular employees have to be modeled as a subclass of the already modeled (probationer) employee class. So, in addition of being an employee (who can go on leave, etc), a titular employee can receive an increasing of his/her rung and can have some administrative responsibilities. More precisely, following the aforementioned step, we present hereafter the structure as well as the associated CO-Net modeling both classes.

```
obj titular is
 extending employee-with-recruitment .
 sort titular, ADV, ADM, TIT, FRM .
  op ⟨_|Rg : _, Adm : _⟩ : Id.emp  nat   string → Local-titular
 (* Local messages *)
  op Tit : Id.emp → TIT.
  op Adv : Id.emp → ADV .
  op Frm : Id.emp → FRM.
endo.
```

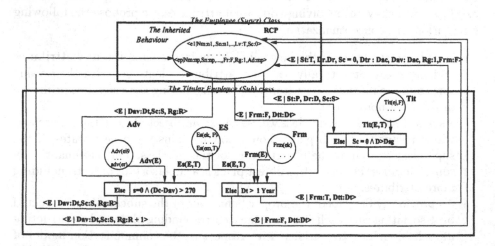

Fig. 5. The Titular Employees as a Subclass of the employee Class

5.2   Interaction between Classes

For interacting independent components, first, we should take into consideration the fact that the internal evolution of each component is ensured by the intra-component evolution pattern specified in figure 4. Second, we should ensure the encapsulation property, that is to say, the internal part of each object state as well as the local messages have to be hidden from the outside; thus only those *explicitly* declared as observed attributes and external messages have to participate in such inter-component communication.

More precisely, as depicted in figure 6 this inter-component interaction may be made explicit as follows: The contact of some external parts of some objects states namely $\langle I_1|attrs\_ob_1\rangle..\langle I_k|attrs\_ob_k\rangle$, that may belong to different classes namely $C_1, ..., C_m$, with some external messages $ms_{i1}, .., ms_{ip}, ms_{j1}, .., ms_{jq}$ defined in these classes and under some conditions on attributes values and parameters messages results in the following:

- The messages $ms_{i1}, .., ms_{ip}, ms_{j1}, .., ms_{iq}$ vanish;
- The state change of some (external parts of) object states participating in the communication, namely $I_{s1}, .., I_{st}$. Change is symbolized by $attrs'_{s1}, .., attrs'_{st}$ instead of $attrs_{s1}, .., attrs_{st}$. The other objects components remain unchanged (i.e. there is no deletion of parts of objects states).
- New external messages (that may involve deletion/creation ones) are sent to objects of different classes, namely $ms'_{h1}, .., ms'_{hr}, ms'_{j1}, .., ms'_{jq}$.

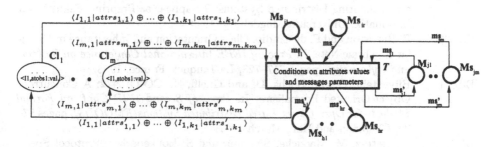

Fig. 6. The Interaction General Model Between classes

6 Conclusion

We proposed an object Petri nets based conceptual model for specifying and validating distributed information systems. The model called CO-Nets is a sound and complete combination of OO concepts and constructions in the ECATNets framework: An algebraic Petri net model mainly characterized by its capability of distinguishing between enabling conditions and destroyed tokens. The semantics of the CO-nets is expressed in rewriting logic allowing us to derive rapid-prototypes using concurrent rewriting in general and the MAUDE language more particularly. Some key features of the CO-Nets approach for specifying complex and distributed information systems are: First, the straightforward modeling of simple and multiple inheritance with the possibility of overriding. Second, the characterization of two communication patterns: an intra-component model for evolving object states in a hierarchy of classes with the possibility of exhibiting intra-object as well as inter-object concurrency and an inter-component communication model for interacting different components that promotes concurrency and preserve the encapsulated features of each components.

The different aspects of the CO-Nets approach have been explained through a simplified but realistic case study dealing with typical staff management system. This case shows, among other, that the CO-Nets conceptual model, with its different abstractions mechanisms, is well suited for dealing with complex distributed information systems applications.

Our future work is to confirm the appropriateness of the CO-Nets for specifying complex distributed and cooperative information systems by leading more complex case studies. Also, we plan for formally integrating property-oriented verification models following mainly the work in [Lec96].

References

[Aou89]   N. Aoumeur. Réalisation d'un Systeme de Gestion du Personnel de l'Université. Memoire d'Ingenieur, Institut d'Informatique, Université D'Oran, 1989.

[Aou99]   N. Aoumeur. Towards an Object Petri Net Based Framework for Modelling and Validating Distributed Systems. To appear as Preprint, Fakultät für Informatik, Universität Magdeburg, 1999.

[BdC93]   E. Battiston and F. de Cindio. Class Orientation and Inheritance in Modular Algebraic Nets. In *Proc. of IEEE International Conference on Systems and Cybernetics*, pages 717–723, Le Touquet, France, 1993.

[Bib97]   Biberstein, O. and Buchs, D. and Guelfi, N. CO-OPN/2: A Concurrent Object-Oriented Formalism. In *Proc. of Second IFIP Conf. on Formal Methods for Open Object-Based Distributed Systems(FMOODS)*, pages 57–72. Chapman and Hall, March 1997.

[BMB93]   M. Bettaz, M. Maouche, Soualmi, and S. Boukebeche. Protocol Specification using ECATNets. *Réseaux et Informatique Répartie*, 3(1):7–35, 1993.

[DJ90]   J. Dershowitz and J.-P. Jouannaud. Rewrite Systems. *Handbook of Theoretical Computer Science*, 935(6):243–320, 1990.

[ECSD98]   H.-D. Ehrich, C. Caleiro, A. Sernadas, and G. Denker. Logics for Specifying Concurrent Information Systems. In J. Chomicki and G. Saake, editors, *Logics for Databases and Information Systems*, chapter 6, pages 167–198. Kluwer Academic Publishers, Boston, 1998.

[EGS92]   H.D. Ehrich, M Gogolla, and A. Sernadas. Objects and Their Specification. In M. Bidoit and C. Choppy, editors, *Proc. of 8th Workshop on Abstract Data*, volume 655 of *Lecture Notes in Computer Science*, pages 40–66. Springer-Verlag, 1992.

[EM85]   H. Ehrig and B. Mahr. Fundamentals of algebraic specifications 1 : Equation and initial semantics. *EATCS Monographs on Theoretical Computer Science*, 21, 1985.

[FJLS96]   B. Freitag, Cliff B. Jones, C. Lengauer, and H. Schek, editors. *Object Orientation with Parallelism and Persistence*. Kluwer Academic Publishers, 1996.

[GD93]   J.A. Goguen and R. Diaconescu. Towards an Algebraic Semantics for the
           Object Paradigm. In *Proc. of 10th Workshop on Abstract Data types*,
           1993.

[GWM+92]   J.A. Goguen, T. Winkler, J. Meseguer, K. Futatsugi, and J.P. Jouannaud.
           Introducing OBJ. Technical Report SRI-CSL-92-03, Computer Science
           Laboratory, SRI International, 1992.

[HK87]   R. Hull and R. King. Semantic Database Modelling : Survey, Applications,
           and Research Issues. *ACM Computing Surveys*, 19(3):201–260, 1987.

[Lak95]   Lakos, C. From Coloured Petri Nets to Object Petri nets. In *Proc. of
           16th Application and Theory of Petri Nets*, volume 935 of *Lecture Notes
           in Computer Science*, pages 278–287. Springer-Verlag, 1995.

[Lec96]   U. Lechner. Object Oriented Specification of Distributed Systems in the
           μ-Calculus and Maude. In J. Meseguer, editor, *Proc. of the First Inter.
           Workshop on Rewriting Logic*, volume 4. Electronic Notes in Theoretical
           Computer Science, 1996.

[Mes92]   J. Meseguer. Conditional rewriting logic as a unified model for concur-
           rency. volume 96 of *Theoretical Computer Science*, pages 73–155, Noord-
           wijkerhout, Netherlands, 1992.

[Mes93]   Meseguer, J. A Logical Theory of Concurrent Objects and its Realization
           in the Maude Language. *Research Directions in Object-Based Concur-
           rency*, pages 314–390, 1993.

[Mil89]   R. Milner, editor. *Communication and Concurrency*. Prentice Hall, 1989.

[Rei85]   W. Reisig. *Petri Nets : An Introduction*. Springer-Verlag, 1985.

[Rei91]   W. Reisig. Petri Nets and Abstract Data Types. *Theoretical Computer
           Science*, 80:1–30, 1991.

Relationship Reification: A Temporal View

Antoni Olivé

Universitat Politècnica de Catalunya
Dept. Llenguatges i Sistemes Informàtics
Jordi Girona 1-3 E08034 Barcelona (Catalonia)
olive@lsi.upc.es

Abstract. Relationship reification is a well-known schema transformation in conceptual modeling of information systems. Traditionally, reification has been studied only for single state conceptual models. We show that these conceptual models and reification are too limited to cope effectively with some modeling situations. On the other hand, very little work has been done on reification in temporal models. In this paper we generalize previous work on reification, and propose three temporal reification kinds. We define the characteristics of the entity types, and of their intrinsic relationship types, produced by each reification kind. The result of our work may be applicable to any temporal conceptual model. We also show, by means of an example, the practical interest of our proposal.

1. Introduction

Relationship reification is a well-known schema transformation in conceptual modeling of information systems. Reification applies to an n-ary ($n \geq 2$) relationship type R and produces a new entity type E, and a set of n relationship types R_i, ($i = 1,...,n$), which connect instances of E with the n participating entities in the corresponding instances of R.

Many conceptual models deal explicitly with reification, and usually their conceptual modeling languages provide specific constructs for showing reification. Among them, we may mention [5,8,10,13,18,20,22]. The name given to reification varies among conceptual models and languages. Some focus on the transformation and call it relationship-to-entity or nominalisation. Others focus on the reified relationship and call it objectified relationship. Finally, others prefer to focus on the result and call it associative entity, association type, association class or relational object type.

The graphical representation of reification also differs among the conceptual languages. For the purposes of this paper we will adopt the representation shown in Figure 1, where a ternary relationship type *Supplies* is reified into entity type *Supply*. Using this representation, the three binary relationship types connecting *Supply* with *Supplier*, *Project* and *Part* are implicit, and not shown in the conceptual schema.

Reification is an information-preserving transformation, in the sense that it does not change the information content of the schema [1,14]. However, reification is necessary when relationships may participate in other relationships, because most

M. Jarke, A. Oberweis (Eds.): CAiSE'99, LNCS 1626, pp. 396-410, 1999.

conceptual models require relationship participants to be entities. On the other hand, reification normalizes any relationship type into a particular form of binary relationship type, which may be very useful for schema analysis and information systems design.

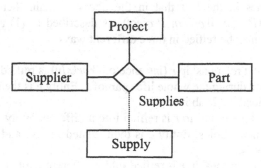

Fig. 1. Graphical representation of reification

Traditionally, reification has been studied only for single state conceptual models, that is, models whose schemes describe the structure and properties of a domain (or information base or database) at a single point of time [3,11]. In this context, application of reification, that we call *static reification*, means that whenever a new relationship is born in the information base, it is reified into an entity at that moment, and it remains in the information base until its corresponding relationship ceases to exist. In the example of Figure 1, there would be an instance of *Supply* for each instance of *Supplies*. [14,15] provide a detailed description of the static reification.

Single state conceptual models and static reification are, of course, very useful in many modeling situations. However, they have their limits, and they are unable to cope effectively with some common modeling situations, where temporal (or multiple states) models and other kinds of reification are needed. To motivate these models and reification kinds, consider a simple domain example, which will be used throughout the paper:

(1) Persons work in projects. A person may work in a project during several non-consecutive temporal intervals. We will assume as base time unit a day. A person may work in any number of projects on the same day. The information system must have available the complete history of projects (which persons have worked in which projects, when, etc.).

(2) A person performs always the same role (project leader, programmer, etc.), and has always the same manager, when he works in a particular project. Both role and manager are independent of when the person works in the project. The role and the manager may be different in other projects the person works in.

(3) During a temporal interval in which a person works in a project, he is working in a task and has a deadline. The task and the deadline are the same during the whole interval. If a person works in a project during two or more temporal intervals, the task and the deadline may be different in each one.

(4) For each day in which a person works in a project, the number of hours worked and the deliverables produced (if any) must be recorded.

Modeling this domain with a single state conceptual model, and applying the static reification, results in a conceptual schema that has several relationship types, and several complex integrity constraints to ensure the integrity of the information base. This affects negatively the quality of the schema.

The problem lies in the fact that in the above domain there is an underlying relationship type (*Person WorksIn Project*), as described in (1) above, whose time-varying instances must be reified in three different ways:

(a) Per life span: a relationship *r* (instance of *WorksIn*) is reified into a single entity *e*, which is the same during the whole life span of *r*. Entity *e* is then related to role and manager, as described in (2) above.

(b) Per interval: a relationship *r* is reified into a different entity *e* for each temporal interval during which *r* holds. Entity *e* is then related to task and date (deadline), as described in (3) above.

(c) Per instant: a relationship *r* is reified into a different entity *e* for each time point in which *r* holds. Entity *e* is then related to integer (number of hours worked) and deliverable, as described in (4) above.

The use of a temporal conceptual model, and the application of the above three temporal reifications would produce a simpler and clearer conceptual schema, as we will show in the rest of this paper.

We note that the problems encountered with the use of single state conceptual models, and the application of static reification, in the above domain, are not due only to the fact that the information system must keep historical information. Exactly the same problems would appear if the conceptual schema had to define the integrity constraints described in (2), (3) and (4) above.

To our knowledge, ERT is the only temporal conceptual model that deals explicitly with reification and provides a language construct for it [18,19]. In ERT, relationships may be time stamped to record their validity period, and their reification produces entities that have the same time stamps. Only one kind of reification is defined, which, as will be seen, corresponds to reification per life span.

The main objective of the work reported here is to study the above kinds of reification, and to characterize them formally, including their temporal aspects. The result of our work is applicable to any temporal conceptual model, such as Telos [9], ERT [18], MADS [16] and others. On the other hand, our work may be of interest to the temporal databases field [17].

The rest of the paper is structured as follows. Sections 2 and 3 describe some temporal features of entity types and relationship types, respectively. The features are used to characterize part of the temporal behavior of entities and relationships. Sections 4, 5 and 6 draw on those features to characterize the result of each reification kind. Section 7 gives the conclusions of the paper, and points out possible extensions.

2. Temporal Features of Entity Types

When we take a temporal view, we observe that entities and relationships are instances of their types at particular time points [4]. We will assume that time points are expressed in a common base time unit, such as second or day. A time point represents an interval in the time axis.

We represent by $E(e,t)$ the fact that entity e is instance of entity type E at time t. For example, $Project(P1,D1)$ means that $P1$ is instance of *Project* at time $D1$ (day in this case). Note that $E(e,t)$ may hold either because e is instance of E at all possible subintervals of t, or because e is instance of E only at one or more subintervals of t. The *population* of E at t is defined as the set of entities that are instance of E at t. The *life span* of entity e in entity type E is the set of time points at which e is instance of E.

The temporal features of entity types in which we are interested characterize the life span of their instances. We draw on the work reported in [2,6,12] to define two orthogonal features of the above set: durability and frequency.

Durability. The durability feature of an entity type has two possible values: instantaneous and durable. We say that entity type E is *instantaneous* if, for all e and t, $E(e,t)$ implies that:
- $E(e,t+1)$ cannot hold, or
- $E(e,t)$ holds only for some subintervals of t.
Otherwise, E is *durable*.

Most entity types are durable. For example, *Project* is durable, because an entity P may be instance of *Project* during two or more consecutive days T and $T+1$, and $Project(P,T)$ may hold for all subintervals of day T. An example of instantaneous entity type may be *Arrival* (of a letter). A fact $Arrival(L,T1)$, meaning that letter L arrives at $T1$, only holds for a subinterval of $T1$, even if the base time unit is second.

If E is a durable entity type, a *classification interval* of e in E is a maximal set of consecutive time points of the life span of e in E. If E is instantaneous, then there is a classification interval of e in E for each time point at which e is instance of E. Figure 2 shows several examples: $[t_a t_d]$ is a classification interval of *Joan* in *Employee*; $[t_a t_s]$ would not be a classification interval because it is not maximal.

The way by which an information system knows a classification interval of e in E depends on the durability of E. If E is durable, the system needs to be told only of the starting and ending times of the interval. If E is instantaneous, the system must be told explicitly of all times at which e is instance of E.

An entity e has one or more classification intervals in E. We denote by $Ci(e,E)$ the set of classification intervals of e in E. For example, in Figure 2 we have $Ci(L,Arrival) = \{[t_y t_y]\}$ and $Ci(E,Employee) = \{[t_1 t_2], [t_4 t_6]\}$. We will also need to use the predicate $IncludedIn(t,ti)$ to indicate that time point t is included in the temporal interval ti. For instance, $IncludedIn(t_a [t_a t_d])$ is true.

Frequency. The frequency feature of an entity type has also two possible values: single and intermittent. We say that entity type E is *single* if all its entities can only be instance of E during one classification interval. Otherwise, E is *intermittent*.

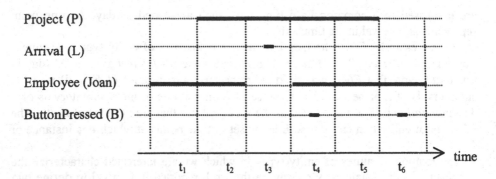

Fig. 2. Examples of classification intervals

Most entity types are single. For example, *Project* is single, if we assume that once a project ceases to exist, it cannot be reincarnated later. An example of instantaneous and single entity type is *Arrival*, since a letter can be instance of it only at a single time point. An example of durable and intermittent entity type could be *Employee*, if we assume that a person can be employed during several intervals. Finally, an example of instantaneous and intermittent entity type could be *ButtonPressed*. A fact *ButtonPressed(B,T1)* means that button B is pressed at time T1. The same button may be pressed several times. Figure 2 shows some classification intervals of one example entity of each of the above types.

3. Temporal Features of Relationship Types

We define in this section some temporal features of relationship types, needed to fully characterize temporal reifications. Other features may be found in [2, 6, 16].

Let R be a relationship type. We denote by $R(P_1{:}E_1,...,P_n{:}E_n)$· the schema of R, where $E_1,...,E_n$ are the participant entity types in R, playing roles $P_1,...,P_n$ respectively. If a role P_i is omitted, it is assumed to be equal to E_i. We represent by $R(e_1,...,e_n,t)$ the fact that entities $e_1,...,e_n$ participate in an instance of relationship type R at time t. We will also say that $(e_1,...,e_n)$ is an instance of R at time t. For example, in *WorksIn(Employee:Person,Project)*, *WorksIn(A1,P1,D1)* represents the fact that *(A1,P1)* is instance of *WorksIn* at time *D1*. Temporal integrity rules require e_i be instance of E_i at time t or before, for $i = 1,..,n$. In the previous example, *A1* must be instance of *Person* at *D1* or before.

We will need to use the classical cardinality constraints [7], defined as follows. The *mapping* constraint between $(P_1,...,P_{i-1},P_{i+1},...,P_n)$ and P_i in $R(P_1{:}E_1,...,P_n{:}E_n)$ is a pair *(min,max)*, with *min, max > 0*, which indicates the minimum and maximum number of instances of E_i that may be related in R with any combination of entities $(e_1,...,e_{i-1},e_{i+1},...,e_n)$ at any time t. The mapping is *functional* if *min = max = 1*.

The *participation* constraint of P_i in $R(P_1{:}E_1,...,P_n{:}E_n)$ is a pair *(min,max)*, with *min, max ≥ 0*, if for each e_i instance of E_i at any time t, the minimum (maximum) number of instances of R in which e_i can participate is *min* (*max*). The participation is *total* if *min > 0*.

The life span of $(e_1,...,e_n)$ in relationship type R, the classification interval of $(e_1,...,e_n)$ in R, and $Ci((e_1,...,e_n),R)$ are defined similarly to as we did for entity types. We also define in a similar way the durability and frequency features for relationship types. We do not reproduce the formal definitions here, but give one example of each of the four combinations, assuming as base time unit a day: *WorksIn (Employee:Person, Project)* could be durable and intermittent; *Has (Person, Name:String)* is durable and single; *Drinks (Person, Bottle)* is instantaneous and single; and *Buys (Person, Product)* is instantaneous and intermittent.

Synchronism. A relationship type $R(P_1:E_1,...,P_n:E_n)$ is *synchronous* if, for $i = 1,...,n$:
$$\forall e_1,...,e_n,t\ (R(e_1,...,e_i,...,e_n,t) \rightarrow E_i(e_i,t))$$
Otherwise, R is *asynchronous*.

In practice, most relationship types are synchronous, and this will be the only case we will assume in this paper. For example, *WorksIn (Employee:Person, Project)* is synchronous. This means that if *(A1,P1)* is an instance of *WorksIn* at time *D1*, then *A1* and *P1* must be instances of *Person* and *Project*, respectively, at *D1*.

Constant relationship type with respect to a participant. A synchronous relationship type $R(P_1:E_1,...,P_n:E_n)$ is *constant* with respect to participant P_i if:

(1) The participation of P_i in R is total.

(2) R is immutable with respect to P_i; that is, if $(e_1,...,e_i,...,e_n)$ is instance of R at t, it will continue to be an instance of R for all times at which e_i is instance of E_i.

(3) R is not insertable with respect to P_i; that is, if $(e_1,...,e_i,...,e_n)$ is instance of R at t, then it must also be an instance of R at the beginning of the life span of e_i in E_i.

For example, *IsWrittenBy (Book, Author:Person)* is constant with respect to *Book*, if we assume that all books have at least one author (1); that the authors of a book cannot be changed (2); and that we cannot add authors to a book (3). Note that *IsWrittenBy* is not constant with respect to *Author*.

Existence dependency. Entity type E_1 is existence dependent of E_2 via a binary relationship type $R(P_1:E_1,P_2:E_2)$ if R is constant with respect to P_1 and the mapping constraint between P_1 and P_2 is functional. This definition generalizes, in a temporal context, the one given in [15].

Existence dependencies are very important because, as we will see in the next sections, any relationship type $R(P_1:E_1,...,P_n:E_n)$ can be reified into a new entity type E and n binary relationship types $R_i(P:E, P_i: E_i)$, such that E is existence dependent of E_i via R_i.

References. Let $R(P:E,P_i:E_i)$ be a binary relationship type. We say that R is a *simple reference* for E if the participation of P in R is total, and the mapping constraint between P_i and P is functional. For example, *Has(Person, Name:String)* is a simple reference for *Person* if all persons have always at least one name, and any *String* can be the name of at most one *Person*.

A set of n ($n \geq 2$) binary relationship types $R_1(P'_1:E,P_1:E_1),...,R_n(P'_n:E,P_n:E_n)$ is a *compound* reference for E if, for $i = 1,...,n$, the mapping constraint between P_i and P'_i is non functional, the participation of P'_i in R_i is total, and

$\forall e,e',e_1,...,e_n,t$ ($R_1(e,e_1,t) \wedge R_1(e',e_1,t) \wedge...\wedge R_n(e,e_n,t) \wedge R_n(e',e_n,t) \rightarrow e = e'$)

For example, the set *{Has(Book,Title:String), IsPublishedBy(Book,Publisher}* is a compound reference for *Book*.

t = 37	.....	t = 96
WorksIn (Pers, Proj) A P1 A P2		WorksIn (Pers, Proj) A P1 B P2
Workday W1 W2 IsDoneBy (Wd, Pers) W1 A W2 A IsWorkedIn (Wd, Proj) W1 P1 W2 P2		Workday W3 W4 IsDoneBy (Wd, Pers) W3 A W4 B IsWorkedIn (Wd, Proj) W3 P1 W4 P2

Fig. 3. Example reification of *WorksIn*

4. Reification per Instant

We introduce the concept of reification per instant by means of an example, before giving its formal definition. Consider relationship type *WorksIn*. The top of Figure 3 gives a sample population at two different instants (days).

Reification per instant of *WorksIn* produces a new entity type, which we call *Workday*. This entity type will have at time t a different instance for each relationship r instance of *WorksIn* at t. This fact is shown in the bottom of Figure 3. Observe that *WorksIn (A,P1)* holds at both $t = 37$ and $t = 96$, and that it originates two different instances of *Workday* (*W1* and *W3*). Instance *W1*, for example, corresponds to the fact that person A works in project $P1$ at time 37.

These instances must be related to the participant entities of the reified relationship, since otherwise we could not establish the correspondence between the entity and the relationship. This is done by means of binary relationships between the new entity and each of the participating entities. We call these relationships intrinsic, since they may be seen as being an intrinsic part of the new entity. In Figure 3 we show the population of the two intrinsic relationship types (*IsDoneBy* and *IsWorkedIn*), which relate *Workday* with *Person* and *Project*, respectively. It is easy to see that we can reproduce any instance of *WorksIn* from a *Workday* entity and the two intrinsic relationships.

Formally, the *reification per instant* of a synchronous relationship type $R(P_1:E_1,...,P_n:E_n)$ is a schema transformation that produces a new entity type E and n intrinsic relationship types $R_i(P:E,P_i:E_i)$, $(i = 1,...,n)$, such that:

(a) E and R_i are instantaneous and single. R_i are synchronous.

(b) Intrinsic relationship types R_i are constant with respect to P.

(c) The mapping constraint between P and P_i in R_i is functional.

(d) There is a one-to-one correspondence between the populations of R and E at any time t:

$$\forall e_1,...,e_n,t\ (R(e_1,...,e_n,t) \rightarrow \exists!e(E(e,t) \wedge R_1(e,e_1,t) \wedge ... \wedge R_n(e,e_n,t)))$$

$$\forall e,e_1,...,e_n,t\ (E(e,t) \wedge R_1(e,e_1,t) \wedge ... \wedge R_n(e,e_n,t) \rightarrow R(e_1,...,e_n,t))$$

The following remarks give the rationale for the definition of the above transformation:

(a) We want the new entities and their intrinsic relationships to hold at one, and only one, time point (see Figure 4).

(b) In this reification kind, condition (b) ensures that entities of the new entity type E must participate in their set of intrinsic relationships.

(c) Each instance of the new entity type participates in only one relationship, in each intrinsic relationship type R_i.

(d) For each instance r of R that holds at a particular time, we want to produce one, and only one, entity, and its set of intrinsic relationships, and all entities must correspond to one, and only one, relationship r.

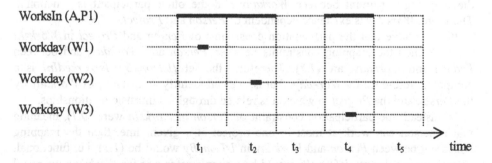

Fig. 4. Example of classification intervals in the reification per instant

The above definition guarantees that we can reproduce (or derive) the instances of R from the instances of E and the instances of its intrinsic relationship types. Additionally, the following properties hold:

(1) E is existence dependent of E_i. This follows from (b) and (c) above.

(2) The participation constraint of P in R_i is $(1,1)$.

(3) The participation constraint of P_i in R_i is the same as its participation constraint in R.

(4) If the participation constraint of P_i in R is (min,max), then the mapping constraint between P_i and P in R_i is (min,max) or, if $min = 0$, $(1,max)$.

(5) If for some R_i the mapping constraint between P_i and P is functional then R_i is a simple reference for E. Otherwise the set $\{R_i,..., R_n\}$ is a compound reference for E.

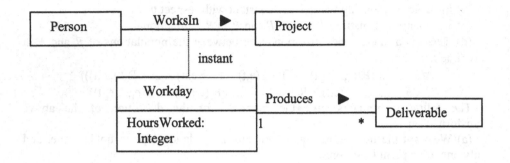

Fig. 5. Reification per instant of *WorksIn*

Application to the example. Applying this definition to our example, we have that reification of *WorksIn* gives entity type *Workday*, and two intrinsic binary relationship types: *IsDoneBy (Workday, Person)* and *IsWorkedIn (Workday, Project)*

Both relationships types are constant with respect to *Workday*. On the other hand, the mapping constraint between *Workday* and the other participant is functional. Therefore, *Workday* is existence dependent of *Person* and *Project*.

If we assume that the participation constraints of *Person* and *Project* in *WorksIn* are $(0, *)$ then the mapping constraints between *Person* and *Workday*, and between *Project* and *Workday*, are $(1, *)$. Therefore, the set $\{IsDoneBy, IsWorkedIn\}$ is a compound reference for *Workday*; that is, we can identify an instance of *Workday* by the *Person* and the *Project* to which it is related through its intrinsic relationships.

If, instead, the participation constraint of *Person* in *WorksIn* were $(0,1)$, meaning that a person can work at most in one project at a given time, then the mapping constraint between *Person* and *Workday* in *IsDoneBy* would be $(1,1)$, i.e. functional. Therefore, in this case *IsDoneBy* would be a simple reference for *Workday*: we could identify an instance of *Workday* by the person to which it is related.

Figure 5 shows the graphical representation of this example. We have added the label 'instant' to the dashed line that represents the reification transformation, to indicate the kind of reification performed.

Figure 5 also shows an attribute of *Workday* (*HoursWorked*, which models the number of hours worked by a person in a project on a particular day), and a relationship type in which it participates (*Produces*, that models the deliverables produced by a person in a project on a particular day).

It is interesting to note that although the result of the reification per instant is always an instantaneous and single entity type, the reified relationship type may have any value in the durability and frequency features: in our example, *WorksIn* is durable and intermittent.

5. Reification per Classification Interval

Reification per classification interval (or, in short, per interval) is the most frequently used. Again, we introduce the concept by means of an example, before giving its formal definition. Consider relationship type *WorksIn*. Reification per interval of *WorksIn* produces a new entity type, which we call now *Assignment*. There will be an instance of *Assignment* for each instance *r* of *WorksIn* and classification interval of *r* in *WorksIn*, *Ci(r,WorksIn)*. That is, if *r* has three classification intervals in *WorksIn*, there will be three instances of *Assignment*. Figure 6 shows an example of classification intervals of a relationship and of the two entities produced. Note the difference with respect to the previous case (Figure 4), where there was one instance for each instant.

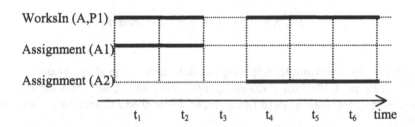

Fig. 6. Example of classification intervals in the reification per interval

Formally, the *reification per interval* of a synchronous relationship type $R(P_1:E_1,...,P_n:E_n)$ is a schema transformation that produces a new entity type E and n intrinsic relationship types $R_i(P:E,P_i:E_i)$, $(i = 1,...,n)$, such that:

(a) E and R_i are single. The value of durability for E and R_i is the same as that of R. R_i are synchronous.

(b) Intrinsic relationship types R_i are constant with respect to P.

(c) The mapping constraint between P and P_i in R_i is functional.

(d) There is a one-to-one correspondence between the populations of R and E at any time t, and there is only one entity for each classification interval of a reified relationship:

$$\forall e_1,...,e_n,t,ti \ (R(e_1,...,e_n,t) \wedge ti \in Ci((e_1,...,e_n),R) \wedge IncludedIn(t,ti)$$
$$\rightarrow \exists!e(E(e,t) \wedge R_1(e,e_1,t) \wedge ... \wedge R_n(e,e_n,t) \wedge ti \in Ci(e,E))$$
$$\forall e,e_1,...,e_n,t,ti \ (E(e,t) \wedge R_1(e,e_1,t) \wedge ... \wedge R_n(e,e_n,t) \wedge ti \in Ci(e,E)$$
$$\rightarrow R(e_1,...,e_n,t) \wedge ti \in Ci((e_1,...,e_n),R))$$

The above definition guarantees that we can reproduce (or derive) the instances of R from the instances of E and the instances of its intrinsic relationship types. It can be seen that properties (1)-(5) of E and R_i, defined in the reification per instant, also hold in this case. Therefore, all properties of the intrinsic relationship types are the same as in the reification per instant, except durability and frequency. Note also that if R is instantaneous, the result of the reification per interval is exactly the same as the one obtained by the reification per instant.

Reification per interval of a relationship type, with frequency single, corresponds to the static reification in single-state conceptual models, mentioned in the Introduction, and characterized in [15]. Therefore, static reification may be seen as a particular case of our temporal reifications.

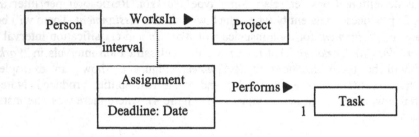

Fig. 7. Reification per interval of *WorksIn*

Application to the example. Applying this definition to the above example, we have that reification of *WorksIn* gives entity type *Assignment*, and two intrinsic binary relationship types: *IsAssignedTo (Assignment, Person)* and *Corresponds (Assignment, Project)*.

Both relationships are constant with respect to *Assignment*. On the other hand, the mapping constraint between *Assignment* and the other participant is functional. Therefore, *Assignment* is existence dependent of *Person* and *Project*.

If we assume that the participation constraints of *Person* and *Project* in *WorksIn* are $(0, *)$ then the mapping constraints between *Person* and *Assignment*, and between *Project* and *Assignment*, are $(1, *)$. Therefore, the set *{IsAssignedTo, Corresponds}* is a compound reference for *Assignment*.

Figure 7 shows the graphical representation of this example. We have added the label 'interval' to the dashed line that represents the reification transformation, to indicate the kind of reification performed.

Figure 7 also shows an attribute of *Assignment* (*Deadline*, which models the planned termination date of the assignment), and a relationship type in which participates (*Performs*, that models the task performed by a person in a project during the assignment). We can now model the property "The task and the deadline are the same during the whole interval", described in the Introduction, by defining *Performs* and *Deadline* constant with respect to *Assignment*.

6. Reification per Life Span

Reification per life span is the last kind of reification we present here. Again, we introduce the concept by means of the example, before giving its formal definition. Consider relationship type *WorksIn*. Reification per life span of *WorksIn* produces a new entity type, which we call now *Participation*. There will be an instance of *Participation* for the whole life span of each instance *r* of *WorksIn*. Figure 8 shows an example of classification intervals of a relationship and of the unique entity produced. Note the difference with respect to the previous cases (Figures 4 and 6).

WorksIn (A,P1)

Participation (Par1)

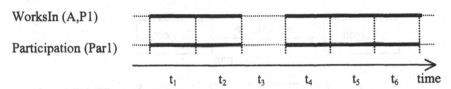

Fig. 8. Example of classification intervals in the reification per life span

Formally, the *reification per life span* of a synchronous relationship type $R(P_1:E_1,...,P_n:E_n)$ is a schema transformation that produces a new entity type E and n intrinsic relationship types $R_i(P:E,P_i:E_i)$, $(i = 1,...,n)$, such that:
(a) The values of durability and frequency for E and R_i are the same as those for R. R_i are synchronous.
(b) Intrinsic relationship types R_i are constant with respect to P.
(c) The mapping constraint between P and P_i in R_i is functional.
(d) There is a one-to-one correspondence between the populations of R and E at any time t, and there is only one entity for all classification intervals of a reified relationship:

$$\forall e_1,...,e_n,t \ (R(e_1,...,e_n,t) \rightarrow$$
$$\exists! e(E(e,t) \land R_1(e,e_1,t) \land... \land R_n(e,e_n,t) \land Ci((e_1,...,e_n),R) = Ci(e,E)))$$

$$\forall e, e_1,...,e_n,t \ (E(e,t) \land R_1(e,e_1,t) \land ... \land R_n(e,e_n,t) \rightarrow$$
$$R(e_1,...,e_n,t) \land Ci(e,E) = Ci((e_1,...,e_n),R)))$$

The above definition guarantees that we can reproduce (or derive) the instances of R from the instances of E and the instances of its intrinsic relationship types. It can be seen that properties (1)-(5) of E and R_i, defined in the reification per instant, also hold in this case. Therefore, all properties of the intrinsic relationship types are the same as in the reification per instant, except the durability and frequency. Note also that if the frequency of R is single, the result of the reification per life span is exactly the same as the one obtained by the reification per interval.

Reification per life span corresponds to the reification defined in ERT [19]. We believe that the other two temporal reifications we have defined here could be also of interest in that temporal conceptual model.

Application to the example. Applying this definition to the above example, we have that reification of *WorksIn* produces entity type *Participation*, and two intrinsic binary relationship types: *IsDoneBy (Participation, Person)* and *ParticipatesIn (Participation, Project)*. Both relationships are constant with respect to *Participation*. On the other hand, the mapping constraint between *Participation* and the other participant is functional. Therefore, *Participation* is existence dependent of *Person* and *Project*. If we assume that the participation constraints of *Person* and *Project* in *WorksIn* are *(0, *)* then the mapping constraints between *Person* and *Participation*, and between *Project* and *Participation*, are *(1, *)*. Therefore, the set *{IsDoneBy, ParticipatesIn}* is a compound reference for *Participation*.

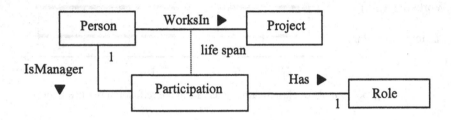

Fig. 9. Reification per life span of *WorksIn*

Figure 9 shows the graphical representation of this example. We have added the label 'life span' to the dashed line that represents the reification transformation, to indicate the kind of reification performed.

The Figure also shows two relationship types in which *Participation* participates. The first *(Has)* is with the *Role* performed in the project, and the second *(IsManager)* is with the *Person* that acts as manager of the participation. We can now model the property "A person performs always the same role and has always the same manager, when he works in a particular project", described in the Introduction, by defining *Has* and *IsManager* constant with respect to *Participation*.

7. Conclusions

We have identified three temporal reifications of relationships in temporal conceptual models. Our work extends current reification theory in conceptual modeling of information systems, which only considers static reification. We have shown that our temporal reifications generalize the static one.

We have defined two new temporal features of entity and relationship types, called durability and frequency, which play a key role in understanding the semantics of the reification.

We have defined formally the characteristics of the new entity type E, and of its intrinsic relationship types $R_i(P:E,P_i:E_i)$, produced by each temporal reification. We have shown that the characteristics of the intrinsic relationship types are the same in all three cases, except for the values of durability and frequency. Table 1 summarizes the values of durability and frequency for the entity and intrinsic relationship types produced by the reification. The main common property of R_i's is that they establish an existence dependency of E with respect to E_i.

Table 1. Durability and Frequency of the reified relationship type, and of the result of the reification

Reified Relationship Type	Reification per instant	Reification per interval	Reification per life span
Instantaneous Single	Instantaneous Single	Instantaneous Single	Instantaneous Single
Instantaneous Intermittent	Instantaneous Single	Instantaneous Single	Instantaneous Intermittent
Durable Single	Instantaneous Single	Durable Single	Durable Single
Durable Intermittent	Instantaneous Single	Durable Single	Durable Intermittent

Relationship reification transforms any relationship type into an equivalent entity type, and a set of intrinsic relationship types, that have particular properties. This fact, we believe, is very important in information systems engineering, because it eases conceptual schema analysis and system design.

We have shown, by means of an example, the application of our temporal reifications, and we have seen that in some modeling situations our reifications produce simpler and more expressive conceptual schemes.

The reification per instant produces a new entity for each instant, which is expressed in the base time unit. In this sense, our work could be extended with a similar reification kind based on time periods coarser than the base time unit. The work [21], done in the temporal databases field, may be relevant for this extension.

Acknowledgments. The author is indebted to Dolors Costal, Juan Ramón López, Joan Antoni Pastor, Maria Ribera Sancho, Ernest Teniente and Toni Urpí, and to the anonymous referees, for their helpful comments. This work has been partially supported by PRONTIC CICYT program project TIC95-0735.

References

1. Batini, C., Ceri, S. and Navathe, S.B. "Conceptual Database Design. An Entity-Relationship Approach", The Benjamin/Cummings Pub. Co., 470 p., 1992.
2. Bergamaschi, S. and Sartori, C "Chrono: A conceptual design framework for temporal entities". 17th International Conference on Conceptual Modeling (ER'98) - Singapore, November 1998, LNCS 1507, pp. 35-50.
3. Boman, M., Bubenko jr. J.A., Johannesson, P. and Wangler, B. "Conceptual Modelling", Prentice Hall, 269 p.,1997.

4. Bubenko, J.A.jr. "The Temporal Dimension in Information Modelling", In "Architecture and Models in Data Base Management Systems", North-Holland, 1977.
5. Cook, S. and Daniels, J. "Designing Object Systems. Object-Oriented Modelling with Syntropy", Prentice Hall, 1994.
6. Costal, D.; Olivé, A. and Sancho, M-R. "Temporal Features of Class Populations and Attributes in Conceptual Models". Proc. 16th. Intl. Conf. On Conceptual Modeling – ER'97, LNCS 1331, pp. 57-70, 1997.
7. Liddle,S.W., Embley,D.W. and Woodfield, S.N. "Cardinality constraints in semanric data models", Data & Knowledge Eng. 11, pp. 235-270, 1993.
8. Martin, J. and Odell, J. "Object-Oriented Methods: A Foundation". Prentice Hall, 412 p., 1995.
9. Mylopoulos, J., Borgida, A., Jarke, M. and Koubarakis, M. "Telos: Representing Knowledge About Information Systems", ACM TOIS, 8,4, pp. 325-362, 1990.
10. Nijssen,G.M. and Halpin, T.A. "Conceptual Schema and Relational Database Design". Prentice Hall, 342 p., 1989.
11. Olivé, A. "A Comparison of the Operational and Deductive Approaches to Conceptual Modelling of Information Systems", Proc. IFIP'86, North-Holland, pp.91-96, 1986.
12. Olivé, A. "On the design and implementation of information systems from deductive conceptual models". Proc. 15th. VLDB, Amsterdam, pp. 3-11, 1989.
13. Rumbaugh, J., Blaha, M., Premerlani, W., Eddy, F. and Lorensen, W. "Object-Oriented Modeling and Design", Prentice Hall, 1991.
14. Rosenthal, A. and Reiner, D. "Tools and Transformations –Rigorous and Otherwise- for Practical Database Design", ACM TODS, 19,2, pp. 167-211, 1994.
15. Snoeck,M. and Dedene,G. "Existence Dependency: The Key to Semantic Integrity Between Structural and Behavioral Aspects of Object Types", IEEE Trans. on Softw. Eng., 24,4, pp. 233-251, 1998.
16. Spaccapietra, S. Parent, C. and Ziményi, E. "Modeling Time from a Conceptual Perspective". CIKM, pp. 432-440, 1998.
17. Tansel,A.U., Clifford,J., Gadia,S., Jajodia, S.,Segev,A. and Snodgrass R. "Temporal Databases. Theory, Design, and Implementation", The Benjamin/Cummings Pub. Co, 1993.
18. Theodoulidis, C., Loucopoulos, P. and Wangler, B. "A Conceptual Modeling Formalism for Temporal Database Applications", Information Systems, 16,4 pp. 401-416., 1991.
19. Theodoulidis, C., Wangler, B. and Loucopoulos, P. "The Entity-Relationship-Time Model", In Loucopoulos, P. and Zicari, R. (eds.). "Conceptual Modeling, Databases and CASE. An Integrated View of Information Systems development", John Wiley and Sons, pp. 87-115, 1992.
20. "UML Notation Guide", Version 1.1, http://www.rational.com/uml. 1997.
21. Wang, X.S., Bettini, C., Brodski, A. and Jajodia, S. "Logical Design for Temporal Databases with Multiple Granularities", ACM TODS, 22,2, pp. 115-170, 1997.
22. Yourdon. "Yourdon Systems Method. Model-Driven Systems development". Yourdon Press. 1993.

Towards a Classification Framework for Application Granularity in Workflow Management Systems

Jörg Becker, Michael zur Mühlen

University of Muenster, Department of Information Systems
Steinfurter Str. 107, D-48149 Muenster, Germany
{isjobe|ismizu}@wi.uni-muenster.de

Abstract. The support of process enactment through the use of workflow management systems has gained considerable attention within the last few years. We develop a classification framework consisting of three different strategies for the use of workflow management systems and outline how these scenarios can be applied in practice. Following the definition of relevant terms in the we identify coordination techniques that are provided by workflow management systems in order to support the automation of business processes. These coordination techniques are evaluated with regard to their dependency on the granularity of applications using the classification framework. The results of this evaluation are compared and an outlook for future research is given.

1   Basic Workflow Geology

For the realization of integrated information systems, several integration perspectives have emerged in the past. Two of these perspectives are the *integration of data*, which is the subject of *data management*, and the *integration of functions* which is part of various *process management*-approaches. A major part of today's business applications satisfies the demands of process orientation only to a minor extent, because they are built as functional program hierarchies and, therefore, are oriented among the fulfillment of single functions. Workflow management systems provide the opportunity to integrate these functionally structured applications into process oriented applications. They guide the user along the business processes to be executed and provide the data and applications that are necessary for the execution of the partial functions.

A *workflow* is the part of a work process that contains the sequence of functions and information about the data and resources involved in the execution of these functions. It is described using a *workflow model*, which usually does not describe the behavior of the single functions or the data to be processed as long as these do not determine the flow of work itself [1]. A *workflow management system* (WfMS) is an information system that enables the execution, coordination and control of workflows. A *workflow application* is the combination of a WfMS and the invoked application systems that is used to support the execution of a work process based on a workflow model [2].

M. Jarke, A. Oberweis (Eds.): CAiSE'99, LNCS 1626, pp. 411-416, 1999.
© Springer-Verlag Berlin Heidelberg 1999

2   Coordination and Efficiency

WfMS support the execution of work processes by the provision of automated coordination mechanisms. Through the reduction of manual coordination and the migration of these coordination mechanisms from existing application systems into the workflow engine WfMS enable a more efficient management and adoption of control mechanisms in enterprises. The coordination mechanisms of a WfMS are outlined in table 1 (cf. [3]) while table 2 shows five efficiency criteria that can be used to measure the efficient execution of business processes (cf. [4]).

Table 1. Coordination Mechanisms of WfMS

Activities	The WfMS automates the transitions between single process activities. The implicit knowledge about the sequence of activities can be handed over to the workflow system entirely (transactional or production workflow) or it can be left in part to the discretion of the workflow participants (ad-hoc or collaborative workflow).
Actors	The WfMS supports the assignment of actors to single process activities according to a set of rules. The coordination instruments used here are the notification and synchronization mechanisms of the work lists.
Data	During the presentation of a workflow activity the WfMS provides the relevant data necessary for the fulfillment of the given task. The efficient supply of data is one of the most important economic arguments for the use of WfMS [5].
Application Systems	During the execution of activities the WfMS provides the actor with the tools necessary for the fulfillment of the given tasks and coordinates the appropriate application systems.
Monitoring and Controlling	WfMS foster the automation of the extraction, analysis and user-appropriate presentation historic data about workflow instances. This data is the main input for early warning mechanism and may serve as a foundation for continuous process improvement [6].

Table 2. Efficiency Criteria for Business Processes

Process Efficiency	Optimization of process criteria such as processing time (to be minimized) or faithfulness to deadlines (to be maximized).
Resource Efficiency	Efficient use of the resources (human resources as well as application systems) available for the execution of processes.
Delegation Efficiency	The proper positioning of the enterprise in its relation to market partners. This includes a reliable prediction of delivery times, transparent communication with suppliers and customers and optimized procurement and distribution processes.
Market Efficiency	Adequate use of the competencies of superior (greater scope of vision along the process) and subordinate (detailed knowledge about single activities) organizational units.
Motivation Efficiency	Motivation of staff to act in a way congruent to the business goals of the enterprise.

3   Application Granularity

An *Invoked Application* is an existing software solution, that is being integrated into one or more activities of a workflow model. The application is executed during the invocation of the workflow activity in order to provide the workflow participant with the tools necessary to fulfill the given task. In this course data can be exchanged between the WfMS and the invoked application. Data affecting the sequence of activities is called *workflow relevant data* while internal data of the single activities is called *application data* (cf. [7]). In most cases application data is not stored in the database of the WfMS, but it is handled by the application system itself. An exception from this approach can be found at some document centric workflow systems.

In the following sections we analyze three different sizes of invoked applications with respect to their economical potential and the implications for the WfMS used. The coarse level of granularity (*rocks*) is formed by activities that call upon complete application systems. The invocation of single modules and function parts of application systems form a medium level of granularity (*stones*), whereas the execution of elementary functions by the WfMS itself forms the finest level of granularity (*sand*).

3.1   Rocks

A coarse application granularity can be observed if a WfMS supports processes at the enterprise level. In this case the invoked application systems are triggered as a whole while only few application data is exchanged between the WfMS and the application systems. The complexity of the business process model is low, because at this high level of abstraction the process model usually consists of a small number of activities. The coordination of activities and the assignment of work to workflow actors play only a minor role within this scenario.

Possible applications that can be linked at a coarse level of granularity are e. g. legacy applications, PPC-systems and other WfMS that control specific parts of a business process. For the supervising WfMS some parts of the typical workflow functionality are less important, e. g. the process of staff resolution. In the "rocks"- scenario the staff resolution mechanism can be used to assign process managers to different sections of an enterprise-wide process. A linking of applications at a coarse level of granularity is useful for those applications whose elementary functions cannot be coordinated by a WfMS sufficiently. For example the PPC-functionality of ex-ante capacity planning and real-time-control is implemented only to a little extent in current WfMS. Therefore, it is easier to integrate the PPC-system as a "black box" into the workflow model, exchanging only start/stop-information, than to emulate these functions using the built-in functionality of a WfMS.

Data consistency is easy to maintain at a coarse level of granularity, because only control information for the invoked applications have to be exchanged (start, stop etc.). Application data is exchanged only in few cases. Component designers for a coarse level of granularity have to provide interfaces that enable the invocation of the application by a WfMS, the querying of the program status and the passing of control data and application data and pointers respectively. The coordination functions of WfMS mentioned in section 2 are of varying importance in this scenario. While the coordination of activities has only little importance due to the few activities in the workflow model, the coordination of application systems is more important. The coordination of actors and the coordination of data are less important due to the high level of abstraction. Moreover, the level of abstraction fosters the use of the audit trail data for controlling purposes at the management level. In order to identify weaknesses in the process this data is less useful, because important information about the elementary functions is missing. Since the WfMS does not deal with application data, security aspects such as the control of data access and the permissions of workflow actors have to be maintained by the application systems themselves.

3.2   Stones

A medium level of granularity can be observed if the WfMS invokes parts of application systems, e. g. transactions of an ERP-software, modules of a legacy system or activity specific parts of a standard application. The granularity of the invoked applications is determined by the size of the functions of the surrounding system (modules, functions, procedures). This is especially true if the WfMS is integrated into the components of a application family (so-called *embedded* WfMS).

Data consistency is much more important at a medium level of granularity than at the "rocks"-level since references to application data may be exchanged more frequently. With the increasing number of activities the complexity of the workflow model increases which in turn leads to an increasing number of control data entities. If the invoked applications do not provide dedicated interfaces for the import and export of data, the WfMS has to perform data conversions as well. The management of data integrity is shifted from the application level towards the level of WfMS.

Due to the increasing complexity at a medium level of granularity the importance of activity coordination increases as well as the importance of the coordination of application systems. The assignment of actors to activities is determined by the division of labor within the single modules, thus, the importance of actor coordination varies. If the an activity is performed by a single actor, traditional staff resolution concepts can be employed. If several actors are involved in the execution of an activity, e. g. if the application system can only be triggered as a whole, the WfMS can only assign a responsible actor to the activity. This can be problematic with respect to the authorization concept. The assignment of an activity to a specific actor does not necessarily ensure that this actor has the necessary privileges at application level to perform the activity in a proper way, e. g. access rights to certain fields in a database management system. The workflow modeler has to ensure that both the role model of the WfMS and the access model of the invoked applications fit together. This may lead to a redundant maintenance of access privileges in both systems.

Information generated with respect to the monitoring and control functions of the WfMS show a medium level of detail within the "stones" scenario. This data is suited for controlling purposes as well as a feedback engineering of process weaknesses. In order to enable a detailed process analysis the audit trail data has to be linked to the application data as described in section 3.1. In addition to interfaces for the exchange of control- and application data, component designers have to provide control mechanisms at different levels of abstraction that enable e. g. the starting of the entire application, the calling of a single module as well as the start of a single transaction.

3.3   Sand

The finest granularity of invoked applications can be observed, if a WfMS controls elementary functions of the invoked applications. In this case the control flow of the applications is no longer part of the process logic. This way the WfMS can be used to bypass the original "hard-coded" control flow within the application system. A precondition for this is the accessibility of the invoked application at an elementary level, e. g. through Remote Function Calls. The integration of existing applications, however, is just one alternative in the "sand"-scenario. Another alternative is the use of a WfMS as a CASE-tool for the design of process-oriented applications. The development of activity specific application components around a central workflow engine leads to the design of a workflow-specific application. Some WfMS provide the user with functions for the development of small applications such as form generators and script languages. In many cases the functionality of these tools is sufficient for the design of an entire workflow application. Within such *integrated workflow applications* the WfMS takes control of the entire data management, because not only workflow relevant data but also application data are exchanged via the interface between the workflow engine and the invoked/integrated applications. Data consistency and integrity have to be maintained by the WfMS entirely. Thus, the relevant data should be stored in a central repository in order to minimize redundancies and other integrity problems. Regarding the actor's permissions the scenario "sand" is less sensitive than the scenario "stones". Here the WfMS has a central control over the access privileges of the users, the access control can be embedded in the role concept of the WfMS.

The importance of activity coordination increases with the increasing complexity of the workflow models. However, the significance of application coordination decreases with every external application that is replaced by a workflow-specific integrated application. The coordination of actors is of increasing importance since the assignment of actors and activities is part of the staff resolution process and maintained entirely within the WfMS. In order to assign process managers to segments of the workflow process proprietary functions of the WfMS have to be employed. With respect to monitoring and controlling the amount of logged audit trail data increases with the complexity of the workflow models. On the one hand, this enables a very detailed monitoring of running workflow instances, thus enhancing the ability to answer to customer and supplier inquiries. With respect to a controlling based on historical workflow data the low degree of abstraction leads to a very large amount of data. Therefore, tools such as data mining systems or process information systems (cf. [8]) should be used in order to analyze the audit trail data.

4 Summary and Outlook

Table 3 summarizes which of the single coordination mechanisms of WfMS are affected by the different levels of application granularity. With a finer granularity the intensity of coordination by the WfMS increases. While at the "rock"-level the linking of entire application systems is the primary focus of the workflow application, at the "sand"-level the WfMS performs an intense coordination at all levels outlined. The more coordination mechanisms are transferred from the application systems and manual actors toward the WfMS, the higher the efficiency benefits resulting from the use of workflow technology are. Therefore, the size of the invoked applications not only determines the process logic of the workflow application but also determines the economical results for the specific enterprise. While the decreasing size of applications increases the coordination intensity this goes along with an increasing complexity of the workflow model and an increasing effort for the implementation of a workflow application. As a result, there cannot be a generally accepted recommendation for the size of the invoked applications.

The linking of "rocks" as well as the coordination of "sand" can be useful in different scenarios. The "stones"-level seems to be more of a problem, because the actor's access rights have to be maintained within the WfMS and the invoked applications. This can lead either to a more detailed modeling of the workflow processes (migration towards the "sand"-scenario) or to a coarse application granularity (migration towards the "rocks"-scenario). Also, a mixture of the scenarios outlined is feasible. Existing larger application systems can be linked using the "rocks"-scenario, ERP-software can be integrated at the "stones"-level, while new applications can be designed using the WfMS as a CASE-Tool.

Table 3. Coordination aspects at different levels of application granularity

	Application level (Rocks)	Module level (Stones)	Function level (Sand)
Coordination of applications	Linking of entire applications	Linking of single functions / modules	Linking of elementary functions
Coordination of activities	Few activities, low complexity of workflow models	Medium number of activities, medium complexity of workflow models	Many activities, highly complex workflow models
Coordination of actors	Assignment of process managers	Assignment of process managers and actors	Assignment of actors
Coordination of data	Exchange of control data. Exchange of references to application data	Exchange of control data. Exchange of references to application data	Exchange of control and application data
Management and control	Monitoring and controlling at a high level of abstraction (management data)	Monitoring and controlling at a medium level of abstraction (middle management data)	Detailed monitoring data, tool support necessary for controlling (data mining)
Data consistency	To be ensured by the application system	To be ensured across system borders	To be ensured by the WfMS

References

1. zur Mühlen, M.: Evaluation of Workflow Management Systems Using Meta Models. In: Sprague, R. (Ed.): Proceedings of the 32nd Hawai`i International Conference on System Sciences (HICSS '99). IEEE, Los Alamitos 1999.
2. Leymann, F. and Roller, D.: Workflow-based Applications. In: IBM Systems Journal, 36 (1997) 1, pp. 102-123.
3. Becker, J.; v. Uthmann, Ch.; zur Mühlen, M.; Rosemann, M.: Identifying the Workflow Potential of Business Processes. In: Sprague, R. (Ed.): Proceedings of the 32nd Hawai`i International Conference on System Sciences (HICSS '99). Springer, Berlin et al. 1999.
4. Theuvsen, L.: Business Reengineering. In: zfbf, 48 (1996) 1, pp. 65-82. (in German)
5. Fisher, L.: Excellence in Practice – Innovation and Excellence in Workflow and Imaging. Lighthouse Point 1997.
6. McLellan, M.: Workflow Metrics – One of the great benefits of Workflow. In: Österle, H. et al. (Eds.): Praxis des Workflow Management. Vieweg, Braunschweig 1996, pp. 301-318.
7. Workflow Management Coalition: Terminology & Glossary. Document Number WFMC-TC-1011. Document Status-Issue 2.0. Brussels 1996.
8. Rosemann, Michael; Denecke, Thomas; Püttmann, Markus: Konzeption und prototypische Realisierung eines Informationssystems für das Prozeßmonitoring und -controlling. Paper Nr. 49, Department of Information Systems, University of Muenster, 1996. (in German)

Adaptive Outsourcing in Cross-Organizational Workflows*

Justus Klingemann, Jürgen Wäsch, and Karl Aberer

German National Research Center for Information Technology (GMD)
Integrated Publication and Information Systems Institute (GMD-IPSI)
Dolivostraße 15, D-64293 Darmstadt, Germany
{klingem,waesch,aberer}@darmstadt.gmd.de

Abstract. The workflow concept has been very successful in streamlining business processes by automating the coordination of activities, but has so far been limited to the use within single organizations. Any attempt to distribute workflows among different organizations has to face the problems posed by the complex relationship among autonomous organizations and their services. To address these problems we propose a service-oriented model for cross-organizational workflows. Modeling the workflow execution as a cooperation of services allows different organizations to interact via well-defined interfaces. We further show how the execution can be optimized by selecting services depending on their contribution to quality criteria of the workflow.

1 Introduction

Competitive markets force companies to minimize their costs while at the same time offering solutions which are tailored to the needs of their customers. This urges organizations to form virtual enterprises by outsourcing activities to external service providers. Hence, business links with other organizations have to be set up and managed. This has to be achieved in a fast and flexible way to guarantee a short time to market while allowing a dynamic reaction to new customer demands and changing offers of service providers in electronic commerce environments.

Information technology has provided different technologies to address these requirements. The workflow concept [1,2,3,4,5] has been very successful in coordinating and streamlining business processes but is so far limited to a single organization. On the other hand, the tremendous growth of global networks like the internet provides the possibility to efficiently exchange data and communicate with a large number of possible service providers. Thus, workflow management systems (WfMS) can limit their scope no longer to a single organization but have to exploit the network infrastructure to cross organizational boundaries.

However, the extension of workflows beyond the borders of a single enterprise raises new challenges. One important challenge is the necessity to choose

* This work has been partially supported by the ESPRIT project CrossFlow (www.crossflow.org). However, it represents the view of the authors.

M. Jarke, A. Oberweis (Eds.): CAiSE'99, LNCS 1626, pp. 417–421, 1999.
© Springer-Verlag Berlin Heidelberg 1999

among different services that potentially satisfy the customers requirements. In particular, it has to be decided which activities or group of activities should be outsourced to which business partners. Relevant criteria with regard to that decision are the required time, cost, or the adherence to domain-specific quality of service parameters.

The autonomy of the participating organizations implies that the initiator of the workflow has only limited control over the outsourced activities. This requires that both sides agree on an interface which allows the service requester to monitor and probably control the outsourced activities to a certain extent.

To address these problems, we propose a service-oriented model for cross-organizational workflows. Modeling the workflow execution as a cooperation of services allows different organizations to interact via well-defined interfaces. We further show how the execution can be optimized by selecting services depending on their contribution to quality criteria of the workflow.

2   A Service-Oriented Model for Cross-Organizational Workflows

In this section, we describe our conceptual model for cross-organizational workflows. However, we confine ourselves to the essential concepts which are necessary to understand the approach presented in this paper. For further details see [6]. We consider a workflow as a collection of activities which are related by certain dependencies. A workflow is modeled as a graph with activities as nodes and edges which represent the control and data flow. In addition, *quality of service (QoS)* parameters are assigned to the workflow, e.g., the maximal duration and the maximal cost allowed for a workflow. Despite these more or less application-independent QoS parameters, domain-specific QoS parameter can exist.

In order to allow the execution of activities at runtime, we need to define a mechanism that assigns activities to particular "agents" that are responsible for the execution of the activity instances. Usually, in intra-organizational workflows, agents are considered to be human beings or computer programs. If a workflow is allowed to span different organizations, there is a third kind of agents that can be involved in the execution of a cross-organizational workflow instance, namely *external service providers*. Therefore, we introduce a *service-oriented model*. We believe that this model is better suited for cross-organizational workflows while at the same time being applicable in ordinary enterprise-wide workflows. The basic entity in our model is a *service*. Informally, a service is an abstract specification of the amount of work that a resource promises to carry out with a specific quality of service. A service specifies which part of a workflow it covers. In general, a service is not restricted to execute a single activity of a workflow, it can span multiple activities. With $A(S)$ we denote the set of activities covered by service S. With each service a *service provider* is associated. This can be either an internal resource or an *external organization*. A service offered by an external organization is called an *external service*. Otherwise, it is called *internal service*.

In contrast to internal services, external services are not executed under the control of the service requester, i.e., the organization that runs and controls the cross-organizational workflow. The service requester has only a limited possibility to get information on the state of an external service execution and to influence this execution. Moreover, the internal work process of an external service might not be known to the service requester due to the autonomy of the service providers. Thus, while they are executed, services have to be treated as "black boxes" from the viewpoint of a service requester. Only the interfaces to and from the services are known by the service requester and which activities are subsumed by the service. This includes a specification how an external service can be invoked, which parameters have to be supplied, etc. Besides the interfaces, a service description contains the quality of service offered by the service provider to the service requester.

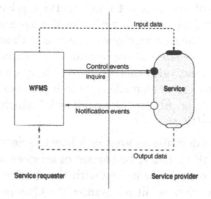

Fig. 1. Interfaces of a service and interaction with the WfMS

Figure 1 illustrates our view on a service. A service S has four interfaces. Two of them (*Input* and *Output*) are concerned with the data flow and two of them (*Control* and *Notification*) are concerned with control flow in form of control and notification events [6]. Control events (specified in the service description) can be sent by the service requester to the service provider in order to influence the processing of the service. Notification events are used to inform the service requester about the state of the processing of the external service. They can be sent as a result of an internal event of the service provider or as a reaction to an inquiry of the service requester.

3 Selection of Services in Cross-Organizational Workflows

In this section, we discuss how services will be selected to execute the activities of the workflow. We assume that all relevant information about services is made available in a *service repository*. Therefore, we do not consider issues like finding out which services are available.

The workflow and its activities have certain QoS parameters. Some of them are *mandatory*, others should be fulfilled as well as possible and are optimized with the following algorithms. For the sake of simplicity, we assume that the latter parameters can be aggregated into a single value which can be used to compare different service offers, i.e., each service S is assigned a value q which we call the *price* of the service. We further assume that this price can be calculated for all services offered. In [7] we have described a technique how a service requester can derive and validate QoS parameters of an offered service based on the observation of previous executions of this service.

Since the control flow part of a workflow specification establishes enabling conditions for activities, it is usually not clear at the start of a workflow which activities actually have to be executed. For example, a workflow can contain branches with alternative sequences of activities for certain parts of the work-flow. Conditions can be evaluated when all necessary parameters are available due to the execution of previous activities. Service selection mechanisms can be differentiated depending on when activities are assigned to services. In this paper, we will consider the case where we assign only those activities to services of which, in the respective state of the workflow, we know that they have to be executed. In [6] we have extended this mechanism to more complex subworkflows which contain decisions yet to be made on which parts of the subworkflow have to be executed. We denote the part of workflow W which can be outsourced at time t as $Outsourcable(W, t)$.

In the following, we describe an approach how to select services for the activities in $Outsourcable(W, t)$. Let Σ be the set of services which offer to cover an appropriate part of the workflow in line with the specification of the workflow. In particular, these services fulfill all mandatory QoS parameters and execute the activities in an execution order that is in line with the workflow specification[1]. Additional restrictions can be included, e.g., the service requester might want to exclude the services of a certain service provider. The problem can then be formulated as finding a set of services from Σ which covers all activities in $Outsourcable(W, t)$ exactly once, while optimizing the non-mandatory QoS parameters. Mathematically, this problem is a minimal weighted exact set cover, i.e., can be formalized as follows: Find a subset O of Σ, that forms an exact cover, i.e., $\bigcup_{S \in O} A(S) = Outsourcable(W, t)$ and $\forall S_i, S_j \in O : A(S_i) \cap A(S_j) = \emptyset$ and such that the *cost* of the cover $\sum_{S_i \in O} q_i$ is minimized. This problem is NP-complete [8,9,10]. However, since the set activities to be outsourced is usually small, we expect that our approach is applicable to many real-world workflows. In [6] we have described an algorithm how to select an optimal choice of services by solving the minimal weighted exact set cover. In the following we will give an example of this approach.

---

[1] Note, that this does not mean that the actual execution order has to be the same as in the workflow specification. Due to the autonomy of the service provider and the resulting limited monotoring capabilities we only require that the execution order cannot be distinguished at the interface of the service.

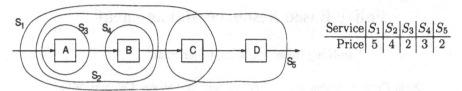

Service	S_1	S_2	S_3	S_4	S_5
Price	5	4	2	3	2

Fig. 3. Services and their
prices

Fig. 2. Services offered for a sub-workflow

Figure 2 shows a simple subworkflow consisting of four activities. We assume that $Outsourcable(W, t) = \{A, B, C, D\}$. There are five services $S_1, \ldots, S_5$ which offer to perform parts of this subworkflow. Figure 3 shows the prices of these services. A correct selection of services would be, for example, $O_1 = \{S_3, S_4, S_5\}$ as each activity is covered by exactly one service. The cost of this selection is 7. Note that the cover $\{S_1, S_5\}$ is not allowed as the activity C is included in both services. However, besides O_1 there exists another exact cover namely $O_2 = \{S_2, S_5\}$ with cost 6. Thus, our algorithm returns O_2 as the optimum. Extensions of this technique for situations in which one activity is allowed to be covered by more than one service are discussed in [6].

References

1. D. Georgakopoulos, M. Hornick, and A. Sheth. An overview on workflow management: From process modeling to workflow automation infrastructure. *Distributed and Parallel Databases*, 3(2), April 1995.
2. G. Alonso, D. Agrawal, A. El Abbadi, and C. Mohan. Functionality and limitations of current workflow management systems. *IEEE Expert Journal*, 12(5), 1996.
3. S. Jablonski and C. Bussler. *Workflow Management — Modeling Concepts, Architecture and Implementation*. International Thomson Computer Press, 1996.
4. A. Dogac, T. Öszu, A. Biliris, and T. Sellis, editors. *Workflow Management Systems and Interoperability*. NATO-ASI Series. Springer Verlag, 1998.
5. A. Cichocki, S. Helal, M. Rusinkiewicz, and D. Woelk. *Workflow and Process Automation - Concepts and Technology*. Kluwer Academic Publishers, 1998.
6. J. Klingemann, J. Wäsch, and K. Aberer. Adaptive outsourcing in cross-organizational workflows. GMD Report 30, GMD — German National Research Center for Information Technology, 1998.
7. J. Klingemann, J. Wäsch, and K. Aberer. Deriving service models in cross-organizational workflows. In *Proceedings of RIDE-Information Technology for Virtual Enterprises*, Sydney, Australia, March 1999.
8. M. R. Garey and D. S. Johnson. *Computers and Intractability — A Guide to the Theory of NP-Completeness*. W. H. Freeman, New York, 1979.
9. R. M. Karp. Reducibility among combinatorial problems. In R. E. Miller and J. W. Thatcher, editors, *Complexity of Computer Computations*, pages 85–103. Plenum Press, New York, 1972.
10. D. S. Hochbaum, editor. *Approximation Algorithms for NP-Hard Problems*. PWS Publishing, Boston, 1997.

Policy-Based Resource Management

Yan-Nong Huan[1] and Ming-Chien Shan[2]

[1]Oracle Corporation, 600 Oracle Parkway, Redwood Shores, California 94065
yahuang@us.oracle.com
[2]Hewlett-Packard Laboratories, 1501 Page Mill Road, 1U-4A, Palo Alto,
California 94304, shan@hpl.hp.com

Abstract. This paper proposes a new method to handle policies in Resource Management of Workflow Systems. Three types of policies are studied including qualification, requirement and substitution policies. The first two types of policies map an activity specification into constraints on resources that are qualified to carry out the activity. The third type of policies intends to suggest alternatives in cases where requested resources are not available. An SQL-like language is used to specify policies. Policy enforcement is realized through a query rewriting based on relevant policies. A novel approach is investigated for effective management of large policy bases, which consists of relational representation of policies and efficient retrieval of relevant policies for a given resource query.

Keywords. Workflow, Resource, Policy, Interval-Based, Query Rewriting.

1. Introduction

An information system is composed of a database system and one or many applications manipulating the database. The database system is a common data repository shared among multiple applications. Besides data, people sometimes move components which seemly belong to applications into the database, so that multiple applications can share common components. In other words, the common components become part of the database's semantics. Active databases are an example of such kind, where dynamic characteristics of data are pushed down to the database, so the data can always behave the same way no matter what applications are.

We are interested in Workflow Management Systems (WFMS) [5], and particularly, in Resource Management (RM) [6] of WFMS. A WFMS consists of coordinating executions of multiple activities, instructing who (resource) do what (activity) and when. The „when" part is taken care of by the workflow engine which orders the executions of activities based on a process definition. The „who" part is handled by the resource manager that aims at finding suitable resources at the run-time for the accomplishment of an activity as the engine steps through the process definition.

Resources of different kinds (human and material, for example) constitute the information system of our interest, their management consists of resource modeling and effective allocation upon users' requests. Since resource allocation needs to follow certain general guidelines (authority, security, for example) - no matter who or what application issues requests: so those general guidelines are better considered as part of the resources' semantics. That is the reason why we are interested in resource

M. Jarke, A. Oberweis (Eds.): CAiSE'99, LNCS 1626, pp. 422-428, 1999.
© Springer-Verlag Berlin Heidelberg 1999

policy management in RM. Resource policies are general guidelines every individual resource allocation must observe. They differ from process specific policies which are only applied to a particular process. The policy manager is a module within the resource manager, responsible for efficiently managing a (potentially large) set of policies and enforcing them in resource allocation.

We propose to enforce policies by *query rewriting*. A resource query is sent to the policy manager where relevant policies are first retrieved, then either additional selection criteria are appended to the initial query (in the case of requirement policies) or a new query is returned (in the case of substitution policies). Therefore, the policy manager can be seen as both a *regulator* and a *facilitator* where a resource query is either „polished" or given alternatives in a controlled way before submitted for actual resource retrieval. By doing so, returned resources can always be guaranteed to fully comply with the resource usage guidelines.

1.1 Design Goals for the Policy Management

Technical issues involved in this study can be presented as the following set of design goals.
1. A simple policy model allowing users to express relationships between an activity and a resource that can be used to carry out the activity;
2. A Policy Language (PL) allowing users to *define* policies; PL must be easy to use and *as close as possible* to SQL;
3. Resource query *enhancement/rewriting*: a major functionality of the policy manager is to enforce policies by enhancing/rewriting the initial resource query;
4. *Efficient* management of policy base: retrieving relevant policies applicable to a given resource query may become time-consuming when dealing with a large policy base, strategies are to be devised to achieve good performance.

1.2 Paper Organization

The rest of the paper is organized in the following way. In Section 2, we give a brief overview of our resource manager, with the purpose of showing how the present research is positioned in its context. In Section 3, three types of policies for resource management are presented and the policy language is illustrated with examples. Some conclusive remarks are drawn in Section 4.

2. Context

In this section, we briefly discuss the context of the present research.

2.1 Architecture

Two main components exist in our Resource Manager (Figure 1). One is the resource manager per se, responsible for modeling and managing resources; the other is the policy manager allowing the user to manage policies. Three interfaces are offered, each obviously requiring a different set of access privileges. The policy language interface allows one to insert new policies and consult existing ones. With the resource definition language interface, users can manipulate both meta and instance resource data. Finally, the resource query language interface allows the user to express resource requests. Upon receiving a resource query, the query processor dispatches the query to the policy manager for policy enforcement. The policy manager first rewrites the initial query based on *qualification policies* and generates a list of new queries. Each of the new queries is then rewritten, based on *requirement policies*, into an enhanced query. The enhanced new queries are finally sent to the resource manager for resource retrieval. In the cases where none of the requested resources is available, the *initial* query is re-sent to the policy manager which, based on *substitution policies*, generates alternatives in the form of queries. Each of the alternative queries is treated as a new query, therefore has to go through both *qualification* and *requirement* policy based rewritings. Then, the policy manager once again sends a list of resource queries to the resource manager. If no relevant resources are found against the rewritten alternative queries, notify the user of the failure. Bear in mind that substitution policies should *not* be used *transitively*.

2.2 Resource and Activity Models

A role is intended to denote a set of capabilities, its extension is a set of resources sharing the same capabilities. In this regard, a role can be seen as a resource type. The resource hierarchy shows resources organized into roles whilst the activity hierarchy describes the classification of activity types.

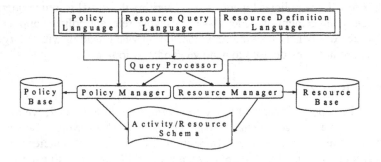

Figure 1: Architecture

Figure 2 shows an example of resource and activity hierarchies. A resource type as well as an activity type is described with a set of attributes, and all the attributes of a parent type are inherited by its child types. In addition to the resource classification, the resource manager holds relationships among different types of resources.

Two possible relationships between resources are exemplified in Figure 3. Note that, like attributes, relationships are inherited from parent resources to child resources. Views may be created on relationships to facilitate query expressions. For example, ReportsTo(Emp, Mgr) is defined as a join between BelongsTo(Employee, Unit) and Manages(Manager, Unit) on the common attribute Unit.

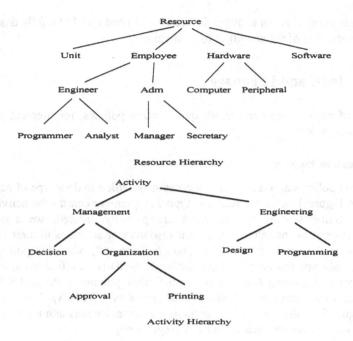

Figure 2: Resource and Activity Classifications

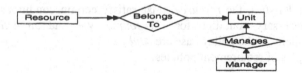

Figure 3: Entity-Relationship Model of Resources

2.3 Resource Query Language

Users can use the resource query language (RQL) to submit resource requests to the resource manager. The language is composed of SQL *Select* statements augmented with activity specifications.

Select	ContactInfo
From	*Engineer*
Where	Location = 'PA'
For	*Programming*
With	NumberOfLines = 35000 And Location = 'Mexico'

Figure 4: Initial RQL Query

Qualify	*Programmer*
For	*Engineering*

Figure 5: Qualification Policy

The query in Figure 4 requests ContactInfo of *Engineer* located in 'PA', for activity *Programming* of 35,000 line code and of location 'Mexico'. Since a resource request is always made upon a known activity, the activity can and should be fully described; namely, each attribute of the activity is to be specified.

3. Policy Model and Language

Three types of policies are considered: qualification policies, requirement policies and substitution policies.

3.1 Qualification Policies

A qualification policy states a type of resources is *qualified* to do a type of activities. The policy in Figure 5 states the resource type *Programmer* can do the activity type *Engineering*. Sinceresources and activities are partially ordered, we allow qualification policies to be inherited from parent resources or activities to their children. Consider a general qualification policy „*Qualify* R *for* A", what this policy really means is any sub-type resource of R (including R itself) is qualified to do any subtype activity of A (including A itself). All qualification policies in the policy base are *Or-related*, and they obey the *Closed World Assumption* (CWA). Namely, if the policy in Figure 5 is the only policy in the policy base, we may assume no resource types other than *Programmer* can do activity *Engineering*.

3.2 Requirement Policies

A requirement policy states that if a *resource* is chosen to carry out an *activity* with specified characteristics, the *resource* must satisfy certain conditions. Therefore, it expresses a necessary condition for a *resource* type and an *activity* type. All requirement policies in the policy base are *And-related*.
Here are examples of requirement policies:

Require	*Programmer*
Where	Experience > 5
For	*Programming*
With	NumberOfLines > 10000

Require	*Employee*
Where	Language = 'Spanish'
For	*Activity*
With	Location = 'Mexico'

Figure 6: Requirement Policies

The first policy in states that if a *Programmer* is chosen to carry out activity *Programming* of more than 10,000 line code, it is required that the *Programmer* have more than 5 year experience.

Given that both the set of resources and the set of activities are partially ordered, the scope of a requirement policy can stretch over resources and activities which are subtypes of the resource and the activity explicitly mentioned in the policy. For example, the second policy in Figure 6 requires the *Employee* be Spanish speaking if (s)he is engaged in activity *Activity* located in Mexico. Since both *Employee* and *Activity* have sub-types in their respective hierarchies (Figure 2), the policy is actually applicable to any pair of resource and activity as long as the resource is a sub-type of *Employee* (including *Employee* itself) and the activity is a sub-type of *Activity* (including *Activity* itself). This gives a great deal of flexibility to expressing requirement policies. The syntax of a general requirement policy is as follows:

Require R
Where   <Where>
For   A
With   <With>

Substitute	*Engineer*
Where	*Location = 'PA'*
By	*Engineer*
Where	*Location = 'Cupertino'*
For	*Programming*
With	*NumberOfLines < 50000*

Figure 7: General Requirement Policy   **Figure 8:** A Substitution Policy

There, *R* is a resource type and *A* is an activity type. <Where> is a SQL *where* clause which can eventually include nested SQL *select* statements. <With> is a restricted form of SQL *where* clause in which no nested SQL statements are allowed. Some more complex policy examples follow,

Require *Manager*
Where   ID = (
Select Mgr
From   ReportsTo
Where Emp = [Requester]
)
For   *Approval*
With   Amount < 1000

Require *Manager*
Where   ID = (
Select   Mgr
From   ReportsTo
Where   level = 2
Start with Emp = [Requester]
Connect by Prior Mgr = Emp
)
For   *Approval*
With   Amount > 1000 And Amount < 5000

Figure 9: Complex Requirement Policies

Both policies in Figure 9 relate resource *Manager* to activity *Approval*. The first states that if the amount requested for approval is less than $1,000, the authorizer should be the manager of the requester. The second policy (a hierarchical sub-query is used) requires that the authorizer be the manager's manager if the requested amount is greater than $1,000 and less than $5,000. Two points are worth mentioning,

1. Nested SQL statement can be used to construct more complex selection criteria.
2. Attributes of the activity can be referenced in constructing selection criteria. To distinguish an attribute of the activity from that of the resource, the former is enclosed between [and]. In the examples of Figure 9, Requester is an attribute of activity *Approval*.

3.3 Substitution Policies

A substitution policy is composed of three elements: a *substituting resource*, a *substituted res*ource and an *activity*; each eventually augmented with descriptions. It states that the substituting resource can replace the substituted resource in the unavailability of the latter, to carry out the activity. Multiple substitution policies are *Or-related*. The policy in Figure 8 states that *Engineers* in PA, in their unavailability, can be replaced by *engineers* in Cupertino to carry out activity *Programming* of less than 50,000 line code. Similar to the requirement policy, the scope of a substitution policy can stretch over resources and activities which are sub-types of the substituted resource and the activity mentioned in the policy. Therefore, the policy in Figure 8 may eventually be applicable to a query looking for a *Programmer* for activity *Programming*.

4. Conclusion

We studied several issues related to resource policies in Workflow Systems. A policy language was proposed allowing users to specify policies of different types. To enforce the policy, a resource query is first rewritten based on relevant policies, before submitted to the resource manager for actual retrieval. The originality of the present work is on the resource policy model, the policy enforcement mechanism and policy management techniques including relational representation of, and efficient access to, a large policy set. A prototype was implemented in Java on NT 4.0, with experimental policies managed in an Oracle database.

References

[1] M. Blaze, J. Feigenbaum and J. Lacy, „Decentralized Trust Management", Proc. of IEEE Symposium on Security and Privacy, Oakland, CA, May 1996.

[2] C. Bufler, „Policy resolution in Workflow Management Systems", Digital Technical Journal, Vol. 6, No. 4, 1994.

[3] C. Bufler and S. Jablonski, „Policy Resolution for Workflow Management Systems", Proc. Of the Hawaii International Conference on System Sciences, Maui, Hawaii, January 1996.

[4] Desktop Management Task Force, „Common Interface Model (CIM) Version 1.0 (Draft)", December 1996.

[5] J. Davis, W. Du and M. Shan, „OpenPM: An Enterprise Process Management System", IEEE Data Engineering Bulletin, 1995.

[6] W. Du, G. Eddy and M.-C. Shan, „Distributed Resource Management in Workflow Environments", Proc. of Database Systems for Advanced Applications (DASFAA), Melbourne, Australia, April, 1997.

Modelling Method Heuristics for Better Quality Products

Naveen Prakash and Ritu Sibal

Division of Computer Engineering
Netaji Subhas Institute of Technology (Formerly DIT)
Kashmere gate, Delhi –110003, India
email : [ritusib, praknav]@hotmail.com

Abstract. Development methods contain heuristics and constraints that help in producing good quality products. Whereas CASE tools enforce method constraints, they rarely support heuristic checking. This paper develops a generic quality model, capable of handling both method constraints and heuristics, which forms the basis of a uniform mechanism for building quality products. The model is metric based, hierarchical in nature, and links metrics to the developmental decisions that are available in a method. The use of this model and the associated quality assessment process is demonstrated through an example of the Yourdon method.

1 Introduction

Broadly speaking, methods provide three features for quality (a) guidelines, (b) method constraints and (c) method heuristics. In supporting the use of methods, CASE tools have particularly looked after method constraint satisfaction. However, it is more difficult to find CASE tools that support heuristic checking. Thus, application engineers are expected to examine products manually and determine whether method heuristics are satisfied or not. The purpose of this paper is to remove this deficiency of CASE tools.

Our approach is based on two assumptions. The first is that a generic solution to the problem of assuring product quality should be found. This genericity is in the sense that both, constraint enforcement as well as heuristic satisfaction can be handled in a uniform manner. The second assumption is that product quality should be metric-based.

A number of metric based quality models [1, 2, 3, 4] have been developed in the area of Software Engineering. These models deal with a given, fixed set of quality factors whereas others [5, 6] cater to only one quality factor. All these models decompose quality factors into quality criteria with which quality metrics are directly associated. In the area of Information Systems also, attempts have been made to develop quality models [7,8]. The former also relies on the decomposition approach. The latter proposes a framework within which quality issues affecting information systems can be formulated and discussed. However, this work is not directly concerned with quality assessment of information system products.

It can be seen that aside from dealing with a model-defined set of quality factors these models do not relate quality factors/criteria to the development process. Thus, it is not known what development decisions affect which factors/criteria in what way.

M. Jarke, A. Oberweis (Eds.): CAiSE'99, LNCS 1626, pp. 429–433, 1999.

As a result, these quality models are stand-alone and divorced from the development activity. Further, none of these models deal with issues of method constraint enforcement, heuristic satisfaction etc. which are interesting in methods.

Thus, the generic quality model developed here must (a) handle different types of quality factors and decompositions and (b) relate development decisions with quality factors/criteria. In [9,10] a method has been viewed as a set of decisions and dependencies between them. The set of decisions has been partitioned into product manipulation and fixed structure enforcement decisions. Product manipulation decisions affect quality factors/criteria whereas fixed structure enforcement decisions determine metric values. Thus, as the product is manipulated, its quality changes and the new product quality can be determined by using fixed structure enforcement decisions. We propose to use this view of decisions in our quality model.

In the next section, we consider heuristics in detail and identify the manner in which we shall represent them. Thereafter, in section III, we present our generic quality model. In section IV the manner in which quality is assured using heuristics is shown through a Data Flow Diagram (DFD) design example.

2   Method Heuristics

When application engineers use heuristics then they may decide that heuristic satisfaction in the product is not mandatory. Thus for example, the number of levels in the specialisation hierarchy in an OMT product may be 4 whereas the corresponding OMT heuristic on specialisation hierarchy suggests that this should be less than 3. Even though the product violates the OMT heuristic, an application engineer may choose to accept this product. This situation is quite different from that in method constraint enforcement where the satisfaction of method constraints in the product is mandatory.

Now, the form of a method heuristic is textual. This is a descriptive statement and therefore, neither amenable to metric based quality calculations nor adequate to form a basis of computer based guidance. In accordance with our interest in metric based quality, we recast a method heuristic as a heuristic function .To do so ,we start by express a method heuristic as

(method concept, metric, operation, value)

where method concept refers to the concept on which the heuristic is defined, metric is the metric used to assess heuristic satisfaction, operation is relational operator and value is the bound within which the metric value should lie. For instance, a design heuristic in the Yourdon method[11] states :

„Avoid Processes that have inputs but no outputs". This means that a process should produce at least one output. This is expressed as

(Process, outpt _cnt, >, 0)

This form is then converted to a heuristic function, $F(H)$. $F(H)$ has two parts to it, a header and a function body. Inside the function body, metric is related to the value through the operation and a Boolean value is returned. This value is checked to ascertain for the satisfaction of the method heuristic.

3   The Generic Quality Model

The central notion (see Fig. 1) of our model is that of a quality requirement. We associate an attribute, *satisfaction*, with the quality requirement which takes the value from the domain {mandatory,optional}. For example, if the quality requirement is a method constraint then its satisfaction attribute has the value mandatory whereas for a heuristic this value is optional.

A quality requirement can be of two kinds, simple or complex. A simple quality requirement cannot be decomposed into simpler requirements whereas a complex quality requirement can be decomposed into simpler ones. Quality requirements are related to one another. One requirement may support another or may be in opposition to it. Thus, when computing the extent to which a requirement has been satisfied, it is necessary to add/subtract the effect of requirements which support/oppose it respectively. This computation is based on the notion of quality metrics.

There are two kinds of metrics, simple and complex. A simple metric is one which can be directly measured in the product whereas a complex metric can only be computed from simpler ones. Clearly, simple metrics supply the 'base' values from which the value of any complex metric is calculated. A metric is associated with every quality requirement.

The value of the metric can be changed by product manipulation decisions. Further, the value of a metric can be checked by a quality enforcement decision which, as defined in [10] returns a value. Based on this value, the application engineer decides which product manipulation decision is to be executed next.

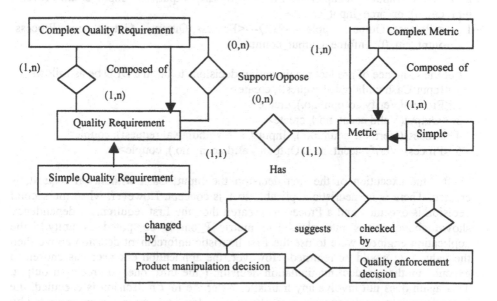

Fig. 1. The Quality Model

4   Using the Quality Model : An Example

In this section, the notions developed in the previous sections will be illustrated through an example. Let us say that we wish to build a DFD. The design heuristics, for DFDs [11] and the function headers are as follows :

1.   (PRODUCT, P_cnt, < , 7)   Process_count(PRODUCT, P_cnt, 7)
2.   (Process, outpt_cnt, > , 0)   Output_count(Process, outpt_cnt, 0)
3.   (Process, inpt_cnt, >, 0)   Input_count(Process, inpt_cnt, 0)

Consider the following product manipulation and heuristic enforcement decisions:

Product manipulation
<Process, create>, <Input, create>, <Output, create>
< Process, Input, couple>, < Process, Output, couple>

Heuristic enforcement
<PRODUCT, Process_count(PRODUCT,P_cnt,7), enforce_Process_count, 7)>
<Process, Output, Output_count(Process, outpt_cnt, 0), enforce_Output_count>
<Process, Input, Input_count(Process, inpt_cnt, 0), enforce_Input_count>

The requirement dependencies between these are as follows:
1.<Process, create>----REQ----<PRODUCT, Process_count(PRODUCT, P_cnt, 7), enforce_Process_count>
2.<Process, Input, couple>---REQ----<Process, Input, Input_count(Process, inpt_cnt, 0), enforce_Input_count>
1.   < Process, Output, couple>---REQ---<Process, Output, Output_count(Process, outpt_cnt, 0), enforce_Output_count>

Let the sequence of product manipulation decisions to build a DFD be as follows:
1.<Input(Cash withdrawal request), create>
2.<Process(Verify account no.), create>
3. <Output(Valid accnt. no.), create>
4.<Process(Verify account no.), Input(Cash withdrawal request), couple>
5.<Process(Verify accnt. no.), Output(Valid accnt. no.), couple>

After the execution of the first decision the Input, Cash withdrawal request, is created. There is no heuristic applicable to this concept. However, when the second decision is executed and a Process is created then the first requirement dependency shown above comes into play. The metric P_cnt is computed as unity.If the application engineer were to use the first heuristic enforcement decision above then the value true would be returned. However, the application engineer has chosen to execute another product manipulation decision (the third one) to create an output. This again does not involve any heuristic. After the fourth decision is executed, the second requirement dependency also comes into play, inpt_cnt is now incremented by one. It can be seen that the application engineer can obtain product quality information while the product is under development.

5   Conclusion

The proposed quality model is generic enough to handle both constraints and heuristics. A prototypical version of the quality enforcement mechanism developed in this paper which shall handle both, constraints and heuristics is under development. The difficult part of our proposals is the generation of method heuristics. We treat this as a part of the method engineering problem and will, in future follow the rule based approach[12] to address it.

References

1.   Boehm B., Brown J., Kaspar J., Lipow M., MacCleod G., & Merrit M., „Characteristics of Software Quality". North Holland.
2.   McCall J., Richards P., & Walters G., „Factors in Software Quality". Vols I, II, III, US Rome Air Development Center Reports NTIS AD/A-049 014, 015, 055.
3.   Gilb T., „Principles of Software Engineering Management", (addison wesley, 1988).
4.   Kitchenham B., „Software quality assurance", Microprocessors and Microcomputers, vol 13, no. 6, 373-381.
5.   Inglis J., „Standard Software Quality Metrics", AT&T Technical Journal, 1986, vol 65, (2), pp 113-118.
6.   Daskalantonakis, MK: „ a Practical View of software Measurement and Implementation experiences Within Motorola" IEEE Transaction on Software Engineering, 1992, vol 18, (11), pp 998-1010.
7.   Delen, GPAJ, Rijsenbrij, DBB: „The Specification Engineering, and Measurement of Information Systems Quality", Journal of systems and Software, 1992, Vol 17, (3), pp 205-217.
8.   Krogstie J., Lindland O., Sindre G., „Towards a deeper understanding of Quality in Requirements Engineering", in „Advanced Information Systems Engineering", Springer 1995.
9.   Prakash N., „Towards a Formal Definition of Methods", Requirements Engineering Journal, Springer.
10.   Prakash N., & Sibal R., „Computer Assisted Quality Engineering : A CASE for Building Quality Products", in First International Workshop on the Many Facets of Process Engineering, Tunis, September, 1997.
11.   Yourdon E., „Modern Structured Analysis", Prentice-Hall.
12.   Prakash N., & Daya Gupta., „An Architecture for a CAME TOOL", in Proceedings of the 8th European-Japanese Conference on Information Modelling and Knowledge Bases, pp 147-179.

Queries and Constraints on Semi-structured Data

Diego Calvanese, Giuseppe De Giacomo, and Maurizio Lenzerini

Dipartimento di Informatica e Sistemistica
Università di Roma "La Sapienza"
Via Salaria 113, 00198 Roma, Italy
lastname@dis.uniroma1.it,
http://www.dis.uniroma1.it/~*lastname*

Abstract. We extend the model for semi-structured data proposed in [4], where both databases and schemas are represented as graphs, with the possibility of expressing different types of constraints on the nodes of the graphs, and defining queries which are used to select graphs from a database. We show that reasoning tasks at the basis of query optimization, such as schema subsumption, query-schema comparison, query containment, and query satisfiability, are decidable.

1 Introduction

The ability to represent data whose structure is less rigid and strict than in conventional databases is considered a crucial aspect in modern approaches to information systems, and is important in many application areas, such as biological databases, digital libraries, and data integration [13, 1, 4, 12, 8].

Recent proposals of models for semi-structured data represent data as graphs with labeled edges, where information on both the values and the schema of data are kept. In particular, we base our work on the BDFS data model [4], where graphs are used to represent both portions of a database (called ground graphs) and schemas. The former have edges labeled by data, and the latter have edges labeled by formulae of a decidable and complete first-order theory $\mathcal{T}$ over a fixed, finite universe $\mathcal{U}$.

A *ground graph* is a rooted connected graph whose edges are labeled with formulae of the form $(self = a)$[1]. A *graph schema* is a rooted connected graph whose edges are labeled with unary formulae of $\mathcal{T}$. Note that a *ground graph* is a special case of *graph schema*. A *semi-structured database* (or simply *database*) is a finite set of graphs (where each one is either a ground graph or a graph schema).

The notion of a ground graph g conforming to a schema S is given in terms of a special relation, called simulation, between the two graphs. Given a ground graph g and a schema S, a *simulation* from g to S is a binary relation $\trianglelefteq$ from the nodes of g to those of S such that $u \trianglelefteq u'$ implies that for each edge $u \xrightarrow{a} v$ in

---

[1] For each constant a of $\mathcal{T}$, $(self = a)(a')$ is **true** if and only if $a = a'$.

M. Jarke, A. Oberweis (Eds.): CAiSE'99, LNCS 1626, pp. 434–438, 1999.

g, there exists an edge $u' \xrightarrow{p} v'$ in S such that $\mathcal{T} \models p(a)$, and $v \trianglelefteq v'$. A ground graph g *conforms to* a schema S, in notation $g \preceq S$, if there exists a *simulation* from g to S such that $root(g) \trianglelefteq root(S)$. Observe that the notion of simulation is less rigid than the usual notion of satisfaction, and suitably reflects the need of dealing with less strict structures of data.

For several tasks related to data management, it is important to be able to check subsumption between two schemas, i.e., to check whether every ground graph conforming to one schema always conforms to another schema. Given two schemas S and S', S' *subsumes* S, in notation $S \sqsubseteq S'$, if for every ground graph g, $g \preceq S$ implies $g \preceq S'$. S' and S are *equivalent* if both $S \sqsubseteq S'$ and $S' \sqsubseteq S$. In [4], an algorithm is presented for checking subsumption (and conformance, being a ground graph a special case of schema). The algorithm essentially looks for the greatest simulation between the nodes of the two schemas, and works in polynomial time with respect to the size of the two schemas.

In [4] the issue of extending the model with different types of constraints is raised. Indeed, in BDFS all the properties of the schema are expressed in terms of the structure of the graph, and the possibility of specifying additional constraints, such as existence of edges, is precluded. In this paper we extend the framework of [4] presenting the following contributions:

- We extend BDFS schemas with constraints (Section 2). The basic idea is to express constraints in terms of formulae associated to nodes of the schema. A formula on a node u imposes a condition that, for every ground graph g conforming to S, must be satisfied by every node of g simulating u. We consider different types of constraints, and we discuss how the expressive power of the constraint language influences the complexity of subsumption checking. In particular, we show that by adding edge-existence and functionality constraints the complexity of subsumption remains polynomial.
- We introduce a basic form of queries (Section 3), called *graph selection queries*, which are used to select graphs from a database The query language presented here represents a basic building block of a full-featured query language and has been designed on one hand to express sophisticated fixpoint properties of graphs, and on the other hand to keep several interesting reasoning tasks decidable. These reasoning tasks, such as comparing queries and schemas or checking containment between queries, are at the basis of query optimization techniques applicable to a more expressive query language.

2   Schemas with Constraints

We address the problem of extending the BDFS data model in order to express constraints on a schema. We conceive a constraint for a schema S as a formula associated to a node u of the schema. The formula is expressed in a certain language $\mathcal{L}$, and its role is to impose a condition that, for every ground graph g conforming to S, must be satisfied by every node of g simulating u.

A *schema with $\mathcal{L}$-constraints*, or simply $\mathcal{L}$-*schema*, is a schema where each node u is labeled by a formula $\mathcal{C}(u)$ of the constraint language $\mathcal{L}$. Given a ground graph g and an $\mathcal{L}$-schema S, a *simulation* from g to S is a binary relation $\trianglelefteq$ from the nodes of g to those of S such that $u \trianglelefteq u'$ implies that (1) u satisfies $\mathcal{C}(u')$, and (2) for each edge $u \xrightarrow{a} v$ in g, there exists an edge $u' \xrightarrow{p} v'$ in S such that $\mathcal{T} \models p(a)$, and $v \trianglelefteq v'$.

Apart from the new definition of simulation, the notions of conformance, subsumption and equivalence remain unchanged. We assume that $\mathcal{L}$ contains the formula $\top$, which is satisfied by every node of every ground graph. Therefore, we can view a ground graph g as an $\mathcal{L}$-schema where $\mathcal{C}(u) = \top$ for every node u of g. Thus, conformance is again a special case of subsumption.

Since constraints may contradict each other, or may even be incompatible with the structure of the graph, the notion of consistency becomes relevant (notice that a ground graph is always consistent). Given an $\mathcal{L}$-schema S, a node $u \in Nodes(S)$ is *consistent* if there is at least one ground graph which conforms to S', where S' is equal to S except that $root(S') = u$. S is *consistent*, if $root(S)$ is consistent. Moreover, two $\mathcal{L}$-schemas S_1 and S_2 are said to be *disjoint*, if there is no ground graph that conforms to S_1 and S_2.

In general, adding constraints to a schema leads to intractability of reasoning [7]. Here we consider a language $\mathcal{L}_l$ that allows for expressing interesting forms of constraints, and for which reasoning remains tractable. The main point is that we allow for expressing only local constraints, i.e., constraints on the edges directly emanating from a node. Formulae in $\mathcal{L}_l$ have the following syntax (γ, γ_1 and γ_2 denote constraints, and p denotes a formula of $\mathcal{T}$):

$$\gamma ::= \top \mid \exists\mathsf{edge}\,(p) \mid \neg\exists\mathsf{edge}\,(p) \mid \exists^{\leq 1}\mathsf{edge}\,(p) \mid \gamma_1 \wedge \gamma_2$$

Intuitively, a constraint of the form $\exists\mathsf{edge}\,(p)$ on a node u, called *edge-existence constraint*, imposes that u has at least one outgoing edge $u \xrightarrow{a} v$ such that $\mathcal{T} \models p(a)$, while a constraint of the form $\exists^{\leq 1}\mathsf{edge}\,(p)$, called *functionality-constraint*, imposes that u has at most one such outgoing edge.

Our main result is that reasoning with schemas with local constraints can be done in polynomial time. In particular:

1. We have devised an algorithm for checking whether an $\mathcal{L}_l$-schema S is consistent. The algorithm is based on a function that first removes the non-existence constraints, and then removes all inconsistent nodes from S. The function runs in time polynomial in the size of S.
2. We have extended the algorithm in [4] in order to deal with local constraints. The basic idea of the algorithm is to look for a simulation between the two schemas by constructing a relation R as the Cartesian product of the two sets of nodes, and then removing from R all the pairs (u, u') for which no relation $\trianglelefteq$ satisfying condition (2) above may exist. The algorithm runs in time polynomial in the size of the two $\mathcal{L}_l$-schemas.
3. We have shown that our technique can also be used to perform in polynomial time the tow following tasks: computing the *Least Upper Bound* (LUB) [4] of two $\mathcal{L}_l$-schemas, and checking whether two $\mathcal{L}_l$-schemas are disjoint.

3 Graph Selection Queries

In general, query languages on semi-structured data are constituted by two components: one for selecting graphs, and another one for restructuring the selected graph to produce the actual answer [5, 3, 9, 2]. Here we introduce a basic form of queries, which we call *graph selection queries (gs-queries)*, which deal only with the selection part. The language of gs-queries allows for expressing sophisticated fixpoint properties of graphs. Furthermore it has been carefully designed in order to keep several interesting reasoning tasks decidable, such as checking query satisfiability, checking containment or disjointness between queries, and comparing queries and schemas.

Observe that the unit retrieved by a gs-query is a graph, whereas there is no means to further manipulate specific data from the retrieved graph (see for example [10]). Therefore our language cannot be considered a full-featured query language, such as UnQL [5], but should rather be regarded as providing basic building blocks for querying semi-structured data, to be exploited in query processing for improving evaluation performance.

In the rest of the paper, we deal only with $\mathcal{L}_l$-schemas, which we simply call schemas. The language for expressing graph selection queries has the following syntax (p denotes a formula of $\mathcal{T}$, n a positive integer, and X a node variable)

$$node\ formulae:\ N ::= X \mid \exists^{\geq n}\mathsf{edge}\,(E) \mid \neg N \mid N_1 \wedge N_2 \mid \mu X.N$$
$$edge\ formulae:\ E ::= p \mid \mathsf{to}(N) \mid \neg E \mid E_1 \wedge E_2$$

with the restriction that every free occurrence of X in $\mu X.N$ is in the scope of an even number of negations[2].

Let g be a ground graph. A *valuation* ρ on g is a mapping from node variables to subsets of $Nodes(g)$. We denote by $\rho[X/\mathcal{N}]$ the valuation identical to ρ except for $\rho[X/\mathcal{N}](X) = \mathcal{N}$. For each node $u \in Nodes(g)$, we define when u *satisfies a node formula* N *under a valuation* ρ, in notation $\rho, u \models N$, as follows:

$$
\begin{aligned}
&\rho, u \models X && \text{iff } u \in \rho(X)\\
&\rho, u \models \exists^{\geq n}\mathsf{edge}\,(E) && \text{iff } \#\{u \xrightarrow{a} v \in Edges(g) \mid \rho, u \xrightarrow{a} v \models E\} \geq n\\
&\rho, u \models \neg N && \text{iff } \rho, u \not\models N\\
&\rho, u \models N_1 \wedge N_2 && \text{iff } (\rho, u \models N_1) \wedge (\rho, u \models N_2)\\
&\rho, u \models \mu X.N && \text{iff } \forall \mathcal{N} \subseteq Nodes(g).\\
&&& \quad (\forall v \in Nodes(g).\rho[X/\mathcal{N}], v \models N \supset \rho[X/\mathcal{N}], v \models X)\\
&&& \quad \supset \rho[X/\mathcal{N}], u \models X
\end{aligned}
$$

where

$$
\begin{aligned}
&\rho, u \xrightarrow{a} v \models p && \text{iff } \mathcal{T} \models p(a)\\
&\rho, u \xrightarrow{a} v \models \mathsf{to}(N) && \text{iff } \rho, v \models N\\
&\rho, u \xrightarrow{a} v \models \neg E && \text{iff } \rho, u \xrightarrow{a} v \not\models E\\
&\rho, u \xrightarrow{a} v \models E_1 \wedge E_2 && \text{iff } (\rho, u \xrightarrow{a} v \models E_1) \wedge (\rho, u \xrightarrow{a} v \models E_2)
\end{aligned}
$$

---

[2] This is the usual *syntactic monotonicity* constraint typical of fixpoint logics, that guarantees the monotonicity of the fixpoint operator.

Given a graph G (either a ground graph or a schema) and a closed node formula N, we say that G satisfies N, in notation $G \sqsubseteq N$, if for every ground graph g conforming to G, $root(g) \models N$. It is easy to see that if g is a ground graph and N is a node formula, then $g \sqsubseteq N$ if and only if $root(g) \models N$.

A graph selection query (gs-query) Q is a closed node formula. The evaluation of Q over a database DB returns the set $Q(DB)$ of all consistent graphs $G \in DB$ such that $G \sqsubseteq Q$. A gs-query Q is satisfiable if there exists a database DB such that $Q(DB)$ is non-empty. Given two gs-queries Q_1 and Q_2, Q_1 is contained in Q_2 if for every database DB, $Q_1(DB) \subseteq Q_2(DB)$, and Q_1 is disjoint from Q_2 if for every database DB, $Q_1(DB) \cap Q_2(DB) = \emptyset$.

On the basis of a polynomial reduction of satisfiability of a gs-query to satisfiability in a variant of modal mu-calculus [11], we were able to prove the following: Checking a gs-query for satisfiability and checking containment and disjointness between two gs-queries are EXPTIME-complete problems [6].

References

[1] S. Abiteboul. Querying semi-structured data. In *Proc. of ICDT-97*, pages 1–18, 1997.

[2] S. Abiteboul, S. Cluet, V. Christophides, T. Milo, and J. S. Guido Moerkotte. Querying documents in object databases. *Int. J. on Digital Libraries*, 1(1):5–19, 1997.

[3] S. Abiteboul, D. Quass, J. McHugh, J. Widom, and J. L. Wiener. The Lorel query language for semistructured data. *Int. J. on Digital Libraries*, 1(1):68–88, 1997.

[4] P. Buneman, S. Davidson, M. Fernandez, and D. Suciu. Adding structure to unstructured data. In *Proc. of ICDT-97*, pages 336–350, 1997.

[5] P. Buneman, S. Davidson, G. Hillebrand, and D. Suciu. A query language and optimization technique for unstructured data. In *Proc. of ACM SIGMOD*, pages 505–516, 1996.

[6] D. Calvanese, G. De Giacomo, and M. Lenzerini. Queries and constraints on semi-structured data. Technical Report 13-98, Dip. di Inf. e Sist., Univ. di Roma "La Sapienza", 1998.

[7] D. Calvanese, G. De Giacomo, and M. Lenzerini. What can knowledge representation do for semi-structured data? In *Proc. of AAAI-98*, pages 205–210, 1998.

[8] M. F. Fernandez, D. Florescu, J. Kang, A. Y. Levy, and D. Suciu. Catching the boat with strudel: Experiences with a web-site management system. In *Proc. of ACM SIGMOD*, pages 414–425, 1998.

[9] M. F. Fernandez, D. Florescu, A. Y. Levy, and D. Suciu. A query language for a web-site management system. *SIGMOD Record*, 26(3):4–11, 1997.

[10] R. Goldman and J. Widom. DataGuides: Enabling query formulation and optimization in semistructured databases. In *Proc. of VLDB-97*, pages 436–445, 1997.

[11] D. Kozen. Results on the propositional μ-calculus. *Theor. Comp. Sci.*, 27:333–354, 1983.

[12] A. Mendelzon, G. A. Mihaila, and T. Milo. Querying the World Wide Web. *Int. J. on Digital Libraries*, 1(1):54–67, 1997.

[13] D. Quass, A. Rajaraman, I. Sagiv, J. Ullman, and J. Widom. Querying semistructured heterogeneous information. In *Proc. of DOOD-95*, pages 319–344. Springer-Verlag, 1995.

A Prototype for Metadata-Based Integration of Internet Sources

Christof Bornhövd and Alejandro P. Buchmann

DVS1, Department of Computer Science, Darmstadt University of Technology,
D-64283 Darmstadt, Germany
{bornhoev,buchmann}@dvs1.informatik.tu-darmstadt.de

Abstract. The combination of semistructured data from different sources on the Internet often fails because of syntactic and semantic differences. The resolution of these heterogeneities requires explicit context information in the form of metadata. We give a short overview of a representation model that is well suited for the explicit description of semistructured data, and show how it is used as the basis of a prototype for metadata-driven integration of heterogeneous data extracted from Web-pages.

1 Introduction

A wide variety of Information is available over the Internet. However, an integration of available data for further *automatic* processing is rarely possible because of a lack of uniform structure and meaning. Semantic context information is, at best, available locally to the institution managing the data source, and is lost when data is exchanged across institutional boundaries. Most sources provide data in semistructured form, and provide no explicitly specified schema with information about the structure and semantics of the data. The following HTML pages from different car reservation systems illustrate this.

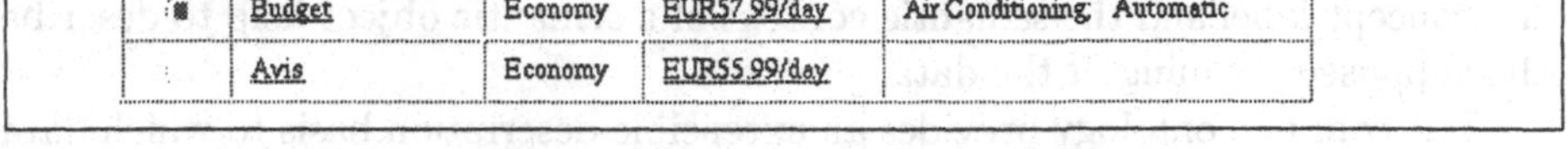

Fig. 1. Reservation System A

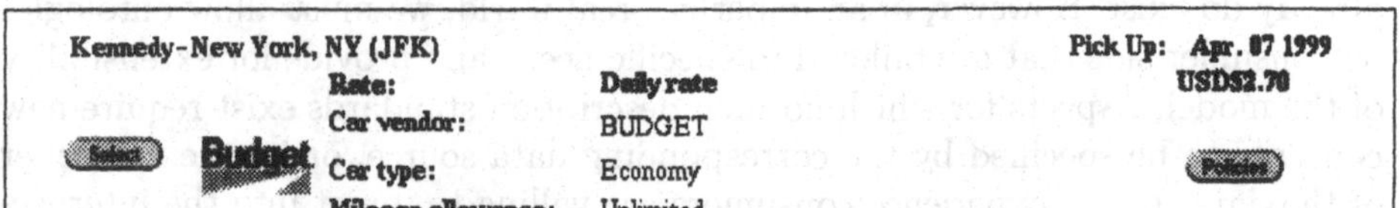

Fig. 2. Reservation System B

M. Jarke, A. Oberweis (Eds.): CAiSE'99, LNCS 1626, pp. 439–445, 1999.
© Springer-Verlag Berlin Heidelberg 1999

To integrate and automatically process these data we must resolve the heterogeneities on the modeling level. This requires explicit knowledge about the structure of and the semantic assumptions underlying the data. For the representation and exchange of this context information [4] we use metadata.

The interpretation of the metadata requires the introduction of a shared vocabulary to reach a common understanding with regard to a given domain. Such a vocabulary is provided by a domain-specific ontology [2,5]. An explicit description of the relationships between the data of a given source and the represented real world phenomenon is established by a reference to the underlying ontology, i.e., by mapping local representation types and terms to semantically corresponding ontology concepts, and adding context information that explicitly describes the underlying modeling assumptions.

In this paper we introduce a representation model that combines the explicit description of modeling assumptions underlying the available data, with concepts of a flexible, self-describing data model suitable for the representation of semistructured data. On the basis of this model we show how data from the Internet can be integrated, and prepared for further automatic processing.

2   MIX – A Metadata Based Integration Model

Our representation model is called *Metadata based Integration model for data X-change*, or MIX for short. MIX is a self-describing data model in the sense of [6], because information about the structure and semantics of the data is given as part of the available data itself, thus allowing a flexible association of context information in the form of metadata.

The model is based on the concept of a *semantic object*. A semantic object represents a data item together with its underlying *semantic context*, which consists of a variable set of meta-attributes (also represented as semantic objects) that explicitly describe implicit modeling assumptions. Our approach is based on the notion of context as proposed in [7,4]. A more comprehensive notion of context can be found in [3].

In addition, each semantic object has a *concept label* associated with it that specifies the relationship between the object and the real world aspects it describes. These concept labels are taken from a commonly known ontology. Thus, the concept label and the semantic context of a semantic object help to describe the supposed meaning of the data.

The common ontology provides an extensible description basis to which data providers and consumers should refer. In specific application domains ontologies already do exist. However, in an imperfect real world, we must allow ontologies on consumer side that are tailored to specific needs and provide for extensibility of the model. Aspects for which no such description standards exist require new concepts to be specified by the corresponding data source, or by the consumer of the data. In our experience consumers are willing to invest into the interpretation of sources and extension of the ontologies if this results in future savings through automatic processing. By providing the means for adding metadata and extending the ontology on the receiver side, we believe that we can claim a reasonable combination of rigor and flexibility that makes the model applicable in real-life situations.

We distinguish between simple and complex semantic objects. *Simple semantic objects* represent atomic data items, such as simple number values or text strings. In contrast, *complex semantic objects* can be understood as heterogeneous collections of semantic objects, each of which describes exactly one attribute of the represented phenomenon. These subobjects are grouped under a corresponding ontology concept. The attributes given for a complex semantic object are divided in those used, similar to a set of key attributes in the relational model, to identify an object of a given concept, and additional attributes that might not be given for all objects of the concept. Attributes used for the identification provide the prerequisite for the identification of semantic objects that represent the same real world phenomenon.

For example, the data given by system A in Fig. 1 may be represented as the complex semantic object $SemObj_A$ of concept *CarOffer* given in Fig. 3. Each offer is identified by the attributes underlined. Additional properties, such as *Extras* are not required for the unique identification and might not be given for each *CarOffer*. In this way, complex semantic objects provide a flexible way to represent data with irregular structure, as it may be given by semistructured sources, or may result from the integration of different heterogeneous data sources.

```
SemObjA = < CarOffer, {
              < Company, "Budget" >,
              < Location, "J.F.Kennedy Int'l. Airport", {<LocationCode, "FullName">} >,
              < VehicleType, "Economy",              {<TypeCode, "FullClassName">} >,
              < DailyRate, 57.99,                     {<Currency, "EUR"> , <Scale, 1>} >,
              < PickUpDay, "07/03/1999",              {<DateFormat, "DD/MM/YYYY">} >,
              < Extras, "Air Conditioned" >,
              < Extras, "Automatic" >
                                                                        } >  } >
SemObjB = < CarOffer, {
              < Company, "Budget" >,
              < Location, "JFK",                      {<LocationCode, "ThreeLetterCode">} >,
              < VehicleType, "Economy",              {<TypeCode, "FullClassName">} >,
              < DailyRate, 52.70,                     {<Currency, "USD"> , <Scale, 1>} >,
              < PickUpDay, "Apr. 07 1999",            {<DateFormat, "Mon. DD YYYY">} >,
              < FreeMiles, "Unlimited" >
                                                                        } >  } >
```

Fig. 3. MIX Representation of Source A and B

For a semantically meaningful comparison of semantic objects we must take their underlying context into consideration. We use *conversion functions* by which semantic objects can be converted among different semantic contexts. These functions can be specified in the underlying ontology, or may be stored in an application-specific conversion library. Based on these mapping functions, semantic objects can be compared by converting them to a common semantic context, and comparing their underlying data values.

The MIX model is capable of representing data from different sources in a uniform way, and on a common interpretation basis. This supports the automatic processing of the data after their integration. Space limitations forced us to describe a short version of MIX. A detailed and formal presentation can be found in [1].

The data provided by the reservation systems introduced in Sec. 1 may be represented as shown in Fig. 3. By avoiding the need to agree on all attributes, both sources can agree on the same meaning for essential aspects of *CarOffer*, even though both sources make different semantic assumptions which result in different semantic contexts for their data.

The process of integrating data represented on the basis of MIX takes place in two steps. First, the semantic objects have to be converted to a common context, which can be specified by the application interested in the data, using appropriate conversion functions.

```
S = {  < LocationCode, "ThreeLetterCode" >,
       < DateFormat, "DD.MM.YYYY" >,
       < TypeCode, "FullClassName" >,
       < Currency, "EUR" >,
       < Scale, 1 >                              }
```

Fig. 4. Common Representation Context

In the second step, semantic objects which represent the same real world object are identified by comparing their identifying attributes, and are fused into a common representation. For example, using context S in Fig. 4, as the common context and conversion functions for the aspects specified in S they may be classified as representing the same offer. Therefore, they are integrated into one semantic object by unification of their attribute sets. Properties described in both objects that are equivalent are represented only once as shown in Fig. 5, where $SemObj_A$ and $SemObj_B$ have been merged into $SemObj_{AB}$.

```
SemObj_AB = < CarOffer, {
             < Company, "Budget" >,
             < Location, "JFK",          {<LocationCode, "ThreeLetterCode">} >,
             < VehicleType, "Economy",   {<TypeCoding, "FullClassName">} >,
             < DailyRate, 57.99,         {<Currency, "EUR">, <Scale, 1>} >,
             < PickUpDay, "07.03.1999",  {<DateFormat, "DD.MM.YYYY">} >,
             < Extras, "Air Conditioned" >,
             < Extras, "Automatic" >,
             < FreeMiles, "Unlimited" >                              } >    } >
```

Fig. 5. Unified MIX Representation

3   Metadata-Based Prototype

To evaluate the MIX model we implemented an application independent Java framework that manages and exchanges semantic metadata. The implementation follows the mediator approach introduced in [9] and is shown in Fig. 6. The bottom layer of the architecture consists of autonomous data sources that may be structured or semistructured. The current prototype supports the mapping of relational databases and XML documents.

Wrappers map local data structures from the source to the concepts specified in the ontology. As stated earlier, the preferred solution is to use standardized ontologies, which exist for some domains, at the source. However, the framework provides the means to extend the ontologies both by the source or the consumer and even to provide an ontology entirely on the consumer side. This makes sense when a consumer interacts regularly with a fixed set of semistructured sources that do not always adhere to an ontology. In the current prototype, data wrappers are implemented as Java classes. These are registered with the federation manager and can be loaded dynamically to transfer data from the source. Wrappers that are not available at the federation manager can be loaded from designated wrapper servers. In this way the architecture allows a flexible management of a large number of data sources that may change frequently.

The federation manager keeps a metadata repository that includes the ontology information as well as information about the wrappers. When the federation manager receives a request the information in this repository is used to identify the appropriate wrapper classes, which are cached by the federation manager. The wrapper classes return semantic objects to the federation manager who converts them to the semantic context specified by the application. Semantically identical objects are fused as explained in Sec. 2. The federation manager then returns the unified semantic objects in the form of Java objects. The application views the data on the level of concepts from a domain-specific ontology without being aware of their local organization.

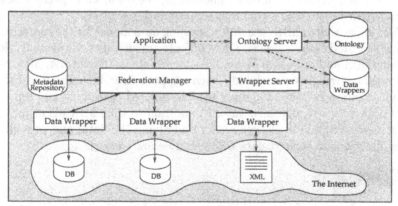

Fig. 6. The MIX Integration Framework

The ontology server stores and manages the domain-specific vocabulary underlying the federation. The concepts of the ontology are given as precompiled Java classes that can be downloaded by the application and the wrappers. To ensure the consistency of the ontology, new concepts are integrated by extending or specializing existing concepts in a predefined way to avoid ambiguous specifications or homonyms. The consistency of a given concept specification is ensured through the language constructs of Java.

To request data, an application builds SQL-like queries using the concepts of the ontology. The federation manager returns semantic objects, i.e. objects that are augmented with metadata. The application can then use these objects without further processing. The connection of an application to the corresponding ontology is established at compile time through the use of import statements which load the necessary concept classes into the local directory path.

As a sample application, the prototype includes an object browser that displays the semantic objects returned by the federation manager and allows the navigation of the object structure. In this way the attributes of complex semantic objects, as well as additional context information can be displayed interactively.

4   Related Research

Because of space limitations we mention only three approaches closely related to MIX. Our concept of a semantic object extends the data model discussed in [7] with regard to complex, maybe irregularly structured data objects. They assume a common vocabulary. MIX makes this vocabulary *explicit* and provides both for the *exchange* of vocabularies, and their *extensibility*.

XML [8] provides a flexible model for the representation and exchange of data similar to MIX. However, XML does not enforce a semantically meaningful data exchange per se, since different providers can define different tags to represent semantically similar information. Furthermore, XML does not support the integration of heterogeneous data. In contrast, MIX supports an explicit representation of semantic differences underlying the data, and specifies how this data may be converted to a common representation.

OEM [6], as well as MIX, is a self-describing data model for the representation of semistructured data. However, OEM objects are identified via system-wide object identifiers, and are based on source-specific labels. In contrast, MIX objects have certain attributes associated which support their identification based on their information content. Finally, OEM is tailored mainly to the representation of data with irregular structure. In addition to this, MIX also supports an explicit representation of the semantics underlying the data, and provides conversion functions to convert data between different contexts.

5   Conclusion

We presented a way of integrating data sources from the Internet which is not claimed to be generally applicable, but provides a fairly simple solution for many application domains. We use MIX in a project for the integration of travel data. The prototype of a Java-based implementation exists for MIX and the MIX integration environment. Current research is concerned with the extension of the representation of conversion functions, and with the extraction of MIX representations for a wider range of semistructured data.

References

1. Bornhövd, C.: *Semantic Metadata for the Integration of Web-based Data for Electronic Commerce*, Proc. Int. Worksh. on E-Commerce and Web-based Information Systems, Santa Clara, 1999
2. Gruber, T.: *Toward Principles for the Design of Ontologies Used for Knowledge Sharing*, International Journal of Human and Computer Studies, 43(5/6), 1995
3. Kashyap, V.; Sheth, A.: *Semantic and Schematic Similarities between Database Objects: A Context-based Approach*, VLDB Journal, 5(4) 1996
4. Madnick, S.E.: *From VLDB to VMLDB (Very MANY Large Data Bases): Dealing with Large-Scale Semantic Heterogeneity*, Proc. VLDB Conf., Zurich, Swizerland, 1995
5. Mena, E.; Kashyap, V.; Illarramendi, A.; Sheth, A.: *Domain Specific Ontologies for Semantic Information Brokering on the Global Information Infrastructure*, Proc. Int. Conf. on Formal Ontology in Information Systems, Trento, Italy, 1998
6. Papakonstantinou, Y.; Garcia-Molina, H.; Widom, J.: *Object Exchange Across Heterogeneous Information Sources*, Proc. Int. Conf. on Data Engineering, Taipei, Taiwan, 1995
7. Sciore, E.; Siegel, M.; Rosenthal, A.: *Using Semantic Values to Facilitate Interoperability Among Heterogeneous Information Systems*, ACM TODS, 19(2), 1994
8. W3C: *Extensible Markup Language (XML) 1.0*, Feb. 10, 1998
9. Wiederhold, G.: *Mediation in Information Systems*, ACM Comp. Surv., 27(2), 1995

Workflow Management Through Distributed and Persistent CORBA Workflow Objects

Mathias Weske

Lehrstuhl für Informatik, Universität Münster
Steinfurter Straße 107, D-48149 Münster, Germany
weske@helios.uni-muenster.de

1 Introduction

Workflow management has gained increasing attention recently as an important technology to improve information system development in flexible and distributed organizations [2,3,8,5]. The WASA project aims at supporting flexible and distributed workflows, using an object-oriented design and the CORBA middleware standard. This paper describes major design goals of WASA$_2$, and it sketches the architecture and implementation of the system based on CORBA workflow objects and CORBA Common Object Services.

2 WASA$_2$ Design Goals

In order to be suitable for a broad spectrum of workflow applications, there are different requirements that have to be met by a workflow management system [6]; we put our emphasis on the topics distribution and scalability, persistency, and flexibility; additional topics are discussed in [9].

Distribution and Scalability Traditionally, workflow management systems are client/server systems such that the server corresponds to a workflow engine, and workflow users access the system using workflow clients as interfaces. Considering workflow executions, this approach can be conceived as distributed since the work performed during the workflow is done in the client side, and typically there are multiple clients involved in a workflow execution. However, as far as controlling the execution of workflows is concerned, the client/server-approach is in fact a centralized one: The workflow engine is a centralized server, which controls the execution of all workflows in a given organization. In large scale workflow applications, the centralized site is likely to receive a heavy load, which may result in performance problems and scalability issues. Besides the fact that the centralized workflow engine can become a performance bottleneck, it is a single point of failure, such that the availability of the workflow application depends on a single site. Regarding performance and fault tolerance issues, for these kind of application it would be much more adequate to use a distributed approach instead of a central one. Thereby we mean that workflow control is performed decentralized, not just workflow executions as is done in today's workflow management systems.

M. Jarke, A. Oberweis (Eds.): CAiSE'99, LNCS 1626, pp. 446–450, 1999.
© Springer-Verlag Berlin Heidelberg 1999

Persistency The success of organizations nowadays relies to a considerable extent on the availability of its information infrastructure. In the database context, this has led to the development of elaborate concurrency control and recovery techniques, aiming at providing execution guarantees in the presence of multiple concurrent users and system failures. Providing this kind of functionality is also important for workflow management systems. In particular, a system failure should not leave running workflow instances and manipulated data in an undefined state. In contrast, up-to-date information on the state of running workflow instances has to be stored in stable storage in order to be able to continue interrupted workflows after the system is restarted. A key prerequisite to develop a fault-tolerant workflow management system which implements a functional workflow restart procedure is to maintain explicit state information of workflow instances and accompanying data on running workflow executions in stable, persistent storage.

Flexibility The first generation of workflow management systems are well suited for modeling and controlling the execution of application processes with a predefined and static structure [3,2]. Adequate support for partially specified or dynamically changing application processes, however, is not provided. This limitation is seen today as one of the main obstacles for the deployment of workflow applications in real-world organization, because workflow users and workflow administrators often encounter situations which have not been foreseen at workflow modeling time and which thus require a dynamic change. As a result, a desirable feature of workflow management systems is to allow structural changes of workflows while they are executing [5,6]; this functionality is known as dynamic change. Allowing rapid changes of workflows increases the competitiveness of an organization significantly.

3   Systems Design

The architecture of the WASA$_2$ prototype consists of three levels (Figure 1): The application level is the top level of the architecture. Users access workflow applications with a graphical user interface (GUI). To perform workflow activities, the GUI can start external applications, as defined in the workflow schema, for instance office applications, existing domain-specific applications or methods provided by business objects. We remark that the graphical user interface is configurable to support the needs of different user groups. In addition, there are integrated tools for the specification of workflow schemas and for monitoring and dynamic modification of workflow instances. In the intermediate level there are facilities used to provide support for workflow applications. Due to the object-oriented approach, on this level there are workflow objects and related objects, as described in the WASA$_2$ workflow meta schema [9]. Business objects also reside on the facility level. Workflow objects, business objects and the graphical user interface communicate through a CORBA Object Request Broker. To implement workflow objects and related objects, CORBA Common

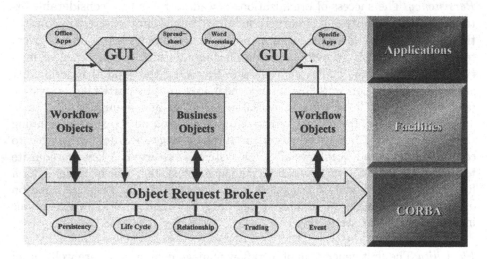

Fig. 1. Architecture of WASA$_2$ system.

Object Services (COS) are used extensively; in the WASA project, we have implemented a number of CORBA COS. Now we describe how the design goals are supported by the WASA$_2$ system.

Distribution and Scalability In WASA$_2$, workflows are executed and controlled fully distributed, using CORBA workflow objects: The execution of a complex workflow starts with the initiation of its sub-workflows. Without going into the technical details, sub-workflow instances are instantiated as CORBA objects, and the control flow and data flow connectors between them are also represented by CORBA objects. The execution is controlled by messages, sent between workflow objects. In particular, to start a sub-workflow, the super-workflow sends a message to that sub-workflow instance. On receipt of that message, the sub-workflow is started. When the sub-workflow instance terminates, it sends a message to each workflow instance, which follows the terminated workflow in control flow, as defined by the respective workflow schema. This procedure continues until the last sub-workflow instance of the complex workflow terminates; this workflow sends a message to the super-workflow. On receipt of that message, the complex workflow is terminated. We mention that workflow objects can reside in different sites of a distributed computing system. By placing workflow objects on different sites (and by adding machines if necessary), the system scales up nicely. The Internet Inter ORB protocol (IIOP) allows the transparent communication of multiple ORBs.

Persistency Persistent workflow objects is the prerequisite for fault tolerant workflow executions. In WASA$_2$, a Persistency Service is used to implement persistent workflow objects. Assume there is a complex workflow instance i with sub-workflow instances j, k, l, to be executed sequentially: i sends a message to

j and waits for the message from l, indicating the successful completion of the complex workflow. Assume the site of i goes down after it sent a start-message to j, and the other workflow instances are in different sites. Then the sub-workflows j, k and l can execute, even though i is currently not available. When l terminates it tries to send a message to i, informing i of its completion. Assuming the site of i is up again at this point in time, the ORB daemon in that site accepts the request. Since the object i is not in main memory, the ORB daemon loads it dynamically from persistent storage using the Persistency Service. Notice that the state of i is valid since the transactional property of the Persistency Services guarantees that i is in a consistent state. After the complex workflow instance i is loaded, the message is sent to i, which resumes execution.

Flexibility WASA$_2$ supports dynamic changes, i.e., the ability to change workflow instances while they execute. As is elaborated in [9], the system determines the set of workflow instances which can be adapted to a particular dynamic change, and it allows to continue workflow instances with the changed workflow schema by changing the instance-of relationship between workflow instance objects and workflow schema objects. We remark that dynamic changes have to be embedded in an organizational framework, which defines who has the ability and competence to change workflow schemas and running workflow instances. The WASA$_2$ system, however, provides the mechanisms to support dynamic modifications on the technical level.

4   Conclusions

Our work is related to the quest of the OMG to define a Workflow Management Facility. However, the Workflow Management Facility proposal [1] stresses runtime interoperability of existing workflow management systems and the ability to use workflow monitoring and auditing tools in these settings [6]. Other approaches to object-oriented workflow management system design include the Meteor$_2$ project at the University of Georgia [7]. In Meteor$_2$, workflow specifications are translated into executable code, which is then executed in a distributed fashion. CORBA is used in the Meteor$_2$ system as a communication infrastructure for distributed workflow executions.

This paper overviews the conceptual foundations and the system design and implementation of WASA$_2$, an object-oriented workflow management system based on CORBA. An in-depth presentation of the conceptual design and implementation of WASA$_2$ can be found in [9]. Key features are reuse of workflow schemas, distributed workflow execution control, persistent workflow executions, and the support for dynamic modifications of running workflow instances with the ability to control the scope of these changes. It is interesting to notice that the requirements as specified in [6] to a large extent are satisfied by the WASA$_2$ system, involving (i) changes of the underlying process model, (ii) composition of reusable business components, (iii) monitoring of process execution, (iv) distribution of a process across business domains and (v) assignment of process steps to workflow participants.

Acknowledgments: The author is thankful to the WASA group at the University of Münster.

References

1. CoCreate Software, Concentus, CSE Systems, Data Access Technologies, Digital Equipment Corp., DSTC, EDS, FileNet Corp., Fujitsu Ltd., Hitachi Ltd., Genesis Development Corp., IBM Corp., ICL Enterprises, NIIIP Consortium, Oracle Corp., Plexus - Division of BankTec, Siemens Nixdorf Informationssysteme, SSA, Xerox: *BODTF-RFP 2 Submission Workflow Management Facility (jointFlow)*. OMG Document bom/98-06-07 (1998)
2. Georgakopoulos, D., Hornick, M., Sheth, A.: *An Overview of Workflow Management: From Process Modeling to Workflow Automation Infrastructure.* Distributed and Parallel Databases, 3:119–153, 1995
3. Leymann, F., Altenhuber, W.: *Managing Business Processes as an Information Resource.* IBM Systems Journal 33, 1994, 326–347
4. OMG: *CORBAServices: Common Object Services Specification.* (available from www.omg.org)
5. Reichert, M., Dadam, P.: *Supporting Dynamic Changes of Workflows Without Loosing Control.* Journal of Intelligent Information Systems, Special Issue on Workflow and Process Management, Vol. 10, No. 2, 1998
6. Schmidt, M.-T.: *Building Workflow Business Objects.* OOPSLA'98 Workshop 8: Business Object Design and Implementation IV: From Business Objects to Complex Adaptive Systems (download from www.jeffsutherland.org/oopsla98/mts.html on 11-11-98)
7. Sheth, A., Kochut, K.J.: *Workflow Applications to Research Agenda: Scalable and Dynamic Work Coordination and Collaboration Systems.* In: Dogac, Kalinichenko, zsu, Sheth (Eds.): Workflow Management Systems and Interoperability. NATO ASI Series, Series F: Computer and Systems Sciences, Vol. 164, 35–60. Berlin: Springer 1998
8. Vossen, G., Weske M.: *The WASA Approach to Workflow Management for Scientific Applications.* In: Dogac, Kalinichenko, zsu, Sheth (Eds.): Workflow Management Systems and Interoperability. NATO ASI Series, Series F: Computer and Systems Sciences, Vol. 164, 145–164. Berlin: Springer 1998
9. Weske, M.: *Design and Implementation of an Object-Oriented Workflow Management System based on CORBA.* Fachbericht Angewandte Informatik und Mathematik 33/98-I, University of Muenster 1998

Component Criteria for Information System Families

Stan Jarzabek

Department of Computer Science, School of Computing
National University of Singapore
Lower Kent Ridge Road
Singapore 119260
stan@comp.nus.edu.sg

Abstract. In this paper, we discuss component technologies in the context of information system (IS) families. An IS family is characterized by common requirements, shared by all the family members, and variant requirements that may differ across family members. Many variant requirements are non-local, i.e., they cannot be confined to a single system component, on contrary, they affect many components in complex ways. An effective generic architecture for an IS family should provide means to handle anticipated and unexpected variant requirements and support evolution of the family over years. In the paper, we illustrate problems that arise in supporting IS families and describe a generic architecture that includes global, cross-component structures to deal with changes during customization and evolution of an IS family.

1 Introduction

An information system (IS) family comprises similar information systems. A family may address a coherent business area (such as payroll or customer order processing) or a certain problem area (such as task management or failure detection). Members of an IS family share common characteristics, but also differ in certain variant requirements. A systematic way to support an IS family is to implement common and variant functions within a generic architecture and then develop individual information systems by customizing and extending the architecture. Many variant requirements for IS families are non-local, i.e., they affect many system components. An effective generic IS architecture should help developers in handling non-local variant requirements. Furthermore, to support evolving business, a generic IS architecture itself must evolve by accommodating new requirements. For the long-term success of an architecture, methods and tools should be provided to keep the complexity of a growing architecture under control. In practice, customizations and evolution of IS family architectures appear to be difficult tasks.

In recent years, Component-based Software Engineering (CBSE) and Distributed Component Platforms (DCP) [6] have received much attention. Component-based systems are built out of autonomous, independently developed runtime components. By conforming to the DCP's interoperability standards, functionality of a component-

M. Jarke, A. Oberweis (Eds.): CAiSE'99, LNCS 1626, pp. 451–455, 1999.

based system can be extended either by adding new components to the system or by replacing a certain component with another one, providing richer functionality. Binary components can be customized using the introspection facility [6]. Component technologies promise to better facilitate reuse and improve software development and maintenance productivity.

In this paper, we shall discuss component technologies in the context of IS families. In our experience, generic IS architectures based on runtime components may not provide sufficient support for customization and evolution. We shall illustrate the problem with an example from our project and outline a possible remedy to the problem.

2   Related Work

The concept of program families was first discussed by Parnas [7] who proposed information hiding as a technique for handling program families. Since then, a range of approaches have been proposed to handle different types of variations (for example, variant user requirements or platform dependencies) in different application domains. Pre-processing, PCL [8], application generators [3], Object-Oriented frameworks [5], Domain-Specific Software Architectures [9], frame technology [2] and, most recently, distributed component platforms – they all offer mechanisms for handling variations that can be useful in supporting IS families.

A software architecture is described by a set of components, externally visible properties of components and component relationships [1]. The rationale for most of the architectures we build is to facilitate reuse – with possible modifications, we wish to reuse an architecture in more than one project. Therefore, most of the architectures really underlie system families rather than a single system. A number of authors advocate clear separation of a construction-time software architecture from it's runtime architecture [1,2,4]. The major concern of construction-time architectures is flexibility, i.e., the ability to customize components to meet variant requirements of products and the ability to evolve the architecture over time to meet changing needs of the business environment. Issues of interest in runtime architectures include allocation of functions to components, deciding which logical components should be packaged into a single executable, parallel execution of components, data communication, invocation of services between components, overall control and synchronization. A generic IS architecture is a software construction-time architecture for supporting an IS family. In a generic IS architecture, some of architecture components may be optional, incomplete or missing. During customization, developers select components and customize them to accommodate specific variant requirements to be implemented in the target information system.

In frame technology [2], a software construction architecture consists of a hierarchy of generic components called frames. A frame is a text (written in any language, such as, for example, IDL™ or Java™) with breakpoints. Frames can be adapted to meet variant requirements of a specific system by modifying frame's code at breakpoints. Frames are organized into frame hierarchies and all the modifications needed to satisfy given variant requirements can be traced from the topmost frame in the hierarchy, called a specification frame. A frame processor is a tool that customizes a frame hierarchy according to directives written in the specification frame and assembles the customized system.

Boca [5] provides a meta-language to define business semantics as a central part of the construction-time architecture. Business components such as customers, orders, employees, hiring and invoicing are specified in the meta-language, separately from the runtime program characteristics. A meta-language provides means for maintaining integrity of requirements for a system family during customization and evolution. Boca supports synthesis of component-based runtime systems from business and implementation-specific component layers. A construction architecture makes it possible to separate business concerns from platform concerns.

3   A Generic IS Architecture Based on Runtime Components

Consider a family of Facility Reservation Systems (FRS). Members of the FRS family include facility reservation systems for offices, universities, hotels, recreational and medical institutions. There are many variant requirements in the FRS domain: In some cases, an FRS should allow one to define facility types (such as Meeting Room and PC) and only an authorized person should be allowed to add new facility types and delete an existing facility type; some FRSes may allow one to view existing reservations by facility ID and/or by reservation date.

During runtime, we want FRSes to consist of three tiers, namely user interface, business logic and a database. Each of these tiers is a component that consists of smaller components, implemented according to standards of the underlying platform (for example, EJB™ or ActiveX™). Suppose we decide to manage an FRS family in terms of runtime components, using one of the available visual environments. A developer should be able to selectively include variant requirements into a custom FRS. To achieve this, all the anticipated variant requirements should be implemented within the relevant components. Most often components affected by variant requirements span all three tiers. A developer might use an introspection facility [6] to customize components. He or she would set component property values to indicate which reservation viewing methods are needed in a target FRS. After customization, components would reveal only the required functions. In the situation of an IS family, this scenario may not work well. Each family member we build will have to include implementation of all the variants, even though some of these variants will never be used. As more and more variants are implemented, components will grow in size. Also, keeping track of how variants affect components must be taken care by developers. Adding new unexpected requirements to the FRS family is not easy, either. If the source code for components affected by new requirements is not available, there is no simple way to implement a new requirement. Developers may need to re-implement affected components, as components cannot be extended in arbitrary ways without the source code. If the source code for relevant components is available, developers could use either inheritance or a suitable design pattern to create new components that would address the new requirement. Visual environments built on top of DCPs support the former solution and some support the latter one (see, for example, the San Francisco framework http://www.ibm.com/Java/SanFrancisco, chapter 8 "Application Development methodology"). While this method of addressing new requirements is sufficient in the rapid application development situation, it presents certain dangers in the context of generic architectures for IS families. Over years of evolution, an architecture may be affected by many new requirements. Implementation of new requirements will add new components (or new versions of old components) to the architecture. As certain requirements may appear in different combinations – we may end up with even more components. As a result, our architecture may become overly complex and difficult to use. These components, growing in size and complexity, have to be included into any information system built based on the architecture, independently of whether the options are need or not. In longterm, accumulative result of this practice is likely to be prohibitive.

4   A Construction-Time Extension of a Runtime Architecture

An architecture based on runtime components does not allow us to exploit software flexibility to its fullest potential [2]. We can alleviate the problems discussed in the last section by designing a generic IS architecture based on construction units that facilitate change better than runtime components. A generic architecture should make it clear how to handle variant requirements and provide a systematic way of extending IS family with new unexpected requirements. While runtime components must be complete executable units, construction units of a generic architecture may be parametarized by variant requirements and may require pre-processing before they can be compiled. Furthermore, construction units may be incomplete in the sense that we may encapsulate different aspects of a system such as business logic, platformdependencies (e.g., event handling code), etc., in separate units. A proper tool will automatically apply a composition operation to combine required construction units into components of a custom system. In the above scenario for supporting an IS family, the emphasis is shifted from ready to use components to the process that produces components from construction units on demand. We think this is essential to keep the complexity of the architecture under control. By studying the customization process for anticipated variant requirements, developers can also better understand how to deal with unexpected requirements that arise during system evolution.

Frame technology [2] directly supports most of the above concepts. It forms a construction environment for managing system families, in particular, it can be applied to component-based systems. In our domain engineering project, we designed a generic FRS architecture as a hierarchy of frames, where frames correspond to components of the FRS runtime architecture. We extended a frame hierarchy with an explicit model of commonalties and variations in the FRS domain, and with a Customization Decision Tree (CDT). A CDT helps understand customizations that lead to satisfying variant requirements. Nodes in the CDT correspond to variant requirements. A script attached to a CDT node specifies customizations of a generic architecture for a given variant requirement. Frame processing is based on a composition operation that can be applied at different levels of abstraction. Before applying a frame processor, we assemble customization scripts from the CDT into a specification frame. The frame processor interprets the specification frame to produce a custom software system, according to a blueprint of its component-based runtime architecture.

5   Conclusions

In the paper, we discussed problems that arise when we base a generic architecture for an IS family on runtime components. As customizations and evolution of an IS family most often affect many runtime components, it is better to base a generic IS architecture on construction units that are designed for the purpose of dealing with changes. Construction units should be parameterized by variant requirements and should partition the implementation space into cohesive, manageable parts that can be combined into custom components using a composition operation and a suitable tool.

Acknowledgments

Thanks are due to Cheong Yu Chye who implemented a generic architecture for the FRS family. I am indebted to Paul Bassett for letting us use the Netron's product Fusion for our projects.

References

1.   Bass, L., Clements, P. and Kazman, R. *Software Architecture in Practice*, Addison-Wesley, 1998
2.   Bassett, P. *Framing Software Reuse - Lessons from Real World*, Yourdon Press, Prentice Hall, 1997
3.   Batory, D et al. "The GenVoca Model of Software-System Generators," *IEEE Software*, September 1994, pp. 89-94
4.   Digre, T. "Business Component Architecture," *IEEE Software*, September/October 1998, pp. 60-69
5.   Johnson, R. and Foote, B. "Designing Reusable Classes," *Journal of Component-Oriented Programming*, June 1988, Vol.1, No.2, pp. 22-35.
6.   Krieger, D. and Adler, R. "The Emergence of Distributed Component Platforms," *IEEE Computer*, March 1998, pp. 43-53
7.   Parnas, D. "On the Design and Development of Program Families," *IEEE Trans. on Software Eng.*, March 1976, p. 1-9
8.   Sommerville, I. and Dean, G. "PCL: a language for modelling evolving system architectures," *Software Engineering Journal*, March 1996, pp.111-121
9.   Tracz, W. Collected overview reports from the DSSA project, Technical Report, Loral Federal Systems – Owego. (1994).

TUML: A Method for Modelling Temporal Information Systems

Marianthi Svinterikou[1], Babis Theodoulidis[2]

[1]Intrasoft, GIS Department, Adrianiou 2, 11525 Athens, Greece
MSSvin@tee.gr
[2] UMIST, Department of Computation, Sackville Street, P.O. Box 88,
Manchester M60 1QD, United Kingdom
babis@sna.co.umist.ac.uk

Abstract. Time is a very important aspect of the real world. The importance of time in database applications has led to work on the extension of existing database technologies in order to handle time efficiently. Nevertheless, little work has been done in the area of temporal application development methods. In this paper we present the Temporal Unified Modelling Language (TUML) method. The TUML method extends the Unified Modelling Language (UML) with the temporal semantics defined in the TAU Temporal Object Model and the process of the Booch method to enable the capturing of the temporal semantics of information during information system development.

1 Introduction

Time is a very important aspect of the real world. Most database applications are temporal in nature, that is, they require the maintenance not only of the current state of the modelled reality, but also past and future states [3]. Examples of such applications include medical-record, accounting, banking, reservation systems, etc.

Management of temporal information is very difficult using conventional databases [3]. Capturing the time-varying nature of an information system is left to the developers of the database applications, leading to ad-hoc solutions that must be reinvented each time a new application is developed [3]. To overcome this, there has been a growing interest in extending conventional database technology with temporal concepts.

Nevertheless, little work has been done in the area of temporal analysis and design methods [5], [8]. These methods provide a set of concepts and a set of graphical notations for representing these concepts that apply to the development of temporal information systems. Moreover, they provide a set of methodological guidelines and rules that facilitate the capture of the temporal semantics of information. However, these methods apply mainly to the analysis phase of system development and do not incorporate all the desirable characteristics of an object-oriented (OO) analysis and design method [6].

M. Jarke, A. Oberweis (Eds.): CAiSE'99, LNCS 1626, pp. 456–461, 1999.
© Springer-Verlag Berlin Heidelberg 1999

The work presented in this paper addresses the lack of such a method by proposing the Temporal Unified Modelling Language (TUML) method. The overall aim is to integrate the areas of OO analysis and design methods and temporal OO databases, to provide an OO analysis and design method that facilitates the modelling of temporal OODBs. TUML is presented as an extension of the Unified Modelling Language [10] with temporal semantics and notation. TUML provides a set of constructs to allow the effective modelling of temporal information. In addition, the associated TUML Process is presented that extends the process of the Booch method [1] to enable the capturing of the temporal semantics of information during information system development.

2 Temporal Unified Modelling Language (TUML)

The Temporal UML is based on semantics defined in the TAU Temporal Object Model [4].

In TUML, the time axis is considered to be *discrete, linear, totally ordered* and *bounded* at both ends. The method adopts the *Gregorian* calendar and supports *absolute* time and multiple granularities. The supported granularities are *year, month, day, hour, minute* and *second*.

The method supports user-defined time, valid time and transaction time (it is a *bitemporal method*). Furthermore, temporal support *is optional,* that is, the designer may choose the temporal support for a TUML model element according to his/her needs. Information may be associated with transaction time, valid time, both or none of them. In addition, TUML supports *property timestamping*.

The set of the instances of the *DataType* UML metaclass includes the following classes (*temporal data types*):
1. *Date* which represents unique points in time
2. *Time* which represents either a unique point in time (for which the date is implicit) or a recurring time point
3. *Timestamp* which represents unique points in time
4. *Interval* which is used to represent a duration of time
5. *Timepoint* which refines the Timestamp type to include granularity
6. *Period* which is used to represent an anchored duration of time, that is, a duration of time with a start and end point
7. *Temporal_Element* which is used to represent a finite union of periods

The properties and operations of these types are defined in [4]. The modeller may choose the precision of user-defined times by selecting an appropriate granularity supported by Timepoint, Period and Temporal_Element. In addition, three special time values are defined named *now, beginning* and *forever* that represent the present, the smallest and greatest time values on the time line respectively.

TUML defines a set of stereotypes that enables the modelling of temporal classes, attributes and associations in a TUML model. These stereotypes are called *temporal stereotypes* and may apply to the *class, attribute* or *association* UML element. The core temporal stereotypes are:

1. <<*transaction time class*>> stereotype denotes that the time period of existence in the database should be kept. The element may only have static and/or transaction time properties.
2. <<*valid time class*>> stereotype denotes that the time period of existence in the modelled reality should be kept. The element may only have static and/or valid time properties.
3. <<*bitemporal time class*>> stereotype denotes that the time period of existence in the database as well as the time period of existence in the modelled reality should be kept. The element may have static, transaction time, valid time and/or bitemporal time properties.
4. <<*transaction time attribute*>> stereotype keeps record of all the values of the attribute that were ever entered in the database as well as the time periods that each of the values was valid.
5. <<*valid time attribute*>> stereotype keeps record of all the values that the attribute ever had in the modelled reality as well as the time periods or timepoints that each of the values was valid.
6. <<*bitemporal time attribute*>> stereotype keeps record of all the values of the attribute that were ever entered in the database and the attribute had in the modelled reality as well as the corresponding time periods.
7. <<*transaction time association*>> stereotype denotes that all the instances of the association that were ever entered in the database should be recorded as well as the time periods that each of the instances exists in the database.
8. <<*valid time association*>> stereotype denotes that all the instances of the association that ever existed in the modelled reality should be recorded as well as the corresponding time periods or timepoints.
9. <<*bitemporal time association*>> stereotype denotes that all the instances of the association that were ever entered in the database and existed in the modelled reality should be recorded as well as the corresponding time periods.

The tagged values and constraints that each temporal stereotype defines for an element, to which it is attached, are given in [6].

3 The TUML Process

The *TUML process* is a set of activities that leads to the orderly construction of the system under development by applying the TUML modelling techniques. The TUML process differs from the Booch process in the following points:

1. The TUML modelling techniques are used for the development of the products of each activity.
2. The TUML macro process is driven by the use cases identified at the early stages of analysis.
3. The activity of *identifying the temporal semantics of classes, objects and relationships* is not defined in the Booch micro process. It follows the activity of identifying the relationships among classes and objects and its definition is the main concern of the TUML process.

The TUML process is *iterative* and *incremental*, that is, the software is developed and released gradually, and each release incorporates more functionality than the previous one, aiming to ultimately meet the requirements of the end user. It allows creativity and innovation within a controlled development process by distinguishing the micro and macro elements of the development process.

During the activity of *Identifying the temporal semantics classes, objects and relationships*, the temporal semantics of the classes and objects that were identified earlier in the micro process are defined. When considering the temporal semantics of the classes in a hierarchy lattice, the development team should start by considering the root of the hierarchy lattice, and then continue by examining the classes all the way down to the leaves. For each class the order of events that take place is [6]:

1. *Identify the temporal semantics of the attributes.*
2. *Identify the temporal semantics of the associations.*
3. *Define the temporal semantics of the class.*
4. *Define the temporal semantics of the classes that belong to the same hierarchy as the class under consideration.*

The methodological rules and guidelines that drive these steps are given in [6]. Early in the development process, valid, transaction and bitemporal classes, attributes and relationships are defined. As development proceeds, the temporal semantics of classes and their properties are re-examined and are refined to include the granularity and type of the valid time timestamp of each valid and bitemporal time information.

During the phase of design, the process considers the issue of the physical deletion of database objects with temporal semantics [6].

The process supports reuse of software development artefacts such as classes, designs, code, etc. and domain analysis i.e. the examination of existing related systems in order to identify the classes and objects common to all applications within a given domain [1]. In addition, it provides support for requirements capture by viewing the system in terms of use cases.

4 An Example

Consider the class diagram shown in Fig. 1(a) as the input to the activity of *identifying the temporal semantics of classes, objects and relationships*. According to the diagram, a person has a name, address, phone number and date of birth. A teacher is a kind of person that has a salary per hour and works for a specific number of hours per month. A teacher may teach to one or more classes and a class may have one or more teachers. A class has a code and a maximum number of students.

Initially, the classes that do not have any superclasses are considered namely the Person and Class. First the attributes of Person are considered with regard to time and as it is decided that Person has only static and valid time attributes, it is defined as a valid time class (Fig. 1(b)). At this point, the attributes of the Class and the association, in which it participates, are considered with regard to time. As Class has only static attributes and a valid time association, it is defined as a valid time class

(Fig. 1(b)). Next the attributes of the Teacher are considered. In addition, for each attribute that Teacher inherits from Person, specialising its temporal semantics is considered. Finally the temporal characteristics of Teacher are defined based on the temporal semantics of its superclass Person, its attributes and association. As Person is a valid time class, its subclasses may be either a valid or a bitemporal time class. Teacher has two bitemporal attributes and is therefore defined as a bitemporal time class (Fig. 1(b)).

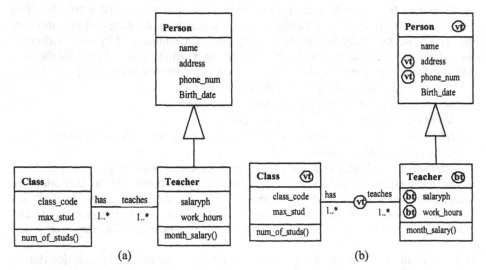

Fig. 1. An example of identifying the temporal semantics of information

5 Conclusions and Future Work

In this paper the language and the process of the TUML method is presented. The TUML method is a temporal OO analysis and design method that addresses the domain of temporal information systems in addition to a wide range of other domains. The method extends from analysis through design to implementation, and consists of the following elements [6]:

1. *The visual language TUML.*
2. *The TUML process.*
3. *The rules and methodological guidelines* for mapping TUML to TAU TODL and *the TODL-specific extensions of TUML* for generating TODL code from TUML diagrams. These TODL-specific rules and guidelines are part of the design and implementation phases of the TUML process.
4. *The TUML Visio stencil,* which is the drawing tool that supports the graphical representation of TUML models.

The work presented in this paper should be extended to incorporate the support of *multiple calendars* and *relative time.* In addition, the mapping of TUML to other temporal OO data models should be considered and work should also focus on the development of a set of tools that will help developers throughout the software development life cycle.

6 Acknowledgements

This work was supported by the Chorochronos project and the Boudouri Institute (Greece). The authors would like to thank John Keane, Ioannis Kakoudakis, Alexandros Vakaloudis and Sofia Svinterikou for their helpful comments on this work.

References

1. Booch, G.: Object-Oriented Analysis and Design with Applications. Benjamin/Cummings Publishing Company, 1994.
2. Jensen, C.S., Cliffrod, J., Elmasri, R., Gadia, S.K, Hayes, P., Jacobia, S. (eds): A Consensus Glossary of Temporal Database Concepts. SIGMOD Record, Vol. 23, (No 1, March 1994, pp. 52-64.
3. Jensen, C. S., Snodgrass, R. T.: Temporal Data Management. Technical Report TR-17, TIMECENTER,1997.Available from http://www.cs.auc.dk/general/DBS/tdb/TimeCenter /publications2.html, Dec. 1997.
4. Kakoudakis, I.: The TAU Temporal Object Model. MPhil Thesis, UMIST, Manchester, UK, 1996.
5. Orci, T.: Course in ORES Methodology. ORES project (ESPRIT P7224 ORES), Royal Institute of Technology, Stockholm, Sweden, 1994.
6. Svinterikou, M.: TUML: A Method for Modelling Temporal Information Systems. MPhil Thesis, UMIST, Manchester, UK, 1998.
7. Theodoulidis, C. I., Loucopoulos, P.: The Time Dimension in Conceptual Modelling. Information Systems, vol. 16, no. 3, 1991, pp. 273-300.
8. Souveyet, C., Deneckere, R., Rolland, C.: TOOBIS Methodology. TOOBIS project, Deliverable T23D1.1, 1997. Available from http://www.di.uoa.gr/~toobis/, Dec. 1997.
9. Snodgrass, R. (ed). The TSQL2 Temporal Query Language. Kluwer Academic Publishers, 1995.
10. Rational Software Corporation, et. al. Unified Modeling Language-Summary. Version 1.1, Sept 1997. Available from http://www.rational.com/uml/1.1/, Dec. 1997.
11. Rational Software Corporation, et. al. Unified Modeling Language-Semantics. Version 1.1, Sept 1997. Available from http://www.rational.com/uml/1.1/, Dec. 1997.
12. Rational Software Corporation, et. al. Unified Modeling Language-Notation Guide. Version 1.1, Sept 1997. Available from http://www.rational.com/uml/1.1/, Dec. 1997.

Beyond Goal Representation: Checking Goal-Satisfaction by Temporal Reasoning with Business Processes

Choong-ho Yi[1] and Paul Johannesson[2]

[1] Department of Information Technology
Karlstad University S-651 88 Karlstad Sweden
e-mail: choong-ho.yi@kau.se
[2] Department of Computer and Systems Sciences
Stockholm University Electrum 230 S-164 40 Kista Sweden
e-mail: pajo@dsv.su.se

Abstract. Most formal approaches to goals proposed within information systems engineering, view goals from the requirements engineering perspective, i.e. for producing future software. Typically, these approaches begin with extracting goals from informal reality and end with representing them in some formal language, leaving the questions arising afterwards unanswered: How can we check whether goals are achieved or not in real business processes? If the goals are not satisfied, why and what to do? This paper presents a formal approach to *representing and reasoning with goals* using a first order many sorted temporal logic, where goals are expressed in terms of actions and static and temporal constraints; the above questions are answered by model theoretic formal reasoning with goals and business processes.

1 Introduction

This paper presents a formal approach to *representing and reasoning with business goals*, an essential aspect in a business enterprise. There are two main differences between previous formal approaches to goals, e.g. [3], [2] and [4], and ours. First, goals there have been viewed from the RE (requirements engineering) perspective, i.e. for producing *future* software, while we approach goals as guiding principles for business activities in an *existing* enterprise. Second, the previous ones mainly begin with extracting goals from informal reality and end with representing them in some formal language, where questions like the following are analysed: What are the goals of an enterprise? How are the actors trying to achieve the goals? How can a goal be decomposed into subgoals? How can a goal be formulated? On the other hand, we start where the others left off, i.e. from formal representation of goals, and proceed to reasoning with them, addressing "post-formulation" questions like the following: Are the goals achieved in the business activities of the enterprise? How can we check it? If goals are not satisfied, why and what to do? The reason we do not consider the topic of goal extraction is not because it is unimportant, but because it has been studied widely elsewhere and our point is to show reasoning with goals.

M. Jarke, A. Oberweis (Eds.): CAiSE'99, LNCS 1626, pp. 462-466, 1999.
© Springer-Verlag Berlin Heidelberg 1999

Most formal approaches within ISE (information systems engineering) do not fit our purpose well, mainly because they are not intended for the same purpose. A natural way to formulate goals of an IS which are highly abstract by nature is, to describe (implement) them in terms of the concepts which are less abstract but reflect the fundamental aspects of the system. *Time, actions* and *states* are such ones, and so should be formalised first in an adequate way. However, 1) time is not considered in, e.g. Z, VDM or Statechart and it is not clear how time can be integrated into them. 2) While in reality actions have duration, i.e. take time, and different actions may have different length of duration, they are often considered without time, e.g. in OASIS, TROLL and ERAE. In other words all actions are understood to be instantaneous, and we cannot express that some business activities (e.g. a supply from USA to Sweden by ship) may take longer time (say, a month) than others (e.g. an order by telephone). 3) In some object-oriented approaches, e.g. TROLL and KAOS, state is defined w.r.t. an object, i.e. state of an object. However, it may cause difficulties when reasoning about several objects at the same time unless all the states of the objects involved are synchronised.

We are using a first order many sorted temporal logic whose semantics has been based on Features and Fluents [6], a framework within the area knowledge representation. The choice of many sorted logic has been motivated to deal with different kinds of concepts effectively, e.g. different object types (e.g. Agent, Product, Item) in a system, properties (e.g. item_of(I,P) meaning "I is an item of product P"), actions (e.g. order(Ag1,Ag2,N,P) meaning "Agent Ag1 orders with reference number N a product P from agent Ag2"), time points, etc, and relationships over them. For example, the predicate holds(Pr,T) over Property×Time states that the property Pr holds at time T, and the predicate occurs(A,T1,T2) over Action×Time×Time states that the action A occurs over the time period T1 (start time) and T2 (end time). Please refer to [7] for a detailed description of the logic.

2 Business Rules

In our approach goals are implemented in terms of *business rules* that prescribe what and how to do in different business situations. These rules are expressed as wffs in the logic. For example, the rule

$$\text{max\_delivery\_time}(7) \equiv \tag{1}$$
$$\text{occurs}(\text{order}(Ag1,Ag2,N,P),T1,T2) \rightarrow$$
$$\exists! I \exists! T3 \exists! T4 \, (\text{holds}(\text{item\_of}(I,P),T3) \land$$
$$\text{occurs}(\text{supply}(Ag2,Ag1,N,P,I),T3,T4) \land T2 \leq T3 \land T4-T2 \leq 7)$$

states that whenever a customer Ag1 orders a product P over [T1,T2], after order is completed (T2≤T3), an item I of the product type is to be delivered exactly once within 7 days (T4-T2≤7), assuming that all time points are expressing dates. Above ∃! is a syntactical abbreviation denoting the quantifier "exactly one", and all free variables are ∀-quantified. The next rule, with all free variables ∀-quantified, states, suppliers Ag1 are expected to stop any more delivery to those customers Ag2 who have not paid for previous shipments within 30 days.

$$\text{stop\_supply\_after}(30) \equiv \qquad\qquad (2)$$
$$\text{occurs}(\text{supply}(\text{Ag1},\text{Ag2},\text{N1},\text{P1},\text{I1}),\text{T1},\text{T2}) \wedge$$
$$\text{occurs}(\text{invoice}(\text{Ag1},\text{Ag2},\text{N1},\text{P1},\text{N2}),\text{T3},\text{T4}) \wedge$$
$$\neg\text{holds}(\text{paid}(\text{Ag2},\text{Ag1},\text{N1},\text{N2}),\text{T4}+30) \wedge \text{T5-T4} >30 \;\rightarrow$$
$$\neg\exists\text{N3}\exists\text{P2}\exists\text{I2}\exists\text{T6}\; \text{occurs}(\text{supply}(\text{Ag1},\text{Ag2},\text{N3},\text{P2},\text{I2}),\text{T5},\text{T6})$$

The agents pair in actions is motivated to describe communications between multiple agents and to trace who is capable of (responsible for) what. Such information may be essential to a business enterprise. The use of explicit time points makes it possible to express action duration and temporal order between actions. Business rules represented as such, i.e. capturing dynamic, static as well as temporal aspects, provide rich expressiveness and flexibility, and are suited for implementing goals.

3 Goals

This section presents a formal approach to answer the "post-formulation" questions raised in Section 1, where goals are viewed as guiding principles for business activities in an existing enterprise. First, we show how goals can be formulated using business rules.

3.1 Implementing Goals Using Business Rules

A characteristic of goals is that they are highly abstract, e.g. customer_satisfied ("the customers should be satisfied"). In order to make such a goal operational, we decompose it into subgoals at a lower level using AND/OR graphs, e.g. AND(prompt_delivery, purchase_on_credit) which means "the customers should get prompt delivery" and "the customers should be allowed to make a purchase on credit". Decomposition process continues until the subgoals can be implemented in terms of business rules described in Section 2. For example, the subgoal prompt_delivery can be implemented by the rule (1), while the rule (2) may be used for, say, the goal measure_against_unpaid, "measures should be taken against the customers who do not pay in time", etc.

3.2 Goals as Guiding Principles for Business Processes

In order to answer the "post-formulation" questions by formal reasoning with business processes, we describe a business process in the language as a set of i) predicates occurs(A,T1,T2) and ii) formulae describing constraints on the action occurrences. The process may exist already in the enterprise, or be proposed as a possible process in the future. An underlying principle is it should be possible to check any goals on any business processes that may take place in the enterprise. Then the main idea behind the reasoning can be summarised as follows: A business goal is satisfied in a business process if at least one *interpretation* I exists which assigns true to both the process and (the business rule implementing) the goal. (An interpretation is a mathematical structure that assigns truth values to each wff in the language. In logic this way of drawing conclusions based on interpretations is called model theory. Please refer to [7] for details on the reasoning not presented here for space reason.) We sketch the idea in three steps with examples below.

1) Let G be an arbitrary goal and let Bp be an arbitrary business process in which we would like to check the goal. For example, consider the goal

$$G\equiv \text{measure\_against\_unpaid}$$

and the process

$$
\begin{aligned}
\text{Bp}\equiv \{\ &\text{occurs(order(ag1, ag3, 1001, p1), 11, 13)}, \\
&\text{occurs(supply(ag3, ag1, 1001, p1, i2), 15, 19)}, \\
&\text{occurs(invoice(ag3, ag1, 1001, p1, 28), 20, 21)}, \\
&\text{occurs(order(ag1, ag3, 1002, p2), 50, 52)}, \\
&\text{occurs(supply(ag3, ag1, 1002, p2, i1), 53, 59)}, \\
&\exists I\ (\text{holds(owner\_of(ag3, I), 15)} \land \neg(I{=}i2))\ \}
\end{aligned}
$$

where ag3 supplies and invoices to ag1 w.r.t. the order #1001; but ag1 places another order #1002 without paying for the previous order and ag3 supplies again; ag3 is to have at least one more item than i2 when he delivers it at time 15.

2) Before checking G on Bp, we need to make sure whether the process may take place successfully, i.e. the preconditions of each action are satisfied when it is evoked and the constraints are satisfied too. Especially, when the process is proposed as future activity. Formally, it is confirmed if at least one interpretation I exists where i) the only actions that may occur are occurs(A,T1,T2) in Bp (to exclude intervention of other actions); ii) I(Bp)= true. We simply establish here it is so with Bp. Continue to 3). If such interpretation doesn't exist, this means the process can not be performed in any way. Go to 1).

3) Check whether the formula

$$\text{impl}(G)= \text{stop\_supply\_after(30)}$$

implementing the goal is true in the interpretation I as well. A yes means, the activities in Bp achieve the goal and may be performed as they are. This is a desirable situation. However, if the formula is not true in I, which is the case with stop_supply_after(30), this means Bp violates G.

In this way we can formally inspect whether goals are/will be achieved in current/future business processes, and give an answer to "How can we check whether goals are achieved or not in real business processes?". At the same time goals are used as *guiding principles for business activities*. That is, when a process turns out to be violating some goal, it can be re-examined concerning the goal. For example, we may find out why the goal G above is not satisfied by the process Bp by tracing the reasons why I(impl(G))= false. Based on the reasons we may even find out how to improve the business process so that it is still performable but satisfies the goal. For example, remove the action occurs(supply(ag3, ag1, 1002, p2, i1), 53, 59) from Bp, meaning that ag3 does not supply. Therefore the question "If the goals are not satisfied, why and what to do?" can be answered. On the other hand, it can be shown that the goal prompt_delivery is achieved in Bp, which means that the process is acceptable w.r.t. the goal.

Yu & Mylopoulos [8] have also suggested to reason with goals. However, their reasoning is done in an informal way and the main purpose with the reasoning is to examine alternative ways to achieve (functional or non-functional) goals in the context of business process reengineering, rather than to check whether goals are attained in business processes.

4 Final Remarks

In this paper we have presented a formal approach to representing and reasoning with goals. Our message was that it is not enough with representing the goals as an essential part of a business enterprise: There should be some systematic way to investigate whether the goals are attained in reality. We have demonstrated how goal satisfaction can be studied by formal reasoning with business processes.

However, much work needs to be done in the future. Goal structure needs to be analysed deeper to consider, e.g. deontic aspects [4], and conflicts between goals. The language should support methods for structuring complex concepts as pointed out by, e.g. [5]. Especially, in order for our approach to be applied in practice, for example, supporting automatic reasoning with business processes, the semantics of the logic should be implemented in some effective algorithms.

References

[1] P. Assenova and P. Johannesson. First Order Action Logic- an Approach for Modelling the Communication Process between Agents. 1st Intl. Workshop on Communication Modeling - The Language/Action Perspective, Eds. F. Dignum, J. Dietz, E. Verharen and H. Weigand, electronic Workshops in Computing, Springer-Verlag, 1996.

[2] A. Dardenne, Van Lamsweerde and S. Fickas. Goal-directed requirements acquisition. *Science of Computer Programming* 20, pp. 3-50, 1993.

[3] E. Dubois. A Logic of Action for Supporting Goal-Oriented Elaborations of Requirements. *ACM SIGSOFT Software Engineering Notes*, Vol. 14, No. 3, pp. 160-168, 1989.

[4] J. Krogstie and G. Sindre. Utilizing deontic Operators in Information Systems Specification. *Requirements Engineering* 1:210-237, 1996.

[5] J. Mylopoulos, A. Borgida, M. Jarke and M. Koubarakis. Telos: Representing Knowledge About Information Systems. *ACM Transactions on Information Systems*, Vol 8, No. 4, pp. 325-362, 1990.

[6] Erik Sandewall. Features and Fluents, A Systematic Approach to the Representation of Knowledge about Dynamical Systems, Oxford University Press, 1994

[7] Choong-ho Yi. PhD thesis manuscript in preparation.

[8] E. Yu and J. Mylopoulos. Using Goals, Rules and Methods to Support Reasoning in Business Process Reengineering. Proc. of the 27th Annual Hawaii Intl. Conf. on Systems Sciences, Vol. 4, pp. 234-243, 1994.

Design the Flexibility, Maintain the Stability of Conceptual Schemas

Lex Wedemeijer[1]

ABP Netherlands, Department of Information Management, P.O.Box 4476,
NL-6401 CZ, Heerlen, The Netherlands
L.Wedemeijer@ABP.NL

Abstract. A well-designed Conceptual Schema should be flexible enough
to allow future change. But current methods for the design and maintenance of Conceptual Schemas are not based on insight into the actual
evolution of the Conceptual Schema over time. The relationships between
the demand of flexibility, the quality aspect stability, and evolution of
the Conceptual Schema are not well understood or investigated. Advance
in current design practices and maintenance of information systems depends on the understanding of the relation between actual properties of
a Conceptual Schema and its evolution.

1   Introduction

Over time, every enterprise and its ways of doing business will change, techno-
logic capabilities will continue to improve, and user demands will change. Hence,
to safeguard business investments, all information systems are demanded to be
flexible. In particular, the Conceptual Schema is required to be flexible, i.e. must
prove to be a sound basis for longterm business support and for a long systems
lifespan.
Figure 1 depicts the ANSI/X3/Sparc 3-schema architecture. According to this,
a well-designed CS satisfies many quality requirements [6]. A common feature
of current design theories and techniques is that the quality of a CS design is
argumented from theoretical principles only, and concerns the design phase only.
All quality aspects of a CS can be established at design time. The one exception
is stability. For that, its operational lifecycle must be considered. No practical
demonstrations of flexibility of a design in the operational phase are to be found
in the literature. This lack is probably due to the difficulties that any research
on operational CSs in a live business environment will encounter.

2   Flexibility of a Conceptuel Schema Design

Intuitively, flexibility means adaptability, responsiveness to changes in the environment [1]. And "more" flexibility will mean a smaller impact of change. A
working definition is:

M. Jarke, A. Oberweis (Eds.): CAiSE'99, LNCS 1626, pp. 467–471, 1999.

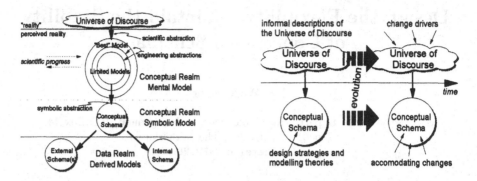

Fig. 1. CS models the perceived UoD (left) and should display joint evolution (right).

> *flexibility is the potential of the Conceptual Schema to accomodate changes in the structure of the Universe of Discourse, within an acceptable period of time*

This definition seems attractive as it is both intuitive and appropriate. It assumes a simple cause-and-effect relation between "structural change" in the UoD and changes in the CS. Also, it prevents inappropriate demands of flexibility on the CS by restricting the relevant environment from which changes stem to the UoD only. Three main design strategies exist that are widely accepted as "good design practices" and that do appear to work. Apart from these, many datamodelling theories exist that claim flexibility. The point is that there is no good understanding of their effectiveness in changing business environments.

Active flexibility or Adaptability is the strategy to improve the design by arranging the constructs of the CS in such a way that it is easy to modify (the *Engineering Abstractions* arrows in fig 1). Notice that no matter how easy the CS *description* can be modified, it is the operational environment that will resist the *implementation* of change. It assumes that certain types of change are easy to accomodate provided the CS is well-arranged, and that any future changes will be of exactly those types. Normalization, modularization, incremental design [3] and the use of component libraries (if applied to reduce the time for response) are based on this strategy. Some related fundamental problems are:

- what principles must be applied to select the right engineering abstractions
- how to detect and resolve conflicts in arranging the constructs
- how to match the perception of reality to a CS that arranges its constructs in special ways

Passive flexibility, or "stabilizing the CS", aims to decrease the need for future change in the CS. The experienced designer uses this strategy when he or she incorporates more requirements into the design than those originating from the current UoD (the *Perceived-Reality* and *Scientific Abstraction* arrows in fig 1). The assumption is that accomodating probable requirements will reduce the need for future change. (Re)use of "proven" designs, Business Data Modelling, the use of component libraries (when taken to represent "good solutions") [2] and many rules-of-thumb [7] are based on passive flexibility. Related problems:

- how far ahead should future requirements be anticipated
- which requirements are relevant, and which are beyond consideration

The *Flexibility by abstraction* strategy puts less information into the CS design, thus making it more abstract. More features of the UoD are deemed "non-conceptual", increasing data independence (as contrasted to *relying* to data independence, which comes under active flexibility). Fundamental in the approach is that it is known which features must be abstracted from. Semantic datamodel theories, and Object-Oriented approaches, are based on this approach that comes under the *Scientific Progress* arrows in fig 1. Related problems to this strategy:

- deciding on the best level of abstraction
- how to transform the abstract CS into workable External and Internal Schemas

Problems with the Concept of Flexibility

There is no way for a designer to pick the best design strategy for a particular business case at hand. One must trust to experience and to state-of-the-art design practices. Further problems in assessing flexibility of a CS design are:

- flexibility is established on the fly. There is no way to verify that a CS has "enough" flexibility, or to discover beforehand that "more" flexibility is needed
- it leaves open what timespan is acceptable to accomodate a change
- it is not a persistent property. A CS that has adapted to many changes in the past may prove to be inflexible the next time.

Nor does the concept of flexibility help to understand the evolution of the CS. The main problem is in its dependence on future events. What is needed is a sound criterium that looks at the actual changes that occur over the operational lifespan of the CS.

3   Change

The CS is a well-defined, formal model that can be studied in isolation from its environment. In contrast, the UoD is informally known, a common understanding of what is "out there". But it can't be caught in formal definitions: any attempt at formalizing the UoD is equal to creating a CS. Over time, the common perception of "reality" will of course evolve as maintenance crews gain experience, employees shift to other jobs, new methods and tools are introduced etc. Although changes in (the perception of) the UoD can only be understood by referring to informal knowledge, there is hope yet. In many business cases, structural change of the UoD can be deduced from informal communications as change requests, project definitions, budget justifications, etc.

A *taxonomy* lists the "elementary" changes that come with a datamodelling theory. But that is syntax only. The semantics of changes in the CS must be established by comparing the current CS description with the previous one, which will encounter serious complications:

- consecutive CS descriptions must be available. This is not usually the case!
- the datamodelling theory must not allow equivalent representations [5]
- the CS description must be faultless. Often, Reverse Engineering is called for
- constructs and constructions in the CS before and after the change must have a recognizable relation, or –even better– preserve their identity.

4   Stability of the Conceptual Schema

As the UoD is bound to change, as people will perceive the UoD in new ways, and as user requirements will change, so the CS must cope with change (Fig. 1). Flexibility is unsuitable to assess this quality aspect, as it depends on future events. Instead, the criterium of stability is proposed. A working definition:

> *a change in the CS is a stable change if it is absolutely necessary to accomodate change in the structure of the UoD*

A CS that changes for any other reason is *unstable*. Generally speaking, while flexibility is a demand that must be met by the designer, stability is proof that it has been delivered. The systems owner should decide on the necessity of the CS change and the spending of vital business resource, weighing it against other pressing business needs. Enterprises try to keep the impact of change as small as possible [4]. This restricts the freedom of choice for the maintenance people as the adapted CS is required to be a good model of the new UoD, and at the same time be "as close to the old CS as possible". This tendency towards stability is evident in the usual demand for compatibility, reducing the need for complex data conversions. Extensibility is a special form of compatibility. Other familiar ways to implement changes in a compatible way are relaxation of database constraints and misuse of data fields. These maintenance strategies are deemed less desirable as they are suspected –but rarely proved– to shorten the lifespan of the CS.

Even if CS changes are detected, it can be difficult to determine if the change is stable. It must be traced back to changes in the UoD, and the following complications might arise:

- lag time between change in the CS and change in the UoD
- update anomaly, if a UoD change causes multiple CS adaptations
- parts of the CS may be invalid; changes to those parts are irrelevant
- user perceptions (the *Mental Model* in fig 1) may change without there being a material change in the way of doing business

Stability or Flexibility

To demand that a new design CS will undergo only stable changes in the future, is equal to demanding its flexibility. But an existing CS can be checked for stability by looking at its changes in the past. The important point is that there is no convincing evidence that correct application of the three design strategies actually does improve the stability of the resulting CS's. To demonstrate effectiveness of the design strategies, changes occuring in operational CS's must be researched, their stability must be determined, and finally, the contribution of the design strategy to that stability must be established.

5   Summary and Conclusion

This paper discussed the problem of determining the flexibility of a CS. From a business point of view, it is important to know in advance whether a proper CS will prove to be flexible enough. Many authors demand that a CS design be flexible, but do not explain their concept of flexibility. They presume that CS changes are driven from the UoD only. State-of-the-art design strategies also claim to promote flexibility, but these claims are all founded on theory, not on proof. The relationship between changes in the UoD and changes in *operational* CS is not well understood. It can only be obtained by researching CS's in their natural environment, the operational business. The research must center on the concept of *stable changes*: changes in the CS that are driven by corresponding changes in the structure of the UoD. Such research will encounter serious difficulties as CS changes are very difficult to observe in real business environments. But it is only through an understanding of this relationship that we can hope to improve current practices.

References

1. Crowe T.J. *Integration is not synonymous with flexibility*, Int. J. of Operations & Production Management vol 12, no 10 (1992) 26–33
2. Di Battista G., Kangassalo H., Tamassia R. *Definition libraries for Conceptual Modelling*, Proceedings of the 7th Int. Conf. on the Entity-Relationship Approach, ed. Batini (1989) Elsevier Science Publishers 251–267
3. Filteau M.C., Kassicieh S.K., Tripp R.S. *Evolutionary Database Design and development in Very Large Scale MIS*, Information & Management vol 15 (1988) 203–212
4. Giacommazzi F., Panella C., Percini B., Sansoni M. *Information systems integration in mergers and acquisitions*, Information & Management vol 32 (1997) 289–302
5. Jajodia S., Ng P.A., Springsteel F.N. *The problem of equivalence for Entity-Relationship diagrams*, IEEE Trans. on Software Engineering vol 9, no 5 (1983) 617–630
6. Kesh S. *Evaluating the quality of Entity Relationship models*, Information and Software Technology vol 37 (1995) 681–689
7. Moody D. *Seven habits of Highly Effective Datamodellers*, Database Programming & Design (1996) 57–64

Metrics for Active Database Maintainability*

Oscar Díaz[1] and Mario Piattini[2]

[1] Departamento de Lenguajes y Sistemas Informáticos,
University of the Basque Country - San Sebastián, Spain
jipdigao@si.ehu.es
[2] Departamento de Informática,
University of Castilla-La Mancha - Ciudad Real, Spain
mpiattini@inf-cr.uclm.es

Abstract. Databases are becoming more complex and it is necessary to measure schemata complexity in order understand, monitor, control, predict and improve software development and maintenance projects. Active databases are a case in point where several reports warned the difficulties to cope with large rule sets. This paper proposes three different metrics for measuring active databases complexity, based on the difficulty to ascertain the causes that make a given rule to be triggered. The measurement theory is used to characterise these metrics.

1 Introduction

Software engineers have been proposing large quantities of metrics for software products, processes and resources. Most of these metrics focus on programme characteristics neglecting databases. This disregard could be explained as databases have been until recently just "simple files/tables" with minor contribution to the complexity of the overall system. With the new database generation however, this is no longer the case. New applications have fuelled the appearance of the "third database generation", where new data types, rules, generalisations, complex objects and functions are being supported within the database realm.

The focus of this paper are active database management systems (DBMS), that is, DBMS that allow the definition and management of event-condition-action rules. This mechanism enables the DBMS to respond automatically to events that are taking place either within or outside the database itself. This mechanism is currently available in a large number of commercial products (Oracle, Sybase, DB2, SQL-Server, Interbase), and rules are reckoned to be useful for a large number of applications. Despite its usefulness, early reports show that a few hundred rules represent a real maintenance problem. Similar disquiet was pointed out at the closing panel at the RIDE-ADS workshop dedicated to Active Database Systems [1]. As these reports suggest, the lack of maintainability is a

---

* This work is partially supported by the MANTICA Project (CICYT/European Union 1FD97-0168).

M. Jarke, A. Oberweis (Eds.): CAiSE'99, LNCS 1626, pp. 472–476, 1999.
© Springer-Verlag Berlin Heidelberg 1999

main obstacle for active system to become widely used. Maintainability is contributed by three factors: understandability, modifiability and testability, which in turn are influenced by complexity [2].

This paper addresses the complexity of large rule sets by means of three measures: the triggering potential, the number of anchors, and the distance of a rule. These measures are characterised using the measurement theory, particularly the formal framework proposed by Zuse [3]. The rest of the paper is organised as follows. Section 2 briefly introduces those aspects of active DBMS significant for this work. Section 3 presents the different complexity measures proposed. We characterise the proposed metrics in Section 4.

2   Characterization of Active Databases

Active DBMS are able to react to significant events. These systems provide a way to describe events and their associated reactions (i.e. the knowledge model) as well as the runtime strategy to process and combine this active behaviour (i.e. the execution model).

A common approach for the knowledge model uses event-condition-action rules (ECA rules) that have an event which describes a happening to which the rule may be able to respond, a condition that examines the context in which the event has taken place, and an action which describes the task to be carried out by the rule if the relevant event has taken place and the condition has evaluated to true. The event part can be a primitive event (e.g. a database operation) or a composite event, i.e., a combination of primitive or composite events. For the purpose of this paper, the cardinality of the rule's event correspond to the number of primitive events that are (either direct or indirectly) referred to in the event part of the rule, regardless of the composite operator used.

The execution model specifies how a set of rules is treated at run-time. Among other aspects, this model includes the coupling mode that determines when the condition (action) is evaluated (executed) relative to the triggering (evaluation) of the event (condition). In this paper, only the immediate coupling mode is considered where the condition (action) is evaluated (executed) immediately after the event (condition). The question of what happens when events occur during the execution of the rule's action is addressed by the cycle policy. This paper, considers a recursive model where events risen during action execution are immediately taken into account. This causes the current rule's action to be suspended, so that any rules monitoring these events can be processed at the earliest opportunity.

Early reports on the use of active systems point out the feeling of lack of control experimented by users. Indeed, the audience at the RIDE-ADS'94 closing panel qualified as infeasible ECA-rule applications which have *more than 7 rules or more than 5 layers of rule triggering* [1]. It is worth noticing that the obstacle identified during this workshop was not the unavailability of appropriate mechanisms, but the complexity of the already available systems.

3   Measures for Active Datatabase Complexity

Design product metrics can be sub-divided into intra-module and inter-module metrics. Likewise, rule complexity can be characterised as intra-rule complexity where the rule in isolation is measure, and inter-rule complexity where the implicit interaction among rules is measure. Experience in building active systems, suggests that it is the degree of interactions rather than the number or complexity of the rules themselves, what affects this sense of lack of control felt by the user. More concretely, two aspects are felt to be specially significant in the interaction of rules: the width and depth of the argumentation. The former reflects the intuition that the larger is the flow of events that conforms the rules circumstance, the more difficult will be to understand these rules. Of course, rules being fired by composite events are potentially more intricate that those with a single event. However, what our experience shows out is that a factor that complicates things even more is when the very same event type that participates in the rule's event is produced in distinct places. This means that the rule's circumstance can raise in different contexts. As a result, the user has a tougher job at ascertaining which of the potential circumstance makes the rule to be triggered. As for the depth of the argumentation, it refers to the intricacy of the line of reasoning that connects the rule with the context where its circumstance has been produced. The depth and number of threads required to encompass the rule's circumstance certainly affects its complexity.

To formalise these intuitions, the notion of a triggering graph is used [4]. A triggering graph is a pair $< S, L >$ where S represent the set of ECA rules, and L is a set of directed arcs where an arc is drawn from Si to Sj if Si's action causes the happening of an event occurrence that participates in Sj's events. This notion of triggering graph is slighted modified for our purposes in two aspects. First, arcs are weighted by the number of potential event occurrences produced by the triggering rule (i.e. Si) that could affect the rule triggered (i.e. Sj's event). Second, the nodes S are extended with the set of transactions T. A transaction is a set of (database) actions where any of these actions could correspond to an event triggering one or more rules. Therefore, T nodes will have outgoing links but never incoming links as we assume that a transaction can never be fired from within a rule's action or another transaction.

The intuitive notions identified previously can now find correspondence as triggering graph measures, namely:

- **NA**, the minimum number of anchors required to encompass the whole set of potential causes of Si. An anchor is a transaction node of the triggering graph which has a link (either direct or transitively) with at least one cause of Si. The intuition is that each of these anchors represents a line of reasoning to be followed to understand the rule's circumstance.
- **D**, the distance which accounts for the length of the longest path that connects Si with any of its anchors. The intuition is that this measure reflects the intricacy of the line of reasoning as the number of inferences which are required to connect the ultimate cause with its effect (i.e. the triggering of Si).

– **TP**, the triggering potential. Given a triggering graph <S,L>, and a node of the graph, rule Si, the number of causes of Si, is the sum of weights of the incoming arcs arriving to Si. The triggering potential for a rule R is the quotient between the number of potential causes of Si, and Si's event cardinality. This measure attempts to reflect the width of Si's circumstance by giving an indication of the potential different circumstances which can make Si to be triggered.

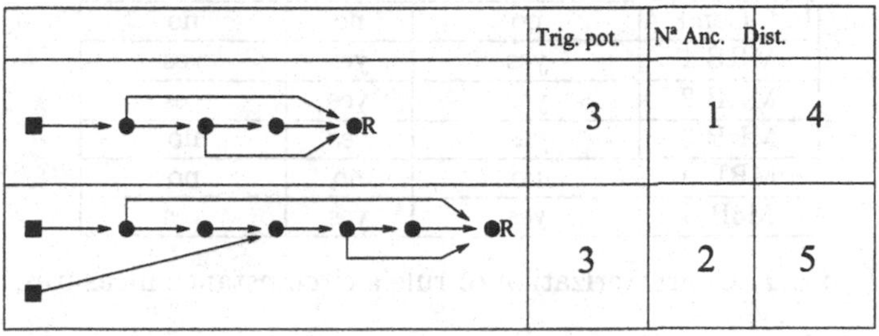

	Trig. pot.	Nᵃ Anc.	Dist.
	3	1	4
	3	2	5

Fig. 1. Measuring different triggering graphs.

Figure 1 illustrates the previous measures for distinct triggering graphs where the event cardinality for rule S is one.

4   Characterization of Active Database Complexity Metrics

The framework described in [3] is used to describe the properties of the metrics defined above. This framework is based on an extension of the classical measurement theory, which gives a sound basis for software measures, their validation and criteria for measurement scales.

For ECA rules, the Empirical Relational System, $A = (S, \bullet >=, o)$ could be defined as follows:

1. S is a non-empty set of rules
2. $\bullet >=$ is the empirical relation "more or equal complex than" on S
3. o is a closed binary (concatenation) operation on S such that concatenation of rules S1(E1, C1, A1) and S2(E2, C2, A2) produces a rule S3, where:
   – event E3 = E1 OR E2
   – condition C3 = (C1 AND e1) OR (C2 AND e2), where ei is a Boolean variable where true (false) indicates the occurrence (absence) of the Ei event
   – action A3 can be defined as: IF e1 THEN A1, IF e2 THEN A2.

Axioms	Anchor Number	Distance	Trig. Potential
Axiom 1	yes	yes	yes
Axiom 2	yes	yes	no
Axiom 3	yes	yes	yes
Axiom 4	yes	yes	yes
Axiom 5	no	yes	no
Axiom 6	no	no	no
Ind. Cond. 1	no	yes	no
Ind. Cond. 2	no	no	no
Ind. Cond. 3	no	yes	no
Ind. Cond. 4	no	no	no
MRB 1	yes	yes	yes
MRB 2	yes	yes	yes
MRB 3	yes	yes	no
MRB 4	no	no	no
M4B 5	yes	yes	yes

Table 1. Characterization of rule's circumstance measures.

The outcome is that the proposed measures do not represent **an extensive structure** but they can be characterised above the ordinal scale by fulfilling some of the properties of modified relations of belief. Table 4 summarises the properties fulfilled by the three metrics following the Zuse framework.

References

[1] J. Widom. Research issues in active database systems: Report from closing panel at ride-ads' 94. In *SIGMOD RECORD*, volume 23 (3), pages 41–43, 1994.
[2] H.F. Li and W.K. Chen. An empirical study of software metrics. *IEEE Trans. on Software Engineering*, 13(6):679–708, 1987.
[3] H. Zuse. *A Framework of Software Measurement*. Walter de Gruyter (Berlin), 1998.
[4] A. Aiken, J.M. Hellerstein, and J. Widom. Static analysis techniqies for predicting the behaviour of active database rules. *ACM Transactions on Databases*, 20(1):3–41, 1995.

Author Index

Springer
and the
environment

At Springer we firmly believe that an international science publisher has a special obligation to the environment, and our corporate policies consistently reflect this conviction.
We also expect our business partners – paper mills, printers, packaging manufacturers, etc. – to commit themselves to using materials and production processes that do not harm the environment. The paper in this book is made from low- or no-chlorine pulp and is acid free, in conformance with international standards for paper permanency.

 Springer

Lecture Notes in Computer Science

For information about Vols. 1–1537
please contact your bookseller or Springer-Verlag